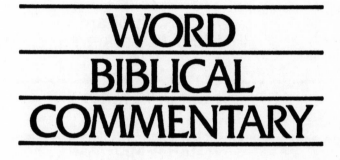

WORD
BIBLICAL
COMMENTARY

WORD
BIBLICAL
COMMENTARY

VOLUME 1

Genesis 1-15

GORDON J. WENHAM

THOMAS NELSON
Since 1798

NASHVILLE   DALLAS   MEXICO CITY   RIO DE JANEIRO

Word Biblical Commentary
GENESIS 1–15
Copyright © 1987 by Thomas Nelson, Inc.

Library of Congress Cataloging in Publication Data
Main entry under title:

Word biblical commentary.

  Includes bibliographies.
  1. Bible—Commentaries—Collected Works.
BS491.2W67   220.7'7   81–71768
ISBN-10: 0849902002 (vol. 1) AACR2
ISBN-13: 9780849902000

Printed in Mexico

Grateful acknowledgment is made for the copyright material used on pp. 162–164 of this volume from James B. Pritchard, ed., *Ancient Near Eastern Texts Relating to the Old Testament*, 2d edition. Copyright 1950, 1955 © 1983 renewed by Princeton University Press. Excerpts, pp. 93–95, reprinted with permission of Princeton University Press.

Scripture quotations in the body of the commentary, unless otherwise indicated, are generally from the Revised Standard Version of the Bible, copyright 1946 (renewed 1973), 1956, and © 1971 by the Division of Christian Education of the National Council of the Churches of Christ in the USA and are used by permission. The author's own translation of the text appears in italic type under the heading *Translation*.

26 27 28 29 30 EPAC 15 14 13 12 11

Contents

Author's Preface

Commenting on Genesis, I have found my mood oscillating between elation and despair. I have been elated at the privilege of writing a commentary on such a central biblical text. I have been driven to despair by the impossibility of doing it justice, let alone dealing adequately with all that others have written about it.

Every commentator stands on the shoulders of his predecessors, and I am personally very indebted to the two modern and exhaustive commentaries of Westermann and Gispen, as well as the numerous monographs and articles on Genesis that have appeared recently. Despite all this help I realize the inadequacy of my work, limited as I am in time, energy, and wisdom. I simply hope that despite its shortcomings this commentary may help some to understand Genesis better.

In writing I have tried to keep three different groups of readers in mind. First are the pastors and laymen whose chief preoccupation is understanding the present text of Genesis. Although the commentary is based on the Hebrew text, I have tried to write the *Comment* and *Explanation* sections so that those who do not know Hebrew may still follow the argument. The *Comment* section attempts to elucidate the basic meaning of the text in its present setting in the book. The *Explanation* gives a broader view of the text, relating it to wider theological discussion and sometimes suggesting its contemporary relevance.

Second, this commentary has in mind the needs of the theological students for whom Genesis is often a set text. Those working on the Hebrew text may find the *Notes* of special interest, for they discuss not only textual criticism and points of Hebrew syntax, but they also parse the trickier verbal forms.

Third, this commentary is intended for biblical scholars, particularly those interested in issues of pentateuchal criticism. In the *Introduction* and the *Form/ Structure/Setting* sections I have surveyed and attempted to evaluate the various positions currently advocated. Though these debates about criticism are often recondite, I believe that their satisfactory resolution may contribute substantially to the accurate exegesis of the text, which should always be the commentator's overriding purpose. The bibliographies are also primarily intended as a scholarly resource. Since Westermann's commentary includes exhaustive lists of material published on Genesis, my bibliographies should be viewed more as a supplement than as a complete listing. Only the most significant earlier publications are cited. Nevertheless, the pace of publication on Genesis has quickened so much recently (on many passages as much has been published since 1970 as in the previous seventy years!), that even with this limitation the bibliographies are lengthy.

Finally, I should like to thank all those who have helped in various ways with the writing of this commentary: the Old Testament editor, John Watts, and the publishers, for entrusting me with the task and keeping me at it; the College of St Paul and St Mary, for allowing me a term's leave of absence spent at Trinity Evangelical Divinity School; that school, for providing a congenial environment in which to work; W. G. Lambert, for his invaluable advice on the relationship of Genesis to ancient Near Eastern tradition and for allowing me to read his forthcoming VTSup article; D. Bryan, for allowing me to read his forthcoming *ZAW* article; T. D. Alexander, N. Kiuchi, and J. G. McGregor, for bibliographical help; G. Eriksson, A. R. Millard, J. Sailhammer, D. T. Tsumura, and my father, J. W. Wenham, whose acute comments on various drafts of the manuscript have greatly improved it; my colleague David Miall, for advice on word processing programs; Mrs Margaret Hardy, for typing it; Mrs Pat Wienandt of Word Publishing, for her careful editing; and last but not least, friends known and unknown, who have prayed for the completion of this commentary. My plan, D.V., is to complete it in one more volume, the introduction of which will discuss issues relating primarily to the patriarchal narratives.

Cheltenham   GORDON J. WENHAM
March 1987

Editorial Preface

The launching of the *Word Biblical Commentary* brings to fulfillment an enterprise of several years' planning. The publishers and the members of the editorial board met in 1977 to explore the possibility of a new commentary on the books of the Bible that would incorporate several distinctive features. Prospective readers of these volumes are entitled to know what such features were intended to be; whether the aims of the commentary have been fully achieved time alone will tell.

First, we have tried to cast a wide net to include as contributors a number of scholars from around the world who not only share our aims, but are in the main engaged in the ministry of teaching in university, college, and seminary. They represent a rich diversity of denominational allegiance. The broad stance of our contributors can rightly be called evangelical, and this term is to be understood in its positive, historic sense of a commitment to Scripture as divine revelation, and to the truth and power of the Christian gospel.

Then, the commentaries in our series are all commissioned and written for the purpose of inclusion in the *Word Biblical Commentary*. Unlike several of our distinguished counterparts in the field of commentary writing, there are no translated works, originally written in a non-English language. Also, our commentators were asked to prepare their own rendering of the original biblical text and to use those languages as the basis of their own comments and exegesis. What may be claimed as distinctive with this series is that it is based on the biblical languages, yet it seeks to make the technical and scholarly approach to a theological understanding of Scripture understandable by—and useful to—the fledgling student, the working minister, and colleagues in the guild of professional scholars and teachers as well.

Finally, a word must be said about the format of the series. The layout, in clearly defined sections, has been consciously devised to assist readers at different levels. Those wishing to learn about the textual witnesses on which the translation is offered are invited to consult the section headed *Notes*. If the readers' concern is with the state of modern scholarship on any given portion of Scripture, they should turn to the sections on *Bibliography* and *Form/Structure/Setting*. For a clear exposition of the passage's meaning and its relevance to the ongoing biblical revelation, the *Comment* and concluding *Explanation* are designed expressly to meet that need. There is therefore something for everyone who may pick up and use these volumes.

If these aims come anywhere near realization, the intention of the editors will have been met, and the labor of our team of contributors rewarded.

General Editors: *David A. Hubbard*
Glenn Barker †
Old Testament: *John D. W. Watts*
New Testament: *Ralph P. Martin*

Abbreviations

BR	*Biblical Research*
BSac	*Bibliotheca Sacra*
BT	*The Bible Translator*
BTB	*Biblical Theology Bulletin*
BWANT	Beiträge zur Wissenschaft vom Alten und Neuen Testament
BZ	*Biblische Zeitschrift*
BZAW	Beihefte zur ZAW
CAD	*The Assyrian Dictionary of the Oriental Institute of the University of Chicago*
CAH	*Cambridge Ancient History*
CBQ	*Catholic Biblical Quarterly*
CBQMS	CBQ Monograph Series
ConB	Coniectanea biblica
CRAIBL	*Comptes rendus de l'Académie des inscriptions et belles-lettres*
CTJ	*Calvin Theological Journal*
CTM	*Concordia Theological Monthly*
CurTM	*Currents in Theology and Mission*
DBSup	*Dictionnaire de la Bible, Supplément*
DBAT	*Dielheimer Blätter zum AT*
DJD	*Discoveries in the Judaean Desert*
EAEHL	*Encyclopedia of Archaeological Excavations in the Holy Land,* ed. M. Avi-Yonah
EE	Enuma Elish
EI	*Ereş Israel*
EgT	*Eglise et Théologie*
EHS	Europäischen Hochschulschriften
EM	*Encyclopedia Miqrait*
EvQ	*Evangelical Quarterly*
EvT	*Evangelische Theologie*
EWAS	T. Muraoka, *Emphatic Words and Structures in Biblical Hebrew*
ExpTim	*Expository Times*
FRLANT	Forschungen zur Religion und Literatur des Alten und Neuen Testaments
GE	Gilgamesh Epic
GKC	*Gesenius' Hebrew Grammar,* ed. E. Kautzsch, tr. A. E. Cowley
GTJ	*Grace Theological Journal*
GTOT	J. Simons, *The Geographical and Topographical Texts of the OT*
GTT	*Gereformeerd Theologisch Tijdschrift*
HAR	*Hebrew Annual Review*
Hen	*Henoch*
HSM	Harvard Semitic Monographs
HTR	*Harvard Theological Review*
HUCA	*Hebrew Union College Annual*
IBD	*Illustrated Bible Dictionary*

IDB	*Interpreter's Dictionary of the Bible*, ed. G. A. Buttrick, 4 vols. (Nashville: Abingdon, 1962)
IDBSup	Supplementary volume to *IDB*
IEJ	*Israel Exploration Journal*
Int	*Interpretation*
ITQ	*Irish Theological Quarterly*
ITS	Innsbrucker theologische Studien
IndTS	*Indian Theological Studies*
IrBS	*Irish Biblical Studies*
JAAR	*Journal of the American Academy of Religion*
JANESCU	*Journal of the Ancient Near Eastern Society of Columbia University*
JAOS	*Journal of the American Oriental Society*
JBC	*The Jerome Biblical Commentary*, ed. R. E. Brown et al.
JBL	*Journal of Biblical Literature*
JCS	*Journal of Cuneiform Studies*
JETS	*Journal of the Evangelical Theological Society*
JJS	*Journal of Jewish Studies*
JNES	*Journal of Near Eastern Studies*
JNSL	*Journal of Northwest Semitic Languages*
Joüon	P. P. Joüon, *Grammaire de l'hébreu biblique* (Rome: Pontifical Biblical Institute, 1947)
JQR	*Jewish Quarterly Review*
JRT	*Journal of Religious Thought*
JSJ	*Journal for the Study of Judaism in the Persian, Hellenistic and Roman Period*
JSOT	*Journal for the Study of the OT*
JSOTSS	*JSOT* Supplement Series
JTS	*Journal of Theological Studies*
KB	L. Koehler and W. Baumgartner, *Lexicon in Veteris Testamenti Libros*, 3d ed.
KD	*Kerygma und Dogma*
Lambdin	T. O. Lambdin, *Introduction to Biblical Hebrew* (New York: Scribner's, 1971)
LD	Lectio divina
LingBib	*Linguistica Biblica*
MDOG	*Mitteilungen der deutschen Orient-Gesellschaft*
MTZ	*Münchener theologische Zeitschrift*
NBD	*New Bible Dictionary*, ed. J. D. Douglas
NedTT	*Nederlands theologisch tijdschrift*
NERTOT	*Near Eastern Texts Relating to the Old Testament*, ed. W. Beyerlin
NICOT	*New International Commentary on the Old Testament*
NorTT	*Norsk Teologisk Tidsskrift*
NRT	*La nouvelle revue théologique*
OBO	Orbis Biblicus et Orientalis
OCCL	*Oxford Companion to Classical Literature*, ed. P. Harvey
Or	*Orientalia*
OTS	*Oudtestamentische Studiën*
POTT	*Peoples of OT Times*, ed. D. J. Wiseman

PWCJS	*Proceedings of the World Congress of Jewish Studies*
RB	*Revue biblique*
Rel	*Religion*
ResQ	*Restoration Quarterly*
RevThom	*Revue thomiste*
RHPR	*Revue d'histoire et de philosophie religieuses*
RivB	*Rivista biblica*
RLA	*Reallexicon der Assyriologie*
RTL	*Revue théologique de Louvain*
SBH	F. I. Andersen, *The Sentence in Biblical Hebrew*
SBLMS	SBL Monograph Series
SBS	Stuttgarter Bibelstudien
SBT	Studies in Biblical Theology
ScEs	*Science et Esprit*
SEÅ	*Svensk exegetisk årsbok*
Sem	*Semitica*
SJLA	Studies in Judaism in Late Antiquity
SJT	*Scottish Journal of Theology*
SR	*Studies in Religion/Sciences religieuses*
ST	*Studia theologica*
StudBT	*Studia Biblica et Theologica*
TA	*Tel Aviv*
TB	*Tyndale Bulletin*
TD	*Theology Digest*
TDNT	*Theological Dictionary of the New Testament*, ed. G. Kittel and G. Friedrich
TDOT	*Theological Dictionary of the Old Testament*, ed. G. J. Botterweck and H. Ringgren
TGl	*Theologie und Glaube*
TGUOS	*Transactions of the Glasgow University Oriental Society*
Them	*Themelios*
THWAT	*Theologisches Handwörterbuch zum Alten Testament*, ed. E. Jenni and C. Westermann
TJ	*Trinity Journal*
TLZ	*Theologische Literaturzeitung*
TQ	*Theologische Quartalschrift*
TRE	*Theologische Realenzyklopädie*
TRev	*Theologische Revue*
TRu	*Theologische Rundschau*
TS	*Theological Studies*
TTZ	*Trierer theologische Zeitschrift*
TV	*Theologia Viatorum*
TZ	*Theologische Zeitschrift*
UF	*Ugarit-Forschungen*
VR	*Vox Reformata*
VT	*Vetus Testamentum*
VTSup	Vetus Testamentum, Supplements
WMANT	Wissenschaftliche Monographien zum Alten und Neuen Testament
WO	*Die Welt des Orients*

WTJ	*Westminster Theological Journal*
ZA	*Zeitschrift für Assyriologie*
ZAW	*Zeitschrift für die alttestamentliche Wissenschaft*
ZTK	*Zeitschrift für Theologie und Kirche*

MODERN TRANSLATIONS

AB	Anchor Bible	NASB	New American Standard Bible
AV	Authorized Version		
JB	Jerusalem Bible	NEB	New English Bible
JPS	Jewish Publication Society of America, *The Holy Scriptures According to the Masoretic Text,* 1917	NIV	New International Version
		RSV	Revised Standard Version
		RV	Revised Version
KJV	King James Version	TEV	Today's English Version

TEXTS, VERSIONS, AND ANCIENT WORKS

G, LXX	Septuagint	Tg. Onq.	*Targum Onqelos*
L	Codex Leningradensis, B19a	Tg. Neof.	*Targum Neofiti*
		Tg. Ps.-J.	*Targum Pseudo-Jonathan*
MT	Masoretic Text	Frg. Tg.	*Fragment-Targum*
NT	New Testament	Vg	Vulgate
OT	Old Testament	α′	Aquila
SamPent	Samaritan Pentateuch	σ′	Symmachus
S	Syriac text	θ′	Theodotion

BIBLICAL AND APOCRYPHAL BOOKS

Old Testament

Gen	Genesis	Isa	Isaiah
Exod	Exodus	Jer	Jeremiah
Lev	Leviticus	Lam	Lamentations
Num	Numbers	Ezek	Ezekiel
Deut	Deuteronomy	Dan	Daniel
Josh	Joshua	Hos	Hosea
Judg	Judges	Joel	Joel
Ruth	Ruth	Amos	Amos
1–2 Sam	1–2 Samuel	Obad	Obadiah
1–2 Kgs	1–2 Kings	Jon	Jonah
1–2 Chr	1–2 Chronicles	Mic	Micah
Ezra	Ezra	Nah	Nahum
Neh	Nehemiah	Hab	Habakkuk
Esth	Esther	Zeph	Zephaniah
Job	Job	Hag	Haggai
Ps(s)	Psalm(s)	Zech	Zechariah
Prov	Proverbs	Mal	Malachi
Eccl	Ecclesiastes		
Cant	Canticles, Song of Solomon		

New Testament

Matt	Matthew	1–2 Thess	1–2 Thessalonians
Mark	Mark	1–2 Tim	1–2 Timothy
Luke	Luke	Titus	Titus
John	John	Phlm	Philemon
Acts	Acts	Heb	Hebrews
Rom	Romans	Jas	James
1–2 Cor	1–2 Corinthians	1–2 Pet	1–2 Peter
Gal	Galatians	1–2–3 John	1–2–3 John
Eph	Ephesians	Jude	Jude
Phil	Philippians	Rev	Revelation
Col	Colossians		

Apocrypha

Add Esth	Additions to Esther	Pr Azar	Prayer of Azariah
Bar	Baruch	Pr Man	Prayer of Manasseh
Bel	Bel and the Dragon	Sir	Ecclesiasticus or The
1–2 Esdr	1–2 Esdras		Wisdom of Jesus Son
4 Ezra	4 Ezra		of Sirach
Jud	Judith	Sus	Susanna
Ep Jer	Epistle of Jeremy	Tob	Tobit
1–2–3– 4 Kgdms	1–2–3–4 Kingdoms	Wis	Wisdom of Solomon
1–2–3– 4 Macc	1–2–3–4 Maccabees		

HEBREW GRAMMAR

abs	absolute	impf	imperfect
acc	accusative	impv	imperative
act	active	ind	indicative
adv acc	adverbial accusative	inf	infinitive
aor	aorist	juss	jussive
apoc	apocopated	masc, m	masculine
c	common	niph	niphal
coh	cohortative	obj	object
conj	conjunction	pass	passive
consec	consecutive	pf	perfect
constr	construct	pl	plural
fem, f	feminine	prep	preposition
fut	future	pron	pronoun
gen	genitive	pronom	pronominal
hiph	hiphil	ptcp	participle
hithp	hithpael	sg	singular
hoph	hophal	subj	subject

MISCELLANEOUS

chap(s).	chapter(s)	J	Jahwist
E	Elohist	JE	Jahwist plus the Elohist
ed(s).	editor(s), edited by	K	Kethib, "written"
ET	English translation	MS(S)	manuscript(s)
Gr.	Greek	P	Priestly Source
Heb.	Hebrew	Q	Qere, to be "read"

Main Bibliography

COMMENTARIES (quoted by author's name alone)

Aalders, G. C. *Genesis I, II.* 5th ed. Korte verklaring der Heilige Schrift. Kampen: Kok, 1974. **Brueggemann, W.** *Genesis.* Interpretation Commentary. Atlanta: John Knox, 1982. **Cassuto, U.** *A Commentary on the Book of Genesis 1–11.* Tr. I. Abrahams. Jerusalem: Magnes, 1961, 1964. **Calvin, J.** *A Commentary on Genesis.* Tr. J. King, 1847. Repr. London: Banner of Truth, 1965. **Cook, F. C.** *Genesis-Exodus.* Speaker's Bible. London: Murray, 1871. **Davidson, R.** *Genesis 1–11, 12–50.* Cambridge Bible Commentary. Cambridge: CUP, 1973, 1979. **Delitzsch, F.** *A New Commentary on Genesis. Vols. 1, 2.* Tr. S. Taylor. Edinburgh: Clark, 1888; repr. Klock, 1978. **Dillmann, A.** *Die Genesis.* Kurzgefasstes exegetisches Handbuch. 6th ed. Leipzig: Hirzel, 1892. **Driver, S. R.** *The Book of Genesis.* 3d ed. Westminster Commentary. London: Methuen, 1904. **Ehrlich, A. B.** *Randglossen zur hebräischen Bibel, vol. 1.* Hildesheim: Olms, 1968 (original edition 1908). **Gibson, J. C. L.** *Genesis I, II.* Edinburgh: St Andrew Press, 1981, 1982. **Gispen, W. H.** *Genesis I–III.* Commentar op het Oude Testament. Kampen: Kok, 1974–83. **Gunkel, H.** *Genesis.* 9th ed. (= 3d ed). Göttingen: Vandenhoeck, 1977 (1910). **Jacob, B.** *Das erste Buch der Tora.* New York: Ktav, 1974 (1934). **Junker, H.** *Das Buch Genesis.* Echter Bibel. 4th ed. Wurzburg: Echter Verlag, 1965. **Keil, C. F.** *The Pentateuch I.* Biblical Commentary. Tr. J. Martin. Repr. Grand Rapids: Eerdmans, n.d. **Kidner, D.** *Genesis: An Introduction and Commentary.* Tyndale OT Commentary. London: Tyndale, 1967. **König, E.** *Die Genesis eingeleitet, übersetzt, erklärt.* Gütersloh: Bertelsman, 1919. **Leibowitz, N.** *Studies in Bereshit.* 4th ed. Jerusalem: World Zionist Organization, 1981. **Procksch, O.** *Die Genesis übersetzt und erklärt.* 2d ed. Leipzig: Deicherische Verlags-buchhandlung, 1924. **Rad, G. von.** *Genesis.* Tr. J. H. Marks and J. Bowden. London: SCM Press, 1972. **Rashi.** *Pentateuch with Rashi's Commentary.* Tr. M. Rosenbaum and A. M. Silbermann. New York: Hebrew Publishing Company. **Sarna, N. M.** *Understanding Genesis.* New York: Schocken Books, 1970. **Skinner, J.** *A Critical and Exegetical Commentary on Genesis.* ICC. 2d ed. Edinburgh: Clark, 1930. **Speiser, E. A.** *Genesis.* AB. New York: Doubleday, 1969. **Spurrell, G. J.** *Notes on the Text of the Book of Genesis.* 2d ed. Oxford: Clarendon Press, 1896. **Vawter, B.** *On Genesis: A New Reading.* Garden City: Doubleday, 1977. **Weinfeld, M.** *Sefer Bereshit.* Tel-Aviv: Gordon, 1975. **Westermann, C.** *Genesis.* 1–11, 12–36, 37–50. Biblischer Kommentar: Altes Testament. Neukirchen: Neukirchener Verlag, 1974–82. Vols. I, II. Tr. J. J. Scullion. London: SPCK, 1984, 1986. (Quotations are usually from Scullion's translation; my own translations are indicated by dual page numbering with German page number first, e.g., 296, ET 217).

OTHER STUDIES

Andersen, F. I. *The Hebrew Verbless Clause in the Pentateuch.* Nashville: Abingdon, 1970. **Dahood, M.** "Northwest Semitic Notes on Genesis." *Bib* 55 (1974) 76–82. **Freedman, D. N.** "Notes on Genesis." *ZAW* 64 (1952) 190–94. **Soggin, J. A.** *OT and Oriental Studies.* BibOr 29. Rome: Biblical Institute Press, 1975. **Speiser, E. A.** *Oriental and Biblical Studies.* Ed. J. J. Finkelstein and M. Greenberg. Philadelphia: University of Pennsylvania, 1967. **Strus, A.** "La poétique sonore des récits de la Genèse." *Bib* 60 (1979) 1–22. **Stuart, D. K.** *Studies in Early Hebrew Meter.* HSM 13. Missoula: Scholars Press, 1976.

GENESIS 1–11

Bič, M. "The Theology of the Biblical Creation Epic." *SEÅ* 28/29 (1963/64) 9–38.
Clark, W. M. "The Animal Series in the Primeval History." *VT* 18 (1968) 433–49.
———. "The Flood and the Structure of the Pre-patriarchal History." *ZAW* 83 (1971)
184–211. **Combs, E.** "The Political Teaching of Gen 1–11." *Studia Biblica 1978*, ed.
E. A. Livingstone. JSOTSS 11. Sheffield: JSOT Press, 1979. 105–10. **Davies, P. R.**
"Sons of Cain." In *A Word in Season: Essays in Honour of W. McKane*, ed. J. D. Martin
and P. R. Davies. JSOTSS 42. Sheffield: JSOT Press, 1986. 35–56. **Drewermann, E.**
Strukturen des Bösen I: Die jahwistische Urgeschichte in exegetischer Sicht. 4 ed. Paderborn:
Schöningh, 1982. **Fenton, T. L.** "Different Approaches of the Biblical Narrators to
the Myth of Theomachy." (Heb.) In *Studies in Bible and the Ancient Near East presented
to S. E. Loewenstamm*, ed. Y. Avishur and J. Blau. Jerusalem: Rubinstein, 1977. 337–
81. **Fretheim, T. E.** *Creation, Fall and Flood.* Minneapolis: Augsburg, 1969. **Gispen,
W. H.** "Exegeten over Gen 1–11." *GTT* 71 (1971) 129–36. **Kapelrud, A. S.** "Die
Theologie der Schöpfung im Alten Testament." *ZAW* 91 (1979) 159–70. **Knight,
G. A. F.** *Theology in Pictures: A Commentary on Gen 1–11.* Edinburgh: Handsel Press,
1981. **Loretz, O.** *Schöpfung und Mythos: Mensch und Welt nach den Anfangskapiteln der
Genesis.* SBS 32. Stuttgart: KBW Verlag, 1969. **Miller, P. D.** *Genesis 1–11: Studies in
Structure and Theme.* JSOTSS 8. Sheffield: JSOT Press, 1978. **Neveu, L.** *Avant Abraham
(Gen 1–11).* Angers: Université Catholique de l'Ouest, 1984. **Niditch, S.** *Chaos to Cosmos:
Studies in Biblical Patterns of Creation.* Chico: Scholars Press, 1985. **Oberforcher, R.**
Die Flutprologe als Kompositionsschlüssel der biblischen Urgeschichte. ITS 8. Innsbruck: Tyrolia Verlag, 1981. **Ruppert, L.** " 'Urgeschichte' oder 'Urgeschehen'? Zur Interpretation
von Gen 1–11." *MTZ* 30 (1979) 19–32. **Scullion, J. J.** "New Thinking on Creation
and Sin in Gen 1–11." *AusBR* 22 (1974) 1–10. **Smith, G. V.** "Structure and Purpose
in Gen 1–11." *JETS* 20 (1977) 307–19. **Stadelmann, L. I. J.** *The Hebrew Conception of
the World: A Philological and Literary Study.* AnBib 39. Rome: Pontifical Biblical Institute,
1970.

Introduction

Name and Contents

BIBLIOGRAPHY

Childs, B. S. *Introduction to the OT as Scripture*. Philadelphia: Fortress Press, 1979. 136–60. **Clines, D. J. A.** *The Theme of the Pentateuch*. JSOTSS 10. Sheffield: JSOT Press, 1979. **Coats, G. W.** *Genesis, with an Introduction to Narrative Literature*. Grand Rapids: Eerdmans, 1983. **Cohn, R. L.** "Narrative Structure and Canonical Perspective in Genesis." *JSOT* 25 (1983) 3–16. **Cross, F. M.** *Canaanite Myth and Hebrew Epic*. Cambridge: Harvard UP, 1973. **Dahlberg, B.** "On Recognizing the Unity of Genesis." *TD* 24 (1976) 360–67. **Davies, P. R.,** and **D. M. Gunn.** "Pentateuchal Patterns: An Examination of C. J. Labuschagne's Theory." *VT* 34 (1984) 399–406. **Labuschagne, C. J.** "The Pattern of the Divine Speech Formulas in the Pentateuch." *VT* 32 (1982) 268–96. ———. "Additional Remarks on the Pattern of the Divine Speech Formulas in the Pentateuch." *VT* 34 (1984) 91–95. ———. "Pentateuchal Patterns: A Reply to P. R. Davies and D. M. Gunn." *VT* 34 (1984) 407–13. ———. "The Literary and Theological Function of Divine Speech in the Pentateuch." *Congress Volume, 1983*. VTSup 36. Leiden: E. J. Brill, 1985. 154–73. **Rendsburg, G. A.** *The Redaction of Genesis*. Winona Lake: Eisenbrauns, 1986. **Robinson, R. B.** "Literary Functions of the Genealogies of Genesis." *CBQ* 48 (1986) 595–608. **Scharbert, J.** "Der Sinn der Toledot-Formel in der Priesterschrift." In *Wort-Gebot-Glaube: FS für W. Eichrodt*, ed. J. J. Stamm and E. Jenni. ATANT 59. Zurich: Zwingli Verlag, 1970. 45–56. **Tengström, S.** *Die Toledotformel und die literarische Struktur der priesterlichen Erweiterungsschicht im Pentateuch*. ConB 17. Lund: Gleerup, 1981. **Weimar, P.** "Die Toledot-Formel in der priesterlichen Geschichtsdarstellung." *BZ* 18 (1974) 65–93. **White, H. C.** "Word Reception as the Matrix of the Structure of the Genesis Narrative." In *The Biblical Mosaic: Changing Perspectives*, ed. R. Polzin and E. Rothman. Philadelphia: Fortress Press, 1982. 61–83. **Witt, D. S. de.** "The Generations of Genesis." *EvQ* 48 (1976) 196–211. **Woudstra, M. H.** "The *Toledot* of the Book of Genesis and Their Redemptive-Historical Significance." *CTJ* 5 (1970) 184–89.

As with the other books of the Pentateuch, the Hebrew title is taken from its opening word בראשית "In the beginning," whereas the English title "Genesis" is a transliteration, via the Vulgate, of the Greek title. Both titles aptly describe the book's contents: it is a book of origins. Greek γένεσις means "origin, source, race, creation." In fact the term is used in the LXX to translate תלדות "generations, family history," a term used repeatedly in the title of each new section of the book, e.g., 2:4; 5:1; 6:9; 11:27 etc. And the Book of Genesis describes in turn the origin of the universe, of mankind, and of the ancestors of the nation of Israel. Indeed, the focus narrows progressively throughout the book.

Chapter 1	—	the origin of the world
2–11	—	the origins of the nations
12–50	—	the origins of Israel

More precisely, the author or final redactor of Genesis has arranged the material so that each new development in the history is introduced by the phrase אלה תלדות "This is the (family) history of." There are ten sections with this heading (eleven if the reduplication of 36:1, 9 are counted separately), with 1:1–2:3 acting as an overture to the whole book.

	1:1–2:3	Prologue
1)	2:4–4:26	History of heaven and earth
2)	5:1–6:8	Family History of Adam
3)	6:9–9:29	Family History of Noah
4)	10:1–11:9	Family History of Noah's sons
5)	11:10–26	Family History of Shem
6)	11:27–25:11	Family History of Terah
7)	25:12–18	Family History of Ishmael
8)	25:19–35:29	Family History of Isaac
9)	36:1–37:1	Family History of Esau
10)	37:2–50:26	Family History of Jacob

Although the same heading "This is the family history of" is used in nearly every case, the sections vary markedly in character. Sections 1, 3, 6, 8, 10 are full and detailed narratives, whereas the other sections are mostly genealogical with few narrative details. Starting with chap. 11, genealogies and narrative sections alternate. Furthermore, despite this editorial leveling, it is obvious that the character of the material in chaps. 1–11 is markedly different from that in chaps. 12 onward. The opening chapters have a universal perspective dealing with all mankind and are obviously related in some way to other oriental traditions about creation, flood, and the origins of arts, crafts, and the nations. Chaps. 12–50, on the other hand, deal almost exclusively with Israelite concerns. They recount the story of the nation's forebears in some detail, mentioning only briefly the origin of some of Israel's closest neighbors, e.g., Moab, Ammon, and Edom.

Finally, in reflecting on the contents of Genesis, it must never be forgotten that it is the first of a five- (or six-) volume work, the Pentateuch (Hexateuch). It gives the background to the history of the exodus from Egypt and the lawgiving at Sinai which are dealt with in great detail in Exodus-Deuteronomy. Whereas according to Genesis' own chronology the first book of the Pentateuch spans some two thousand years, the next four cover a mere one hundred and twenty. This helps to put Genesis into perspective. It does not stand on its own, but rather contains essential background for understanding those events which constituted the nation of Israel as the LORD's covenant people. It would therefore not be surprising to find adumbrations of the later national history in the story of the patriarchs. In turn, too, the primeval history (chaps. 1–11) must be seen in this perspective. It is also essentially preparatory in function and puts the patriarchs into their cosmic context. The God who called Abraham was no local divinity but the creator of the whole universe. The succession of catastrophes that befell humanity prior to Abraham's call show just why the election of Abraham, and in him, Israel, was necessary.

Text of Genesis

BIBLIOGRAPHY

TEXT AND VERSIONS OF GENESIS

Good editions of the Hebrew text and most of the early translations of Genesis are now available.

Hebrew
Masoretic Text (MT)

Eissfeldt, O. *Liber Genesis: Biblia Hebraica Stuttgartensia.* Stuttgart: Deutsche Bibelstiftung, 1969.

Samaritan Pentateuch (SamPent)

Gall, A. F. von. *Der hebräische Pentateuch der Samaritaner.* Giessen: Töpelmann, 1914–18.

Greek—Septuagint (LXX or G)

Wevers, J. W. *Genesis.* Septuaginta. Vetus Testamentum Graece Auctoritate Academiae Scientiarum Gottingensis editum I. Göttingen: Vandenhoeck & Ruprecht, 1974.

Latin—Vulgate (Vg)

Weber, R. *Biblia Sacra iuxta Vulgatam Versionem I.* Stuttgart: Württembergische Bibelanstalt, 1969.

Syriac—Peshitta (S)

Boer, P. A. H. de. *The OT in Syriac according to the Peshitta Version. I: Genesis* (based on material collected and studied by T. Jansma). Leiden: Brill, 1977.

Aramaic—Targum Onqelos (Tg. Onq.)

Sperber, A. *The Bible in Aramaic. I: The Pentateuch according to Targum Onkelos.* Leiden: Brill, 1959.

Targum Neofiti (Tg. Neof.)

Diez Macho, A. *Neofyti I: Targum Palestinense MS de la Biblioteca Vaticana. I: Genesis.* Madrid: Consejo Superior de Investigaciones Científicas, 1968.

Fragment-Targums (Frg. Tgs.)

Klein, M. L. *The Fragment-Targums according to their Extant Sources.* AnBib 76. Rome: Biblical Institute Press, 1980.

Targum Pseudo-Jonathan (Tg. Ps.-J.)

Clarke, E. G. *Targum Pseudo-Jonathan of the Pentateuch: Text and Concordance.* Hoboken: Ktav, 1984. **Ginsburger, M.** *Thargum Jonathan ben Usiel zum Pentateuch.* Berlin: 1903. **Rieder, D.** *Pseudo-Jonathan: Targum Jonathan ben Uziel on the Pentateuch Copied from the London MS.* Jerusalem: Salomon, 1974.

Genesis Apocryphon (Gen. Ap.)

Avigad, N., and **Y. Yadin.** *A Genesis Apocryphon: A Scroll from the Wilderness of Judaea.* Jerusalem: Magnes Press, 1956.

Samaritan Targum

Tal, A. *The Samaritan Targum of the Pentateuch: A Critical Edition. Pt. 1: Genesis, Exodus.* Tel Aviv: Tel Aviv University, 1980.

TEXT-CRITICAL STUDIES

Aberbach, M., and **B. Grossfeld.** *Targum Onkelos to Genesis.* New York: Ktav, 1982. **Albrektson, B.** "Reflections on the Emergence of a Standard Text of the Hebrew Bible." *Congress Volume, 1977.* VTSup 29. Leiden: E. J. Brill, 1978. 49–65. **Barthélemy, D.** "History of Hebrew Text." *IDBSup* 878–84. **Bowker, J. W.** *The Targums and Rabbinic Literature.* Cambridge: CUP, 1969. **Cross, F. M.** *The Ancient Library of Qumran and Modern Biblical Studies.* 2d ed. New York: Doubleday, 1961. ———, and **S. Talmon.** *Qumran and the History of the Biblical Text.* Cambridge: Harvard UP, 1975. **Fitzmyer, J. A.** *The Genesis Apocryphon of Qumran Cave 1: A Commentary.* BibOr 18A. 2d ed. Rome: Biblical Institute Press, 1971. **Skehan, P. W.** "Texts and Versions." *JBC* 2:361–67. **Waltke, B. K.** "The Samaritan Pentateuch and the Text of the OT." In *New Perspectives on the Old Testament,* ed. J. B. Payne. Waco: Word, 1970. 212–39. **Wevers, J. W.** *Text History of the Greek Genesis.* Mitteilungen des Septuaginta-Unternehmens. Göttingen: Vandenhoeck & Ruprecht, 1974. **Würthwein, E.** *The Text of the Old Testament.* Tr. E. F. Rhodes. London: SCM Press, 1980.

The text on which this commentary is based is the traditional Masoretic Text (MT), preserved in the great majority of mediaeval biblical manuscripts. The particular edition used here, *Biblia Hebraica Stuttgartensia (BHS)* 1977, reproduces the Leningrad manuscript B19[A] which dates from the eleventh century A.D. Another Hebrew tradition, the Samaritan Pentateuch (SamPent), is available in the critical edition of A. von Gall (1914–18). The most important non-Hebrew witness to the text of Genesis is the Septuagint (LXX), which in the case of the Pentateuch was a Greek translation made in the third century B.C. and preserved in many Christian manuscripts mostly from the fourth century A.D. onwards. It has complicated textual problems of its own, but J. Wevers has recently published a critical edition. Other less important translations of the Hebrew that need to be consulted include the Peshitta (S) (the Syriac translation), the various Aramaic targums (Tg), and the Latin Vulgate (Vg).

Despite the relative lateness of the main MT manuscripts, it is universally recognized that the MT of Genesis has preserved one Hebrew text with remarkable fidelity from pre-Christian times. This conclusion, reached originally by comparing the MT with other versions, was confirmed by the discovery of the Dead Sea Scrolls. Fragments of fifteen manuscripts of Genesis have been found at Qumran dating from about the first century B.C. These show few variants from the traditional text. Readings agreeing with the LXX are rare, suggesting that the text of Genesis was already standardized in this era. Fragments of Genesis were also discovered at Masada (pre-A.D. 73), one at Murabaat (pre-A.D. 135) and another at Nahal Hever. The Qumran and Murabaat fragments are partially published in *DJD* 1–5. For further details see P. W. Skehan, *JBC* 2:564–66. Also among the Qumran manuscripts was found an Aramaic paraphrase of Gen 12–14 called the Genesis Apocryphon (see Avigad [1956] and Fitzmyer, [1971]).

These newer discoveries have led to renewed confidence in the relative antiquity and general superiority of the Masoretic Text. Waltke (1970) showed again that the Samaritan Pentateuch (SamPent) represents a revision of the MT, in which Hebrew grammar is modernized and linguistic, historical, and theological problems are eased or brought into line with sectarian ideology. He argues that much of this revision dates from about the fifth century B.C. and that the MT textual tradition must therefore be earlier. Similarly, the Septuagint, which sometimes has readings in common with SamPent, reflects a later variant Hebrew tradition at some points and is most useful as a witness to the understanding of Genesis current among Egyptian Jews in the third century B.C. (e.g., 3:15; chap. 5; 15:6).

In general, then, the commentator must proceed to establish the text of Genesis eclectically, that is, by examining each particular case on its own merits. Usually the MT offers the most trustworthy text, but the SamPent and versions need to be consulted constantly just in case they offer superior readings, as perhaps at 4:8.

Genesis in Recent Research

BIBLIOGRAPHY

Armerding, C. E. *The Old Testament and Criticism.* Grand Rapids: Eerdmans, 1983. **Clements, R. E.** "Pentateuchal Problems." In *Tradition and Interpretation,* ed. G. W. Anderson. Oxford: Clarendon Press, 1979. 96–124. **Eissfeldt, O.** *The Old Testament: An Introduction.* Tr. P. R. Ackroyd. Oxford: Blackwell, 1965. **Fohrer, G.** *Introduction to the Old Testament.* Tr. D. Green. London: SPCK, 1970. **Gunneweg, A. H. J.** "Anmerkungen und Anfragen zur neueren Pentateuchforschung." *TRu* 48 (1983) 227–53; 50 (1985) 107–31. **Rad, G. von.** *Die Priesterschrift im Hexateuch literarisch untersucht und theologisch gewertet.* BWANT 65. Stuttgart: Kohlhammer, 1934. **Rendtorff, R.** "The Future of Pentateuchal Criticism." *Hen* 6 (1984) 1–14. ———. *The Old Testament: An Introduction.* Tr. J. Bowden. London: SCM Press, 1985. **Robinson, A.** "Process Analysis Applied to the Early Traditions of Israel." *ZAW* 94 (1982) 549–66. **Ruppert, L.** "Die Aporie der gegenwärtigen Pentateuchdiskussion und die Joseferzählung der Genesis." *BZ* 29 (1985) 31–48. **Schmid, H. H.** "Auf der Suche nach neuen Perspektiven für die Pentateuchforschung." *Congress Volume, 1980.* VT Sup 32. Leiden: E. J. Brill,

1981. 375–94. **Schmitt, H.-C.** "Der Hintergründe der 'neuesten Pentateuchkritik' und der literarische Befund der Josefgeschichte Gen 37–50." *ZAW* 97 (1985) 161–79. **Seters, J. van.** "Recent Studies in the Pentateuch: A Crisis in Method." *JAOS* 99 (1979) 663–72. **Soggin, J. A.** *Introduction to the OT.* Tr. J. Bowden. London: SCM Press, 1976. **Tengström, S.** *Die Hexateucherzählung: Eine literaturgeschichtliche Studie.* ConB 7. Lund: Gleerup, 1976. **Thompson, R. J.** *Moses and the Law in a Century of Criticism since Graf.* VTSup 19. Leiden: Brill, 1970. **Volz, P.,** and **W. Rudolph.** *Der Elohist als Erzähler: Ein Irrweg der Pentateuchkritik?* BZAW 63. Giessen: Töpelmann, 1933. **Westermann, C.** *Genesis 1–11/Genesis 12–50.* Erträge der Forschung. Darmstadt: Wissenschaftliche Buchgesellschaft, 1972/1975.

Genesis, as anyone with the slightest acquaintance with Old Testament scholarship knows, is central to every theory of pentateuchal criticism. These theories have been and continue to be the subject of an endless stream of monographs and articles, as well as being summarized in every introduction to the OT and many a Genesis commentary. It is not my purpose here to tread the same ground yet again. (For surveys of these areas see, for example, the OT Introductions listed in the bibliography, and also the works by Clements, Thompson, and Westermann. Westermann's commentary also contains numerous excursuses outlining changing critical approaches to different parts of Genesis.) Rather, my aim is to draw attention to some of the more significant recent critical work on Genesis, so that the reader has a clear general perspective on the issues raised. But I shall begin by putting the present discussions in context by sketching briefly the regnant critical view and its precursors, for some modern scholarship is reacting against the traditional consensus and in some cases resurrecting ideas last entertained seriously in the nineteenth century.

For the best part of a century following the publication of J. Wellhausen's works *Die Komposition des Hexateuchs* (1876–77; 4th ed., Berlin: de Gruyter, 1963) and *Prolegomena zur Geschichte Israels* (Berlin: Reimer, 1878), there has been a widespread critical consensus about the composition of the Pentateuch. According to this view, the Pentateuch is composed of four distinct sources: J (10/9th century), E (9/8th century), D (7th century), P (6/5th century). These sources were successively amalgamated, culminating in the composition of the existing Pentateuch in about the fifth century B.C. As far as Genesis is concerned, it was compiled from three main sources: J (comprising about half of the material), E (about a third), and P (about a sixth). These sources were distinguished on five main criteria: different names of the deity (J speaks of Yahweh, the LORD, E and P of Elohim, God); duplicate narratives (e.g., different accounts of creation, Gen 1 and 2; repetition within the flood story, Gen 6–9; doublets within the patriarchal narratives, cf. 12:10–20 with chap. 20); different vocabulary (J "cuts" covenants, P "establishes" covenants); different style (J and E contain vivid narrative, P is repetitious and fond of genealogies); and finally, different theologies (according to P, God is remote and transcendent; in J and E, God is anthropomorphic, etc.).

Though this view was very widely accepted from about 1878 to 1970, there have been significant dissenters at various points. For example, Gunkel postulated two Js, a view echoed later by O. Eissfeldt (1965) and G. Fohrer

(1970), who distinguished L or N sources alongside J. G. von Rad (1934) subdivided P into two, while P. Volz and W. Rudolph denied the distinction of an E source alongside J (1933). There have, of course, been those who have entirely rejected these source-critical analyses and the dates assigned by them. The valuable commentaries of Jacob (1934) and Cassuto (1944) dispense completely with the sources JEP and attempt to understand Genesis as a coherent unity.

Before the Wellhausenian consensus emerged in the late nineteenth century, there had been more than a hundred years of critical debate about Genesis and its sources. Though some of the more obvious differences within Genesis were quickly discerned and ascribed to different sources, there was much discussion about the relationship between the sources and their relative dating. Should one regard the sources as lengthy documents which have been successively combined by a series of editors who did little but weave the sources together? This type of view became dominant with Wellhausen and is known as a *documentary* hypothesis. Or should one hold that essentially the Pentateuch grew like a snowball from one main source that subsequent editors have expanded down the centuries, adding extra material either from other traditions or from the editor's imagination to fill out the details in the original source? This type of approach is known as a *supplementary* hypothesis. Thirdly, *fragmentary* hypotheses were advocated. According to this type of theory, the Pentateuch was composed of a large number of relatively short sources. These short stories were strung together by an editor or editors to form the long narrative that constitutes our present Pentateuch. In recent years, fragmentary or supplementary hypotheses have increasingly been preferred to explain the composition of other biblical books, e.g., Judges, Samuel, Kings. A variety of discrete sources (fragments) is postulated to have been incorporated into the Book of Kings, ranging from extracts from the royal archives to prophetic legends. These have been put together by one or more editors with deuteronomic inclinations (deuteronomists). It is held that they have strung together the fragments, adding their own interpretative comments at the beginning and end of each fragment, sometimes putting their own theological reflection into the mouths of the leading actors in the story. It is this sort of approach to the composition of the Pentateuch that was widely supported in the pre-Wellhausenian era and is being resurrected by some modern pentateuchal critics.

Finally it may be noted that before Wellhausen there was much more uncertainty about the dating of the sources. The earliest critics held that the sources of Genesis were pre-Mosaic and that Moses was the editor of Genesis. Subsequent writers tended to prefer a later date for the composition of Genesis, usually in the early monarchy period. But they mostly put the sources in an order different from that of Wellhausen: many of the most eminent nineteenth-century writers (e.g., Stähelin, Ewald, Tuch, Nöldeke, Riehm, Hupfeld) held that the J material represented the latest material to be written: what is now known as P and E antedated J. And even after the Wellhausenian revolution, A. Dillmann, still one of the most useful nineteenth-century commentators, persisted in dating J after P.

Having outlined the traditional critical view of Genesis and some of its

forerunners, I now propose to outline some of the new hypotheses that have
been advanced since 1970. To simplify the discussion I shall look at recent
discussions as they affect each source in turn—first J, then E, then P—and
finally I shall outline modern methods of literary criticism and their impact on the study of Genesis. Inevitably this approach will involve a certain
amount of duplication as changing views of E, for example, affect understandings of J, but I hope this method will make for a clearer presentation
of significant trends in scholarship than would a mere chronological account.

J (The Yahwistic Source)

BIBLIOGRAPHY

Alexander, T. D. *A Literary Analysis of the Abraham Narrative in Genesis.* Ph.D. Diss.:
Queen's University of Belfast, 1982. ———. "Gen 22 and the Covenant of Circumcision." *JSOT* 25 (1983) 17–22. **Coats, G. W.** *From Canaan to Egypt: Structural and Theological Context for the Joseph Story.* CBQMS 5. Washington: Catholic Biblical Association,
1976. **Lohfink, N.** *Die Landverheissung als Eid.* SBS 28. Stuttgart: Katholisches Bibelwerk, 1967. **Lubsczyk, H.** "Melchizedek: Versuch einer Einordnung der Melchisedek-
Perikope (Gen 14) in den jahwistischen Erzählzusammenhang." In *Einheit in Vielfalt:
Festgabe für H. Aufderbeck,* ed. W. Ernst and K. Feiereis. Leipzig: St. Benno Verlag,
1974. 92–109. **Radday, Y. T.,** and **H. Shore.** *Genesis: An Authorship Study.* AnBib 103.
Rome: Biblical Institute Press, 1985. **Rendtorff, R.** *Das überlieferungsgeschichtliche Problem des Pentateuch.* BZAW 147. Berlin: de Gruyter, 1976. **Rose, M.** *Deuteronomist und
Jahwist: Untersuchungen zu den Berührungspunkten beider Literaturwerke.* ATANT 67. Zu-
rich: Theologischer Verlag, 1981. **Schmid, H. H.** *Der sogenannte Jahwist: Beobachtungen
und Fragen zur Pentateuchforschung.* Zurich: Theologischer Verlag, 1976. **Schmidt, L.**
"Überlegungen zum Jahwisten." *EvT* 37 (1977) 230–47. **Schmidt, W. H.** "Ein Theologe
in salomonischer Zeit? Plädoyer für den Jahwisten." *BZ* 25 (1981) 82–102. **Schmitt,
H. C.** *Die nichtpriesterliche Josephsgeschichte: Ein Beitrag zur neuesten Pentateuchkritik.*
BZAW 154. Berlin: de Gruyter, 1980. ———. "Redaktion des Pentateuch im Geiste
der Prophetie." *VT* 32 (1982) 170–89. **Seters, J. van.** *Abraham in History and Tradition.*
New Haven: Yale UP, 1975. ———. *In Search of History: Historiography in the Ancient
World and the Origins of Biblical History.* New Haven: Yale UP, 1983. **R. Smend.** *Die
Entstehung des Alten Testaments.* Stuttgart: Kohlhammer, 1979. **Vorländer, H.** *Die Ents-
tehungszeit des jehowistischen Geschichtswerk.* EHS 23:109. Frankfurt: Lang, 1978. **Why-
bray, R. N.** "The Joseph Story and Pentateuchal Criticism." *VT* 18 (1968) 522–28.
———. *The Making of the Pentateuch: A Methodological Study.* JSOTSS 53. Sheffield:
JSOT Press, 1987.

In the kaleidoscope of new pentateuchal hypotheses the existence of J
remains one of the few points of agreement conceded by nearly everyone.
R. Rendtorff, *Das überlieferungsgeschichtliche Problem des Pentateuch* (1976), is
the one significant dissenter. He doubts the existence of any source documents
running all through the Pentateuch, preferring a traditio-historical approach.
This is akin to the older fragmentary or supplementary hypothesis which
held that the Pentateuch stories grew as they were retold and were linked
by editors. But since the material ascribed to J is heterogeneous, Rendtorff

does not think one hand can be credited with arranging it, so it is wiser to give up talking about J altogether.

Most scholars, however, have been proceeding in the opposite direction to Rendtorff, at least as far as J is concerned. More of Genesis is being credited to J than under the Wellhausenian consensus. For example, Gen 15 was traditionally divided between J and E, but N. Lohfink (1967) was one of the first to argue that it was almost entirely J's reworking of earlier tradition, a position followed by J. van Seters (1975) and Coats (1983). Gen 14 is usually considered a stray boulder within Genesis, but again Lohfink, Lubsczyk (1974), Vawter (1977), and Coats (1983) have argued that although it may have been independent once, it is now clearly part of J's story of Abram and Lot (cf. Gen 13, 18–19), so it should not be viewed as an insertion into Genesis long after J; rather the account antedates J. The similarity of the style of Gen 14 to other J narratives has been demonstrated by Radday (1985). J. van Seters (1975), while rejecting this last point, has argued for an even larger J. He has argued firmly for a supplementary hypothesis to explain the growth of the Abraham stories. A very brief account of Abraham's life was expanded further by adding parts of chaps. 20–21 (traditionally E). But the definitive redaction of Gen 12–25 was the responsibility of J, who added much new material (usually ascribed to J and E). Everything but the P material and chap. 14, according to van Seters, can be attributed to J. Following van Seters, Westermann denies the presence of a separate E source in Gen 12–25, while Coats (1983) thinks it likely that chaps. 21–22, usually ascribed to E, more likely come from J. Alexander (1982) has gone even further, arguing that there is only one main editor of Gen 12–25, namely, J. He argues that even the P sections, e.g., Gen 17 and 23, have been edited by J; for example, the sacrifice of Isaac (chap. 22) presupposes the account in Gen 17.

In other parts of Genesis there is a similar tendency to maximize J at the expense of E. Whybray (1968) argued that the Joseph story is a substantial unity, which, says Coats (1976, 1983), is mostly the work of J (1983). Westermann, however, while admitting the basic unity of the Joseph story, holds that its author is not identical with J, though he worked in the same period, because the literary techniques used in Gen 37–45 are different from other sections of Genesis ascribed to J. H. C. Schmitt (1980) favors a van Seters–type approach to the Joseph and Jacob stories, viz., an original Judah source, expanded by the Reuben material E, and then edited by J. More radical still, Rendsburg (1986) argues that one editor—whether J or P is a matter of indifference—is responsible for compiling the whole of Genesis in the united monarchy period. Whybray (1987) has defended a similar view, though he dates the composition of Genesis much later.

Alongside the strong tendency in recent writing to give J an even bigger role in the composition of Genesis than Wellhausen allowed, there is a somewhat weaker party arguing that J is much later than the tenth century B.C. H. H. Schmid (1976), M. Rose (1981), R. Smend (1984), for example, want to date J in the late monarchy period mainly on grounds of its affinities with deuteronomic literature. Similarly, van Seters (1975; cf. Whybray [1987]) posits the composition of J in about the sixth century on literary and archeological grounds. But his arguments on the dating of J have carried less conviction than his remarks about its extent.

E (The Elohistic Source)

BIBLIOGRAPHY

Craghan, J. F. "The Elohist in Recent Literature." *BTB* 7 (1977) 23–35. **Jenks, A. W.** *The Elohist and North Israelite Traditions.* SBLMS 22. Missoula: Scholars Press, 1977. **Klein, H.** "Ort und Zeit des Elohisten." *EvT* 37 (1977) 247–60. **Portnoy, S. L.,** and **D. L. Petersen.** "Genesis, Wellhausen and the Computer: A Response." *ZAW* 96 (1984) 421–25. **Radday, Y. T., H. Shore, M. A. Pollatschek,** and **D. Wickmann.** "Genesis, Wellhausen and the Computer." *ZAW* 94 (1982) 467–81. **Weimar, P.** *Untersuchungen zur Redaktionsgeschichte des Pentateuch.* BZAW 146. Berlin: de Gruyter, 1977. **Wenham, G. J.** *"Genesis: An Authorship Study* and Current Pentateuchal Criticism." *JSOT* (forthcoming). **Zenger, E.** "Auf der Suche nach einem Weg aus der Pentateuchkrise." *TRev* 78 (1982) 353–62.

E has become very much the Cinderella of the pentateuchal sources in recent criticism. J's growth has been largely at the expense of E, as the above discussion indicates. (See especially the work of van Seters, Westermann, and Coats). For van Seters the E material has become one of the sources utilized by J or J's own material; at any rate no E material is of later date than J. Westermann and Coats, on those occasions where they admit the existence of E material independent of J, tend to view it as a later expansion of the existing J narrative. In other words, some of the E material is seen by them not as constituting a separate source document but as a supplement to J. At these points they are advocating a supplementary theory.

This tendency among leading source critics to merge the J and E sources has received significant support from the computerized statistical linguistic studies of Radday (1982, 1985). Using a battery of linguistic criteria (word length, grammatical features, transition frequencies) and a variety of statistical analyses, Radday and his collaborators were able to distinguish differences of style within Genesis. They observed that human and divine speeches reported in Genesis differed in style from each other and from the narrator's style. This was something overlooked by previous studies. And certain passages, e.g., Gen 5 and 11, stood out as quite distinctive. These stylistic distinctions clearly must be ascribed to differences in genre: speech, narrative, and genealogy inevitably utilize different styles.

But appeal is also usually made to stylistic differences to distinguish the sources J, E, and P in Genesis. Here, however, no significant difference in style between J and E was detected when Radday compared similar genres of material. A marked difference in style between J and P was noted, though Radday thinks this may be ascribed to differences in genre: P's lists are bound to differ stylistically from J's or E's narratives. He notes that in Gen 2–11 the narrative styles of J and P are often quite similar.

Before embracing these results too quickly, however, one should be aware of the limitations of this approach (cf. Portnoy and Petersen, 1984). First, the stylistic identity of J and E need not indicate identity of authorship: identity of authorship is the simplest, most economical hypothesis, but stylistic uniformity could indicate that all Hebrew prose writers adopted a very uniform stereotyped style of writing within a particular genre. Second, statistical analysis requires longish sections of text (at least 200 word samples) to make a judgment. Thus, distinguishing an editorial comment from a narrative or list used by the editor is beyond the power of this method. Statistical studies may provide a rough sketch map of the problem, not a detailed guide. So while Radday's work points to J and E's having a unified origin, it does not demonstrate this unequivocally. Whether such a view ultimately prevails depends on critics being persuaded that passages traditionally ascribed to different sources make good, coherent sense when read as a unity.

Though E seems to be making an exit from Genesis there are some recent studies which presuppose it. One may cite Jenks (1977), Weimar (1977), Klein (1977), and Zenger (1982) among recent studies, as well as many articles and most introductions to the OT. So E could yet make a comeback.

P (The Priestly Source)

BIBLIOGRAPHY

Haran, M. *Temples and Temple Service in Ancient Israel.* Oxford: Clarendon Press, 1978. ———. "Behind the Scenes of History: Determining the Date of the Priestly Source." *JBL* 100 (1981) 321–33. **Hildebrand, D. R.** "A Summary of Recent Findings in Support of an Early Date for the So-called Priestly Material in the Pentateuch." *JETS* 29 (1986) 129–38. **Hurvitz, A.** *A Linguistic Study of the Relationship between the Priestly Source and the Book of Ezekiel: A New Approach to an Old Problem.* Paris: Gabalda, 1982. **Kikawada, I. M.,** and **A. Quinn.** *Before Abraham Was: The Unity of Genesis 1–11.* Nashville: Abingdon Press, 1985. **Külling, S. R.** *Zur Datierung der "Genesis-P-Stücke," namentlich des Kapitels Genesis 17.* Kampen: Kok, 1964. **Milgrom, J.** *Studies in Cultic Theology and Terminology.* SJLA 36. Leiden: Brill, 1983. **Rendsburg, G. A.** "Late Biblical Hebrew and the Date of 'P'." *JANESCU* 12 (1980) 65–80. ———. "A New Look at Pentateuchal HWꞋ." *Bib* 63 (1982) 351–69. **Weinfeld, M.** *Deuteronomy and the Deuteronomic School.* Oxford: Clarendon Press, 1972. ———. "Old Testament—The Discipline and Its Goals." *Congress Volume, 1980.* VTSup 32. Leiden: Brill, 1981. 423–34. **Zevit, Z.** "Converging Lines of Evidence Bearing on the Date of P." *ZAW* 94 (1982) 481–511.

Of all the pentateuchal sources, P was the most precisely defined, and disagreements about its limits were minor. Though less material in Genesis is ascribed to P than to J or E, it occurs mostly in discrete blocks; whole chapters, e.g., 1, 5, 17, 23, are ascribed to P. Close interweaving of P with other sources, e.g., as in Gen 6–9, is unusual. It has also, since Wellhausen, been regarded as the latest of the sources, though many earlier scholars regarded it as earlier than J.

By and large, most scholars have been content with this traditional view of P as a late documentary source. However, questions have been raised in three areas. Is all the P material from the same source? Is P a document or is it an editorial layer? Here again the suggestion of a supplementary hypothesis is reappearing. Finally, is P a late source from exilic times, or does it come from much earlier? Especially in connection with P's cultic regulations, several recent works have argued that P reflects first-temple practice and must come from that period. We shall examine these points in turn.

The analysis of the flood story in Gen 6–9 into J and P used to be hailed as "a masterpiece of modern criticism" (Gunkel). However, several studies (see bibliography of 6:9–9:29; Anderson [1978], Wenham [1978], Longacre [1979], recently followed by Kikawada [1985], Larsson [1985], and Rendsburg [1986]), independently argued for the literary integrity of these chapters, which makes their dissection into two parallel accounts much more problematic. Attempts to reassign other parts of P to other sources have been rare: most striking is Rendtorff's (1976) assault on the assumption that Gen 23 belongs to P, and Radday's (1982, 1985) questioning of the methods used to identify P: the latter holds that genre differences are a sufficient explanation of the stylistic differences between J and P.

More widespread doubts have been expressed about whether P constitutes an independent document, or whether it is really little more than editorial additions to an earlier J or JE document. Cross (1973) holds that P was never an independent narrative document, but just a later edition of the JE Pentateuch. Rendtorff (1976) too inclines to see the P material in terms of editorial additions. Tengström (1981) also argues that P is essentially an editorial layer: he even finds evidence of P's rearranging material that is usually considered pure J. However, he does not think P was the main editor of the Pentateuch.

Finally, the date of P has been debated. Most of those arguing for P's antiquity have arrived at their conviction on the basis of the cultic regulations found in Exodus to Numbers: they hold that the institutions of P simply do not fit what is known of the post-exilic period (e.g., Weinfeld, [1972], Haran [1978], Milgrom [1983]). Others, though, have proposed an early date of P on the basis of its language (e.g., Rendsburg [1980, 1982], Hurvitz [1982], Zevit [1982]). Few of these writers give detailed attention to the date of the P material found in Genesis: it is just a corollary of their view that if the cultic laws in P date from the monarchy period so do the narratives found in Genesis. This would make P of similar age to J. Finally, two works arguing that P is even earlier may be noted. Külling (1964) showed in detail the weakness of the standard arguments for a late date of P in Genesis, though his proofs of its second-millennium origin are less cogent. Recently Alexander (1982, 1983) has argued that Gen 22 (J or E) presupposes Gen 17 (P), which suggests to him that at least some of P antedates J.

The New Literary Criticism

BIBLIOGRAPHY

Alonso Schökel, L. "Of Methods and Models." *Congress Volume, 1983.* VTSup 36. Leiden: Brill, 1985. 3–13. **Alter, R.** *The Art of Biblical Narrative.* New York: Basic Books, 1981. **Berlin, A.** *Poetics and Interpretation of Biblical Narrative.* Sheffield: Almond Press, 1983. **Fishbane, M.** *Text and Texture.* New York: Schocken, 1979. **Fokkelmann, J. P.** *Narrative Art in Genesis.* Assen: Van Gorcum, 1975. **Good, E. M.** *Irony in the Old*

Testament. London: SPCK, 1965. **Licht, J.** *Storytelling in the Bible.* Jerusalem: Magnes Press, 1978. **McEvenue, S. E.** *The Narrative Style of the Priestly Writer.* AnBib 50. Rome: Biblical Institute Press, 1971. **Redford, D. B.** *A Study of the Biblical Story of Joseph.* VTSup 20. Leiden: Brill, 1970. **Sternberg, M.** *The Poetics of Biblical Narrative.* Bloomington: Indiana UP, 1985. **Strus, A.** *Nomen-Omen.* AnBib 80. Rome: Biblical Institute Press, 1978. **Weiss, M.** *The Bible from Within.* Jerusalem: Magnes Press, 1984. **Williams, J. G.** *Women Recounted: Narrative Thinking and the God of Israel.* Sheffield: Almond Press, 1982. **Zakovitch, Y.** *"For Three . . . and for Four": The Pattern of the Numerical Sequence Three-Four in the Bible.* (Heb.) Jerusalem: Makor, 1979.

While traditional critical views of JEDP have been under debate using traditional critical methods of argument, a quite fresh look at Genesis has come from scholars concerned to appreciate it as a piece of literature in its own right. This is part of a strong interest in biblical narrative and its techniques that has come to the fore in the last decade. Clearly biblical storytellers were masters of the craft: even in translation the story of Joseph or Ruth or the parables of Jesus grip their hearers when read with sensitivity. What the secret of their craft was has barely been explored till recently; now there are so many studies that it is hard to keep up.

Good (*Irony in the Old Testament* [1965]) was a forerunner of the present wave of interest in storytelling technique. Among recent general studies of this area are Licht (1978), Alter (1981), Berlin (1983), and Sternberg (1985), all of which illustrate their discussions from Genesis. Several monographs and theses have been devoted to explicating the narrative structure of parts of Genesis itself: for example, the Joseph story has been discussed in these terms by Redford (1970) and Coats (1976); the Jacob stories by Fokkelmann (1975) and Fishbane (1979); the Abraham cycle by Alexander (1982); the P material by McEvenue (1971); paronomasia and proper names by Strus (1978); and women by Williams (1982). Clines's *The Theme of the Pentateuch* (1978) is a particularly significant work which attempts to discover a theme or themes that unite the whole of the present Pentateuch. Clines argues that its theme is the partial fulfillment of the promises of blessing made to the patriarchs. All the material found in the present Pentateuch is included to show the gradual fulfillment of these promises: even the primeval history serves this end by showing man's need for divine blessing, a blessing that will ultimately restore man to what God intended when he created him. Besides these major studies, there has been a torrent of articles exploring the art and meaning of the Genesis stories from the perspective of the new literary criticism. Such has been the enthusiasm for this approach to Scripture that three new journals (*Semeia, JSOT, Prooftexts*) emphasizing these disciplines have been founded recently.

Though some of these literary studies have dealt with the interpretation of long, extended narratives, much attention has been paid to examining short stories and episodes within them. The use of dialogue and direct speech, techniques of mimesis and scenic composition, type scenes and key words, exact repetition and repetition with variation, the fondness for groups of three, the use of chiasmus and parallel-panel writing—all these devices and many others are the central concerns of the new literary criticism. Many of these points had been observed before in haphazard fashion by both medieval and more modern commentators such as Gunkel and Cassuto. Modern writers, though, are attempting to make these observations more thorough and systematic.

What most sets this approach apart from earlier critical writing, however, is its concentration on the present final form of the text. Without denying the presence of sources within the narrative, the new literary critic wants to understand how the final editor viewed his material and why he arranged it in the way he did. The new criticism aims to understand texts synchronically, that is, as coherent pieces of work written at a particular time; the older source criticism tended to think diachronically, that is, it asked how and when a work came into existence, what its sources were, and so on. This change in biblical study from the older diachronic approach to the modern synchronic approach mirrors a similar change of approach in linguistics. Until about fifty years ago, linguistics concentrated on language change, etymology, and grammatical and semantic innovation from one period to another. Modern linguistics is much more interested in exploring the nature of a particular language or dialect, with the problems of formulating its grammatical structure and defining the meaning of its words. Clearly, synchronic and diachronic approaches to languages and literatures are both valid and complementary. It is right both to explore the history of a language and the particular form it takes at one point in its history. Of necessity, though, synchronic study must take priority. One must understand a particular grammatical form or word in one dialect before comparing it with another. The same is true of texts. It is valid to interpret Chronicles or Luke as documents in their own right. It is equally valid to examine the writers' methods diachronically by seeing how they have used their putative sources, Kings and Mark. Many modern writers on Genesis would say that a similar relationship exists between the source-critical theories that led to the identification of JEDP and modern literary interpretation of the text of Genesis. Literary criticism tells us what the stories meant to the final editor; source criticism, how he composed Genesis.

Evaluation of Current Critical Positions

This brief survey of the current discussion of Genesis has shown how some of the most deeply rooted convictions of the critical consensus have been challenged in recent years. The extent and date of J, the existence of E, the date of P, even the standard criteria for source division have been questioned. This is certainly not the first time since Wellhausen that these theories have been rejected by some commentators, but in the past, rejection has usually come from orthodox Jews, conservative Christians, or others on the fringes of mainstream scholarship. The striking thing about the current debate is that it emanates from within the heart of critical orthodoxy; indeed the protagonists of new positions include some of the most respected names in pentateuchal scholarship. However, the present ferment among scholars working on the Pentateuch should not be misinterpreted. The typical OT introduction or critical commentary on Genesis tends to assume the JEDP theory in a fairly traditional form, and it still forms the heart of most lecture courses on the Pentateuch. No new consensus has evolved to replace Wellhausen's basic theory, so it still continues to be assumed by many scholars, though there is now widespread recognition of the hypothetical character of the results of modern criticism. Rendtorff (BZAW 147 [1976] 169) has observed: "We possess hardly any reliable criteria for the dating of pentateuchal literature. Every dating of the pentateuchal 'sources' rests on purely hypothetical assumptions, which ultimately only have any standing through the consensus of scholars." W. H. Schmidt laments the breakup of the consensus in his introduction: "How united was OT scholarship for so long, how deeply divided now! The change has come about at some vital points; what was more or less self-evident and undisputed has become doubtful . . . the connection of Deuteronomy with Josiah's reform, the early date of the Yahwist. Even the legitimacy of source division in the Pentateuch is contested" (*Einführung in das Alte Testament*, [Berlin: de Gruyter, 1979] v–vi). H. C. Schmid (1985) has distinguished four major approaches with minor variations current in Germany. This situation is one in which there is no king in OT scholarship. Everyone is doing what is right in his own eyes!

Writing a commentary on Genesis is thus a particularly awkward assignment at the moment. Discretion dictates a low profile. The safe option would be simply to list the various critical opinions and let the reader make up his own mind about the analysis and date of the sources and their redaction. I hope my statement of the various options under the heading *Form/Structure/ Setting* before each chapter is full and fair enough for this purpose. Yet since in the course of my study I have come to certain critical conclusions, albeit very hesitantly and tentatively, it has seemed sensible to put my own conclusions here. At least then readers may more easily discount my bias when working on the detailed parts of the commentary. I shall therefore review in turn the relationship of the new literary criticism and traditional source criticism, the number and extent of the sources, and finally their date and the date of Genesis.

Literary and Source Criticism

We have already observed that while some scholars are using the insights of literary criticism to revise the conclusions of the older source criticism, others are trying to maintain the JEDP analysis and graft onto them literary-critical approaches as a route to interpreting Genesis in its final form.

It is hypothetically possible that all the traditional source-critical theories about the composition of Genesis could coexist quite happily with the new literary approach. The JEDP theory explains how Genesis was written; the new literary criticism explains how the final editor understood and arranged his material. This is the position adopted by many devotees of the new criticism. But in fact this view is oversimple. There is some tension between the older source criticism and the newer literary criticism, because some of the old criteria for source division are seen quite differently by literary critics. Repetition, duplicate narratives, varying names of God, and other changes in vocabulary were typically seen as marks of different sources. But according to literary theory, such features may not be signs of a change of author but of the skill of one sophisticated author intent on holding his hearer's attention by recapitulating the story at key points (repetition) and by introducing subtle variation (contradictions). Van Seters and Coats in particular have allowed the insights of literary criticism to influence their source-critical judgments. Van Seters (1975) states explicitly that apparent duplication of narratives or changes in divine name are not sure guides to source analysis. He has sought to formulate new criteria for distinguishing sources within Genesis, following in the earlier footsteps of Redford (1970).

So in certain areas literary criticism is consciously affecting source-critical judgments. But it seems likely that this also may be happening at a less conscious level. One of the clear trends in source criticism is to magnify J at the expense of the other sources, and this may be partly due to commentators beginning to read Genesis holistically rather than as a collection of independent and poorly connected sources. But as yet this tendency is rather haphazard. Westermann and Coats, for example, while often making good use of literary methods, fail to read Genesis as a coherent unity. Rather they still see it as two works (J and P) running in tandem. They use one part of J to elucidate other parts of J, and parts of P to elucidate other P passages, but hardly ever is a J passage used to explain the meaning of a P passage or vice versa. This is a methodological blind spot. If a final redactor of Genesis worked with at least two sources J and P, he must have seen connections between the pieces of J and P that he arranged next to each other. It is the commentator's first duty to understand the present form of the text, what Genesis meant to its final editor or author. Then the commentator may embark on the task of defining the pre-existing sources used by the final editor and what they meant. This is a more hazardous operation since there is a greater element of conjecture involved. "The starting point should be the completed literary entities, i.e., the OT itself and its parts. From them one can then work backwards and ask questions about the redaction and the literary sources used by them. . . . From the relatively certain one can work back to the relatively uncertain. . . . The distinction between the certain and the uncertain has often been culpably neglected in OT scholarship in recent decades" (R. Smend, *Enstehung*, 11).

Our commentary therefore aims to discuss first what is certain, namely, the present form of the text, before tackling the less certain issues of sources and their redaction. This approach is not only sounder from the point of view of literary method, but also theologically. For at least two millennia, the Synagogue and then the Church read only the final form of the text. The final form was seen as the canonical and inspired text, on which the godly meditated and modeled their lives. The JEP versions of Abraham's life or the story of creation were known only as they were combined. It is the final text of Genesis that has inspired the faithful down the ages and fueled the imagination of poets and other writers, so it is essential to begin here.

Source Criticism

BIBLIOGRAPHY

Jacobsen, T. *The Sumerian King List.* Chicago: University of Chicago Press, 1939.
————. "The Eridu Genesis." *JBL* 100 (1981) 513–29. **Kikawada, I. M.** "Literary
Convention of the Primeval History." *AJBI* 1 (1975) 3–21. **Lambert, W. G.** "Babylonien
und Israel." *TRE* 5 (1979) 67–79. ————, and **A. R. Millard.** *Atrahasis.* Oxford: Clarendon Press, 1969. **Matouš, L.** "Die Urgeschichte der Menschheit im Atrahasis-Epos
und in der Genesis." *ArOr* 37 (1969) 1–7, 148. **Miller, P. D.** "Eridu, Dunnu, and
Babel: A Study in Comparative Mythology." *HAR* 9 (1985) 227–51. **Poebel, A.** *Historical
Texts.* Publications of the Babylonian Section, The University Museum 4.1. Philadelphia: University Museum, 1914. **Savasta, C.** "Alcune considerazioni sulla lista dei
discendenti dei figli di Noè." *RivB* 17 (1969) 89–102, 337–63. **Shea, W. H.** "A Comparison of Narrative Elements in Ancient Mesopotamian Creation-Flood Stories with Gen
1–9." *Origins* 11 (1984) 9–29. **Wenham, G. J.** "The Religion of the Patriarchs." In
Essays on the Patriarchal Narratives, ed. A. R. Millard and D. J. Wiseman. Leicester:
IVP, 1980. 157–88.

Recent scholarship has shown a marked preference for a simpler source-
critical analysis of Genesis. This is most obvious in the tendency to eliminate
the E source and to view the Joseph story as a substantial unity. And this is
a trend with which this commentary identifies. Literary explanations of doublets, variation of divine names, and to some extent theological emphases tend
to make redundant, if not implausible, many of the traditional arguments
for source analysis. Furthermore, the general parallel between Gen 1–11
and the Sumerian flood story and the particular Babylonian parallels with
the flood story suggest that the thematic unity of this biblical material antedates J or P. Most of the narratives in Genesis are so vivid and well told
that it seems high-handed to deny their substantial unity and split them up
into various much less fetching parts.

Nevertheless, within the gripping narratives that characterize most of the
book, certain sections stand out as quite different: the genealogies in chaps.
5 and 11, the table of nations in chap. 10, and the war against the eastern
kings in chap. 14 have a totally different feel about them. It seems likely
that they come from a source or sources different from the surrounding
materials. (Most of chaps. 5, 10, and 11 are traditionally P, and 14 is un-
attached). And when Gen 1–11 is compared with chaps. 12–50, a striking
difference emerges: chaps. 1–11 are full of parallels with Near Eastern tradition, so that it looks as though Genesis is reflecting these oriental ideas both
positively and negatively. But chaps. 12–50 are quite different. Abraham
and his descendants are the exclusive concern of these chapters: there is no
suggestion that the patriarchal stories are adaptations of well-known oriental
sagas, even though they occasionally mention customs and legal usages attested in other oriental texts. It therefore looks as though in the pre-literary
phase Gen 1–11 had a quite different tradition history from chaps. 12–50.
The opening chapters use and modify stories well diffused throughout the
ancient world, whereas the patriarchal stories with their focus on the origins
of the nations may be presumed to have been passed down within the

Israelite tribes. It seems likely then that a number of written and oral sources were used to compile Genesis.

Defining and identifying these sources is much more difficult. Ockham's razor "Do not multiply entities beyond necessity" and C. S. Lewis's complaint that biblical critics claim to see fern seed when they cannot spot an elephant ten yards away make me very cautious about complex source-critical analyses. That Genesis makes use of multiple sources is doubtless true, but it is much more difficult to be very specific about where one source ends and another source or editor begins.

This makes me dubious about the traditional documentary analysis that divides Genesis into three continuous strands, J, E, and P. As already pointed out, the existence of E is now widely questioned. This seems to me right. But I also doubt the view that J and P are two continuous written sources in their own right, or that P is an editorial layer grafted onto J. If we are to think in terms of two sources, J and P, it seems to me that their chronological order should be reversed, P being the earlier source and J the later one. This view was widely held before Wellhausen (P was described as the *Urschrift*, "original text"), and modern arguments for the relative antiquity of P (especially if they were combined with those for a later date of J) show that the sequence of P before J is not out of the question.

These general considerations, however, are not decisive in my judgment. It is the literary evidence of distinctly P passages that points most clearly toward P's priority. Here I shall refer briefly to the most striking passages; they are discussed more fully in the body of the commentary. Throughout Gen 5–11 it appears that J comments have been appended to P texts. Westermann observes this feature in the flood story. He notes that the P sections are by and large long blocks and the J passages seem to be inserted into them. He says that "J has been worked into P's basic material" (1:396). Because he assumed the priority of J, Westermann failed to draw the obvious conclusion from his observation.

Clearer still is the evidence of chap. 5. Here a very coherent genealogy usually ascribed to P is interrupted by a clearly J comment on Noah's name (5:29). J features are also in evidence in the introduction to the genealogy (5:1–2) and in the immediately following passage (6:1–8). On this view J has taken the genealogy (possibly P) added his own introduction and conclusion, and inserted a comment about the key figure in the genealogy.

Similarly, in the table of the nations, chap. 10, a fairly compact list of nations usually ascribed to P (10:2–7, 20, 22–23, 31–32) has been broken up by longish J additions (10:8–19, 21, 24–30). They are good reasons for holding with Savasta (1969) that J's editorial activity in Gen 10 is even more extensive than this conventional analysis suggests (see *Form/Structure/Setting* on 10:1–33). On Savasta's analysis it is clear that J is the final editor of Gen 10, but even on the conventional analysis it looks probable. J's additions to P reflect his special interest in Israel's neighbors, viz., the Egyptians, Canaanites, Assyrians, and Arabian tribes. What is more, these J insertions seem to reflect J's interest in the curse of Ham found in 9:25–27. Chap. 10 is arranged to illustrate its implications. Finally, the editorial unit 10:1–11:9 is again closed by a J passage, the tower of Babel episode, 11:1–9. The pattern of working here is similar to that in 5:1–6:8, and suggests that both reflect the same editorial hand.

To sum up: Within Genesis 2–11 it is agreed that J is the major contributor of material. Furthermore, it appears that J arranges and comments on material conventionally assigned to P, and this suggests that J is a later writer than P. However, that is not to say that J himself created the overall plot of these chapters.

Within Gen 1–11 at least, a good case can be made for supposing that both the basic outline of the primeval history and many elements within the stories existed prior to the major editorial work of J. This proto-J material consists not only of many elements conventionally ascribed to P but also parts of J itself. This is most clearly seen in the flood story. If the final form of the story, the P version, and the J version are compared with the Gilgamesh epic's account of the flood, it is apparent that the final form of the narrative is closer to the Gilgamesh version than the latter is to J or P. This implies (see Wenham [1978] and detailed discussion on chaps. 6–9) that the final editor of Gen 6–8 had before him a flood story containing much of J and P. It seems unlikely that he combined J and P himself, as the usual theory maintains, because the basic outline of the flood story in Genesis was already known in the second millennium b.c. in other parts of the ancient orient.

What is true of the flood story is true also of the basic plot of Gen 1–11. Pre-biblical accounts of primeval history include features from both the J and P parts of Gen 1–11.

In fact, the Atrahasis epic from the early second millennium shows that the basic plot of Gen 1–11 was already known then. The Atrahasis epic tells of the creation of mankind, then of various divine judgments on him, culminating in the flood which destroyed all but Atrahasis and his family, who escaped in a boat. As in Genesis they offer a sacrifice on leaving the ark. Clearly the Atrahasis epic shows that creation and flood were already part of a coherent story of world origins before Genesis was composed, but Kikawada's attempt (1975, 1985) to demonstrate that in overall structure Gen 1–11 parallels Atrahasis is not strong. He would like to show that Gen 1–11 (J and P) is a unity because of these extrabiblical parallels. But Atrahasis suggests rather that either J or P or J and P have second-millennium precursors.

More interesting in showing that Gen 1–11 (J and P) is a thematic unity are the observations of Matouš (1969) and Jacobsen (1981) who have, apparently independently, argued that the Sumerian flood story, renamed by Jacobsen the "Eridu Genesis," parallels P's version of Gen 1–11 very closely. Since the Sumerian flood story is roughly contemporary with Atrahasis, this led Matouš to argue for an early date for P, in the second millennium. He held J was later. However, Jacobsen does not draw such conclusions, since a copy of a bilingual version of the flood story from the seventh century b.c. is also known.

Jacobsen's reconstruction of the Sumerian flood story does not in our estimation support the view that it only parallels P: as Shea (1984) and Miller (1985) have noted, several features relate more closely to J. Jacobsen reconstructs his "Eridu Genesis" on the basis of the sole surviving tablet of the Sumerian flood story. This comes from Nippur and dates from *ca.* 1600 b.c.

The gaps in this tablet he supplements from another Sumerian text from Ur of approximately the same date (according to Jacobsen) and a much later (*ca.* 700 B.C., so Lambert) bilingual text from Ashurbanipal's library. What he calls the "Eridu Genesis" is thus a composite of three different texts. Even without supplementation from the other texts, the parallels between Gen 1–9 and the Sumerian flood story are clear: if Jacobsen's reconstruction is correct, the parallels in structure are quite close, as the following table shows.

Lines 1–36 (lost)	told of the creation of man and the animals, man's sad plight, no irrigation canals, no clothes, no fear of wild	(cf. Gen 1)
	animals, such as snakes	(cf. Gen 2–3)
37–50	The plan of the goddess Nintur (mother of mankind) to end man's nomadic exis-	(cf. Gen 3:20; 4:1)
	tence	(cf. Gen 4:1–16)
51–85 (lost)	The failure of Nintur's plan The establishment of kingship	
86–100	Building of first cities, includ-	
	ing Eridu	(cf. Gen 4:17–18)
	Establishment of worship	(cf. Gen 4:26)
101–134 (lost)	List of antediluvian kings	(cf. Gen 5)
	Man's noise	(cf. Gen 6:1–8)
135–260	The flood	(cf. Gen 6:9–9:29)

Three points should be made about this reconstruction. First, the aptness of the title "Eridu Genesis" is questionable; though the tradition may go back to the city of Eridu, there is no evidence that the text was either composed or copied there. I shall therefore continue to use the conventional title for the work, the Sumerian flood story. Second, the suggested content of lines 1–36 is uncertain. Given the reference to the creation of man and the animals in ll.47–50, ll.1–36 must have contained reference to this. Whether they also included a description of man's sad plight, his lack of clothes, the absence of irrigation canals, and no fear of wild animals, is more conjectural. Certainly the Ur tablet mentions these points, and they are well paralleled elsewhere, but that is not to say that the Sumerian flood story must have mentioned them at this point. Finally, the list of antediluvian kings that Jacobsen hypothesizes were mentioned in ll.101–34, is a strong possibility, though not proven. Earlier Lambert (*TRE* [1979] 75) had more cautiously suggested something similar. The fact that the antediluvian prologue to the Sumerian king list mentions the same five cities as those mentioned in the Sumerian flood story, ll.93–97, makes the suggestion an attractive one, as does their mention in the late Ashurbanipal tablet, but that does not conclusively prove that the full list of antediluvian kings appeared in the older Sumerian flood story. That this section contained a reference to man's noise which provoked the flood seems likely. (Cf. A 1.352–59.)

It it not my purpose here to evaluate the significance of this very important text for the interpretation of Gen 1–11. As Jacobsen points out the message of Gen 1–11 is very different from the Sumerian story despite many general points of similarity in the plot. What is interesting for the present is to note that no later than 1600 B.C. a story of origins was known in Mesopotamia that bears a striking resemblance to Genesis as it now stands. This makes it unlikely that the Genesis account was created by some editor who knitted together two independent Hebrew versions of origins (J and P). The outline of the plot antedates the work of the Hebrew writer. We therefore believe that the final editor, J, had before him an outline of primeval history, an abbreviated version of our present Gen 1–11, which he reworked to give the present form of text.

Poebel, the first editor of the Sumerian flood story suggested that it may have formed the prologue to a complete history of Babylon from the beginning to the first dynasty of Babylon (2000–1600 B.C.). In this case, as Miller (*HAR* 9 [1985] 234) observes: "The Eridu Genesis would provide an even more extensive analogue to the biblical narrative which, via genealogies (Gen 10) plus additional stories (i.e., Gen 11:1–9 and beyond) continues from the story of origins on down into later times, that is, to the present when the narrative came into being." But no literary texts have yet been discovered that make the Sumerian flood story part of a history of Mesopotamia from creation to the first dynasty of Babylon. The Sumerian king list, in the most complete version, the Weld-Blundell text, does include the list of antediluvian kings, then a mention of the flood, and the postdiluvian kings down to the Isin-Larsa period *ca.* 1980 B.C. First-millennium versions of the king list add yet later kings to the list. The normative character of the Sumerian king list within Mesopotamian thought is confirmed finally by the use that the Greek writer Berossus (*ca.* 300 B.C.) makes of this tradition. So certainly from the late third millennium B.C., attempts were made in Mesopotamia to write its history from antediluvian times to the present. Of course, the biblical Genesis has a quite different center of interest from Sumero-Babylonian tradition and places an entirely different interpretation on these primeval events, yet, as in the flood story, Gen 1–11 does seem to bear witness to an outline of earliest antiquity common to Babylon and Israel.

The patriarchal narratives again provide evidence for holding that J is the last major redactor of this material, whether individual stories are ascribed to J, E, or P. We have already noted how van Seters (1975) and Schmitt (1980) tend to make J the last major editor of the Abraham and Joseph stories, the subsequent contributions of P being quite minor. However, there are grounds here too for holding that the P sections antedate J's editorial activity (Wenham, "The Religion of the Patriarchs"). Throughout these stories the divine name "Yahweh" appears more frequently in the narrative sections than in the dialogue; and it is particularly noticeable that "Yahweh" is used at the beginning and end of scenes, which suggests that their editor was J. A number of other problems concerning the history of patriarchal religion admit of relatively straightforward solution if J is seen as the last of the sources rather than the first (e.g., Exod 6:3.) It has also been noted that Gen 22 (J-edited) seems to tell of the ratification of the covenant promise in Gen 17 (P; Alexander, 1983).

All these considerations seem to point toward J's being the last major redactor of the Genesis traditions. Who and what preceded him is much more difficult to say. Should one postulate a documentary source like P that

J subsequently expanded? Some of the literary evidence cited above is compatible with such a view. However, the P material is often so sketchy that it hardly seems a viable entity in its own right. Further, it contains such diverse material (cf. chap. 5 with chap. 17) that to ascribe them both to the same document, while possible, only introduces an unnecessary extra stage into the history of the tradition. It would be easier to see chaps. 5 and 17 as separate sources, "fragments," in their own right. Both could have been taken over and used directly by J. Similarly, there is a vast amount of material in J that seems unlikely to have been invented by him, however much he edited it, and it is possible that it too is based on a diversity of sources (cf. chaps. 2–3, 14, 24). In short, if the J material goes back to a variety of fragmentary sources, and the material conventionally called P also derives from a diversity of sources, may it not be possible to see Genesis as basically the work of J who used a number of relatively short sources to compose his volume? In Gen 1–11 we suggested that one major source (proto-J) has been expanded by J to form the present text. We argued this on the basis of Mesopotamian parallels. Rendtorff has posited a similar situation with each of the other major blocks of material—the Abraham stories, the Jacob stories, and the Joseph story. A primitive account of each of these patriarchs has been expanded by various editors and then linked up. Rendtorff's scheme, though, is relatively complicated and hard to prove because, unlike the primeval history, there are no extrabiblical accounts of the patriarchs. His refusal to identify the editor with J is also unsatisfactory. Nevertheless it does seem right to look again at the old documentary hypothesis and reconsider a fragmentary and supplementary view of the composition of Genesis while holding onto J as the most significant editor of the book. Whether the sources used by J were written or oral is moot. Genesis is a written work but one designed for oral recitation. How far its oral qualities are the work of J's genius, or how far it reflects the materials he used, is again difficult to say.

Date

BIBLIOGRAPHY

See also bibliography on J.

Bimson, J. J. *Redating the Exodus and Conquest.* JSOTSS 5. Sheffield: JSOT Press, 1978. **Lambert, W. G.** "Babylonien und Israel." *TRE* 5 (1979) 67–79. ———. "Old Testament Mythology in Its Ancient Near Eastern Context." VTSup (forthcoming). **Mazar, B.** "The Historical Background of the Book of Genesis." *JNES* 28 (1969) 73–83. **Millard, A. R.,** and **D. J. Wiseman.** *Essays on the Patriarchal Narratives.* Leicester: IVP, 1980. **Thompson, T. L.** *The Historicity of the Patriarchal Narratives.* BZAW 133. Berlin: de Gruyter, 1974. **Wenham, G. J.** "The Date of Deuteronomy: Linch-Pin of Old Testament Criticism." *Them* 10.3 (1985) 15–20; 11.1 (1985) 15–18.

The date of J is another very moot question. For most of this century the consensus has been that it is a tenth-century work dating from the reigns of

David and Solomon. In favor of a view that places the composition of J in the tenth century B.C. it was argued (1) that the prophetic passages in Genesis (e.g., about the borders of Israel, 15:18–21, and the rise of the Davidic monarchy 49:10; cf. chap. 38) point to such a date; (2) that the genealogical relationships between the patriarchs (e.g., Esau and Jacob) mirror the political alliances between Israel and its neighbors in the tenth century B.C.; (3) that the narratives reflect a period when tribal divisions were important but not bitter, and when northern sanctuaries, e.g., Bethel and Shechem, were still regarded as respectable, attitudes which changed radically in the southern kingdom after the division of the monarchy; and finally, (4) that the wealth and culture of the united monarchy age make it a likely period in which to compile a history of national origins. These considerations, it was held, pointed to a *terminus ad quem* for J of about 900 B.C.

Although a tenth-century date for J was part of standard critical theory, it was not held that J was invented then. Rather, J rests on much older traditions that reflect accurately the situation in the early second millennium B.C. The names of the patriarchs are typical of this period; the legal customs, especially in the area of family law, reflect the practice of the second millennium; the religious outlook and practices of the patriarchs fit this period too. So although J was regarded as a relatively late composition, nearly a thousand years after the events it describes, it was surprisingly reliable where it could be checked. But as Rendtorff (1976) has pointed out, this was just a consensus: there are really very few clear indications of the material's date. As already mentioned, there have been several attempts to date J another half a millennium later (see bibliography on J). But the archeological evidence for a late date is not very convincing either, nor do the literary arguments for a late date, J's affinity with Deuteronomy, really carry conviction. Again the date of Deuteronomy is largely a matter of consensus rather than proof, and even if its usual date is correct, one might suggest that J inspired Deuteronomy's language and ideology. And though Genesis and Deuteronomy share a common belief in the divine gift of the land of Canaan and in the LORD's unique covenant relationship with Israel, at other points they are ideologically poles apart. Genesis portrays the patriarchs living fairly harmoniously with the Canaanites, worshiping at their holy places, and indeed from time to time the LORD calls himself El, the supreme God of the Canaanite pantheon. Deuteronomy, on the other hand, is passionately opposed to allowing the Canaanites to live alongside Israel and insists on their destruction and particularly the destruction of their shrines and all their religious practices. These differences of emphasis surely suggest that Genesis and Deuteronomy are addressing quite different situations, rather than that both come from the same circle of writers working in the late seventh/early sixth centuries B.C. At least the protagonists of J's lateness have not proved that Deuteronomic ideas influenced J rather than vice versa. So there is no good reason to date J later than the united monarchy period.

Whether it need be as late as this is uncertain. Though the archeological arguments for the early second millennium origin of the material (historical traditions, patriarchal names, legal customs, and so on) are not as strong as once held (here Thompson's [1974] treatment is judicious), most of the patriarchal material looks more at home in the second millennium than in the first (see Millard and Wiseman [1980]).

The same may be said of the relationship of Gen 1–11 to antecedent Near Eastern tradition. Lambert (*TRE* 5 [1979] 70–71) has observed that it is most unlikely that the Mesopotamian traditions reflected in these chapters were transmitted to Israel after the second millennium B.C. If knowledge of these ideas does not go back to the patriarchs—the simplest hypothesis—the most likely period for the Hebrews to have become aware of them is the Amarna period (*ca.* 1400 B.C.) and shortly afterwards. In this era Mesopotamian culture was widely diffused in the West (a fragment of the Gilgamesh epic has been found at Megiddo and a piece of a flood story at Ras Shamra). But in the twelfth century, the invasions of the sea-peoples in the West and the Aramaeans in the East broke up this international cultural interchange, so that it seems unlikely that the Hebrews would have absorbed Mesopotamian ideas after this upheaval. Lambert holds that it is particularly unlikely that the Jews would have accepted aspects of Babylonian mythology during the exile. The time span was too short, and the spiritual leaders of the Jews, e.g., Ezekiel and Ezra, were aggressively opposed to syncretism in all its forms: that, they held, was why Israel succumbed to the Babylonians. It is most unlikely that they should have incorporated Mesopotamian mythology, even reinterpreted monotheistically, into their Scriptures in such an environment. Furthermore, Genesis' knowledge of Mesopotamian ideas is too vague and diffuse to suggest that it had been acquired by a Jewish exile undergoing a crash course in Babylonian mythology at some scribal school. Though Genesis often addresses topics similar to those in Babylonian sources, the story line and the names are usually quite different. This suggests that, as far as Gen 1–11 is concerned, the point of contact between Israel and Babylon lies far back in the distant past, not in the sixth century B.C., and that these similarities arise from oral transmission, not through Hebrews studying Mesopotamian literature.

We have noted that the overall structure of the material in Gen 1–11 finds its closest parallels in the Sumerian flood story and the Sumerian king list, and in the Atrahasis epic, all dated to 1600 B.C. or earlier. But, clearly, Genesis could not have been written until after Joseph, indeed until after the exodus, since Genesis is the first volume of the Pentateuch. And as we shall argue, Genesis is not merely an extrinsic prologue to the other books of the Pentateuch; many of its stories from chap. 1 onward look forward to institutions of the Mosaic era. So on a conventional date for the exodus and conquest, which is again controversial (Bimson, 1978), Genesis could not have been put into literary form before about 1250 B.C. nor much after 950 B.C. Certain well-known post-Mosaica in Genesis do point to a later revision of the material, if an early date within this time span is preferred. (The references to Canaanites [13:7], Ur of the Chaldees [15:7], and kings in Israel [36:31] are the most obvious late features.) Whether this late reviser is to be identified with J or someone else is unclear. But whether a very early date, e.g., thirteenth century, for J, the main redactor of Genesis, or a later date, e.g. tenth century, makes relatively little difference to the question of the reliability of the traditions enshrined in Genesis. At least four hundred years separate the origins of the latest traditions of Genesis from the time they were committed to writing by J or proto-J. This is an enormous time span for oral tradition to be accurately preserved. That these stories, at least where they can be checked, do seem to reflect accurately the situation in about the early second millennium speaks highly of the reliability of that tradition.

Theology of Genesis 1–11

To deal adequately with the theology of Gen 1–11 would require a book of its own. Here my aim is much more modest, to discuss very briefly the theological relationship of these chapters, first, to ancient Near Eastern ideas, second, to Gen 12–50 and the rest of the Pentateuch, and finally, to modern thought. I hope thereby to help readers orient themselves to the material in the commentary that follows, so that he or she may be able to distinguish the wood from the trees, that is, to pick out the larger theological principles from the minutiae of detailed exegesis. Modern man makes assumptions about the world that are completely different from those of the second millennium B.C. Consequently when we read Genesis, we tend to grab hold of points that were of quite peripheral interest to the author of Genesis and we overlook points that are fundamental. By looking at the oriental background and the place of Gen 1–11 within the whole book, we hope to escape this particular pitfall and understand Genesis as it was originally intended.

An examination of the relationship between Gen 1–11 and earlier oriental tradition sheds much light on the background to biblical thought and highlights the distinctiveness of its message. Though Genesis shares many of the theological presuppositions of the ancient world, most of the stories found in these chapters are best read as presenting an alternative world-view to those generally accepted in the ancient Near East. Gen 1–11 is a tract for the times, challenging ancient assumptions about the nature of God, the world, and mankind.

Though Christian theologians have devoted most of their attention to Gen 1–11 or more precisely Gen 1–3, the rest of the book has been comparatively neglected, although it is about four times as long as the opening chapters. The balance of material in Genesis shows where the editor's interest lies, with the patriarchs rather than with the primeval history. Clearly Gen 1–11 serves simply as background to the subsequent story of the patriarchs, and their history is in turn background to the story of Israel's exodus from Egypt and the lawgiving at Sinai which forms the subject matter of Exodus to Deuteronomy. But is the primeval history related simply to emphasize the need for a new beginning with the patriarchs, to show that because sin has such disastrous consequences God must step in to restore the situation? Or do these chapters of Genesis not only disclose man's sinfulness, but the divine ideals for mankind which one day will be achieved when the promises to Abraham and his seed are fulfilled? It is this sort of question that needs further discussion, if we are to grasp the author's intention in writing these chapters.

My overriding goal, like that of most academic commentators, is thus to discover the original meaning of Genesis, what it meant to its final editor and its first readers. An understanding of ancient oriental mythology is essential if we are to appreciate the points Gen 1–11 was making then, as too is a grasp of the relationship between its opening chapters and the patriarchal narratives. But we modern readers with a world-view molded by modern science find it hard to relate Genesis to the rest of our thinking. It is my conviction that many of our problems are caused by misunderstanding the original intentions of Genesis. When the editor's major points are grasped, many of the clashes between his world-view and ours are eliminated. Nevertheless, problems do remain, and it is the purpose of the final section of this introduction to list some possible approaches to their resolution.

Gen 1–11 and the Ancient Near East

BIBLIOGRAPHY

See also chapter bibliographies.

Albertz, R. "Die Kulturarbeit im Atramhasis im Vergleich zur biblischen Urgeschichte." In *Werden und Wirken des Alten Testaments: FS für C. Westermann,* ed. R. Albertz. Göttingen: Vandenhoeck & Ruprecht, 1979. 38–57. **Albright, W. F.** "The Babylonian Matter in Gen 1–11." *JBL* 58 (1939) 91–103. **Attridge, H. W.,** and **R. A. Oden.** *Philo of Byblos: The Phoenician History.* CBQMS 9. Washington: Catholic Biblical Association of America, 1981. **Dijk, J. van.** "Existe-t-il un 'poème de la création' sumérien?" In *Kramer Anniversary Volume: Cuneiform Studies in Honor of S. N. Kramer,* ed. B. L. Eichler, J. W. Heimerdinger, and A. W. Sjöberg. AOAT 25. Neukirchen: Neukirchener Verlag, 1976. 125–33. **Drews, R.** "The Babylonian Chronicles and Berossus." *Iraq* 37 (1975) 39–55. **Ebach, J. H.** *Weltentstehung und Kulturentwicklung bei Philo von Byblos.* Stuttgart: Kohlhammer, 1979. **Finkel, I. L.** "Bilingual Chronicle Fragments." *JCS* 32 (1980) 65–80. **Finkelstein, J. J.** "The Antediluvian Kings: A University of California Tablet." *JCS* 17 (1963) 39–51. **Frymer-Kensky, T.** "The Atrahasis Epic and Its Significance for Our Understanding of Gen 1–9." *BA* 40 (1977) 147–55. **Grønbaek, J. H.** "Baal's Battle with Yam—A Canaanite Creation Fight." *JSOT* 33 (1985) 27–44. **Hallo, W. W.** "Antediluvian Cities." *JCS* 23 (1970) 57–67. **Harrelson, W.** "The Significance of Cosmology in the Ancient Near East." In *Translating and Understanding the Old Testament: Essays in Honor of H. G. May,* ed. H. T. Frank and W. L. Reed. Nashville: Abingdon Press, 1970. 237–52. **Heidel, A.** *The Gilgamesh Epic and Old Testament Parallels.* 2d ed. Chicago: University Press, 1949. **Kapelrud, A. S.** "Baal, Schöpfung und Chaos." *UF* 11 (1979) 407–12. ———. "Creation in the Ras Shamra Texts." *ST* 34 (1980) 1–11. **Kikawada, I. M.** "The Double Creation of Mankind in 'Enki and Ninmah,' 'Atrahasis I, 1–351' and 'Gen 1–2.' " *Iraq* 45 (1983) 43–45. **Killmer, A. D.** "The Mesopotamian Concept of Overpopulation and Its Solution as Reflected in Mythology." *Or* 41 (1972) 160–77. **Kümmel, H. M.** "Bemerkungen zu den altorientalischen Berichten von Menschenschöpfung." *WO* 7 (1973–74) 25–38. **Lambert, W. G.** "A New Look at the Babylonian Background of Genesis." *JTS* 16 (1965) 287–300. ———. "New Evidence for the First Line of *Atrahasis.*" *Or* 38 (1969) 533–38. ———. "A New Fragment from a List of Antediluvian Kings and Marduk's Chariot." In *Symbolae Biblicae et Mesopotamicae F. M. T. de L. Böhl dedicatae,* ed. M. A. Beek, A. A. Kampman, C. Nijland, and J. Ryckmans. Leiden: Brill, 1973. 271–80. ———. "New Fragments of Babylonian Epics." *AfO* 27 (1980) 71–82. **Margalit, B.** "Weltbaum and Weltberg in Ugaritic Literature: Notes and Observations on RŠ 24.245." *ZAW* 86 (1974) 1–23. ———. "The Ugaritic Creation Myth: Fact or Fiction." *UF* 13 (1981) 137–41.

Millard, A. R. "A New Babylonian 'Genesis' Story." *TB* 18 (1967) 3–18. **Moran, W. L.** "The Creation of Man in Atrahasis 1:192–248." *BASOR* 200 (1970) 48–56. ————. "Atrahasis: The Babylonian Story of the Flood." *Bib* 52 (1971) 51–61. **Neiman, D.** "The Supercaelian Sea." *JNES* 28 (1969) 243–49. **Notter, V.** *Biblischer Schöpfungsbericht und ägyptische Schöpfungsmythen.* SBS 68. Stuttgart: KBW Verlag, 1974. **O'Brien, J.,** and **W. Major.** *In the Beginning: Creation Myths from Ancient Mesopotamia, Israel and Greece.* Chico: Scholars Press, 1982. **Oden, R. A.** "Transformations in Near Eastern Myths: Gen 1–11 and the Old Babylonian Epic of Atrahasis." *Rel* 11 (1981) 21–37. ————. "Divine Aspirations in Atrahasis and in Gen 1–11." *ZAW* 93 (1981) 197–216. **Ohler, A.** "Die biblische Deutung des Mythos: Zur Deutung von Gen 1–3." *TRev* 66 (1970) 177–84. **Oswalt, J. N.** "The Myth of the Dragon and Old Testament Faith." *EvQ* 49 (1977) 163–72. **Otzen, B., H. Gottlieb,** and **K. Jeppesen.** *Myths in the Old Testament.* London: SCM Press, 1980. **Pettinato, G.** "Die Bestrafung des Menschengeschlechts durch die Sintflut." *Or* 37 (1968) 165–200. **Picchioni, S. A.** *Il Poemetto di Adapa.* Budapest: 1981. **Rapaport, I.** *The Babylonian Poem "Enuma Elish" and Genesis Chapter One.* Melbourne: Hawthorn Press, 1979. **Reiner, E.** "The Etiological Myth of the 'Seven Sages.'" *Or* 30 (1961) 1–11. **Ringgren, H.** "Remarks on the Methods of Comparative Mythology." In *Near Eastern Studies in Honor of W. F. Albright,* ed. H. Goedicke. Baltimore: Johns Hopkins Press, 1971. 407–11. **Roberts, J. J. M.** "Myth *versus* History: Relaying the Comparative Foundations." *CBQ* 38 (1976) 1–13. **Sjöberg, A. W.** "Eve and the Chameleon." In *In the Shelter of Elyon: Essays in Honor of G. W. Ahlström,* ed. W. B. Barrick and J. R. Spencer. JSOTSS 31. Sheffield: JSOT Press, 1984. 217–25. **Soden, W. von.** " 'Als die Götter (auch noch) Mensch waren.' Einige Grundgedanken des altbabylonischen Atramhasis-Mythus." *Or* 38 (1969) 415–32. ————. "Grundsätzliches zur Interpretation des babylonischen Atramhasis-Mythus." *Or* 39 (1970) 311–14. ————. "Der Mensch bescheidet sich nicht: Überlegungen zu Schöpfungserzählungen in Babylonien und Israel." In *Symbolae biblicae et mesopotamicae: F. M. T. de Liagre Bohl dedicatae.* Leiden: Brill, 1973, 349–58. ————. "Die erste Tafel des altbabylonischen Atramhasis-Mythus: 'Haupttext' und Parallelversionen." *ZA* 68 (1978) 50–94. ————. "Konflikte und ihre Bewältigung in babylonische Schöpfungs- und Fluterzählungen." *MDOG* 111 (1979) 1–33. ————. "Mottoverse zu Beginn babylonischer und antiker Epen, Mottosätze in der Bibel." *UF* 14 (1982) 235–39. **Tobin, T. H.** *The Creation of Man: Philo and the History of Interpretation.* CBQMS 14. Washington: Catholic Biblical Association of America, 1983. **Veenker, R. A.** Gilgamesh and the Magic Plant. *BA* 44 (1981) 199–205. **Wakeman, M. K.** *God's Battle with the Monster: A Study in Biblical Imagery.* Leiden: Brill, 1973. **Wilson, R. R.** *Genealogy and History in the Biblical World.* New Haven: Yale UP, 1977.

Gen 1–11 as we read it is a commentary, often highly critical, on ideas current in the ancient world about the natural and supernatural world. Both individual stories as well as the final completed work seem to be a polemic against many of the commonly received notions about the gods and man. But the clear polemical thrust of Gen 1–11 must not obscure the fact that at certain points biblical and extrabiblical thought are in clear agreement. Indeed Genesis and the ancient Near East probably have more in common with each other than either has with modern secular thought.

It has already been mentioned that Gen 1–9 records a bare outline of world history from its creation to the flood that finds a parallel in the Atrahasis epic and even more strikingly in the Sumerian flood story. Within this bare outline the stories of the flood in Gilgamesh (perhaps borrowed from a lost

edition of the Atrahasis epic) and in Gen 6–9 are astonishingly similar. This
is not to say that the writer of Genesis had ever heard or read the Gilgamesh
epic: these traditions were part of the intellectual furniture of that time in
the Near East, just as most people today have some idea of Darwin's *Origin
of Species* though they have never read it.

Not only does Genesis share a common outline of primeval history with
its neighbors, it also concurs with contemporary culture on various other
points. Both agreed that an invisible supernatural world existed; that a God
or gods existed; were personal; could think, speak, and communicate with
men; indeed control human affairs. Genesis also agreed with oriental theology
that man is more than material: he has a spiritual divine dimension. Atrahasis
tells of man being made out of the mixture of clay and the flesh and blood
of a dead god (A 1.208–60). This parallels Gen 2:7 where the LORD creates
man out of the dust of the earth and breathes into him the divine breath of
life. Similarly, Egyptian texts speak of man being made in the image of God
(cf. Gen 1:26–27). Creation as an act of separation between light and darkness,
land and sea, and by the word of God all find parallels in Near Eastern
theology (see Westermann 1:25–47).

These similarities between biblical and non-biblical thinking, however, are
overshadowed by the differences. Jacobsen points out that despite Genesis's
"probable dependency on the Mesopotamian version of origins" we must
also note how decisively these materials have been transformed in the biblical
account, altering radically their original meaning and import.

> The "Eridu Genesis" takes throughout . . . an affirmative and optimistic view
> of existence: it believes in progress. Things were not nearly as good to begin with
> as they have become since. . . .
> In the biblical account it is the other way around. Things began as perfect
> from God's hand and grew then steadily worse through man's sinfulness until
> God finally had to do away with all mankind except for the pious Noah who
> would beget a new and better stock.
> The moral judgment here introduced, and the ensuing pessimistic viewpoint,
> could not be more different from the tenor of the Sumerian tale; only the assurance
> that such a flood will not recur is common to both (*JBL* 100 [1981] 529).

It is striking that Jacobsen arrives at this contrast by comparing the "Eridu
Genesis," his expanded flood story, with P, which is generally seen as much
more optimistic about the human situation than J. But the biblical Genesis
as it stands contains all sorts of other episodes illustrating man's sinfulness:
the fall (chap. 3), Cain and Abel (chap. 4), the sons of God (6:1–4), the
curse of Ham (9:20–29), and the tower of Babel (11:1–9). These incidents,
when added to the P outline of world history, make the situation even blacker
and the contrast with the Sumerian flood story even more stark. Genesis is
flatly contradicting the humanistic optimism of Mesopotamia: humanity's situation in its view is hopeless without divine mercy.

Many of the individual episodes in Gen 1–11 may be seen to have a distinctly
polemical thrust in their own right, particularly against the religious ideas
associated most closely with Mesopotamia. For example, Gen 11:1–9, the
tower of Babel story, is a satire on the claims of Babylon to be the center of

civilization and its temple tower the gate of heaven (EE 6:50–80): Babel does not mean gate of God, but "confusion" and "folly." Far from its temple's top reaching up to heaven, it is so low that God has to descend from heaven just to see it! (11:4–9).

Babylonians and Canaanites practiced cult prostitution and sacred marriage, a fertility rite in which it is commonly supposed that the gods had sexual union with women. These rites were believed to promote the well-being of the nation by securing the fertility of the soil. Gen 6:1–8, however, looks on such customs with absolute horror: instead of promoting mankind's prosperity they prompted God to send the flood which destroyed all life, except Noah's family and the animals he brought into the ark.

Mesopotamian accounts of the flood not only provide some of the closest parallels between the Bible and oriental literature, they also paint a completely different picture of the relationship between the human and divine worlds. They tell that the flood was sent by the gods piqued at man's noisiness and overpopulation of the earth. The Babylonian "Noah" escaped because he happened to worship a god who did not support the flood decision. Once started, the flood was beyond the gods' control, and they were terrified by it. In the closing scene, Enlil, the most powerful god, turns up at the sacrifice and is surprised to find "Noah" still alive. Genesis, while preserving a substantially similar story, paints a very different portrait of the actors involved. There is only one God, who is both omniscient and omnipotent. The flood is sent by his command and is totally under his control. Whereas the Mesopotamian gods destroyed mankind out of caprice and their "Noah" just happened to be lucky enough to worship the right deity, Genesis declares that man's wickedness provoked the flood and that Noah was saved because he was righteous, a point demonstrated by his behavior throughout the flood. Finally, whereas after the flood the Mesopotamian deities looked for means to limit population growth, the LORD positively encouraged it. Noah, like Adam, was told, "Be fruitful and multiply" (Gen 9:1, 7; cf. 1:28).

In a similar way it seems that Gen 1–3 takes up ideas current in the ancient world and comments on them. Gen 1 again affirms the unity of God over against the polytheisms current everywhere else in the ancient Near East. In particular it insists that the sun, moon, stars, and sea monsters—powerful deities according to pagan mythology—are merely creatures. It may well be that Gen 1:1, "God created the heavens and the earth," is affirming the creation of matter over against the widely held view of the time that matter was eternal and that creation just involved the ordering of pre-existing matter. (See further discussion on 1:1.) Certainly Genesis gives man a very different place in the created order from that given him by oriental mythology. Man was according to this view created by the gods as an afterthought to supply the gods with food (A 1.190–91; EE 6:35–37). Gen 1 paints a quite contrary picture. Man is the climax of creation, and instead of man providing the gods with food, God provided the plants as food for man (1:29). The same theme of the LORD's concern for man's welfare is very apparent in Gen 2. Here he first creates man, then provides him with a garden to dwell in, with animals as his companions, and last of all, a wife. Finally, according to one Babylonian tradition, the seventh, fourteenth, nineteenth, twenty-first, and twenty-eighth days of each month were regarded as unlucky: Genesis, however, declares the seventh day of every week to be holy, a day of rest consecrated to God (2:1–3).

Gen 2–3 lacks good oriental parallels, though Jacobsen holds that the Sumerian flood story began by telling of an era when men went naked and enjoyed peace with other men and the animals. This was viewed not as an idyllic age but as a miserable, poverty-struck existence from which the goddess Nintur rescued humankind. The closest comparison that can be made is with the Adapa myth (*ANET*, 100–103). Adapa (note the similarity of the name to the name *Adam*) was probably the first of the seven sages of Mesopotamia. One day Adapa was summoned to heaven and there offered the bread and water of life, but he declined, having previously been warned by his personal god to reject such an offer. If we read the fall story in the light of this parallel, we see that Genesis could be saying that the first man, far from demonstrating his wisdom by obeying God, showed his sinfulness by doing what had been forbidden. Certainly Gen 2–3 puts early man's exploits in a very negative light when compared with the Sumerian tradition.

The ancient oriental background to Gen 1–11 shows it to be concerned with rather different issues from those that tend to preoccupy modern readers. It is affirming the unity of God in the face of polytheism, his justice rather than his caprice, his power as opposed to his impotence, his concern for mankind rather than his exploitation. And whereas Mesopotamia clung to the wisdom of primeval man, Genesis records his sinful disobedience. Because as Christians we tend to assume these points in our theology, we often fail to recognize the striking originality of the message of Gen 1–11 and concentrate on subsidiary points that may well be of less moment. But an examination of the wider context of Gen 1–11 within the book itself, and the structure of these chapters, does, I believe, emphasize the centrality of these themes in the opening chapters.

Gen 1–11 and the Rest of the Book

BIBLIOGRAPHY

Brueggemann, W. "David and His Theologian." *CBQ* 30 (1968) 156–81. ———. "The Kerygma of the Priestly Writers." *ZAW* 84 (1972) 397–414. **Clines, D. J. A.** "Theme in Gen 1–11." *CBQ* 38 (1976) 483–507. **Crüsemann, F.** "Die Eigenständigkeit der Urgeschichte." In *Die Botschaft und die Boten, H. W. Wolff FS*, ed. J. Jeremias and L. Perlitt. Neukirchen: Neukirchener Verlag, 1981. 11–29. **Dumbrell, W. J.** *Covenant and Creation*. Exeter: Paternoster, 1984. **Gross, H.** "Der Universalismus des Heils: A. Nach der biblischen Urgeschichte Gen 1–11." *TTZ* 73 (1964) 145–53. **Gunneweg, A. H. J.** "Urgeschichte und Protevangelion." In *Sola Scriptura*. Göttingen: Vandenhoeck & Ruprecht, 1983. 83–95. **Lohfink, N.** "Die Priesterschrift und die Geschichte." VTSup 29 (1978) 189–225. **Lubsczyk, H.** "Elohim beim Jahwisten." VTSup 29 (1978) 226–53. **Rendtorff, R.** "Gen 8:21 und die Urgeschichte des Jahwisten." *KD* 7 (1961) 69–78. **Steck, O. H.** "Gen 12:1–3 und die Urgeschichte des Jahwisten." In *Probleme biblischer Theologie: FS für G. von Rad*, ed. H. W. Wolff. Munich: Kaiser Verlag, 1971. 525–54. **Wolff, H. W.** "**Das Kerygma des Jahwisten.**" *EvT* 24 (1964) 73–98. ET: *Int* 20 (1966) 131–58.

Of the fifty chapters of Genesis only eleven are devoted to the primeval history: this indicates where the book's main interest lies—with the patriarchs, the forefathers of the nation. Gen 1–11 gives the background to the call of Abraham in two main ways. First, it discloses the hopeless plight of mankind without the gracious intervention of God. Second, it shows how the promises made to the patriarchs fulfill God's original plans for humanity.

The opening chapters of Genesis describe an avalanche of sin that gradually engulfs mankind, leading first to his near-annihilation in the flood, and second, to man's dispersal over the face of the earth in despair of achieving international cooperation. Gen 3 describes how man's first sin led to alienation between husband and wife and expulsion from the presence of God in Eden. Chap. 4 tells how Cain murdered his brother Abel and how Cain's descendants further degraded mankind by their barbaric behavior. Chap. 6, the sexual union of women with the sons of God, is the last straw; the ultimate boundary between deity and the human family is breached, and the first creation returns to the watery chaos that characterized the earth before the separation of land and sea.

Noah, in many respects a second Adam, head of the new humanity and recipient of the renewed commission to fill the earth and subdue it, makes a more promising start. He is portrayed as an exemplary doer of the law, righteous and perfect in his generation. Yet he succumbs to wine, and his son Ham acts most dishonorably toward his father Noah, attracting to himself and his descendants a curse that was to be reflected in their future history. For from Ham descended Israel's arch-foes, such as Egypt, Assyria, and the Canaanites (9:24–27; 10:6–20). Finally, the tower of Babel demonstrates the folly of the most illustrious civilization and religious system of the day. Their attempt to reach up to heaven is the acme of folly and prompts mankind's dispersal over the face of the globe. Without the blessing of God the situation of humanity is without hope: that seems to be the chief thrust of the opening chapters of Genesis.

But the promises first made to Abraham in 12:1–3 begin to repair that hopeless situation. The fivefold blessing here counteracts the five curses that have been pronounced earlier. What is more, the promise of land, nationhood, the presence of God, and blessing to the nations restores what has been lost by man through his misbehavior recorded in Gen 3–11. In the beginning man had been told to be fruitful and multiply: the Abrahamic promises mean that at least one nation is going to achieve that goal. Man had been told to subdue the earth. From Abraham are to come kings and princes (17:6, 20). The LORD God created Adam a garden in which he enjoyed the intimate presence of God: Abraham is likewise promised land and an intimate covenant relationship in which the LORD would be their God, and they would be his people. Finally, the Abrahamic covenant will not just benefit Abraham and his descendants, but in him all the nations of the earth shall find blessing. Sin had apparently frustrated God's purposes for mankind: the promises give hope that they may indeed be realized. The primeval history thus explains the significance of the patriarchal story: though apparently of little consequence in the world of their day, the patriarchs are in fact men through whom the world will be redeemed. The God who revealed himself to them was no mere tribal deity but the creator of the whole universe.

Within the perspective of Genesis as a whole, the primeval history serves to enhance our appreciation of the patriarchs and their calling. Conversely, the patriarchal story, coming as it does as a sequel to the primeval history, helps us to understand the latter too. If the message of Genesis is essentially one of redemption, Gen 3–11 explains why man needs salvation and what he needs to be saved from. Chaps. 1–2, in describing the original state of the world, also describe the goal of redemption, to which ultimately the world and humanity will return when the patriarchal promises are completely fulfilled.

Gen 1–11 and Modern Thought

BIBLIOGRAPHY

The literature here is too enormous to list. However, helpful orientation to some of the main issues is provided by the following:

Blocher, H. *In the Beginning.* Leicester: IVP, 1984. **Hayward, A.** *Creation and Evolution.* London: SPCK, 1985. **Pollard, W. G.** "Science and the Bible." *IDB Sup* 789–94. **Poole, M. W.** *Creation or Evolution: A False Antithesis?* Oxford: Latimer House, 1987.

Modern commentators on Genesis face a problem unknown to past generations, the possibility of being charged with using sexist language if they speak of "man" or "mankind," terms central to chaps. 1–11 of this book. I deeply sympathize with feminist concern that certain terms may enshrine and help perpetuate male oppression of women. But I believe in this case their fears are misplaced. Words are not univocal like scientific symbols, but they have a variety of meanings. The context makes clear which meaning is intended. In traditional English, and particularly British, usage (see the standard Oxford dictionaries) the primary meaning of "man" is "human being" or "human race," and a hearer or reader generally understands the term in this way, unless the sentence in which "man" is used clearly demands the sense "adult male." Similarly, "mankind" always means "the human race, humanity" unless it is explicitly and most unusually contrasted with "womankind." Since all works on English style insist that it is better to use the short and simple word than the longer, more obscure term, I have preferred for the most part to retain "man" and "mankind" rather than adopt alternative terms such as "persons," "human being," or "humankind." Not only do I believe that classic English usage is more accurate and elegant, but "man" has just the versatility required to express Hebrew *ʾadam*, whose meaning stretches from "the human race" to "Adam," the first adult male. The fluidity of the Hebrew term is thus nicely matched in English "man" as traditionally understood, whereas modern alternatives like "person" or "human being" do not correspond so well to Hebrew *ʾadam*.

But the most serious problem for the modern reader of Genesis is to know how to relate Genesis 1–11 to current scientific and historical knowledge. The issues here are so vast, that I can only point to some of the many studies available (see bibliography) and urge that Genesis be read on its own terms, not on ours.

If it is correct to view Gen 1–11 as an inspired retelling of ancient oriental traditions about the origins of the world with a view to presenting the nature of the true God as one, omnipotent, omniscient, and good, as opposed to the fallible, capricious, weak deities who populated the rest of the ancient world; if further it is concerned to show that humanity is central in the divine plan, not an afterthought; if finally it wants to show that man's plight is the product of his own disobedience and indeed is bound to worsen without divine intervention, Gen 1–11 is setting out a picture of the world that is at odds both with the polytheistic optimism of ancient Mesopotamia and the humanistic secularism of the modern world.

Genesis is thus a fundamental challenge to the ideologies of civilized men and women, past and present, who like to suppose their own efforts will ultimately suffice to save them. Gen 1–11 declares that mankind is without hope if individuals are without God. Human society will disintegrate where divine law is not respected and divine mercy not implored. Yet Genesis, so pessimistic about mankind without God, is fundamentally optimistic, precisely because God created men and women in his own image and disclosed his ideal for humanity at the beginning of time. And through Noah's obedience and his sacrifice mankind's future was secured. And in the promise to the patriarchs the ultimate fulfillment of the creator's ideals for humanity is guaranteed.

These then are the overriding concerns of Genesis. It is important to bear them in mind in studying its details. Though historical and scientific questions may be uppermost in our minds as we approach the text, it is doubtful whether they were in the writer's mind, and we should therefore be cautious about looking for answers to questions he was not concerned with. Genesis is primarily about God's character and his purposes for sinful mankind. Let us beware of allowing our interests to divert us from the central thrust of the book, so that we miss what the LORD, our creator and redeemer, is saying to us.

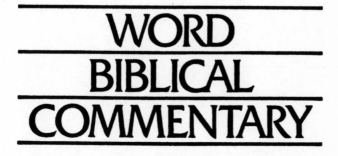

WORD
BIBLICAL
COMMENTARY

Genesis 1-15

In the Beginning (1:1–2:3)

Bibliography

(See also the Main Bibliography and the Genesis 1–11 bibliography.)

Anderson, B. W. "A Stylistic Study of the Priestly Creation Story." In *Canon and Authority,* ed. G. W. Coats and B. W. Long. Philadelphia: Fortress Press, 1977. 148–62. ———. *Creation in the OT.* Philadelphia: Fortress, 1984. **Auzou, G.** *Au commencement Dieu créa la monde.* Paris: Editions du Cerf, 1973. **Bauer, B.** "Der priesterliche Schöpfungshymnus in Gen 1." *TZ* 20 (1964) 1–9. **Beauchamp, P.** *Création et séparation.* Paris: Desclée, 1969. **Beyer, K.** "Althebräische Syntax in Prosa und Poesie." In *Tradition und Glaube, K. G. Kuhn FS,* ed. G. Jeremias, H. W. Kuhn, and H. Stegemann. Göttingen: Vandenhoeck und Ruprecht, 1971. 76–96. **Blenkinsopp, J.** "The Structure of P." *CBQ* 38 (1976) 275–92. **Cook, J.** "Gen 1 in the Septuagint as an Example of the Problem: Text and Tradition." *JNSL* 10 (1982) 25–36. **Cross, F. M.** "The 'Olden Gods' in Ancient Near Eastern Creation Myths." In *Magnalia Dei: The Mighty Acts of God. Essays on the Bible and Archaeology in Memory of G. E. Wright,* ed. F. M. Cross, W. E. Lemke, and P. D. Miller. Garden City: Doubleday, 1976. 329–38. **Dantinne, E.** "Création et séparation." *Le Muséon* 74 (1961) 441–51. **Day, J.** *God's Conflict with the Dragon and the Sea.* Cambridge: CUP, 1985. **Doukhan, J.** *The Literary Structure of the Genesis Creation Story.* Ph.D. Diss.: Andrews University, 1978. **Fisher, L. R.** "Creation at Ugarit and in the Old Testament." *VT* 15 (1965) 313–24. **Garbini, G.** "The Creation of Light in the First Chapter of Genesis." *PWCJS* 5 (1971) 1–4. **Gordon, C. H.** "Build-Up and Climax." In *Studies in Bible and the Ancient Near East Presented to S. E. Loewenstamm,* ed. Y. Avishur and J. Blau. Jerusalem: Rubinstein, 1978. 29–34. **Hasel, G. F.** "The Significance of the Cosmology in Gen 1 in Relation to Ancient Near Eastern Parallels." *AUSS* 10 (1972) 1–20. ———. "The Polemic Nature of the Genesis Cosmology." *EvQ* 46 (1974) 81–102. **Heidel, A.** *The Babylonian Genesis.* 2d ed. Chicago: University Press, 1954. **Hermant, D.** "Analyse littéraire du premier récit de la création." *VT* 15 (1965) 437–51. **Herrmann, S.** "Die Naturlehre des Schöpfungsberichtes." *TLZ* 86 (1961) 413–24. **Holwerda, D.** "The Historicity of Genesis 1–3." *Reformed Journal* 17.8 (1967) 11–15. **Kapelrud, A. S.** "The Mythological Features in Genesis 1 and the Author's Intentions." *VT* 24 (1974) 178–86. **Koole, J. L.** "Het Litterair Genre van Genesis 1–3." *GTT* 63 (1963) 81–122. **Kselman, J. S.** "The Recovery of Poetic Fragments from the Pentateuchal Priestly Source." *JBL* 97 (1978) 161–73. **Landes, G. M.** "Creation Tradition in Prov 8:22–31 and Gen 1." In *A Light unto My Path: Old Testament Studies in Honor of J. M. Myers,* ed. H. N. Bream, R. D. Heim, and C. A. Moore. Philadelphia: Temple UP, 1974. 279–93. **Lane, W. R.** "The Initiation of Creation." *VT* 13 (1963) 63–73. **Lella, A. A. di.** "Gen 1:1–10: A Formal Introduction to P's Creation Account." In *Mélanges bibliques et orientaux en l'honneur de M. Delcor,* ed. A. Caquot, S. Légasse, and M. Tardieu. AOAT 215. Kevelaer: Butzon and Bercker, 1985. 127–37. **Loader, J. A.** "Onqelos Gen 1 and the Structure of the Hebrew Text." *JSJ* 9 (1978) 198–204. **Loewenstamm, S. E.** "The Seven-Day-Unit in Ugaritic Epic Literature." *IEJ* 15 (1965) 122–33. **Loretz, O.** "Wortbericht-Vorlage und Tatbericht-Interpretation im Schöpfungsbericht Gen 1:1–2:4a." *UF* 7 (1975) 279–87. **Lubsczyk, H.** "Wortschöpfung und Tatschöpfung." *BibLeb* 6 (1965) 191–208. **Nielsen, E.** "Creation and the Fall of Man." *HUCA* 43 (1972) 1–22. **Pasinya, L. M.** "Le cadre littéraire de Gen 1." *Bib* 57 (1976) 225–41. **Payne, D. F.** *Genesis 1 Reconsidered.* London: Tyndale, 1964. **Ricoeur, P.** "Sur l'exégèse de Gen 1:1–2:4a." In *Exégèse et herméneutique,* ed. R. Barthes. Paris:

de Seuil, 1971. 67–84. **Sailhammer, J.** "Exegetical Notes: Gen 1:1–2:4a." *TJ* 5 (1984) 73–82. **Schmid, H.** "Die 'Mutter-Erde' in der Schöpfungsgeschichte der Priesterschrift." *Judaica* 22 (1966) 237–43. **Schmidt, W. H.** *Die Schöpfungsgeschichte der Priesterschrift.* 2d ed. WMANT 17. Neukirchen: Neukirchener Verlag, 1967. **Siegwalt, G** "L'actualité de Gen 1." *RHPR* 59 (1979) 319–25. **Ska, J. L.** "Séparation des eaux de la terre ferme dans le récit sacerdotal." *NRT* 103 (1981) 512–32. **Southwell, P. J. M.** "Gen 1 Is a Wisdom Story." *Studia Evangelica.* Texte und Untersuchungen 126 (1982) 467–82. **Steck, O. H.** *Der Schöpfungsbericht der Priesterschrift.* Göttingen: Vandenhoeck und Ruprecht, 1975. **Ultvedt, A. W.** "Genesis 1 og dens litteraere kilder." *NorTT* 81 (1980) 37–54. **Weinfeld, M.** "God the Creator in Genesis 1 and in the Prophecy of Second Isaiah." (Heb.) *Tarbiz* 37 (1967/68) 105–32. ———. "Sabbath, Temple and the Enthronement of the LORD—The Problem of the Sitz im Leben of Genesis 1:1–2:3." *Mélanges bibliques et orientaux en l'honneur de M. Henri Cazelles,* ed. A. Caquot and M. Delcor. AOAT 212. Kevelaer: Verlag Butzon und Bercker, 1981. 501–12. **Wifall, W.** "God's Accession Year According to P." *Bib* 62 (1981) 527–34. **Wyatt, N.** "Killing and Cosmogony in Canaanite and Biblical Thought." *UF* 17 (1986) 375–81. **Young, E. J.** "The Days of Genesis." *WTJ* 25 (1962/63) 1–34, 143–71. **Zimmerli, W.** "Der Mensch im Rahmen der Natur nach den Aussagen des ersten biblischen Schöpfungsberichtes." *ZTK* 59 (1979) 139–58.

Translation

¹*In*[a] *the* [b]*beginning God created the heaven and the earth.*
²*Now the earth was total chaos,*[b] *and darkness covered the deep and the Wind of God hovered*[c] *over the waters.*[a] ³*Then God said, "Let there be*[a] *light," and there was*[b] *light.* ⁴*And God saw*[a] *that the light*[b] *was good, and God made a division*[c] *between the light and the darkness.* ⁵*God*[a] *called the light day and the darkness he called night.*[a] *There was evening and morning, a first*[b] *day.*
⁶*Then God said, "Let there be a firmament in the midst of the waters and let there be a divider*[a] *between the waters."* ⁷*So God made*[a] *the firmament, and he divided the waters under the firmament from the waters above the firmament*[b] *and it was so.*[b] ⁸*God called the firmament heaven.*[a] *There was evening and morning, a second day.*
⁹*Then God said, "Let the waters under the heaven gather*[a] *in one place*[b] *and let the dry land appear."*[c] *And it was so.*[d] ¹⁰*God*[a] *called the dry land earth and the gathering of the waters he called seas.*[a] *And God saw that it was good.* ¹¹*Then God said, "Let the earth make itself green*[a] *with grass, with seed-bearing*[b] *plants, with*[c] *fruit trees bearing fruit according to their types with their seed in them on the earth." And it was so.* ¹²*So the earth produced*[a] *grass, seed-bearing plants according to their types, fruit trees with their seed in them according to their types. And God saw that it was good.* ¹³*There was evening and morning, a third day.*
¹⁴*Then God said,* [a]*"Let there be lights*[a] *in the firmament of the heaven*[b] *to divide*[c] *the day from the night, and let them be for signs, for fixed times, for days and years.* ¹⁵*Let them be for lights in the firmament of the heaven to give light*[a] *on the earth." And it was so.* ¹⁶*God made two large lights, the larger*[a] *light to rule*[b] *the day and the smaller*[a] *light to rule*[b] *the night, and also the stars.* ¹⁷*God placed*[a] *them in the firmament of the heaven to give light on the earth,* ¹⁸*to rule*[a] *the day and the night, and to divide the light from the darkness. And God saw that it was good.* ¹⁹*There was evening and morning, a fourth day.*

²⁰ *Then God said,* ᵃ *"Let the waters swarm with swarming things, living creatures, and let birds fly* ᵃᵇ *about over the earth across the firmament of the heaven."*ᶜ ²¹ *So God created the great sea monsters and all the moving living creatures with which the waters swarm according to their types, and all the winged birds according to their types. And God saw that it was good.* ²² *Then God blessed* ᵃ *them (saying)* ᵇ ᶜ *"Be fruitful and multiply* ᶜ *and fill the waters in the seas, and let the birds multiply* ᵈ *on earth."* ²³ *There was evening and morning, a fifth day.*

²⁴ *Then God said "Let the earth produce* ᵃ *living creatures according to their types: cattle, creeping things, and wild animals* ᵇ *according to their types." And it was so.* ²⁵ *So God made the wild animals according to their types, the cattle according to their types, and everything that creeps on the ground according to its type. And God saw that it was good.* ²⁶ *Then God said, "Let us make man in our image* ᵃ *according to our likeness, that they may rule* ᵇ *the fish of the sea, and the birds of the sky, and the cattle, and all the earth, and all creeping things that creep on the earth."* ²⁷ *So* ᵃ *God created man in his image,* ᵇ *in the image of God he created him:* ᶜ *male and female he created them.* ᵈ

²⁸ *And God blessed them* ᵃ *and God said to them,* ᵃ ᵇ *"Be fruitful, and multiply* ᵇ *and fill* ᶜ *the earth and subdue* ᶜ *it and rule* ᶜ *the fish of the sea, the birds of the sky* ᵈ *and every living creature* ᵉ *that moves on the earth."* ²⁹ *Then God said, "Since* ᵃ *I have given you every seed-bearing plant which is on the surface of the whole earth and every fruit tree* ᵇ *bearing seed, you may have it for food.* ³⁰ *So may* ᵃ *all the wild land animals, and all the birds of the sky, and all creeping things* ᵇ *on the earth which have the breath of life in them; all the vegetative plants are for food."* *And it was so.* ³¹ *And God saw all that he had made that* ᵃ *it was really very good. There was evening and morning, the sixth day.*

²:¹ *So the heaven and the earth and all their host were finished.* ᵃ ² *On the seventh* ᵃ *day God had finished* ᵇ *his work which he did, and he rested on the seventh day from all his work which he did.* ³ *God blessed the seventh day and hallowed* ᵃ *it, for in it he rested from all his work which God had created by making* ᵇ *it.*

Notes

1.a.-2.a. The syntactic relationship of v 1 to v 2 is problematic. This translation takes v 1 to be a main clause and v 2 as circumstantial to v 3 (*SBH*, 79, 85–86). For fuller discussion see *Comment*.

1.b. Heb. lacks the def art in בראשית (lit., "in beginning") but "in the beginning" is an acceptable translation (Joüon, 137k). Omission of the def art is regular in temporal phrases and does not necessarily indicate that ראשית should be taken as constr (cf. Isa 46:10; Prov 8:23).

2.b. On translation see *Comment* on ובהו. N.B. pointing of ו to join paired terms (GKC, 104g).

2.c. Fem sg piel ptcp רחף "hovering."

3.a. 3 masc sg juss היה "to be."

3.b. Waw consec + 3 masc sg juss (shortened impf) of היה.

4.a. Waw consec + 3 masc sg juss (shortened impf) of ראה "to see."

4.b. Lit., "the light that (it was) good." With verbs of perception the subj is regularly anticipated by making it the obj of the verb (Joüon, 157d; cf. Gen 6:2). On the translation of כי טוב see J. L. Kugel, *JBL* 99 (1980) 433–35, and J. G. Janzen, *JBL* 102 (1983) 99–106.

4.c. Waw consec + 3 masc sg short impf hiph of בדל "to separate."

5.a-a. Chiasmus of verb and indir obj "call-light // darkness-call" used to express unity of the two acts of naming (*SBH*, 129).

5.b. The cardinal "one" may be used for the ordinal "first" in Heb. and Akk. (Speiser, 6; cf. Gen 2:11).

6.a. Hiph ptcp בדל "dividing, separating" following the verb "to be" expresses continuing future action (GKC, 116r; Joüon, 121e). Alternatively the ptcp may be viewed as a virtual noun in parallel to "firmament," so that "Let there . . . between the waters" is a pair of conjoined precative clauses (SBH, 105).

7.a. Waw consec + 3 masc sg short impf עשה "to make."

7.b-b. G transposes this phrase to the end of v 6, which would be more normal (cf. vv 9, 11, 16,. etc.). It is characteristic of G to standardize the formulae (Beauchamp, Création, 26–32).

8.a. G inserts "And God saw that it was good." An inept attempt at standardization (cf. vv 4, 10, 12, etc.) because (a) the heavens were not complete till day 4, and (b) the addition mars the sevenfold use of the formula in the MT.

9.a. 3 masc pl impf niph קוה "to gather."

9.b. For מקום "place" G reads συναγωγήν "place of assembly." This would seem to be a fair translation of מקום, though some suggest it presupposes Heb. מקוה "gathering" (cf. T. L. Fenton, VT 34 [1984] 438–45).

9.c. 3 fem sg impf niph ראה "to see."

9.d. G adds "And the water which was below the heaven gathered to their places and the dry land appeared," characteristically conforming to the standard pattern by adding the execution formula absent from MT.

10.a-a. Chiasmus of verb and indir obj (cf. v 5).

11.a. 3 fem sg juss hiph דשא "sprout, grow green."

11.b. Ptcp hiph זרע "to bear seed."

11.c. SamPent, G, S, Vg add "and" before "fruit trees." This reading implies that עשב "plants" and עץ "tree" are included in דשא "grass," whereas without "and," "grass," "plants," "trees" could be mutually exclusive categories. The former interpretation is probably correct (see Comment), although the MT reading may be preferable as the more difficult. Waltke (217) notes SamPent tends to eliminate asyndetic constructions.

12.a. Waw consec + 3 fem sg impf hiph יצא "to go out"; hiph "bring out."

14.a-a. Sg verb with pl subj. Frequent where predicate precedes subj (GKC, 145o).

14.b. SamPent, G add "to shine upon the earth and." Typical harmonizing addition. MT to be retained.

14.c. Inf constr hiph בדל.

15.a. Inf constr hiph אור "to be light."

16.a. Lit., "large" "small." The use of the simple adjective to express the comparative and superlative is normal Heb. (cf. 19:31, 34, etc.; GKC, 133f.)

16.b. Constr ממשלה "rule."

17.a. Waw consec + 3 masc sg impf נתן "to give."

18.a. Inf constr משל "to rule."

20.a-a. Chiastic sentence indicating creation of birds and fishes to be "distinct but concomitant" acts (SBH, 105–6); cf. vv 5, 10.

20.b. 3 masc sg impf polel עוף "to fly."

20.c. G adds "and it was so," characteristically conforming the use of this phrase to the standard formula, but spoiling the sevenfold appearance of the phrase in the MT.

22.a. Waw consec + 3 masc sg impf piel ברך "to bless."

22.b. Inf constr אמר "to say" introduces direct speech (cf. Lambdin, 49.)

22.c-c. Hendiadys (SBH, 117), i.e., "Be abundantly fruitful." 2 masc pl impv פרה "be fruitful," רבה "multiply."

23.d. SamPent reads full impf ירבה for MT apocopated (juss) ירב (cf. Waltke, 214–15).

24.a. Cf. n. 12.a.

24.b. Normal constr of חיה is חית; cf. v 25. This form with additional (paragogic) waw occurs in six other poetic passages (e.g., Isa 56:9). GKC, 90k, and Joüon, 93r, suggest it is the remains of an old case ending. SamPent reads חית, as elsewhere omitting the paragogic waw (cf. Waltke, 217.)

26.a. SamPent, G, Vg insert "and." MT may stand, specifying apposition.

26.b. 3 masc pl impf רדה "rule." Impf preceded by simple waw as here expresses purpose (GKC, 109f; Lambdin, 119.)

27.a-b-c-d. Three clauses in apposition: b-c in epic apposition to a-b, and c-d specifying apposition to b-c (*SBH*, 55.)

28.a-a. G "saying" assimilating to v 22 (cf. Vg).

28.b-b. Hendiadys (cf. v 22).

28.c-c. The impvs here express promise (GKC, 110c.)

28.d. G, S insert "and all cattle"; G also adds "and all the earth." Unnecessary harmonistic additions. MT is preferable.

28.e. SamPent unnecessarily inserts def art (GKC, 117c.)

29.a. הנה introduces a clause giving ground for subsequent action (Lambdin, 169–70.)

29.b. SamPent regularizes by omitting def art before "tree."

30.a. *Pace BHS*, no emendation required. V 30 carries on sense from v 29.

30.b. SamPent inserts def art.

31.a. והנה frequent after verbs of seeing in case of "excited perception" (D. J. McCarthy, *Bib* 61 [1980] 332–33). As in v 4 the object of perception is anticipated in the main clause.

2:1.a. Waw consec + 3 masc pl impf pual כלה "to finish" used to sum up or recapitulate a narrative; cf. 23:20 (GKC, 111k; Joüon, 118i).

2.a. SamPent, G, S read "6th day." An interpretation designed to avoid any suspicion that God was active on the 7th day. *Tg. Onq.* also has this concern and uses different verbs for finishing in vv 1–2 (B. Grossfeld, *JJS* 24 [1973] 176–78). For reasons given in the comment on this verse a pluperfect translation "had finished" may be justified here, which avoids the problem felt by the versions.

2.b. Waw consec + 3 masc sg impf piel כלה.

3.a. Waw consec 3 masc sg impf piel קדש "be holy."

3.b. Lit., "to work, do" (ל + inf constr עשה; cf. לאמר "saying"; GKC, 114o; Joüon, 124o n.).

Form/Structure/Setting

Gen 1 (more precisely 1:1–2:3) is the majestic opening chapter of both the Hebrew and the Christian Bible. It introduces the two main subjects of Holy Scripture, God the Creator and man his creature, and sets the scene for the long tale of their relationship. It is at the same time the opening of the Torah, or Pentateuch, the first five books of the Canon, which relate the origins of the people of Israel. Although Torah is customarily translated "Law," this conveys too narrow a conception of what the Torah is. Rather Torah is "a unique combination of story and commandment that makes a fundamental statement about what God expects by saying as forcefully as possible what the people of God is" (Coats, 321). The narratives in Genesis teach ethics and theology just as much as do the laws and theological sermons found elsewhere in the Pentateuch, and for this reason these also belong to the Torah.

More immediately, Gen 1 introduces the primeval and patriarchal histories that constitute the Book of Genesis. The relationship of Gen 1–11 to Gen 12–50 on the one hand and its relationship to ancient Near Eastern tradition on the other have already been briefly discussed in the introduction. Here it is necessary to focus more closely on 1:1–2:3, which stands apart from the narratives that follow in style and content and makes it an overture to the whole work.

1:1–2:3 form the first section of Genesis; the second starts with 2:4. 2:1–3 echoes 1:1 by introducing the same phrases but in reverse order: "he created," "God," "heavens and earth" reappear as "heavens and earth" (2:1) "God" (2:2), "created" (2:3). This chiastic pattern brings the section to a neat close which is reinforced by the inclusion "God created" linking 1:1 and 2:3.

The correspondence of the first paragraph, 1:1–2, with 2:1–3 is underlined by the number of Hebrew words in both being multiples of 7. 1:1 consists of 7 words, 1:2 of 14 (7 x 2) words, 2:1–3 of 35 (7 x 5) words. The number seven dominates this opening chapter in a strange way, not only in the number of words in a particular section but in the number of times a specific word or phrase recurs. For example, "God" is mentioned 35 times, "earth" 21 times, "heaven/firmament" 21 times, while the phrases "and it was so" and "God saw that it was good" occur 7 times.

The majority of modern scholars hold that the opening section of Genesis ends with 2:4a, not 2:3. The vocabulary of v 4a is typical of P, to which 1:1–2:3 is also conventionally assigned; therefore v 4a must go with what precedes it, not what follows. It is, however, recognized that it is most anomalous for "This is the story of" (2:4) to conclude a section: everywhere else in Genesis (e.g., 5:1, 11:27) it introduces a major new development in the story. Furthermore, the tight chiastic structure of 2:4 (see below on 2:4) makes it unlikely that the sources split in the middle of the verse. For these reasons the opinion of Jacob, Cassuto, Cross (*Canaanite Myth*, 293–325) and Tengström (*Toledotformel*, 54–58) that 2:3 closes the opening section of the book and that 2:4 opens the next section is the basis of the ensuing exposition.

The arrangement of 1:1–2:3 is itself highly problematic. Briefly, the eight works of creation are prompted by ten divine commands and executed on six different days. Many attempts have been made to discover a simpler, more symmetrical arrangement underlying the present scheme. None of these suggestions has proved persuasive. More objective are the efforts of Cassuto, Beauchamp, and Pasinya to explicate the present form of the text.

Gen 1 is characterized by a number of recurrent formulae: (1) announcement of the commandment, "And God said" (10 times; vv 3, 6, 9, 11, 14, 20, 24, 26, 28, 29); (2) order, e.g. "Let there be . . ." (8 times; vv 3, 6, 9, 11, 14, 20, 24, 26); (3) fulfillment formula, e.g. "And it was so" (7 times; vv 3, 7, 9, 11, 15, 24, 30); (4) execution formula or description of act, e.g. "And God made" (7 times; vv 4, 7, 12, 16, 21, 25, 27); (5) approval formula "God saw that it was good" (7 times; vv 4, 10, 12, 18, 21, 25, 31); (6) subsequent divine word, either of naming or blessing (7 times; vv 5 [2 times], 8, 10 [2 times], 22, 28); (7) mention of the days (6/7 times; vv 5, 8, 13, 19, 23, 31 [2:2]). It is worth noting that although there are ten announcements of the divine words and eight commands actually cited, all the formulae are grouped in sevens. Indeed, the fulfillment formula is omitted in v 20, the description of the act in v 9, and the approval formula in vv 6–8. In each case LXX adds the appropriate formula, but it is characteristic of P to indulge in "dissymmetric symmetry" (McEvenue, *Narrative Style*, 113–15), and these additions obscure the sevenfold patterning of this section.

The narrative structure also highlights the third and the sixth days of creation. Both days have a double announcement of the divine word "And God said" (vv 9, 11, 24, 26) and the approval formula twice (vv 10, 12, 25, 31), so that they correspond to each other formally. But there is also a correspondence in the contents of the days. Day 3 deals with the creation of the land and plants, while day 6 deals with the animals that live on the land and man, and God permits them to eat the plants. Similar correspondences link days 1 and 4: day 1 mentions the creation of light, day 4 the creation of the light-producing bodies. Day 2 discusses the creation of the sky, day 5 the birds of heaven. Diagrammatically this may be represented as follows:

Day 1	Light	Day 4	Luminaries
Day 2	Sky	Day 5	Birds and Fish
Day 3	Land (Plants)	Day 6	Animals and Man (Plants for food)
		Day 7	Sabbath

The narrative has two poles, heaven and earth (1:1, 2:1), and its focus moves from heaven to earth, finishing with a close-up on man (vv 26–30). This shift of focus is again reflected in the arrangement of the creative acts.

Day 1	heaven	
Day 2	heaven	
Day 3		earth
Day 4	heaven	
Day 5		earth
Day 6		earth

Day 4 is, of course, half way through the week and, as Beauchamp (*Création*, 94) has shown, is elaborately constructed in a palistrophic pattern of terms introduced by the preposition "to." (See *Comment* on vv 14–18.)

Such crossover patterns are quite common in the OT, and it is very fitting that there should be one at this midpoint of the creation narrative. Its presence suggests the author was particularly interested in the work of the fourth day of creation. The sun, moon, and stars dictate the seasons, days, and years, and the narrative's focus on their function is appropriate in an account of creation that allocates the work of creation and God's rest on the Sabbath to the days of the week.

However, 2:1–3, the account of the seventh day, stands apart from the standard framework of each of the other six days. The terms "heaven and earth," "God," "create" reappear in the reverse order to that of 1:1, and this inverted echo of the opening verse rounds off the section. The threefold mention of the seventh day, each time in a sentence of seven Hebrew words, draws attention to the special character of the Sabbath. In this way form and content emphasize the distinctiveness of the seventh day.

It has often been argued that the present text of 1:1–2:3 is based on a brief source, describing creation merely in terms of divine actions (*Tatbericht*). This account was subsequently expanded by including divine commands (*Wortbericht*) as a prelude to the divine activity. Westermann and W. H. Schmidt (*Schöpfungsgeschichte*) exemplify this approach.

The hypothesis that Gen 1 rests on an earlier written source describing only divine actions has been thoroughly discussed by O. H. Steck (*Schopfungsbe-*

richt). He concludes that the *Tatbericht* is too fragmentary ever to have existed as an independent literary entity and that various features in the present narrative which Schmidt would describe as later literary developments cannot be separated from the earliest *Tatbericht* material. At most the *Tatbericht* was an idea in the author's mind when he wrote Gen 1. Beauchamp (*Création*) adopts a similar approach. Loretz (*UF* 7 [1975] 279–87) on the other hand argues that a poetic *Wortbericht* was the basis of the present form of the chapter. While he is right to draw attention to various poetic features of Gen 1 (see below), the seven-strophe poem that he reconstructs as the original *Wortbericht* is too fragmentary and uneven to be plausible.

Another source-critical theory sometimes held in conjunction with the *Tatbericht* view (e.g., W. H. Schmidt, *Schöpfungsgeschichte*) holds that Gen 1 either used the Babylonian creation story, *Enuma elish*, or at least is generally dependent on Mesopotamian traditions. Indeed, this used to be the consensus view: from Gunkel, *Schöpfung und Chaos*, 1895, to Speiser in 1964, it was repeatedly asserted that Gen 1 is indebted to *Enuma elish*. Speiser (10), following Heidel (*Babylonian Genesis*, 129), noted a number of parallels between *Enuma elish* and Gen 1 that could suggest dependence of the latter on the former, e.g., creation of light, firmament, dry land, luminaries, and the divine rest on the seventh day. All advocates of this view noted that the overall purpose of *Enuma elish* and many of its details were quite different from those of Gen 1. *Enuma elish* is concerned with glorifying Marduk and justifying his supremacy in the Babylonian pantheon. The creative acts of this god constitute very minor illustrations of his power: His victory over Tiamat is central to *Enuma elish*, whereas in Genesis, of course, God's work of creation is the central theme of chap. 1. Nevertheless, scholars felt that because Genesis evidently knew some form of the Mesopotamian flood story, the slight points of contact with *Enuma elish* suggested a similar relationship in the accounts of creation.

However, Lambert (*JTS* 16 [1965] 287–300) pointed out that there were decisive objections to postulating the dependence of Gen 1 on *Enuma elish*. The latter text does not represent normative Mesopotamian cosmology. "It is a sectarian and aberrant combination of mythological threads woven into an unparalleled composition . . . not earlier than 1100 B.C." (291). Many of the supposed parallels between *Enuma elish* and Genesis are commonplaces in many Near Eastern cosmologies, e.g., the watery origin of the world and the separation of land, while the creation of man and the rest of the gods is mentioned in other earlier Babylonian sources, such as the Epic of Atrahasis, *ca.* 1600 B.C. The relative lateness of *Enuma elish* in Lambert's opinion also tells against its being a source of Genesis.

Subsequent discussion of the relationship between Babylonian thought and Genesis has therefore concentrated on the Atrahasis epic. A stronger case can be made for asserting a relationship between Genesis and Atrahasis in that Atrahasis also presents primeval history as a sequence of creation–divine displeasure–flood. In other words this, the standard Babylonian account of creation, sees creation as a prelude to the flood, just as Gen 1–11 does. Nevertheless, it is still quite improbable that there is direct literary dependence of Genesis on Atrahasis. The general thrust and the various details of the narrative are too different to make this probable. The similarities can be explained by the origin of both accounts in neighboring countries in roughly the same chronological period.

Herrmann (1961), Kilian (1966), Notter (1974), and Ultvedt (1980) have argued that closer parallels are to be found in Egyptian literature. Notter notes many motifs in a wide variety of Egyptian texts which resemble features in Gen 1 and 2, e.g., the creation of chaos as the first step, the concept of a firmament, the making of man in God's image, man being made from clay and then inspired by God, the symbolism of sevens. Notter is not claiming that any of the Egyptian material he cites served as a direct source of Gen 1, simply that the writer was quite familiar with Egyptian ideas of creation. However, Ultvedt argues that Gen 1 must be dependent on the cosmogony expressed in the Teaching of King Merikare (21st century B.C.) which he suggests was probably known to the Hebrew writer in a Phoenician version. Ultvedt holds there is no evidence for supposing Genesis to have been dependent on Mesopotamian sources, least of all *Enuma elish*. These writers underline the tenousness of the relationship between Mesopotamian and Hebrew tradition. But it is doubtful whether the parallels cited actually demonstrate dependence on Egyptian sources.

Furthermore, the known links of the Hebrew patriarchs with Mesopotamia and the widespread diffusion of cuneiform literary texts throughout the Levant in the Amarna period (late 15th century) make it improbable that the writers of Genesis were completely ignorant of Babylonian and cognate mythology. Most likely they were conscious of a number of accounts of creation current in the Near East of their day, and Gen 1 is a deliberate statement of Hebrew view of creation over against rival views. It is not merely a demythologization of oriental creation myths, whether Babylonian or Egyptian; rather it is a polemical repudiation of such myths.

Hasel (1972, 1974) detects five areas in which Gen 1 appears to be attacking rival cosmologies. First, in some Near Eastern cosmogonies, dragons *tnn* are rivals whom the Canaanite gods conquer, whereas in Gen 1:21 the great sea monsters are just one kind of the aquatic animals created by God. Second, these cosmogonies describe the struggle of the gods to separate the upper waters from the lower waters; but Gen 1:6–10 describes the acts of separation by simple divine fiat. Third, the worship of the sun, moon, and stars was current throughout the ancient orient. Genesis pointedly avoids using the normal Hebrew words for sun and moon, lest they be taken as divine, and says instead God created the greater and the lesser light. Fourth, Babylonian tradition sees the creation of man as an afterthought, a device to relieve the gods of work and provide them with food. For Genesis, the creation of man is the goal of creation and God provides man with food. Finally, Genesis shows God creating simply through his spoken word, not through magical utterance as is attested in Egypt. There thus runs through the whole Genesis cosmology "a conscious and deliberate anti-mythical polemic" (Heidel, *Babylonian Genesis*, 91). The author of Gen 1 therefore shows that he was aware of other cosmologies, and that he wrote not in dependence on them so much as in deliberate rejection of them.

Extrabiblical creation stories from the ancient Near East are usually poetic, but Gen 1 is not typical Hebrew poetry. Indeed, some writers endeavoring to underline that Gen 1 is pure priestly theology insist that it is not poetry at all. There is no "hymnic element in the language" (von Rad, 47). On the other hand, Gen 1 is not normal Hebrew prose either; its syntax is distinctively different from narrative prose. Cassuto (1:11 [1961]), Loretz (1975) and Kselman (1978) have all pointed to poetic bicola or tricola in Gen 1, while admitting that most of the material is prose. It is possible that these poetic fragments go back to an earlier form of the creation account, though, as Cassuto observes, "it is simpler to suppose . . . the special importance of the subject led to an exaltation of style approaching the level of poetry" (1:11).

Gen 1 is unique in the Old Testament. It invites comparison with the psalms that praise God's work in creation (e.g., 8, 136, 148) or with passages such as Prov 8:22–31 or Job 38 that reflect on the mystery of God's creativity. It is indeed a great hymn, setting out majestically the omnipotence of the creator, but it surpasses these other passages in the scope and comprehensiveness of vision. In that it is elevated prose, not pure poetry, it seems unlikely that it was used as a song of praise as the psalms were. Rather, in its present form it is a careful literary composition introducing the succeeding narratives.

According to Westermann, it is a "majestic festive overture to P" (1:129; cf. ET, 93). It introduces the great train of events that began with creation, leads on to the call of the patriarchs and the exodus from Egypt and climaxes with the law-giving at Sinai and the establishment of worship in the tabernacle. Though at first sight Gen 1 is far removed from the cultic concerns that figure so prominently in P, it does serve to reinforce the significance and privilege of worship. The God whom Israel adores and whose law she obeys is the almighty Creator of heaven and earth.

In its present setting Gen 1:1–2:3 serves as a splendid introduction to the book of Genesis as a whole. It declares that the God of Abraham, Isaac, and Jacob is no mere localized or tribal deity, but the sovereign LORD of the whole earth. The apparently petty and insignificant family stories that occupy the bulk of the book are in fact of cosmic consequence, for God has chosen these men so that through them all the nations of the earth should be blessed.

The careful symmetries and deliberate repetitiveness of the chapter reveal more than a carefully composed introit to the book of Genesis; they speak of a God who creates order by his very word of command. Gen 1 is more than a repudiation of contemporary oriental creation myths; it is a triumphant invocation of the God who has created all men and an invitation to all humanity to adore him who has made them in his own image.

Sub-Bibliography on 1:1–3

(See also the Main Bibliography and the Gen 1–11 bibliography.)

Andreasen, N. E. "The Word 'Earth' in Gen 1:1." *Origins* 8 (1981) 13–19. **Blythin, I.** "A Note on Gen 1:2." *VT* 12 (1962) 120–21. **Caquot, A.** *In Principio: Interprétations des premiers versets de la Genèse.* Paris: Centre d'Études des Religions du Livre, 1973. **Duchesne-Guillemin, J.** "Gen 1:2c, Ugarit et l'Egypte." *CRAIBL* (1982) 512–25. **Eichrodt, W.** "In the Beginning." *Israel's Prophetic Heritage: Essays in Honor of J. Muilenburg,* ed. B. W. Anderson and W. Harrelson. New York: Harper and Row, 1962. 1–10. **Fisher, L. R.** "An Ugaritic Ritual and Gen 1:1–5." *Mission de Ras Shamra* 17. *Ugaritica* 6 (1969) 197–205. **Friedman, T.** "The Breath of God Hovered over the Water (Gen 1:2)." (Heb.) *BMik* 25 (1980) 309–12. **Görg, M.** "Tohû wabohû—ein Deutungsvorschlag." *ZAW* 92 (1980) 431–34. ———. "Zur Ikonographie des Chaos." *BN* 14 (1981) 18–19. **Gross, W.** "Syntaktische Erscheinungen am Anfang althebräischer Erzählungen: Hintergrund und Vordergrund." VTSup 32 (1981) 131–45. **Hasel, G. F.** "Recent Translations of Gen 1:1: A Critical Look." *BT* 22 (1971) 154–67. **Humbert, P.** "Encore le premier mot de la bible." *ZAW* 76 (1964) 121–31. **Jansma, T.** "Some Remarks on the Syro-Hexaplaric Reading of Gen 1:2." *VT* 20 (1970) 16–24. **Jongeling, B.** "Some Remarks on the Beginning of Gen 1:2." *Folia Orientalia* 21 (1980) 27–32. **Junker, H.** "In Principio Creavit Deus Coelum et Terram." *Bib* 45 (1964) 477–90. **Kilian, R.** "Gen 1:2 und die Urgötter von Hermopolis." *VT* 16 (1966) 420–38. **Luyster, R.** "Wind and Water: Cosmogonic Symbolism in the Old Testament." *ZAW* 93 (1981) 1–10. **Marzel, Y.** "Light and Lights (Gen 1:2–19)." (Heb.) *BMik* 28 (1982/83) 156–61. **Naor, N.** "In the Beginning He Created—Of Creation?" (Heb.) *BMik* 16 (1971) 306–11. **Orlinsky, H. M.** "The Plain Meaning of Gen 1:1–3." *BA* 46 (1983) 207–9. **Payne, D. F.** "Approaches to Gen 1:2." *TGUOS* 23 (1969–70) 61–71. **Ridderbos, N. H.** "Gen 1:1 und 2." *OTS* 12 (1958) 214–60. **Schäfer, P.** "Zur Interpretation von Gen 1:1 in der rabbinischen Literatur." *JSJ* 2 (1971) 161–66. **Smith, P. J.** "A Semotactical Approach to the Meaning of the Term *rûaḥ ĕlōhîm* in Gen 1:1." *JNSL* 8 (1980) 99–104. **Waltke, B. K.** "The Creation Account in Gen 1:1–3." *BSac* 132 (1975) 25–36, 136–44, 216–28, 327–42; 133 (1976) 28–41. **Young, E. J.** "The Interpretation of Gen 1:2." *WTJ* 23 (1960/61) 151–78.

Comment

1–3 "In the beginning God created." The stark simplicity of this, the traditional translation, disguises a complex and protracted debate about the correct interpretation of vv 1–3. Four possible understandings of the syntax of these verses have been defended.

1. V 1 is a temporal clause subordinate to the main clause in v 2: "In the beginning when God created . . ., the earth was without form . . . ."

2. V 1 is a temporal clause subordinate to the main clause in v 3 (v 2 is a parenthetic comment). "In the beginning when God created . . . (now the earth was formless) God said . . . ."

3. V 1 is a main clause, summarizing all the events described in vv 2–31. It is a title to the chapter as a whole, and could be rendered "In the beginning God was the creator of heaven and earth." What being creator of heaven and earth means is then explained in more detail in vv 2–31.

4. V 1 is a main clause describing the first act of creation. Vv 2 and 3 describe subsequent phases in God's creative activity. This is the traditional view adopted in our translation.

Theologically these different translations are of great consequence, for apart from #4, the translations all presuppose the existence of chaotic pre-existent matter before the work of creation began. The arguments for and against these translations must now be reviewed.

#1 was first propounded by Ibn Ezra but has attracted little support since, apart from Gross (VTSup 32 [1981] 131–45). Though NEB and NAB appear to adopt this translation, by placing a period at the end of v 2, they probably regard the main clause as "God said" in v 3, i.e., option 2. It is the least likely interpretation in that v 2 is a circumstantial clause giving additional background information necessary to understanding v 1 or v 3 and therefore either v 1 or v 3 must contain the main clause.

#2 was first propounded by Rashi, though there are hints in rabbinic texts that it may have been known earlier (Schäfer, 162–66). More recent defenders include Bauer, Bayer, Herrmann, Humbert, Lane, Loretz, Skinner, and Speiser, as well as RSV mg., NEB, NAB, and TEV.

This interpretation begins with the observation that the first word בראשית, literally, "in beginning," does not have the definite article. It may therefore be construed as a construct and the whole clause may then be translated, "In the beginning of God's creation of heaven and earth." In this type of construction the verb is usually in the infinitive (בְּרֹא) whereas here it is perfect (בָּרָא, "he created"). However, this is not without parallel; cf. Hos 1:2 (F. I. Andersen and D. N. Freedman, *Hosea*, AB24 [Garden City: Doubleday, 1980] 153.)

In support of this being the right interpretation of v 1 the following arguments are also cited. First, ראשית "beginning" rarely, if ever, has the absolute sense: it means "formerly," "firstly," not "first of all." Second, Gen 2:4b, usually regarded as the start of the second account of creation, begins, literally, "in the day of the making by the LORD God of heaven and earth." Third, *Enuma elish* and the Atrahasis epic both begin with a similar dependent temporal clause. However, the majority of recent writers reject this interpretation for the following reasons:

First and fundamental is the observation that the absence of the article in בראשית does not imply that it is in the construct state. Temporal phrases often lack the article (e.g., Isa 46:10; 40:21; 41:4, 26; Gen 3:22; 6:3, 4; Mic 5:1; Hab 1:12). Nor can it be shown that ראשית may not have an absolute sense. It may well have an absolute sense in Isa 46:10, and the analogous expression מראש in Prov 8:23 certainly refers to the beginning of all creation. The context of בראשית standing at the start of the account of world history makes an absolute sense highly appropriate here. The parallel with Gen 2:4b disappears, if, as argued below, the next section of Genesis begins with 2:4a, not 4b. As for the alleged parallels with Mesopotamian sources, most of those who acknowledge such dependence point out that better parallels with extra-biblical material may be found in Gen 1:2–3 than in 1:1. The first verse is the work of the editor of the chapter; his indebtedness to earlier tradition first becomes apparent in v 2.

On these grounds most modern commentators agree that v 1 is an independent main clause to be translated "In the beginning God created . . . ." However, within this consensus there is still dispute as to the relationship between v 1 and vv 2–3. The majority (Driver, Gunkel, Procksch, Zimmerli, von Rad, Eichrodt, Cassuto, Schmidt, Westermann, Beauchamp, Steck) adopt the view that Gen 1:1 is essentially a title to what follows. 1:1 is in a chiastic correspondence to 2:4a (create, heavens and earth // heavens and earth, create), and these two clauses thus frame the intervening account. This argument proves little, although it could also be argued that the closing words of 2:3, "which God created," make a telling inclusion with 1:1. On this view, vv 2–30 expound what is meant by the verb "create" in v 1. Creation is a matter of organizing pre-existing chaos. The origin of the chaos is left undiscussed, and given the background of oriental mythology, it may be presumed to be eternal.

In support of this view it is urged that only it does justice to the exact wording of v 1. The traditional interpretation supposes that God first created chaos and then ordered it, whereas elsewhere Scripture speaks of God creating order, not chaos (e.g., Isa 45:18). Even here the text says God created "heaven and earth," which most naturally denotes the whole ordered cosmos. The strength of these arguments depends on the exact interpretation of the terms in v 1, and this will be discussed below. Here it suffices to observe that if the creation of the world was a unique event, the terms used here may have a slightly different value from elsewhere. Furthermore, Gunkel argued that there is a contradiction between vv 1 and 2, if v 1 is merely a title. How can God be said to create the earth (v 1), if the earth pre-existed his creative activity (v 2) as this view implies? A diachronic literary explanation is usually advanced, namely, that v 1 is a later addition to an earlier source: Gen 1:1 is P's own interpretative comment on the traditional material in vv 2–3. Before Genesis reached its present final form, the account simply spoke of God addressing a dark chaotic world (cf. vv 2–3). Then the author or editor of Genesis prefaced this older version with v 1, stating that "In the beginning God created the heaven and the earth." The contradiction between v 1 and vv 2–3 is thus explained in terms of a reviser's not integrating his remarks adequately with earlier material. However, a text ought to be interpreted synchronically as well, i.e., in its total final form. This tends to support the traditional view, for it is preferable to suppose that the editor did not leave obvious contradictions within his work.

Finally, interpretation #4, the traditional view, still has many adherents. The versions and Masoretic pointing imply this was the standard view from the third century B.C. (LXX) through to the tenth century A.D. (MT). Modern advocates include Wellhausen (*Die Composition des Hexateuchs*), König, Heidel, Kidner, Ridderbos, Young, Childs (*Myth and Reality in the Old Testament* [London: SCM, 1960] 31–43), Hasel, Gispen, and Notter.

The antiquity of this interpretation is the greatest argument in its favor: those closest in time to the composition of Gen 1 may be presumed to be best informed about its meaning. However, Hasel has argued that this interpretation becomes the more likely since it is apparent that vv 2–3 are not a straight borrowing of extrabiblical ideas. Mesopotamian sources formulate their descriptions negatively—"When the heaven had *not* yet been named"—whereas v 2 is positive, "the earth was total chaos." In other words, it looks as though vv 2–3 were composed by the writer responsible for v 1, and not simply borrowed from a pre-biblical source. This makes it most natural to interpret the text synchronically, i.e., v 1: first creative act; v 2: consequence of v 1; v 3: first creative word. Notter (23–26) points out that the idea that a god first created matter, the primeval ocean, and then organized it, has many Egyptian parallels. Whether this, the traditional understanding of these verses, does justice to the exact wording of Genesis must now be investigated.

1 ראשית "beginning" is an abstract noun etymologically related to ראש "head," and ראשון "first." In temporal phrases it is most often used relatively, i.e., it specifies the beginning of a particular period, e.g., "From the beginning of the year" (Deut 11:12) or "At the beginning of the reign of" (Jer 26:1). More rarely, as here, it is used absolutely, with the period of time left unspecified; only the context shows precisely when is meant, e.g., Isa 46:10. "Declaring the end from the beginning and from ancient times (מקדם) things not yet done" (cf. Prov 8:22). The contexts here and in Gen 1 suggest ראשית refers to the beginning of time itself, not to a particular period within eternity (cf. Isa 40:21; 41:4; H. P. Müller, *THWAT* 2:711–12).

By prefixing ראשית "beginning" with the preposition ב "in" Genesis makes its first two words begin identically, for ברא also spells "he created." Whether this is mere coincidence or literary conceit is open to question. The literary craftsmanship employed elsewhere in the chapter perhaps makes the latter likely. Elsewhere in these opening chapters ברא is always employed in close proximity to ברך "to bless" (1:21/22; 1:27/28; 2:3/3; 5:1–2/2;) suggesting that creation and blessing are linked in the divine purpose, a purpose eventually to be realized through Abra[ha]m (12:1–3) whose name (אברהם) consists of the same three letters + hm. (So D. F. Pennant, *Bib,* forthcoming.)

ברא "he created." The verb is used in both the qal and niphal. An etymological connection with the piel בֵּרֵא "to cut," "split" (e.g.,Josh 17:15) is doubtful. It is particularly easy to read English notions of creation into the Hebrew verb, given the theological importance of the idea. It is therefore vital to examine usage carefully to determine its meaning. First, it should be noted that God, the God of Israel, is always subject of ברא. Creation is never predicated of pagan deities. Second, the text never states what God creates out of. Third, the most frequently named products of creation are man, (e.g., 1:27), and unexpected novelties (e.g., Num 16:30; Isa 65:17); more rarely mentioned are the sea monsters (Gen 1:21), mountains (Amos 4:13), and animals (Ps 104:30).

It is therefore clear that ברא is not a term exclusively reserved for creation out of nothing. For example, it can be used of the creation of Israel (Isa 43:15). Nevertheless, as with the word "create" in English, there is a stress on the artist's freedom and power—the more so in the Hebrew as the word is used solely for God's activity. W. H. Schmidt (*Schöpfungsgeschichte,* 166–67) correctly points out that though ברא does not denote *creatio ex nihilo,* it preserves the same idea, namely, "God's effortless, totally free and unbound creating, his sovereignty. It is never mentioned what God created out of."

That God did create the world out of nothing is certainly implied by other OT passages which speak of his creating everything by his word and his existence before the world (Ps 148:5; Prov 8:22–27) (Ridderbos, *OTS* 12 [1958] 257). Though such an interpretation of Gen 1:1 is quite possible, the phraseology used leaves the author's precise meaning uncertain on this point.

אלהים "God." "The first subject of Genesis and the Bible is God" (Procksch, 438). The word is the second most frequent noun in the OT. It is derived from the common Semitic word for god *il.* As here, Hebrew generally prefers the plural form of the noun, which except when it means "gods," i.e., heathen deities, is construed with a singular verb. Though the plural has often been taken to be a plural of majesty or power, it is doubtful whether this is relevant to the interpretation of אלהים. It is simply the ordinary word for God: plural in form but singular in meaning.

Strictly speaking, אלהים is an appellative, that is, it can be used of any deity. It is not a personal name, such as Yahweh, El Shaddai, Marduk, or Chemosh. Nevertheless, as with the English word "God," it often acts almost as a proper name. Certainly in this chapter אלהים is a more appropriate word to use than יהוה (the LORD): it implies that God is the sovereign creator of the whole universe, not just Israel's personal God (H. Ringgren, *TDOT* 1:267–84; W. H. Schmidt, *THWAT* 1:153–67).

It is important to appreciate the fact that Hebrew אלהים is not simply synonymous with English "God." Thanks to secularism, God has become for many people little more than an abstract philosophical concept. But the biblical view avoids such abstractions. Westermann points out: "God in Gen 1 is one who acts and speaks." His reality is seen in his acts; he is not an entity who can be conceived of apart from his works (139; cf. ET, 100).

השמים ואת הארץ "the heaven and the earth." It is characteristic of many languages to describe the totality of something in terms of its extremes, e.g., "good and bad," "big and little," etc. Here we have an example of this usage to define the universe (cf. J. Krašovec, *Der Merismus im Biblisch-Hebräischen und Nordwestsemitischen,* BibOr 33 [Rome: Biblical Institute Press, 1977] 16–25).

On its own שמים means "sky" or "heaven," i.e., the abode of God, while ארץ denotes the "earth, world," which is man's home. But in the OT, as well as in Egyptian, Akkadian, and Ugaritic, "heaven and earth" may also be used to denote the universe (M. Ottosson, *TDOT* 1:389–91; Stadelmann, *Hebrew Conception of the World,* 1–2; Gen 14:19, 22; 24:3; Isa 66:1; Ps 89:12).

Gen 1:1 could therefore be translated "In the beginning God created everything." Commentators often insist that the phrase "heaven and earth" denotes the completely ordered cosmos. Though this is usually the case, totality rather than organization is its chief thrust here. It is therefore quite feasible for a mention of an initial act of creation of the whole universe (v 1) to be followed by an account of the ordering of different parts of the universe (vv 2–31). Put another way, ארץ may well have a different meaning in vv 1 and 2. Compounded with "heaven" it designates the whole cosmos, whereas in v 2 it has its usual meaning "earth." According to Stadelmann (*Hebrew Conception of the World,* 127), "the term ארץ means primarily the entire area in which man thinks of himself as living, as opposed to the regions of heaven or the underworld." The very different contexts show that it is wrong to identify the sense of ארץ in v 1 with its sense in v 2 too precisely (cf. N. E. Andreasen, *Origins* 8 [1981] 13–19).

2 והארץ "Now the earth." "And" + noun (= earth) indicates that v 2 is a disjunctive clause. It could be circumstantial to v 1 or v 3, but for reasons already discussed (see above, pp. 11–13) the latter is more probable. V 2 therefore describes the state of the earth before the first divine command in v 3. For similar constructions cf. 3:1; 4:1, etc.

תהו ובהו "Total chaos" an example of hendiadys, literally, "waste and void." תהו "waste" has two main senses, either "nothingness" (e.g., Isa 29:21) or, as here, "chaos, disorder," most frequently of the untracked desert where a man can lose his way and die (Deut 32:10; Job 6:18). This frightening disorganization is the antithesis to the order that characterized the work of

creation when it was complete. Here and in Isa 34:11 and Jer 4:23 תהו is
coupled with בהו "void," where, as the context shows, the dreadfulness of
the situation before the divine word brought order out of chaos is underlined.

The same point is made in another powerful image in the next clause,
"darkness covered the deep." חשׁך "darkness" is another evocative word in
Hebrew. If light symbolizes God, darkness evokes everything that is anti-
God: the wicked (Prov 2:13), judgment (Exod 10:21), death (Ps 88:13). Salvation is described as bringing light to those in darkness (Isa 9:1, etc.). But
whereas darkness is opaque to man, it is transparent to God (Ps 139:12).
Indeed God can veil himself in darkness at moments of great revelation (Deut
4:11; 5:23; Ps 18:12). There is therefore an ambiguity in this reference to
darkness covering the deep. *Prima facie*, it is just another description of the
terrible primeval waste, but it could hint at the hidden presence of God
waiting to reveal himself.

תהום "deep," "deep waters" occurs 36 times in the OT. Its basic meaning,
"deep water," is found in many passages. "Deep water" can threaten life in
that a man may drown in it (Exod 15:8), but it can also assure the continuance
of life in the dry climate of the Near East (Gen 49:25; Deut 8:7). In a small
number of passages, including this one, תהום is identified with the primeval
ocean that is supposed to surround and underlie the earth (e.g., Gen 7:11).
But there is no hint in the biblical text that the deep was a power, independent
of God, which he had to fight to control. Rather it is part of his creation
that does his bidding (cf. Ps 104:6; Prov 8:27–28).

Gunkel suggested that Hebrew תהום was to be identified with Tiamat,
the Babylonian goddess, slain by Marduk, whose carcass was used to create
heaven and earth. He saw in Gen 1:2 an allusion to the Mesopotamian creation
myths. Though Otzen (*Myths in the OT*, 33–34) has reaffirmed this connection,
Heidel (*Babylonian Genesis*, 98–101) showed that a direct borrowing is impossible. Both Hebrew and Babylonian *Ti'amat* are independently derived from
a common Semitic root. Westermann justly states that the OT usage of תהום
"does not allow us to speak of a demythologizing of a mythical idea or name
as do many commentaries. When P inherited the word תהום, it had long
been used to describe a flood of waters without any mythical echo" (1:105).
That is not to say that this verse shows no connection with other oriental
concepts of creation. In ancient cosmogonies a reference to a primeval flood
is commonplace (Westermann, 1:105–6). But the word תהום is not an allusion
to the conquest of Tiamat as in the Babylonian myth.

"And the Wind of God hovered over the waters." There is deep disagreement among modern commentators as to the correct interpretation of this
phrase. On the one hand von Rad, Speiser, Schmidt, Westermann, and NEB
see this as simply a description of the primeval chaos and therefore translate
it "a mighty wind swept over the surface of the waters." On the other hand,
Cassuto, Kidner, and Gispen, as well as older commentators such as Gunkel,
Skinner, and Procksch prefer the traditional translation: "The Spirit of God
was moving . . . ," while Ridderbos and Steck think "the breath of God" a
preferable translation. The dispute centers on the two words in the phrase
רוח אלהים. רוח can mean "wind" or "spirit." אלהים almost always means
"God," but in a few passages it does appear to be used as an alternative to a
superlative; hence the proposed rendering "mighty wind."

Commentators are, however, agreed on the syntactic function of this clause. It parallels "the earth was total chaos" and "darkness covered the deep." Indeed, "deep" and "waters" are virtually synonymous here. V 2 therefore consists of three parallel clauses describing the situation prior to the divine fiat in v 3. Since clauses 1 and 2 describe a situation of black chaos, a similar picture must be conveyed by the third clause, argue Westermann and Schmidt. A reference to the Spirit of God in such a context is inappropriate. Since אלהים can be used to express the superlative, the translation "great wind" is preferable.

However, reducing אלהים simply to a superlative seems unlikely in this chapter, which elsewhere always uses it to mean God. Furthermore, nowhere else in Scripture does the phrase רוח אלהים or רוח יהוה ever mean "great wind": it always refers to the Spirit or Wind of God. Thus the phrase must be taken to involve some manifestation of God, whether as wind, spirit, or breath (cf. R. Luyster, *ZAW* 93 [1981] 1–10). This is not necessarily in total contrast to the first two clauses mentioning chaos and darkness, for darkness is ambivalent; as mentioned above, at times it is synonymous with all that is anti-God, but it may also be his hiding place. It is impossible to make a firm choice between "wind," "breath," and "spirit" as translations of רוח in this case, but the verb "hovering," used in conjunction with it, does perhaps fit "wind" better than either "spirit" or "breath." Admittedly מרחפת "hovering" has been used to justify some less probable views. For example, Syriac *raḥep* can mean "brood over" or "incubate," so it has been suggested we have here a picture of the Spirit incubating the world egg, a notion found in some Phoenician cosmologies. But this seems unlikely. Deut 32:11 is the only other passage in the OT where רחף (piel) is found. Here it describes the action of an eagle hovering over its young before it flies off. *rḥp* is also found in Ugaritic to describe birds' flight. Beauchamp (*Création*, 172–86) observes that רחף would also aptly describe the motion of the wind, and it is for this reason I have adopted the rendering "Wind of God" as a concrete and vivid image of the Spirit of God. The phrase does really express the powerful presence of God moving mysteriously over the face of the waters. Beauchamp helpfully compares the description of the divine chariot to "a stormy wind" guided by the spirit (Ezek 1:4, 12, 20) and the references to wisdom watching over God's creative activity (Prov 8 and Job 38) to this passage in Genesis. Though it cannot be proved that this is exactly what Gen 1:2 intends to say, these interpretations could be evoked by the image of the Wind of God hovering and ready for action.

3–5 record the first of the ten words of creation. These verses contain the seven standard formulae that comprise the description of each stage of creation: 1) announcement, "God said"; 2) command, "let there be"; 3) fulfillment, "it was so"; 4) execution, "light"; 5) approval, "saw . . . good"; 6) subsequent word, "God called"; 7) day number. In fact, it is the only occasion where all seven elements are present in simple sequence (Beauchamp, *Création*, 28). It is therefore here that we must examine the basic elements of the formulae, as well as the ingredients peculiar to the first day.

3 "God said." This formula occurs ten times in this chapter (cf. vv 6, 9, 11, 14, 20, 24, 26, 28, 29). Though it is of course taken for granted throughout the OT that God speaks, אמר "to say" is used here in a more pregnant sense than usual. It is a divine word of command that brings into existence what it expresses. Throughout Scripture the word of God is characteristically both creative and effective: it is the prophetic word that declares the future and helps it come into being. But in this creation narrative these qualities of the divine word are even more apparent (cf. S. Wagner, *TDOT* 1:336; Westermann, 1:110–12).

"Let there be light." The second formal element is the divine fiat itself, usually a jussive as here (cf. vv 6, 9, 14, etc.), but once a cohortative "let us" (v 26).

אוֹר "light." Light is the first of the creator's works. "Light manifests most adequately the divine operation in a world which, without it, is darkness and chaos" (Stadelmann, *Hebrew Conception of the World*, 49). Though it is not itself divine, light is often used metaphorically for life, salvation, the commandments, and the presence of God (Ps 56:14; Isa 9:1; Prov 6:23; Exod 10:23). It is the antithesis, literally and metaphorically, of חֹשֶׁךְ "darkness"; cf. *Comment* on 1:2. There is no problem in conceiving of the creation of light before the heavenly bodies (vv 14–19). Their creation on the fourth day matches the creation of light on the first day of the week. But the existence of day and night (v 5) before the creation of the sun is more difficult to understand on a purely chronological interpretation of this account of creation. The implications of this and other features of this account are discussed more fully in the *Explanation* section.

"And there was light.": the fulfillment formula. In its other six occurrences in this chapter (vv 7, 9, 11, 15, 24, 30) the formula is "And it was so." The exact echoing of the command here emphasizes the total fulfillment of the divine word.

4 "God saw that the light was good.": the approval formula. This statement also occurs seven times in this chapter (cf. vv 10, 12, 18, 21, 25, 31). God the great artist is pictured admiring his handiwork. This account of creation is a hymn to the creator: creation itself bears witness to the greatness and goodness of God. It may be noted that light, not darkness, is noted as good: God is, as it were, prejudiced in favor of light.

טוֹב "good." This very common Hebrew adjective has a broad range of meaning, as does the English term. Primarily, it draws attention to an object's quality and fitness for its purpose. But the Hebrew term as used by the Israelites is more closely related to the mind and opinion of God than is the English word. God is preeminently the one who is good, and his goodness is reflected in his works (Ps 100:5; cf. I. Höver-Johag, *TDOT* 5:296–317; H. J. Stoebe, *THWAT* 1:652–64).

"God separated. . . ." Usually this formulaic element, execution of the divine word, precedes the formula of appreciation, "God saw" (cf. 12, 16–18, 21, 25), but a certain flexibility within the refrains is characteristic of the style of this account. "Separated," וַיַּבְדֵּל. Separation is one of the central ideas in this chapter. God separates darkness and light, upper and lower waters, day and night (vv 6, 7, 14, 18). Elsewhere separation almost becomes synonymous with divine election (Lev 20:24; Num 8:14; Deut 4:41; 10:8; 1 Kgs 8:53). And Israel is expected to become as discriminating as her LORD in distinguishing between clean and unclean, holy and profane (Lev 10:10;

20:25). In separating light and darkness, there is probably a hint of the divine preference for the former; and possibly the upper waters bringing the rain were regarded as more valuable than sea water (B. Otzen, *TDOT* 2:1–3; Beauchamp, *Création*, 235–39).

5 "God called." On the chiasmus in this verse, see *Notes*. Seven times a subsequent divine word either of naming (vv 5 [2 times], 8, 10 [2 times]) or blessing (vv 22, 28) follows an act of creation. God names the heavens, the earth, and the seas, as well as day and night. In other ancient cosmologies, e.g., *Enuma elish*, creation is coupled with naming. In the OT, to name something is to assert sovereignty over it; cf. 2:20; 2 Kgs 23:34; 24:17. Here darkness, though not said to have been created, is still named by God. Giving names also defines roles, and the naming of day and night here is an aspect of separating darkness and light.

"There was evening and morning, a first day." This formula closes the account of each day's activity (vv 8, 13, 19, 23, 31; cf. 2:2). Probably the mention of the evening before morning reflects the Jewish concept that the day begins at dusk, not at dawn. Though the OT may be interpreted to mean that the new day begins at dawn, less difficulties are posed by the evening theory (cf. H. R. Stroes, *VT* 16 [1966] 460–75). On this view, the first day began in darkness (v 2) and ended, after the creation of light, with nightfall, the start of the second day.

But Westermann (1:115) is no doubt right to insist it is the division of time into days that is the narrator's chief concern: he is not much concerned whether a day consists of a period of darkness followed by a period of light or *vice versa*. The pattern of six days of similar acts followed by a change on the seventh day is well attested in Mesopotamian and Ugaritic literature (cf. Loewenstamm, *IEJ* 15 [1965] 121–33, and Young, *WTJ* 25 [1962/63] 144–47).

יוֹם "day." There can be little doubt that here "day" has its basic sense of a 24-hour period. The mention of morning and evening, the enumeration of the days, and the divine rest on the seventh show that a week of divine activity is being described here. Elsewhere, of course, "in the day of" and similar phrases can simply mean "when" (e.g., 2:4; 5:1, etc.). Ps 90:4 indeed says that a thousand years are as a day in God's sight. But it is perilous to try to correlate scientific theory and biblical revelation by appeal to such texts. Rather, it is necessary to inquire more closely into the literary nature of Gen 1 and whether chronological sequence and scientific explanation are the narrator's concern. These questions will be discussed briefly below under *Explanation*.

6–8 All the standard formulaic elements are found in this description of the divine works on the second day, except for the appreciation formula, possibly omitted because the separation of the waters was not completed till the following day (v 10).

6 "Firmament," רָקִיעַ. Its function is defined in the second clause, "a divider between the waters," i.e., the firmament separates the water in the sky from the seas and rivers. In v 8 it is called "heaven." Put another way, the firmament occupies the space between the earth's surface and the clouds. Quite how the OT conceives the nature of the firmament is less clear.

The word is derived etymologically from רקע to "stamp, spread" (Ezek 6:11; Isa 42:5). In Exod 39:3 it means "to spread by hammering," (piel). Job 37:18 speaks of the skies being "spread out hard as a molten mirror." The noun is rare outside Gen 1. Ezek 1:22 and Dan 12:3 describe the firmament as shiny. Such comments may suggest that the firmament was viewed as a glass dome over the earth, but since the most vivid descriptions occur in poetic texts, the language may be figurative. Certainly Gen 1 is not concerned with defining the nature of the firmament, but with asserting God's power over the waters. The separation of heaven and earth is a familiar theme in ancient cosmologies, but the control of the waters appears to be peculiar to *Enuma elish* and Genesis. There is also the implication that heaven itself was created by God: it is not an aspect of God.

7 The verbal repetition highlights the correspondence between the word of command and its fulfillment. This is further underlined by the clause "And it was so," which elsewhere in this chapter precedes the detailed description of the fulfillment of the divine word (vv 11–12, 15–16, 24–25). "The formula lets the narrator bring out and underline for his reader or listener the inner connection between word and event" (Steck, *Schöpfungsbericht*, 36).

9–13 The narrative moves from the creation of light by which the works of God are seen, through heaven, the throne of God, to earth, the abode of man. With the establishment of land and sea the basic parameters of human existence in time and space are complete. But unlike the works of the first two days, the work of the third involved no new creation, but more an organization of existing material.

9–10 Two works took place on the third day: separation of the land and sea, and the creation of the plants. This means most of the standard formulae are repeated, e.g., "It was so," "God saw . . . good" (vv 9, 11, 10, 12). LXX's attempt to add missing formulae in v 10 is probably not original (see *Notes*).

The "one place" is in contrast to an implied "every place" when the waters covered the whole earth. It is not that the OT envisages all the water being gathered into a single ocean, as the mention of seas in v 10 makes clear. Whereas we view the continents as islands surrounded by oceans, the phraseology here suggests they saw the world as dry land with seas in it (cf. Schmidt, *Schöpfungsgeschichte*, 106). It was God's power that had limited the waters to certain areas (cf. Jer 5:22). When these great acts of separation were finished, God's glory was again apparent: "It was good." In the flood, the bounds established at creation were overstepped, and death and chaos returned.

11–13 The emergence of plants. The major question in these verses is the relationship between דשא "grass," עשב "plants," and עץ "trees." At first glance, this terminology suggests three distinct types of vegetation, and this is how Gispen (1:57) understands these terms. However, though דשא usually just means grass, it here appears to be a broader term that includes both "plants" and "trees." In favor of the latter interpretation, both "plants" and "trees" are qualified as self-propagating, "seed-bearing," "bearing fruit," whereas דשא has no such qualification. Plants and trees are mentioned in vv 29–30, but not the grass. This bipartite classification appears to be the understanding of the earliest versions (see *Notes*) and is the view of most modern commentators.

12 "According to their types." מִין "type" is a common word in lists, especially in priestly material (cf. vv 21, 24–25; 6:20; 7:14; Lev 11:14–29; Deut 14:13–18). There runs through this chapter a concern with definitions and divisions. God has created different types of plants and given them the power to reproduce: "seed bearing, fruit bearing." There is a givenness about time and space which God has ordered by his own decree. The different species of plant and animal life again bear testimony to God's creative plan. The implication, though not stated, is clear: what God has distinguished and created distinct, man ought not to confuse (Lev 19:19; Deut 22:9–11). Order, not chaos, is the hallmark of God's activity. This chapter is as much concerned with the implications of God creating the world as with the how and why of creation. Modern readers tend to be preoccupied with scientific and historical questions about the origins of the world, whereas the OT in describing how our world came to be is at the same time suggesting a moral stance to be adopted toward the natural order. Things are the way they are because God made it so, and men and women should accept his decree.

14–19 The creation of the sun, moon, and stars is described at much greater length than anything save the creation of man. The description is also quite repetitive. The fullness of the description suggests that the creation of the heavenly bodies held a special significance for the author and possibly that a variety of sources underlie the account. Schmidt (*Schöpfungsgeschichte*, 109–17) argues that these verses offer the clearest support for his view that an older *Tatbericht* (vv 16–18a) has been supplemented by a later *Wortbericht* (14–15), a view endorsed by Westermann (1:128–29).

The most obvious reason for the detail in the fourth day's description is the importance of the astral bodies in ancient Near Eastern thought. In neighboring cultures, the sun and the moon were some of the most important gods in the pantheon, and the stars were often credited with controlling human destiny (cf. Hasel, *AUSS* 10 [1972] 12–15). So there is probably a polemic thrust behind Genesis' treatment of the theme. This comes out in several ways.

First, the sun, moon, and stars are created by God: they are creatures, not gods. And with creatureliness goes transience; unlike the Hittite sun-god, they are not "from eternity." Second, the sun and moon are not given their usual Hebrew names שֶׁמֶשׁ and יָרֵחַ here, which might suggest an identification with Shamash the sun god or Yarih the moon god. Instead they are simply called "the larger" and "the smaller light." Third, the sun and moon are simply assigned the role of lighting the earth and ruling the day and night, as the surrogates of God. This is quite a lowly function by ancient Near Eastern standards, though Marduk does something similar in appointing stations for the great gods in EE 5.1–22. Finally, the stars, widely worshiped and often regarded as controllers of human destiny, are mentioned almost as an afterthought: they too are merely creatures.

There is, it is true, a certain amount of repetitiousness in the account of the fourth day, but the very repetition makes for a well-organized concentric structure (Cassuto, 1:42–43; Beauchamp, *Création*, 92–97; Steck, *Schöpfungsbericht*, 105). Its main elements consist of a list of functions:

A   to divide the day from the night (14a)

B   for signs, for fixed times, for days and years (14b)

C   to give light on the earth (15)

D   to rule the day (16a)   ⎱ God made the

D'   to rule the night (16b) ⎰ two lights

C'   to give light on the earth (17)

B'   to rule the day and the night (18a)

A'   to divide the light from the darkness (18b)

The fulfillment of the divine commands in vv 14–15 is recorded in reverse order in vv 17–18. The creation of the sun and moon is mentioned at the center of the pattern (v 16). Structure inversions of this sort, palistrophes, are a common feature of Hebrew prose (cf. S. E. McEvenue, *Narrative Style*, 157–58). The threefold function of the heavenly bodies, to "divide," to "rule," and to "give light," are thus each mentioned twice, so as to underline their real function. Within these five verses ל "to" occurs eleven times, defining the role of the sun and moon. Yet at the same time, there are slight variations between command and fulfillment (cf. A/A' B/B') which adds interest to the account. Given the subtlety of this composition, it becomes difficult to maintain that the original core of this narrative was a *Tatbericht* in vv 16–18 to which vv 14–15 (*Wortbericht*) are a later supplement. Rather it is a homogeneous unity, bringing out the characteristic concerns of the author and demonstrating through the structure of the narrative itself the sovereign power of the divine word in creation. At most, the so-called *Tatbericht* is the germinal idea from which the narrator has constructed the present account (Beauchamp).

14 Outside Gen 1 מאור "light, lamp" is always used in the Pentateuch to designate the sanctuary lamp in the tabernacle: only two other passages, Ezek 32:8; Ps 74:16 use it of the heavenly lights. "To divide the day from the night"; cf. v 18b, "the light from the darkness." Astronomical knowledge makes it difficult to conceive of the existence of day and night before the creation of the sun, but Cassuto argues that the Hebrews did not make an absolute connection between daylight and the sun. At dusk and dawn the world is light even though the sun is below the horizon. This verse, though, affirms the relationship between sun and daylight for all time from the creation of the sun on the fourth day. It must therefore be supposed that the first three days were seen as different: then light and darkness alternated at God's behest.

"for signs . . . years." Two problems are posed by this phrase: the syntactical relationship between the terms, and their precise meaning. "Signs, fixed times and days" are all prefixed by ל "for," whereas "years" lacks the preposition. Commentators agree that "days and years" go together, for ל governs both "days" and "years." The relationship between signs and fixed times is more difficult. Speiser regards it as hendiadys, "mark the fixed seasons," i.e., "signs of fixed times." Westermann and Steck argue that "signs" covers two sub-categories: (a) "fixed times" and (b) "days and years." As vegetation was subdivided into plants and trees (vv 11–13), so the sun and moon determine the festival seasons and the chronological periods. Yet a third possibility (e.g., Gispen and many early commentators) is to take אוֹת "sign" as a special celestial sign, whether it be a rainbow (Gen 9:12) or some omen (Isa 38:7). In this case we would have a threefold categorization: (a) heavenly portents, (b) festal seasons, (c) days and years.

There is insufficient evidence to decide among these rival interpretations, but the second possibility seems simpler than the other two. What is clear is the importance attached to the heavenly bodies' role in determining the seasons, in particular in fixing the days of cultic celebration. This is their chief function. Beauchamp (*Création,* 113–16) has suggested that by mentioning "fixed times" on the fourth day of creation, the author is hinting that Wednesday was often a day on which great festivals, and in particular, New Year's Day, always fell. This is not the case with the standard Jewish calendar, but it would be so if the calendar mentioned in the Book of Jubilees and probably used at Qumran by some first-century Jews is presupposed here. But whether this calendar was known to the author of Genesis is moot (cf. Wenham, *VT* 28 [1978] 343–45 and our discussion of the flood chronology below).

15 "Let them be for lights." A similar tautology appears in Num 15:39: "It (the tassel) shall be for a tassel." The tautology serves to emphasize the function of the luminaries "to give light" and to discount any notion of their divinity. Its awkward avoidance of the terms "sun and moon" also highlights the anti-mythical thrust of the passage.

16–19 The exact fulfillment of the divine command is here recorded in the standard stereotyped phrases. The chiastic patterning of the command and its fulfillment has already been noted. This, the fourth day, is the only day on which no divine word subsequent to the fulfillment is added. On days 1–3 this divine word names the created objects (vv 5, 8, 10); on days 5–6 the creatures are blessed (vv 22, 28). The omission may be just elegant stylistic variation, or it may be a deliberate attempt to avoid naming "sun" and "moon" with their connotations of deity.

20–23 Just as the creation of the heavenly bodies on the fourth day corresponds to the creation of light on the first day of creation, so the creation of birds and fishes on the fifth day matches the division of the waters by the firmament on the second day. The standard formulae reappear except for "and it was so." Though LXX includes this phrase, it is unlikely to be original, for its inclusion disturbs the sevenfold patterning (cf. above). This is the first time the additional divine word takes the form of a blessing (v 22, cf. 28) instead of a naming (vv 5, 8, 10). Schmidt again wishes to find a *Tatbericht* in v 21 to which a *Wortbericht* has been appended in v 20. Westermann (1:134–35) rejects this, preferring to regard the mention of the birds as a later addition to an account which originally dealt only with sea creatures, but he admits that this supplementation must have taken place very early in the tradition.

20 "Swarm with swarming things." As in v 11 ("grow green with grass") we have a verb (שָׁרַץ) used with its cognate noun (שֶׁרֶץ). Usually this stem refers to movement, especially the swift chaotic hither-and-thither motion of small animals such as insects, mice, and fish (Lev 11 passim), but it carries with it overtones of abundant fertility (e.g., Exod 1:7). "Here, in the command of God, who is communing with Himself, it refers also to large creatures, for vis-à-vis the Creator, they are all equally small" (Cassuto, 1:48).

"Living creatures" (נפש חיה) in apposition to "swarming things." This comprehensive term is used here of water creatures, in v 24 of land animals, in 9:10 of birds and land animals, and 9:16 of man and animals; in other words, of all animate creation in which there is "the breath of life" (נפש חיה; 1:30).

"Fly about." The use of the polel עופף instead of the qal עוף "fly" again suggests swarming-type motion.

"Across the firmament." From the ground, birds appear to fly against the background of the sky. This is one of the indications in the narrative that it is written from the perspective of a human observer.

21 "God created the great sea monsters." This is the first time ברא has been used since v 1, and it is probably significant that תנין "sea monsters" are picked out for special mention. In the OT תנין can mean "snake" (Exod 7:9) or "crocodile" (Ezek 29:3) or other powerful animal (Jer 51:34). Isa 27:1; 51:9; Ps 74:13 and Job 7:12 apparently use the language of Canaanite myth to describe God's victory over his foes, and it may well be that this verse mentions that the great sea monsters were created by God precisely to insist on his sovereignty over them. They are not rivals that have to be defeated, just one of his many creatures (cf. Ps 148:7).

22 "God blessed them." Note how here and in 1:28; 2:3; 5:2 a statement about God's blessing, ברך, immediately follows a mention of his creating, ברא. Divine blessing continues God's benevolent work in creation, and the writer exploits the verbal similarity between the terms to draw attention to their theological relationship. The blessing of God is one of the great unifying themes of Genesis. God blesses animals (1:22), mankind (1:28), the Sabbath (2:3), Adam (5:2), Noah (9:1), and frequently the patriarchs (12:3; 17:16, 20, etc.). God's blessing is most obviously visible in the gift of children, as this is often coupled with "being fruitful and multiplying." But all aspects of life can express this blessing: crops, family, and nation (Deut 28:1–14). Where modern man talks of success, OT man talked of blessing.

Though God's blessing can be simply evident in a man's happy and successful life (e.g., 24:35), it is always regarded as the result of a divine promise of blessing. The word of blessing, whether pronounced by God or man, guarantees and effects the hoped-for success. So here the words of command "be fruitful and multiply" carry with them the divine promise that they can be carried out. Once uttered, the word carries its own life-giving power and cannot be revoked by man (cf. 27:27–40). Genesis may be described as the story of the fulfillment of the divine promises of blessing. The earth is filled with animals and man and filled a second time following the flood. The patriarchs, despite initial infertility, have many children and in spite of many foolish acts enjoy great prosperity.

Within these promises, that of being fruitful and multiplying, פרו ורבו, is central (cf. 1:28; 9:1, 7; 17:6, 20; 28:3; 41:52; 48:4). If God's blessing is in one sense a perpetuation of God's creative activity, it also enables man to imitate God by procreating. It is possible that the Hebrew writer is deliberately exploiting the phonetic similarity of the terms "bless" ברך, "be fruitful" פרה, "multiply" רבה, and "create" ברא, as well as their ideological connections by juxtaposing them in these verses.

For fuller discussion see J. Scharbert, *TDOT* 2:279–308; C. A. Keller and G. Wehmeier, *THWAT* 1:353–76; J. Scharbert, *Solidarität in Segen und Fluch im AT und in seiner Umwelt*, BBB 14 (Bonn: Hanstein Verlag, 1958); C. Westermann, *Blessing in the Bible and the Life of the Church* (Philadelphia: Fortress, 1978).

24–31 Once again the creative acts on this the sixth day correspond to those of three days earlier. On the third day (vv 9–13) the land was made to appear and vegetation started to grow. On the sixth day the land animals were created and the vegetation was assigned to them as food. But whereas the words of the third day are described quite succinctly, those of the sixth are set out more fully than any other. This fullness of description reflects the importance of the events on this day, for in it creation reaches its climax in the formation of man in the divine image. The comment at the end too reinforces the point: "God saw . . . that it was really very good" (v 31). All the standard formulaic elements are included; indeed, four divine speeches are recorded (vv 24, 26, 28, 29), twice as many as on any other day (cf. Exod 16:22–29 where the LORD supplies twice as much manna as on other days). Maybe there is a hint of divine urgency to complete everything before the Sabbath.

Once again Schmidt has attempted to distinguish an original *Tatbericht* (v 25) of the creation of animals from subsequent additions in v 24 that constitute a *Wortbericht*. However, in the creation of man he reckons that all the present material reflects later interpretation, and therefore two accounts cannot be distinguished here.

24 "Let the earth produce"; cf. v 12 where on the third day the earth produces (hiphil יצא) grass, thus underlining the parallel between the works of the two days. Like fish, birds (1:21), and humans (2:7), the land animals are living creatures (see *Comment* on 1:21), here divided into three categories: "cattle" (בהמה), "creeping things" (רמש) and "wild animals" (חיתו־ארץ). The Hebrew terminology is more fluid than this translation suggests. Though בהמה most often denotes large domesticated animals and חיה wild animals, either term can stand for all the animal kingdom as opposed to mankind. Here, though, the animal world is being classified into three main groups, a favorite device of Hebrew writers and legislators: domestic, wild, and small animals. The last named "creeping things" refers to mice, reptiles, insects, and any other little creatures that keep close to the ground.

25 "So God made the wild animals . . ., the cattle . . ., and everything that creeps on the ground." Note the chiasmus between command (v 24) and fulfillment:

A   cattle and creeping things

B   wild animals

B¹   wild animals

A¹   cattle . . . creeping things

The absence of a blessing on the land animals has often been commented on. Whereas birds and fish (v 22) and man (v 28) are blessed and told to be fruitful, no such command is given to the animals. Of the suggested explanations, two seem plausible: either the land animals are not told to multiply lest they compete with man and endanger his survival (cf. Exod 23:29; Lev 26:22; Jacob, 56) or more probably, because the blessing on man (v 28) covered all the works of the sixth day, including the land animals (so most recently Westermann, 1:141–42).

Sub-Bibliography on 1:26–28

(See also the Main Bibliography and the Gen 1–11 bibliography.)

Ahuviah, A. "In the Image of God He Created Him." (Heb.) *BMik* 30 (1984/85) 361–91. **Angerstorfer, A.** "Hebräisch *dmwt* und aramäisch *dmw(t)*: Ein Sprachproblem der Imago-Dei-Lehre." *BN* 24 (1984) 30–43. **Barr, J.** "The Image of God in the Book of Genesis—A Study of Terminology." *BJRL* 51 (1968–69) 11–26. **Barthélemy, D.** "'Pour un homme', 'pour l'homme' ou 'Pour adam'?" In *De la Tôrah au Messie: Études offertes à H. Cazelles*, ed. M. Carrez, J. Doré and P. Grelot. Paris: Desclée, 1981. 47–53. **Bird, P. A.** "Male and Female He Created Them." *HTR* 74 (1981) 129–59. **Clines, D. J. A.** "The Image of God in Man." *TB* 19 (1968) 53–103. ———. "The Etymology of Hebrew *ṣelem*." *JNSL* 3 (1974) 19–25. **Cook, J. I.** "The Old Testament Concept of the Image of God." In *Grace upon Grace: Essays in Honor of L. J. Kuyper*, ed. J. I. Cook. Grand Rapids: Eerdmans, 1975. 85–94. **Creager, H. L.** "The Divine Image." In *A Light unto My Path: Old Testament Studies in Honor of J. M. Myers*, ed. H. N. Bream, R. D. Heim, and C. A. Moore. Philadelphia: Temple UP, 1974. 103–18. **Dequeker, L.** "'Green Herbage and Trees Bearing Fruit' (Gen 1:28–30; 9:1–3): Vegetarianism or Predominance of Man over the Animals?" *Bijd* 38 (1977) 118–27. **Dion, P. E.** "Ressemblance et Image de Dieu." *DBSup* 10, fasc. 55 (1981) 365–403. ———. "*Image* et *ressemblance* en araméen ancien (Tell Fakhariyah)." *ScEs* 34 (1982) 151–53. **Dohmen, C.** "Die Statue von Tell Fecherije und die Gottebenbildlichkeit des Menschen: Ein Beitrag zur Bilderterminologie." *BN* 22 (1983) 91–106. **Fossum, J.** "Gen 1:26 and 2:7 in Judaism, Samaritanism and Gnosticism." *JSJ* 16 (1985) 202–39. **Gilbert, M.** "Soyez féconds et multipliez (Gen 1:28)." *NRT* 96 (1974) 729–42. **Gross, W.** "Die Gottebenbildlichkeit des Menschen im Kontext der Priesterschrift." *TQ* 161 (1981) 244–64. **Hasel, G. F.** "The Meaning of 'Let Us' in Gen 1:26." *AUSS* 13 (1975) 58–66. **Horowitz, M. C.** "The Image of God in Man—Is Woman Included?" *HTR* 72 (1979) 175–206. **Houston, W. J.** "'And Let Them Have Dominion . . .': Biblical Views of Man in Relation to the Environmental Crisis." *Studia Biblica 1978*, ed. E. A. Livingstone. JSOTSS 11. Sheffield: JSOT Press, 1978. 161–84. **Jobling, D.** "And Have Dominion . . .: The Interpretation of Gen 1:28 in Philo Judaeus." *JSJ* 8 (1977) 50–82. **Kline, M. G.** "Creation in the Image of the Glory-Spirit." *WTJ* 39 (1977) 250–72. **Loewenstamm, S. E.** "Beloved Is Man in That He Was Created in the Image." In *Comparative Studies in Biblical and Ancient Oriental Literatures*. AOAT 204. Kevelaer: Butzon and Bercker, 1980. 48–50. **Loretz, O.** *Die Gottebenbildlichkeit des Menschen*. Munich: Kösel-Verlag, 1967. **Mettinger, T. N. D.** "Abbild oder Urbild? 'Imago Dei' in traditionsgeschichtlicher Sicht." *ZAW* 86 (1974) 403–24. **Miller, J. M.** "In the 'Image' and 'Likeness' of God." *JBL* 91 (1972) 289–304. **Ockinga, B.** *Die Gottebenbildlichkeit im Alten Ägypten und im AT*. Wiesbaden: Harrassowitz, 1984. **Otto, E.** "Der Mensch als Geschöpf und Bild Gottes in Ägypten." In *Probleme biblischer Theologie: FS für G. von Rad*, ed. H. W. Wolff. Munich: Kaiser Verlag, 1971. 335–48. **Qoler, Y.** "Creation of Man." (Heb.) *BMik* 28 (1982/83) 223–29. **Rordorf, B.** "'Dominez la terre' (Gen 1:28): Essai sur les résonnances historiques de ce commandement biblique." *BCPE*

31 (1979) 5–37. **Sawyer, J. F. A.** "The Meaning of בצלם אלהים ('In the Image of God') in Gen 1–11." *JTS* 25 (1974) 418–26. **Stamm, J. J.** "Zur Frage der Imago Dei im AT." In *Humanität und Glaube: Credenkschrift für K. Guggisberg,* ed. U. Neuenschwander. Bern: Haupt, 1973. 243–50. **Wildberger, H.** "Das Abbild Gottes." *TZ* 21 (1965) 245–59. **Ziegenaus, A.** "Als Mann und Frau erschuf er sie' (Gen 1:27): Zum sakramentalen Verständnis der geschlechtlichen Differenzierung des Menschen." *MTZ* 31 (1980) 210–22.

26–30 With the creation of man the creation account reaches its climax. We have observed how the acts of creation most germane to human existence— the earth, man's home (vv 9–13), the sun and moon that determine his life cycle (vv 14–19)—were described more fully than other less vital aspects of the created order. But now with man's creation, the narrative slows down even more to emphasize his significance.

26a	Announcement in the first person of God's intention
26b	Purpose of man's creation: to rule the earth
27	Creation of man
28	Blessing on man: to breed and rule the earth
29	Assignment of food to man
30	and to the animals

26 "Let us make man in our image according to our likeness." In the vast amount of literature that this statement has generated, discussion has focused on three main issues:

1. Why does God speak in the plural (us/our)? Why did he not say, "Let me make man in my image?" Such a reinterpretation appears to have been suggested by some early translators (Clines, *TB* 19 [1968] 62).

2. What is the force of the prepositions "in" (ב) and "according to" (כ) in this passage?

3. What is meant by "image" and "likeness"? Is there any difference between the terms here?

We shall review the various issues in turn.

The use of the plural

(a) From Philo onward, Jewish commentators have generally held that the plural is used because God is addressing his heavenly court, i.e., the angels (cf. Isa 6:8). Among recent commentators, Skinner, von Rad, Zimmerli, Kline, Mettinger, Gispen, and Day prefer this explanation. Westermann thinks such a conception may lie behind this expression, but he really regards explanation (e) below as adequate.

(b) From the Epistle of Barnabas and Justin Martyr, who saw the plural as a reference to Christ (G. T. Armstrong, *Die Genesis in der alten Kirche* [Tübingen: Mohr, 1962] 39; R. McI. Wilson, "The Early History of the Exegesis of Gen 1:28," *Studia Patristica* 1 [1957] 420–37), Christians have traditionally seen this verse as adumbrating the Trinity. It is now universally admitted that this was not what the plural meant to the original author.

(c) Gunkel suggested that the plural might reflect the polytheistic account taken over by P, though he recognized that this could not be P's view. As shown above, Gen 1 is distinctly antimythological in its thrust, explicitly rejecting ancient Near Eastern views of creation. Thus modern commentators are quite agreed that Gen 1:26 could never have been taken by the author of this chapter in a polytheistic sense.

(d) Some scholars, e.g., Keil, Dillmann, and Driver, have suggested that this is an example of a plural of majesty; cf. the English royal "we." It refers to "the fullness of attributes and powers conceived as united within the Godhead" (Driver, 14). Joüon's observation (114e) that "we" as a plural of majesty is not used with verbs has led to the rejection of this interpretation.

(e) Joüon (114e) himself preferred the view that this was a plural of self-deliberation. Cassuto suggested that it is self-encouragement (cf. 11:7; Ps 2:3). In this he is followed by the most recent commentators, e.g., Schmidt, Westermann, Steck, Gross, Dion.

(f) Clines (*TB* 19 [1968] 68–69), followed by Hasel (*AUSS* 13 [1975] 65–66) suggests that the plural is used because of plurality within the Godhead. God is addressing his Spirit who was present and active at the beginning of creation (1:2). Though this is a possibility (cf. Prov 8:22–31), it loses much of its plausibility if רוח is translated "wind" in verse 2.

The choice then appears to lie between interpretations (a) "us" = God and angels or (e) plural of self-exhortation. Both are compatible with Hebrew monotheism. Interpretation (e) is uncertain, for parallels to this usage are very rare. "If we accept this view, it will not be for its merits, but for its comparative lack of disadvantages" (Clines *TB* 19 [1968] 68). On the other hand, I do not find the difficulties raised against (a) compelling. It is argued that the OT nowhere else compares man to the angels, nor suggests angelic cooperation in the work of creation. But when angels do appear in the OT they are frequently described as men (e.g., Gen 18:2). And in fact the use of the singular verb "create" in 1:27 does, in fact, suggest that God worked alone in the creation of mankind. "Let us create man" should therefore be regarded as a divine announcement to the heavenly court, drawing the angelic host's attention to the master stroke of creation, man. As Job 38:4, 7 puts it: "When I laid the foundation of the earth . . . all the sons of God shouted for joy" (cf. Luke 2:13–14).

If the writer of Genesis saw in the plural only an allusion to the angels, this is not to exclude interpretation (b) entirely as the *sensus plenior* of the passage. Certainly the NT sees Christ as active in creation with the Father, and this provided the foundation for the early Church to develop a trinitarian interpretation. But such insights were certainly beyond the horizon of the editor of Genesis (cf. W. S. LaSor, "Prophecy, Inspiration and *Sensus Plenior*," *TB* 29 [1978] 49–60).

The prepositions ב *and* כ *("in," "like")*

The prepositions ב "in, by" and כ "as, like" are not exact synonyms, though their semantic fields do overlap (cf. BDB, 88–91, 453–55). But in this verse, the early translators and most modern commentators agree that ב "in" is virtually equivalent to כ "like, according to." However, Wildberger (*THWAT* 2:559), Clines, and Gross have attempted to prove that ב here has the rarer meaning "in the capacity of," as in Exod 6:3, "I appeared to Abraham ב (as) El-Shaddai." Thus Clines can argue that man was not created as an imitation of the divine image but to *be* the divine image.

However, the interchangeability of the prepositions ב and כ in Gen 5:1, 3, especially in connection with the words "image" and "likeness" makes this view untenable (Mettinger, *ZAW* 86 [1974] 406, and Sawyer, *JTS* 25 [1974] 421). ב here means "according to, after the pattern of." A closely parallel usage is to be found in Exod 25:40 (cf. 25:9), where Moses is told to build the tabernacle "after the pattern" (בתבנית). For these reasons the traditional interpretation of ב as "in" = "like" appears to be justified here. "According to our likeness" therefore appears to be an explanatory gloss indicating the precise sense of "in our image."

"Image" and "likeness"

The rarity of צלם "image" in the Bible and the uncertainty of its etymology make the interpretation of this phrase highly problematic. Of its 17 occurrences, 10 refer to various types of physical image, e.g., models of tumors (1 Sam 6:5); pictures of men (Ezek 16:17); or idols (Num 33:52); and two passages in the Psalms liken man's existence to an image or shadow (Ps 39:7; 73:20). The other five occurrences are in Gen 1:26,27; 5:3; 9:6.

Etymology may sometimes help to define a word's meaning, especially where it is so obvious that the native speaker is aware of similar sounding words with similar meanings. Unfortunately this is not the case here. Two suggestions have been made as to the etymology of צלם: that it comes from a root meaning "to cut" or "hew," attested in Arabic, or from a root attested in Akkadian and Arabic, "to become dark." The former fits the idea of physical image quite well, but insofar as there is no verb in biblical Hebrew from this root which would have clarified what it meant to the native speaker, its meaning must have been as opaque to them as it is to us.

"Likeness," דמות, on the contrary, is transparent in its meaning. It has an ending typical of an abstract noun and is obviously related to the verb דמה "to be like, resemble." The noun can be used to denote a model or plan (1 Kgs 16:10). Most of its 25 occurrences are to be found in Ezekiel's visions, e.g., 1:5, where it could be aptly rendered "something like"; RSV "the likeness of." Both terms, צלם and דמות, are found together in a ninth-century old Aramaic inscription from Tell Fakhariyeh to describe the statue of King Haddu-yisi, the oldest pairing of these terms yet known in Aramaic (Dion, *ScEs* 34 [1982] 151–53).

But in what does the "image" and "likeness" consist? Five main solutions have been proposed.

a) "Image" and "likeness" are distinct. According to traditional Christian exegesis (from Irenaeus, *ca.* 180 A.D.), the image and the likeness are two distinct aspects of man's nature. The image refers to the natural qualities in man (reason, personality, etc.) that make him resemble God, while the likeness refers to the supernatural graces, e.g., ethical, that make the redeemed godlike.

While these distinctions may be useful homiletically, they evidently do not express the original meaning. The interchangeability of "image" and "likeness" (cf. 5:3) shows that this distinction is foreign to Genesis, and that probably "likeness" is simply added to indicate the precise nuance of "image" in this context.

b) The image refers to the mental and spiritual faculties that man shares with his creator. Intrinsically this seems a probable view, but it is hard to pin down the intended qualities. Among the many suggestions are that the image of God resides in man's reason, personality, free-will, self-consciousness, or his intelligence. Owing to the sparsity of references to the divine image in the OT, it is impossible to demonstrate any of these suggestions. In every case there is the suspicion that the commentator may be reading his own values into the text as to what is most significant about man. For these reasons, most modern commentators have either abandoned the attempt to define the image, assuming that its nature was too well known to require definition, or they look for more specific clues in Genesis as to how the image was understood.

c) The image consists of a physical resemblance, i.e., man looks like God. In favor of this interpretation is the fact that physical image is the most frequent meaning of צֶלֶם, and that in Gen 5:3 Adam is said to have fathered Seth "after his image," which most naturally refers to the similar appearance of father and son. P. Humbert (*Études sur le récit du paradis*, 153–63) insisted that this was all Genesis meant, Gunkel and von Rad that it was at least part of its meaning. Nevertheless, the OT's stress on the incorporeality and invisibility of God makes this view somewhat problematic (cf. Deut 4:15–16). The difficulty is increased if, as is usually the case, the material is assigned to the late P source, for this would be too gross an anthropomorphism for exilic literature. And if, as is widely believed, the "image of God" terminology is based on Egyptian and possibly Mesopotamian thinking, it should be noted that the image of God describes the king's function and being, not his appearance in these cultures. Furthermore, it is argued that the OT does not sharply distinguish the spiritual and material realms in this way. The image of God must characterize man's whole being, not simply his mind or soul on the one hand or his body on the other. Finally, it may be noted that the ancient world was well aware, partly through the practice of sacrifice, that physiologically man had much in common with the animals. But the image of God is something that distinguishes man from the animal kingdom. The case for identifying the image of God with man's bodily form or upright posture is therefore unproven.

d) The image makes man God's representative on earth. That man is made in the divine image and is thus God's representative on earth was a common oriental view of the king. Both Egyptian and Assyrian texts describe the king as the image of God (see Ockinga, Dion, Bird). Furthermore, man is here bidden to rule and subdue the rest of creation, an obviously royal task (cf. 1 Kgs 5:4 [4:24], etc.), and Ps 8 speaks of man as having been created a little lower than the angels, *crowned* with glory and made to *rule* the works of God's hands. The allusions to the functions of royalty are quite clear in Ps 8. Another consideration suggesting that man is a divine representative on earth arises from the very idea of an image. Images of gods or kings were viewed as representatives of the deity or king. The divine spirit was often thought of as indwelling an idol, thereby creating a close unity between the god and his image (Clines, *TB* 19 [1968] 81–83). Whereas Egyptian writers often spoke of kings as being in God's image, they never referred to other people in this way. It appears that the OT has democratized this old idea. It affirms that not just a king, but every man and woman, bears God's image and is his representative on earth.

Westermann has objected to the idea that man is the divine representative on earth. It is meaningful to speak of an individual king as a divine surrogate, but not of a large class or of mankind in general. Nor does he think it is compatible with P's theology to say with W. H. Schmidt (*Schöpfungsgeschichte*, 144), "God is proclaimed, wherever man is. . . . Man is God's witness." P makes a sharp distinction between the divine and human realms, which an assertion of the representative nature of man will blur.

These objections show a failure to understand the nature of biblical symbolism. Quite frequently a class of objects may represent an individual, e.g., sacrificial animals represent Israel. And while it would be too much simply to equate God and his representative, man, recognition of his mediating position between God and the rest of creation is quite consonant with biblical symbolism. In a similar way, the high priest represents Israel to God and God to Israel. The ritual system of the OT is not just concerned with establishing the gulf between God and man, but with ways of bridging the gap.

e) The image is a capacity to relate to God. Man's divine image means that God can enter into personal relationships with him, speak to him, and make covenants with him. This view, most eloquently propounded by K. Barth (*Church Dogmatics*, III.1.183–87), is also favored by Westermann. He holds that the phrase "in our image" modifies the verb "let us make," not the noun "man." There is a special kind of creative activity involved in making man that puts man in a unique relationship with his creator and hence able to respond to him. But the "image of God" is not part of the human constitution so much as it is a description of the process of creation which made man different.

If attention is limited to passages discussing the creation of man in God's image, Westermann's view is tenable, for "in our (his) image" is always mentioned in connection with making or creating man. However, passages like 5:3 and Exod 25:40 suggest that "in the image" describes the product of creation rather than the process. Man is so made that he resembles the divine image. Even if Westermann were correct and "in the image" characterized the process of creation, the question about the consequence of the special process would still arise. What are the distinctive qualities of man which result from his creation in the divine image? Certainly a capacity to relate to God covers many aspects of his being listed under b) and d), but the vagueness of the idea may make it less useful than some of the alternatives.

The above survey indicates the difficulty of determining what Genesis understands by the image of God. None of the suggestions seem entirely satisfactory, though there may be elements of truth in many of them.

The strongest case has been made for the view that the divine image makes man God's vice-regent on earth. Because man is God's representative, his life is sacred: every assault on man is an affront to the creator and merits the ultimate penalty (Gen 9:5–6). But this merely describes the function or the consequences of the divine image; it does not pinpoint what the image is in itself.

Second, it must be observed that man is made "*in* the divine image," just as the tabernacle was made "*in* the pattern." This suggests that man is a copy of something that had the divine image, not necessarily a copy of God himself. Exod 25:9, 40 states that the earthly tabernacle was modeled on the heavenly, and Mettinger (*ZAW* 86 [1974] 410–11) argues that Genesis, in speaking of men being made in God's image, is comparing man to the angels who worship in heaven. Man's similarity to them consists in their similar function: both praise God either on earth or in heaven (Mettinger, 411). Furthermore, angels are pictured as ruling the nations on God's behalf (Deut 32:8), just as man is appointed to rule the animal kingdom.

But even if angels bear the divine image, we are still left with isolating what it is that God, the angels, and men have in common that constitutes the divine image. A study of the verbs that are used of both God and man would help to identify some of those features. Both God and man see, hear, speak. Man dies but God does not. God creates but man does not. God cannot be seen, and so on. And of course, both God and man rest on the seventh day (2:1–3). While these continuities between God and man do not exhaust the notion of the divine image, they do suggest areas of similarity that perhaps the biblical writers were referring to when they used this term. (See further J. F. A. Sawyer, *JTS* 25 [1974] 418–26.)

אדם "man" in Gen 1–4 is usually preceded by the definite article "the man," except when preceded by an inseparable preposition such as ל "to" (2:20; 3:17, 21). In omitting the article with the preposition ל, אדם behaves like אלהים "God." In chap. 5 אדם is used without the article as a personal name "Adam," but from 4:1 and 4:25 it is evident that even with the article "Adam" may be the better translation, just as האלהים may well be translated "God," e.g., 22:1 (cf. Cassuto, 1:166–67). This fluidity between the definite and indefinite form makes it difficult to know when the personal name "Adam" is first mentioned (LXX 2:16; AV 2:19; RV and RSV 3:17; TEV 3:20; NEB 3:21). The very indefiniteness of reference may be deliberate. אדם is "mankind, humanity" as opposed to God or the animals (איש is man as opposed to woman). Adam, the first man created and named, is representative of humanity (cf. *TDOT* 1:75–87; *THWAT* 1:41–57). (For a diachronic explanation of the variant spellings in chaps. 2–3 see Barthélemy, 1981).

27 Whereas v 26 used the anarthrous אדם, here in v 27 the definite article האדם is used, and clearly mankind in general, "male and female," not an individual, is meant. The fulfillment of the divine command is recorded in three brief sentences specifying the most significant aspects of human existence:

> So God created man in his own image,
> in the image of God he created him:
> male and female he created them.

The three clauses are in apposition. The first two are arranged chiastically and emphasize the divine image in man, while the third specifies that women also bear the divine image (on apposition clauses cf. *SBH*, 55). The midrashic suggestion "that man as first created was bisexual and the sexes separated afterwards is far from the thought of this passage" (Skinner, 33). The expression "male and female" is most frequent in legal texts, and highlights rather the sexual distinctions within mankind and foreshadows the blessing of fertility to be announced in v 28.

28 God's blessing on mankind is like that pronounced on the animals in v 22. Like the animals man is to "be fruitful and multiply." But whereas v 22 simply gives a command, this verse adds "and God said to them," thus drawing attention to the personal relationship between God and man. Furthermore, man is told to "subdue and rule" the earth and its animal inhabitants, thereby fulfilling his role as God's image-bearer on earth (cf. v 26). But the focus in Genesis is on the fulfillment of the blessing of fruitfulness. This command, like others in Scripture, carries with it an implicit promise that God will enable man to fulfill it. It is repeated to Noah after the flood (9:1), and the patriarchs too are reminded of this divine promise (17:2, 20: 28:3; 35:11). The genealogies of Gen 5, 9, 11, 25, 36, 46 bear silent testimony to its fulfillment, and on his deathbed Jacob publicly notes the fulfillment of the divine word (48:4; cf. 47:27).

Here, then, we have a clear statement of the divine purpose of marriage: positively, it is for the procreation of children; negatively, it is a rejection of the ancient oriental fertility cults. God desires his people to be fruitful. His promise makes any participation in such cults or the use of other devices to secure fertility not only redundant, but a mark of unbelief (cf. Gen 16; 30:14–15).

God's purpose in creating man was that he should rule over the animal world (v 26). Here this injunction is repeated and defined more precisely. "Rule the fish of the sea, the birds of the sky and every living creature . . . on earth." Because man is created in God's image, he is king over nature. He rules the world on God's behalf. This is of course no license for the unbridled exploitation and subjugation of nature. Ancient oriental kings were expected to be devoted to the welfare of their subjects, especially the poorest and weakest members of society (Ps 72:12–14). By upholding divine principles of law and justice, rulers promoted peace and prosperity for all their subjects. Similarly, mankind is here commissioned to rule nature as a benevolent king, acting as God's representative over them and therefore treating them in the same way as God who created them. Thus animals, though subject to man, are viewed as his companions in 2:18–20. Noah, portrayed as uniquely righteous in 6:9, is also the arch-conservationist who built an ark to preserve all kinds of life from being destroyed in the flood (6:20; 7:3).

29–30 God's provision of food for newly created man stands in sharp contrast to Mesopotamian views which held that man was created to supply the gods with food (A.1.339). Westermann (1:163–64) cites other texts to show that there was a widespread belief in antiquity that man and the animals were once vegetarian. The prophets' expectation that one day "the lion shall eat straw like the ox" (Isa 11:7; 65:25; cf. Hos 2:20 [2:18]) is often thought to reflect this idea; the new age will be a return to paradise. V 29 permits man to eat plants and fruit, but the animals may only eat plants (30). 9:3 explicitly gives man the right to eat meat. "Every moving thing that is alive shall be yours to eat; like the green vegetation I gave you, I have given you everything."

Gen 1, however, does not forbid the consumption of meat, and it may be that meat eating is envisaged from the time of the fall. Man is expected to rule over the animals. The LORD provided Adam with garments of skin (3:21). Abel kept and sacrificed sheep (4:2–4), and Noah distinguished clean and unclean animals (7:2). Gispen may therefore be correct in suggesting that 9:3 is ratifying the post-fall practice of meat-eating rather than inaugurating it.

31 "And God saw all that he had made that it was really very good." The appreciation formula (cf. 4, 10, 12, 18, 21, 25) is here modified in three ways to emphasize the perfection of the final work. First, it is applied to the whole creation, "all that he had made," instead of just to individual items. Second, instead of the usual word for "that," כי, used before (e.g., v 4), here והנה "that . . . really" is used, suggesting God's enthusiasm as he contemplated his handiwork. Third, the finished whole is said to be "very good," not merely "good." The harmony and perfection of the completed heavens and earth express more adequately the character of their creator than any of the separate components can. The special character of the sixth day, the day on which creation was complete, is perhaps hinted at by the grammar of the concluding formula ". . . the sixth day," for days 2–5 always use the same formula, "day, Xth," but here the definite article is added to the ordinal "day, *the* sixth," phraseology also used in connection with the Sabbath, e.g., 2:3: "day, *the* seventh."

Sub-Bibliography on 2:1–3

(See also the Main Bibliography and the Gen 1–11 bibliography.)

Andreasen, N. E. A. *The Old Testament Sabbath.* Missoula: Scholars Press, 1972. **Bettenzoli, G.** "La tradizione del *šabbāt.*" *Hen* 4 (1982) 265–93. **Gordon, C. H.** "Asymmetric Janus Parallelism." *EI* 16 (1982) 80–81. ———. "The Seventh Day." *UF* 11 (1979) 299–301. **Grossfeld, B.** "Targum Onkelos and Rabbinic Interpretation to Gen 2:1, 2." *JJS* 24 (1973) 176–78. **Newman, A.** "Gen 2:2: An Exercise in Interpretative Competence and Performance." *BT* 27 (1976) 101–4. **Robinson, G.** "The Idea of Rest in the OT and the Search for the Basic Character of Sabbath." *ZAW* 92 (1980) 32–42. **Siker-Gieseler, J. S.** "The Theology of the Sabbath in the OT: A Canonical Approach." *StudBT* 11 (1981) 5–20. **Toeg, A.** "Gen 1 and the Sabbath." (Heb.) *BMik* 18 (1972) 288–96.

2:1–3 In form and content the seventh day differs sharply from the preceding six. But this is no reason for making a break in the account between 1:31 and 2:1 as the medieval chapter division suggests. These verses make a beautifully arranged conclusion to the account of creation, echoing and balancing the opening verses. 2:1, mentioning "heaven and earth," and 2:3, "which God created," are linked chiastically with 1:1, and 2:2–3 with its threefold mention of God's resting on the seventh day focus on the unique character of that day. (For further discussion see Cassuto 1:12–15, 60–70.)

1 "The heavens and the earth and all their host." The stars (Deut 4:19) and, more rarely, the angels (1 Kgs 22:19) are the host of heaven. Probably only the former are meant here. But the "host of earth" never occurs anywhere else, and here it must refer to everything created on earth. This verse then serves as a summary conclusion to chap. 1.

2 "God had finished his work . . . on the seventh day." To say that God finished work on the seventh day might seem to imply that he was working on that day. For this reason some versions and modern commentators changed "seventh" to "sixth" (Newman, *BT* 27 [1976] 101–4). This spoils the threefold repetition of "seventh" in vv 2–3, and it overlooks the exact nuance of כלה "and he had finished." Elsewhere in the Pentateuch, e.g., Gen 17:22; 49:33; Exod 40:33, the phrase indicates that the action in question is past, and a pluperfect is used in English translations. There is no implication in the Hebrew of 2:2 that God was working on the seventh day before he finished.

מלאכה "work" occurs three times in vv 2–3. It is the ordinary word for human work (cf. 39:11; Exod 20:9), and it is therefore a little unexpected that the extraordinary divine activity involved in creating heaven and earth should be so described. It may be, as Westermann suggests (1:170), that this word has been deliberately chosen to hint that man should stop his daily work on the seventh day. The phraseology of Exod 40:33, "And Moses finished the work," is particularly close to this verse and suggests that the erection of the tabernacle is being compared to God's creation of the world.

"He rested" שבת has three closely related senses: "to cease to be," "to desist from work," and "to observe the sabbath." It is clear that the second sense is central here, though since God abstained from work on the seventh day, subsequently called the Sabbath, the sabbatical idea is also near at hand. Nevertheless it is striking that the Sabbath is not mentioned by name. Cassuto (1:65–68) suggests that this is because the Babylonians termed the fifteenth day of the month, the day of the full moon, *Šapattu;* so Genesis, not wishing to confuse the two, avoids the term. A less likely possibility is that the word might have been taken to mean "Saturn" as in later post-biblical Hebrew (Gordon, *UF* 11 [1979] 300) and was therefore shunned, just as the terms "sun" and "moon" are in v 16. At any rate, in Mesopotamia the 7th, 14th, 19th, 21st and 28th days of each month were regarded by some as unlucky. It seems likely that the Israelite Sabbath was introduced as a deliberate counter-blast to this lunar-regulated cycle. The Sabbath was quite independent of the phases of the moon, and far from being unlucky, was blessed and sanctified by the creator. Cassuto's interpretation is attractive in the light of the possible polemic against Near Eastern practices elsewhere in chap. 1, but it remains unprovable. Stolz has suggested that the observance of the Sabbath developed out of major festivals, which often lasted seven days, and the custom of making the final day of a festival into a Sabbath was subsequently put on a weekly basis (Stolz, *THWAT* 2:863–69). Again, this schema is conjectural. It could well be argued that the custom of forbidding work on the seventh day of a festival was an extension of the sabbatical principle rather than its origin. (For further discussion see R. de Vaux, *Ancient Israel,* 475–83; N. E. A. Andreasen, *The OT Sabbath* [Missoula: Scholars Press, 1972]; see also *IDBSup*, 760–62; *THWAT* 2:863–69.)

Exod 16:22–30 suggests that Israel first learned about the Sabbath in the wilderness, though Exod 20:8, like this passage, asserts that the Sabbath idea is as old as creation itself. In observing the seventh day as holy, man is imitating his creator's example.

3 Though the seventh day is not called the Sabbath, God "blessed" it and "hallowed" it. These are striking terms to apply to a day. Biblical usage generally restricts blessing to animate beings—God, men, animals and so on—and it is not immediately obvious in what sense a day can be blessed (cf. 1:22, 28). Divine blessing on men and animals leads to fruitfulness and success, and it is paradoxical that the day on which God refrains from creative activity is pronounced blessed. Partly the Sabbath is blessed by being "hallowed," but there is also the suggestion that those who observe the Sabbath will enjoy divine blessing in their lives.

Similarly, it is unusual for a day to be "hallowed," that is, made or declared holy. The piel of קדש is usually factitive, though here it may be declarative. Places, people, and religious objects may be hallowed, but apart from the Sabbath, only in Neh 8:9, 11 is a festival day called holy. God is holy: holiness is the essence of his character. Anything else that is described as holy in the OT derives its holiness from being chosen by God and given to him in the correct prescribed manner (see G. J. Wenham, *Leviticus*, 18–27). The seventh day is the very first thing to be hallowed in Scripture, to acquire that special status that properly belongs to God alone. In this way Genesis emphasizes the sacredness of the Sabbath. Coupled with the threefold reference to God resting from all his work on that day, these verses give the clearest of hints of how man created in the divine image should conduct himself on the seventh day.

"Which God had created by making it" is an expansion of the usual phrase "the work which he did" (2:2). The insertion of "God created" into the phrase produces slightly ungainly Hebrew, but more significantly harks back to 1:1, resulting in a fine inclusion indicating that the first section of Genesis ends here. The combination of the verbs ברא "to create" and עשה "to make" covers all of God's creative activity in the six days, reminding the reader of all that has been achieved. Its very brevity evokes the silent awe that is appropriate before the grandeur of the work that has been accomplished.

Explanation

Simple and majestic, dignified yet unaffected, profound and yet perfectly clear, Genesis makes a superb introduction not only to the Book of Genesis itself but to the whole of Scripture.

V 1 sets the tone and states the theme of all that follows: "In the beginning God created the heaven and the earth." God is the author of the whole world: "heaven and earth" here mean everything, owe their existence to the divine will. His sovereignty is made visible in the things that exist. God alone "creates" in the full sense of that word, molding all things to fulfill his inscrutable purposes.

The power and inscrutability of God are again emphasized by the Wind of God hovering over the dark waters of chaos. The three parallel clauses of v 2 describe the state of the earth before the creation of light—already the focus is narrowing from the entire universe in v 1 to earth in v 2 to man in v 26—and it would be possible to regard these clauses as virtually synonymous. But it is better to see them as forming a progression from the wholly negative "the earth was total chaos" through the mysterious and ambiguous darkness (is it shrouding only the earth or does it veil the divine presence as well?), to the still allusive Wind of God that is nevertheless pregnant with creative power.

Suddenly the tempo changes. In a mere six words the creation of light is described. The separation of light from darkness and their naming follow in quick succession.

Though this is narrative, it is highly stylized: every phrase in day one becomes a formula that is reused in the subsequent days. This reuse is far from mechanical. Though the formulaic elements in the account of each day's activities are substantially the same, omission and expansion of individual parts of the formula sustain variety and interest. While the creation of light and the firmament on days 1 and 2 are described quite succinctly, those aspects of the environment described in days 3 to 5 that affect man more closely—plants, sun and moon, and the animals—take up proportionately more narrative space, and the creation of man himself and the definition of his role is the fullest account of all. The creation of man in the divine image is without doubt the focal point of Gen 1, the climax of the six days' work.

But it is not its conclusion. The only connection the seventh day has with the preceding days is sequence. Its character and formulae set it apart from the preceding six days. It is pre-eminently the day God ceased his creative work: of all the days the seventh is the only one blessed and sanctified. Its different literary form sets it apart in the narrative, just as the divine rest and sanctification set it apart in fact.

Viewed with respect to its negatives, Gen 1:1–2:3 is a polemic against the mythico-religious concepts of the ancient Orient. If, with traditional exegetes, we understand 1:1 to assert that God created the whole universe, by implication out of nothing, this is a rejection of the common notion that matter pre-existed the gods' work of creation. The polemic intent of Genesis is even more clear in its handling of the sea monsters and the astral bodies: for this writer they are not gods who compete with Yahweh; they are merely his creatures who display his power and skill. The concept of man here is markedly different from standard Near Eastern mythology: man was not created as the lackey of the gods to keep them supplied with food; he was God's representative and ruler on earth, endowed by his creator with an abundant supply of food and expected to rest every seventh day from his labors. Finally, the seventh day is not a day of ill omen as in Mesopotamia, but a day of blessing and sanctity on which normal work is laid aside.

In contradicting the usual ideas of its time, Gen 1 is also setting out a positive alternative. It offers a picture of God, the world, and man which has become so much part and parcel of the Judaeo-Christian tradition that analysis is very difficult. For this very reason it is important to attempt such an analysis. Four things stand out.

(1) God is without peer and competitor. He does not have to establish his

power in struggle with other members of a polytheistic pantheon. The sun
and moon are his handiwork, not his rivals. His word is supreme: a simple
fiat is sufficient. He speaks and it is done. Word and deed reveal his omnipotence. Although the Hebrew verb "create" does not necessarily connote *creatio
ex nihilo,* the overall thrust of the narrative implies that God had this ability:
the idea of a demiurge modeling pre-existing matter is far removed from
this account. While God has no equals, Gen 1:26, "Let *us* make man," and
maybe 2:1, "all their host," do seem to presuppose the existence of other
angelic beings, but this is quite distinct from polytheism. In keeping with its
earthly/human orientation the story says nothing about the origin of the
angels.

(2) God is more than creator, he is law-giver. He divides the light from
darkness and the land from sea, and he names them. He appoints the stars
for signs and for fixed times. The animate creation is told to be fruitful and
multiply. Man is to subdue the earth, and the seventh day is hallowed. God
sets bounds for the natural order and specifies the roles of the species within
it. With this goes the corollary that all creatures will fulfill their divinely
appointed role only if they adhere to God's directive.

(3) The world reflects its creator. Genesis, by focusing in turn on different
yet representative areas of life, announces that each is created by God and
obeys God. The immediate fulfillment of each command and the refrain
"And it was so" emphasize the subjection of creation. The refrain "And God
saw that it was good" and the concluding statement "God saw all that he
had made that it was really very good" bring out the perfection of creation
and its conformity to the divine will. The waters will remain separate from
the earth, the light from the darkness. The sun will rule the day and the
moon and stars the night. The plants will bear seed and the animals be
fruitful and multiply. In so fulfilling the divine purpose, "the heavens declare
the glory of God and the firmament shows his handiwork" (Ps 19:1).

(4) Finally, this chapter discloses man's true nature. He is the apex of the
created order: the whole narrative moves toward the creation of man. Everything is made for man's benefit, most obviously the plants assigned to him
to eat (v 29). While man shares with plants and animals the ability to reproduce
himself, he alone is made in the divine image and is instructed to subdue
the earth. The image of God means that in some sense men and women
resemble God and the angels, though where the resemblance lies is left unde-
fined in this chapter. The divine image does enable man to be addressed
directly by his creator and makes him in a real sense God's representative
on earth, who should rule over the other creatures as a benevolent king.
Finally, as the creator rested on the seventh day from all his work, so Genesis
2:1–3 implies man should also take a break from his labors. If the other
parts of creation were designed for man's benefit, so too was the Sabbath.

Gen 1 has been called a festive overture to P, for it introduces themes
that are characteristic of and developed in much greater detail in other priestly
material later in the Pentateuch. By tracing back to creation the classificatory
system among plants and animals, the Sabbath, and the origins of divine
blessing, the writer is giving these institutions the authority of primeval antiquity. Though there is little in the chapter that relates directly to worship,
the prime interest of the P material, the references to the fixed times (v 14),

and to the seventh day (2:1–3) may be construed as hints of the editor's preoccupation with the cult.

While the existence of a P document or editorial layer remains speculative, there is no doubt as to the present function of Gen 1. It heads the Book of Genesis, indeed introduces the Pentateuch and the whole canon. The musical metaphor of an overture could, I think, be extended to cover these much more extensive units of tradition. For Gen 1 stands apart from them, yet also introduces them. From Gen 2:4 onward, sacred history in Genesis is unfolded in ten cycles, each headed by the phrase "this is the family history of." The absence of this heading in Gen 1:1 and the distinctive style of the chapter sets it off from what follows. Yet here the great themes, or at least the presuppositions of the subsequent narratives, are made explicit. If the divine word established the world in the beginning, it will become clear that the same word governed and directed the subsequent unfolding of sacred history. Man created in the divine image is expected to imitate God in his daily life: how far he conforms to this ideal is the story not only of Genesis but of the rest of Scripture. God is here portrayed as a benevolent creator concerned for man's welfare, creating man in his own image, blessing him, and giving him instruction. That man can enjoy fellowship with God, obey him, and be blessed by him are the presuppositions of all the subsequent narratives. In all these ways Gen 1 forms a strikingly beautiful prelude to the rest of Genesis.

Any attempt to trace the subsequent use of this chapter in Scripture would be most unsatisfactory just because its themes and motifs are so pervasive and its theology so fundamental to the biblical world-view. Here we have some of the principal themes of biblical theology displayed in epigrammatic brevity: there these simple but far-reaching affirmations have become the presuppositions of the rest of the sacred story. Gen 1 formed the basis of the first article of the Christian creed, "I believe in God the Father, maker of heaven and earth." In more recent times Gen 1 provided the intellectual underpinning of the scientific enterprise. Its assumption of unity and order underlying the manifold and seemingly capricious phenomena of experience rests on Gen 1's assertion of the one almighty God who created and controls the world according to a coherent plan. Only such an assumption can justify the experimental method. Were this world controlled by a multitude of capricious deities, or subject to mere chance, no consistency could be expected in experimental results and no scientific laws could be discovered.

It has been unfortunate that one device which our narrative uses to express the coherence and purposiveness of the creator's work, namely, the distribution of the various creative acts to six days, has been seized on and interpreted over-literalistically, with the result that science and Scripture have been pitted against each other instead of being seen as complementary. Properly understood, Genesis justifies the scientific experience of unity and order in nature. The six-day schema is but one of several means employed in this chapter to stress the system and order that has been built into creation. Other devices include the use of repeating formulae, the tendency to group words and phrases into tens and sevens, literary techniques such as chiasm and inclusio, the arrangement of creative acts into matching groups, and so on.

If these hints were not sufficient to indicate the schematization of the six-day creation story, the very content of the narrative points in the same direction. In particular, evening and morning appear three days before the sun and moon, which are explicitly stated to be for "days and years" (v 14). Also, this chapter stands outside the main historical outline of Genesis, each section of which begins, "This is the (family) history of." (Cf. 2:4; 6:9). As we have said, it is an overture to the rest of the story and therefore does not stand foursquare with the rest of Genesis, to be interpreted according to precisely the same criteria. Finally, at best, all language about God is analogical. Words used to describe him and his acts must inevitably be human words, but they do not have quite the same meaning when applied to him as when they refer to men. In speaking of God as father, we do not assign him all the attributes of human fatherhood. Similarly, in speaking of his creating the world in six days, we do not identify his mode of creation with human creativity nor need we assume his week's work was necessarily accomplished in 144 hours. By speaking of six days of work followed by one day's rest, Gen 1 draws attention to the correspondence between God's work and man's and God's rest as a model for the Sabbath, but that does not necessarily imply that the six days of creation are the same as human days.

The Bible-versus-science debate has, most regrettably, sidetracked readers of Gen 1. Instead of reading the chapter as a triumphant affirmation of the power and wisdom of God and the wonder of his creation, we have been too often bogged down in attempting to squeeze Scripture into the mold of the latest scientific hypothesis or distorting scientific facts to fit a particular interpretation. When allowed to speak for itself, Gen 1 looks beyond such minutiae. Its proclamation of the God of grace and power who undergirds the world and gives it purpose justifies the scientific approach to nature. Gen 1, by further affirming the unique status of man, his place in the divine program, and God's care for him, gives a hope to mankind that atheistic philosophies can never legitimately supply.

The Garden of Eden (2:4–3:24)

Bibliography

(See also the Main Bibliography and Gen 1–11 bibliographies)

Alonso-Schökel, L. "Sapiential and Covenant Themes in Gen 2–3." *TD* 13 (1965) 3–10. **Alster, B.** "Enki and Ninhursag." *UF* 10 (1978) 15–27. **Andreasen, N. E.** "Adam and Adapa: Two Anthropological Characters." *AUSS* 19 (1981) 179–94. **Ashbel, D.** "The Four Rivers Leaving Eden." (Heb.) *BMik* 15 (1969/70) 100–104. **Auffret, P.** *La sagesse a bâti sa maison.* OBO 49. Fribourg: Editions Universitaires, 1982. 23–68. **Bailey, J. A.** "Initiation and the Primal Woman in Gilgamesh and Gen 2–3." *JBL* 89 (1970) 137–50. **Baker, J.** "The Myth of Man's 'Fall'—A Reappraisal." *ExpTim* 92 (1981) 235–37. **Beattie, D. R. G.** "What Is Gen 2–3 About?" *ExpTim* 92 (1980) 8–10. ———. "'Peshat' and 'Derash' in the Garden of Eden." *IrBS* 7 (1985) 62–75. **Beeston, A. F. L.** "One Flesh." *VT* 36 (1986) 115–17. **Bergmeier, R.** "Zur Septuagintaübersetzung von Gen 3:16." *ZAW* 79 (1967) 77–79. **Bing, J. D.** "Adapa and Immortality." *UF* 16 (1984) 53–56. **Boomershine, T. E.** "The Structure of Narrative Rhetoric in Gen 2–3." *Semeia* 18 (1980) 113–29. **Bravmann, M. M.** "Concerning the Phrase 'And shall cleave unto his wife.'" *Muséon* 85 (1972) 269–74. ———. "The Original Meaning of '. . . A Man Leaves his Father and Mother' (Gen 2:24)." *Muséon* 88 (1975) 449–53. **Brinktrine, J.** "Gen 2:4a: Überschrift oder Unterschrift?" *BZ* 9 (1965) 277. **Brueggemann, W.** "Of the Same Flesh and Bone (Gen 2:23a)." *CBQ* 32 (1970) 532–42. ———. "From Dust to Kingship." *ZAW* 84 (1972) 1–18. **Buccellati, G.** "Adapa, Genesis and the Notion of Faith." *UF* 5 (1973) 61–66. **Burns, D. E.** "Dream Form in Gen 2:4b–3:24: Asleep in the Garden." *JSOT* 37 (1987) 3–14. **Castellino, G.** "Les origines de la civilisation selon les textes bibliques et les textes cunéiformes." *Congress Volume, 1956.* VTSup 4. Leiden: Brill, 1957. 116–37. **Charbel, P. A.** "Gen 2:18–20: Una polemica sottintesa dello Jahwista." *BeO* 22 (1980) 233–35. **Clark, W. M.** "A Legal Background to the Yahwist's Use of 'Good' and 'Evil' in Gen 2–3." *JBL* 88 (1969) 266–78. **Clines, D. J. A.** "The Tree of Knowledge and the Law of Yahweh." *VT* 24 (1974) 8–14. **Coats, G. W.** "The God of Death: Power and Obedience in the Primeval History." *Int* 29 (1975) 227–39. **Combs, E.,** and **Post, K.** "Historicity and Necessity: Death in Genesis and the *Chāndoyga Upanishad.*" *SR* 9 (1980) 41–52. **Coppens, J.** "La nudité des protoplastes." *ETL* 46 (1970) 380–83. **Couffignal, R.** *Le drame de l'Eden: le récit de la Genèse et sa fortune littéraire.* Toulouse: Université Toulouse-le Mirail, 1980. ———. "Guides pour l'Eden: Approches nouvelles de Gen 2:4–3." *RevThom* 80 (1980) 613–27. **Culley, R. C.** "Action Sequences in Gen 2–3." *Semeia* 18 (1980) 25–33. **Davidsen, O.** "The Mythical Foundation of History: A Religio-Semiotic Analysis of the Story of the Fall." *LingBib* 51 (1982) 23–36. **Dockx, S.** *Le Récit du Paradis.* Paris: Duculot, 1981. **Dubarle, A. M.** *Le Péché originel dans l'écriture.* LD 20. 2d ed. Paris: du Cerf, 1967. **Ellington, J.** "Man and Adam in Gen 1–5." *BT* 30 (1979) 201–5. **Feilschuss-Abir, A. S.** "'Da werden eure Augen geöffnet und ihr werdet sein wie Gott, wissend Gutes und Böses (Gen 3:5).'" *TGl* 74 (1984) 190–203. **Foh, S. T.** "What Is the Woman's Desire?" *WTJ* 37 (1974/75) 376–83. **Fraine, J. de.** *La Bible et l'origine de l'homme.* Bruges: Desclée, 1961. **Fuss, W.** *Die sogenannte Paradieserzählung.* Gütersloh: Gerd Mohn, 1968. **Gerleman, G.** "*Adam* und die alttestamentliche Anthropologie." *Die Botschaft und die Boten.* FS für H. W. Wolff, ed. J. Jeremias and L. Perlitt. Neukirchen: Neukirchener Verlag, 1981. 319–33. **Gese, H.** "Die bewachte Lebensbaum und die Heroen: zwei mythologische Ergänzungen zur Urgeschichte der Quelle J." In *Wort und Geschichte: FS für K. Elliger*. AOAT 18. Kevelaer: Butzon and Bercker, 1973. 77–85. **Gilbert, M.** "Une seule chair (Gen 2:24)." *NRT* 100 (1978) 66–89. **Gispen, W. H.** "Gen 2: 10–14." *Studia Biblica et Semitica: FS für T.C. Vriezen*. Wageningen: Veenman, 1966. 115–24. **Görg, M.** "Wo lag das Paradies?" *BN* 2 (1977) 23–32. ———. "Ein architectonischer Fachausdruck in der Priesterschrift: zur Bedeutung von 'eden.'" *VT* 33 (1983) 334–38. **Granot, M.** "For Dust Thou Art." (Heb.) *BMik* 17 (1971/1972) 310–19. **Grant, A. M.** "Adam and Ish: Man in the Old Testament." *AusBR* 25 (1977) 2–11. **Grelot, P.** "Réflexions sur le problème du péché originel." *NRT* 89 (1967) 337–75, 449–84. **Gross, H.** "Theologische Exegese von Gen 1–3." In *Mysterium Salutis II*, ed. J. Feiner and M. Lohrer. Einsiedeln: 1967. 421–39. **Haag, E.** *Der Mensch am Anfang: Die alttestamentliche Paradiesvorstellung nach Gen 2–3*. Trier: Paulinus, 1970. **Haag, H.** *Biblische Schöpfungslehre und kirchliche Erbsündenlehre*. SBS 10. Stuttgart: Katholisches Bibelwerk, 1966. ———. "Die Komposition der Sündenfall-Erzählung." *TQ* 146 (1966) 1–7. **Habel, N. C.** "Ezekiel 28 and the Fall of the First Man." *CTM* 38 (1967) 516–24. **Hauser, A. J.** "Genesis 2–3: The Theme of Intimacy and Alienation." In *Art and Meaning: Rhetoric in Biblical Literature*, ed. D. J. A. Clines, D. M. Gunn, A. J. Hauser. JSOTSS 19. Sheffield: JSOT Press, 1982. 20–36. **Hendel, R. S.** "'The Flame of the Whirling Sword': A Note on Gen 3:24." *JBL* 104 (1985) 671–74. **Hidal, S.** "The Land of Cush in the Old Testament." *SEÅ* 41–42 (1976–77) 97–106. **Humbert, P.** *Études sur le récit du paradis et de la chute dans la Genèse*. Neuchâtel: Université, 1940. **Jaroš, K.** "Die Motive der heiligen Bäume und der Schlange in Gen 2–3." *ZAW* 92 (1980) 204–15. **Jobling, D.** "The Myth Semantics of Gen 2:4b–3:24." *Semeia* 18 (1980) 41–49. ———. "Myth and Its Limits in Gen 2:4b–3:24." In *The Sense of Biblical Narrative: Structural Analyses in the Hebrew Bible II*. JSOTSS 39. Sheffield: JSOT Press, 1986. 17–43. **Joines, K. R.** "The Serpent in Gen 3." *ZAW* 87 (1975) 1–11. **Kikawada, I. M.** "Two Notes on Eve." *JBL* 91 (1972) 33–37. ———. "The Irrigation of the Garden of Eden." *Actes du 29e Congrès international des Orientalistes Études Hébraiques* 1975. 29–33. **King-Farlow, J.,** and **D. W. Hunt.** "Perspectives on the Fall of Man." *SJT* 35 (1982) 193–204. **Koole, J. L.** "De Stamvader (Gen 1–3)." *Schrift en uitleg: Studies aangeboden aan W. H. Gispen*. Kampen: Kok, 1970. 79–94. **Köster, H. M.** *Urstand, Fall und Erbsünde in der katholischen Theologie unseres Jahrhunderts*. Regensburg: Friedrich Pustet, 1981. **Kruse, H.** "Vorstufen der Erbschuldlehre." *MTZ* 20 (1969) 288–314. **Kutsch, E.** "Die Paradieserzählung Gen 2–3 und ihr Verfasser." In *Studien zum Pentateuch: FS für W. Kornfeld*, ed. G. Braulik. Vienna: Herder, 1977. 9–24. **Lamberg-Karlovsky, C. C.** "Dilmun: Gateway to Immortality." *JNES* 41 (1982) 45–50. **Landy, F.** "The Song of Songs and the Garden of Eden." *JBL* 98 (1979) 513–28. **L'Hour, J.** "Yahweh Elohim." *RB* 81 (1974) 524–56. **Lipinski, E.** "Garden of Abundance, Image of Lebanon." *ZAW* 85 (1973) 358–59. ———. "Ancient Types of Wisdom Literature in Biblical Narrative." In *Essays on the Bible and the Ancient World III: I. L. Seeligman Volume*, ed. A. Rofé and Y. Zakovitch. Jerusalem: Rubinstein's Publishing House, 1983. 39–55. **Lohfink, N.** "Gen 2f als 'geschichtliche' Ätiologie." *Scholastik* 38 (1963) 321–34. ———. "Wie sollte man das Alte Testament auf die Erbsünde hin befragen?" In *Zum Problem der Erbsünde: Theologische und philosophische Versuche*. Essen: Ludgerus Verlag, 1981. 9–52. **Loretz, O.** *Schöpfung und Mythos, Mensch und Welt nach den Anfangskapiteln der Genesis*. SBS 32. Stuttgart: Katholisches Bibelwerk, 1968. **McKenzie, J. L.** "The Literary Characteristics of Gen 2–3." *TS* 15 (1954) 541–72. **Mayes, A. D. H.** "The Nature of Sin and Its Origin in the Old Testament." *ITQ* 40 (1973) 250–63. **Mendenhall, G. E.** "The Shady Side of Wisdom: The Date and Purpose of Gen 3." In *A Light unto My Path: Old Testament Studies in Honor of J. M. Myers*, ed. H. N. Bream, R. D. Heim, and C. A. Moore. Philadelphia: Temple UP, 1974. 319–34. **Merode, M. de.** "'Une aide qui lui corresponde': L'exégèse de Gen 2:18–24 dans les écrits de l'A.T., du judaisme et du NT." *RTL* 8 (1977) 329–52.

Metzger, M. *Die Paradieserzählung: Die Geschichte ihrer Auslegung von J. Clericus bis W. M. L. de Wette.* Bonn: Bovier, 1959. **Meyers, C. L.** "Gender Roles and Gen 3:16 Revisited." In *The Word of the Lord Shall Go Forth: Essays in Honor of D. N. Freedman,* ed. C. L. Meyers and M. O'Connor. Winona Lake, IN: Eisenbrauns, 1983. 337–54. **Mikaelsson, L.** "Sexual Polarity: An Aspect of the Ideological Structure in the Paradise Narrative, Gen 2:4–3:24." *Temenos* 16 (1980) 84–91. **Millard, A. R.** "The Etymology of Eden." *VT* 34 (1984) 103–6. **Müller, H. P.** "Mythische Elemente in der jahwistischen Schöpfungserzählung." *ZTK* 69 (1971) 259–89. **Naidoff, B. D.** "A Man to Work the Soil: A New Interpretation of Gen 2–3." *JSOT* 5 (1978) 2–14. **Neiman, D.** "Gihon and Pishon: Mythological Antecedents of the Two Enigmatic Rivers of Eden." *PWCJS* 1 (1977) 321–28. **Neveu, L.** "Le paradis perdu: recherches sur la structure littéraire de Gen 2:4b–3:24." *Impacts* 4 (1982) 27–74. **Nielsen, E.** "Sur la théologie de l'auteur de Gen 2–4." In *De la Tôrah au Messie: Études offertes à H. Cazelles,* ed. M. Carrez, J. Doré, P. Grelot. Paris: Desclée, 1981. 55–63. **Pearce, E. K. V.** *Who Was Adam?* Exeter: Paternoster, 1970. **Patte, D.,** and **J. F. Parker.** "A Structural Exegesis of Gen 2 and 3." *Semeia* 18 (1980) 55–75. **Reiser, W.** "Die Verwandschaftsformel in Gen 2:23." *TZ* 16 (1960) 1–4. **Roth, Y.** "The Intentional Double-Meaning Talk in Biblical Prose." (Heb.) *Tarbiz* 41 (1972) 245–54. **Rosenberg, J. W.** "The Garden Story Forward and Backward: The Non-Narrative Dimension of Gen 2–3." *Prooftexts* 1 (1981) 1–27. **Rouillard, H.** "Les feintes questions dans la Bible." *VT* 34 (1984) 237–42. **Ruppert, L.** "Die Sündenfallerzählung (Gen 3) in vorjahwistischer Tradition und Interpretation." *BZ* 15 (1971) 185–202. **Saebo, M.** "Die hebräischen Nomina 'ed und 'ēd—Zwei sumerisch-akkadische Fremdwörter?" *ST* 24 (1970) 130–41. **Sasson, J. M.** "*wĕlōˁ yitbōšāšû* (Gen 2:25) and Its Implications." *Bib* 66 (1985) 418–21. **Scharbert, J.** *Prolegomena eines Alttestamentlers zur Erbsündenlehre.* Freiburg: Herder, 1968. ———. "Quellen und Redaktion in Gen 2:4b–4:16." *BZ* 18 (1974) 45–64. **Schildenberger, J.** "Ist die Erzählung von Sündenfall ein Gleichnis?" *Erbe und Auftrag* 49 (1973) 142–47. **Schmidt, W. H.** *Die Schöpfungsgeschichte der Priesterschrift: Zur Überlieferungsgeschichte von Gen 1:1–2:4a und 2:4b–3:24.* WMANT 17. 2d ed. Neukirchen-Vluyn: Neukirchener Verlag, 1967. **Seethaler, P.-A.** "Kleiner Diskussionsbeitrag zu Gen 3:1–5." *BZ* 23 (1979) 85–86. **Shea, W. H.** "Adam in Ancient Mesopotamian Traditions." *AUSS* 15 (1977) 27–41. **Ska, J. L.** "'Je vais lui faire un allié qui soit son homologue' (Gen 2:18): A propos du terme *ezer* -'aide.'" *Bib* 65 (1984) 233–38. **Speiser, E. A.** "ED in the Story of Creation." In *Oriental and Biblical Studies,* 19–22. ———. "The Rivers of Paradise." In *Oriental and Biblical Studies,* 23–34. **Steck, O. H.** *Die Paradieserzählung.* BibS 60. Neukirchen: Neukirchener Verlag, 1970. **Stitzinger, M. F.** "Gen 1–3 and the Male/ Female Role Relationship." *GTJ* 2 (1981) 23–44. **Stoebe, H. J.** "Sündenbewusstsein und Glaubensuniversalismus, Gedanken zu Genesis 3." *TZ* 36 (1980) 197–207. **Stolz, F.** "Die Bäume des Gottesgartens auf dem Libanon." *ZAW* 84 (1972) 141–56. **Thompson, P. E. S.** "The Yahwist Creation Story." *VT* 21 (1971) 197–208. **Trible, P.** *God and the Rhetoric of Sexuality.* Philadelphia: Fortress, 1978. **Trudinger, L. P.** "'Not Yet Made' or 'Newly Made': A Note on Gen 2:5." *EvQ* 47 (1975) 67–69. **Tsevat, M.** "The Two Trees in the Garden of Eden." (Heb.) *N. Glueck Memorial Volume.* Jerusalem: Israel Exploration Society, 1975. 40–43. ———. "Der Schlangentext von Ugarit." *UF* 11 (1979) 759–78. **Tsukimoto, A.** "'Der Mensch ist geworden wie unsereiner'—Untersuchungen zum zeitgeschichtlichen Hintergrund von Gen 3:22–24 und 6:1–4." *AJBI* 5 (1979) 3–44. **Tucker, G.** "The Creation and the Fall: A Reconsideration." *LTQ* 13 (1979) 113–24. **Tur-Sinai, N. H.** "Jhwh Elohim in der Paradies-Erzählung Gen 2:4b–3:24." *VT* 11 (1961) 94–99. **Vermeylen, J.** "Le récit du paradis et la question des origines du pentateuque." *Bijd* 41 (1980) 230–50. **Vogels, W.** "L'être humain appartient au sol: Gen 2:4b–3:24." *NRT* 105 (1983) 515–34. **Wallace, H. N.** *The Eden Narrative.* HSM 32. Atlanta: Scholars Press, 1985. **Walsh, J. T.** "Gen 2:4b–3:24: A Synchronic

Approach." *JBL* 96 (1977) 161–77. **Wambacq, B. N.** "Or tous deux étaient nus . . . (Gen 2:25)." In *Mélanges B. Rigaux,* ed. A. Descamps and A. de Halleux. Gembloux: Duculot, 1970. 547–56. **Watson, P.** "The Tree of Life." *ResQ* 23 (1980) 232–38. **Wenham, G. J.** "Sanctuary Symbolism in the Garden of Eden Story." *PWCJS* 9 (1986) 19–25. **White, H. C.** "Direct and Third Person Discourse in the Narrative of the 'Fall.'" *Semeia* 18 (1980) 92–106. **Wifall, W.** "The Breath of His Nostrils: Gen 2:7b." *CBQ* 36 (1974) 237–40. **Williams, A. J.** "The Relationship of Gen 3:20 to the Serpent." *ZAW* 89 (1977) 357–74. **Williams, J. G.** "Genesis 3." *Int* 35 (1981) 274–79. **Woudstra, M. H.** "The Story of the Garden of Eden in Recent Study." *VR* 34 (1980) 22–31. **Wright, G. E.** "Women and Masculine Theological Vocabulary in the Old Testament." In *Grace upon Grace: Essays in Honor of L. J. Kuyper,* ed. J. I. Cook. Grand Rapids: Eerdmans, 1975. 64–69. **Wyatt, N.** "Interpreting the Creation and Fall Story in Gen 2–3." *ZAW* 93 (1981) 10–21. **Young, E. J.** *Genesis 3.* London: Banner of Truth, 1968. **Zaclad, J.** "Création, péché originel et formalisme." *RHPR* 51 (1971) 1–30.

Translation

⁴*This*[a] *is the history of the heaven and the earth when they were created,*[b] *on the day the* LORD *God made*[c] *earth and heaven.*

⁵*No*[a] *shrub of the plain had yet*[b] *grown in the earth, nor had any plant of the plain yet*[b] *sprung up, because the* LORD *God had not made it rain on the earth and there was no man to till the land.* ⁶*But*[a] *the fresh water ocean used to rise*[b] *from the earth and water*[c] *the whole surface of the land.* ⁷*Then the* LORD *God shaped*[a] *man from*[b] *the dust of the land and blew*[c] *into his nostrils the breath of life and man became*[d] *a living creature.* ⁸*The* LORD *God planted*[a] *a garden in Eden in the east and placed*[b] *the man there whom he had formed.* ⁹*And the* LORD *God made all kinds*[a] *of trees to sprout*[b] *from the land, trees desirable*[c] *to look at and good to eat;* [d]*the tree of life was in the middle of the garden and also the tree of the knowledge*[e] *of good and evil.*[d]

¹⁰*Now*[a] *there was a river flowing*[b] *out of Eden to water*[c] *the garden, and from there it divided*[d] *and became*[e] *four branches.* ¹¹*One is named*[a] *Pishon: it goes round all the land of Havilah, where there is gold.* ¹²*The gold*[a] *of that*[b] *land is good.*[c] *There too is bdellium and onyx stone.* ¹³*The second river is named Gihon: it goes round all the land of Kush.* ¹⁴*The third river is named Tigris: it runs to the east of Ashur. And the fourth river is the Euphrates.*

¹⁵*Then the* LORD *God took*[a] *man and put*[b] *him in the garden of Eden to till it*[c] *and guard it.*[c] ¹⁶*The* LORD *God commanded*[a] *man: "You may freely*[b] *eat of every garden tree,* ¹⁷*but* [a]*from the tree*[a] *of the knowledge of good and evil never eat,*[b] *for on the day you do,*[c] *you will certainly*[d] *die."*

¹⁸*The* LORD *God thought, "It is not good for man to be*[a] *alone. Let me*[b] *make him a helper, matching him."* ¹⁹*So the* LORD *God shaped*[a] *from the land* [b]*all kinds of wild animals of the plain and birds of the sky and brought*[c] *them to man to see what he would call them.*[d] *And whatever man called* [e]*a living creature,*[e] *that was its name.* ²⁰*Man gave names to all the cattle, to*[a] *the birds of the sky and all the wild animals of the plain, but no helper was found*[b] *for man,*[c] *matching him.*

²¹*Then the* LORD *God made a heavy sleep to overcome*[a] *man and he fell asleep. Then he took*[b] *one of his ribs and closed up the flesh in its place.*[c] ²²*The* LORD

God then built^a the rib he had taken from man into a woman and brought^b her to man. ²³Then man said, "This time! This is bone of my bones and flesh of my flesh! ^aThis shall be called^b a woman, for from a man^c was she taken,^d this one!"^a ²⁴Therefore a man forsakes^a his father and mother and sticks to his wife and they^b become one flesh. ²⁵The two of them, man and his wife, were nude, but they were not ashamed.^a

^{3:1}Now^a the snake was more shrewd than all the wild animals of the plain which the LORD God had made.^a He^b said to the woman, "Has^c God really said you must not^d eat from any^d of the trees in the garden?" ²The woman said to the snake, "We may^a eat of the fruit of the trees in the garden, ³but of the fruit of the^a tree in the middle of the garden God has said, 'Do not eat of it and do not touch^b it lest you die.'"^c ⁴The snake said to the woman, "You will not^a certainly die. ⁵But^a God knows that on the day you eat of it your eyes will be opened^b and you will become like God, knowing good and evil."

⁶Then the woman saw^a that the tree was good to eat and that it was a delight to the eyes and the tree^b was desirable^c to give one insight. So she took some of its fruit, ate it, and also gave^d it to her husband with her and he^e ate. ⁷Then the eyes of both of them were opened,^a and they realized they were nude, and they sewed fig leaves^b together and made themselves loincloths. ⁸Then they heard the sound of the LORD God walking^a to and fro in the garden in the breeze of the day, and man^b and his wife hid^c from the LORD God among the trees of the garden.

⁹Then the LORD God called to man and said to him, "Where^a are you?" ¹⁰He said, "I heard your voice in the garden. I was afraid^a because I was naked, so I hid."^b ¹¹He said, "Who told^a you that you were naked? Have you^b eaten of the tree which I ordered you not to eat?" ¹²Man said, "It was the woman you gave to me who gave me of the tree and I ate."^a ¹³Then the LORD God said to the woman, "What^a have you done?" The woman said, "The snake^b fooled^c me and I ate."

¹⁴Then the LORD God said to the snake,

"Because^a you have done this,

^byou are more cursed than ^call domesticated animals and^c all wild animals;
on your belly you must go, and you must eat dust all the days of your life.^b

¹⁵I shall put hostility between you and the woman, between your offspring and her offspring.

He will batter^a your head^b and you will batter^a his heel."^b

^{16a}To the woman he said,

"I shall greatly multiply^b your pains and your pregnancies;^c
in pain^d you will bear^e children;
your urge will be to your husband,
but he shall rule over you."

¹⁷To man^a he said,

"Because you have obeyed your wife and eaten from the tree which I commanded you, 'Do not eat of it,'
the land is cursed because of you;
in pain you will eat^b of it all the days of your life.

¹⁸It will bring^a up thorns and thistles for you,
and you will eat the plants of the plain.

¹⁹By the sweat of your brow you shall eat bread

until you return to the land from which you were taken,[a]
for you are dust[b] *and to dust you must return."*

²⁰ Man named his wife Eve, because she was the mother of all living. ²¹ Then
the LORD God made for man[a] and his wife tunics of skin and clothed[b] them.

²² The LORD God said, "Since[a] man has become like one[b] of us, knowing good
and evil, now lest he reach out and take from the tree of life as well and eat and
live[c] for ever"—[d] ²³ The LORD God sent[a] him out of the garden of Eden to till the
land from which he was taken.[b] ²⁴ He drove[a] out man and stationed[bc] to the east
of the garden of Eden[d] the cherubim and the flame of a revolving[e] sword to guard
the way to the tree of life.

Notes

4.a. G reads "This is the book of" for MT "This/these," אלה, assimilating the formula to
5:1. MT is preferable.

4.b. The minuscule ה in בהבראם "when they were created" (niph inf + 3 masc pl suffix)
in some MSS leads *BHS* to propose reading the qal בבראם "when (God) created them." MT
may be retained.

4.c. G S SamPent *Tg. Neof.* have instead of "earth and heaven" the more usual order "heaven
and earth." This rearrangement mars the elaborate chiasmus of v 4 in MT:

> a   heaven
> b   earth
> c   created
> c′   made
> b′   earth
> a′ heaven

5.a. Vv 5–6 are conjoined circumstantial clauses preparing for the action in v 7. According
to *SBH* (86) they modify the inf constr "made" in v 4, but it would be simpler to regard them
as simply episode-initial as in 3:1 (cf. *SBH*, 79).

5.b. טרם "not yet" is followed by impf (BDB, 382b).

6.a. "but": antithetic use of ו following negative (*SBH*, 183).

6.b. Impf in past contexts expresses duration (GKC, 107b,d).

6.c. Cf. previous note. Pf (hiph שקה) + waw consec expressing duration (GKC, 112d).

7.a. Main verb following circumstantial clauses in vv 5–6 (waw consec + 3 masc sg impf qal
יצר).

7.b. Verbs of making take a double object, the artifact "man" and the material "dust" (GKC,
117hh).

7.c. Waw consec + 3 masc sg impf qal, נפח.

7.d. היה ל "become" (BDB, 226a; Lambdin, 56).

8.a. Waw consec + 3 masc sg impf qal נטע.

8.b. Waw consec + 3 masc sg impf qal שים

9.a. Waw consec + 3 masc impf hiph צמח "to sprout."

9.b. כל before indefinite noun may mean "all kinds of" (GKC, 127b); cf. Gen 4:22; 24:10.

9.c. Niph ptcp חמד with gerundive sense: "desirable, pleasant" (GKC, 116e).

9.d-d. This clause is probably circumstantial to the preceding clause "the LORD . . . kinds
of tree," and with vv 11–14 it gives a description of the garden (*SBH*, 87).

9.e. דעת "knowledge." Though a substantivized inf from ידע, it may still take a dir obj
"good and evil" (GKC, 115d; Joüon, 124j); cf. Jer 22:16.

10.a. On the syntactic function of vv 10–14, cf. n. 9.d-d above; alternatively these verses
could be episode-initial (*SBH*, 82).

10.b. The ptcp "flowing," the subsequent impf 10.d (3 masc sg impf niph פרד), and pf
with waw 10.e draw attention to the continuity of the actions (GKC, 107d, 112e).

10.c. Inf constr hiph שקה.

10.d. See n. 10.b.

10.e. See n. 10.b.

11.a. On the syntax of naming, cf. *SBH,* 33–34.

12.a. וְזָהַב "And the gold"; the hatef vowel instead of וְזָהָב is prompted by the וֹ before initial sibilant (GKC, 10g).

12.b. הוא stands for הוּא ("that" masc sg) or הִיא ("that" fem sg) in the Pentateuch, the punctuation making it clear when it is, as here, to be read as fem (a so-called *qere perpetuum,* GKC, 32l). For a possible historical explanation of the form as a mark of early Heb see G. A. Rendsburg, *Bib* 63 (1982) 351–69.

12.c. SamPent characteristically inserts "very"; cf. Waltke, 221.

15.a. Waw consec + 3 masc sg impf qal לָקַח "to take."

15.b. Waw consec + 3 masc sg impf hiph נוח "to rest" + 3 masc sg obj suffix.

15.c. Fem suffix agreeing with Eden (Gispen, 1:121), or possibly אֲדָמָה "land" added to inf constr of עבד and שׁמר.

16.a. Waw consec + 3 masc sg impf (apocopated) piel of צוה "to command."

16.b. Inf abs emphasizes permissive nuance of impf (Joüon, 113l).

17.a-a. The antithesis with the previous verse is emphasized by placing "from the tree" before the verb (*SBH,* 182).

17.b. לא + impf for permanent prohibitions (GKC, 107b; Lambdin, 114); cf., Exod 20:4–17.

17.c. Inf constr אכל "to eat" + 2 masc sg suffix.

17.d. Inf abs מות with finite verb (תמות impf) makes statement very emphatic, lit., "you shall dying die" (GKC, 113l-n; A. B. Davidson, *Hebrew Syntax* [Edinburgh: T. & T. Clark, 1894] 86a).

18.a. Inf constr, היה.

18.b. G and Vg have pl, "Let us make," assimilating this to 1:26. The mappiq in ה in *BHS* following codex Leningrad B19ᴬ is unusual and not followed by most MSS.

19.a. SamPent and G insert "still, again" (עוֹד, ἔτι), harmonizing with 1:21, 25 perhaps.

19.b. SamPent inserts definite obj marker: typical (Waltke, 221).

19.c. Waw consec + 3 masc sg impf hiph of בוא.

19.d. Lit., "him" (לוֹ). Sg refers to collectives mentioned earlier (GKC, 145m).

19.e-e. Regarded as gloss by *BHS* and some commentators, but the suggestion lacks textual support.

20.a. Some MSS, G S Tg Vg, add "all." The MT and SamPent omission of "all" is the harder reading (cf. "all cattle, all the wild animals") and to be preferred.

20.b. Lit., "he found." Impersonal use of 3 masc sg qal instead of passive construction.

20.c. With inseparable preps הָאָדָם, "man" is pointed without the def art; cf. 3:17 and *Comment* on 1:26. This pointing suggests that the Masoretes wanted to understand the personal name Adam.

21.a. Waw consec + 3 masc sg impf hiph נפל "to fall."

21.b. Cf. n. 2:15.a.

21.c. On תחת SamPent has more usual suffix יה. MT is using suffix נה, common on verbs (GKC, 103d).

22.a. Waw consec + 3 masc sg impf (apoc) בנה.

22.b. Cf. n. 2:19.c.

23.a-a. Note the chiastic construction "This : woman // man : this."

23.b. 3 masc sg impf niph קרא "to call."

23.c. SamPent G Tg read "her man" (i.e., "from her husband"). Retain MT.

23.d. 3 fem sg pf qal passive לֻקָח, not pual (Joüon, 58a; Lambdin, 253). On punctuation of this form see GKC, 52d.

24.a. Impf for repeated customary action (GKC, 107g). Pointing יַעֲזָב, not יַעֲזֹב, because of maqqeph.

24.b. SamPent G S Tg Vg add "the two of them," probably by assimilation to v 25.

25.a. 3 masc pl impf hithpolel (בושׁ), reciprocal meaning "be ashamed before one another" (GKC, 72m).

3:1.a-a. Episode-initial circumstantial clause (*SBH,* 79).

1.b. G S add "the snake."

1.c. *BHS* suggested addition of interrogative ה = הַאַף. Unnecessary. On כי אף as interrogative, see Joüon, 157aN; BDB, 65a; *EWAS,* 142–43.

1.d. כל . . . לא = "not . . . any" (GKC, 152b).

2.a. Impf with permissive sense (GKC, 107s).

3.a. SamPent adds הזה "this."

3.b. 2 masc pl impf qal נגע "touch."

3.c. Note the spelling תמתון instead of the usual תמתו. The extra "n," paragogic nun, is found on impf pl endings especially in older parts of the OT (GKC, 47m; Spurrell, 36–38).

4.a. It is usual for the negative לא to come between the inf abs and the finite verb, not before both inf and verb as here. The only other examples of this word order are Amos 9:8; Ps 49:8. It is probably to echo 2:17 (GKC, 113v). Cassuto (1:146) suggests that it is the antithesis of v 4 to v 3 that prompts this word order here.

5.a. כי; probably antithetic "but" after preceding negative (SBH, 184; Gispen, 1:137; cf. BDB, 474a).

5.b. Waw consec + 3 pl pf niph פקח "open" (of eyes).

6.a. Waw consec + 3 fem sg impf (apoc) qal ראה "to see."

6.b. G Vg omit "the tree."

6.c. See n. 2:9.c.

6.d. Waw consec + 3 fem sg impf qal נתן "to give."

6.e. SamPent G read "they."

7.a. Waw consec + 3 fem pl impf niph פקח.

7.b. SamPent characteristically reads pl עלי for MT עלה collective (Waltke, 218–19).

8.a. Hithp ptcp הלך; "walk to and fro."

8.b. SamPent omits def art.

8.c. Waw consec + 3 masc sg impf hithp חבא "to hide." Notice the sg verb with pl ("they") subj. With a multiple subj, the verb often agrees with first noun (GKC, 146f).

9.a. איה "where" + 2 masc sg suffix "you."

10.a. S reads "I saw," i.e., ואראַ instead of MT ואירא, waw consec + 1 sg impf qal ירא "fear."

10.b. Waw consec + 1 sg impf niph חבא.

11.a. 3 masc sg pf hiph נגד "tell."

11.b. Joüon (161b) understands the interrogative ה as exclamatory and suggests translating "You have eaten then . . . !"

12.a. Pausal form 1 sg impf qal אכל; cf. v 13 (GKC, 68e).

13.a. זאת "this" is an enclitic, making the question sound more shocked (GKC, 136c, 148b; EWAS, 134–37).

13.b. The subj here is emphasized by its preverbal position (GKC, 142a; cf. EWAS, 32).

13.c. 3 masc sg pf hiph נשא + 1 sg suffix.

14.a. It is unusual for a כי (because) clause to precede main clause; cf. v 17. When the causal clause precedes the main clause, it underlines its importance. The more important clause comes first (Joüon, 170n).

14.b. It is typical for a curse to consist of one or more sentences in apposition, the general first statement in precative mood followed by detailed predictions in indicative mood; cf. v 17; 4:11; 9:26 (SBH, 54).

14.c-c. There is no need to regard this phrase as a gloss, pace BHS.

15.a. Impf qal שוף + object suffixes.

15.b. Accs specifying site of battering (GKC, 117ll).

16.a. SamPent G S insert "and." Retain MT.

16.b. Inf abs + 1 sg impf hiph רבה.

16.c. SamPent has commoner spelling of this word, והריונך. G apparently has different reading; see BHS.

16.d. SamPent has different spelling, בעצבון.

16.e. 2 fem sg impf qal ילד.

17.a. BHS repoints unnecessarily; cf. n. 2:20.c.

17.b. On hatef patah under כ see GKC, 10g.

18.a. Cf. n. 2:9.a.

19.a. Qal passive; cf. n. 2:23d.

19.b. The predicate "dust" precedes the subj "you," as is usual in classifying clauses (F. I. Andersen, Verbless Clause, 42–45, 90). It is not to emphasize the predicate.

21.a. On punctuation, cf. n. 2:20.c.

21.b. Waw consec + 3 masc sg impf hiph לבש + 3 masc pl suffix.

22.a. On הן/הנה "since," see Lambdin, 169–71.

22.b. In constr state before prep מן (GKC, 130a).

22.c. Waw consec + 3 masc sg pf חיה "live"; cf. GKC, 76i.

22.d. Aposiopesis; the sentence is left unfinished. The expected cohortative "let us send him out" is omitted here, and converted into simple narrative in v 23. In that the next verse begins a different construction, the transition is sometimes termed "anacolouthon."

23.a. Waw consec + 3 masc sg impf piel שלח + 3 masc sg obj suffix.

23.b. Cf. nn. 2:23.d, 3:19.a.

24.a. Waw consec + 3 masc sg impf piel גרש "expel."

24.b. Waw consec + 3 masc sg impf hiph שכן "dwell."

24.c. G inserts "him."

24.d. G inserts "and he placed." These G additions make man live east of Eden as opposed to the cherubim; cf. 4:16.

24.e. Fem sg hithp ptcp הפך "turn."

Form/Structure/Setting

The opening clause "This is the history of X" is everywhere else in Genesis a heading to a cycle of narratives (e.g., 6:9; 11:27; 37:2) or to a genealogy (e.g., 5:1; 25:12). Elsewhere, however, X is always a personal name—Adam, Noah, Ishmael—whereas here X is the heavens and the earth, so many commentators ancient and modern have regarded v 4a not as a heading to what follows, but as a postscript to what precedes it, the account of creation in Gen 1:1–2:3. It is argued that 2:4a makes a neat *inclusio* with 1:1.

It seems preferable, though, to regard 2:4 as fulfilling its usual function here, that is, as a heading to the narratives in chaps. 2–4 (cf. Jacob, Cassuto, Cross, Woudstra, Tengström, Childs). This allows full weight to be given to the chiastic structure of the verse and the usual meaning of תולדות "history" (see *Comment* below). If, further, this clause is editorial rather than derived from the P source, another problem with the conventional critical view is obviated, namely, that in P we must suppose the consecutive use of two nearly identical phrases, 2:4a and 5:1, the first as a subscript to the account of creation and the second as a heading to the family history of Adam. But if this formula is always a heading, we have here the editor introducing the first block of narratives about the primeval history of mankind: the stories of Adam and his sons.

Within this editorially demarcated unit of 2:5–4:26, three quite distinct narratives are apparent: the garden of Eden, 2:5–3:24; the murder of Abel, 4:1–16; Cain's family, 4:17–26. The garden of Eden story is in its present form a highly organized unit, though again it is often surmised that originally separate tales have been fused to form the present narrative. Some of the main source-critical analyses of this material are discussed below.

The garden story itself falls into two halves, 2:5–25 (the creation of man and his wife) and 3:1–24 (the temptation and fall from the garden). Both parts are introduced by episode-initial circumstantial clauses, 2:5–6 and 3:1a. Chap. 2 further subdivides into (a) the creation of man and the garden, vv 5–17; and (b) the creation of woman, vv 18–25. It is less easy to define subunits within chap. 3, and commentators who attempt this task have suggested a variety of analyses. The majority make a division between vv 7 and 8, but the use of a waw consecutive "heard," without an explicit noun subject, ties the verses too closely together to make this division probable.

The analysis of Walsh (*JBL* 96 [1977] 161–77), followed with refinements by Auffret (*La sagesse*, 25–67), offers less problems than the alternatives and is the basis of the following discussion. The narrative falls into seven scenes: "scenes are those smaller parts of a narrative differentiated by change of actors, situation or activity" (Gunkel, 34.)

1)	2:5–17	Narrative	God the sole actor: man present but passive
2)	2:18–25	Narrative	God main actor, man minor role, woman and animals passive
3)	3:1–5	Dialogue	Snake and woman
4)	3:6–8	Narrative	Man and woman
5)	3:9–13	Dialogue	God, man and woman
6)	3:14–21	Narrative	God main actor, man minor role, woman and snake passive
7)	3:22–24	Narrative	God sole actor: man passive

Each scene is carefully constructed, and there are such elaborate interconnections between the scenes "that the deletion of any part of the text (except, perhaps, 2:10b–14) would have significant repercussions for the whole passage" (Walsh, *JBL* 96 [1977] 171–72). The tight structuring of the account is most apparent in the balance between the opening and closing scenes, and in its use of inversion. Thus scene 1 matches scene 7; scene 2, scene 6; scene 3, scene 5; while scene 4 constitutes the centerpiece of the narrative when the couple eat of the forbidden fruit.

Scenes 1 and 7 are alike in that both are narratives with God as the all-important actor: though man is present in both, he is completely passive. The vocabulary of the two scenes is distinctive: the phrases "on the east," "tree of life," "garden of Eden," "till," and "guard" are found only in these scenes. Finally, there is an inversion between them. In scene 1 man is made from "the dust of the land" and placed in the garden (vv 7–8), whereas in the final scene man is driven from the garden, by implication back to the dust of the land from which he was taken (v 23; cf. 19).

Scenes 2 and 6 correspond in that only in these two scenes are four actors present: God, the man, the woman, and the animals (in scene 6 and elsewhere in the narrative the serpent represents the animals). In both scenes, God is the principal actor, and the action takes place within the garden. Each scene is concerned with relationships between man and the rest of creation. Scene 2 describes the ideal: the animals were created to be man's companions, and woman is his perfect partner. But scene 6 portrays the actual situation: perpetual conflict between man and the serpent, and frustration in relations between the sexes. Yet both scenes assert the same hierarchy among the creatures. God the creator is supreme. Man comes next: his superiority to the animals is indicated by giving them names. Similarly, man's authority over woman is implied in his twofold naming of her (2:23; 3:20), but her superiority to the animals is manifest for only she is a perfect match for man. Finally both scenes end with statements about woman's role as wife and mother (2:24; 3:20) and about clothing (2:25; 3:21).

Both scenes 3 and 5 are essentially dialogues about eating the fruit of the tree and its consequences. Both take place inside the garden, though not at its center: the woman talks of the tree "in the middle of the garden" evidently implying they are some distance from it, and in scene 5 the guilty couple are pictured as having fled from the tree of knowledge and as hiding elsewhere in the undergrowth. In the third scene the serpent and the woman make three comments about the tree, whereas in the fifth God puts three questions to the man and his wife.

Scene 4 stands apart from the rest of the narrative. Here the human actors are alone: neither God nor the serpent is mentioned. They are now at the heart of the garden standing before the tree of knowledge. It is here that the woman decides to follow the snake's advice and ignore the divine command, and likewise the man accepts the fruit proffered by his wife in defiance of the divine will. The hierarchy of authority established in scene 2 and reaffirmed in scene 5 is overturned. God-man-woman-animal in scene 2 becomes snake-woman-man-God in scene 4. The order of creation is totally inverted. Not only is the scene the centerpiece of the narrative, but the crucial words "and he ate" are themselves sandwiched between a twofold mention of the desired effects of the fruit: its ability to open eyes and to give knowledge.

The whole narrative is therefore a masterpiece of palistrophic writing, the mirror-image style, whereby the first scene matches the last, the second the penultimate and so on: ABCDC'B'A'. This device is well attested in Genesis, e.g., 6–9, 17, 18–19, and elsewhere in the OT. Not only does the literary structure move in and out in this fashion, but so does the action: it commences outside the garden, the dialogues are conducted within the garden, and the decisive act of disobedience takes place at its very center. Similarly, the palistrophic structure of the flood story matches the movement in the events described: the rise and fall of the waters, the entry and emergence from the ark, and so on.

Earlier critical work concentrated on attempting to identify the sources behind Gen 2–3. (For a history of this research see Westermann, 1:186–90). It was often argued on the basis of the unusual combination of the two names of God (Yahweh Elohim) and of apparent doublets within the story, e.g., the two trees, the double naming of Eve, the twofold expulsion from Eden, that two literary sources had been combined to produce the present account. Since Humbert (*Études sur le récit du paradis*, 1940) dismissed this approach, it has been generally given up. Fuss (*Die sogenannte Paradieserzählung*, 1968) and Scharbert (*BZ* 18 [1974] 45–64) attempted to revive it, but they are untypical. The critical consensus is that these chapters are almost entirely the work of the Yahwist, who is regarded as the main author of Genesis.

It has, however, been suggested that the Yahwist utilized earlier shorter tales that he has modified and combined to form the present narrative. McKenzie (*TS* 15 [1954] 541–72) proposed that three tales underlie the existing story: an account of the creation of woman, an account of the woman's sin, and an account of the man's sin. Westermann argues that two narratives have been combined: the first dealing with the creation of mankind (chap. 2) and the second depicting the fall (chap. 3). Steck (*Paradieserzählung*, 58–

65) prefers a simpler traditio-critical approach. He suggests that one short tale (*Paradiesgeschichte*) relating how man alone lived in the garden and was subsequently expelled has been drastically reworked by the Yahwist to form the present narrative (*Paradieserzählung*). In any case, so many features of the narrative—the creation of woman, the serpent's temptation, the tree of life, and the curses—are ascribed to J, that it becomes essentially J's composition. Attractive though such hypotheses are, they must, in the absence of any sources where the stories occur independently, remain conjectural, and it would certainly be unwise to base an exegesis of these chapters on guesses as to how the writer has modified his putative sources. The present form of the material is the surest guide to his intentions.

Less problematic is the relationship of this account to other Near Eastern material. In the *Introduction* (pp. xxxvii–xlii) I have already drawn attention to the similarities in outline between the accounts of primeval antiquity in Gen 1–11 and Mesopotamian tradition, particularly the Atrahasis epic and the Sumerian flood story. These begin to be obvious in Gen 2. The Sumerian flood story apparently began with an account of the creation of man and the animals, (cf. Gen 2:7,19) and told of the difficulties of agriculture (cf. 2:5) and man's nakedness (2:25). The Atrahasis epic is more fully preserved at this point and tells of the lesser gods working as common laborers to dig the irrigation canals (A 1:1–49; cf. Gen 2:5). To relieve them, man was created out of clay and the blood of a god (A 1:210–41; cf. Gen 2:9). In fact, seven pairs of men and women were created, thus instituting marriage (A 1:251–300; cf. Gen 2:20–25).

It is interesting that there are these points of comparison between Mesopotamian tradition and Genesis, but the stories in which they occur are very different. However, many of the other motifs within Gen 2–3 do have oriental parallels. Sumerian tradition told of a paradise island on Dilmun at the head of the Persian Gulf (C. C. Lamberg-Karlovsky, *JNES* 41 [1982] 45–50), with an abundance of life-giving water springing out of the earth (Enki and Ninhursag, 55–59; *ANET*, 38; P. Attinger, *ZA* 74 [1984] 1–52). Similarly, Ugaritic mythology also affirmed that El lived "at the sources of the two rivers, in the midst of the two oceans" (Aqht A.6.48, *ANET*, 152; cf. Wallace, *Eden Narrative*, 76). This shows that the idea of a well-watered paradise where the gods dwelt was a common motif in the ancient Orient. It is often affirmed that the notion of plants that could confer immortality was well known in antiquity, but Sjöberg, in *The Shelter of Elyon*, 219–21, has shown that the evidence is very tenuous. Very interestingly, the Epic of Gilgamesh (11:280–90) links a serpent with such a life-giving plant. Having acquired this plant, Gilgamesh left it beside a well while he went to bathe, but a snake appeared and ate it. Egyptian (cf. V. Notter, *Biblischer Schöpfungsbericht*, 148–51) as well as Mesopotamian sources (A 1:203; G 1:33–35) say man was molded from clay.

But the most striking comparison is with the Adapa myth which, though of Mesopotamian origin, was also found at Tell el-Amarna in Egypt (translation, *ANET*, 101–3). Adapa is phonetically close to Adam and he is also known to be the first of the seven sages (*apkallus*) of Mesopotamia, who were contemporaries of the antediluvian kings (see E. Reiner, *Or* 30 [1961] 1–11; R. Borger,

JNES 33 [1974] 183–96). Adapa was summoned to heaven where he was interrogated by the god Anu and invited to eat of the bread of life and water of life. But Adapa declined having been briefed in advance by his personal god Ea not to accept such an offer. Adapa was then allowed to return to earth. (Cf. the articles of G. Buccellati, *UF* 5 [1973] 61–66; N. E. Andreasen, *AUSS* 19 [1981] 179–94; J. D. Bing, *UF* 16 [1984] 53–56). Though at first sight this looks like a close parallel to the Genesis story, the context of the Adapa myth is quite different, and the obedience of Adapa contrasts with the disobedience of Adam.

In all these cases there is no evidence of simple borrowing by the Hebrew writer. It would be better to suppose that he has borrowed various familiar mythological motifs, transformed them, and integrated them into a fresh and original story of his own. Whereas Adapa heeded the word of the god Ea and did not eat the forbidden fruit, Adam and Eve rejected the LORD's command and followed the serpent. In the Gilgamesh epic the snake devoured the plant of rejuvenation: in Genesis no one is said to have consumed it. The Atrahasis epic (1:208–50) mentions that man was created out of clay mixed with the blood of a god, indicating that man is partly physical, partly divine. Genesis puts the same idea into different images: man was made from the dust of the ground, and then God breathed into him the breath of life. In Mesopotamian thought, man worked so that the gods could rest. Gen 2 gives no hint of this approach: God worked until all man's needs were satisfied. The God of Genesis is totally concerned with man's welfare. Man is to be more than a tiller of the ground; his need is for companionship, a lack which the creator is anxious to fill. The treatment of earlier oriental tradition in these chapters bears comparison with their use in chap. 1. But whereas in chap. 1 there was a distinctively polemical thrust challenging the accepted mythology of creation in the ancient Near East, this note is muted in chaps. 2 and 3. Rather the writer appears to be using and adapting earlier motifs in a free and creative way to express his vision of reality. The particular combination of ideas in Gen 2–3 according to McKenzie "is due entirely to the creative imagination of the writer, and they indicate his capacity to assemble scattered strands from many sources into a compactly unified narrative" (*TS* 15 [1954] 569). Thus divine truths about man and his relationships with his Creator and his fellow creatures are presented in a vivid and memorable way.

Traditionally these chapters have been assigned to the J source. The vivid narrative style, the anthropomorphic view of God, who molds man like a potter and walks in the garden, and the use of the divine name Yahweh are all accounted hallmarks of the Yahwist's style. More recently, Tengström (*Toledotformel*) and Dockx (*Récit du paradis*) have detected the hand of the final editor of Genesis at various points in these chapters. Vermeylen (*Bijd* 41 [1980] 230–50) believes he can detect a deuteronomistic reworking of J, while Wyatt (*ZAW* 93 [1981] 10–21) draws attention to points of contact in vocabulary between Gen 2–3 and exilic literature. However, the few words or phrases on which these theories of late composition rest do not necessitate such a conclusion. It may be a matter of chance, but the possibility that Gen 2–3 influenced later biblical literature cannot be excluded. Similarly, just because the garden of Eden narrative uses many symbols at home in the priestly account of the tabernacle does not show that Gen 2–3 should be ascribed to P, but that the different blocks of material within the Pentateuch are not so distinct as often supposed (cf. Wenham, 1986).

The nature of the material in these chapters has been the topic of prolonged discussion among commentators. Whereas the layman tends to see the issue in simple categories of myth or history, theologians have for various reasons tended to avoid this polarization. Gunkel spoke of Gen 2–3 as "faded myth" because he recognized the difference between the presentation of divine activity in Genesis and other Near Eastern mythology. The uniqueness and sovereignty of God in Genesis give reports of his deeds a quite different quality from the myths of ancient polytheism. Von Rad and Westermann call Gen 2–3 simply narrative (*Erzählung*), and Coats calls it a tale.

Similarly, Otzen (*Myths in the Old Testament*, 25) states, "The narratives in the opening chapters of Genesis do not have the character of real myths." But the garden of Eden story does fulfill functions often associated with myths in other cultures. It explains man's present situation and obligations in terms of a primeval event which is of abiding significance. Marriage, work, pain, sin, and death are the subject matter of this great narrative. And this narrative is replete with powerful symbols—rivers, gold, cherubim, serpents and so on—which hint at its universal significance.

Yet for the author of Genesis it is clear "that here a factual report is meant to be given about facts which everyone knows and whose reality no one can question" (von Rad, 75). The introductory formula "This is the history of the heaven and the earth" (2:4) not only links this cycle of narratives with those which follow (e.g., 5:1 or 11:27), but implies that the characters who appear in Gen 2 and 3 are as real as the patriarchs.

But to affirm that Gen 2–3 is "a factual report" is not to say it is history, at least history in the normal meaning of the term. For Gunkel it could not be history, because he considered that in scholarly historical writing God could never appear as a prime cause of events but only as the ultimate reality behind all events, thus apparently ruling out the possibility of divine miracles and similar supernatural interventions. Less question-begging is the view that Gen 2–3, because it is dealing with events before written records began, could at best be described as pre-history. But whether even this term is an apt definition of the nature of the material in these chapters is a matter of debate. In discussing the parallel Near Eastern material, Jacobsen (*JBL* 100 [1981] 528) has coined the term "mytho-historical," in that Atrahasis and the Sumerian flood story are relating stories about the gods and men sequentially and in terms of cause and effect. The same is true of Genesis, though as often observed, the more obviously mythical features have been eliminated, so if "mytho-historical" is not considered an apt description, perhaps "proto-historical" story or tale would be preferable.

In attempting to define the nature of the story in these chapters, discussion has focused on the processes of their composition. If earlier commentators tended to think in terms of the writer of Genesis putting into words a vision of the garden which was disclosed to him, or recording a primeval tradition for posterity, modern writers (e.g., Dubarle, Alonso-Schökel, Lohfink) prefer to think in terms of divine inspiration working through the author's creative imagination. It is a characteristic of biblical theology to look for the cause of present calamities in the sins of former generations. It is suggested that under the guidance of the Spirit the author of these chapters identified the origin of the problems that beset all mankind—sin, death, suffering—with a primeval act of disobedience of the first human couple. Whereas a modern writer might have been happy to spell this out in abstract theological terminology— God created the world good, but man spoiled it by his disobedience—Genesis puts these truths in vivid and memorable form in an absorbing yet highly symbolic story. It is argued that such an understanding of the story's composition can account for its use of mythological motifs from neighboring peoples and its points of connection with other parts of the OT, particularly the covenant and wisdom traditions. The validity of this hypothesis, like most critical suggestions, remains open to debate, but its validity or otherwise in no way impairs the inspired truth of the present narrative.

Comment

2:4 This verse serves both as a title to 2:5–4:26 (see previous section on *Form/Structure/Setting*) and as a link with the introduction 1:1–2:3. The first and second halves of the verse are tied together with deliberate use of chiasmus: A, "heaven"; B, "earth"; C, "created"—C', "made"; B', "earth"; A', "heaven." The word order in the second half of the verse is particularly unusual in that "earth" precedes "heaven." "Heaven" and "earth" are frequently paired in the OT, but elsewhere "heaven" comes first: the one other exception is Ps 148:13, which appears to be alluding to this passage. It looks as though the writer has intentionally inverted the usual word order here to link the two parts of the verse together. The opening clause "This . . . the heaven and the earth when they were created" forms a looser chiastic inclusion with 1:1, "God created the heaven and the earth," thus binding 1:1–2:3 to the succeeding narratives. The pairing of "create" and "make" takes up the two key descriptions of divine activity in chap. 1.

"This is the history of": אלה תולדות. Elsewhere in Genesis (cf. 6:9, 10:1, etc.) this is translated "This is the family history of" and it always announces a new section of narrative, which makes it natural to suppose that it fulfills the same function here rather than serving as colophon to what precedes. This is confirmed by the etymology and usage of תולדות. It is derived from ילד "to bear," hence the older translation "generations." But this translation can mislead, for "the generations of X" are those whom X produces, not the ancestors of X. In the patriarchal narratives, "This is the family history of X" typically heads a section, which commences with the death of X's father and closes with X's own death. Thus "This is the family history of Ishmael" takes up the story of Ishmael after Abraham's death and ends with a mention of Ishmael's death (25:12–18; cf. 25:19–35:29). The heading covers the period when X was head of the patriarchal extended family, which may be identified with Hebrew מולדת "kindred" (cf. Wenham, *Leviticus*, 255–57). But though the named old man X is nominally in charge of the group, it is his sons who make the running and are the chief actors in the stories. Thus "this is the family history of Isaac" (25:19) heads the Jacob and Esau stories, while "this is the family history of Jacob" (37:2) introduces the Joseph cycle.

In the section Gen 2–11 the same logic applies in 6:9. "This is the family history of Noah" spans the period between the death of the last of the antediluvian patriarchs and the death of Noah, but it is used more loosely elsewhere in the primeval history. However, it is clear that in all cases "the family history of X" describes what X and his descendants did, not the origins of X. Here by analogy the term is applied to the heavens and the earth, and therefore "must describe that which is generated by the heavens and the earth, not the process by which they themselves are generated" (Skinner, 41). In other words, 2:4 makes an excellent title for what follows, but in no way can it be regarded as a postscript to what precedes it.

"On the day the LORD God." Commentators who regard v 4b as the start of the J source draw attention to the verbal parallel with the opening line of *Enuma elish*. *Enuma* means "when, in the day." The use of cognate conjunctions in the Hebrew of Genesis and the Akkadian of *Enuma elish* is likely to be mere chance. The probability that Gen 2:4 is alluding to Babylonian sources is further diminished once the literary integrity of the verse is admitted. A closer parallel is 5:1–2, which combines the syntactical forms of 2:4 with the ideas of 1:26–27.

"The LORD God" יהוה אלהים: This particular divine title occurs only once in the Pentateuch outside Gen 2–3, in Exod 9:30. Within these two chapters it is used consistently, apart from 3:1–5 in the dialogue between the snake and the woman. There (3:1–5) in conversation they simply use the ordinary word for divinity אלהים "God," not his personal name יהוה "Yahweh" that was unique to Israel. Genesis in other passages uses either אלהים or יהוה, singly, not combined as here. Yahweh passages are generally assigned to the J (Yahwistic) source, and Elohim passages to either P (priestly source, e.g., chap. 1) or E (Elohistic source). Here we have the unique phenomenon of a passage assigned to J, using יהוה אלהים or אלהים by itself. The strangeness of the phenomenon has taxed the imagination of literary critics and exegetes alike, for whether one accepts the usual documentary analysis or not, the commentator must still explain why here the editor of this finely constructed tale has forsaken his usual policy of using one name or the other and instead uses both together.

The view that Gen 2–3 has been compiled from two parallel sources, one using "Yahweh" and the other "Elohim," finds little favor today, though Fuss and Scharbert have attempted to revive it. Westermann, following many earlier commentators, prefers to see the composite divine name as redactional. An earlier form of the narrative spoke simply of "Yahweh"; "Elohim" was introduced to emphasize the identity of the God of Gen 2 with the God of Gen 1. Westermann points out that this redactor may also have had a theological purpose behind his coinage: to insist that God as revealed in this story is both creator of the universe and God of Israel. A quite different suggestion is that of Tur-Sinai (*VT* 11 [1961]), followed by Speiser and Gispen, who regard the double name as evidence that Gen 2–3 rests on a Mesopotamian original. Akkadian puts determinatives before nouns to indicate their class.

Thus the names of gods are preceded by the determinative "god," and so "the LORD God" means "the God Yahweh."

These theories have been examined in detail by J. L'Hour (*RB* 81 [1974] 524–56). He points out that the redactional theories do not explain why it is only here in Genesis that "Yahweh Elohim" occurs, and twenty times at that. It is usually assumed that the redactor worked late in Israelite history when it was self-evident to everyone that Yahweh was divine. At this period it was neither necessary nor useful to create an idiosyncratic form of the divine name to make such a point. Nor can the redactional hypothesis explain the use of "Elohim" by itself in 3:1–5. The latter point also tells against Tur-Sinai's suggestion that a Mesopotamian document underlies Gen 2–3, not to mention the fact that the total story in Gen 2–3 is quite different from any Near Eastern text so far discovered.

On the basis of an examination of the twenty examples of the use of "Yahweh Elohim" in Gen 2–3 and its sixteen occurrences elsewhere in the OT, L'Hour argues that the Yahwistic author has deliberately used this form to express his conviction that Yahweh is both Israel's covenant partner and the God (Elohim) of all creation. Other early examples of its use (Exod 9:30; 2 Sam 7:25; Ps 72:18; 84:12) all seem to be making this point. This is most obvious in Exod 9:30, where the seventh plague of hail is designed to prove to Pharaoh that Yahweh is not merely Israel's national deity but the sovereign God who controls all creation. It is because "Yahweh Elohim" expresses so strongly the basic OT convictions about God's being both creator and Israel's covenant partner that the serpent and the woman avoid the term in their discussion. The god they are talking about is malevolent, secretive, and concerned to restrict man: his character is so different from that of Yahweh Elohim that the narrative pointedly avoids the name in the dialogue of 3:1–5. L'Hour's theory is not completely new (cf. Delitzsch, Cassuto, Westermann, and E. Haag), but he has given a more convincing justification for it than any previous writer.

5 "No shrub of the plain had yet grown in the earth." This is the first of four conjoined circumstantial clauses describing the situation prior to God's creation of man in v 7. But the interpretation of vv 5–6 is difficult. Some commentators (e.g., Gunkel, Driver, Zimmerli, Schmidt) regard v 5 as describing the whole earth as a desert, J's equivalent of P's watery chaos in 1:2. Others (e.g., Keil, Jacob, Cassuto) argue that the creation of chap. 1 is presupposed and therefore 2:5–6 are stating what agricultural land was like before man started farming. A third view (e.g., E. Haag, Steck, Westermann) argues that the main interest is to contrast the situation before man's arrival (2:5–6) with that after his creation and disobedience (3:17–24). If, as argued above, 2:4 is a title to 2:5–4:26, the first suggestion, that it is describing a desert, has least to commend it. But since it cannot be ruled out that the writer of Genesis may have wished to offer two images of the chaos that preceded creation, each view must be examined carefully.

Three geographic terms appear in vv 5–6: "plain" (שדה), "earth" (ארץ), and "land" (אדמה); and two terms for vegetation: "shrub" (שיח) or "plant" (עשב). The geographic terms have a wide variety of meanings; indeed, they are interchangeable in some contexts and therefore difficult to define. However, in these chapters they appear to be used with their most usual senses. Evidently "earth" is the broadest term for the land surface of our planet; whereas "land" comprises but a part of the earth. "Earth" (ארץ) is contrasted with heaven (2:4). On it the plants grow and the rain falls (2:5). From the "earth" (ארץ) the water rises to water the "land" (אדמה; 2:6). More precisely "land" appears to be agricultural land which consists of dust (2:7) and which it is man's duty to till (2:5; 3:17; 4:2). Man's especially close relationship to the land is seen in his creation from its dust (2:7). Over against the cultivated land stands the open uncultivated "plain," שדה, home of wild animals (2:19, 20; 3:1, 14) and plants (2:5; 3:18). In the "plain" one pastures the flocks (4:8). Man's life is a struggle to bring more "plain" under cultivation and conversely to prevent land being reduced to "plain" (3:17–18). (On these terms see further *TDOT* 1:88–98, 388–405; *THWAT* 1:57–60, 228–36; Stadelmann, *Hebrew Conception of the World*, 126–38).

The distinction between "shrub" (שיח) and "plant" (עשב) seems to lie in whether they may be eaten or not. "Shrub," a rare term, seems to denote the low bushy plants characteristic of the arid areas bordering on the fertile crescent (21:15; Job 30:4,7), whereas "plant" covers wild and cultivated plants that may be eaten (cf. 1:29, 30; 3:18).

Gen 2:5 therefore distinguishes two types of land: open, uncultivated "plain" or "field," the wilderness fit only for animal grazing, and the dusty "land" where agriculture is possible with irrigation and human effort. As Castellino has pointed out, this fits in well with a Mesopotamian setting for Gen 2–4 and ties in with the Akkadian distinctions between "earth," *erṣetu,* "land," *mātu,* and "field," *ṣēru* (VTSup 4 [1957] 116–37). But at this stage there was not any sort of vegetation, for there had been no rain to make the desert bloom and there was no man to work the agricultural land.

6 "But the fresh water ocean used to rise from the earth and water the whole surface of the land." Here again a Mesopotamian background seems likely. In this area agriculture was totally dependent on controlling the annual floodwaters of the Tigris and Euphrates. The Hebrew word אד "fresh water ocean" only occurs here in this sense: in Job 36:27 it apparently denotes water coming down from the sky, whereas here it is said to rise from the earth. The old translations (LXX, Vg, S) all translate אד as "spring," and this fits in with the more likely etymology of the word from Sumerian/Akkadian, *id,* which represents the cosmic river (M. Saebo, *ST* 24 [1970] 130–41). This derivation poses less problems than the alternative etymology favored by E. A. Speiser (*BASOR* 140 [1955] 9–11), KB 11 from Akkadian *edû* "flood," "outburst of subterranean water," or Dahood's (*CBQ* 43 [1981] 534–38) derivation from Eblaite *i-du* "rain-cloud."

Whatever the origin of the word, the concept of an underground stream watering the earth is attested in Sumerian mythology: "From the mouth 'whence issues the waters of the earth' . . . brought her sweet water from the earth . . . her furrowed fields and farms bore her grain" (Enki and Ninhursag, 55–61; *ANET,* 38). But Saebo (*ST* 24 [1970] 136) points out that any mythical overtones of the term ID in Sumerian have been completely eliminated in the Hebrew account: אד is just a great spring fed from the subterranean ocean.

If there was such an abundant water supply for the land (v 6), why did v 5 convey the impression of an arid wilderness barren through lack of rain? Gunkel, Schmidt, Westermann ascribe vv 5 and 6 to different sources in an attempt to resolve the apparent conflict. But this is to belittle the competence of the author of this chapter, who would not be expected to introduce an isolated sentence into his narrative that conflicts with the context. Besides, he returns to the same idea in v 10a, "a river flowing out of Eden to water the garden." It is preferable to follow Castellino and Gispen, who put down the lack of vegetation on the land to man's absence. Without man to irrigate the land, the spring was useless. "When set against the conditions of Mesopotamia, specially the South, everything becomes at once quite natural" (Castellino, VTSup 4:120).

7 "Then the LORD God shaped man from the dust of the land." The focus on man and his relationship to the land in vv 5–6 is but a prelude to man's (אָדָם) creation from the land (אֲדָמָה). Though אדמה is grammatically the feminine form of אדם, it is doubtful whether there is any etymological connection between the two words. It is sometimes suggested that both terms are derived from אָדֹם "red." the color of man's skin and also the earth. This too seems improbable. Certainly, however, there is a play on the two terms אדם and אדמה, to emphasize man's relationship to the land. He was created from it; his job is to cultivate it (2:5, 15); and on death he returns to it (3:19). "It is his cradle, his home, his grave" (Jacob).

This play on similar sounding words, paronomasia, is a favorite device of Hebrew writers (cf. 2:23), and many other phonetic allusions to 'ādām "man" have been noted in these chapters. Strus (*Nomen-Omen*, 114–20) points out that the whole story reverberates with allusions to the word 'ādām, and to the name of Eve ḥawwāh, just as the flood story has many puns on Noah's name. Besides 'ādāmāh and 'ēden (Eden), qedem, qidmat (East), tardēmāh (heavy sleep), and môt tāmût (you shall certainly die) seem to make allusion to 'ādām. The terms ḥayyîm ḥayyāh (life, living, wild animal) audibly resemble the name of Eve. For a discussion of the meaning of האדם and האדמה, see *Comment* on 1:26 and 2:5.

"Shaped," יצר: The present participle of this verb means "potter" (e.g., Jer 18:2), and it may well be that the image of a potter shaping his clay lies behind this description of man's creation, even though "dust of the land" is not the normal material a potter works with. Though turning pots may often be a tedious, repetitive work, these are not the overtones of יצר, as a look at the other uses of the word reveals. "Shaping" is an artistic, inventive activity that requires skill and planning (cf. Isa 44:9–10). Usually the verb describes God's work in creation. God has "shaped" the animals (2:19), Leviathan (Ps 104:26), the dry land (Ps 95:5), the mountains (Amos 4:13), and the future course of history (Isa 22:11, Jer 33:2). Preeminently, God's shaping skill is seen in the creation of man, whether it be from dust as here or in the womb (Isa 44:2, 24) or in shaping human character to fulfill a particular role (Isa 43:21; 44:21).

"Dust," עפר: That man was created from the dust is alluded to in many parts of the OT (Job 10:9; Isa 29:16; Ps 90:3; 104:29, etc). The idea is also commonplace outside the OT. The Gilgamesh Epic (1:34) tells how the goddess

Aruru created Enkidu from clay. Egyptian monuments portray the god Khnum making man out of clay. The classical myths tell of Prometheus creating the first man from soil and water (Ovid, *Metamorphoses* 1.82; Juvenal 14:35). It is evident then that Genesis is here taking up a very ancient tradition of the creation of man and is giving these old ideas its own distinctive flavor.

"Blew into his nostrils the breath of life." Man is more than a God-shaped piece of earth. He has within him the gift of life that was given by God himself. The biblical writer was not alone in the ancient world in rejecting a reductionist view of man which sees him as simply an interesting collection of chemicals and electrical impulses. Other peoples too regarded man as constituted of clay plus a divine element. The Babylonians spoke of man as a mixture of clay and the blood of a god (e.g., A 1:208–50). The Egyptians held that men had souls like the gods (F. Maass, *TDOT* 1:78). Similarly, Prometheus made man's body from clay and gave it life with divine sparks (Dillmann, 54–55).

"Blew," נפח, suggests a good puff such as would revive a fire (Isa 54:16; Hag 1:9). The closest parallel is Ezek 37:9 where the prophet is told to blow on the recreated bodies to resuscitate them, and then, filled with wind/spirit (רוח), they stood alive. It is the divine inbreathing both here and in Ezek 37 that gives life.

"The breath of life" (נשמת חיים) is different from the word for "spirit" (רוח) in Ezekiel. Indeed נשמה and רוח sometimes occur in parallel (e.g., Job 27:3; Isa 42:5) suggesting a near synonymity. In fact נשמה "breath" is a narrower and rarer term than רוח "wind, spirit." "Breath," the ability to breathe, is a key characteristic of animal life as opposed to plant life. The flood destroyed "everything which has the breath of life in its nostrils" (7:22). Frequently, however, "breath" is more restrictive: to have breath is to be human (Josh 11:11; Isa 2:22), though it can of course be used analogically of the breath of God, e.g., 2 Sam 22:16. So when this verse says God blew into man's nostrils the breath of life, it is affirming that God made him alive by making him breathe.

As a result of this divine inbreathing, man became a "living creature" (נפש חיה). This phrase is used again of the land animals and birds in 2:19; 9:9; and in 1:20 it is also used of sea creatures. The term נפש is one of the most common words in the OT (754 occurrences), and it has a wide range of meaning—"appetite, throat, person, soul, self, corpse," among others. There have been many attempts to define and interpret the word, and often this particular verse is said to give a special insight into Hebrew psychology. (For discussion see C. Westermann, *THWAT* 2:71–96; E. Jacob, *TDNT* 9:618–31; H. W. Wolff, *Anthropology of the Old Testament* [London: SCM, 1974] 10–25; W. H. Schmidt, "Anthropologische Begriffe im AT," *EvT* 24 [1964] 374–88).

It tends to be overlooked in such discussions, however, that this verse says man became a נפש חיה a "living creature," not merely נפש "creature." The adjective is significant in the phrase: implicitly this "living creature" is being contrasted with a dead one, e.g., Num 5:2; 6:6, 11. Given the other uses of the phrase נפש חיה in Gen 1, 2, 9, it seems unlikely that 2:7, "man became a living creature," means any more than the TEV rendering "and the man began to live." By blowing on the inanimate body made from the earth, God made man come alive. It is not man's possession of "the breath of life" or his status as a "living creature" that differentiates him from the animals (*pace* T. C. Mitchell, *VT* 11 [1961] 186). Animals are described in exactly the same terms. Gen 1:26–28 affirms the uniqueness of man by stating that man alone is made in God's image and by giving man authority over the animals. There may be a similar suggestion here, in that man alone receives the breath of God directly (cf. 2:7 and 2:19). Man's authority over the animals is evident in that he is authorized to name them.

8 "The LORD God planted a garden in Eden in the east." The use of the waw-consecutive here suggests the garden was "planted" after man was formed: a pluperfect sense, "had planted" (with Vg, Jacob), though possible, is unlikely. As Westermann observes, the establishment of the garden for man more closely parallels the provision of food for him in 1:29 than the creation of the plants in 1:12–13. גן "garden" is an enclosed area for cultivation (cf. vv 5, 15): perhaps we should picture a park surrounded by a hedge (cf. 3:23). This seems to be the understanding of the early versions which translate גן as "paradise," a Persian loan word, originally meaning a royal park.

"In Eden" is the only occurrence of this phrase. Elsewhere the phrase is either "garden of Eden" (e.g., 2:15; 3:23, 24) or simply Eden (4:16; Isa 51:3, etc.). The use of the preposition "in" shows that Eden is understood as the name of the area in which the garden was planted. Its situation is then defined by reference to the author's position "in the east," i.e., east of the Land of Israel. מקדם "in the east" does sometimes mean "in ancient times" (e.g., Isa 45:21; 46:10), and though this interpretation was followed by many of the early translations (α', σ', θ', Vg, S) the context and 11:2 make it unlikely here. "In the east" appears to locate Eden somewhere in Mesopotamia or Arabia.

Such a location would be confirmed if it were demonstrable that עדן "Eden" were derived from Akk. *edinu*, Sum. *edin*, "plain, steppe" (so Speiser and Weinfeld). But this is etymologically difficult (Westermann, Gispen), while Cassuto's attempt to derive it from a Ugaritic noun "moisture" seems to rest on a misunderstanding of the Ug *'dn* (cf. Aisleitner no. 2011 and J. C. de Moor, *The Seasonal Pattern in the Ugaritic Myth of Ba'lu,* AOAT 16 [Neukirchen-Vluyn: Neukirchener Verlag, 1971], 148–49).

It is simpler to associate Eden with its homonym "pleasure, delight" (2 Sam 1:24; Jer 51:34, Ps 36:9). Whenever Eden is mentioned in Scripture it is pictured as a fertile area, a well-watered oasis with large trees growing (cf. Isa 51:3; Ezek 31:9, 16, 18; 36:35, etc.), a very attractive prospect in the arid East. (For confirmation of this interpretation, cf. the newly discovered old Aramaic root *'dn*, "enrich" [A. R. Millard, *VT* 34 (1984) 103–6]). This lush fecundity was a sign of God's presence in and blessing on Eden. E. Haag (*Mensch am Anfang,* 26–27) suggests "in the east" evokes the same ideas. For in the east the sun rises, and light is a favorite biblical metaphor for divine revelation (Isa 2:2–4; Ps 36:10). So it seems likely that this description of "the garden in Eden in the east" is symbolic of a place where God dwells. Indeed, there are many other features of the garden that suggest it is seen as an archetypal sanctuary, prefiguring the later tabernacle and temples. But the mention of the rivers and their location in vv 10–14 suggests that the final editor of Gen 2 thought of Eden also as a real place, even if it is beyond the wit of modern writers to locate.

9–15 These verses elaborate on the summary statement of v 8.

9 "The LORD God made all kinds of trees to sprout from the land." Note that the trees, like man in v 7 and the animals in v 19, are created from the "land." Some commentators regarded the mention of the trees as sources of food as characteristic of man's diet before the fall: he was reduced to eating other plants by the curse of 3:22. It is more likely that trees make a garden. Nevertheless, the remark that they were "pleasant to look at and good to eat" emphasizes the abundance of God's provision.

"The tree of life was in the middle of the garden and also the tree of the knowledge of good and evil." The present narrative describes two trees in the middle of the garden, but since this passage explicitly locates the tree of life at the center, and 3:3 locates the other there, it is surmised that this is evidence of the reworking of the earlier *Paradiesgeschichte* which knew only one tree. This could be corroborated by the awkward way "the tree of the knowledge of good and evil" is tacked on in this verse. Nevertheless, Dillmann pointed to other sentences where a phrase is tacked on at the end as here (e.g., 1:16; 34:29; Num 13:23) and also pointed out that the tree of life is an essential mark of a perfect garden where God dwells, so that it is unlikely to be secondary either. Furthermore, in terms of the symbolism of this story, both trees correspond to items found in or near the center of Israelite worship (see below).

Trees as a symbol of life are well known in the Bible. The Gilgamesh epic also mentions that its hero found in a deep well a plant that would confer "youth in old age" (11:268–89). Gen 3:22 notes that this tree too would also confer life on those who ate its fruit. Proverbs describes wisdom (3:18), the fruit of the righteous (11:30), a desire fulfilled (13:12), and a gentle tongue as a tree of life: in other words, they give fullness of life to their owners. In Scripture, trees, because they remain green throughout the summer drought, are seen as symbolic of the life of God (e.g., Ps 1:3; Jer 17:8). Abraham prayed by a tamarisk he planted (21:33), and green trees were a regular feature of the so-often-denounced Canaanite shrines (e.g., Deut 12:2). Furthermore, it seems likely that the golden candlestick kept in the tabernacle was a stylized tree of life: the falling of its light on the twelve loaves of the presence symbolized God's life sustaining the twelve tribes of Israel (Exod 25:31–35; Lev 24:1–9 [see C. L. Meyers, *The Tabernacle Menorah*, ASOR DS 2 (Missoula: Scholars Press, 1976) 174–81]).

"The tree of the knowledge of good and evil" is found only in this story, and it is much more difficult to establish its significance. Yet it is most important to try, for it is a key phrase in the narrative, occurring twice in the opening scene, 2:9, 17; once in the first dialogue, 3:5; and finally once again in the closing scene, 3:22.

Two initial points can be made. First, it seems likely that since eating the fruit of the tree of life would have led to immortality, so eating the fruit of the other tree would lead to a knowledge of good and evil too (3:22). Second, we must attempt to establish the meaning of "knowing good and evil" by examining the use of the phrase as a whole here and in other passages, not simply by looking at its component parts.

Suggested interpretations of the phrase "knowing good and evil" include:

1. "The knowledge of good and evil" is simply a description of the consequences of obeying or disobeying the commandments (so Kidner and Gispen). Man would have known good had he obeyed the command: he knows evil as a result of disobedience. "The tree plays its part in the opportunity it offers, rather than the qualities it possesses; like a door whose name announces only what lies beyond it" (Kidner, 63).

Valid as this observation is, it is inadequate. As the tree of life offered immortality, so this tree offered knowledge appropriate only to the divine (3:5, 22). Furthermore, this explanation does not fit Deut 1:39 and 2 Sam 19:36 [35], which observe that neither the very young nor the elderly know good and evil.

2. "Knowledge of good and evil" means moral discernment, knowing the difference between right and wrong. Last advocated by Budde (1883), this interpretation is not taken seriously by modern commentators, because, given the narrator's assumptions, it is absurd to suppose man was not always expected to exercise moral discretion or that he acquired such a capacity through eating the fruit.

3. "Knowledge of good and evil" means sexual knowledge (e.g., Weinfeld). Though this explanation suits the situation of the elderly and the young, it is incongruous in its present context. In Gen 1 and 2 there is no hint that sexual knowledge is reserved for God, or that it was wrong for man (cf. 1:28; 2:18–25). "This explanation then is quite untenable" (Westermann, 1:243).

4. "Knowledge of good and evil" means omniscience (von Rad; cf. Wallace, *Eden Narrative*, 128). "Good and evil" here stand for the parts which make up the whole, just as the phrase "heaven and earth" means the universe. Though God enjoys omniscience, and the narrative suggests that the woman hoped to gain great knowledge (3:6), it is clear that the man and woman who ate the fruit did not acquire omniscience as a result, merely shame and a recognition of their nakedness (3:7–8).

5. "Knowledge of good and evil" is wisdom (Cassuto, Westermann, Vawter; cf. Clark). It offered "insight" השכיל (3:6). At first sight this interpretation appears as unlikely as moral discernment. It is easy to see that God has wisdom and that children lack it, but more difficult to see why it was forbidden to man. The acquisition of wisdom is seen as one of the highest goals of the godly according to the Book of Proverbs. But the wisdom literature also makes it plain that there is a wisdom that is God's sole preserve, which man should not aspire to attain (e.g., Job 15:7–9, 40; Prov 30:1–4), since a full understanding of God, the universe, and man's place in it is ultimately beyond human comprehension. To pursue it without reference to revelation is to assert human autonomy, and to neglect the fear of the LORD which is the beginning of knowledge (Prov 1:7). "For the Yahwist the only proper posture of man if he would be truly wise and lead a full life is faith in God and not a professed self-sufficiency of knowledge. It is in this latter acceptation, then,

that man is forbidden 'the tree of the knowledge of good and bad'" (Vawter, 73). This interpretation appears to be confirmed by Ezek 28, the closest parallel to Gen 2–3, which in highly mythological language describes how the king of Tyre was expelled from Eden for overweening pride and claiming himself to be "wise as a god" (28:6, 15–17). Approaching the issue from a different direction, Clark (*JBL* 88 [1969] 266–78) has come to similar conclusions: he points to the use of the phrase "good and evil" in legal contexts to describe legal responsibility. In Gen 2–3 he suggests J is using it for moral autonomy, deciding what is right without reference to God's revealed will. This is confirmed by the allusions to Gen 2–3 in Ps 19:8–10 [7–9] where the law is compared to the tree of knowledge: the law makes wise the simple and enlightens the eyes (cf. Gen 3:6; see D. J. A. Clines, *VT* 24 [1974] 8–14).

In the garden, the revealed law of God amounted to the warning "Do not eat this tree" on pain of death. In later Israel, many more laws were known, and those who flouted them incurred the divine curse and risked death. Since the law was God-given, it could not be altered or added to by man (Deut 4:2); thus human moral autonomy was ruled out (Josh 4:7). In preferring human wisdom to divine law, Adam and Eve found death, not life. In the tabernacle, the inviolability of the law was symbolized by storing the tables of the law inside the ark itself, the sacred throne of God, guarded and out of sight in the innermost holy of holies, for to see or to touch the ark brought death (Exod 40:20; Num 4:15, 20.)

10–14 The narrative flow is here interrupted with details about the rivers of the garden. This break has led most modern commentators to conclude that these verses at least reflect a different source from the rest of the chapter. Some older writers suggested these verses are a late interpolation into J, whereas recent opinion inclines to see them as an early tradition incorporated by J. The main argument for their antiquity is the description of the Tigris flowing east of the city of Ashur (v 14), which may indicate that it is an old geographical note, possibly dating from the era when Ashur was capital of Assyria. To see this passage as an old note integrated into the present narrative is also preferable grammatically in that v 10 is a circumstantial clause conjoined to v 9b (see *SBH*, 87). Furthermore, as we shall argue below, the symbolism of these verses coheres well with the rest of the chapter. Westermann suggests that these geographical notes function rather like the genealogies (e.g., Gen 10) in that they serve to relate present realities, well-known nations and rivers, to their ultimate sources in primeval history.

10 "There was a river flowing out of Eden." The participle יֹצֵא is tenseless and therefore could be translated "is flowing" (so Westermann), but grammatically, given the context, a continuous past is required (cf. Joüon, 154d). The phraseology suggests that the river rose in Eden and then flowed into the garden to water it. However, if Eden and the garden were believed to be coterminous, the river must have risen in the garden. According to v 6, the fresh-water ocean waters the earth. Here it is said that the river waters the garden, probably implying that the river itself is fed by this subterranean ocean.

"And from there," i.e., after leaving the garden, "it divided and became four branches." "Branches," literally, "heads" (רָאשִׁים): more commonly small tributaries join up to form a larger river. Its division into four streams may suggest the idea of completeness and the universality of the river, something made the more probable by the mention of the two great rivers of Mesopotamia in v 14. The picture of a great river flowing out of Eden is akin to Ps 46:5, "There is a river whose streams make glad the city of God," and Ezekiel's description of the eschatological Jerusalem from which a great river will flow to sweeten the Dead Sea (Ezek 47:1–12). In every case the river is symbolic of the life-giving presence of God.

11 The identity of Pishon and Gihon (v 13), is problematic. Probably the words are descriptive: Pishon "the leaper" comes from פּישׁ "to leap," and Gihon "the springer out," from גיח "to break out." There is no consensus about which rivers are meant.

The Pishon is mentioned only here in the OT. It has been identified with the Indus (e.g., Dillmann, Delitzsch), the Ganges (Josephus), one of the rivers of Arabia (KB, Faisan) or a river of Mesopotamia (Speiser, *Oriental Studies*, 31–34).

"The Land of Havilah, where there is gold" is mentioned in several other passages (cf. 10:7, 29; 25:18; 1 Sam 15:7; 1 Chr 1:9, 23). These suggest that Havilah is in Arabia: Simons (*GTOT*, 40–41) and Gispen think it comprises all Arabia. Certainly Arabia was a source of gold in ancient times. On this basis the Pishon must either be identified with an Arabian river, or with the Persian Gulf and Red Sea "which goes round all the land of Havilah."

12 "Bdellium," a transliteration via Greek βδέλλιον of Hebrew בדלח (Akk. *budulḫu*), is a translucent aromatic substance to which the manna is compared in Num 11:7. Jacob and Cassuto follow the LXX ἄνθραξ in supposing that some precious stone is meant here. This would fit in with the mention of gold and onyx stone, and Ezek 28:13 with its catalog of jewels in the garden of Eden.

"Onyx stone." It is uncertain if this traditional English translation following Greek and Latin versions is correct. Hebrew שׁהם may be cognate with Akkadian *sāmtu*, but this too has not been certainly identified. Modern suggested translations for the Hebrew include "carnelian" (NEB, *EM* 7:526–27), "lapis lazuli" (Speiser), and "chrysoprase" (Gispen). Whatever the correct identification of the "onyx stone," they were widely used in decorating the tabernacle and temple (Exod 25:7; 1 Chr 29:2) and in the high-priestly vestments (Exod 28:9, 20). The names of the twelve tribes of Israel were engraved on two onyx stones, set in gold, and attached to the shoulder of the ephod (Exod 28:9–14). "Pure gold" (note Gen 2:12: "the gold of that land is good") was widely used in covering the sacred furniture, such as the ark, altar of incense, lampstand, in the holiest parts of the tabernacle. Paradise in Eden and the later tabernacle share a common symbolism suggestive of the presence of God.

13 "Gihon . . . Cush." Gihon is the name of Jerusalem's principal spring, the virgin's spring (cf. 1 Kgs 1:33, 38). But it seems unlikely that this could be described as "going round all the land of Cush." It is the mention of the land of Cush which has led most ancient and modern commentators to identify this Gihon with the Nile. Usually Cush refers to the land of Ethiopia (e.g., Isa 20:3, 5; Jer 46:9), but in Gen 10:8 it means the Cassites, the successors to the old Babylonian empire who were at home in the hills of western Iran. Speiser and Weinfeld have argued that the land of Cush is the land of the Cassites and that the Gihon is one of the rivers or canals of Mesopotamia. This makes it easier to envisage a point where all the rivers met, possibly in the mountains of Armenia or at the head of the Persian gulf, but since it is only in Gen 10:8 that Cush may be equated with the Cassites, this view has difficulties.

14 The Tigris and the Euphrates create no problems of identification, but the remark that the Tigris runs to the east of Ashur raises questions. It seems that Ashur here means the old capital city of Assyria, not the whole country, as it usually does in Hebrew. For the territory of Assyria lies on both sides of the Tigris, whereas the river itself runs east, or in front of the city (the Hebrew קִדְמַת means either "east of" or "in front of"). After 1400 Ashur was no longer the political capital of Assyria, so Gunkel and Westermann conclude that this is proof of the antiquity of this tradition in Genesis. However, since Ashur remained the most important religious city of the region, we cannot be so dogmatic. It may be mere coincidence, but it may be noted that very near the beginning of the Atrahasis epic (1:25) both the Tigris and the Euphrates are mentioned.

THE LOCATION OF EDEN

The geographic location of Eden has been debated at great length but quite inconclusively. The general setting as described in vv 5–8 favors a Mesopotamian site. In Eden a great river rises, and after leaving the garden, splits up into four rivers including the Tigris and Euphrates. On this basis alone we should conclude that Eden lies somewhere in Armenia near the sources of the Tigris and Euphrates. And this is a long-established, widely held view. It is, however, complicated by the mention of the Pishon flowing round Havilah (Arabia?) and the Gihon flowing round Cush (Ethiopia or western Iran?). An easy solution is to put the confusion down to the hazy geographical knowledge of the ancients. They imagined all these rivers did join up somewhere. Fewest problems are posed by the view of Haupt (see Driver, 58) and Speiser that the garden was located near the head of the Persian Gulf. Here three of the rivers converge, and if the fourth is an Arabian stream or the Persian Gulf itself, all four meet. According to Mesopotamian mythology, the island of Dilmun (Bahrain) at the northern end of the gulf was a paradise isle, a land of life and immortality, where thousands of people from surrounding areas were buried, perhaps in an attempt to ensure eternal life (cf. C. C. Lamberg-Karlovsky, *JNES* 41 [1982] 45–50). The greatest difficulty with this view is that, according to Genesis, the rivers as they flow from Eden split into four, whereas on Speiser's location they flow toward Eden to converge there (cf. Driver, 39). Speiser does not face this problem, but is this perhaps yet another example of the way in which Genesis takes up old mythological motifs, radically transforming them to suit its purposes? Maybe the reversed flow of the rivers suggests that paradise is beyond man's present experience. Their names affirm that there was a garden there, but maybe the insoluble geography is a way of saying that it is now inaccessible to, even unlocatable by, later man (cf. 3:24).

15 Here the writer picks up the narrative thread from v 8 by repeating some of the same phraseology, a characteristic device of Hebrew narrative signaling the end of a digression (S. Talmon, *Scripta Hierosolymitana* 27 [1978] 9–26). Here is added that man's job in the garden is "to till it and guard it."

עבד "to serve, till" is a very common verb and is often used of cultivating the soil (2:5; 3:23; 4:2, 12, etc.). The word is commonly used in a religious sense of serving God (e.g., Deut 4:19), and in priestly texts, especially of the tabernacle duties of the Levites (Num 3:7–8; 4:23–24, 26, etc.). Similarly, שמר "to guard, to keep" has the simple profane sense of "guard" (4:9; 30:31), but it is even more commonly used in legal texts of observing religious commands and duties (17:9; Lev 18:5) and particularly of the Levitical responsibility for guarding the tabernacle from intruders (Num 1:53; 3:7–8). It is striking that here and in the priestly law these two terms are juxtaposed (Num 3:7–8; 8:26; 18:5–6), another pointer to the interplay of tabernacle and Eden symbolism already noted (cf. *Ber. Rab.* 16:5).

It should be noted that even before the fall man was expected to work; paradise was not a life of leisured unemployment. Both *Enuma elish* and the Atrahasis epic also speak of man being created to work to relieve the gods (EE 6:33–36; A 1.190–97). But the biblical narrative gives no hint that the creator is shuffling off his load onto man: work is intrinsic to human life.

16–17 The narrative continues with a recounting of God's bountiful provision for mankind and at the same time provides a vital clue to understanding the tragedy in chap. 3.

In 2:9 it was said that the garden contained trees good to eat; now explicit permission is given to eat of them all save the tree of knowledge. This "again reveals the abundance of [God's] fatherly care" (von Rad, 80). The prohibition applies simply to one of the two special trees; evidently man was allowed to eat of the tree of life if he wanted.

17 The restriction is blunt and firm. "Never eat," literally, "you shall not eat," resembles in its form the ten commandments: לא "not" followed by the imperfect is used for long-standing prohibitions; cf. "Do not steal, murder," etc. (Exod 20:3–17). To it is appended a motive clause: "for on the day you do (eat), you will certainly die" (cf. Exod 20:5, 7, 11), a characteristic feature of Hebrew law (cf. B. Gemser, "Motive Clause in Old Testament Law," VTSup 1 [1953] 50–66). It is not, as Westermann (1:225) maintains, the characteristic formulation for the death sentence in legal texts. They use infinitive plus hophal [יומת] "he shall be put to death," whereas here we have infinitive plus qal [תמות] "you will die." This is the form characteristic of divine or royal threats in narrative and prophetic texts (e.g., 20:7, 1 Sam 14:39, 44; 22:16; 1 Kgs 2:37, 42; 2 Kgs 1:4, 6; Ezek 33:8, 14). These parallels show that the fruit of the tree was not poisonous, as occasionally suggested. The death sentence demonstrates God's seriousness in prohibiting access to the tree. The parallels also show that Speiser (cf. Cassuto) is unjustified in retranslating "you will certainly die" by "you shall be doomed to die" (15).

The text is a straightforward warning that death will follow eating. Nor can the contradiction between this warning, the snake's remarks (3:4), and the conclusion of the story be resolved by retranslating "on the day" as "when." Though this phrase can mean vaguely "when" (cf. 2:4; 5:1), it tends to emphasize promptness of action (e.g., Num 30:6, 8, 9, etc.), especially in the closely similar passage (1 Kgs 2:37, 42). Whether the serpent was right to dismiss the divine warning, here so emphatic and explicit, as mere bluff will be discussed below.

18 "The LORD God thought, 'It is not good for man to be alone. Let me make him a helper matching him.'" For the first time since chap. 1 God speaks, or thinks; אמר can have both senses. Just as the creation of mankind (1:28) was preceded by divine self-deliberation, "Let us make man" (1:26), so here the need for the creation of woman is adumbrated by God, "It is not good for man to be alone." Against the sevenfold refrain of "and God saw that it was (very) good" in chap. 1, the divine observation that something was not right with man's situation is startling. It alerts the reader to the importance of companionship for man. He needs a "helper matching him" (18, 20). Elsewhere עזר "helper/help" usually refers to divine assistance, but it is used in three prophetic passages of military aid (Isa 30:5; Ezek 12:14; Hos 13:9). To help someone does not imply that the helper is stronger than the helped; simply that the latter's strength is inadequate by itself (e.g. Josh 1:14; 10:4, 6; 1 Chron 12:17, 19, 21, 22). The compound prepositional phrase "matching him," כנגדו, literally, "like opposite him" is found only here. It seems to express the notion of complementarity rather than identity. As Delitzsch (1:140) observes, if identity were meant, the more natural phrase would be "like him," כמוהו. The help looked for is not just assistance in his daily work or in the procreation of children, though these aspects may be included, but the mutual support companionship provides.

"Two are better than one . . . for if they fall one will lift up his fellow" (Eccl 4:9–10; cf. Prov 31:10–31).

Despite God's identification of man's need, there is a delay in his provision: contrast the instantaneous fulfillment of the divine word in chap. 1. This hold-up creates suspense. It allows us to feel man's loneliness. All the animals are brought before him, and we see him looking at each one in the hope it would make a suitable companion for man. *Ber. Rab.* 17:5 pictures the animals passing by in pairs and man commenting, "Everything has its partner but I have no partner."

The pathos is heightened in the narrative's emphasis on the fact that the animals, like man (v 7), are shaped from the land (v 19), and, like him, are "living creatures." Furthermore, the word for "animal" and "living," *ḥayyāh*, anticipates "Eve," *ḥawwāh*. Though in Hebrew these creatures' names sound so similar to Eve's, they are not what man is looking for. Despite man's superiority to the other creatures, demonstrated by his naming of them (to give a name to something is to assert authority over it; cf. 1:26, 28), no suitable helper is found. Once again the narrative is laying the ground for chap. 3, establishing man's place in the world, a little lower than the angels and a little higher than the animals. Compared with the comprehensive lists of animals in chap. 1, these short summaries just mention those that might be considered possible companions for man—(wild) animals and birds in v 19 and cattle (i.e., domesticated animals), birds, and wild animals in v 20. Fish obviously could not qualify as man's helpmeet. It would seem that the addition of "cattle" in v 20 is deliberate: probably they are simply included in the wild animals in the previous verse. But they are specially mentioned in v 20 because they are the most likely candidates for man's companion and yet they are sadly inadequate.

21–25 The creation of woman from man's rib supplies what was missing for his perfect happiness. Five short clauses in vv 21–22 describing God's work complete the description of the task of finding a companion for man begun in v 18. His success is rapturously acclaimed in the poetic outburst in v 23. Indeed, the whole account of woman's creation has a poetic flavor: it is certainly mistaken to read it as an account of a clinical operation or as an attempt to explain some feature of man's anatomy (cf. von Rad, Procksch). Rather, it brilliantly depicts the relation of man and wife. "Just as the rib is found at the side of the man and is attached to him, even so the good wife, the *rib* of her husband, stands at his side to be his helper-counterpart, and her soul is bound up with his" (Cassuto, 134). The idea that woman was made out of man's rib, because "rib," *ti*, and "life," *til*, are similar sounding Sumerian words seems farfetched and presupposes an extraordinary knowledge of Sumerian by a Hebrew (cf. W. G. Lambert, *TRE* 5 [1975] 72–73). Matthew Henry's comment comes closer to the spirit of the text. "Not made out of his head to top him, not out of his feet to be trampled upon by him, but out of his side to be equal with him, under his arm to be protected, and near his heart to be beloved." Charming though this picturesque tale is, it should be borne in mind that it has a more serious purpose than entertainment. Here the ideal of marriage as it was understood in ancient Israel is being portrayed, a relationship characterized by harmony and intimacy between the partners. The destruction of this relationship is described in the following chapters, but like other aspects of man's existence set out in Gen 1–2, the first days of the first marriage remain a goal to which Israel hoped to return when the promises to Abraham were fulfilled. The story therefore needs to be closely read, for in its often poetic phraseology are expressed some of the Old Testament's fundamental convictions about the nature and purpose of marriage.

21 "Then the Lord God made a heavy sleep overcome man." "Heavy sleep," תרדמה, is often divinely induced sleep (cf. Isa 29:10; 1 Sam 26:12) and the occasion for divine revelation (Gen 15:12; Job 4:13). Possibly sleep is mentioned here because God's ways are mysterious and not for human observation (Dillmann, von Rad) or because to imagine man conscious during the operation would destroy the charm of the story (Cassuto). Certainly the remark about closing up the flesh afterwards must be ascribed to the narrator's concern with the beauty of the occasion.

22 "The Lord God then built the rib . . . into a woman." "Built" (בנה): only here and in Amos 9:6 is this verb used of God's creative activity, though in Akkadian and Ugaritic it is the regular term for creation.

When man woke up, God "brought her to the man." The God-created partner is introduced to man by the creator himself. The man's passivity in

the match-making process is notable, but fits easily into a society where arranged marriages were the norm.

23 In ecstasy man bursts into poetry on meeting his perfect helpmeet.
The verse is traditionally scanned into a two-beat tricolon and a three-beat
bicolon, literally:

This, this time,	2	(4 syllables)
(is) bone of my bones	2	(6 ")
and flesh of my flesh	2	(7 ")
This shall be called woman	3	(7 ")
for from man was taken this	3	(7 ")

In these five short lines many of the standard techniques of Hebrew poetry
are employed: parallelism (lines 2–3; 4–5), assonance and word play (woman/
man); chiasmus (ABC/C′B′A′) (lines 4–5, "this . . . called woman" // "man-
. . . taken this"); and verbal repetition: by opening the tricolon and bicolon
with "this" and then by concluding with the same word the man's exclamation
concentrates all eyes on this woman.

The first three lines are a poetic formulation of the traditional kinship
formula. For example, Laban said to his nephew Jacob, "You are my bone
and my flesh" (29:14; cf. Judg 9:2; 2 Sam 5:1; 19:13–14 [12–13]). Whereas
English speaks of blood relationships, Hebrew spoke of relatives as one's
"flesh and bone." It is often suggested that the story of woman's creation
from man's rib illustrates the meaning of this traditional kinship formula.
"The first man could employ . . . (these) words in their literal connotation:
actually bone of his bones and flesh of his flesh!" (Cassuto, 1:136). This
formula sets man and woman on an equal footing as regards their humanity,
yet sets them apart from the animals (vv 19–20; cf. 1:26–28).

"This shall be called a woman, for from a man was she taken." The last
two lines are a typical example of Hebrew naming. Despite their similarity,
it is doubtful whether there is any etymological connection between אִשָּׁה
(ʾiššāh) "woman" and אִישׁ (ʾîš) "man." (But see S. Qogut, *Tarbiz* 51 [1982]
293–98 for possible link.) Frequently Hebrew folk etymologies offer a wordplay on the circumstances of the person's birth (cf. 4:1, 25; 17:17, 19; 29:32–
30:24, etc.). Here the first man names the first woman in a similar fashion.
Though they are equal in nature, that man names woman (cf. 3:20) indicates
that she is expected to be subordinate to him, an important presupposition
of the ensuing narrative (3:17).

24 "Therefore a man forsakes his father and his mother." This is not a
continuation of the man's remarks in v 23, but a comment of the narrator,
applying the principles of the first marriage to every marriage.

"Forsakes," יַעֲזֹב. The traditional translation "leaves" suggests that the man
moves from his parents and sets up home elsewhere, whereas in fact Israelite
marriage was usually patrilocal, that is, the man continued to live in or near
his parents' home. It was the wife who left home to join her husband. So it
is preferable here to translate עזב as "forsake." Israel is bidden not to forsake
the poor and the Levite, or the covenant (Deut 12:19; 14:27; 29:24). On
the other hand, God promises not to forsake Israel (Deut 31:8; Josh 1:5).

These examples show that forsaking father and mother is to be understood in a relative sense, not an absolute sense; cf. Hos 6:6, "I desire mercy and not sacrifice," or our Lord's remarks about hating father and mother, wife and children in Luke 16:26. On marriage a man's priorities change. Beforehand his first obligations are to his parents: afterwards they are to his wife. In modern Western societies where filial duties are often ignored, this may seem a minor point to make, but in traditional societies like Israel where honoring parents is the highest human obligation next to honoring God, this remark about forsaking them is very striking.

"And sticks to his wife." This phrase suggests both passion and permanence should characterize marriage. Shechem's love of Dinah is described as "his soul stuck to Dinah" (Gen 34:3). The tribes of Israel are assured that they will stick to their own inheritance; i.e., it will be theirs permanently (Num 36:7, 9). Israel is repeatedly urged to stick to the LORD (Deut 10:20; 11:22; 13:5, etc.). The use of the terms "forsake" and "stick" in the context of Israel's covenant with the LORD suggests that the OT viewed marriage as a kind of covenant.

"They become one flesh." This does not denote merely the sexual union that follows marriage, or the children conceived in marriage, or even the spiritual and emotional relationship that it involves, though all are involved in becoming one flesh. Rather it affirms that just as blood relations are one's flesh and bone (cf. *Comment* on v 23), so marriage creates a similar kinship relation between man and wife. They become related to each other as brother and sister are. The laws in Lev 18 and 20, and possibly Deut 24:1–4, illustrate the application of this kinship-of-spouses principle to the situation following divorce or the death of one of the parties. Since a woman becomes on marriage a sister to her husband's brothers, a daughter to her father-in-law, and so on, she cannot normally marry any of them should her first husband die or divorce her. (See G. J. Wenham, *The Book of Leviticus*, 253–61, and *idem, JJS* 30 [1979] 36–40). The kinships established by marriage are therefore not terminated by death or divorce.

25 "The two of them . . . were nude, but they were not ashamed." This verse has an important narrative function. It closes scene 2, thereby creating a parallel with the end of scene 6 in 3:21, and it also explains the background to many of the actions in chap. 3. After eating the forbidden fruit, the couple notice their nakedness, make fig-leaf aprons, cover themselves, and hide in the bushes when they hear God approaching (3:7–11). 2:25 points out that originally men did not react this way: "They were not ashamed." The Hebrew root בוֹשׁ "to be ashamed" does not carry the overtones of personal guilt that English "shame" includes. Hebrew can speak of "shame" triggered by circumstances completely extrinsic to the speaker (Judg 3:25; 2 Kgs 2:17). Perhaps then it might be better to translate here, "they were unabashed" or "they were not disconcerted." They were like young children unashamed at their nakedness.

Some writers (e.g., Wambacq, *Mélanges B. Rigaux* [1970] 547–56; and E. Haag, *Mensch am Anfang*, 50) see nakedness as a symbol of poverty and need and suggest that feelings of sexual guilt had nothing to do with it. The LORD's subsequent provision of clothing (3:21) paralleled his earlier provision of food (2:19; 2:9), food and clothing being man's fundamental needs. Attractive though this argument is, it hardly does justice to the clause "but they were not ashamed," which surely suggests that primeval man had all he required. Nor as Coppens points out (*ETL* 46 [1970] 380–83) does it sit well with Gen 9:20–27 and its fundamental assumption that it is grossly indecent to uncover one's sexual organs, or the law's insistence that priests must not expose their privy parts when offering sacrifice (contrast Sumerian custom; Exod 20:26; 28:42–43). It would seem much more probable then that Gen 3 is explaining why man must wear clothes, rather than that 2:25 is idealizing nudity. 2:25 reiterates the contentment of the couple with God's provision and fills in the background detail just enough for the understanding of chap. 3.

3:1–5 The third scene opens with a circumstantial clause describing the snake as "more shrewd than all the wild animals of the plain which the LORD God had made." The rest of the scene is dialogue between the snake and the woman (cf. scene 5, vv 9–13). Now, explicit characterization of actors in the story is rare in Hebrew narrative, so it seems likely that in noting the snake's shrewdness the narrator is hinting that his remarks should be examined very carefully. He may not be saying what he seems to be saying. Perhaps we should not take his words at their face value as the woman did.

1 "Now the snake was more shrewd than all the wild animals." "Shrewd" עָרוּם is an ambiguous term. On the one hand it is a virtue the wise should cultivate (Prov 12:16; 13:16), but misused it becomes wiliness and guile (Job 5:12; 15:5; cf. Exod 21:14; Josh 9:4). The choice of the term עָרוּם "shrewd" here is one of the more obvious plays on words in the text; for the man and his wife have just been described as עָרֹם "nude" (2:25). They will seek themselves to be shrewd (cf. 3:6) but will discover that they are "nude" (3:7, 10).

The snake is here described as one of "the wild animals which the LORD God had made." Why, it is often asked, did a snake appear and tempt the woman? Very diverse answers have been offered, though none appear entirely satisfactory. Early Jewish and Christian commentators identified the snake with Satan or the devil, but since there is no other trace of a personal devil in early parts of the OT, modern writers doubt whether this is the view of our narrator. It is often asserted that the serpent is the symbol of the Canaanite fertility cults, and that therefore Gen 3 illustrates the choice before Israel—should they obey Yahweh or follow Baal? But as Westermann observes, it hardly seems likely that Gen 3 would have mentioned the LORD God's creating the snake if it was supposed to represent the archenemy of the true faith. It has also been pointed out that in the ancient Orient snakes were symbolic of life, wisdom, and chaos (K. R. Joines, *ZAW* 87 [1975] 1–11), all themes that have points of contact with the present narrative, though whether this is sufficient explanation of a snake's presence here is doubtful. It may be that we have here another transformation of a familiar mythological motif. The Gilgamesh Epic relates how Gilgamesh found a plant through which he could avoid death. Unfortunately while he was swimming in a pond a snake came out and swallowed the plant, thereby depriving him of the chance of immortality. Here in Genesis we have a quite different story, but once again a snake, man, plants, and the promise of life are involved, though here man loses immortality through blatant disobedience, whereas in the epic that loss seems to be just a matter of bad luck. Furthermore, it may be noted that according to the classification of animals found in Lev 11 and Deut 14, the snake must count as an archetypal unclean animal. Its swarming, writhing locomotion puts it at the farthest point from those pure animals that can be offered in sacrifice. Within the world of OT animal symbolism a snake is an obvious candidate for an anti-God symbol, notwithstanding its creation by God. In one way, a dead animal, which is even more unclean than any living creature, would be a better anti-God symbol, yet it would be quite absurd to have a corpse talk. So for any Israelite familiar with the symbolic values of different animals, a creature more likely than a serpent to lead man away from his creator could not be imagined. The serpent Leviathan, mentioned in Ugaritic mythology, is also referred to in Isa 27:1 (cf. Job 26:13) as a creature destroyed by God, further evidence of the familiar association in biblical times of serpents and God's enemies.

The serpent begins by asking an apparently innocent question, "Has God really said . . .?" However, in the very first words אף כי "really," there is possibly a touch of scepticism or at least surprise, which carries through into "you must not eat from *any* of the trees," a total travesty of God's original generous permission (2:16). Yet taken as a question, the snake's remark appears ingenuous enough. But how, the narrator expects us to ask, did the snake know anything about God's command? If he heard that command, why has he so grossly distorted it? Thus in his very first words the snake's shrewdness is illustrated. Furthermore, in describing God simply as God (אלהים) instead of as the LORD God, which is characteristic of the rest of Gen 2–3, there is a suggestion of the serpent's distance from God. God is just the remote creator, not Yahweh, Israel's covenant partner (cf. *Comment* on 2:4).

2–3 The woman corrects the snake, but not quite accurately. Whereas the LORD had said, "You may freely eat of *every* garden tree," she omits "every," saying simply, "We may eat of the fruit. . . ." She also adopts the snake's description of the LORD God, describing him simply as "God," and most significantly, she adds to the ban on eating of the tree of knowledge a prohibition on even touching it "lest you die." These slight alterations to God's remarks suggest that the woman has already moved slightly away from God toward the serpent's attitude. The creator's generosity is not being given its full due, and he is being painted as a little harsh and repressive, forbidding the tree even to be touched. Indeed, the way "lest you die" follows "touch" suggests that not just eating it but touching it may be lethal.

4–5 It is in the snake's reply that we appreciate why he is called shrewd. His words sound like a sharp rejection of God's. "You will not certainly die," he says, "but God knows that on the day you eat of it your eyes will be opened and you will become like God." And yet, greatly to our surprise (for biblical narrative generally adopts a divine or prophetic perspective), his remarks are apparently vindicated. The man and his wife do not die, at least not until Adam reached the ripe age of 930 years (5:5)! While v 7 notes that their eyes were opened and in v 22 God says, "Man has become like one of us, knowing good and evil." On first reading at least, God seems to have tried to deceive his creatures by issuing threats he subsequently did not fulfill. The snake told the truth, not the LORD God.

But as commentators have often pointed out, the snake was uttering half-truths. There is a subtle ambiguity in his words which warrants describing him as "shrewd." Furthermore, as Gunkel (17) notes: "It is very neat, that the snake never directly demands that they should eat—he understands the art of seduction." The ambiguity is clearest in the serpent's claim that their eyes will be opened. They were indeed, but with more than a touch of pathos and irony the story continues: "they realized they were nude"! Similarly, becoming "like God, knowing good and evil," only serves to separate them from him. On hearing him approach, they hide among the bushes and they are expelled from the garden. The snake's promises have come true but in a very different way from the way one might have expected, had they come from God.

Similarly, there is undoubtedly a double-entendre in his opening remark "You will not certainly die." This English translation, like the original Hebrew, is ambiguous; does it mean "Certainly you will not die" or "It is not certain that you will die?" The latter understanding is preferred by Vawter (78). Roth (*Tarbiz* 41 [1972] 245–54), on the other hand, calls attention to the unusual Hebrew word order (usually the "not" comes between the verb and infinitive absolute; the only parallels to this order are Ps 49:8 and Amos 9:8) and thinks the ambiguity means the hearer must choose between taking it as "No: you will certainly die" or "You will certainly not die." Yet another possibility that has been suggested is that the snake is simply denying the woman's incorrect addition to God's words, namely, that touching the tree will kill. Or, finally, it could be that the snake is partially quoting God's words in 2:17, "you will certainly die," by prefacing them with "not" and then going on to give a different divine motivation. So we might render his words "Not 'certainly die,' but God knows . . . you will become like God, knowing good and evil."

Finally, it may be that just as the other two serpentine remarks about opening eyes and becoming like God can be understood in two ways, there are two meanings of "you shall die." We have seen that the garden of Eden narrative is full of symbols suggesting the presence of God and his life-giving power—trees, gold, rivers, and jewels used to adorn the holy of holies. In Israelite worship, true life was experienced when one went to the sanctuary. There God was present. There he gave life. But to be expelled from the camp, as lepers were, was to enter the realm of death. Those unfortunates had to behave like mourners, with their clothes torn and their hair disheveled (Lev 13:45). If to be expelled from the camp of Israel was to "die," expulsion from the garden was an even more drastic kind of death. In this sense they did die on the day they ate of the tree: they were no longer able to have daily conversation with God, enjoy his bounteous provision, and eat of the tree of life; instead they had to toil for food, suffer, and eventually return to the dust from which they were taken. A parallel to this idea of death before death is to be found in the story of Saul. As far as Samuel was concerned,

Saul "died" when he rejected the word of the Lord at Gilgal. So Samuel mourned for him (1 Sam 15:35–16:1). And evidently the narrator shared Samuel's perspective, for he states, "and Samuel did not see Saul again until the day of his death," although he relates another encounter between Samuel and Saul in 1 Sam 19:24. Evidently this did not count, for Saul was as good as dead, though his physical death was to be delayed some years.

Seen in this light, the snake was indeed shrewd. He told no outright lies, merely highly suggestive half-truths. At face value they contradicted God's warnings about the inevitability of death, but at a deeper level the latter were vindicated.

6–8 Here in the central scene the narrative reaches its climax. Here Hebrew prose style is seen to be at its most effective. With remarkable brevity, compared with the long-winded descriptions that precede it and the recriminations that follow, the fatal steps are described in a series of eleven *waw*-consecutive clauses that suggest the rapidity of the action—"she saw," "she took," "she gave. . . ." We have already noted (see *Form/Structure/Setting*) how the scenes themselves are arranged in a concentric palistrophic pattern (ABCDCBA). Within this central scene, the same device is used; the midpoint "and he ate" employs the key verb of this tale—"eat." On either side we have the woman's hopes of eating, "good to eat," "delight to the eyes," "giving insight," balanced by its effects, "eyes opened," "knowing they were nude," "hiding in the trees." These contrasts are deliberately drawn. The woman's inflated expectations of the wisdom she will acquire are hinted at in v 6. Then the actual consequences, mentioned in a very matter-of-fact way, are so comic as to be hilarious, were it not for the seriousness of the subject.

Walsh (*JBL* 96 [1977] 161–77) has already drawn attention to the inversion of roles that characterizes this narrative: how the man listens to his wife instead of God, the woman to the creature, and so on. The very phraseology of these verses strengthens his observations. Actions hitherto characteristic of the creator are now ascribed to the woman. She "saw *that* the tree was *good*," clearly echoing the refrain of Gen 1, "God saw . . . that it was good." In chap. 2 it is the Lord God who *takes* the man and the rib (15, 21, 22, 23); here she takes the fruit. Hitherto it has been God who has made all that man requires; now man and wife attempt to make loincloths (1:7, 11, 26, 31; 2:18; etc.). The human pair are shown usurping divine prerogatives as well as explicitly disobeying God's express word. When God makes the couple clothes of skin in 3:21, this is both an act of grace and a reassertion of the creator's rights.

6 "Then the woman saw that the tree was good to eat and . . . a delight to the eyes" (cf. 2:9). In the woman's eyes, the forbidden tree is now like the other trees. It was also "desirable to give one insight." This is preferable to the "desirable to look at" of Vg, S, Gunkel, and Skinner, who, prompted by 2:9, would ascribe a rare, if not unparalleled, meaning to השכיל, which otherwise has to do with understanding. The woman's covetousness is described in terminology that foreshadows the tenth commandment. "Delight," תאוה, and "desirable," נחמד, are from roots meaning "to covet" (Deut 5:21; cf. Exod 20:17). She "gave it to her husband with her": this last phrase emphasizes the man's association with the woman in the eating (cf. 6:18; 7:7; 13:1). Indeed, his eating is the last and decisive act of disobedience, for immediately the consequences of their sin are described.

7 "Then the eyes of both of them were opened" combines phrases from 2:25 and 3:5. The snake's prediction is literally fulfilled, but their vision is somewhat of a letdown: "They realized they were nude, and they sewed fig leaves together." "Fig leaves" were probably used because they are the biggest leaves available in Canaan, though their heavy indentations must have made them less than ideal for a covering!

"Loincloths" חגרת: elsewhere used of a belt (1 Kgs 2:5; 2 Kgs 3:21; Isa 3:24). The usual term for loincloth is אזור. Perhaps again the skimpiness of their clothing is being emphasized. Though somewhat ineffective, these actions suggest urgency and desperation; the innocent serenity of 2:25 is shattered. But who are the couple trying to hide from? From each other or from God? Certainly their behavior before meeting God shows (*pace* Westermann, 1:253) that they had a sense of guilt before he addressed them (so Drewermann, 79).

8 "They heard the sound of the LORD God walking to and fro in the garden in the breeze of the day." The description of Eden with its trees, rivers, gold, and so on emphasized God's presence there. Therefore it seems likely that it was not unusual for him to be heard walking in the garden "in the breeze of the day," i.e., in the afternoon when cool breezes spring up and the sun is not so scorching. Maybe a daily chat between the Almighty and his creatures was customary. The term "walking" (hithpael participle of הלך) is subsequently used of God's presence in the Israelite tent sanctuary (Lev 26:12; Deut 23:15 [14]; 2 Sam 7:6–7) again emphasizing the relationship between the garden and the later shrines. It is not God's walking in the garden that was unusual, but the reaction of man and his wife. They "hid . . . among the trees of the garden." The same phrase, "man and his wife," last occurred in 2:25: "The two of them, man and his wife, were nude, but they were not ashamed." A more complete transformation could not be imagined. The trust of innocence is replaced by the fear of guilt. The trees that God created for man to look at (2:9) are now his hiding place to prevent God seeing him.

9–13 Scene 5 constitutes a divine inquest into the proceedings. Here the actors are addressed in the opposite order to their appearance in the preceding scene: man, woman, snake. The original order reappears in scene 6 when the curses on the snake, the woman, and the man are pronounced (3:14–19). Here the sins of the various characters are elicited from their own lips. But there is a certain gentleness about the inquisition. Delitzsch (1:157) remarks, "It was God their creator, who now as God the redeemer was seeking the lost." By reverting to the term "the LORD God" from v 8 (cf. "God" in vv 1b–5), the narrator hints that God can still be man's covenant partner as well as his creator and judge.

9 Nevertheless, the brusque "the LORD God *called*" suggests the Judge of the whole earth is calling man in order to demand an account of his conduct (Cassuto, 1:155). Other enraged suzerains introduce their complaints by calling on their covenant partners for explanation (Pharaoh, 12:18; Abimelech, 20:9; 26:9–10). "And said to him": as Cassuto observes, this shows that the LORD knew where the man was, and that the following question, "Where are you?," is essentially rhetorical. אַיֵּה "where?" is often used in this way in poetry, e.g., Isa 33:18; 36:19; Ps 42:4, 11 [3, 10], and a very close parallel is found in Gen 4:9, where "Where is Abel your brother?" is followed by "Listen, your brother's blood is crying to me from the land," showing that God knows perfectly well what has happened to Abel. This interpretation of the verse as merely rhetorical is already presupposed in the Pseudo-Jonathan and Neofiti targums' lengthy paraphrase of the question, and Justin's dialogue 99 (Bowker, *The Targums and Rabbinic Literature*, 127). It has been followed by Rashi and more modern commentators such as Jacob, Cassuto, Gispen, though many, following Gunkel, have supposed that it was a real question and that God did not know where the couple were hiding. They see this as showing the primitive, childlike quality of the story. God is not pictured as an omniscient creator, but, just like a man looking for a friend, he really wanted to find out where they were. But this seriously underestimates our narrator's subtlety and skill. Certainly he portrays Adam and Eve as somewhat naive and childish in their game of hide and seek. Just as a parent who sees where his children are hiding may shout out, "Where are you?," in effect inciting them to come out, so does God. And, with Cassuto, we presume that this is what happened here: the couple emerge shamefaced from the trees. Their reply to God's inquiry shows that they understood the question as an invitation to come out and explain their behavior.

10 "He said, 'I heard your voice in the garden. I was afraid because I was naked, so I hid.'" Not only are the actors introduced in reverse sequence, but the divine cross-examination elicits an account of their deeds that goes back over them in reverse order. In language reminiscent of v 8, man first mentions his hiding among the trees. "He does not dare lie before his Creator, but he is not yet willing to avow his sin; hence he strives to turn the conversation to another subject, the last thing that happened *after* his transgression." He then offers an excuse for hiding himself—"because I was naked" (cf. v 7)— "without perceiving that his very excuse provides evidence of his misdeed" (Cassuto, 1:156).

11 "Who told you . . . ? Have you eaten . . . ?" These further questions are not those of an ignorant inquirer. Their very formulation suggests the all-knowing detective who by his questioning prods the culprit into confessing his guilt.

12 "It was the woman you gave to me who gave me of the tree and I ate." The man's reply goes over the events described in v 6. As people are wont in such situations, the man tries to excuse himself by blaming the woman and implying that it was really God's fault for giving him this woman. Here the divisive effects of sin, setting man against his dearest companion (cf. 2:23) and alienating him from his all-caring creator, are splendidly portrayed. "This too is characteristically human: people are inclined to justify their conduct by pointing to the circumstances and fate that God has allotted them in life" (Cassuto, 1:157). God's silence indicates his rejection of this plea.

13 "What have you done?" Finally the woman is questioned. Once again the form of the question "What . . . done?," spoken in a shocked tone (see

n. 13.a.), and the information already given by the man in the preceding
verse show that it is rhetorical. Once again the guilty party attempts to shift
the blame onto someone else, this time the serpent: "The snake fooled me
and I ate." Already the peace that characterized man's original relationship
with the animals is shattered. Sin has put alienation between God and man,
between men and women, and between animals and men. Yet the goal of
universal peace is not forgotten (cf. Isa 11:6–9).

14–21 But the serpent is given no chance to reply. God pronounces a
series of curses on those involved, addressing in turn snake, woman, and
man. This constitutes the sixth scene. In the passivity of the creatures vis-à-
vis the creator it matches the second scene (2:18–25), and like it, closes with
man naming his wife (2:23; 3:20).

The curses (vv 14–19) are rhythmical, though the meter is irregular and
they contain clauses in prose that make the rhythms still more uneven. Westermann and Steck believe that the earlier version of the story moved directly
from the divine interrogation to the expulsion from the garden and that
the curses represent an addition by J from another source. On such a hypothesis
the curses offer a peculiarly illuminating insight into the editor's view. But
as we have already observed, if various sources have been used, they have
been well integrated here and elsewhere in the story.

14–15 The curse on the snake. V 14, omitting the prose introduction
"Because you have done this, you are more cursed than all domesticated
and all wild animals," may be scanned as a pair of three two-beat lines: "On
your belly you must go and you must eat dust all the days of your life."
The introductory "Because you have done this" echoes v 13, while "You are
more cursed (אָרוּר)" than "all wild animals" echoes 3:1, "the snake was more
shrewd (עָרוּם) than all the wild animals . . .," in sound as well as phraseology.
Note that the causal clause "Because you have done this" precedes the main
clause, stressing the significance of the act (cf. n. 14.a.)

Only here and in 4:11 does God actually use this traditional formula "Cursed
are you"; elsewhere some third person pronounces the curse (e.g., Deut 28:16).
"To curse" is the antonym of "to bless" (cf. Gen 12:3). In the Bible, to curse
means to invoke God's judgment on someone, usually for some particular
offense. Thus various grave but secret sins, for which it would be difficult
to secure conviction in court, are cursed in Deut 27:15–26. Those cursed
may expect all kinds of misfortune to befall them; where a modern would
describe someone as unlucky, biblical man would call him "cursed." Though
curses were often held to be automatically effective (Num 22:6), they were
in fact dependent on the divine will for their effect. What is striking is that
here God himself pronounces the curse: its effectiveness is thus completely
guaranteed. The characteristic behavior of snakes—crawling, eating dust—
pursued by man, is proof that this curse was fulfilled.

מִן "more than." On the strength of the root meaning of מִן "from," commentators have often read into this remark proof that the snake was somehow
separated from other creatures, even אָרַר "to curse" being reinterpreted to
mean "ban, separate" (e.g., Speiser, Westermann, Vawter, and *TDOT* 1:409).
This seems unnecessary. מִן is often used in comparatives to mean "than,"
and the close parallel with 3:1 makes this much the most likely construction

here (so NEB, Cassuto, Weinfeld). "This does not necessarily imply that the other animals are also cursed, any more than the words 'subtle above all the beasts' imply that all other beasts are subtle" (E. W. Hengstenberg, *Christology of the OT*, 1 [1858]:14).

"On your belly you must go." The only parallel to this phrase is Lev 11:42, which brands all such creatures as unclean. It is doubtful whether this implies that snakes once had legs to walk with like other animals, an idea expressed in *Tg. Ps.-J*, Josephus, *Ant.* I.1.50 and *Gen. Rab.* 20:5, and periodically since. Rather, "the narrator . . . contemplates the present behavior of the snake and sees in it a divine curse" (Gunkel, 20). Sjöberg (*In the Shadow of Elyon*, 222–23) suggests this shows that the snake was actually a chameleon, which has legs and travels on its belly.

"Eat dust." This is not to say that snakes live on dust, rather it is figurative for abject humiliation, especially of enemies (cf. Ps 72:9; Isa 49:23; Mic 7:17).

"All the days of your life." Here the snake and his descendants are merged. The humiliation will endure for the lifetime of this snake, and that of all his successors, as v 15 makes plain.

Sub-Bibliography on 3:15

Aberbach, M., and **B. Grossfeld**. *Targum Onkelos to Genesis*, 37. **Gallus, T.** *Die "Frau" in Gen 3:15*. Klagenfurt: Carinthia, 1979. **Görg, M.** "Das Wort zur Schlange (Gen 3:14f.): Gedanken zum sogenannten Protoevangelium." *BN* 19 (1982) 121–140. **Hengstenberg, E. W.** *Christology of the Old Testament*, vol. 1. Tr. T. Meyer. Edinburgh: Clark, 1858. 4–20. **LaSor, W. S.** "Prophecy, Inspiration and *Sensus Plenior*." *TB* 29 (1978) 49–60. **Lipinski, E.** "Études sur des textes 'messianiques' de l'A.T." *Sem* 20 (1970) 41–57. **Martin, R. A.** "The Earliest Messianic Interpretation of Gen 3:15." *JBL* 84 (1965) 425–27. **McNamara, M.** *The New Testament and the Palestinian Targum to the Pentateuch.* AnBib 27. Rome: Pontifical Biblical Institute, 1966. 217–22. **Michl, J.** "Der Weibessame (Gen 3:15) in spätjüdischer und frühchristlicher Auffassung." *Bib* 33 (1952) 371–401, 476–505. **Rüger, H. P.** "On Some Versions of Gen 3:15, Ancient and Modern." *BT* 27 (1976) 105–10. **Szabo, A.** "Nunquam Retrorsum: zur Frage des Protoevangeliums: Gen 3:15." *Judaica* 35 (1979) 120–24. **Wifall, W.** "Gen 3:15—A Protoevangelium?" *CBQ* 36 (1974) 361–65. **Woudstra, M. H.** "Recent Translations of Gen 3:15." *CTJ* 6 (1971) 194–203.

15 Metrically this verse may be scanned as four two-beat lines and two three-beat lines.

> I shall put hostility
> between you and the woman,
> between your offspring
> and her offspring.

"Hostility" [איבה]: Both this context and other passages suggest that long-lasting enmity is meant (cf. Num 35:21–22; Ezek 25:15; 35:5). The human race, "her offspring," and the serpent race, "your offspring," will be forever at loggerheads. Those who had been in league against their creator will from now on be fighting against each other, a motif that reappears in the tower of Babel story (11:1–9). It is not simply a case of God versus the snake in perpetuity, but of mankind versus the snake as well (cf. Isa 11:8).

He will batter your head
and you will batter his heel.

The translation of this curse is extraordinarily problematic, because the root
שׁוּף "batter, crush, bruise" occurs only here and in two other difficult poetic
passages: Ps 139:11, Job 9:17. There is a similar root, שׁאף, which sometimes
means "crush," e.g., Amos 2:7, and sometimes "gasp for, long for," e.g.,
Jer 14:6. It is therefore often surmised that שׁוּף has both meanings as well.
There is no agreement among ancient versions or modern commentators,
however, as to which meaning is appropriate in which clause in Gen 3:15.
The majority of modern writers believe that the sense is the same in both
clauses, more preferring the interpretation "crush, batter" (e.g., Westermann,
Gispen, Weinfeld, Speiser, Driver, Skinner, Keil) to the alternative "strive
after" (Steck, Jacob; cf. LXX). A minority prefer to see a wordplay between
two different meanings, the woman's seed "crushing" the serpent, and the
serpent "craving" the man's heel (so Cassuto, Kidner, Procksch; Vg, Tg).
    Despite these long discussions, etymology makes little difference to the
understanding of the passage. Close attention to grammar and context is
more important. The imperfect verb is iterative. It implies repeated attacks
by both sides to injure the other. It declares lifelong mutual hostility between
mankind and the serpent race. Of more moment for interpretation is the
question whether one side will eventually prove victorious in the battle, or
whether the contest will be never-ending.
    On the face of it, the saying looks like a mere etiology. It is an explanation
of why men try to kill snakes, and why snakes try to bite men; Gen 2–3 is a
myth explaining the present human situation. It is also argued that the order
of clauses ending with "you shall batter his heel" does not favor eventual
human victory (so Skinner).
    On the other hand, it must be remembered that this is a curse on the
serpent, not on mankind, and something less than a draw would be expected.
Furthermore, the serpent is in a tactically weaker situation, being able only
to strike at man's heel, while man can crush its head. And what is more
decisive, this story is not just an etiology, a just-so story explaining why snakes
are so unpleasant; many elements in it are highly symbolic, and the dialogue
between snake and woman employs ambiguity and innuendo with great subtlety. If elsewhere in the narrative we have double-entendre and symbolic
language, it would be strange for it to disappear here, so that the serpent is
just a snake and not an anti-God symbol. Once admitted that the serpent
symbolizes sin, death, and the power of evil, it becomes much more likely
that the curse envisages a long struggle between good and evil, with mankind
eventually triumphing. Such an interpretation fits in well with 4:7 where
Cain is warned of sin lurking to catch him, but is promised victory if he
resists.
    Certainly the oldest Jewish interpretation found in the third century B.C.
Septuagint, the Palestinian targums (Ps.-J., Neof., Frg.), and possibly the Onqelos targum takes the serpent as symbolic of Satan and look for a victory over
him in the days of King Messiah. The NT also alludes to this passage, understanding it in a broadly messianic sense (Rom 16:20; Heb 2:14; Rev 12),

and it may be that the term "Son of Man" as a title for Jesus and the term "woman" for Mary (John 2:4; 19:26) also reflect this passage (Gallus; cf. Michl). Certainly, later Christian commentators, beginning with Justin (*ca.* A.D. 160) and Irenaeus (*ca.* 180), have often regarded 3:15 as the Protoevangelium, the first messianic prophecy in the OT. While a messianic interpretation may be justified in the light of subsequent revelation, a *sensus plenior*, it would perhaps be wrong to suggest that this was the narrator's own understanding. Probably he just looked for mankind eventually to defeat the serpent's seed, the powers of evil.

16 The sentence on the woman is traditionally scanned as a seven-beat line and a four-beat line. Alternatively it could be 4, 3, 2, 2.

> I shall greatly multiply your pains and your pregnancies;
> in pain you will bear children.

It should be noted that neither the man nor the woman are cursed: only the snake (v 14) and the soil (v 17) are cursed because of man. The sentences on the man and woman take the form of a disruption of their appointed roles. The woman was created to be man's helper and the mother of children (cf. 2:18, 23–24). The first part of her judgment is that maternity will be accompanied by suffering. "Your pains and your pregnancies" is probably hendiadys for "your pains of pregnancy." "To be a joyful mother of children" (Ps 113:9), preferably a large family, was a sure sign of God's blessing (cf. Pss 127, 128). Yet the pain of childbirth, unrelieved by modern medicine, was the most bitter known then (cf. Mic 4:9–10; Isa 13:8; 21:3). "In pain you will bear children." Neither the word used here for "pain," עֶצֶב, nor the earlier one, עִצְּבוֹן, is the usual one for the pangs of childbirth. Cassuto plausibly suggests this term has been deliberately chosen by way of a pun on עֵץ "tree," as if to say the *tree* brought *trauma*.

> Your urge will be to your husband,
> but he shall rule over you.

Here it is more difficult to grasp the author's precise intention. Evidently he does not regard female subordination to be a judgment on her sin. In that woman was made from man to be his helper and is twice named by man (2:23; 3:20) indicates his authority over her. It is therefore usually argued that "rule" here represents harsh exploitive subjugation, which so often characterizes woman's lot in all sorts of societies. "'To love and to cherish' becomes 'To desire and to dominate'" (Kidner, 71). Women often allow themselves to be exploited in this way because of their urge toward their husband: their sexual appetite may sometimes make them submit to quite unreasonable male demands. Once again woman's life is blighted at the most profound level.

Susan Foh (*WTJ* 37 [1974/75] 376–83) has, however, argued that the woman's urge is not a craving for her man whatever he demands but an urge for independence, indeed a desire to dominate her husband. Such an interpretation of "urge" is required in the very closely parallel passage in 4:7, where sin's urge is said to be for Cain, but he must master it. Here in 3:16 woman's desire for independence would be contrasted with an injunction to man to master her. There is a logical simplicity about Foh's interpretation that makes it attractive, but given the rarity of the term "urge" (תשוקה, apart from Gen 3:16 and 4:7 occurring only in Cant 7:11), certainty is impossible.

17–19 The sentence on the man is the longest and fullest, since he bore the greatest responsibility in following his wife's advice instead of heeding God's instructions personally given to him. The length of the curses has led some commentators to suggest that two versions have been combined here, but Westermann's view that one traditional curse formula, 17b–19b, has been expanded by prose additions in 17a and 18b and a proverb in 19c has fewer difficulties.

17 "To man" or "Adam." Many commentators believe this is the first instance of "Adam" being used as a personal name; cf. *Comment* on 1:26.

"Because you have obeyed your wife." Note that, as in v 14, the causal clause precedes the main clause, emphasizing the relative importance of the former (cf. n. 14.a.). Obeying his wife rather than God was man's fundamental mistake. שמע לקול, literally, "listen to the voice of," is an idiom meaning "obey"; cf. 16:2; Exod 18:24; 2 Kgs 10:6 (BDB, 1034a).

"Eaten." Five times in three verses is eating mentioned. Man's offense consisted of eating the forbidden fruit; therefore he is punished in what he eats. The toil that now lies behind the preparation of every meal is a reminder of the fall and is made the more painful by the memory of the ready supply of food within the garden (2:9).

"The land is cursed." אדמה, "land" one of the key words of the narrative (cf. 2:5–7, 19) is mentioned at the beginning and close of the curse "until you return to the land" (v 19), thereby forming an inclusion. Land blessed by God is well-watered and fertile (Deut 33:13–16; cf. Gen 2:8–14), so that when cursed it lacks such benefits (cf. v 18).

"In pain [עצבון] you will eat." Note the similar terminology in v 16. As woman is doomed to suffer in her fundamental role as wife and mother, man will be similarly afflicted in his basic role as farmer and food-producer (cf. 2:15).

"All the days of your life"; cf. v 14. These phrases link the sentence on the man to that pronounced on the snake and the woman. As the curse on the ground foreshadows the problems discussed in the next verse, so "all the days of your life" hints at their limited lifespan made explicit in v 19.

18 The phrase "It will bring up thorns and thistles" stands in contrast to 2:5, 9, where the same root צמח "spring up, sprout" is used. The same combination of "thorns and thistles" growing up in desolate places is found in Hos 10:8. "Plants of the plain"; cf. 2:5 and 1:11–12. Here it probably covers both wild and cultivated plants in contrast to the fruit-bearing trees of the garden supplied by the Lord God for their sustenance, already giving a hint that they will soon be leaving the garden.

19 "By the sweat of your brow." Work itself is not a punishment for sin. Man was placed in the garden to cultivate it (2:15). Rather it was the hardship and frustration that attended work that constitutes the curse. "As for man, his punishment consists in the hardship and skimpiness of his livelihood, which he must now seek for himself. The woman's punishment struck

at the deepest root of her being as wife and mother; the man's strikes at
the innermost nerve of his life: his work, his activity, and provision for sustenance" (von Rad, 93–94).

"Until you return to the land from which you were taken for you are
dust." Here much of the phraseology of man's creation is picked up. Man
was "shaped from the *dust* of the land" (2:7); now he must return to *dust*.
Woman was *taken* out of man (2:23) as man was *taken* from the ground (3:19).
Man's lifelong struggle for survival will eventually end in death. Most commentators have taken this curse as confirmation of the death-threat announced
in 2:17 on those who eat of the forbidden tree. However, some have disputed
this (notably Skinner and Westermann, and more guardedly, Gunkel and
Jacob). They argue that the parallels between this verse (3:19) and 2:7 suggest
that death is "part of the natural order of things—the inevitable 'return' of
man to the ground whence he was taken" (Skinner, 83). They point out
that the story does not say man would have lived forever if he had not eaten.
"Death is therefore not punishment for man's transgression; it is the limitation
of the toil of human work" (Westermann, 1:363; cf. ET 267).

While commentators must always seek to free themselves from their own
dogmatic prejudices in recovering the original sense of the text, it is doubtful
whether Skinner and Westermann are justified in this instance. Though there
are close parallels between 2:7 and 3:19, the omissions are significant, most
obviously the absence of any mention of the breath of life which had made
man a living creature. Furthermore, the curse has already mentioned a change
in man's feeding arrangements, suggesting that he would no longer enjoy
access to the tree of life. Finally, and most decisively, the sentence on man
is introduced in v 17 by an exact though incomplete quotation of the original
prohibition not to eat of the tree of knowledge (2:17).

The narrator, who according to Westermann added 3:17a to the older
curse formulae, must have expected the listener to complete the quotation of 2:17 and to be looking for a confirmation of the threat of death in
the curses. But he holds this back to v 19, when at last man is explicitly
told that he will return to the land: "for you are dust and to dust you
must return," a remark that is echoed in many biblical passages, e.g., Job
10:9; 34:15; Ps 103:14; Eccl 12:7, etc. In this way the original threat is
endorsed.

It is nevertheless striking that life and death are not mentioned in so
many words in Gen 3:17–19; the return to dust is presented as inevitable,
rather than as an immediate consequence in the death penalty which 2:17
led us to expect. Just as the remarks about toiling for food suggest that
exclusion from the garden is imminent, so does the ultimacy of death, for
obviously man could expect to live forever if he were free to eat of the tree
of life. It may be then that the narrator avoids life-and-death language in
this verse, because for him only life in the garden counts as life in the fullest
sense. Outside the garden, man is distant from God and brought near to
death. The warnings about returning to dust eventually hint that a drastic
change will shortly overtake the man.

20–21 Like the second scene (2:18–25), this, the penultimate scene, has
the man's naming of his wife and a mention of their clothing. These remarks

therefore serve to enhance the balance of the scenes and help to explain
the sequence of thought.

20 "Man named his wife Eve." "Eve" (חַוָּה, *ḥawwāh*) is very like the Aramaic
word (חִיוְיָא, *ḥiwyāʾ*) "serpent," so some early Jewish commentators and some
twentieth-century writers have suggested that this is what the man meant.
He was rebuking his wife for deceiving him by calling her "serpent." The
following remark, "because she was the mother of all living," is then seen as
a punning reinterpretation of the name by the narrator. However, though
it is likely that the comment comes from the narrator, for Adam would not
have used the past tense "she *was* the mother," the etymology associating
Eve with serpent is improbable (A. J. Williams, *ZAW* 89 [1977] 357–74),
More likely חוה is a by-form of חיה and means "life" (BDB, 295b); at least
this is how LXX translates "Eve," *Zoe*—"life," and it fits in with the explanation
offered in the text itself.

What prompted the man to call his wife "Life" especially at this juncture
in the story? It comes immediately after the curses announcing man's mortality
(v 19), the pains of childbirth (v 16), and the struggle of the woman's seed
with the snake (v 15). Any of these curses could furnish the cue for the
naming of the woman "Eve," but whether it represents an act of faith on
the man's part (so Keil, Delitzsch, von Rad, Steck) is more doubtful.

21 "Then the LORD God made for man and his wife tunics of skin." As
God's final kindness toward man in the garden (cf. 2:8, 15, 19, 22), his provision
of clothes is obviously of great significance (cf. Jacob). Clothing, besides its
obvious protective function, is one of the most pervasive of human symbols
through which a person's position and role in society is signaled.

"Tunics of skin." A tunic (כתנת), the basic outer garment worn next to
the skin, was a long shirt reaching the knees or ankles (for illustrations see
NBD, 324–25; *ANEP*, figs. 1–66). Whereas the human couple could only
produce inadequate loincloths (3:7), God provided them with a proper outfit.

"Of skin." This is the more natural understanding of the Hebrew construction (cf. "linen tunic," "linen turban," etc., Exod 28:39), and is followed by
LXX and most modern commentators. However, *Tgs. Onk.* and *Neof.*, Junker,
and Haag (*Mensch am Anfang*, 68) prefer the translation "for their skin," i.e.,
to cover their nakedness. Though this was doubtless the divine intention,
the usual translation is preferable.

"Clothed them" (hiph לבש). This form of the verb has two main uses:
either of kings' clothing honored subjects (e.g., Gen 41:42; 1 Sam 17:38),
or for the dressing of priests in their sacred vestments, usually put on by
Moses. Frequently he clothes them in their tunics (e.g., Exod 28:41; 29:8;
40:14; Lev 8:13). Here again the terminology of the garden of Eden runs
closely parallel to the vocabulary associated with worship in the tabernacle.
The law particularly insists that Israelite priests, unlike their Sumerian counterparts, must cover their private parts when approaching the altar (Exod 20:26;
28:42). Indeed, the ordinary Israelite is urged to exercise discretion in relieving
himself because God walks in the camp (Deut 23:13–15 [12–14]). It therefore
follows that in Eden, the garden of God, man and woman must be decently
clad, so God clothes them himself. Yet prior to their disobedience, they,
and apparently God, had been quite unconcerned about their nakedness

(2:25; cf. 3:11). In this context God's provision of clothes appears not so much an act of grace, as often asserted, but as a reminder of their sinfulness (cf. Calvin, 1:182). Just as man may not enjoy a direct vision of God, so God should not be approached by man unclothed.

(On the symbolism of clothing see E. Haulotte, *Symbolique du vêtement selon la Bible* [Paris: Aubier, 1966].)

22–24 This, the seventh scene, matches the first (2:5–17) in that God is the sole actor and man is only passive. Some terms are peculiar to both scenes 1 and 7: "in the east," "garden of Eden," and "tree of life." The action in both crosses the boundary between the land and the garden, whereas in the intervening scenes all the action has taken place within the garden. This recall of the opening scene gives a roundness and completeness to the narrative, but it also serves to point up more sharply and poignantly just what man has lost. In scene 1 the garden was planted for man (2:8); he was allowed to eat of the tree of life (2:9, 16–17); and his job was to till and guard it (2:15). The writer expatiates on the rich lushness of the garden of Eden in leisurely detail, so as to emphasize that it was man's perfect home, where he enjoyed peace with God. In comparison, in scene 7 man's expulsion from the garden is described almost abruptly, as we learn that he will no longer have access to the tree of life; instead of man guarding the garden, armed cherubim will be stationed there to keep him out. Finally, he who was appointed to till the garden will till the land instead, thereby foreshadowing the fulfillment of the curse "until you return to the land from which you were taken, for you are dust and to dust you must return" (3:19).

22 "Since man has become like one of us, knowing good and evil." Here the LORD acknowledges that the snake's promise (3:5) has been in one sense partially fulfilled. They may not have become "like God" himself, but they have become like "one of us," that is, like the heavenly beings, including God and the angels (cf. *Comment* on 1:26), insofar as man now knows good and evil. (On the knowledge of good and evil see *Comment* on 2:9.) In no other regard has man become like God or the angels. In particular, he does not possess immortality. To forestall any attempt to gain it, God says, "Now lest he reach out and take from the tree of life . . . ." The sentence ends in mid-air, leaving the listener to supply the rest of God's thoughts, e.g., "Let me expel him from the garden." This device of aposiopesis is very unusual in reporting divine speech in Hebrew. Usually the narrators like to report the exact and complete fulfillment of God's words. Here the omission of the conclusion conveys the speed of God's action. He had hardly finished speaking before they were sent out of the garden.

"Take from the tree of life" seems to imply that while he was in the garden man could have eaten of the tree, but he had not.

23 "Sent him out." There is probably deliberate word play with "reach" in v 22. The same root (חלש) is used. God forestalls man's next step towards self-divinization by his own preemptive first strike (cf. 11:7–9).

24 "He drove out." This is a stronger term than "send out," used in v 22. It is often used in the Pentateuch of the expulsion of the inhabitants of Canaan (e.g., Exod 23:28–31). It is coupled with "send out" in Exod 6:1; 11:1, and in each case it adds emphasis. "God did not just *send him forth*, an act that would not have precluded all possibility of his returning, but *He drove him out*—completely" (Cassuto, 1:173). There is thus no need to postulate the existence of two sources behind vv 23 and 24.

"Stationed," literally, "caused to camp," שׁכן (qal), is particularly associated with God's camping in the tabernacle among his people (e.g., Exod 25:8). The piel nearly always has this sense (e.g., Deut 12:11; Jer 7:3), whereas the hiphil used here sometimes does (e.g., Josh 18:1), although it has other uses too. The word's cultic overtones are further reinforced by the presence of the cherubim, human-headed winged lions, the traditional guardians of holy places in the Near East. The Hebrew word כרבים is probably borrowed from the Akkadian *kurību*. In Israel pictures of cherubim adorned the walls of the tabernacle and temple (Exod 26:31; 1 Kgs 6:29), a pair of solid cherubim formed the throne of God on the ark (Exod 25:18–22), and a very large pair guarded the inner sanctuary of the temple (1 Kgs 6:23–28).

"The flame of a revolving sword." This phrase is without exact parallel in the OT, but fire is a regular symbol of the presence of God, especially in judgment (e.g., Exod 19:18; Ps 104:4). "Revolving," מתהפכת, is the hithpael participle of הפך "to turn," hence "to turn itself." It is used of the cake which "rolled" into the camp of Midian in Judg 7:13. Gese (*FS K. Elliger*, 80–81) suggests the image is that of forked lightning, zigzagging to and fro. At any rate, the idea is clear: a revolving or zigzagging sword, especially one wielded by angels, is one that is sure to hit and bring death (cf. Num 22:23, 31, 33). "To guard the way to the tree of life": as already noted (cf. *Comment* on 2:9), the golden candlestick in the tabernacle represented both the tree of life and the presence of God.

"East of the garden." Why should the cherubim be stationed here? Evidently, as Cassuto (1:174) notes, because "there, apparently, was the entrance" to the garden. Again one is reminded of the orientation of the tabernacle and temple, which were entered from the east.

Thus in this last verse of the narrative there is a remarkable concentration of powerful symbols that can be interpreted in the light of later sanctuary design. Other features of this garden—rivers, gold, precious stones—that are similarly evocative were mentioned in the first scene. These features all combine to suggest that the garden of Eden was a type of archetypal sanctuary, where God was uniquely present in all his life-giving power. It was this that man forfeited when he ate the fruit.

Explanation

In this, the first story in the Bible, Hebrew narrative art is seen at its highest. The exquisite charm with which the tale unfolds serves only to deepen the tragedy that is related, while the apparent naïveté of the style disguises a richness of theological reflection that philosophers and theologians have not exhausted. And perhaps this is the greatest tribute that can be paid to the writer: he communicates to all—young and old, the educated and the unsophisticated. He describes God's relations with men, not in high-flown abstract theological jargon that needs special linguistic aptitudes and a long training to acquire, but in a simple vocabulary drawn from peasant life. Yet the ideas he puts so clearly in story form have theological ramifications that have stretched the minds of the greatest thinkers down the ages.

The story is headed by a well-structured title in v 4, "This is the history of . . . ," which covers all the material in chaps. 2–4. This title includes the divine epithet "the LORD God," which is characteristic of chaps. 2–3, but of nowhere else in Genesis. Usually one or the other name is used, but here the two are combined, suggesting no doubt that this story reveals both God's character as sovereign creator of the universe (God) and his intimate covenant-like relationship with mankind (the LORD).

Both traits are prominent in the first scene (2:5–17) which shows the LORD God creating man and a perfect environment for him. It discloses God's sovereignty over man his creature and his loving concern for his well-being. The setting of the action appears to be southern Mesopotamia. In this region the "field" is an arid desert if it does not rain, and the agricultural "land" is equally barren, despite the ample supplies of fresh water, without man to irrigate it.

The LORD God therefore molded man out of the dust of the land. But man's nature is more than modeled clay: he owes his life to the inbreathing of breath from God. Whereas the exact nature of this inbreathing has been a subject of detailed discussion, it is not the present concern of Genesis. The story hurries on to describe the marvelous garden or park in the land of delight (Eden) which the creator prepared for man to dwell in, full of trees, water, and precious stones. These details suggest that not only man but God dwelt there as well, a point confirmed later in the story (3:8), for these are symbols of God's life-giving presence.

Two trees are singled out for special mention—the tree of life, which confers immortality, and the tree of the knowledge of good and evil, which gives access to wisdom. Contrary to expectation, man is allowed to eat of the tree of life, but not of the tree of wisdom, for that leads to human autonomy and an independence of the creator incompatible with the trustful relationship between man and his maker which the story presupposes. Man is placed in the garden to till it and guard it, just as in later days the Levites were instructed to guard the tabernacle. Man's labor in the garden is indeed a kind of divine service, for it is done for God and in his presence. Only one restriction is placed on man's freedom: he is forbidden to eat of the tree of knowledge. If he does, he will immediately die.

Continuing the theme of God's fatherly concern for man, the second scene (2:18–25) opens with his observation that "it is not good for man to be alone" and the decision to make a helper who matches him. The phraseology suggests the partner is to complement man, not to be identical with him. To accentuate man's need for human companionship, the animals are created and brought near for man to name. Yet though they are so close to man in many ways, like man, shaped from the land and called "living creatures," they fail to meet his real need.

Only woman fits the bill, because she is made of man's rib. She is thus declared in her essential nature to be the equal of man, even though created as his helper and complement. Furthermore, this account of woman's origin explains the experience of every couple that in marriage they become related to each other as though they were blood relatives: "they become one flesh." Indeed, the marriage bond is even stronger than that between parent and child, for "a man forsakes his father and mother and sticks to his wife," an astounding declaration in a world where filial duty was the most sacred obligation next to loyalty to God.

Given the presuppositions of ancient Israel, the next comment is almost as surprising: they "were nude, but they were not ashamed." The couple's unself-consciousness about their lack of clothing stands in stark contrast to their later ludicrous efforts to hide themselves in the trees and to clothe themselves with fig leaves. It is also quite out of keeping with the usual attitude to nakedness attested in the Old Testament: that, in general, nakedness is shameful and therefore to be avoided, particularly by those approaching God in worship or other sacred duties. Yet here in the garden which is full of symbols of the divine presence, where God himself regularly comes to meet with them, they were nude but unashamed. Since the relationships between man and wife and between them and their creator are unclouded by sin, there is no need for them to cover up. The fullness of their fellowship is here most vividly expressed.

In the third scene, the temptation scene (3:1–5), the mood changes. Harmony gives way to discord, mutual trust to suspicion. The entrance of the snake, an archetypal unclean creature though created by God, is disturbing in itself. The remark about his shrewdness adds to the sense of unease. Yet on the surface the conversation between the snake and the woman is smooth and urbane. The snake's opening question appears to be innocent curiosity. He never tells the woman to disobey God and eat from the tree. He cannot even be accused of lying: in the most literal sense all his words prove true, although at a more profound level they are totally misleading.

Yet in the very opening question, "Has God really said . . . you must not eat from any of the trees?", there are several clues that should alert listeners less naïve than Eve to the serpent's sinister intentions. First, the snake speaks boldly of "God" (the distant creator) instead of "the LORD God" (creator and covenant partner) used elsewhere in these chapters. Second, though God allowed men to eat freely of all the trees save one, the snake asks whether God had forbidden men to eat from every tree. How did he know about the prohibition at all, and then get it so wrong? The very way the question is put suggests malevolent intent. But Eve appears quite oblivious of these dangerous nuances and simply corrects the snake's mistakes: "God allows us to eat of all the trees except one which we cannot even touch lest we die." But in her words we have the first hints of her distancing herself from her creator. While openly acknowledging his bounty in allowing them to eat most of the trees, she adopts the snake's less friendly title of "God" instead of "the LORD God," and adds that he is perhaps a little harsh imposing the death penalty for merely touching a tree.

To this the serpent confidently replies, "You will not certainly die. But God knows. . . ." Though this looks like a brazen, bare-faced lie on first sight, for it is in flat contradiction with the divine warning (2:17) with which the author and reader of Genesis automatically identify, it is in fact a much more subtle remark. For evidently the man and woman do not die immediately;

their eyes are opened (3:7), and God himself comments that they have "become like one of us" (3:22). Perhaps the serpent was right after all: the creator was simply trying to retain their allegiance by exploiting their naïveté. The very way the story is told forces the reader to ask again what God meant by "dying" and what the serpent meant, and what the significance was of their "eyes being opened" and "becoming like God." The apparent duplicity of the creator in this story involves the listener in a way that a less awkward narrative would not. If it was as improbable to the narrator as to the listener that God was wrong and the snake was right, what did God mean? We are therefore compelled to read the rest of the story more carefully to find out.

The narrative does not immediately offer a solution. Instead it moves briskly to describe the act of disobedience. Substituting her own values of what is good for the norms revealed by the Almighty, the woman proceeds to follow the snake's suggestion instead of the explicit divine prohibition. Her husband too falls in with her instead of heeding God. As the snake promised, their eyes were opened, but all they saw was their nakedness and their unfitness to meet their creator.

Confronted and interrogated by God, they are made to confess their disobedience, though they try to minimize their culpability by suggesting that someone else is more to blame (3:9–13).

Then follows the verdict and sentence of the divine judge. In turn each is condemned to some permanent disadvantage in life. So characteristic of human existence are these features that modern man tends to regard them as simply inevitable: the posture of snakes, the pain of childbirth, and the labor to produce enough food. But against the background of Gen 1, which ended by stating that everything that God had made was very good, these phenomena pose problems and demand explanation.

The snake, who had earlier been described as more shrewd than the other animals, is now decreed to be more cursed than any. Sentenced to grovel in the dust forever, he moves with an uncouth gait that marks his humiliation and his alienation from the rest of creation. In particular, snakes will fight a running battle with mankind as each tries to destroy the other. In that in vv 14–15 the serpent and not man is cursed, the implication is that man may expect ultimate victory in the struggle.

Woman too is sentenced to pain and frustration at the center of her existence, in her distinctive role as wife and mother. In traditional societies, a woman longed to be the mother of a large family, but the more children she wanted, the more pregnancies and painful labors she had to undergo. Though woman was created to be man's companion, she is told that her desire for independence will conflict with his demand for submission. Under the curse, those who were created to be one flesh will find themselves tearing each other apart.

Finally, man, who had enjoyed a carefree existence in a garden designed for his benefit, is warned that he too will have to toil to sustain himself and ultimately will return to the dust from which he was made. Physical death is therefore man's eventual destiny, however hard he tries to avoid the fact. The divine curse thus explains man's mortality, just as much as it accounts for the pains of childbirth and the snake's movements.

Apparently then, man did not die on the day he ate of the tree. But in the closing verses of the chapter, sanctuary symbolism and language reappear (3:21–24). God clothes the human couple and then expels them through the east-facing entrance to the garden where cherubim are stationed to guard the tree of life. These features anticipate the design of the tabernacle and the regulations associated with it. Like the garden of Eden, the tabernacle was a place where God walked with his people. To be expelled from the camp of Israel or to be rejected by God was to experience a living death; in both situations gestures of mourning were appropriate (Lev 13:45–46; Num 5:2–4; 1 Sam 15:35). The psalmists, too, held that in the house of God men could "drink from the river of the delights [עֵדֶן], for with thee is the fountain of life" (Ps 36:9–10 [8–9]). Only in the presence of God did man enjoy fullness of life. To choose anything else is to choose death (Prov 8:36). The expulsion from the garden of delight where God himself lived would therefore have been regarded by the godly men of ancient Israel as yet more catastrophic than physical death. The latter was the ultimate sign and seal of the spiritual death the human couple experienced on the day they ate from the forbidden tree.

Gen 2–3, then, offers a paradigm of sin, a model of what happens whenever man disobeys God. It is paradigmatic in that it explains through a story what constitutes sin and what sin's consequences are. The essence of man's first sin was his disobedience to the only divine command he had received: not to eat of the tree of knowledge. The consequences of his actions are both physical—toil, pain, and death—and spiritual—alienation from God. The spiritual consequences follow the act of disobedience immediately, but the physical penalties—pain, suffering and death—may take longer to become evident.

As a paradigm of sin this model would be equally at home in any of the great theological traditions of the Old Testament. The covenant theology expressed most clearly in Deuteronomy insists that disobedience to God's commandments brings the curse and ultimately death (e.g., Deut 30:15–19). The prophets similarly harp on this theme (e.g., Isa 24:4–6; Jer 21:8). It is just as central in the wisdom tradition too: "There is a way which seems right to a man, but its end is the way to death" (Prov 14:12; 16:25). It is therefore somewhat surprising that there is no certain use of this garden of Eden story elsewhere in the OT, for the interpretation of Hos 6:7 is problematic. However, in Ezek 28:12–20 there appears to be a poetic variant on the story relating how the king of Tyre once dwelt in Eden and was expelled for his sin. Whether this is an independent account of the fall or a free poetic application to the Tyrian king is uncertain, but it certainly underlines the compatibility of its theology with prophetic principle.

In later Jewish and, particularly, Christian theology the story becomes very important. According to Ecclus 25:24, "Woman is the origin of sin, and it is through her that we all die"; Rom 5:12, "Sin came into the world through one man and death through sin"; and 4 Ezra 7:118, "O Adam, what have you done? Your sin was not your fall alone; it was ours also, the fall of your descendants." The sin of the first man was more than a paradigm of every sinner's experience; it was indeed the first sin, which has had dire consequences for the whole human race. Subsequent sinners have not had the same advantages as Adam in Eden. Building on Paul's exposition of Gen 3, the Christian doctrines of original sin and guilt have been developed.

Other commentators, especially Jews, prefer to see Gen 3 as simply paradigmatic: Adam's transgression did not have the dire consequences alleged by St. Paul. Rather, as the *Apocalypse of Baruch* (early 2nd century A.D.) 54:19 puts it: "Adam is therefore not the cause, save only of his own soul, but each of us has been the Adam of his own soul."

To explore the ramifications of these very different theologies is beyond the scope of an exegetical commentary. But one may inquire which view is closer to the Genesis writer's own understanding. Does he offer any clues as to whether he regards the story he relates as merely paradigmatic, or in some sense as a real event in primeval history? The symbolic dimensions of the story linking the garden with the later sanctuaries support a paradigmatic reading. Water, gold, jewels, cherubim and so on link the garden of Eden with the tabernacle and temples described later. The curses pronounced on the guilty for disobeying the divine instructions anticipate those pronounced on those who disregard the law. These elements give the story a universalistic flavor, or at least a pan-Israelite setting. "Adam" is every man in Israel.

Yet other features of the narrative point in a more historical direction. The heading of the story, "This is the history of," links Gen 2–4 with the subsequent narratives of Noah, Abraham, Jacob, and the other great figures from Israel's past. The ensuing story of Cain and Abel and especially the genealogy of chap. 5, linking Adam with Noah, shows that the author understood the earliest stories to be about real people. Within the story itself there are features suggesting that the actions described have consequences stretching far beyond the lifetime of the participants. The curse on the snake that makes him crawl on the ground and makes him man's inveterate enemy is not something that every man rediscovers when he disobeys his creator. It is rather part of the present situation which everyone takes for granted. Similarly, pain, toil, and death are surely viewed by the author as part of his human inheritance and not to be ascribed to his personal sin: they are blamed on the first couple's disobedience. Most obviously, the expulsion from the garden indicates an irreversible change in man's situation. Cain and Abel begin their lives outside Eden, not inside. Cain's own sin drives him farther from Eden, but he never enjoys his parents' initial privilege. Finally, when set against the affirmation of Gen 1:31 that everything God made was very good, it seems likely that chaps. 2–3 are explaining why the world fails to exhibit that perfection today.

For these reasons I prefer to view Gen 2–3 as both paradigmatic and protohistorical. It is paradigmatic in that it offers a clear and simple analysis of the nature of sin and its consequences, albeit in rich and symbolic language. Disobedience to the law of God brings physical pain and suffering and alienation from him. This is indeed the experience of every man. In this sense the story is paradigmatic. But in all societies, and especially the tightly knit family society of ancient Israel, the behavior of parents has great impact on their children for good or ill. It therefore follows that the disobedience of the first couple from whom Genesis traces the descent of the whole human race must have had grave consequences for all mankind. In this sense, then, the story offers a protohistorical account of man's origins and his sin.

The First Human Family (4:1–26)

Bibliography

(See also the Main Bibliography and Gen 1–11 Bibliography)

Bassler, J. M. "Cain and Abel in the Palestinian Targums: A Brief Note on an Old Controversy." *JSJ* 17 (1986) 56–64. **Beltz, W.** "Religionsgeschichtliche Anmerkungen zu Gen 4." *ZAW* 86 (1974) 83–86. **Ben Yashar, M.** "Sin Lies for the Firstborn." (Heb.) *BMik* 7 (1963) 116–19. ———. "Zu Gen 4:7." *ZAW* 94 (1982) 635–37. **Borger, R.** "Gen 4:1." *VT* 9 (1959) 85–86. **Castellino, G. R.** "Gen 4:7." *VT* 10 (1960) 442–45. **Dietrich, W.** "'Wo ist dein Bruder?' Zu Tradition und Intention von Gen 4." *Beiträge zur Alttestamentlichen Theologie: FS für W. Zimmerli*, ed. H. Donner, R. Hanhart, and R. Smend. Göttingen: Vandenhoeck, 1977. 94–111. **Enslin, M. S.** "Cain and Prometheus." *JBL* 86 (1966) 88–90. **Fraade, S. D.** *Enosh and His Generation.* SBLMS 30. Chico: Scholars Press, 1984. **Gabriel, J.** "Die Kainitengenealogie: Gen 4:17–24." *Bib* 40 (1959) 409–27. **Gevaryahu, H. M. Y.** "The Punishment of Cain and the City Which He Built." (Heb.) *BMik* 13 (1967) 27–36. **Golka, F. W.** "Keine Gnade für Kain: Gen 4:1–16." *Werden und Wirken des Alten Testaments: FS für C. Westermann*, ed. R. Albertz. Göttingen: Vandenhoeck, 1979. 58–73. **Gruber, M. I.** "The Tragedy of Cain and Abel: A Case of Depression." *JQR* 69 (1978) 89–97. **Hauser, A. J.** "Linguistic and Thematic Links between Gen 4:1–16 and Gen 2–3." *JETS* 23 (1980) 297–305. **Heyde, H.** *Kain, der erste Jahwe-Verehrer.* Arbeiten zur Theologie 23. Stuttgart: Calwer Verlag, 1965. **Klemm, P.** "Kain und die Kainiten." *ZTK* 78 (1981) 391–408. **Krinetzki, G.** "Prahlerei und Sieg im alten Israel (Gen 4:23f etc.)." *BZ* 20 (1976) 45–58. **Levin, S.** "The More Savory Offering: A Key to the Problem of Gen 4:3–5." *JBL* 98 (1979) 85. **Levine, E.** "The Syriac Version of Gen 4:1–16." *VT* 26 (1976) 70–78. **Loewenclau, I. von.** "Gen 4:6–7—eine jahwistische Erweiterung." *Congress Volume, 1977.* VTSup 29. Leiden: Brill, 1978. 177–88. **Mellinkoff, R.** *The Mark of Cain.* Berkeley: University of California Press, 1981. **Miller, J. M.** "The Descendants of Cain: Notes on Gen 4." *ZAW* 86 (1974) 164–74. **Miller, P. D.** "Eridu, Dunnu and Babel: A Study in Comparative Mythology." *HAR* 9 (1985) 227–51. **Mutius, H. G. von.** "Gen 4:26, Philo von Byblos und die jüdische Haggada." *BN* 13 (1980) 46–48. **Ramoroson, L.** "A propos de Gen 4:7." *Bib* 49 (1968) 233–37. **Riemann, P. A.** "Am I My Brother's Keeper?" *Int* 24 (1970) 482–91. **Rüterswörden, U.** "Kanaanäisch-städtische Mythologie im Werk des Jahwisten: Eine Notiz zu Gen 4." *BN* 1 (1976) 19–23. **Sandmel, S.** "Gen 4:26b." *HUCA* 32 (1961) 19–29. **Schunck, K. D.** "Henoch und die erste Stadt: eine textkritische Ueberlegung zu Gen 4:17." *Hen* 1 (1979) 161–65. **Sioni, Y.** "Un Verset difficile à traduire." *AMIF* 21 (1972) 990–1004. **Waltke, B. K.** "Cain and His Offering." *WTJ* 48 (1986) 363–72. **Willi, T.** "Der Ort von Gen 4:1–6 innerhalb der althebräischen Geschichtsschreibung." In *Essays on the Bible and the Ancient World III: I. L. Seeligman Volume*, ed. A. Rofé and Y. Zakovitch. Jerusalem: Rubinstein's Publishing House, 1983. 99–113. **Wöller, U.** "Zu Gen 4:7." *ZAW* 91 (1979) 436. ———. "Zu Gen 4:7." *ZAW* 96 (1984) 271–72. **Vermes, G.** "The Targumic Versions of Gen 4:3–16." *Post-Biblical Jewish Studies.* SJLA 8. Leiden: Brill, 1975. 92–126.

Translation

[1] *Now* [a] *man knew Eve his wife.* [a] *She conceived,* [b] *gave birth* [c] *to Cain and said: "I have gained a man with* [d] *the* LORD'S *help."* [2] *She again* [a] *gave birth* [b] *to his brother* [c] *Abel.*

^d*Abel became a shepherd of the flock but Cain became a tiller of the land.*^d
³*After a year*^a *Cain brought*^{ab} *some produce of the land as an offering to the* LORD. ⁴*Abel*^a *also*^b *brought*^a *some firstlings of his flock and*^c *their*^d *fat portions.*
^e*The* LORD *paid attention*^f *to Abel and his offering.*^e ⁵*But* ^a*to Cain and his offering he paid no attention.*^a *So Cain was very angry*^b *and his face fell.*^c

⁶*Then the* LORD *said to Cain: "Why are*^a *you*^b *angry and why has*^a *your face fallen?* ⁷*Is there not forgiveness*^a *if you do well?*^b *And*^c *if you do not do well,*^b *sin is crouching*^d *at the door. Its*^e *urge is for you, but you must*^f *rule over it."*^e

⁸*Cain said to his brother.*^a *When they were*^b *in the field, Cain rose*^c *up against Abel his brother and killed him.*

⁹*Then the* LORD *said to Cain, "Where*^a *is Abel your brother?" And he said, "I do not know.*^b *Am*^c *I my brother's keeper?"* ¹⁰*He said, "What have you done? Listen, your brother's blood*^a *is crying*^a *to me from the land.* ¹¹*And now you are* ^a*cursed from*^a *the land which has opened its mouth to receive your brother's blood from your hand.* ¹²*When you till the land, it will no longer*^a *give*^b *you its strength. You shall be a* ^c*wandering vagrant*^c *in the earth."* ¹³*Cain said to the* LORD, *"My punishment is* ^a*too great to bear.*^a ¹⁴*Since*^a *you have today driven*^b *me from the surface of the land and I must*^c *hide from your face and become a* ^d*wandering vagrant*^d *in the earth,* ^e*anyone who finds me*^e *will kill me."*

¹⁵*The* LORD *said to him: "This being so,*^a *whoever*^b *kills Cain shall be punished*^c *sevenfold."*^d *So the* LORD *placed*^e *a sign for Cain so that* ^f*whoever found him*^f *would not attack*^g *him.* ¹⁶*Then Cain left the* LORD's *presence and dwelt in the land of wandering* ^a*east of Eden.*^a

¹⁷*Then Cain knew his wife. She conceived*^a *and gave birth*^b *to Enoch. He*^c *was building*^c *a city and Enoch*^d *called the city after his son's name.* ¹⁸*To Enoch was born*^a *Irad.* ^b*Irad fathered Mehuya'el.*^{cb} ^b*Mehiya'el*^c *fathered Methushael.*^b ^b*Methushael fathered Lamek.*^{bd} ¹⁹*Lamek took*^a *two wives:* ^b*Adah was the name of the first, Zillah the name of the second.*^b ²⁰*Adah gave birth*^a *to Yabal:* ^b*he became father of those who dwell*^c *in tents with herds.*^{db} ²¹*His brother's name was Yubal:* ^a*he became father of all who play the lyre and pipe.*^a

²²*Zillah*^a *also gave birth to Tubal-Cain,*^a ^b*father of all who sharpen copper and iron.*^b *Tubal-Cain's sister was Naamah.* ²³*Lamek said to his wives:*

"Adah and Zillah, hear^a *my voice*
Wives of Lamek, attend^b *to my words.*
Truly^c *I have killed a man for*^d *bruising me,*
        a youth for^d *hitting me.*
²⁴*Truly*^a *Cain will be avenged*^b *sevenfold,*^c
but Lamek seventy-sevenfold."^d

²⁵*Then Adam knew his wife again. She gave birth*^a *to a son and she called*^b *his name Seth "because*^c *God has set me other offspring instead of Abel, because Cain killed him."* ²⁶*Also*^a *to Seth a son was born.*^b *He called his name Enosh. At that time*^c *people began*^d *to call on*^e *the name of the* LORD.

Notes

1.a-a. Episode-initial circumstantial clause; cf. 3:1 (*SBH*, 79).
1.b. Waw consec + 3 fem sg impf (apoc) הרה.
1.c. Waw consec + 3 fem sg impf ילד.

1.d. Versional variants (G διὰ; Vg *per*; *Tg. Onq.* קֹדֶם מִן) reflect the difficulty of MT אֵת, not different Hebrew text. See *Comment* for further discussion.

2.a. Waw consec + 3 fem sg impf hiph יֹסֶף. On this usage, cf. Lambdin, 238–39.

2.b. לְ + inf constr יָלֵד.

2.c. Repetition of object marker אֵת before noun in apposition is more common when noun of nearer definition precedes a proper name (GKC, 131h).

2.d-d. First pair of a string of chiastic clauses in 4:2–5. Note Hebrew word order "became (A) Abel (B) . . . Cain (B′) became (A1′)." Chiasmus (ABB′A′) is used to set events alongside each other as equal and contemporary (*SBH*, 122).

3.a-a. Chiastic with v 4 "brought Cain . . . Abel brought" cf. n. 2.d.

3.b. Waw consec + 3 masc sg impf hiph בוֹא.

4.a-a. Chiasmus with v 3 "brought Cain."

4.b. Literally "he also": גַם emphasizes the similarity between Cain and Abel's acts. Both brought gifts (*SBH*, 158).

4.c. "And" may here have explanatory force: "i.e., their fat portions" (GKC, 154aN).

4.d. Pl suffix הֶן- written defectively; cf. 1:21. Three Cairo Geniza fragments, SamPent have more usual plene form יהֶן-.

4.e-e. Chiasmus with v 5: "to Cain . . . no attention."

4.f. Waw consec + 3 masc sg impf (apoc) שָׁעָה; cf. v 5.

5.a-a. Chiasmus with v 4 "paid attention to Abel" (*SBH*, 129, 182).

5.b. Waw consec + 3 masc sg impf (apoc) חָרָה. Impersonal construction "it was angry to Cain" (BDB, 354a; GKC, 144b).

5.c. Waw consec + 3 masc pl impf נָפַל.

6.a. Perfects describing past events with continuing effects (Joüon, 112e).

6.b. לָךְ "to you (masc sg)" in pause.

7. SamPent supports MT. Versional differences, e.g., G "Is it not so that if you offer correctly, but do not cut it up correctly, you have sinned?" point to the difficulties in the Heb., but do not offer a superior text. See *Comment* for further discussion.

7.a. Inf constr נְשֹׂא "lift up, forgive."

7.b. 2 masc sg impf hiph יטב.

7.c. *SBH*, 114, suggests that "and" here carries over the sense of the opening interrogative הֲלֹא and translates "and does not sin crouch at the door, if you do not do well?"

7.d. רֹבֵץ: apparently masc sg ptcp "crouching," but grammatically it should agree with חַטָּאת fem "sin." Possibly רֵבֶץ "crouching" derives from Akk. *rābiṣu* "demon," or is a masc noun "croucher."

7.e. ו "It(s)" is masc suffix and must refer to רבץ masc "crouching," not fem "sin."

7.f. "Must rule," lit., "will rule." Impf used with impv meaning (Joüon, 113m).

8.a. SamPent adds נֵלְכָה הַשָּׂדֶה "let us go into the field" and this is supported by the ancient versions except *Tg. Onq.* and S, which says "let us go down into the valley." The clause may have been omitted in MT because of homoeoteleuton with "in the field." But the difficulty of MT may have prompted the expansion found in the other texts.

8.b. Inf constr הִיה + בְּ + 3 masc pl suffix.

8.c. Waw consec + 3 masc sg impf קוּם.

9.a. אֵי; SamPent has commoner form אַיֵּה.

9.b. Pf with present meaning (GKC, 106g).

9.c. הֲ introduces open questions, or, as here, questions expecting the answer "no" (GKC, 150d).

10.a. SamPent has singulars דַּם צֹעֵק for MT plurals, דְּמֵי צֹעֲקִים, thereby ensuring agreement between "voice" and "crying" (cf. Waltke, *New Perspectives*, 218). In MT the pl ptcp agrees with "blood"; דָּמִים is "plural of collective genitive" (Gispen, 1:176). GKC, 146b, and von Rad translate קוֹל "voice" as "Hark." דָּמִים pl used for spilt blood (BDB, 196–97; Joüon, 136b).

11.a-a. Or "more cursed than"; cf. 3:14 and see *Comment* below.

12.a. תֹסֶף: usually taken to be 3 fem sg juss hiph יסף "to add, do again." More probably 3 fem sg impf qal יֹסֵף (Joüon, 75f.); cf. Num 22:19; Joel 2:2. On construction, see Lambdin, 238–39.

12.b. תֵּת inf constr נתן.

12.c-c. Qal ptcp of נוּע "move, wave"; נוּד "wander."

13.a-a. מִן "from" + inf constr נְשֹׂא "to lift up." On construction מִן = "too" (GKC, 133c).

14.a. For הן "since," BDB, 243, cf. usage of הנה (Lambdin, 169–71).

14.b. 2 masc sg pf piel גרש. Perfect for a present instantaneous act felt to be already past (Joüon, 112f).

14.c. 1 sg impf niph סתר. Impf used with impv sense; cf. n. 7.f. and Joüon, 113m.

14.d-d. Cf. n. 12.c-c.

14.e-e. Qal ptcp מצא + 1 sg suffix, lit., "my finder."

15.a. BDB, 487a; cf. F. J. Goldbaum, *JNES* 23 (1964) 132–35. G S Vg evidently read לא כן "not so," an emendation widely adopted.

15.b. For this translation of כל + ptcp, cf. Joüon, 139h; Wenham, *TB* 22 (1971) 95–102.

15.c. 3 masc sg impf נקם "to avenge" (usually supposed to be hophal, but more likely qal passive; cf. Joüon, 58).

15.d. שבעתים looks like a dual form (i.e., two sevens). It is more probably seven (fem) שבעת + adverbial ending *ām)ayim*. Means "seven times" (Joüon, 100o; cf. GKC, 134r).

15.e. Waw consec + 3 masc sg impf שים.

15.f-f. Cf. n. 14.e-e.

15.g. Inf constr hiph נכה.

16.a-a. Acc of place (Joüon, 126h).

17.a,b. Cf. 4:1.

17.c-c. היה + ptcp for continuing action in past time (Joüon 121f); cf. 37:2; 39:22. The pointing בנה, not construct בנה, suggests our translation rather than "he became a city-builder"; cf. 4:2.

17.d. It is unusual for the subject "Enoch" to be so distant from the verb. It may be a misplaced gloss on "his son's name." See *Comment.*

18.a. Waw consec + 3 masc sg impf niph ילד used impersonally, allowing a dir obj "Irad" marked by preceding את (GKC, 121a,b; Joüon, 128b).

18.b-b. Three disjunctive clauses, pseudo-circumstantial, quite anomalous syntactically. Each clause would be expected to begin with ויולד or וילד; cf. *SBH*, 87–88.

18.c. Note variant spellings in MT: מחייאל/מחויאל. Most versions harmonize the two spellings. With C, S, *Tg. Neof., Ps.-J.*, Vg, "Mehuyael" seems more probable than SamPent G "Mehiyael," but it may be that MT's mixed reading is the oldest; so Cassuto, 1:232–33.

18.d. לְמֶךְ: pausal form of Lemek, hence usual English transliteration.

19.a. Cf. n. 2:15a.

19.b-b. On this construction see *SBH*, 32–33.

20.a. Cf. n. 4:1.c.

20.b-b. Clause in apposition to and explaining first half of verse, *SBH*, 59.

20.c. ישב "dwell in, inhabit" may be transitive; here followed by object "tent," GKC, 117 bb; cf. Ps 22:4.

20.d. Lit., "and herds." The syntax is problematic. "Herds" is either dependent on "father" or "dwelling." The former makes him the first owner of herds, the latter the first dweller with herds. With Dillmann and Skinner our translation adopts the second view. A similar construction, zeugma, is found in vv 21,22.

21.a-a. Explanatory apposition clause; cf. v 20b.

22.a-a. Circumstantial clause, chiastic with v 20a "gave birth Adah. . . . Zillah gave birth" suggests contemporaneity, reinforced by "also," גם־היא (*SBH*, 158).

22.b-b. Difficult. Lit., "a sharpener, all who work copper and iron." MT is supported by SamPent and other early versions except *Tg. Onq., Ps.-J.*, which emend or attest a different text. For לטש כל־חרש these targums seem to read אבי כל־לטש "father of all who sharpen" or אבי כל־חרש "father of all who work." This parallels vv 20, 21, "father of tent dwellers, father of lyre players," and אבי כל חרש is adopted by *BHS*, Westermann, Weinfeld, as original. With Gunkel, Freedman (*ZAW* 64 [1952] 192), and Wilson (*Genealogy and History*, 144), it would seem that the rarer term לטש was the original reading, later replaced by the more common חרש. Then the two readings were combined, omitting the vital אבי "father of" to form our present text. (On the phenomenon of double readings see S. Talmon, *Textus* 1 [1960] 144–84; *Scripta Hierosolymitana* 8 [1961] 335–83).

23.a. 2 fem pl impv שמע written defectively without final ה (GKC, 46f).

23.b. 2 fem pl impv hiph אזן.

23.c. On כי as emphatic exclamation cf. J. Muilenburg, *HUCA* 32 (1961) 135–60.

23.d. Lit., "for my wound/my strike." On this use of ל see BDB, 514b.

24.a. Cf. n. 23.c.
24.b. Cf. n. 15.c.
24.c. Cf. n. 15.d.
24.d. On the use of the cardinal 77 for the multiplicative "77 times" cf. GKC, 134r; Joüon, 142q.
25.a. Cf. n. 1.c.
25.b. SamPent "he called," assimilating to v 26a.
25.c. G Vg Tg add "saying/she said" before or after "because."
26.a. Comparing Seth to Adam, cf. vv 4, 22 (*SBH*, 157–58).
26.b. 3 masc sg pf qal passive, Joüon, 58a.
26.c. אז "then" usually followed by impf, here by pf to stress action really past (GKC, 107c).
26.d. 3 masc sg pf hoph חלל "to begin." Here a passive used impersonally, "people began" (GKC, 144k). SamPent (Vg) defective spelling החל "he began." G mistranslates "he hoped." The targums see here a reference to the introduction of idolatry, understanding חלל "to pollute."
26.e. בשם "on the name of." ב expresses not the instrument but the close relationship between caller and called on; H. D. Preuss, *THWAT* 2:673.

Form/Structure/Setting

The story of Adam's descendants (Gen 4) is, as already observed, part of the larger editorial unit encompassed by Gen 2:4–4:26. The coherence of this block of material is indicated by the opening heading "This is the history of the heaven and the earth" and by the use of numerical symmetry within it. Throughout the Pentateuch, the sevenfold use of divine speech formulae is commonplace (Labuschagne, *VT* 32 [1982] 268–96), and within this chapter the number seven is clearly significant (cf. vv 15, 24). Unusually full details about Lamek, the seventh generation from Adam (18–24), may illustrate another convention associated with biblical genealogies, a tendency to draw attention to the seventh generation (Sasson, *ZAW* 90 [1978] 171–85). Indeed various keywords in the narrative appear a multiple of seven times. Within 4:1–17, "Abel" and "brother" occur seven times, and "Cain" fourteen times. Within the whole of 2:4–4:26, ארץ "earth," not "land of," is mentioned seven times, אדמה "land" fourteen times, and "God" "the LORD" or "The LORD God" some thirty-five times, exactly matching the thirty-five occurrences of "God" in 1:1–2:3. The last verse of chap. 4, "At that time people began to call on the name of the LORD," thus contains the seventieth mention of the deity in Genesis and the fourteenth use of the key word "call" (cf. Labuschagne, *VT* 32 [1982] 270).

The arrangement of the material in this chapter exemplifies patterns found elsewhere in Genesis. First, the genealogy of Adam to Lamek (1–18) is interrupted by a long narrative digression describing the struggle between Cain and Abel. In similar fashion, the story of Noah is sandwiched between 5:32 and 9:28–29, stereotyped formulae previously used in the genealogy of 5:3–31 to note births and deaths. Second, the story of Cain and Abel contains many thematic and structural parallels with chap. 3 (see below). Third, it is characteristic of Genesis to trace mankind's descent from Adam in a series of bifurcations. Typically a man has two or three sons (e.g., Abraham—Ishmael, Isaac; Isaac—Jacob, Esau; Noah—Shem, Ham, and Japheth), and it is usually the younger son who receives God's favor, not the elder who might by right have been expected to enjoy such a privilege. So here Adam has three sons—Cain, Abel, and Seth. Cain, the eldest boy, has his sacrifice rejected, whereas

Abel's is acceptable. When Abel is killed, God's blessing cannot rest on Cain, so Seth becomes father of the chosen line.

Finally, Genesis always records the descendants of the unfavored sons before the elect line. The genealogies of Japheth and Ham precede that of Shem (chap. 10); Ishmael's genealogy precedes Isaac's (25:12–34); and Esau's, Jacob's (chaps. 36–37). So here the genealogy of Cain precedes Seth's (4:17–5:32). At first sight, there is unexpected duplication in the genealogy of Seth: it begins in 4:25 and resumes in 5:3. However, Genesis regularly has such anticipations of the new section at the close of the preceding section: they act like colophons, as trailers for the sequel. Thus the next main section, 5:1–6:8, closes with remarks anticipating divine judgment and the salvation of Noah (6:5–8), the theme of 6:9–9:29; 9:19 adumbrates the spread of Noah's descendants throughout the world (see 10:1–11:9); 11:26 anticipates 11:27–25:11; 25:11 introduces 25:19–35:29. In all these respects chap. 4 is entirely typical of the editorial techniques used throughout Genesis, and its present form must owe much to the final editor (cf. Tengström, *Toledotformel*, 57).

Chap. 4 has been correctly characterized by Westermann as an expanded genealogy of Adam, in which the principal expansions concern Cain's relations with Abel in 3–16 and Lamek's matrimonial affairs 19–24. It falls into three main sections:

1–16 Cain and Abel
17–24 Cain's descendants
25–26 Seth's family

Each section opens similarly "Man/Cain/Adam knew his wife. She conceived, gave birth to . . . and she said (called) . . .," v 1; cf. vv 17, 25. These parallel formulas show that the Cainite genealogy (vv 17–24) is a continuation of the genealogy begun in 4:1–2, while the subtle switch from הָאָדָם with the article "man" in v 1 to אָדָם without it, "Adam," in v 26 prepares the way for the genealogy in chap. 5, which also uses the anarthrous form "Adam." Further proof of the homogeneity of chap. 4's genealogy is the way participial phrases are used to describe the pursuits of the men named: Abel, "shepherd of the flock"; Cain, "tiller of the land" (v 2); Enoch (Cain), "building a city" (v 17); Yabal, "dweller in tents" (v 20; cf. 21, 22). "The two portions of the genealogy thus seem to have been shaped by the same hand and clearly belong together. For this reason it is unlikely that the parts circulated separately in their present forms. At the same time, the beginning of the genealogy in 4:1–2 and the description of the two brothers clearly form the introduction to the following story (4:3–16) and cannot now be separated from it. This fact would suggest that the whole of chap. 4 is a literary unit and would make it even more difficult to argue that any of the components in their present forms ever circulated separately" (Wilson, *Genealogy*, 157).

If modern opinion tends to view chap. 4 as a coherent unity, this was not true of earlier writers (e.g., Dillmann, Gunkel, Driver, Skinner). They pointed to the following inconsistencies between vv 1–16 and the rest of the chapter, which, they argued, showed the existence of two sources within J. Vv 12–16 make Cain a perpetual wanderer, but according to v 17 he builds a city. Abel was the first shepherd (v 2), but Yabal was the father of herdsmen (v 20). People did not start to call on the name of the LORD till Enoch's day (v 26), but Yahweh is frequently mentioned in vv 2–16.

While some of these points may reflect the diversity of traditions available to the editor, it is evident that he cannot have regarded them as glaring contradictions or he would not have juxtaposed them in this fashion. Indeed, some of the supposed differences are open to straightforward exegetical explanation; see *Comment* below. Most modern writers are therefore happy to ascribe the whole chapter to J, despite the uncharacteristic use of "Elohim" in v 25.

The attribution of this chapter to J rests positively on its frequent use of the divine name "The LORD" and on the similarity of its language and ideas to chaps. 2–3, and negatively on the different style of the genealogy here from that in chap. 5 (usually ascribed to P). The relationship between these genealogies is discussed under *Form/Structure/Setting* in chap. 5. Noting the transitional nature of 4:25–26 which links chaps. 4 and 5, Coats argues that these verses have been inserted by the editor who amalgamated J and P. This seems likely, but if the P material antedated J, J could still be regarded as the author or redactor responsible for the whole of chap. 4.

Attempts to pin down the sources used by J in this chapter are just as elusive as in chaps. 2–3. Dietrich (*Beiträge zur alttestamentliche Theologie*, 94–111) has attempted to isolate the pre-J traditions used in vv 2–16, but the absence of any close extrabiblical parallels in this story, except for the common "hostile brothers" motif, makes attempts to distinguish source and editor unconvincing. It is worth noting, however, that the text of the Sumerian flood story begins with the birth goddess Nintur declaring her intention to end mankind's nomadic existence, settle them in cities, and establish centers of worship (39–43). Obviously the goddess's plan did not succeed right away, perhaps through lack of human leadership, for when the text resumes it tells that kingship has been instituted, worship is being offered, and the first cities have been built (86–100). Because he compared the Sumerian flood story only with the P material in Genesis, Jacobsen overlooked the remarkable similarities with Gen 4, which also tells of early man's nomadic plight (vv 11–16), the building of the first city, probably called Irad (cf. Eridu; see comments on vv 17–18), and the establishment of worship (v 26). Biblical scholars have often held that these three motifs of nomadism, city-building, and worship go back to originally independent traditions and were combined by the biblical writer. The Sumerian flood story suggests rather that they already belonged together in early tradition. P. D. Miller (*HAR* 9 [1985] 238–40) has noted another possible link between Genesis and Mesopotamian tradition in the Harab myth.

As at other points, though, Genesis puts a different slant on these developments in primeval history. Nomadism according to the Sumerian flood story is a plight from which the gods rescued man; according to the Bible a nomadic existence was a judgment imposed on the first murderer. This contrast fits in with the overall optimism of Mesopotamia which believes in human progress over against the biblical picture of the inexorable advance of sin (cf. *Introduction*, 5:1). It would seem likely that the other human achievements listed here—

farming, metalwork, and music—are also seen by Genesis as somehow under the shadow of Cain's sin. But tracing these arts and crafts back to primeval times was not unique to Israel. Mesopotamian tradition tells of seven *apkallus*, sages who lived before the flood and taught man the arts of civilization. (For further discussion, see *Comment* on vv 17–24.) Thus, as in chaps. 2–3, the stories in this chapter seem to be aware of older Near Eastern traditions, but in retelling them, Genesis completely transforms them and offers an entirely fresh interpretation of them.

In determining the character of the stories in this chapter, a comparison with Gen 2–3 is most instructive. Structurally, thematically, and verbally there are close parallels between the Cain and Abel pericope (4:2b–16) and the garden of Eden story in Gen 2–3. First, this section falls into five major scenes with alternating narrative and dialogue.

1)	2b–5	Narrative	Cain, Abel main actors; Yahweh passive.
2)	6–7	Dialogue	Yahweh questioning Cain.
3)	8	(Dialogue) narrative	Cain and Abel alone.
4)	9–14	Dialogue	Yahweh and Cain.
5)	15–16	Narrative	Yahweh active, Cain passive.

As in the previous story, scenes 1 and 5 correspond to each other, as do scenes 2 and 4, while the decisive event, here the murder of Abel, constitutes the central scene 3. Both scenes 1 and 5 show Cain approaching God, first in sacrifice and then in prayer, and in both scenes being rebuffed by God. Between the two scenes there is an inversion. In the first scene Cain brings a sacrifice to God; in the last he goes away from the presence of God. Scenes 2 and 4 correspond in both being dialogues between the LORD and Cain, though Cain's replies to the divine questions in scene 2 are unrecorded. In both scenes God asks Cain two essentially rhetorical questions, double-barreled in vv 6–7, simple in vv 9–10. In the second scene sin is pictured as an animal waiting to devour Cain: in the fourth the land has opened its mouth to receive Abel's blood.

Not only is the overall pattern of this story similar to the account of the fall, but many of the scenes are closely parallel. The central scene in each case is a terse description of the sin (3:6–8 // 4:8) which contrasts strikingly with the long dialogues before and afterwards. The following scene in each case where God investigates and condemns the sin is remarkably similar: cf. "Where is Abel your brother? // Where are you?" 4:9; 3:9; "What have you done?" 4:10; 3:13; "You are cursed from the land," cf. "You are more cursed than all domesticated animals; The land is cursed because of you" 4:11; 3:14, 17. Also cf. 4:12 with 3:17–19. The marking of Cain (4:15) is clearly analogous with the clothing of Adam and Eve (3:21). Both stories conclude with the transgressors leaving the presence of God and going to live east of Eden (4:16; cf. 3:24).

It is not merely the structure of the stories that run parallel, but there are interesting cross-linkages. For instance, in Hebrew, God's warning to Cain "Its urge is for you, but you must rule over it" is even closer to the curse on Eve than is suggested by the English "Your urge will be to your husband,

but he shall rule over you" (4:7; 3:16). After God asked Adam, "Where are
you?," Adam replied, "I heard your voice." After questioning Cain similarly,
God says, "Listen [literally, "the voice of"] your brother's blood is crying to
me" (3:10 // 4:10). Finally, according to 3:24, the LORD "drove man out of
the garden," and Cain's complaint is similar: "You have driven me from the
surface of the land" (4:14). For other verbal and thematic connections between
the stories, see Hauser (*JETS* 23 [1980] 297–305) and *Comment* below.

These similarities between chaps. 3 and 4 confirm that the former should
be read as a paradigm of human sin. Fratricide illustrates in a different way
how sin works. Yet the differences between the two stories must not be overlooked either. Whereas in chap. 2 there is no sense of alienation between
man and God to start with, in chap. 4 this is present from the outset because
the LORD does not accept Cain's sacrifice. If the two temptation scenes are
compared, differences spring readily to the eye. Eve has to be persuaded to
disregard the creator's advice by the serpent (3:1–5), but Cain is not dissuaded
from his murderous intention by his creator's appeal (4:6–7). Finally, when
God pronounces sentence on Adam, Eve, and the serpent, they accept it
without demur (3:14–20), but Cain protests that he is being treated too harshly
(4:14). Clearly, then, though the writer of Genesis wants to highlight the
parallels between the two stories, he does not regard the murder of Abel
simply as a rerun of the fall. There is development: sin is more firmly en-
trenched and humanity is further alienated from God.

The parallels between chaps. 3 and 4 are also important for determining
the character of the Cain and Abel story. They show that Genesis understands
Cain and Abel to be individuals belonging to primeval history, not personifica-
tions of tribes or peoples, as sometimes maintained. Westermann observes
that all exegetes have recognized that, as it stands, Genesis presupposes the
individuality of Cain and Abel: only at an earlier stage in the tradition have
some writers affirmed that they may have represented tribes. Furthermore,
the absence of any close parallels to the story weakens the case for supposing
that a collective interpretation of these figures preceded Genesis' own protohistorical understanding of their roles. (For an attempt to revive the collective
interpretation, see W. Dietrich, *Beiträge,* 94–111).

Comment

1–2 These verses constitute the opening of the genealogy of Adam via
Cain which continues in 17–26 after the digression about the murder of
Abel in vv 3–16. Like chap. 3, the new episode opens with a circumstantial
clause. The word order with the subject preceding the verb marks a new
beginning, not a special emphasis on the man (e.g., Cassuto, Gispen). Nor
does it justify translating "knew" as a pluperfect "had known" with the implication that Adam "knew" his wife before he left the garden of Eden (e.g.,
Rashi, Jacob). Though he may have done, this construction does not require
such an interpretation.

1 "Man knew." Like English "know," Hebrew יָדַע is a very broad term.
Primarily, it covers knowledge acquired through the senses, experience that
can be passed on to others, and practical knowledge. Here it is euphemistic

for sexual intercourse, a usage common to the OT and other Semitic languages (e.g., 4:17; 19:5, 8; 24:16, etc.; Akk. *idû, lamādu*; Arab. *ʿarafa*), and though some have maintained that this special use of the word is a key to its usual meaning, this is unlikely (see W. Schottroff, *THWAT* 1:682–701, *pace* Speiser, Westermann). For the sequence "know, conceive, give birth" cf. 4:17; cf. also 16:4, 11; 19:35–38; 21:2; 29:32–35; 30:3–5, 16–19; 38:2–5.

"Cain . . . I have gained a man." This translation aims to draw attention to the assonance in the Hebrew between "Cain"/*qayin* and "I have gained"/*qānîtî*. Other key phrases in the story also seem to make phonetic allusions to the name Cain—"Cain arose" קַיִן וַיָּקָם, v 8 (cf. *yqm // qyn*); " . . . Cain will be punished/avenged sevenfold," קַיִן יֻקַּם שִׁבְעָתָיִם, v 15; and similarly, v 24). Echoes of Cain's name reverberate through this story, just as in other passages names of the leading characters are often alluded to in the narratives about them (cf. Adam in chap. 2; Abram in chap. 12, etc.; Strus, *Nomen-Omen*, 172–74).

The etymology of Cain's name offered in the text is "poetic," as there is no intrinsic connection between קַיִן and קָנָה. In this respect it resembles the etymologies of Seth, 4:25; Noah, 5:29; Levi, 29:34; Judah, 29:35, etc. (Strus, *Nomen-Omen*, 65–67). The historical etymology of Cain is obscure. It has often been explained as "smith," or "metalworker" on the basis of Arabic *qaynun* and Aramaic קִינָאָה (cf. "Qenan," Gen 5:12–14). In support of this derivation, v 22, which speaks of Tubal-Cain as the father of metalworkers, and 2 Sam 21:16, where the Hebrew word קַיִן means "a lance," i.e., "something worked in metal," are appealed to. Arguing in a slightly different direction, Cassuto thinks the proper name "Cain" must mean "something worked, i.e., a creature." But really, as Westermann says, there is too little information to be sure about the original meaning of the name.

קָנִיתִי אִישׁ אֶת־יהוה "I have gained a man with the LORD's help." "Every word of this little sentence is difficult" (von Rad, 103). First, there is the problem of the meaning of קָנָה "gain." Then, it is peculiar to call a baby boy "a man." Finally, the last phrase, אֶת־יהוה, is very strange. Is אֶת the definite object marker? In that case we ought to translate "I have acquired a man the LORD." Or is it a preposition that normally means "with," as our translation assumes?

קָנָה means "acquire, buy" (e.g., 25:10; 33:19) more commonly than "to create" (e.g., 14:19, 22). Given the preoccupation of Gen 1–3 with creation, the rarer meaning would seem more appropriate here. However, the existence of second-millennium names such as *itti-ili ašamšu* ("I bought him from God") gives the edge to the other translation as it also explains the problematic preposition אֶת, though מֵאֵת "from" would have been more idiomatic Hebrew (R. Borger, *VT* 9 [1959] 85–86). Nevertheless, connections with the earlier story cannot be eliminated. אִישׁ "man" is used nowhere else to describe a baby boy. Its use here is most probably to be explained as an allusion to 2:23, "from a man she was taken." Building on this and other links with the preceding narratives and on the interpretation of קָנָה as "create," Cassuto and Westermann interpret Eve's remark as a shout of triumph at putting herself on a par with Yahweh as creator: "I have created a man equally with the LORD." Westermann admits, though, that if this was Eve's meaning, she should have said "as [כ] the LORD." On the other hand, it is also unparalleled for את to mean "with the help of." So some have suggested repointing it את "sign of" and translating "I have gained a man the sign of the LORD" (e.g., P. A. H. de Boer, *NedTT*, 31 [1942] 197–212). Some read it as the object marker and translate "I have gained a man, the LORD," i.e., Cain is the son of God promised in 3:15 (so Luther and early Lutheran exegetes [T. Gallus, *Die "Frau" in Gen 3:15*, 31–32]). Yet the majority of commentators have argued that since it is a regular feature of the promises to the patriarchs that God will be with them, implicitly to help them, it is justified here to translate את "with the help of" (cf. 21:20; 26:3, 24; 28:15; 31:3; 39:2).

For these reasons it seems more likely that Eve meant "I have gained a man with the LORD's help" than "I have created a man as the LORD (has done)." Nevertheless there is an ambiguity about her expression which may suggest that she covertly compared her achievement with Yahweh's greater works and hoped that he would be with her son.

2 This verse nicely links the genealogy of Adam (vv 1, 17 f.) to the story of Cain and Abel (vv 3–16). In particular, the definitions of the brothers' tasks (using present participles), "shepherd of the flock/tiller of the land," link this verse with vv 17, 20, 21. Simultaneously the chiastic construction "became Abel : Cain became" integrates it with the string of similarly constructed clauses in vv 3–5 (cf. *Notes*). The description of the birth of Esau and Jacob follows a similar pattern to this verse.

Birth of two sons	4:1, 2a	25:24–26
Naming of son(s)	4:1b	25:15b, 26b
Calling of sons	4:2b	25:27

However, there is no indication that Cain and Abel, unlike Esau and Jacob, were twins. Certainly Abel is the younger brother, a significant theological point.

"Abel" (Hebrew הבל). Unlike the case with Cain, no explanation of his name is given by his mother. It is improbable that it was derived from Akk. *aplu*, "son." Probably its meaning was too obvious to warrant comment. הבל means "breath" or "vanity" (Eccl 1:2). "Man is a like a breath, his days are like a passing shadow" (Ps 144:4; cf. Job 7:16). Abel's name thus alludes unwittingly to the fate in store for him, that his life will be cut short. His junior status and the remark that "he became a shepherd" may also adumbrate the Lord's preference for him. For although Adam was appointed to till the ground (2:15), the elect patriarchs' preferred profession was shepherding (47:3) as David's was later (1 Sam 16:11). Though the eldest son had certain legal privileges (see, e.g., 25:32; 27:1–40; Deut 21:15–17), the biblical narratives regularly show God's choice falling on the younger brother (e.g., Isaac, not Ishmael; Jacob, not Esau; Ephraim, not Manasseh; David, the youngest son of Jesse). Already in this verse, then, there are hints that Abel is the elect younger brother.

2b–5 These verses constitute the first scene in the Cain and Abel story. Like the final scene (15–16), it is pure narrative. But whereas in the first scene Cain and Abel are the principal actors and God is in the background, in the last scene, Cain is passive and God is the sole actor. The chiastic linkage between clauses in this scene is remarkable. Abel–Cain : Cain–Abel : Abel–Cain; see *Notes* on vv 2–5.

3 To link this verse chiastically with the preceding, Cain's offering is mentioned first. Westermann sees the opening phrase "After a year" (which, with most commentators, he translates "after some time") as a clear indicator that the story of Cain and Abel has been inserted from another story that related some previous episode in their careers. This may well be so, but it must remain conjecture.

"After a year," ויהי מקץ ימים. ימים, lit., "days," can refer to an indefinite period, short or long (see, e.g., 24:55; 40:4) or specifically to a year (Lev 25:29; 1 Sam 1:21, etc.). It seems slightly more natural with Jacob, Junker, and a few rabbinic commentators to take it in its precise sense "a year" in this context. Nearly always the introductory phrase "after" (ויהי מקץ) is followed by a precise period of time (as, e.g., in 8:6; Exod 12:41). Second, it seems natural to suppose that at the end of the agricultural year sacrifices would have been brought. As soon as their labors had borne fruit they brought appropriate offerings.

"Brought" (ויבא): often used in cultic texts for the offering of sacrifice, e.g., Lev 2:2, 8. "Offering" (מנחה) is a term in secular texts for gifts used to win the favor of the great (e.g., 32:14, 19; 43:11). In cultic texts it usually denotes grain offerings as opposed to animal sacrifice (e.g., Lev 2), though it occasionally covers the latter as well (e.g., 1 Sam 2:17, 29). Though the narrower sense aptly suits Cain's offering, the following verse uses it in the wider sense to describe Abel's offering of animals.

4 Abel's offering corresponds to his vocation as a shepherd. It may not be coincidence that Adam's second son offers firstlings (first-born animals) whereas Cain, the older son, offers neither firstlings nor firstfruits. Note the association of the first-born with firstlings in Exod 22:28–29 [29–30]; 34:19–20. The law is insistent that all firstlings must be offered in sacrifice or redeemed. The first-born by right belong to God. So human first-born must be redeemed. Israel as a nation is described as God's first-born (Exod 13:2, 12–15; 4:22; M. Tsevat, *TDOT* 2:121–27). In all animal sacrifices the fat was burnt, because it too belonged to the LORD, being regarded as the choicest part of the animal (Lev 3:16; Deut 32:38; Ps 147:14; G. Münderlein, *TDOT* 4:391–97). The very positive connotations of "firstlings" and "fat" in the OT support the view of Keil, Delitzsch, Cassuto, Speiser, Kidner, and rabbinic commentators that Abel offered the pick of his flock to the LORD.

וישע "Paid attention to"; cf. Akk *šeû* "look closely into," Speiser; "seek, recognize" (poetic), *AHW* 1224–25; used also in Exod 5:9; Ps 119:117. How Cain and Abel recognized divine approval is unclear. As early as Theodotion (who translates וישע ἐπύρισεν "he burnt") it has been understood that divine fire burnt up Abel's offering but not Cain's (cf. Lev 9:24; Judg 6:21; 1 Kgs 18:38). This explanation is as good as any, but Genesis is more interested in the fact of divine approval than in how it was shown.

5 "But to Cain and his offering he paid no attention." The verse begins with the final member of the chiastic chain, "Cain and his offering," corresponding to "Abel and his offering" in v 4b.

"Cain was very angry." "Very" indicates the intensity of Cain's passion; being "very angry" is often a prelude to homicidal acts (cf. 34:7; 1 Sam 18:8; Neh 4:1; cf. Num 16:15; 2 Sam 3:8). "His face fell": cf. v 6 and for a similar expression using the hiphil, Job 29:24; Jer 3:12.

Why Cain's offering should have been rejected while Abel's was accepted has occasioned much perplexity. At least five different types of explanation have been offered. (1) God prefers shepherds to gardeners (Gunkel). This seems improbable in the light of 2:15 where Adam was appointed to till the soil. (2) Animal sacrifice is more acceptable than vegetable offerings (Skinner, Jacob). While blood sacrifices were obviously regarded as more valuable, every stratum of the law recognizes the propriety and necessity of grain offerings as well. (3) God's motives are inscrutable: his preference for Abel's sacrifice reflects the mystery of divine election (von Rad, Vawter, Golka, and apparently Westermann). Clearly the preference for Abel does anticipate a frequent pattern in Genesis of the choice of the younger brother (cf. Jacob/Esau, Isaac/Ishmael, etc.), but this type of explanation should only be resorted to if the text gives no other motives for divine action. (4) Inspired by Heb 11:4, "By faith Abel offered to God a more acceptable sacrifice than Cain," some commentators (e.g., Calvin, Dillmann, Driver, König) suggest that it was the differing motives of the two brothers, known only to God, that accounts for their different treatment. (5) The commonest view among commentators, ancient and modern, is that it was the different approach to worship that counted and that this was reflected in the quality of their gifts. Whereas Cain offered simply "some produce of the land," Abel offered the choicest animals from his flock, "firstlings" and "their fat portions." The sacrificial law underlines frequently that only perfect, unblemished animals may be offered in sacrifice (Lev 1:3; 22:20–22, etc.). "I will not offer burnt offerings to the LORD . . . that cost me nothing" (2 Sam 24:24). Since this is the first account of sacrifice in the OT we might well expect an allusion to this fundamental principle in this story.

6–7 The second scene corresponds to the fourth (vv 9–14) and consists of dialogue between God and Cain. Both scenes open with God asking two questions, and both close with two divine statements about Cain's fate. They differ in that in the second scene Cain's responses are not recorded.

6 "Why are you angry and why has your face fallen?" God's questions, echoing v 5, are somewhat like the snake's in 3:1 in character. In both cases the questioners know the answer to their own question, but whereas the snake's was designed to lead man into sin, God's were intended to provoke a change of heart.

7 "Is there not forgiveness." "The most obscure verse in Genesis" (Procksch). Because of its grammatical improprieties and its unusual terminology, commentators are forced to choose between emendation and positing a rare meaning for רבץ "crouching." To compound the problems, other words are of uncertain meaning. Of the various suggestions the following present the least difficulty:

Ben Yashar (*BMik* 7 [1963] 116–19; *ZAW* 94 [1982] 635–37) suggests new meanings for the nouns שׂאת "forgiveness" and פתח "door." The former he translates "first-born's dignity" (cf. 49:3), and the latter, "first-born"; cf. the

phrase "to open the womb" (29:31; 30:32). So he translates the whole verse:
"Is it not this way? If you do well, there is the honour due to the first-born.
If you do not do well, sin crouches [reading תרבץ] for the first-born." In
other words, Cain, the first-born, has special responsibilities, especially in
worship. If he carries them out, he will enjoy the privileges associated with
his primacy.

Though this interpretation is quite compatible with biblical thinking, it
seems precarious in that it postulates new meanings for two words and a
textual emendation (תרבץ 3 fem sg impf for רבץ). Then Ben Yashar maintains
that "His/its urge . . . you must rule over him/it" refers to Cain dominating
Abel, which does not seem to follow on very easily from the previous clauses.

Ramaroson (*Bib* 49 [1968] 233–37) observed that the present formulation
of the divine speech is rhythmically unbalanced as well as grammatically un-
sound (see *Notes*). It falls into three lines:

"Is there not forgiveness, if you do well?"   3 beats
"And if you do not do well, sin is crouching at the door"   5 beats
"Its desire is for you, but you must rule over it"   4 beats

Ramaroson suggests that a scribe has by accident transposed sin from the
first to the second line. Originally it read:

הלא אם־תיטיב שאת חטאת   "Is there not forgiveness of sin, if you do well?"
ואם לא תיטיב לפתח רבץ   "If you do not do well, the croucher (demon) is at the
                           door."
ואליך תשוקתו ואתה תמשל־בו   "Its desire is for you, but you must rule over it."

On this rearrangement, there are now four beats per line; the "it(s)" in the
third line must refer to "the croucher" (masculine participle) and not to sin
which is feminine; and the lack of concord between sin (f) and crouching is
eliminated. In adopting the translation "croucher, demon" from Akk. *rābiṣu*
for רבץ, Ramaroson is following a suggestion first proposed by Lenormant
in 1880 and subsequently adopted by many commentators (cf. *AHW*, 935b).

Substantially similar interpretations of the verse's syntax and meaning are
offered by Cassuto, Speiser, Westermann, Gispen, and Vawter, but without
rearranging the word order. These commentators argue that רבץ is a masculine noun to which the suffixes ו "it(s)" in the final line refer. However, if
the sentence is not rearranged à la Ramaroson, the meaning of שאת "forgiveness" becomes uncertain. The word comes from the root נשא "to lift up,"
which is a broad term whose precise meaning can only be determined by
the context. Here it may refer to (1) God's forgiving Cain (*Tg. Onq.*); (2)
God's receiving Cain and his offering (Vg, S, rsv, neb, Calvin, König, Kidner)
or (3) Cain's subjective feelings, i.e., exaltation as opposed to his fallen face
(vv 5–6; so Speiser, Delitzsch, Keil, Dillmann, Driver, von Rad, Westermann)
or (4) Cain's posture—"upstanding," not crouching like sin; so Cassuto. In
that the primary contrast in the divine interrogation is between שאת and
חטאת רבץ, the traditional interpretations (1 and 2), referring שאת to God's
forgiveness or acceptance of Cain, seem more probable than a mere reference

to Cain's feelings or posture. Nevertheless, there may be a secondary allusion to v 6, "Why has your face fallen?" for if Cain were forgiven or accepted, he might well have felt exalted too.

"Sin is crouching." רבץ "crouching" is frequently and plausibly identified with Akk *rābiṣu*, denoting various officials and also demons, especially those that guard entrances to buildings. Here then sin is personified as a demon crouching like a wild beast on Cain's doorstep.

"Its urge is for you, but you must rule over it"; cf. 3:16 and *Comment* there.

8 This is the central scene, with Cain and Abel the only actors. The awefulness of the deed is accentuated by the stark brevity of the description and the twice-repeated "his brother." "Cain said to his brother": whether by accident or design, Cain's words to his brother are unrecorded. They may have dropped out through homoeoteleuton (see *Notes*) or been deliberately suppressed so as to focus complete attention on the action. Some commentators accept the originality of SamPent, "let us go out into the field"; others have emended or reinterpreted ויאמר "and (Cain) said," to eliminate the need for any words to follow. Gunkel proposes the emendation וימר, and Golka (*C. Westermann FS*, 63) proposes ויתמרמר "and (Cain) was angry." Cassuto cites a cognate Arabic root to show ויאמר here means "and (Cain) made a *rendez-vous*" with Abel. Dahood (*Bib* 61 [1981] 90–91) compares Ugaritic *'amr* and Akkadian *amāru* "to see" and translates "Cain was watching for his brother Abel." It is as easy to suppose that Cain's words were never included: the terseness conveys the feel of the story hastening to its climax; cf. 3:22–23.

"When they were in the field." שדה "field, plain." On this term see 2:5. In the law the circumstance that a crime is committed "in the field," i.e., out of range of help, is proof of premeditation; cf. Deut 22:25–27. "Cain rose up": note the assonance in Hebrew, *wayyāqom qayin*.

"Killed him" הרג is used particularly of ruthless violence by private persons, BDB, 247; cf. H. F. Fuhs, *TDOT* 3:447–57.

9–14 The fourth scene, like the second, is a dialogue between the LORD and Cain. But whereas in vv 6–7 Cain's replies are unrecorded, here they are given in full. The divine interrogation of Cain and the subsequent pronouncement of curses resemble the similar treatment of Adam. (Cf. 4:9 // 3:9; 4:10 // 3:13; 4:11 // 3:14,17; 4:12 // 3:17–19). Many of the key words of chap. 3 reappear here too: ידע "know," שמר "guard," ארור "cursed," אדמה "land," גרש "drive" (cf. Hauser, *JETS* 12 [1980] 297–305).

9 God's opening question, "Where is Abel your brother?" like 3:9, is essentially rhetorical, for God knows where Abel is (v 10). It invites Cain to acknowledge his responsibility for his "brother." Note again how the story repeatedly draws attention to the fraternal relationship.

When Adam was challenged, he at least told the truth if not the whole truth (3:10), but Cain tells a bare-faced lie, "I do not know," and follows it up with an impertinent witticism, "Am I my brother's keeper?" Since Abel kept sheep and שמר is a term for shepherds (cf. Exod 22:6, 9; 1 Sam 17:20) Cain's reply could be paraphrased "Am I the shepherd's shepherd?" It may well be that Cain is overstating his responsibility toward his brother in order to deny it completely, for no man is called on in the OT to act as another's keeper (so P. A. Riemann, *Int* 24 [1970] 482–91). "To keep" a man would involve keeping an eye on him all the time, which could be somewhat intrusive. Yet biblical law expects a man's brother to be the first to assist him in time of trouble (Lev 25:48). Cain might not have expected to "keep" Abel, but as his brother he certainly should have been ready to act as redeemer and to avenge his blood when he was murdered (Num 36:12–28). His outright denial of responsibility shows he is "much more hardened than the first human pair" (von Rad, 106).

10 With God's pronouncement of Cain's guilt the narrative reaches its real climax. Though the external events climax in the murder, "the narrator has portrayed the deed so tersely that he has succeeded in shifting the real weight of the action to [this] sentence" (Westermann, 1:305).

"What have you done?": cf. 3:13.

"Listen," קול, literally, "voice of." Used similarly in Isa 13:4; 52:8; Jer 10:22; 50:28.

"Your brother's blood is crying to me." The four Hebrew words used hardly require comment. Compressed into them is a whole theology whose principles inform much of the criminal and cultic law of Israel. Life is in the blood (Lev 17:11), so shed blood is the most polluting of all substances. Consequently, unatoned-for murders pollute the holy land, making it unfit for the divine presence. To prevent such a catastrophe, the cities of refuge were established (Num 35:9–34; Deut 19:1–13). In cases where the murderer could not be traced, the rite prescribed in Deut 21:1–9 had to be carried out. Because man is made in God's image, homicide must be avenged (Gen 9:5). Here Abel's blood is pictured "crying" to God for vengeance. צעק "cry" is the desperate cry of men without food (Gen 41:55), expecting to die (Exod 14:10), or oppressed by their enemies (Judg 4:3). It is the scream for help of a woman being raped (Deut 22:24, 27). It is the plea to God of the victims of injustice (Exod 22:22[23], 26[27]). The law, the prophets (Isa 19:20; cf. 5:7), and the psalms (34:18[17]; 107:6, 28) unite with narratives like this (cf. 2 Sam 23; 1 Kgs 21) to assert that God does hear his people's desperate cries for help.

11 "And now" ועתה (cf. 3:22) generally introduces an ethical consequence of a preceding statement (cf. K. A. Brongers, *VT* 15 [1965] 289–99).

"You are cursed from the land." The parallel with 3:14 prompted *Tg. Onq., Ber. R.*, Rashi to translate "you are more cursed than the land." Most modern commentators suggest that it means you are cursed *away from* the land, i.e., you are banished from the cultivated area (אדמה) that was man's original home (cf. 2:5) to the uncultivated steppe. Cassuto prefers to give the phrase the same sense as in v 10. As the blood of Abel cried from the ground, so the curse arises from the ground to convict Cain. It may be that both ideas are reflected in the phrase (cf. Jacob). In Gen 3 man is not cursed, only the ground and the serpent, so cursing Cain is a serious development. Certainly there is an element of mirroring punishment in the curse pronounced on Cain: "Cain had tilled the land. He had offered the fruit of the land, and given the land his brother's blood to drink: but from the land the blood cries against him, for which the land refuses him its fruit, so he is banned from the land" (Gunkel, 45).

"The land which has opened its mouth"; cf. the description of the earth swallowing up Korah (Num 16:30, 32; Deut 11:6) or vomiting out the Canaanites for their sins (Lev 18:28). Cassuto suggests that "the land" is here a name of the underworld, Sheol, often pictured as swallowing the dead (cf. Isa 5:14; Hab 2:5).

12 Whereas 3:17–19 warned of the hard labor that man would face in tilling the soil, "When you till the land, it will no longer give you its strength" (cf. Job 31:39) implies that its yields would be minimal for Cain.

His lack of success as a farmer may have been one reason why Cain became a "wandering vagrant." Only here and in v 14 are these two similar-sounding participles paired together, literally, "wandering" (cf. Ps 109:10; Lam 4:14–15) and "fluttering" (Prov 26:2). Cain is not being condemned to a Bedouin-like existence; the terminology is too extreme to describe such a life-style. Rather it seems likely that the curse on Cain reflects the expulsion from the family that was the fate in tribal societies of those who murdered close relatives. Normally murders were avenged by the nearest male relative (cf. Num 35:9–28), but where fraternal loyalties conflicted, expulsion was an alternative punishment (cf. 2 Sam 13:34–14:24; cf. H. M. Y. Gevaryahu, *BMik* 13 [1967] 29–31). "To be driven away from the land" (cf. v 14) is to have all relationships, particularly with the family, broken. Moreover, it is to have one's relationship with the LORD broken (Coats, 65).

13 "My punishment is too great to bear." Though G, Vg, Jacob, Cassuto translate "my iniquity is too great to be forgiven," this does not appear to be the meaning of the phrase עון נשא, literally, "to carry iniquity/punishment" (Lev 16:22), when applied to ordinary men. When men "bear iniquity," they must pay the penalty for their sin whatever it may be (e.g., Lev 5:1, 17; Num 5:31). However, when God bears iniquity, that means forgiveness for the sinner; hence the translation "forgiving iniquity" (Exod 34:7; Hos 14:3). When priests and Levites "bear iniquity" (Num 18:1, 23), they may be paying the price of their own failings or those of the people. But in the case of Cain it seems clear that he is referring to the consequences of his iniquity, which he finds intolerable (cf. Golka, *C. Westermann FS*, 67–68).

14 "Since you have today driven me from the surface of the land and I must hide from your face and become a wandering vagrant." These words sum up what Cain finds intolerable about his fate. The first three clauses repeat the divine curses on Cain, slightly modifying the phraseology of v 12. Cain introduces clear echoes of chap. 3 as he likens his expulsion (גרש) from the face of the ground to Adam and Eve's expulsion from Eden (3:24). Like them he must "hide" (different Hebrew roots) from the face of the LORD (3:8). He seems to be suggesting that he is being driven even further from the divine presence symbolized by the garden than his parents were. As a perpetrator of a homicide, he would have liked to have returned to Eden, for if it may be regarded as the archetype of later sanctuaries, he could have taken refuge there (Exod 21:14; 1 Kgs 2:28). It may be too that there is an analogy in Absalom's action in going to sacrifice at Hebron when he returned from exile after killing his brother Amnon (2 Sam 15:7–9). It might have been expected that he should have paid his vow at the national sanctuary in Jerusalem, but he went to Hebron instead. Gevaryahu (*BMik*

13 [1967] 34) has noted that in Greece murderers were prohibited from worshiping in their home shrine.

Alienation from God leads to fear of other men (cf. Job 15:20–25). Certainly it is the fear of retribution that is the heart of Cain's complaint "Anyone who finds me will kill me." Whom he feared has perplexed commentators, since according to the Genesis account there was no one else around but his parents. This may indicate that the story of Cain and Abel was originally independent of the stories in chaps. 2 and 3. However, it is unlikely that the editor was unaware of the problem created by juxtaposing chaps. 3 and 4 in this way (cf. Westermann, Gunkel). Most probably he envisaged other descendants of Adam seeking to avenge Abel's death.

15–16 In this the final scene God is active and Cain passive. The LORD reaffirms the sentence on Cain to a wandering existence away from Eden, but Cain is reassured that he will be protected from blood vengeance himself. Indeed, a premature death would cut short his sentence, so it is hardly right to see these verses as a lightening of it (Jacob, and Golka, *C. Westermann FS*, 58–73 are to be followed here).

"Whoever kills Cain shall be punished sevenfold." For this type of case-law construction, cf. Exod 22:18 [19] (cf. also 21:12, 15–17; G. J. Wenham, "Legal Forms in the Book of the Covenant," *TB* 22 [1971] 95–102). The root "punish," נקם, may be used for retaliatory killing (e.g., Exod 21:20–21).

"Sevenfold." This could mean that Cain's killer and six of his relatives will die, but this seems unlikely with God as its agent. Another suggestion first made in *Tg. Onq.* (and taken up by Rashi, Ibn Ezra) is that it means to the seventh generation from Adam (i.e., Lamek; cf. v 24) or the seventh from Cain, i.e., Tubal-Cain and the flood (Jacob, hesitantly). Most probably it is a poetic turn of speech meaning full divine retribution; cf. Ps 12:7[6]; 79:12; Prov 6:31. Seven is of course a sacred number frequently used in OT rituals.

"The LORD placed a sign for Cain." The nature of Cain's sign or mark has been the subject of endless inconclusive speculation (cf. Westermann's excursus, 1:312–14, and R. Mellinkoff, *The Mark of Cain*). Signs (cf. F. J. Helfmeyer, *TDOT* 1:167–88) are typically given to men to assure them of God's goodwill toward them and take a variety of forms (e.g., rainbow, circumcision, a fulfilled prophecy or miracle: 9:12; 17:11; Exod 3:12; Isa 7:11), so various suggestions have been made along these lines to identify the sign given to Cain. In this case the sign deters would-be attackers, and this has led the majority of writers to conclude that the mark of Cain must be something about him that shows he has divine protection, e.g., a tattoo, special hairstyle, or the like. *Ber Rab.* 22:12 ingeniously combines both ideas of the meaning of "sign" by suggesting that the sign for Cain was a dog which accompanied him on his wanderings: the dog served to reassure Cain of God's protection and scared off any assailants! But for this idea there is as little proof as for any of the other suggestions. The simplest suggestion is that of P. A. H. de Boer (*NedTT* 31 [1942] 210) that the sign for Cain is simply his name (*qayin*), which sounds somewhat like *yuqqam* "shall be punished"; cf. *Notes* on v 1. His very name hints at the promise of divine retribution on his attackers. It could be objected that quite a different explanation of the name Cain has already been given at his birth, but renaming or reinterpreting an existing name is a regular feature of Hebrew narrative (17:5, 15). Nevertheless, the text here gives barely a hint that this was the writer's intention. So the precise nature of the sign remains uncertain, but its function is clear. As the clothing given to Adam and Eve after the fall (3:21) served to remind them of their sin and God's mercy, so does the mark placed on Cain: "As a protective device against potential enemies it may stay death; in that sense, the anticipated punishment is softened. But at the same time it serves as a constant reminder of Cain's banishment, his isolation from other people" (Coats, 65).

16 The story that began with the attempt by Cain and Abel to draw near to God through sacrifice ends in Cain's "leaving the LORD's presence" and living "east of Eden," presumably even farther from the garden of "delight" from which his parents had been expelled. Like the account of the fall (chap. 3), this story concludes by underlining the truth that sin separates man from God and that God's judgments are carried out. Cain lives in a land whose very name (נוד *nod* means "wandering") reminds him of the divine sentence that he would become a "wandering vagrant." It is uncertain where the Hebrews located this land, but that is immaterial to the story and its interpretation.

17–24 Here the genealogical structure of the account becomes apparent again. V 17 could have immediately followed v 2 had not the long digression about Abel's murder been included at this point. Vv 17–24 include several brief comments on the vocations of Cain's descendants (e.g., 17b, 20b, 21, 22), but the only lengthy digression is the song of Lamek (23–24) in which he shows that he has all the violent traits of his forefather Cain. It may be noted that these comments cluster around Enoch and Lamek, the only two men in this genealogy whose names reappear in the genealogy of Adam via Seth. Apparently to make sure that the two Enochs and the two Lameks are not confused, both genealogies give more detail about these individuals than the others in these lists. For the most part, the other antediluvians remain simply names. The general similarity of style with the rest of chap. 4 persuades most commentators that J is again responsible for editing this section. But whereas no good parallels to the Cain and Abel story are known, this list of antediluvian heroes who founded the arts of human civilization, city-building, herding, metal-working, music, etc., does have counterparts in other ancient oriental tradition. Parallels with the Sumerian flood story have already been mentioned under Form/Structure/Setting. Mesopotamian sources make occasional mention of seven *apkallus* who lived before the flood. The older texts are not explicit about the precise skills of these *apkallus*, but the oldest *apkallu* was called Adapa and is associated with Eridu, generally regarded in Mesopotamian tradition as the first city to be founded. The later writer Berossus claims that this first sage, Oannes (Adapa), rose from the sea and taught man the arts of writing, agriculture, and city-building. He was followed by six others who also rose from the sea. Phoenician tradition preserved by Philo of Byblos also knew of a number of gods or supermen who brought to earth various technical and magical skills. (See R. R. Wilson, *Genealogy and History,* 149–58;, also works by E. Reiner, R. Borger, J. J. Finkelstein, H. W. Attridge, and R. A. Oden in bibliographies.)

The parallels between Gen 4:17–26 and extrabiblical traditions are not close enough to suggest direct borrowing by Genesis from the extant sources. It is possible, though, that the biblical writer knew these old ideas and wanted to comment on them: he held that technology was a human achievement, not the gift of the gods (so Cassuto). Indeed, by linking urbanization and nomadism, music and metalworking to the genealogy of Cain, he seems to be suggesting that all aspects of human culture are in some way tainted by Cain's sin: "By virtue of being Cain's descendants, the people named in the genealogy all inherit his curse. Thus the Cainite genealogy becomes part of the Yahwist's account of man's increasing sin" (Wilson, *Genealogy and History*, 155).

17 "Then Cain knew his wife. She conceived and gave birth to Enoch." Note the closely parallel phraseology in 4:1, 25. "Enoch": three others bear this name in the OT—a son of Yered (5:18–24), a son of Midian (25:4), and Reuben's eldest son (46:9). Interestingly, Reuben was Jacob's eldest son, just as Cain was Adam's; thus both Adam's and Jacob's eldest grandsons were called Enoch. Etymologically, Enoch may come from the root חנך "to train," or "to dedicate." Relying on the first meaning of the root Noth (*Die israelitischen Personnamen*, 228) translates Enoch "learned, clever," but the context suggests the alternative "dedication": Enoch is the dedicator of cities.

"Was building a city." On the unusual Hebrew punctuation of "building" see *Notes*. The major problem posed by this verse is the identity of the builder: is it Cain or Enoch? The former is usually supposed because of the final word in the verse, "after his son's name, Enoch." However, the supposition that Cain built the first city comes, strangely, after his condemnation to a wandering life in the immediately preceding verses. And were it not for the mention of Enoch at the end of v 17, the subject of "he was building a city" would naturally be Enoch as elsewhere in this chap (vv 2, 21). For this reason, various emendations have been proposed to smooth the text. Following Budde, Procksch and Westermann suggest that the verse be translated "He (i.e., Enoch) became a builder of a city and he called the name of the city after his own name [reading שְׁמוֹ (his name) for שֵׁם בְּנוֹ (his son's name)] Enoch." This allows a progression in the genealogy from Cain, the first farmer, to Enoch, the first city-builder. Enoch is again made the builder by Cassuto's suggestion (followed by Wilson *Genealogy and History* 139–40, and Sasson, *ZAW* 90 [1978] 174), which holds that the final word "Enoch" is a misplaced gloss. The sentence then reads, "He was building a city and he called the city after his son's name" (i.e., Enoch called the city Irad [cf. v 18], not Enoch). It is pointed out that this understanding gives a double play on words between "building," בֹּנֶה, and "his son," בְּנוֹ, and between "city," עִיר, and "Irad," עִירָד. Furthermore, the name of this city sounds very like "Eridu," which Mesopotamian tradition held to be the oldest city in the world. Why "Enoch" should have been added remains unclear. It may have been the error of a copyist, who possibly intended "Enoch" to be the subject of the verb "he called," though it is quite unusual for a subject to be so far from the verb.

18 "To Enoch was born Irad." The meaning of the name "Irad" is quite uncertain. On the basis of Arabic cognates it has been suggested it means "bird," "wild ass," "strength," or "reed hut." It has been identified with the place names "Arad" and "Eridu." But its origin may be pre-Semitic (cf. J. Gabriel, "Die Cainitengenealogie," *Bib* 40 [1959] 409–27, on this whole section).

"Mehuya'el/Mehiyael." Two alternative spellings of the same word (cf. "Peniel/Penuel," 32:31–32 [30–31]) and again of uncertain meaning. Suggestions include "blotted out by God"; "God gives life"; "priest of God."

"Methushael." Here the majority of modern commentators suggest the name means "man [*mutu*] of [*ša*] God [*ilu*]," but it may be based on *mutu* ("man") *š'l* ("to ask" or "Sheol"), hence "man of the underworld," "man of desire," or even "man of prayer."

"Lamek." Like "Abel" for *hebel*, "Lamek" is the pausal form of *"Lemek,"* but unlike "Abel," not certainly of Hebrew derivation. It may be connected with Sumerian *lumga*, a title of Ea, as patron deity of song and music, but this is very doubtful. Other suggestions based on Arabic include "strong youth" or "oppressor." Lamek, as the seventh from Adam, occupies a significant place in the genealogy, so more details of his life are noted about him than about his immediate ancestors (Sasson, *ZAW* 90 [1978] 171–85). His violent life-style strongly recalls that of his forefather Cain.

19–22 Segmentation of a family tree into three male lines at the end of a period is attested elsewhere in Genesis, e.g., Noah's sons in 5:32, Terah's in 11:26. Polygamy too is frequent among the patriarchs (e.g., Abraham, Esau, Jacob). So, as with Cain and Abel, this story has a number of features typical of later narratives. It may therefore be wrong to argue that because the first polygamist in Scripture was an unsavory character, Genesis is thereby condemning the practice of polygamy itself. It is more concerned with illustrating how all human activity, including marriage, is affected by sin. Nevertheless, the fact that Gen 2 pictures the ideal relationship between man and woman may suggest that the author regards monogamy as the norm and that Lamek's bigamy reflects one aspect of his decline from the creator's pattern for human life.

19 "Adah." The name probably means "ornament," or "pretty." It is also the name of one of Esau's wives (36:2).

"Zillah." Usually interpreted as "shadow," perhaps alluding to the relief given by shade in a hot climate (צל "shadow, protection"). Cassuto and Westermann prefer to derive the name from צלצל "to tinkle" and see in the name "an allusion to the sweetness of the human voice." If this be correct, the names of the two women form an excellent parallel, pointing to the two charming feminine attributes mentioned in Cant 2:14: "a sweet voice and a pretty face" (Cassuto, 1:234). "Probably the holy author wanted to show Lamek as a person who had succumbed to sensuality" (Gabriel, *Bib* 40 [1959] 417).

20–22 The names of Lamek's children—Yabal, Yubal, and Tubal-Cain— all appear to be derived from the same Hebrew word, יָבֻל "produce," presumably alluding to their inventiveness. However, the precise difference between the different names is obscure. Jacob thinks that they may also be intended as echoes of Abel (הבל). Cassuto observes that each of their professions or names apparently alludes paronomastically to their forefather Cain (קין): Yabal is connected with cattle (מקנה); Yubal is linked with music, and laments (קינות) are often mentioned in the OT; finally, Tubal-Cain incorporates Cain's name in his.

Giving two children in a family similar-sounding names is well attested in the OT, e.g., Medan/Midian, 25:2; Ephah/Epher, 25:4; Ishvah/Ishvi, 46:17; Oholah/Oholibah, Ezek 23:4.

20 "Yabal . . . became father of those who live in tents with herds." On the construction see *Notes*. Yabal is thus the father of the Bedouin lifestyle. He did not merely reestablish Abel's pastoral work. Abel shepherded צאן "sheep and goats," but Yabal tended מקנה "herds": that term covers all animals that are herded—sheep, goats, cattle, asses, or camels (47:16–17; Exod 9:3). Whereas Abel merely lived off his flocks, Yabal could trade with his beasts of burden, and this represents cultural advance (cf. Gabriel, *Bib* 40 [1959] 422).

Philo of Byblos states that Amynos and Magos were the first to live in villages and rear sheep (Eusebius, *Praeparatio Evangelii,* 1.10.13; Attridge and Oden, *Philo of Byblos,* 45).

21 "Yubal . . . father of all who play the lyre and pipe," i.e., the first musician. His very name "Yubal" sounds like *yôbēl* (יוֹבֵל) the ram's horn blown to mark the year of Jubilee and other great religious occasions (Exod 19:13; Lev 25:9–10; Jos 6:5; Gabriel, *Bib* 40 [1959] 417). The lyre and pipe are "the oldest and simplest musical instruments" (Skinner, 119). The lyre כנור was a stringed instrument played with the hand (1 Sam 16:23) and was used for both sacred and secular music. The pipe עוגב is mentioned more rarely, usually in parallel with lyres (Job 21:12; 30:31), and seems to have been a reed or Pan's pipe. Westermann's assertion that it was never used in worship is contradicted by Ps 150:4. For illustrations see E. Werner, "Musical Instruments," *IDB* 3:469–76; "Music and Musical Instruments," *IBD* 1031–40. The brotherhood of Yabal and Yubal may suggest an association of music with nomadism similar to that attested in classical mythology, where the shepherd god Pan invented the pipe.

22 "Tubal-Cain, father of all who sharpen copper and iron." On the difficult textual problem see the notes.

"Tubal-Cain." The double-barreled name has led to the suspicion that Cain is a gloss (e.g., Procksch). But it is unnecessary to eliminate "Cain" here; the name probably means "smith" (cf. *Comment,* v 1) and anticipates the more explicit remarks about his metalworking skill that follow. Cain could have been added to Tubal's name to distinguish him from the other Tubal, son of Japhet, mentioned in various places (10:2; 1 Chr 1:5; Isa 66:19; Ezek 27:13, etc.).

"Tubal." The name, probably from the same root יבל as that of his half-brothers Yabal and Yubal, is of uncertain meaning.

לטש "sharpen" is used only here and in 1 Sam 13:20; Ps 7:13 [12]; 52:4 [2]; Job 16:9. "Copper and iron": נחשת covers both copper and its alloys, such as bronze. Since copper was the first metal to be worked, from about the fourth millennium B.C., it is appropriately mentioned before iron, first smelted in the second millennium. The mention of ironworking so early in history would be anachronistic, so it has been suggested that the cold forging of meteoric iron, which was practiced very early, is meant (cf. *NBD*, 825, 1302). However, this is hardly the most natural rendering of "sharpen." Rather Westermann seems right that the intention of the passage is simply to note the origin of metalworking in general, not to date the introduction of particular metals. Philo Byblius notes that two brothers discovered iron and how to process it (Eusebius, *Preparatio Evangelii*, 1.10.11).

"Naamah": "pleasant." This is also the name of Rehoboam's mother (1 Kgs 14:21). Why she should be picked out for special mention remains obscure. Some Jewish traditions associate her with singing and identify her as Noah's wife (cf. Cassuto). Wilson (*History and Genealogy*, 144) suggests the narrator simply wished to offer a balanced genealogy by noting that both Lamek's wives had two children.

23–24 The song of Lamek. Along with the invention of music (v 21) went the composition of poetry. This is a superb example of an early Hebrew poem using a variety of literary devices to maximum effect. Note the parallelism: "Adah and Zillah" // "wives of Lamek"; "Hear my voice" // "Attend to my words" (cf. Isa 28:23; 32:9; Ps 17:6); "a man" // "a youth"; "bruising me" // "hitting me" (Exod 21:25, Isa 1:6); "sevenfold" // "seventy-sevenfold." Rhyme is unusually prominent: many words end with or include the vowel *î*, "my, me," emphasizing Lamek's cruel egotism. Metrically, there are three bicola: 4:4 in 23a, 3(4):2 in 23b; and 3:3 in 24. Counting syllables of the MT gives 10:10/8:8/9:8. D. K. Stuart's reconstruction of the archaic pronunciation gives 9:9/7:7/7:7 (*Studies in Early Hebrew Poetry*, 97). But its disciplined form only accentuates the barbarity of the message: Lamek is even more depraved than his forefather Cain.

23 Though his words "I have killed . . ." are usually understood as a boast about what he has done, Westermann, relying on a supposed original nomadic setting, argues that this is a threat: "I should kill a man.   . ." In its present context, however, illustrating the character of Lamek, it seems more likely that it is meant as a boast. "I have killed a man for bruising me, a youth for hitting me" should probably be taken as two ways of describing the same incident rather than as two separate incidents. "Youth" (ילד), usually translated "child," in fact covers a person up to about forty years of age (1 Kgs 12:8, 10; cf. 1 Kgs 14:21; Dan 1:4) as opposed to old men whose strength has declined.

24 "Truly Cain will be avenged sevenfold, but Lamek seventy-sevenfold." It is unusual in poetry to have two consecutive clauses introduced by כי, "Truly." Westermann therefore suggests that this line represents J's expansion of the original song and serves to connect it not simply with the genealogy but with the Cain and Abel story (cf. 4:15). As this line scans easily, it may be too hasty to conclude that the author could not have found it in his source. Certainly it rounds off the Cainite genealogy dramatically and effectively. If Adah and Zillah watched with pride as their sons developed husbandry, music, and metalworking, they listened with horror to their husband's violent blood lust. Lamek's seventy-sevenfold vengeance stands in contrast with the law of talion which limits retaliation to exact equivalence (Exod 21:25 "bruise for bruise," "hit for hit" echoes the terminology of Gen 4:23 exactly). By placing this comment at the end of the story of Cain, the editor suggests that all his descendants are under judgment and hints at the disaster to come.

25–26 These verses provide a smooth transition between the history of Cain's family and the genealogy of Seth that follows. For the third time we hear of Adam (or Cain) knowing his wife and of her giving birth to a son and naming him (cf. 4:1, 17). Once again we are reminded that Cain killed Abel. But these verses also pave the way for chap. 5. Here for the first time אָדָם "Adam" appears alone without being preceded by the definite article or a preposition. This is why it is here taken as a proper name and not generically as "(the) man." This anarthrous use anticipates 5:1–6 which speaks of Adam, not "man." And it is also quite characteristic of one section in Genesis to introduce the subject matter of the following section (cf. 6:5–8 introducing Noah and the flood story). Here 4:25–26 anticipates 5:1–6:8.

To appreciate the precise force of these remarks about Seth's birth (vv 25–26) they must be compared with what is said about the two earlier births and their aftermath (vv 1–16, 17–24). Compared with these two gloomy tales, this brief introduction to the line of Seth offers two rays of hope: the explanation of Seth's name and men calling on the name of the LORD.

25 "She called his name Seth." Though Eve's explanation of Seth's name suggests it is derived from the verb שִׁית "to place, put" there may be no etymological connection, simply paronomasia (so A. Strus, *Nomen-Omen*, 66); cf. the explanation of Cain's name, 4:1. But many commentators have accepted a derivation from "to place" and suggest Seth means "substitute." There is certainly no connection between Seth and the tribe of Shut mentioned in Num 24:17.

"Because God has set me other offspring." This attempt to bring out Eve's pun on Seth's name obscures the allusion to 3:15, which states, "I shall put [set] hostility between your *offspring* and her *offspring*." Furthermore, Eve's comment contrasts with her remark in 4:1: "I have gained a man with the LORD's help." Is there significance in her substituting "offspring" for "man" and "God" for "LORD"? Jacob and Cassuto see Eve as less proud and triumphant at the birth of Seth than at that of Cain. Gispen suggests that by speaking of God rather than Yahweh, Eve is celebrating God's creative power: her earlier remark tended to show her on intimate terms with the LORD. Cassuto suggests that Eve is mourning the fate of her first two sons and therefore sees God as the remote and distant creator rather than as the LORD, a name affirming his intimacy with man. The word "offspring" rather than "man" may suggest she hoped for a line of children from Seth such as the rest of Genesis describes.

"Instead of Abel, because Cain killed him." Jacob (151) says: "She can as little forget the murdered as the murderer, for both were her children and in one sentence she mentions the name of all three sons."

26 "He called his name Enosh." For the first time the father rather than the mother names the child (cf. 4:1, 25). "Enosh," like "Adam," can be used either as a proper name (as here and in 5:6–12) or just as a word for "man." It occurs 42 times with the meaning "man," only in poetic texts, whereas אָדָם "man" appears 554 times. Often it suggests man's weakness, mortality, and distance from God (e.g., Ps 103:15; 33:12, 26). But it may also be used in quite a general neutral sense (e.g., Ps 104:15; Job 28:13), and it is hard to distinguish any semantic difference between אָדָם and אֱנוֹשׁ (cf. F. Maas, *TDOT* 1:345–48; C. Westermann, *THWAT* 1:41–57).

"At that time people began to call on the name of the LORD." Reviewing the variety of interpretations which this simple statement has spawned,

S. Sandmel said that his article might be called "a history of reading difficulties into a text" ("Genesis 4:26b," *HUCA* 32 [1961] 19[–29]). Early Jewish exegetes understood הוחל "began" to have its other common meaning, "polluted," and therefore held that this sentence was referring to the introduction of idolatry. But this is unlikely, given the succeeding phrase "on the name of the LORD." "To call on the name of the LORD" is used elsewhere in Genesis of the patriarchs 12:8; 13:4; 21:33; 26:25, and it seems to be an umbrella phrase for worship, most obviously prayer and sacrifice. On this view Gen 4:26 is noting the origin of regular divine worship, just as the preceding verses have noted the origins of farming, music, and metallurgy. Though Cain and Abel offered sacrifice, this verse notes its reintroduction on a regular basis (cf. the other reintroductions in 9:20; 10:8). Many commentators have attached special significance to the mention of the LORD here: they interpret it to mean "This was the first time men began to address God in prayer as the LORD." It is said that whereas E (Exod 3:14–15) and P (Exod 6:3) date the introduction of the name "Yahweh" to the time of Moses, here J brings it back to primeval times. However, this view is not tenable for the following reasons: First, J has already allowed Eve to mention Yahweh's name in 4:1 in a prayerlike exclamation, so J can hardly be supposed to be laying stress on the newness of the name in Enosh's time. Second, as Westermann points out, such an interpretation puts the historical remarks in Exodus on a par with the stories in Gen 1–11. These stories are concerned with universal human institutions and experiences, not with a particular event in the history of Israel. It makes better sense to take this remark as a comment on the fact that all nations worship, not as a comment on the name under which they worship God. Third, it is dubious whether even in the patriarchal narratives the phrase "call on the name of the LORD" means that they were worshiping him as Yahweh. A careful reading of Gen 12–50 suggests that the narrators do not imply that the name "Yahweh" was known before Moses (see G. J. Wenham, in *Essays on the Patriarchal Narratives,* 157–88). With Delitzsch, König, and Westermann it seems wisest to regard this verse as simply noting the beginning of public worship, a conclusion that receives further support from the Sumerian flood story, which mentions the building of the first cities and the establishment of worship in the pre-flood era. "He regularly performed to perfection the august divine services and offices" (line 90).

Explanation

Gen 4 concludes the story of mankind that was cut off in the flood, a tale that opened with Gen 2:4, "This is the history. . . ." With the aid of a genealogy from Adam to Lamek, the seventh generation, it traces the development of technology and arts on the one hand and the growth of violence on the other. Only in the last two verses introducing the descendants of Seth do we have glimmers of hope, for from him, as chap. 5 will describe, descended Noah, the survivor of the flood, and it was in Enosh's day that the public worship of God was reintroduced. "At that time people began to call on the name of the LORD."

The genealogical framework of this chapter as well as the introductory formula in 2:4 which covers 2:4–4:26 shows that the editor considers his account protohistorical: he is describing real individuals from the primeval past whose actions are significant for all mankind. Yet he makes it just as plain by his long digressions about Cain and Lamek that his stories are paradigmatic. Like those in Gen 3, they describe patterns of behavior into which every man is likely to lapse, and they stand as warnings to all who are tempted to disregard God's laws.

The paradigmatic character of these stories is most clear in the account of Cain and Abel. In structure and phraseology there are many close parallels with the story of the fall. Just as Gen 3 describes how sin disrupts the relationships between man and wife, God and man, Gen 4:2–16 explains how sin introduces hate between brothers and separation from God. Yet there is also progression between the stories: Cain is portrayed as a much more hardened sinner than his father. Adam merely ate a fruit given him by his wife; Cain murdered his brother. Cain rejects the divine entreaty and then grumbles about his sentence. And this pattern is repeated with Lamek, who arrogantly asserts, "Cain will be avenged sevenfold, but Lamek seventy-sevenfold."

In similar fashion to Gen 2–3, Gen 4 expresses through narrative principles that are of fundamental importance in biblical law. The description of the garden of Eden evokes the imagery of the tabernacle and suggests that fullness of life is to be found only in the presence of God. Similarly, the acceptance of Abel's sacrifice in contrast to the rejection of Cain's is not just an illustration of the election of the younger brother, but emphasizes that only those who offer the best in their sacrifices are acceptable to God. A cardinal demand of the law is that sacrificial animals must be unblemished, a principle reaffirmed by prophets such as Malachi, 1:6–14. The blood of Abel crying to God introduces a theme that reappears frequently in story, law, psalms, and prophecy. God cares about the death of the innocent: their blood pollutes the holy land (6:11–12; 18:20; 1 Kgs 21; Exod 20:13; Num 35:9–34; Ps 37; Isa 5:7; Luke 18:7–8; Rev 6:9–10).

Again the unbridled vengeance of Lamek stands in ferocious contrast to the strict justice of the law of talion. Where Lamek claimed to have killed a man for bruising him and a youth for hitting him, Exod 21:20–25 says "eye for eye . . . bruise for bruise, hit for hit." Without the protection of the law, Gen 4 implies, even the able-bodied, let alone the weak, will be at the mercy of men like Lamek.

Finally, within the OT perspective it is interesting that "calling on the name of the LORD" is linked to the line of Seth. For from Seth descended Noah, and from him ultimately the patriarchs, who are several times said to have called on the name of the LORD (12:8; 13:4; 21:33; 26:25).

The NT makes less use of these narratives in Gen 4 than of the preceding ones. It interprets them in a quite straightforward fashion, seeing in them real characters whose examples should still guide Christian conduct. Abel is the first martyr for righteousness' sake (Matt 23:35; cf. 5:10–12). His sacrifice was more acceptable than Cain's because it was offered in faith, a quality he shared with the other saints of the old covenant (Heb 10:4). His blood pleaded for vengeance, but the sprinkled blood of Jesus "speaks more graciously than the blood of Abel" (Heb 12:24). If Abel should be a model for believers,

Cain's behavior must be avoided (Jude 11). 1 John 3:11–15 brings both themes together. "This is the message which you have heard from the beginning, that we should love one another, and not be like Cain who was of the evil one and murdered his brother. And why did he murder him? Because his own deeds were evil and his brother's righteous. Do not wonder, brethren, that the world hates you. . . . Anyone who hates his brother is a murderer, and you know that no murderer has eternal life abiding in him."

Adam's Family Tree (5:1–32)

Bibliography

(See also the Main Bibliography and the Gen 1–11 bibliography.)

Barnouin, M. "Recherches numériques sur la généalogie de Gen 5." *RB* 77 (1970) 347–65. **Borger, R.** "Die Beschwörungsserie *Bît Mēseri* und die Himmelfahrt Henochs." *JNES* 33 (1974) 183–96. **Bryan, D. T.** "A Reevaluation of Gen 4 and 5 in the Light of Recent Studies in Genealogical Fluidity." *ZAW*, forthcoming. **Egerton, F. N.** "The Longevity of the Patriarchs: A Topic in the History of Demography." *Journal of the History of Ideas* 27 (1966) 575–84. **Fraenkel, D.** "Die Überlieferung der Genealogien Gen 5:3–28 und Gen 11:10–26 in den 'Antiquitates Iudaicae' des Flavius Josephus." In *De Septuaginta: Studies in Honour of J. W. Wevers*, ed. A. Pietersma and C. Cox. Mississauga: Benben Publications, 1984. 175–200. **Green, W. H.** "Primeval Chronology." *BSac* 47 (1890) 285–303. **Hartman, T. C.** "Some Thoughts on the Sumerian King List and Gen 5 and 11B." *JBL* 91 (1972) 25–32. **Hasel, G. F.** "The Genealogies of Gen 5 and 11 and Their Alleged Babylonian Background." *AUSS* 16 (1978) 361–74. **Klein, R. W.** "Archaic Chronologies and the Textual History of the Old Testament." *HTR* 67 (1974) 255–63. **Luke, K.** "The Genealogies in Gen 5." *IndTS* 18 (1981) 223–44. **Malamat, A.** "King Lists of the Old Babylonian Period and Biblical Genealogies." *JAOS* 88 (1968) 163–73. ———. "Tribal Societies: Biblical Genealogies and African Lineage Systems." *Archives européennes de Sociologie* 14 (1973) 126–36. ———. "Longevity: Biblical Concepts and Some Ancient Near Eastern Parallels." *AfO* Beiheft 19 (1982) 215–224. **Naor, M.** "Sons of Seth and Sons of Cain." (Heb.) *BMik* 18 (1972–73) 198–204. **Savasta, C.** "L'Età dei Patriarchi Biblici in un recente Commento à Gen 1–11." *RivB* 19 (1971) 321–25. **Schmitt, A.** "Die Angaben über Henoch: Gen 5:21–24 in der LXX." *Forschung zur Bibel* 1 (1972) 161–69. ———. "Entrückung-Aufnahme-Himmelfahrt: Untersuchung zu einem Vorstellungsbereich im AT." *Forschung zur Bibel* 10 (1973) 152–193. ———. "Zum Thema Entrückung im AT." *BZ* 26 (1982) 34–49. **Walton, J.** "The Antediluvian Section of the Sumerian King List and Gen 5." *BA* 44 (1981) 207–8. **Wilson, R. R.** "The Old Testament Genealogies in Recent Research." *JBL* 94 (1975) 169–89. **Zachmann, L.** "Beobachtungen zur Theologie in Gen 5." *ZAW* 88 (1976) 272–74.

Translation

[1] *This[a] is the book of the family history of Adam.[a] On the day God created[b] Adam, [c]in the likeness of God he made him.[c]* [2a]*Male and female he created them.[a] Then he blessed them and called their name Adam[b] on the day they were created.[c]* [3]*Adam lived[a] 130[b] years and then fathered[c] a child[d] in[e] his own likeness and according[e] to his image, and he called his name Seth.* [4]*Adam's years after he had fathered[a] Seth came to 800,[b] fathering sons and daughters.* [5]*Adam's whole life which he lived[a] lasted 930 years; then he died.[b]*

[6]*Seth lived 105 years, and then fathered Enosh.* [7]*Seth lived 807 years after he had fathered Enosh fathering sons and daughters.* [8]*Seth's whole life lasted 912 years; then he died.*

[9]*Enosh lived 90 years, and then fathered Qenan.* [10]*Enosh lived 815 years after he had fathered Qenan fathering sons and daughters.* [11]*Enosh's whole life lasted 905 years; then he died.*

¹²*Qenan lived 70 years, and then fathered Mahalalel.*ᵃ ¹³*Qenan lived 840 years after he had fathered Mahalalel fathering sons and daughters.* ¹⁴*Qenan's whole life lasted 910 years; then he died.*

¹⁵*Mahalalel lived 65 years and then fathered Yared.*ᵃ ¹⁶*Mahalalel lived 830 years after he had fathered Yared fathering sons and daughters.* ¹⁷*Mahalalel's whole life lasted 895 years and then he died.*

¹⁸*Yared lived 162 years and then fathered Enoch.* ¹⁹*Yared lived 800 years after he had fathered Enoch fathering sons and daughters.* ²⁰*Yared's whole life lasted 962 years; then he died.*

²¹*Enoch lived 65 years and then fathered Methuselah.* ²²*Enoch walked*ᵃ *with God*ᵇ *for 300 years after he had fathered Methuselah fathering sons and daughters.* ²³*Enoch's whole life lasted*ᵃ *365 years.* ²⁴*Then Enoch walked with God and was not,*ᵃ *because God took him.*

²⁵*Methuselah lived 187 years and fathered Lamek.* ²⁶*Methuselah lived 782 years after he had fathered Lamek fathering sons and daughters.* ²⁷*Methuselah's whole life lasted 969 years; then he died.*

²⁸*Lamek lived 182 years and fathered a son.*

²⁹*He called his name Noah, commenting, "May this one bring*ᵃ *us relief from our work and from the pain of our hands because of*ᵇ *the land which the* LORD *has cursed."*ᶜ ³⁰*Lamek lived 595 years after he had fathered Noah fathering sons and daughters.* ³¹*Lamek's whole life lasted*ᵃ *777 years; then he died.*

³²*Noah was 500 years old, and he fathered Shem, Ham, and Japhet.*

Notes

1.a-a. The title to the section is in apposition to following clauses: *SBH*, 54.

1.b. Inf constr of ברא, lit., "in day of God creating Adam."

1.c-c. Clause in apposition to and explaining previous one: *SBH*, 55.

2.a-a. Apposition clause to preceding. For similar construction to 5:1–2, cf. 1:27.

2.b. Or "man"; cf. *Comment* on v 2.

2.c. Cf. n. 2:4b.

3.a. Waw consec + 3 masc sg impf (apoc) חיה.

3.b. G 230. On the recurrent textual variants in the ages of the patriarchs see *Excursus*.

3.c. Waw consec + 3 masc sg impf hiph ילד.

3.d. "A child" is not in the text: *BHS* suggests that בן "son" has been omitted. But MT may be retained. "The usage is absolute, since an immediate object would have been stylistically awkward; the implied object is ילד child" (Speiser, 40).

3.e. Some MSS reverse the prepositions ב and כ assimilating to 1:26. The present reading may be retained.

4.a. Inf constr hiph ילד + 3 masc sg suffix.

4.b. G 700. Note that G, SamPent and MT differ frequently on the ages of the antediluvians. For a discussion of the textual problems, see *Excursus*.

5.a. חי "he lived": 3 masc sg pf חיה.

5.b. Waw consec + 3 masc sg impf (pausal) מות.

12.a. G Μαλελεήλ, also in vv 13–17.

15.a. Yared is pausal form of Yered, the normal form of the name found in vv 16–20. Cf. Lamek, pausal form of Lemek.

22.a. Waw consec + 3 masc sg impf hithp הלך; cf. 3:8.

22.b. Some MSS of G, Vg add "and Enoch lived," assimilating to standard formulation of the chapter. Retain MT.

23.a. MT here has sg ויהי "and it was" instead of pl ויהיו "and they were" found elsewhere in the chapter, vv 5, 8, 11, etc. SamPent also has pl and may be followed, though MT is not grammatically impossible (GKC, 145q, 146c).

24.a. אין "there is not" + 3 masc sg suffix; cf. 42:13, 36.

29.a. 3 masc sg impf piel נחם + 1 pl suffix.
29.b. מ "from" or "because of" (BDB, 579–80).
29.c. 3 masc sg pf piel ארר + 3 fem sg suffix.
31.a. SamPent ויהיו "and they were"; cf. 23a.

Form/Structure/Setting

The introductory formula "This is the book of the family history of Adam" (5:1; cf. 2:4; 6:9; 10:1; etc.) indicates that a new section of Genesis begins here. Many commentators assume that it concludes with 5:32. But Cassuto is correct to maintain that since the next introductory formula "This is the family history of Noah" does not occur till 6:9, the section must end at 6:8. Other considerations support this conclusion. First, 5:32 is an inappropriate point to end a section, in view of the fact that every preceding paragraph has gone on to tell how much longer the patriarch lived. It just leaves the story hanging, whereas 6:8, "Noah found favor in the eyes of the LORD," makes a better ending to a section. Second, if the whole section runs from 5:1 to 6:8, certain key words occur a significant number of times, i.e., multiples of 7 or 6 (cf. *Form/Structure/Setting* on 4:1–26). "Adam/the man" occurs in total 14 times, 7 times with the article, 7 times without. "God" occurs 14 times. "Make" and "create" together total 7 times; "the LORD," 6 times; "sons," 12 times; "daughters," 12 times; the root ילד "to bear" or "to father," 30 times. Finally, in its present form 5:1–3 provides a retrospective summary of the preceding section, 2:4–4:26, while 6:5–8 acts as a prospective trailer for the flood story 6:9–9:29. This pattern of retrospect–new material–prospect is characteristic of the organization of the sections in Genesis as defined by the introductory phrase "This is the family history of. . . ."

Within this long section the material is quite diverse:

5:1–32—Genealogy of Adam to Noah
6:1–4 —The angel marriages
6:5–8 —God's plan to destroy mankind except for Noah.

Because 6:1–8 is so different from what precedes it, we shall postpone further discussion of it until we have completed commenting on chap. 5.

5:1–32 falls into ten paragraphs:

5:1–5	Adam	5:18–20	Yared
5:6–8	Seth	5:21–24	Enoch
5:9–11	Enosh	5:25–27	Methuselah
5:12–14	Qenan	5:28–31	Lamek
5:15–17	Mahalalel	5:32	Noah

Most paragraphs follow exactly the same form:

a) A lived x years, and then fathered B.
b) A lived y years after he had fathered B, fathering sons and daughters.
c) A's whole life lasted x + y years; then he died.

Exactly the same formulae are used in the genealogy of Shem in 11:10–26, but (c), the third element, summing up the patriarch's life, is omitted there.

In chap. 5 there is a slight deviation from this standard pattern in the case of four of the patriarchs.

Adam (vv 3–5) is prefaced by a summary of the creation of man (vv 1–2). And v 3b instead of saying "and then fathered Seth" states "and then fathered a child in his own image and according to his likeness, and he called his name Seth." 5a adds "which he lived" after "Adam's whole life."

Enoch, the seventh in the list (vv 21–24) is described as "walking with God" and "being taken" instead of "living" and "dying" (vv 22, 24).

The pattern for Lamek, the ninth in line, also deviates slightly from the norm by including his hopes about his son Noah in v 29. Instead of simply saying "and fathered Noah," vv 28b–29 continue "and fathered a son. He called his name Noah, commenting, 'May this one bring us relief from our work . . . which the LORD has cursed.'"

Finally, the comment on Noah (v 32) starts slightly differently: "Noah was 500 years old" instead of "Noah lived 500 years." Then it mentions the birth of three sons instead of the usual one, and the formula is not completed till 9:29, which reads "Noah's whole life lasted 950 years; then he died."

The distinctive style of this genealogy has led most commentators to suppose that chap. 5 has a source different from the material immediately preceding and following it. This conclusion is endorsed by Y. Radday's statistical tests (*Genesis: An Authorship Study*, 185–86). Furthermore, the heading "This is the book of the family history" tends to support the idea that a literary document is being quoted, for it is only here that *a book* is mentioned. Elsewhere the phrase is always "This is the family history of . . . ." So von Rad and Cross (*Canaanite Myth and Hebrew Epic*, 302) argue that there was a *Toledot* book from which P drew all his genealogical material. Other commentators (e.g., Gunkel, Westermann, and S. Tengström, *Die Toledotformel*, 71) hold that ספר should not be translated "book" but "record, account," without the implication that a written source is being quoted. However, this is not the natural way to understand ספר: elsewhere it always seems to refer to an independent written document. Nor does it adequately explain why only here is the phrase "book of the family history" used. If the editor did not intend to imply he was quoting from a written source, his usual introductory formula "This is the family history . . ." would appear quite adequate. Thus it seems probable that a *Toledot* book is being quoted here and in 11:10–26, but its precise contents remain conjectural. Whereas von Rad restricted it to the genealogical notices in P, Weimar would expand it to include parts of P's narrative as well (*BZ* 18 [1974] 84–87).

The regular structure of the genealogy allows its original form to be reconstructed quite easily and the editorial modifications to be distinguished with some confidence. For example, 5:1–2 not only summarizes 1:1–2:3, especially 1:27–28, but in its chiastic construction and use of key words ("make," "create," "day of") closely resembles 2:4. 5:3b echoes both 1:26–27 and 4:25. The phraseology of 5:22, 24, "walking with" (hithpael הלך), most closely parallels 6:9, "Noah walked with God," though the same verbal form is used of the LORD walking in the garden in 3:8. 5:29, Lamek's hopes for his son Noah, explicitly refers to the curse of the ground in 3:17. Finally, the opening statement about Noah in 5:32 has been split off from its conclusion in 9:28–29 by the insertion of the flood story in chaps. 6–9. Apart from the extra details about Adam and Noah, the first and last members of the genealogy, the only other irregularities in it concern Enoch (vv 22, 24) and Lamek (v 29), the two antediluvians whose names also appear in Cain's genealogy (4:17–24). In both chapters it seems that the editor gives extra information about these figures in order that the Cainite Enoch would not be confused with the Sethite, or the Cainite Lamek with his Sethite counterpart.

On the traditional documentary hypothesis most of these editorial changes are ascribed to P, for the most obvious connections in 5:1–3 are with 1:1–2:4a, which is assigned to the P source. However, 5:29, pointing back to 3:17 and mentioning "the LORD" by name, has to be ascribed to J. It is often suggested that it derives from the lost ending of J's genealogy of Seth. Its insertion into the late P genealogy has to be ascribed to an even later redactor. Tengström (*Toledotformel*), following Cross (*Canaanite Myth*, 293–325), argues that P is not a source, simply a supplementer and editor of J. Indeed, Tengström suggests that P is responsible for the shape of Gen 2–4 as well as Gen 1. In this way he can account for the close parallels between 5:1–2 and 2:4. 2:4a is conventionally ascribed to P and 2:4b to J. Though Tengström does not say so, the identification of the editor of Gen 2–4 (conventionally J) with the editor of Gen 5 (P) would also account for the presence of J elements in Gen 5, i.e., vv 3b and 29, and for the splicing of the flood story into the genealogy of Seth, i.e., between 5:32 and 9:28. This technique is also used in the genealogy of Cain (4:3–16 being spliced between 4:2 and 17). Finally, it would account for the presence of J material in 6:1–8 at the end of the section headed by 5:1: "This is the book of . . . ," and the conformity of 5:1–6:8 with the overall design of material found elsewhere in Genesis.

To sum up, most of 5:1–6:8 derives from an earlier source, the *Toledot* book. Various editorial modifications to this source are apparent and are typical of other parts of Genesis. Some of these changes (e.g., 5:3b, 29; 6:1–8) are conventionally ascribed to J, so it is likely that J was the editor responsible for the final form of this section rather than P. Parallels between the genealogies in Gen 4 and 5 have long been noted. The three-member genealogy of Seth in 4:25–26 acts as a trailer to the full ten-member genealogy in 5:1–32. It has also been observed that the last seven members of Sethite genealogy in 5:12–32 parallel the genealogy of Cain in 4:17–18.

Gen 5		*Gen 4*		*Gen 4*	
		Sethite line		*Cainite line*	
1	Adam	25	Adam	1	Adam
6	Seth	26	Seth		
9	Enosh	26	Enosh		
12	Qenan קינן			17	Cain קין
15	Mahalalel מהללאל			17	Enoch
18	Yared ירד			18	Irad עירד
21	Enoch			18	Mehuya'el מחויאל
25	Methuselah מתושלח			18	Methusha'el מתושאל
28	Lamek			18	Lamek
32	Noah			20	Yabal, Yubal, Tubal-Cain

To be precise: of the six names mentioned in 4:17–18, two, Enoch and Lamek, reappear in 5:12–28, and only Lamek appears at the same point in the geneal-

ogy, i.e., as penultimate member. If, however, Mahalalel changes places with
Enoch in Gen 5, or Enoch changes with Mehuya'el in 4:17–18, there would
be a sequence of similar-sounding names in both chapters. This has led most
commentators to conclude that here are two alternative versions of the same
genealogy. Nevertheless, it is clear that there cannot have been any direct
borrowing from 4:17–18 for use in 5:12–28 or vice versa: for apart from
the difference in order already mentioned, four of the six names require
the change or addition of at least one consonant to make them identical. If
then 4:17–18 and 5:12–28 witness to a common genealogy, it existed long
before the literary composition of Gen 4–5 (J. M. Miller, "The Descendants
of Cain," *ZAW* 86 [1974] 164–73). However, R. R. Wilson (*Genealogy and
History,* 166–204) has pointed out that peoples often retain variant genealogies
alongside each other without sensing any contradiction between them. Certainly the editor of Genesis did not regard these genealogies as identical:
not only do both have different starting points (Cain and Seth) and different
conclusions (Tubal-Cain and Noah), but Enoch and Lamek, the only identical
names within the two genealogies, are distinguished by additional biographical
details which show that they were regarded as different people. The morpho-
logical similarity of the other names could be explained as easily by assimilation
between the genealogies, a phenomenon attested in Mesopotamian texts dealing with primeval history (J. J. Finkelstein, *JCS* 17 [1963], 50, n.41; W. W.
Hallo, *JCS* 23 [1970] 63–64), as by positing a common source for the names
(cf. D. Bryan).

Comparison of the genealogies in the present setting in Genesis indicates
that the editor saw them as distinct. The different style suggests that they
probably derive from distinct sources. But this is not to say that they must
have been first brought together by the editor of Genesis, for once again
the Sumerian flood story may have discussed similar topics to Gen 4 and 5
in the same order.

We earlier noted the parallels between Gen 4 and the Sumerian flood
story—the references to nomadism, city-building, and the institution of public
worship. The Sumerian flood story, as reconstructed by Jacobsen on the basis
of the bilingual version from Ashurbanipal's library, next goes on to mention
the nine kings who reigned before the flood. These kings all reigned an
exceptionally long time, up to 64,000 years! The first two kings reigned in
Eridu (cf. Gen 4:18) and the last was called Ziusudra, the Sumerian name
for the survivor of the flood. For these reasons this list of seven to ten (the
number varies in different texts) antediluvian kings has often been compared
with Gen 5. What is new about Jacobsen's Sumerian flood story is that its
sequence of material follows much the same order as that found in Gen 4–
5.

As already observed, Jacobsen's Sumerian flood story involves a certain
amount of conjectural reconstruction, but the Sumerian king list certainly
does present a similar sequence to that attested in Gen 5, 6–9, 11, viz.: list
of very long-lived antediluvians, flood, list of shorter-lived postdiluvians. In
particular, the marked resemblances between Gen 5, with its list of ten generations from Adam to Noah and the eight, nine, or ten (depending on the
version) kings of the Sumerian king list who reigned before the flood have
often been noted.

Nevertheless, it is as important to note the differences as the similarities between Gen 5 and Sumerian tradition (cf. G.F. Hasel, *AUSS* 16 [1978] 361–74). The names are quite different. The genealogies have different starting points: the first king, not the first man. The king lists concern length of reign, not length of life. The reigns recorded in the Sumerian king list are much longer than the lives of the biblical heroes—of the order of fifty times longer. And the purpose of the lists is very different: the Sumerian king list, to which this list of antediluvians is often prefaced, is designed to justify one city's claim to leadership of Mesopotamia, whereas the biblical genealogy has a world-wide perspective, tracing as it does the history of humanity from its creation in Adam to its sole survivor Noah and his family. In these respects there is a clear contrast between Gen 5 and the antediluvian prologue to the Sumerian king list that makes direct dependence most improbable. Rather, the contacts between Mesopotamian and Hebrew tradition must have occurred far back in the process of oral transmission between one culture and the other.

Within the book of Genesis itself more light is shed on the function of Gen 5 by comparing it with the genealogies of Cain and Seth found in Gen 4. Chap. 4 described the growing power of sin from Adam via Cain, culminating in the viciousness of Lamek. It also traced early developments in culture and technology but suggested that all were tainted by the effects of human sin. Chap. 5 on the other hand records God's blessing of mankind; man multiplies, "fathering sons and daughters." Through sexual intercourse the divine image is transmitted from generation to generation. The statement in 4:26 "At that time people began to call on the name of the LORD" gave a hint that the Sethite line would be blessed. The same hope is expressed in 5:29 when Lamek says of Noah, May this one comfort us and relieve us of the effects of the LORD's curse. But of course any optimism engendered by chap. 5 is dashed by chap. 6. There the abuse of sexuality leads into the decree of the flood. Lamek's hopes for mankind were not fulfilled as he expected. Instead of mankind's being comforted by Noah, Noah is the only survivor of the cataclysm. The genealogy in chap. 5 thus serves to link the first founder of humanity, Adam, with its refounder, Noah. The long period of peace and apparent prosperity described in this chapter serves to make the sequel in 6:1–8 the more surprising and shocking, just as the creation stories in Gen 1–2 make the fall in chap. 3 the more poignant.

Comment

1 "This is the book of the family history of Adam." A heading like this introduces each new section in Genesis (cf. 2:4; 6:9), but only here is a book mentioned.

On תולדת "family history" see *Comment* on 2:4. According to the MT chronology, Adam lived to see Lamek, Noah's father (see *Excursus*). So the usage of the phrase with Adam is comparable with that found in the patriarchal stories, where it introduces an epoch in which the figure named, e.g., Isaac, Jacob, is head of the family.

"Book" ספר covers anything from a short legal document, e.g., Deut 24:1, to a written document of some length (Deut 31:24, 26). The reference to a book is reminiscent of the mention of "The Book of the Wars of the LORD" (Num 21:14) or "the Book of Jashar" (Josh 10:13; 2 Sam 1:18) and suggests that a written source is being quoted here. However, what "the book . . . of Adam" contained is uncertain. According to Weimar it included much of P (*BZ* 18 [1974] 86–87), but von Rad limited it to the genealogical and chronological data of P. At the very least it contained the genealogy of chap. 5, and probably 11:10–26, which appears to be the continuation of chap. 5.

1b–2 This editorial summary of what has gone before is characteristic of Genesis. Its elevated prose style is akin to that of Gen 1, to which it most clearly refers, but in structure and terminology its closest parallel is Gen 2:4. Note that both passages have a similar chiastic structure (ABCCBA). Both pair "making" and "creating" at the midpoint (CC) of the construction. Finally, both have the phrase "when they were created" (niphal infinitive ברא with 3rd plural suffix), the only places where this phrase is attested.

A	On the day God created	Cf. 2:4:	A	The heaven
B	Adam		B	and the earth
C	In the likeness of God he made him		C	when they were created
C	Male and female he created them		C	on the day the LORD God made
	[he blessed them and called their name]			
B	Adam		B	earth and
A	On the day they were created		A	heaven

In grammatical arrangement 5:1–2 thus bears a striking similarity to the first heading of Gen 2:4, but in content these verses reproduce the subject matter of 1:26–28 with some abbreviation. "So God created man in his image, in the image of God he created him: male and female he created them. And God blessed them, and God said to them: 'Be fruitful and multiply.'" Some slight changes of terminology may be noted: "make" for "create" and "likeness" for "image." The blessing of God is referred to, but not elaborated as in 1:28: "Be fruitful and multiply." However, the whole genealogy in chap. 5 illustrates the fulfillment of this blessing.

2 "Called their name Adam." Nowhere in chaps. 1–3 does God give mankind a name, although "man," literally, "the man" (האדם), is often mentioned. But from 4:25 to 5:6 the anarthrous form אדם "Adam," the proper name, is used. However, such a translation here is jarring in English: the generic "man" runs more smoothly and most commentators adopt the generic term here. The problem really lies in our transliteration of the Hebrew names: if we used "Man" for "Adam" and "man" for "mankind," our translation could oscillate between "Man" and "man" as easily as Hebrew does between האדם and אדם. Since in vv 1 and 3 the personal name "Adam," "Man," is clearly intended and v 2 actually speaks of giving a name, the older translations, LXX, Vg, and AV, are correct in understanding the personal name "Adam" here despite the incongruity of its apparently referring to both sexes.

3–5 Note the first example of the standard formulae for giving biographi-

cal details; cf. 6–8, 9–11, etc. See above, *Form/Structure/Setting*. On the ages
of the antediluvians see *Excursus*.

3 "Adam . . . fathered a child in his own likeness and according to his
image." This verse makes the point that the image and likeness of God which
was given to Adam at creation was inherited by his sons. It was not obliterated
by the fall. Note that, compared with 1:26, the prepositions ב "in" and כ
"according to" are reversed, suggesting their semantic interchangeability when
used with the nouns "image" and "likeness" (cf. *Comment* on 1:26).

5 "Adam's whole life which he lived lasted 930 years." The summary
statement about Adam differs from the later ones in two minor ways. First,
it adds the phrase "which he lived," also used of Abraham in 25:7. Second,
it puts the hundreds (900) before the tens (30), whereas the other summaries
have the reverse order. Jacob suggests that these differences emphasize the
length of Adam's life, which according to the MT chronology would have
been witnessed by all the antediluvians up to Lamek, and the fact of his
death.

6–8 "Seth": cf. *Comment* on 4:25.

9–11 "Enosh": cf. *Comment* on 4:26.

12–14 "Qenan." The name is mentioned only here. Usually it is interpreted as a variant form of Cain. Cf. *Comment* on 4:1.

15–17 "Mahalalel." Obviously a Hebrew name meaning either "Praise
of God" or "Praising God." A Judaean had this name (Neh 11:4).

18–20 "Yared." A name of uncertain meaning and derivation. It could
be derived from Hebrew ירד "to go down" and therefore mean "going down,"
or from Akkadian *wardu* "servant," or, less likely, from the Arabic word for
"courageous" (so L. Kopf, *VT* 8 [1958] 179). Another Yared is mentioned in
1 Chr 4:18.

21–24 "Enoch": on the name cf. *Comment* on 4:17. In biblical genealogies
the seventh member is often specially favored, and Enoch, the seventh from
Adam, conforms to this pattern (J. M. Sasson, *ZAW* 90 [1978] 171–85). Unlike
the other antediluvians who "live" and "die," Enoch "walked with God and
was not, because God took him." These extra details also serve to distinguish
him from Cain's son Enoch (4:17).

22 "Walked with God" is a phrase used twice of Enoch, here and in v
24, and once of Noah, in 6:9. Later patriarchs "walked before" God (17:1;
24:40; 48:15) and the Lᴏʀᴅ God walked in the garden of Eden (3:8). The
priests were expected to walk with God (Mal 2:6) and Micah 6:8 describes
this as God's basic requirement for all persons, though here the verb הלך is
used in the qal, not the hithpael. Clearly, then, the phrase suggests a special
intimacy with God and a life of piety. This is not to say the other antediluvians
mentioned in this chapter were godless: they all represent the chosen line
of Seth and include Enosh and Noah as well. The double repetition of the
phrase "walked with God" indicates Enoch was outstanding in this pious
family.

23 "365 years" is the shortest life-span of any of the antediluvians. It is
usually supposed that Enoch's age must be related to the number of days in
a solar year. Westermann suggests that the number shows that "his life-span
was a full rounded whole that could be short because it did not end with

death" (1:358) L. Zachmann (*ZAW* 88 [1976] 272–74) rejects this idea, however, and thinks that Enoch was removed from earth early to spare him contact with the sinful world.

24 "and was not": Enoch disappeared from the earthly scene. Sometimes the phrase is a poetic euphemism for death, e.g., Ps 39:14[13]; 103:16; Job 7:21; 8:22. But here it stands in contrast to the usual phrase "then he died," which shows that Enoch did not experience a normal death. This is confirmed by the final remark, "because God took him," a phrase used of Elijah's translation to heaven in a chariot of fire (2 Kgs 2:1, 5, 9, 10). The Gilgamesh epic (11:196) also speaks of the gods taking Utnapishtim, the survivor of the flood, to enjoy immortality at the mouth of the rivers.

Other oriental and classical parallels to the idea of pious men being taken directly to heaven are known, e.g., Adapa, Aeneas, Heracles (A. Schmitt, *Forschung zur Bibel* 1 [1972] 161–69). It has also been observed that the seventh antediluvian king according to Berossus and one version of the Sumerian king list was also recipient of divine mysteries. This parallels Enoch's intimacy with God. But the most striking parallel to Enoch, the seventh antediluvian patriarch, is to be found in a text published by Borger (*JNES* 33 [1974] 183–96), which describes the seventh of the ancient sages as Utuabzu "who ascended to heaven." Utuabzu was advisor to Enmeduranki, the seventh antediluvian king. Later Jewish tradition (cf. the book of Enoch) developed stories about Enoch that elaborated his significance. To stop such ideas *Tg. Onq.* goes so far as to assert that "the LORD caused him to die" (see J. W. Bowker, *The Targums and Rabbinic Literature*, 143–50). In contrast to these extra- and post-biblical views Gen 5:22–24 is very restrained. It may well be that while acknowledging the truth that Enoch was very devout and did not see death, these verses are trying to counteract these ancient speculations about great men of the past.

25–27 "Methuselah" means "man of [Akk. *mutu*, "man"] Shelah" (cf. 4:18). The meaning of "Shelah" is uncertain. It may be a place name, a name of an underworld god (so M. Tsevat, *VT* 4 [1954] 41–49), or mean simply "missile." "Shelah" is found as a personal name in 10:24; 11:12–15.

28–31 "Lamek": cf. *Comment* on 4:18. Note that the additional information about the two Lameks ensures that they are not confused, despite their identical names.

29 "He called his name Noah, commenting, 'May this one bring us relief from our work and from the pain of our hands.'" Noah (literally, "rest") is one of the central figures in Genesis. His name and its poetic etymology introduce some of the verbal motifs and theological themes that will dominate the next four chapters. As is often the case in the OT, the etymology is not scientific; it is simply associated with the name because of its similar sound. Here "He will bring us relief," יְנַחֲמֵנוּ, echoes the נח of Noah (the final vowel û is akin to ô in Noah) and rhymes with the next Hebrew word, מִמַּעֲשֵׂנוּ "from our work," and, more loosely, with "our hands." The terms for "rest," "relief/repentance," "work/making ark," "the land," נח, נחם, עשה, ארץ, are all important in the next few chapters and are associated with Noah's mission (cf. A. Strus, *Nomen-Omen*, 66, 158–62). Most obviously, Lamek's remarks look back to the curse on the land (3:17); cf. *Comment* on 3:16–17. But the very terminology he uses obliquely hints at Noah's future achievements, namely, his construction of the ark (6:14–22) and his planting of a vineyard (9:20). Lamek's remarks find a more distant parallel in the Atrahasis epic where the gods send various plagues on earth, culminating in the flood, in an attempt to stop the noise made by mankind.

This verse breaks the regular pattern of the genealogy, and it is therefore most likely an editorial insertion into "the book of the family history of Adam" (5:1). This view is supported by the way the text anticipates the thematic motifs of chaps. 6–9. On the basis of its allusion to 3:17 it is usually held to derive from the J source, though as Westermann observes, it is hard to envisage a suitable context for it in J. I prefer to ascribe it to the final editor.

30, 32 Strus (*Nomen-Omen,* 217) detects loose paronomasia between "Noah" and "500" (נ ח // חמש), just as his name is later associated with violence (חמס 6:11,13).

32 Here the genealogy diverges from its standard form by mentioning the birth of three sons, as the Shemite genealogy does in 11:26. Adam, Noah, and Terah are not only distinctive in heading the great epochs of world history portrayed in Genesis, they all also father three sons. The other slight difference is that the verse opens "Noah was 500 years old" instead of the usual "Noah lived 500 years." This change perhaps highlights the link between "Noah" (נח) and "500 years old" (בן חמש מאות). The genealogy does not conclude until 9:29, being interrupted by the account of the flood.

"Shem, Ham, and Japhet": the three sons of Noah, who accompanied him into the ark, with him survived the flood (6:10; 7:13; 9:18) and founded the three great divisions of mankind (10:1–32).

The etymology and meaning of their names is obscure. S. N. Kramer's suggestion that "Shem" may be derived from Sumerian "Kengir" (sometimes read "S[h]umer"), their term for southern Mesopotamia (*The Sumerians* [Chicago: University Press, 1963] 297–99) is unlikely. But since "Shem" (שם) means simply "name," "reputation," or "fame," this may be how his name was understood; "Perhaps Noah wanted to express through this name his anticipation that his son would make a name for himself" (Gispen, 1:213).

"Ham" may be related to Ḥammu (as in Hammurapi) a West Semitic sun-god (so KB, 312). In Hebrew "Ham" (חם) means "hot." It may be that Ham's name looks forward to his improper behavior toward his father (9:20–27), which is a type of the heated sexual conduct of his descendants. For the root חם of sexual passion, cf. Isa 57:5.

"Japhet": as with Abel and Lamek, it is customary to use the pausal form of the name instead of Jephet. Japhet may be linked etymologically with Greek Ἰάπετος, one of the Titans. 9:27 connects Japhet with the verb פתה "to make broad." Possibly, "May (God) enlarge (him)." See further on 9:27; 10:2.

Explanation

The explanation of this chapter is included with that on the next section, 6:1–8.

Excursus: The Ages of the Antediluvians

Gen 5 presents two very intractable problems. First, and more obviously, these patriarchs age extraordinarily slowly. All are at least sixty-five years old when their first child is born, and most are approaching a thousand when they die! How are these very long life-spans to be explained? Second, the three oldest textual witnesses, the Masoretic (MT), the Samaritan Pentateuch (SamPent) and the Greek Septuagint (LXX) disagree at many points about the ages of these antediluvian patriarchs. This makes it difficult to determine the earliest reading.

These questions would be hard to unravel on their own: unfortunately the longevity question is intertwined with the text-critical, and the date of the flood is also a factor complicating the issue. Insofar as it is possible, these problems will be looked at separately. First the textual evidence will be discussed, then the ages of the men themselves.

Each patriarch's life is summarized in Gen 5 according to the following formula:

> A lived x years and then fathered B
> A lived y years after he had fathered B
> A's whole life lasted x + y years.
>
> x = patriarch's age when his first child was born
> y = number of years from birth of first child to patriarch's death
> x + y = patriarch's age at death

The different figures for x, y, and x + y in the MT, SamPent, and LXX are summarized in the table on the following page.

Using the figures from this table, we can calculate how many years after the creation of Adam a patriarch died. The patriarchs' dates of death are given in the fourth box. The year of the flood can also be calculated by adding up all the figures in the first column (x) and adding 100 (Noah was 500 years old when his children were born and 600 when the flood came).

It then appears that according to the MT the flood came in the year 1656. It also appears that all Noah's ancestors died before 1656, except Methuselah, who died that year. Did he die in the flood?

According to the Samaritan Pentateuch, the flood occurred in 1307. This lower figure is reached by the SamPent's having made the patriarchs Yared, Methuselah, and Lamek much younger when their first child was born. Accordingly all three, Yared, Methuselah and Lamek died in 1307, the year of the flood.

According to the best MSS of LXX, the flood occurred in 2242. This figure is arrived at by LXX's making most of the patriarchs father their first child 100 years later than the MT does. None of Noah's ancestors die in 2242, the year of the flood, but Methuselah lives to 2256, 14 years afterward! Not surprisingly, many texts of the LXX follow the MT figures and make Methuselah die before the flood.

Which of these chronologies is closest to the original? There is no consensus on this issue, except that the LXX looks secondary. The regular lengthening, usually by 100 years, of the period till the birth of the patriarch's first son and the corresponding contraction of his subsequent years of life looks artificial. When the LXX was being translated in Egypt, there was great interest among Egyptian Jews in chronological issues, and it seems likely that these patriarchal ages were adjusted by translators to compete with Egyptian claims about the antiquity of mankind.

Where MT and SamPent agree against LXX, they are to be followed. But with three patriarchs—Yared, Methuselah, and Lamek—MT disagrees with SamPent,

	MT			SamPent			LXX			Patriarch's date of death		
	First child born	Other years	Age at death									
	x	y	x + y	x	y	x + y	x	y	x + y	MT	SamPent	LXX
Adam	130	800	930	130	800	930	230	700	930	930	930	930
Seth	105	807	912	105	807	912	205	707	912	1042	1042	1142
Enosh	90	815	905	90	815	905	190	715	905	1140	1140	1340
Qenan	70	840	910	70	840	910	170	740	910	1235	1235	1535
Mahalalel	65	830	895	65	830	895	165	730	895	1290	1290	1690
Yared	162	800	962	62	785	847	162	800	962	1422	1307	1922
Enoch	65	300	365	65	300	365	165	200	365	987	887	1487
Methuselah	187	782	969	67	653	720	167	802	969	1656	1307	2256
Lamek	182	595	777	53	600	653	188	565	753	1651	1307	2207
Noah	500	—	—	500	—	—	500	—	—	—	—	—
Till the flood	100	—	—	100	—	—	100	—	—	—	—	—
Year of flood	1656	—	—	1307	—	—	2242	—	—	—	—	—

x = patriarch's age when his first child was born

y = number of years from birth of first child to patriarch's death

x + y = patriarch's age at death

and it is not clear which readings are to be preferred. Chronological schematization has been detected behind both sets of figures. If this can be demonstrated, it might imply that neither set is original.

Cassuto (1:255–65) believed in the originality of the MT. He pointed out that all the MT figures are multiples of 5 with occasionally the addition of 7 or 14 (e.g., 182 = 175 [35 x 5] + 7). He did not observe, though, that all the SamPent figures are multiples of 5 with occasionally the addition or *subtraction* of 7 (e.g., 53 = 12 x 5 - 7).

Dillmann favored the originality of the SamPent figures. He pointed out that according to the SamPent the age at which the patriarchs fathered their first child and their total life spans drop steadily from generation to generation, whereas there are several hiccups in the ages according to MT. He also thought it was easier to explain the origin of the MT and LXX figures on the assumption of the SamPent's originality than on the basis of the MT's originality.

R. W. Klein (*HTR* 67 [1974] 255–63) has adopted an eclectic approach to these figures. On Yared he argues that MT and LXX's agreement about his total life span of 962 years is to be preferred to SamPent's 847. The latter figure has been adjusted to make Yared die before the flood. However, Klein thinks that it seems more likely that Enoch was born when Yared was 62 (SamPent) than when he was 162 (MT, LXX), because LXX consistently raises these figures by 100. Similarly, 100 years should be deducted from the LXX ages of Methuselah and Lamek at the birth of their firstborn to arrive at the original readings (67 [= SamPent] and 88).

Klein thinks SamPent has reduced Methuselah's age at death (969 per MT, LXX) to 720 to make him die before the flood. The total life span of Lamek is most likely to be 753 (so LXX), as SamPent's 653 is again reduced to ensure Lamek's death before the flood, and MT's 777 seems to be related to his 77-fold vengeance; cf. 4:24.

Klein therefore reconstructs the table as follows:

	x	*y*	*x + y*	*Date of Death*
Adam	130	800	930	930
Seth	105	807	912	1042
Enosh	90	815	905	1140
Qenan	70	840	910	1235
Mahalalel	65	830	895	1290
Yared	62	900	962	1422
Enoch	65	300	365	887
Methuselah	67	903	969	1556
Lamek	88	665	753	1407
Noah	500			
Flood	1342			

On this reconstruction, Yared, Methuselah and Lamek survived the flood, as well as Noah. When this was noted, the different versions adopted different methods of eliminating the problem. SamPent reduced the age at which the offending patriarchs died. MT increased the age at which the offending patriarchs fathered their first child, and LXX was adjusted by increasing the age at which all the patriarchs fathered their first child.

Klein's reconstruction is interesting, but not compelling. Would the editor of Genesis have overlooked the fact that three ancestors of Noah survived the flood as well as Noah and his sons? Admittedly, 4:17–22 might be taken to imply that the sons of Lamek who founded the techniques of civilization somehow survived the flood. But it is precarious to argue that the "fathers" of these arts must have a continuous line of successors right through the period of the flood. The Sumerian king list envisaged kingship's being cut off in the flood and "lowered again from heaven" afterward. Maybe the Sumerian flood story thinks in similar terms about the skills of the pre-flood city-builders. Their skills have been revived in the post-flood era. Klein's reconstructed chronology also makes Yared and Methuselah live much longer after the birth of their firstborn than the other patriarchs.

It may therefore be concluded that there is no obvious answer to the text-critical problems posed by these chapters. The LXX appears to have least in its favor, but whether the SamPent, MT or some other scheme is the most primitive is hard to tell.

Whichever figures are correct, the problems posed by this chapter are formidable for anyone who wishes to relate them to history. The longevity of these patriarchs is unparalleled in modern times, while the date for the creation of Adam (ca. 4004 B.C.) implied by their genealogy and the subsequent data (e.g., 11:10–26) in Genesis is hard to correlate with archeological discoveries about the origins of mankind and his civilization.

Much ingenuity has been devoted to these problems but without conspicuous success. It is often suggested that the years of Gen 5 may have been much shorter than ours, perhaps equivalent to a month or two. But the flood story makes it quite clear that the years of Genesis were about 360 days. Furthermore, if the ages of the patriarchs are reduced, then the creation of Adam must be more recent than 4004.

Another suggestion (W. H. Green, *BSac* [1890] 285–303) is that the genealogy is not intended to be complete, that generations have been omitted, and therefore it should not be used for chronological purposes. However, the Hebrew gives no hint that there were large gaps between father and son in this genealogy. 4:25 makes it clear that Seth was Adam and Eve's third son. At the other end of the genealogy, Lamek comments on Noah's birth, and Ham, Shem, and Japhet were contemporaries of their father. It therefore requires special pleading to postulate long gaps elsewhere in the genealogy.

Attempts to explain the great ages of the patriarchs by reference to ancient Near Eastern parallels are also disappointing. J. Walton (*BA* 44 [1981] 207–8) suggested that the sum total of the Genesis patriarchs' ages from Seth to Lamek, 6,700 years, can be derived from the Sumerian king list. According to one text of this list, eight antediluvian kings reigned for 241,200 years. Walton postulates that these Sumerian figures were written in sexagesimal notation and were misinterpreted by Hebrew scribes working on a decimal system. But Walton's hypothesis explains only the totals (even here his mathematics seems dubious), not the individual ages of the patriarchs or the age at which they fathered their first-born.

Whereas Walton suggested that the Hebrew chronologist was working to the base ten, Cassuto in his commentary suggested that the Hebrew figures are in fact related to the sexagesimal system. The ages of the patriarchs tend either to be exact multiples of 5 years (60 months) or multiples of 5 + 7 (in the case of Methuselah + 14). Furthermore, he calculated that the period of the first world from creation to the end of the flood is 60 myriad (600,000) days less 14 years. Though Cassuto's arithmetical observations, are interesting they do nothing to explain the ages of particular patriarchs.

Barnouin (*RB* 77 [1970] 347–65) has made the bravest attempt to confront this issue. He believes that the ages of the antediluvians can be related to various astronomical periods such as the number of days or weeks in the year or the synodic periods of the planets (i.e., the time it takes for a planet to return to the same point in the sky). These astronomical periods were known to the Babylonians, and a sexagesimal arithmetic, he maintains, would have made the calculations quite easy.

Barnouin notes the obvious point that Enoch lived 365 years, which he supposes represents the perfect span of life.

Furthermore, if the figures in column 1 (x Adam → x Lamek) and the figures in column 2 (y Adam → y Lamek) are each divided by 60, and the remainders added together, the sum of the remainders is 365! As for the patriarchs' ages at death, these can be related to synodic periods: e.g., Lamek's 777 = synodic period of Jupiter + synodic period of Saturn; Yared's 962 = synodic period of Venus + synodic period of Saturn. He shows how other patriarchal ages can be generated similarly.

Barnouin's mathematics is impressive and the coincidences he finds are striking, even if he sometimes resorts to approximations. However, he offers no explanation of why the writer of Genesis should want to relate the ages of the patriarchs to synodic periods and the like, merely suggesting that they express the orderliness of life before the flood and convey the passage of time in those distant years.

To date, then, no writer has offered an adequate explanation of these figures. If they are symbolic, it is not clear what they symbolize. If they are to be taken literally, we are left with the historical problems with which we began. The majority of commentators therefore just offer some general observations of a more theological nature. This genealogy is designed to show how the divine image in which Adam was created was passed on from generation to generation, and that the divine command to be fruitful and multiply (1:28) was fulfilled. Many ancient peoples have held that in primitive antiquity men lived much longer than at present: the Sumerians believed the pre-flood kings reigned for thousands of years, and according to the Lagash king list, babies were kept in diapers for a hundred years! (Jacobsen, *JBL* 100 [1981] 520–21). It may be that Gen 5 is reflecting such ideas and suggesting that the history of mankind stretches back into an inconceivably distant past. Cassuto, though, sees in the ages of the patriarchs, relatively low when contrasted with the enormous reigns of Sumerian kings, another aspect of anti-Mesopotamian polemic. The Hebrew writer was intent on scaling down the alleged ages of man's earliest forebears. Though they lived a long time, none reached a thousand years, which in God's sight is but an evening gone (cf. Ps 90:4). Gispen suggests that these figures are designed to show that though the narrative is dealing with very distant times, it is a sort of history, and that however long men lived, they were mortal.

These seem better approaches to these great ages than the attempts to find symbolic or historical truths in the precise ages of the patriarchs. Could it be that the precision of the figures conveys the notion that these patriarchs were real people, while their magnitude represents their remoteness from the author of Genesis? Even if we know that twenty centuries is really too short for the period from the creation of man to the call of Abraham, it still feels a very long time to anyone who tries to think himself back through such a period, as anyone who tries to do this for the years from the present to the time of Christ will quickly discover.

Spirit-Human Marriages and Their Aftermath (6:1–8)

Bibliography

Alexander, P. S. "The Targumim and Early Exegesis of 'Sons of God' in Gen 6." *JJS* 23 (1972) 60–71. **Bartelmus, R.** *Heroentum in Israel und seiner Umwelt.* ATANT 65. Zurich: Theologischer Verlag, 1979. **Boer, P. A. H. de.** "The Son of God in the Old Testament." *OTS* 18 (1973) 188–207. **Cassuto, U.** "The Episode of the Sons of God and the Daughters of Man." In U. Cassuto, *Biblical and Oriental Studies* I. Jerusalem: Magnes Press, 1973. 17–28. **Clines, D. J. A.** "The Significance of the 'Sons of God' Episode (Gen 6:1–4) in the Context of the 'Primeval History' (Gen 1–11)." *JSOT* 13 (1979) 33–46. **Dexinger, F.** *Sturz der Göttersöhne oder Engel vor der Sintflut?.* Vienna: Herder, 1966. **Emanueli, M.** "The Sons of God Took Wives Whomever They Chose." (Heb.) *BMik* 20 (1974) 150–52. **Eslinger, L.** "A Contextual Identification of the *bene ha'elohim* and *benoth ha'adam* in Gen 6:1–4." *JSOT* 13 (1979) 65–73. **Gemeren, W. A. van.** "The Sons of God in Gen 6:1–4." *WTJ* 43 (1981) 320–48. **Hanson, P.** "Rebellion in Heaven: Azazel and Euhemeristic Heroes in 1 Enoch 6–11." *JBL* 96 (1977) 195–233. **Hendel, R. S.** "Of Demigods and the Deluge: Toward an Interpretation of Gen 6:1–4." *JBL* 106 (1987) 13–26. **Houtman, C.** "Het verboden huwelijk: Gen 6:1–4 in haar context." *GTT* 76 (1976) 65–75. **Kline, M. G.** "Divine Kingship and Gen 6:1–4." *WTJ* 24 (1963) 187–204. **Kurtz, J. H.** *Die Söhne Gottes in 1 Mos 6:1–4 und die sündigenden Engel.* Mitan: Neumann's Verlag, 1858. **Loretz, O.** "Aspeckte der kanaanäischen Gottes-So[ö]hn[e]-Tradition im Alten Testament." *UF* 7 (1975) 586–89. **Marrs, R.** "The Sons of God." *ResQ* 23 (1980) 218–24. **Naor, M.** "The Nephilim were in the Earth." (Heb.) *BMik* 11 (1965) 26–33. **Petersen, D. L.** "Gen 6:1–4, Yahweh and the Organization of the Cosmos." *JSOT* 13 (1979) 47–64. **Scharbert, J.** "Traditions- und Redaktionsgeschichte von Gen 6:1–4." *BZ* 11 (1967) 66–78. **Schlisske, W.** *Gottessöhne and Gottessohn im Alten Testament.* BWANT 97. Stuttgart: Kohlhammer, 1973. **Schreiner, J.** "Gen 6:1–4 und die Problematik von Leben und Tod." *De la Tôrah au Messie: Études offertes à H. Cazelles,* ed. M. Carrez, J. Doré and P. Grelot. Paris: Desclée, 1981. 65–74. **Wifall, W.** "Gen 6:1–4—A Royal Davidic Myth?" *BTB* 5 (1976) 294–301.

Translation

[1] When [a] man began [b] to multiply [c] on the land, and when [a] daughters were born [d] to them, [2] the sons of the gods saw [a] that the daughters of man were good [a] and they took wives for themselves from any [b] they chose. [3] Then the LORD said: "My spirit shall not remain [a] in man for ever, because [b] he is flesh: his days shall be one hundred and twenty years." [4] The [a] Nephilim were in the earth in those days, and also afterwards: [a] whenever the sons of the gods went [b] in to the daughters of man, they bore [c] them children. They are the warriors from olden times, the famous men.

[5] Then the LORD saw [a] that the evil of man was great in the earth and every idea of the plans of his mind was nothing but [b] evil [c] all the time. [c] [6] The LORD regretted [a] that he had made man in the earth. He felt [b] bitterly indignant about it. [7] The LORD said, "I shall wipe out man whom I have created from the land, man, land animals, creeping creatures, and birds of the sky, for I regret [a] that I made them." [8] But [a] Noah found favor in the eyes of the LORD. [a]

Notes

1.a-a. כִּי governs both clauses, cf. 27:30 (*SBH*, 86–87).
1.b. 3 masc sg pf hiph חלל.
1.c. Inf const רבב.
1.d. 3 pl qal passive ילד, cf. 4:26 (Joüon, 58a; Lambdin, 253).
2.a-a. Cf. 1:4 for a similar construction: the subject of the subordinate clause "daughters" is anticipated by being made object of the main clause (Joüon, 157d).
2.b. For this use of כל cf. 7:22; 9:10; Lev 11:32 (Joüon, 133e).
3.a. 3 masc sg impf qal ידון; for meaning see *Comments*.
3.b. בשׁגם "because," either a compound particle + בְּ "in" = שׁ "which," + גם "also" or inf const שׁגג "to make a mistake" + ם "their" + בְּ prefix "in" = "when they make a mistake." The former is more likely, cf. the similar compound באשׁר "because" (39:9,23)
4.a-a. Conjunctionless apposition is used for parenthetical comments (*SBH*, 37).
4.b. Impf for repeated action (GKC, 107e).
4.c. Pf consec after preceding frequentative impf (GKC, 112e).
5.a. Waw consec + 3 masc sg impf (apoc) ראה.
5.b. רק means here "nothing but" (*SBH*, 175) or "altogether" (*EWAS*, 131).
5.c-c. For this translation cf. Joüon, 139g.
6.a. Waw consec + 3 masc sg impf niph נחם.
6.b. Waw consec + 3 masc sg impf hithp עצב.
7.a. 1 sg pf niph נחם.
8.a-a. Episode-final circumstantial clause (*SBH*, 80–81, 180).

Form/Structure/Setting

6:1–8 falls into two paragraphs—vv 1–4, divine-human intermarriage, and vv 5–8, intimation of total destruction—which conclude the whole section 5:1–6:8, "the family history of Adam." Though 6:1–8 appears to have little connection with the preceding genealogy, it is in fact closely integrated with it. Those key words which appear in multiples of six or seven in 5:1–6:8 are well represented here: "man," "the LORD," "God," "sons," "daughters," "make," "create" (see above on 5:1–32, *Form/Structure/Setting*).

In content, 6:1–8 takes up the subject matter of chap. 5. 6:1 introduces the story of the "daughters" often mentioned in passing in chap. 5 despite their apparent irrelevance to the genealogical line. Now they become the focus of attention. Indeed, the opening phrase "When man began to multiply" could refer to the whole process of multiplication recorded in 5:1–32, while the closing sentence about Noah in 6:8 links this paragraph to the close of the genealogy in 5:29–32.

Gen 6:5–8 makes a typical conclusion to one of the larger sections in Genesis in that it rounds off one stage of the story and adumbrates the next. It acts as a trailer to the flood story. By focusing on God's "making" and "creating man" in 6:6, 7 and 5:1, 2, it also forms a loose inclusion with the opening paragraph 5:1–5.

The contents of 6:5–8 are arranged in a rough palistrophe:

A The LORD sees mankind, 6:5
B The LORD regrets, 6:6
C The LORD says "I shall wipe out," 6:7
B' because I regret
A' The LORD sees Noah, 6:8

Structurally, the divine decree of destruction in 6:7 is here the focus of the paragraph. Yet the last remark, "Noah found favor in the eyes of the LORD," which looks forward to the next narrative, is just as significant.

Strus (*Nomen-Omen*) points out that the key words in 6:5–8 make paronomastic allusion to the name of Noah. The consonants (נ ח) or similar sounds are to be found in "regretted" (נחם), 6:6, 7 (here God's attitude stands in bitter contrast to the hopes expressed at Noah's birth: "May this one bring us relief" [נחם, 5:29]); "wipe out" (מחה) and "favor, grace" (חן), 6:8. Strus (*Nomen-Omen*, 158–59) says: "The biblical author connects three concepts with Noah's name: to regret, to wipe out, and grace. The organization of the composition shows that these concepts follow each other and form a climax.

> God regrets creating man
> God intends to wipe man out from the face of the land
> God spares Noah who has found grace in his eyes."

Because Noah's name is alluded to from the very first mention of God's regret and of his plan to wipe out man, the divine decree is always tinged with a glimmer of hope.

In chaps. 2–3 the close relationship between man (אדם) and the land (אדמה) was established. This relationship is recalled in 6:1, "When man began to multiply (on the face of) the land," but the destruction announced in 6:7 ruptures this connection: "I shall wipe out man . . . from (the surface of) the land." The second of the two paragraphs deliberately echoes the preceding one in other ways, creating some interesting inversions.

6:2	The sons of the gods see . . .	the daughters . . .	are good
6:5	The LORD sees	the thoughts	are evil
6:3	The LORD said, "my Spirit . . . in man for ever"		
6:7	The LORD said, "I shall wipe out man"		

It may well be that Noah, who found favor in the LORD's eyes (6:8), stands in contrast to the warriors of olden days in 6:4.

Further confirmation of the unity of the two paragraphs is provided by the fact that source critics, who ascribe the genealogy in 5:1–32 to P, apart from glosses, usually ascribe them both to J. It is almost always held, however, that in 6:1–4 J is largely reproducing earlier tradition, while 6:5–8 contains more editorial comment interpreting the theological significance of the flood.

More recent critical studies have put forward modifications to this view. Westermann suggests that 6:1–2, 4 derive ultimately from Canaanite sources. He notes parallels between vv 1–2 and 12:10–20 and 2 Sam 11–12, other accounts of powerful men marrying beautiful women to whom they had no right, and argues that it should be seen as a narrative like others in the primeval history, not simply as etiological myth. But since Gen 12 and 2 Sam 12 both conclude with a divine intervention curbing the transgression, he suggests that an earlier version of 6:1–4 must have contained a similar remark that has now been replaced by J's own comment in 6:3.

Others have argued that since 6:1–4 does not appear to be integral to J or to P, it ought to be ascribed to an editorial layer. P. Weimar (BZAW 146,

35–39) and J. Schreiner (*De la Tôrah au Messie* [1981] 65–74) argue that it comes from the JE redactor (late 8th century), while J. Scharbert (*BZ* 11 [1967] 66–78) prefers to associate it with P and the final redaction of the Pentateuch. Houtman (*GTT* 76 [1976] 65–75) has also pointed out that it barely makes sense except in its present context.

In 6:5–8 Westermann suggests that the repetitions (e.g., "regret" 6:6, 7) represent some of J's additions to the original tradition (6:5a, 7a): "The LORD saw that the evil of man was great in the earth, And the LORD said, 'I shall wipe out man from the land.'" J reinforced the stress on the sinfulness of man by adding 5b, and by his comment about God's regrets in vv 6–7, introduced the idea of God as a reluctant judge. Strus (*Nomen-Omen*, 159, n. 95) observes that this theological interest is also reflected in the name "Noah" and its associated words "grace," "regret," "wipe out." Finally, it is widely held that "whom I have created" and "man, land animals . . . birds of the sky" is an editorial addition of priestly origin that reflects the phraseology of Gen 1.

In 6:1–8 we are therefore confronted with similar phenomena to those in 5:1–32, but in reverse. Chap. 5 can be described as "basically P with J glosses" whereas 6:1–8 can equally be described as "mainly J with P glosses." This underlines the difficulty with the traditional analysis. As argued earlier, I should prefer to identify the P and J glossators with the final editor of Genesis. On this basis 6:1–2, 4, 5a, 7a[8] might reflect the traditions he received, and 6:3, 5b, 6, 7b might be his own theological commentary on them.

In the quest for pre-Israelite sources used by J or the editor of Genesis, Near Eastern literature gives relatively little help. Stories of the flood generally begin by telling of a divine decree behind the events. The reference to the multiplication of humanity (6:1) has parallels in the Atrahasis epic (1:353; 2:1, 1–2). But the reasons for the divine decision are completely different (see further on 6:9–9:29). In particular, neither the Atrahasis epic nor the Sumerian flood story mentions intermarriage between the gods and men at this point.

Marriages between men and the gods are a well-known feature of Greek, Egyptian, Ugaritic, Hurrian, and Mesopotamian theology (cf. Westermann, 1:379–81; Drewermann, *Strukturen des Bösen*, 1:171–76). The heroic figure of Gilgamesh was held to be descended from such a union. His divine parentage endowed him with incredible energy, but not immortality.

So it is clear that even if specific sources for Gen 6:1–8 cannot be identified, Genesis is making use of well-known oriental ideas. Indeed, at this point Genesis comes closer to myth than anywhere else, for it is describing acts of godlike figures. Yet the description of their activity is so brief, and they and their offspring are so subordinated to the judgment of Yahweh, that the old tradition has been effectively demythologized. It is another narrative in the primeval history that, like the accounts of the creation and the fall, describes distant events that determine the character of mankind's present existence.

Comment

1 "When man began to multiply on the land." This clause describes an ongoing situation, the multiplication of humanity, that forms the background of the new action in v 2. Other examples of this use of ויהי כי are to be seen in 26:8; 27:1; Exod 1:21; 13:15. This clause points back to the first command given to mankind, "be fruitful and multiply," and also to the close connection between "man" (האדם) and "the land" (האדמה), which was noted earlier (cf. 2:5, 7; 3:17). Here אדם is prefixed with the article ("the man") as is normally the case in chaps. 2–4, in contrast to the anarthrous proper name "Adam" used in 4:25–5:5.

"And when daughters were born to them." Unusually for Hebrew word order, the subject of this clause, "daughters," here precedes the verb and so throws it into prominence. Chap. 5 described how man created in God's image as male and female multiplied "bearing sons and daughters" (5:4, 7,-10, 13, etc). But whereas in chap. 5 the male descendants were the center of attention, here the daughters are highlighted.

It should also be noted that in the Atrahasis epic the multiplication of mankind is mentioned shortly before the divine decree to send a catastrophic flood.

When the land extended and the peoples multiplied.
The land was bellowing like a bull (A 2:1,2–3).

"The sons of the gods" or "the sons of God." בני־האלהים could be translated either way. Job 1:6; 2:1 lend support to the latter, while Pss 29:1; 89:7 make the former possible. However, it is the nature of "the sons of the gods/God," that has perplexed commentators. Three main kinds of interpretation are offered by modern exegetes. First, "the sons of the gods" are nonhuman, godlike beings such as angels, demons, or spirits. Second, "the sons of the gods" are superior men such as kings or other rulers. Third, "the sons of the gods" are godly men, the descendants of Seth as opposed to the godless descendants of Cain.

The "angel" interpretation is at once the oldest view and that of most modern commentators. It is assumed in the earliest Jewish exegesis (e.g., the books of 1 Enoch 6:2ff; Jubilees 5:1), LXX, Philo (*De Gigant* 2:358), Josephus (*Ant.* 1.31) and the Dead Sea Scrolls (1QapGen 2:1; CD 2:17–19). The NT (2 Pet 2:4, Jude 6, 7) and the earliest Christian writers (e.g., Justin, Irenaeus, Clement of Alexandria, Tertullian, Origen) also take this line.

Modern scholars who accept this view advance three main reasons for supporting it. First, elsewhere in the OT (e.g., Ps 29:1, Job 1:6) "sons of God" refers to heavenly, godlike creatures. Second, in 6:1–4 the contrast is between "the sons of the gods" on the one hand and "the daughters of man" on the other. The alternative interpretations presuppose that what Gen 6 really meant was that "the sons of some men" married "the daughters of other men." The present phrase "sons of God" is, to say the least, an obscure way of expressing such an idea. It is made the more implausible by 6:1 where "man" refers to all mankind. It is natural to assume that in v 2 "daughters of man" has an equally broad reference, not a specific section of the human race. Finally, it is pointed out that in Ugaritic literature "sons of God" refers to members of the divine pantheon, and it is likely that Genesis is using the phrase in a similar sense.

The royal interpretation was introduced into Jewish exegesis about the middle of the second century A.D., partly, it seems, out of conviction that angels could not indulge in sexual intercourse and partly to suppress speculation about them (P. S. Alexander, *JJS* 23 [1972] 60–71.) It subsequently became the most usual rabbinic view and has a number of Christian advocates as well (e.g., F. Dexinger, *Sturz der Gottersöhne*; M. G. Kline, *WTJ* 24 [1963] 187–204). D. J. A. Clines (*JSOT* 13 [1979] 35) suggests a combination of the angelic and royal interpretations: the sons of God may be "*both* divine beings *and* antediluvian rulers."

In support of this view it is pointed out that judges are apparently identified with gods and the sons of the Most High in Ps 82. Certainly the Davidic king is called God's son in 2 Sam 7:14 and Ps 2:7 and at Ugarit King Keret is described as El's son. On this interpretation the kings were guilty of an abuse by marrying "whoever they chose," i.e., compelling women to join their polygamous harems. It is urged that only an interpretation which identifies "sons of God" with men as opposed to angels can explain why men are judged for the intermarriages that occurred.

The Sethite interpretation, for a long time the preferred Christian exegesis, again because it avoided the suggestion of carnal intercourse with angels, has few advocates today. In support of this view it was pointed out that the Sethites are the chosen line from whom Noah is descended, and that elsewhere in the Pentateuch the elect nation Israel is called God's son (Exod 4:22; Deut 14:1).

L. Eslinger (*JSOT* 13 [1979] 65–73) has reversed the identifications, claiming that the Cainites are the "sons of God" and that the Sethites are the daughters of men, for in 4:19–24 it is Cain's descendant Lamek who is the polygamist and it is the Sethites of chap. 5 who have sons and *daughters*. Furthermore he notes that the description of the sin of the sons of God, "they saw . . . good . . . took," echoes Eve's archetypal sin, so that they must be regarded as the sinful line, i.e., the Cainites. Though Eslinger has observed interesting echoes of the fall in Gen 6:2, he offers no explanation of why the wicked Cainites should be called "sons of God." Nor do his other arguments carry conviction.

Given the variety of ways in which "sons of the gods" has been understood, it is hard to know which sense is correct—angelic, royal or traditional Sethite. In the light of Canaanite usage and of passages such as Job 1:6, it seems most likely that the "angelic" interpretation is to be preferred. Much of the objection to this view would be eliminated if the term "angel" were avoided and a more ambivalent term such as "spirit" were used instead. In Job 1 and 2, "the Satan" appears as one of "the sons of God" and is a highly malevolent member of the heavenly court. This OT picture of the heavenly council, in which the LORD chairs a committee of "the sons of God" (cf. Ps 82), parallels Canaanite descriptions of the heavenly pantheon, whose gods often enjoy sexual intercourse. It seems likely, then, that Genesis believed the sons of God could have acted similarly. If the modern reader finds this story incredible, that reflects a materialism that tends to doubt the existence of spirits, good or ill. But those who believe that the creator could unite himself to human nature in the Virgin's womb will not find this story intrinsically beyond belief.

"Saw that the daughters of man were good and they took wives for themselves from any they chose." Some commentators have argued that the very phraseology used to describe these unions condemns them. It is suggested that rape or polygamy is implied by this description. However, this cannot be sustained. Cassuto correctly insists that these words can apply to perfectly proper marriages: "The passage contains not a single word . . . alluding to rape or adultery or any act against the LORD's will" (1:294). Westermann argues that the parallels in 12:10–20 and 2 Sam 11 show that seeing and taking a woman is automatically condemned, and such a condemnation may be inferred here. But again his conclusion is unjustified. The Pharaoh and David were condemned because they committed adultery with other men's wives; there is no hint of that here.

One must look behind the specific terms used to discover the reason for the condemnation in this case. The sequence of "saw . . . good . . . took" parallels most closely the terminology in 3:6 and suggests the sinfulness of the action of the sons of God. When the woman saw and took, she transgressed a boundary set by the LORD. The essence of Adam's sin was to acquiesce in his wife's transgression by eating the fruit she gave him. Here the fault of the daughters of man lies presumably in their consenting to intercourse with "the sons of the gods." It ought also to be borne in mind that the girls' fathers would also have been implicated, since, if there was no rape or seduction, their approval to these matches would have been required. The obvious avoidance of any terms suggesting lack of consent makes the girls and their parents culpable, the more so when the previous chapter has demonstrated that mankind was breeding very successfully on its own.

This story may also be, as Drewermann (181–83) suggests, a polemic against the fertility cults which often included sacred marriages between the gods and men. Certainly, the OT law strongly condemns all attempts at crossbreeding of species. Mixed crops are prohibited, and mixed clothing (Lev 19:19; Deut 22:9–11). Copulating with animals is a capital offense (Lev 20:16) and marrying non-Israelites is also outlawed (Deut 7:3). It therefore follows that unions between the "sons of the gods" and human women must be at least as reprehensible, for in this case both parties must know it is against the will of the creator who made the world so that everything should reproduce "according to its kind" (1:11–12, 21, 24–25).

3 "Then the LORD said," as in v 7 and 3:22, introduces God's thoughts to himself.

"My spirit shall not remain in man for ever." Almost every word in this statement has been the subject of controversy, though there are signs of an emerging consensus among recent commentators.

It is relevant to note first of all the similarity with 3:22, "[lest he] live for ever." This implies that the divine-human intercourse was, like eating the tree of life, intended to procure eternal life for man. This attempt to usurp what belongs to God alone is therefore condemned. Instead human life is limited to a maximum of 120 years.

"My spirit." Though Skinner argued this referred "to the divine substance common to Yahweh and the angels" (145), it seems much more likely that it denotes the life-giving power of God, on which every creature is entirely dependent for its life. It is called the "breath of life" (2:7) or "the spirit of life" (6:17; 7:15) and the phrase "my spirit" is used again in Ezek 37:14.

"Remain," זון, is a hapax legomenon that has been variously understood. However, the early translators (G, Vg) seem to have been confirmed by modern etymological research. Cassuto pointed to cognates in Akkadian, Aramaic, Arabic, and late Hebrew which all support the meaning "abide, remain."

"For ever." Context dictates this translation rather than "never again" which Jacob argues for on grounds of word order (cf. Jer 3:12). To say "My spirit shall never more remain in man" would imply that the spirit of life is to be immediately withdrawn and that all men would die. Translating "My spirit shall not remain for ever" implies a limit on human life without being specific. Only later by mentioning 120 years is the limit specified.

"Because he is flesh." On "because" see Notes. "Flesh," בשר, is one of the most significant anthropological terms in the OT (for fuller discussion see N. P. Bratsiotis, TDOT 2:317–32; H. W. Wolff, Anthropology of the OT; J. Scharbert, Fleisch, Geist und Seele im Pentateuch [SBS 19 Stuttgart: Katholisches Bibelwerk, 1967]). Its basic meaning is "flesh," "body." The "flesh" stands in contrast to the "blood" which represents the "life" or "soul" of the creature (9:4; Lev 17:11). Animals, like men, are described as "flesh" (7:21), but God never is. Compare Isa 31:3 where "man" and "flesh" are set over against "God" and "spirit." Without the continual indwelling of the Spirit, the flesh perishes and man returns to the dust (Job 34:14–15; cf. Gen 2:7; 3:19; Isa 40:7). Sometimes "flesh" refers to man's moral weakness and propensity to sin (cf. Gen 6:12), but here the primary reference must be to man's mortality and his total dependence on God's power to survive.

"His days shall be one hundred and twenty years." In the immediate context of Gen 6:1–4 the meaning of this remark appears quite obvious: from now on nobody shall live to more than 120 years of age. However, within the wider setting of Genesis this interpretation is problematic, for Noah and many of his descendants live hundreds of years (Gen 11). Even Abraham lived to 175; Isaac, to 180; and Jacob, to 147 years. On the other hand, according to 5:32, Noah was 500 years old when he fathered Ham, Shem, and Japhet, and 600 years old when the flood began (7:6), so some commentators (e.g., Keil, König, Kidner) have suggested that 120 years represents a period of grace before the flood. It may be, however, that the author thought of the 120 years as a maximum life-span that was only gradually implemented; cf. the slow-acting curses of Eden 3:16–19. In the post-flood period, the recorded ages steadily decline (chap. 11), and later figures very rarely exceed 120. After the time of Jacob, the longest-lived include Joseph (110, Gen 50:26), Moses (120, Deut 34:7), and Joshua (110, Josh 24:29). Only Aaron (123, Num 33:39) exceeds 120.

4 The relationship of this verse to the preceding verses is problematic. It appears to be going back to the spirit-human marriages of vv 1–2, but it is not clear what the relationship is between the Nephilim and these unions, nor can we be certain what is meant by "in those days and also afterwards." Some have ascribed the obscurity to the insertion of v 3 by the editor, between v 2 and v 4. Westermann suggests that v 4 may be an independent tradition that has been tacked on. But whatever the redactional processes, the present text is what must be explained, and it seems wisest to accept the consensus that v 4 is simply continuing the subject of vv 1–3.

"The Nephilim were in the earth in those days." The only other biblical reference to the Nephilim is Num 13:33. The Israelite spies said they saw the Nephilim, who were so tall that they felt as small as grasshoppers. LXX and Vg also understand them to be giants. Indeed their term, *gigantes*, suggests they understood the Nephilim to be the offspring of the "angel" marriages, for in Greek mythology the *gigantes* were the product of the union of earth and heaven. And this is the way most modern commentators understand the term.

The etymology of "Nephilim" is obscure. If Ezek 32:20–28 is alluding to Gen 6:1–4, it seems likely that he connected the Nephilim with נפל "to fall." There he repeatedly speaks of גבורים "the warriors," the same term as here, who have fallen in battle and who now inhabit Sheol. Similarly the *gigantes* of Greek mythology were defeated and imprisoned in the earth.

"In those days" refers to the pre-flood period when the events described in vv 1–3 took place. "And also afterwards" is a parenthetic comment reminding the reader that giants were still around in the post-diluvian period (Num 13:33). However, to avoid the implication that the race of giants survived the flood, or that "angel" marriages continued after it, rabbinic commentators preferred to suppose that "and also afterwards" refers to the period of grace before the flood. But this seems strained, as the following sentence implies continued visits by "angels to mortal wives" (Skinner, 147).

"Whenever the sons of the gods went in to the daughters of men, they bore them children." Though it is not impossible to translate this as a simple past event "When they went in . . ." etc., it is more natural (with Skinner, König, Gispen) to take the imperfect "went" and perfect preceded by *waw* ("bore . . . children") as frequentative. To "go in to" is a frequent euphemism for sexual intercourse (cf. 30:16; 38:16).

"They are the warriors from olden times." "They" refers to the Nephilim. "Warriors": cf. the same term in 10:8–9; Ezek 32:21, 27.

"From olden days" (עולם) defines long periods of time past or future. When such times are of unlimited duration, "eternity" may be an appropriate translation; cf. לעולם "forever." But here the reference is simply to remote antiquity; cf. Josh 24:2; 1 Sam 27:8; Isa 63:16.

"Famous men." Despite their origin and their fame, the Nephilim were only human.

5–8 Though these verses are often regarded as the prologue to the flood story, it is better, as argued above, to view them as the final paragraph of 5:1–6:8. But, as often in Genesis, the conclusion of one section hints at themes to be developed in the next. Here Noah, the hero of 6:9–9:29, is introduced; a divine decree of destruction is announced, although without any indication of how it will be executed; and finally, there are numerous hints that the judgment will be tinged with mercy.

Theologically, this paragraph is also of great moment. Being largely the formulation of the editor of Genesis (cf. above on *Form/Structure/Setting*, von Rad and Westermann), it gives important insights into the theology of the writer. Here in prophetic fashion the narrator interrupts his report of the divine motives that underlie the decree of destruction (6:5a, 7) in order to highlight in particular man's depravity (6:5b) and God's reluctance to punish (6:6).

5 "The LORD saw" is used in other passages to introduce a decisive divine intervention (6:12; 29:31; Exod 2:25; 3:4; 4:31, etc.). "It does not denote sudden perception but the consideration of a state of affairs that had long been in existence, and on account of which a decision has to be taken" (Cassuto, 1:302; cf. 30:1, 9; 50:15). Here the phrase clearly recalls the refrain of chap. 1, "God saw that it was good," and its climax, "God saw *all* that he had made . . . that it was really very good" (1:31). The contrast could hardly be more absolute: "The LORD saw that the *evil* of man was great in the earth and *every* idea of his mind was nothing but *evil all* the time." Note the twice-repeated כל ("all/every") and רע ("evil"). This verse also stands in ironic contrast with the sons of God *seeing* the *good* daughters of men who had *multiplied* רב (cf. רַבָּה "great") on the earth, 6:1–2.

A relatively bland statement about the greatness of human evil is supplemented by a very explicit analysis of its nature and origin: "Every idea of the plans of his mind was nothing but evil all the time." Similar phrases to "idea of the plans of his mind" reappear in 8:21; 1 Chr 28:9; 29:18. "Idea," יצר: what is molded and created by the mind. The verb יָצַר is to mold as a potter does; cf. Isa 29:16; Gen 2:7, 8. "Plan, thought," מחשבה, often suggests thinking ahead. "Mind," לב, literally, "heart," is the center of the human personality in biblical anthropology, where will and thought originate (Prov 4:23); it is not merely the source of the emotions as in English. This text asserts that every human thought from its inception is intrinsically "evil," רע, (cf. Prov 15:26), a comprehensive and general term of condemnation, especially for things disapproved of by God (cf. H. J. Stoebe, *THWAT* 2:794–803). Few texts in the OT are so explicit and all-embracing as this in specifying the extent of human sinfulness and depravity (cf. Ps 14:1–3; 51:3–12 [1–10]; Jer 17:9–10). But that sin has its root in man's thought world is certainly a commonplace of biblical ethics (cf. "You shall not covet," Exod 20:17).

6 "The LORD regretted (נחם) that he had made (עשה) man in the earth. He felt bitterly indignant about it (עצב)." These three key roots have been used in 5:29 by Lamek when naming Noah: "May this one bring (נחם) us relief from our work (מעשה) and the pain (עצבון) of our hands." An English translation cannot bring out the ironic punning of the Hebrew text. Lamek's hopes for consolation by Noah correspond to the creator's disappointment with his creation.

"Regret" or "repent" may suggest a mere change of attitude, but when God "repents," he starts to act differently. Here and in 1 Sam 15:11 and Jer 18:10 he regrets some good thing he has done for his people, whereas in Exod 32:12, 14; 2 Sam 24:16; Amos 7:3, 6 he repents of some evil he is carrying out. That God should change his mind might lead to his being accused of capriciousness, which Scripture firmly denies: "God is not a son of man that he should repent" (Num 23:19; cf. 1 Sam 15:29). Such remarks obviously raise various questions for the doctrine of divine sovereignty and its correlate human responsibility, but theological systematization is hardly the concern of the biblical narrators. For them divine repentance is a response to man's changes of heart, whether for better or worse.

"He felt bitterly indignant." The root עצב is used to express the most intense form of human emotion, a mixture of rage and bitter anguish. Dinah's brothers felt this way after she was raped; so did Jonathan when he heard Saul planned to kill David; and David reacted similarly when he heard of Absalom's death (34:7; 1 Sam 20:34; 2 Sam 19:3[2]). A deserted wife feels this way (Isa 54:6). The word is used of God's feelings in only two other passages (Ps 78:40; Isa 63:10). Only here is the verb supplemented by the phrase "to his heart" (in our translation "bitterly"), underlining the strength of God's reaction to human sinfulness.

7–8 "I will wipe out" (מחה) is used of erasing names from records (e.g., Exod 17:14; 32:32–33) and wiping plates (2 Kgs 21:13). Since water was sometimes used for achieving this result (Num 5:23), the very word chosen perhaps hints at how the complete annihilation of mankind will be secured (cf. its threefold use later in the story, at 7:4, 23). The elaboration of the divine decree against "whom I have created from the land, man, land animals, creeping creatures and birds . . . I made them" makes the point that the flood reverses God's great act of creation. The very terminology reflects the account of Gen 1 (cf. 1:20, 24–30).

Yet though a more catastrophic sentence is hard to imagine, it is tinged with a glimmer of hope: the very terms used to pronounce it, "regret" (נחם) and "wipe out" (מחה), make paronomastic allusion to "Noah" (נח), the man who "found favor (חן) in the eyes of the LORD." "To find favor" is a formal expression often used when someone is making a request of a superior (e.g., 33:8, 10) or when someone in authority helps someone without status (39:4). It is sometimes used in prayer when men are asking favors of God (e.g., 18:3; Exod 33:12, 13, 16), but it is very rare for it to be said outright that a man has found favor in God's sight. One such example is Moses (Exod 33:17). This sentence therefore puts Noah on a par with Moses as one of the greatest saints of the old covenant and of course leads us to expect that Noah will escape the coming cataclysm.

Thus this final paragraph (6:5–8) of the second great section of Genesis introduces us to the theme of the section (6:9–9:29), the universal judgment from which Noah alone will be saved. 5:1–6:8 began with creation and closes with a warning that this creation will be destroyed. The world is going to be reduced to a watery chaos before a new start can be made.

Explanation

Gen 5:1–6:8 could be described as the story of the old world, the world before the flood. It begins with the creation of Adam, traces the multiplication of his descendants, and concludes with the announcement of the total annihilation of every living creature. Chap. 5 links these two primal events, creation and the flood, by a genealogy of ten patriarchs. Within the time-scale of Genesis, this chapter covers the longest period in world history. But apart from the first man, Adam, and the last antediluvian, Noah, of whom much more is related elsewhere, this chapter says remarkably little about these ancient heroes, simply that these men were born, fathered children, and then died in their turn.

The only personal details, the age at which they fathered their first child and their age at death, have perplexed and embarrassed later writers. Yet

these specific details serve to remind the reader that there were real human
people made in God's image who lived before the flood. Their great ages
express the remoteness of the times in which they lived. If post-enlightenment
readers delight in chronological computations with a view to demonstrating
the implausibility of Genesis' timescale, these interests are far removed from
the intention of Genesis. The ages attributed to these men of old convey
their remoteness from the writer's own age and yet their reality. As in later
Israel a man's age at the birth of his first child and at his death was considered
important, so it was also before the flood. And though these pre-flood men
lived a very long time, none reached even a thousand years, which is a mere
day in the light of God's eternity. All except Enoch died, showing that though
they inherited Adam's likeness, they also suffered the inexorable judgment
on his sin.

A belief in the longevity of our forefathers was widespread in antiquity.
Likewise, it was widely held that the occasional man escaped death and was
translated to heaven. According to Genesis, Enoch achieved this not by heroic
efforts, but because of his piety: "he walked with God," something every
devout Israelite was expected to do. His fate hints at a life beyond this, a
life that is to be preferred to the present, which, as Noah's father observed,
is dogged by hard work, pain, and the curse upon the land. The shortness
of Enoch's life must in the context of his piety and Lamek's comments be
regarded as a reward or a blessing, not a misfortune.

The transformation of oriental theology found in chaps. 1–5 continues
in 6:1–4. Stories of superhuman demigods like Gilgamesh were a commonplace, and intercourse with the divine was regularly sought in the fertility
cults of Canaan and the sacred marriage rites of Mesopotamia. Through
such procedures men sought to achieve enhanced earthly life and even eternal
life. But to Hebrew thinking such ideas were utterly abhorrent. Within the
earthly realm the creator's categories must not be transgressed. Each species
had been created to propagate itself "according to its type." Thus crossbreeding
of cattle, intermarriage with foreigners, even plowing with teams of different
types of animals or wearing garments of mixed cloth was forbidden by the
law. How much worse was this breach of the boundary between the earthly
and heavenly realms. It seems that the sons of the gods must be understood
as spiritual beings akin to angels or demons. Though some have regarded it
as unfair that mankind should have been punished for this transgression
which was provoked by the initiative of spirits, the narrative gives no hint
that seduction or rape was involved. These unions are described in terms
befitting perfecly normal marriages, which presupposes that the fathers of
the girls gave their free assent to the arrangements. In biblical times a man
might propose, but it was certainly the girl's father who disposed when it
came to matrimony. The narrator evidently pictures the girls' fathers encourag-
ing these unions, just as it was presumably fathers who pushed their daughters
to participate in the fertility cults. So, as in Gen 3, we have the temptation
to sin coming from outside man, but his freely given consent brings him
under judgment.

As often in Scripture the punishment is made to fit the crime. Grasping
at immortality through these liaisons, man is sentenced to live a maximum

of 120 years, roughly a sevenfold reduction over the average lifespan of the antediluvians. Though some of Noah's immediate descendants live longer than this, their lives are much shorter than the pre-flood patriarchs. The Pentateuch shows that by the time of Moses one hundred and twenty was regarded as the greatest age a man could hope to reach.

But this sentence did not deter some from continuing to ignore divine displeasure by perpetuating these strange unions: "Also afterwards . . . the sons of the gods went into the daughters of man." This situation reveals the full extent of man's depravity: "Every idea of the plans of his mind was nothing but evil all the time." It also reveals the intensity of God's abhorrence of man's attitudes and actions: "The LORD regretted that he had made man in the earth. He felt bitterly indignant about it." In other words, he felt the bitter rage of someone whose closest friend had been terribly wronged. This is the anger of someone who loves deeply. It spurs on to drastic action, in this case nothing less than God's destruction of his creatures "man, animals, creeping creatures and birds."

But even in the way the sentence of utter destruction is couched, with its pre-echoes of Noah's name, there are glimmers of hope. The close of the first chapter of mankind's history is so phrased as to indicate that it will not be the last, for "Noah found favor in the eyes of the LORD." The full consequences of the divine decision are worked out in the next section of Genesis, the story of the flood, which marks the end of the old humanity and the beginning of the new. Noah, the righteous survivor of the old world, will be the founder of the new epoch.

The brevity with which Gen 5 deals with such a long period in the life of mankind has led to its comparative neglect in later theology. Luke (3:37–38), using this genealogy, traces the ancestry of Christ back to Adam to show he was not only the son of Adam, but also the son of God. The mysterious fate of Enoch led to much speculation among later Jewish writers. For Heb 11:5–6, Enoch is one of the great examples of men of faith: "By faith Enoch was taken up so that he should not see death" (cf. Sir 44:16; 49:14). The race of supermen, the offspring of these mixed marriages, also excited interest (cf. Bar 3:26–28; Sir 16:7; Wis 14:6). 2 Pet 2:4 uses the judgment that befell these angels according to tradition as a warning for his readers: "If God did not spare the angels when they sinned, but cast them into hell . . .": cf. Jude 6. So then this section displays all those features typical of other parts of the primeval history. It offers a vivid picture of a lost world, a world destroyed by the flood. The great age of the antediluvians points up their distance from us, but their names and precise chronology remind us that these almost-forgotten souls have by their actions affected the present. If the majority of them stand as a grim warning of the consequences of disobeying the divine decrees, the examples of Enoch and Noah encourage the faithful to walk with God whatever the cost.

The Story of Noah   (6:9–9:29)

Bibliography

(See also Main Bibliography and Gen 1–11 bibliography)

Anderson, B. W. "From Analysis to Synthesis: The Interpretation of Gen 1–11." *JBL* 97 (1978) 23–39. **Barnard, A. N.** "Was Noah a Righteous Man?" *Theology* 84 (1971) 311–14. **Baumgarten, J. M.** "Some Problems of the Jubilees Calendar in Current Research." *VT* 32 (1982) 485–89. **Ben-Uri, A. M.** "Noah's Ark: An Example of Construction Language in the Law." (Heb.) *BMik* 17 (1971) 24–31. **Brueggemann, W.** "Kingship and Chaos." *CBQ* 33 (1971) 317–32. **Clark, W. M.** "The Righteousness of Noah." *VT* 21 (1971) 261–80. ———. "The Flood and the Structure of the Pre-patriarchal History." *ZAW* 83 (1971) 184–211. **Clines, D. J. A.** "Noah's Flood: The Theology of the Flood Narrative." *Faith and Thought* 100 (1972–73) 128–42. **Cryer, F. H.** "The Interrelationships of Gen 5:32; 11:10 and 7:6 and the Chronology of the Flood." *Bib* 66 (1985) 241–61. **Fritz, V.** "'Solange die Erde Steht'—Vom Sinn der jahwistischen Fluterzählung in Gen 6–8." *ZAW* 94 (1982) 599–614. **Gunn, D. M.** "Deutero-Isaiah and the Flood." *JBL* 94 (1975) 493–508. **Kessler, M.** "Rhetorical Criticism of Gen 7." In *Rhetorical Criticism: Essays in Honor of J. Muilenburg*, ed. J. J. Jackson and M. Kessler. Pittsburg: Pickwick Press, 1974. 1–17. **Kselman, J. S.** "A Note on Gen 7:11." *CBQ* 35 (1973) 491–93. **Larsson, G.** "Chronological Parallels between the Creation and the Flood." *VT* 27 (1977) 490–92. ———. "The Documentary Hypothesis and the Chronological Structure of the OT." *ZAW* 97 (1985) 316–33. **Lemche, N. P.** "The Chronology in the Story of the Flood." *JSOT* 18 (1980) 52–62. **Lewis, J. P.** *A Study of the Interpretation of Noah and the Flood in Jewish and Christian Literature.* Leiden: Brill, 1968. **Loewenstamm, S. E.** "The Flood." *Comparative Studies in Biblical and Ancient Oriental Literatures.* AOAT 204. Kevelaer: Butzon and Bercker, 1980. 93–121. ———. "Die Wasser der biblischen Sintflut: ihr Hereinbrechen und ihr Verschwinden." *VT* 34 (1984) 179–84. **Longacre, R. E.** "The Discourse Structure of the Flood Narrative." *JAAR* 47 Sup (1979) 89–133. **McEvenue, S. E.** *The Narrative Style of the Priestly Writer.* AnBib 50. Rome: BIP, 1971. **Mallowan, M. E. L.** "Noah's Flood Reconsidered." *Iraq* 26 (1964) 62–82. **Morawe, G.** "Erwägungen zu Gen 7:11 und 8:2: Ein Beitrag zur Überlieferungsgeschichte des priesterlichen Flutberichtes." *Theologische Versuche* 3 (1971) 31–52. **Müller, H. P.** "Das Motiv für die Sintflut." *ZAW* 97 (1985) 295–316. **Muraoka, T.** "Hebrew Philological Notes." *AJBI* 5 (1979) 88–104. **Oberforcher, R.** *Die Flutprologe als Kompositionsschlüssel der biblischen Urgeschichte: Ein Beitrag zur Redaktionskritik.* ITS 8. Innsbruck: Tyrolia Verlag, 1981. **Patten, D. W.** "The Biblical Flood: A Geographical Perspective." *BSac* 128 (1971) 36–49. **Pearce, E. K. V.** "The Flood and Archaeology." *Faith and Thought* 101 (1974) 228–41. **Petersen, D. L.** "The Yahwist on the Flood." *VT* 26 (1976) 438–46. **Raikes R. L** "The Physical Evidence for Noah's Flood." *Iraq* 28 (1966) 52–63. **Rendtorff, R.** "Gen 8:21 und die Urgeschichte des Jahwisten." *KD* 7 (1961) 69–78. **Sasson, J. M.** "Word Play in Gen 6:8–9." *CBQ* 36 (1974) 165–66. **Schlosser, J.** "Les Jours de Noé et de Lot." *RB* 80 (1973) 13–36. **Steck, O. H.** "Gen 12:1–3 und die Urgeschichte des Jahwisten." *Probleme biblischer Theologie: G. von Rad FS*, ed. H. W. Wolff. Munich: Kaiser Verlag, 1971. 525–54. **Ullendorff, E.** "The Construction of Noah's Ark." *Is Biblical Hebrew a Language?* Wiesbaden: Harrassowitz, 1977. 48–49. **Weinfeld, M.** "Gen 7:11; 8:1–2 against the Background of Ancient Near Eastern Tradition." *WO* 9 (1978) 242–48. **Wenham, G. J.** "The Coherence of the Flood Narrative." *VT* 28 (1978) 336–48. **Wöller, V.** "Zur Übersetzung von כִּי in Gen 8:21 und 9:6." *ZAW* 94 (1982) 637–38.

Translation

6:9 *This is the family history of Noah.* ᵃ*Noah was a righteous man. He was blameless among his contemporaries. Noah walked*ᵇ *with God.*ᵃ ¹⁰*Noah fathered*ᵃ *three sons, Shem, Ham and Japhet.*

¹¹ *The earth was ruined*ᵃ *in God's sight and the earth was filled*ᵃ *with violence.* ¹² *God saw the earth; it was really*ᵃ *ruined because all flesh had ruined its way on the earth.*

¹³ *Then God said to Noah, "The end of all flesh has been determined*ᵃ *by me, because the earth is full*ᵇ *of violence because of them, so* ᶜ*I am about to*ᶜ *ruin*ᵈ *them with*ᵉ *the earth.* ¹⁴ ᵃ*Make*ᵇ *yourself an ark of gopher wood.*ᵃ *You shall make the ark with reeds*ᶜ *and seal it inside and out with pitch.* ¹⁵ *This is how you are to make it:* ᵃ*the length of the ark shall be three hundred cubits, its breadth fifty cubits, and its height thirty cubits.*ᵃ ¹⁶ *You shall make a roof for the ark and complete*ᵃ *it* ᵇ*to a cubit upwards.*ᵇ *You shall put a door in the side of the ark. Lower, second, and third decks you shall make.*

¹⁷ *"I myself*ᵃ *am about to bring*ᵇ *the flood, water*ᶜ *over the earth, to ruin*ᵈ *all flesh in which there is the spirit of life beneath the heaven.* ᵉ*Everything on earth will expire.*ᵉ ¹⁸ *But I shall confirm*ᵃ *my covenant with you, and* ᵇ*you will enter the ark, you,*ᶜ *your sons, your wife, and your sons' wives.*ᵇ ¹⁹ ᵃ*At the same time you shall bring*ᵇ *into the ark to stay alive*ᶜ *with you some of every living thing,*ᵈ *some of all flesh, pairs*ᵉ *of everything:*ᵃ ᶠ*they shall be male and female.*ᶠ ²⁰ *Some of the birds according to their types, some of the land animals according to their types,* ᵃ*some of all the creeping things that creep on the earth according to their types, pairs of everything will come to you to stay alive.* ²¹ *But as for you,*ᵃ *take and store some of every edible*ᵇ *food, so that you and they will have it to eat."*

²² *Noah did exactly as God commanded him,* ᵃ*so he did.*ᵃ

7:1 *The* Lord ᵃ *said to Noah: "Enter the ark, you and all your household, because you* ᵇ *I have seen are righteous before me in this generation.* ² *You must take seven pairs,* ᵃ*man and wife,*ᵃ *of all clean domesticated animals and one pair,*ᵇ *man and wife, of animals which are not clean;* ³ *also seven pairs, male and female, of the* ᵃ*birds of the sky to preserve*ᵇ *descendants over the whole earth.* ⁴ *For in*ᵃ *seven days' time I am about to make it rain*ᵇ *on the earth for* ᶜ*forty days and forty nights.*ᶜ *I shall wipe out all existence that I have made from the surface of the land."*

⁵ *So Noah did exactly as the* Lord *commanded him.* ⁶ ᵃ*Now Noah was six hundred years old*ᵃ ᵇ*when the flood came,*ᵇ ᶜ*water on the earth.*ᶜ ⁷ *So* ᵃ*Noah entered*ᵃ *the ark, his sons, his wife and his sons' wives as well, because of the waters of the flood.* ⁸ *Some of the clean land animals and some of the land animals that are not clean and some of the birds and* ᵃ*everything that creeps on the earth* ⁹ *came to Noah in the ark in pairs, male and female, as God*ᵃ *had commanded Noah.*

¹⁰ *In seven days the waters of the flood came upon the earth.* ¹¹ *In the six hundredth year*ᵃ *of Noah's life, in the second month on the seventeenth*ᵇ *day of the month, on that very day all the springs of the great deep burst open and the windows of heaven were opened.* ¹² *Heavy rain fell on the earth forty days and forty nights.* ¹³ *On this very day, Noah, and Shem and Ham and Japhet, Noah's sons, Noah's wife, and the three*ᵃ *wives of his sons with them*ᵇ *entered the ark,* ¹⁴ *they and all the wild animals according to their types, all the domesticated animals according*

to their types and all the creeping things which creep on the earth according to their types, all birds according to their types, [a]every small bird and winged creature.[a] [15]So[a] there came in to Noah into the ark pairs of all flesh[a] in which there was the spirit of life. [16]Those who entered were [a]male and female of all flesh: they entered[a] as God had commanded him. Then the LORD shut him in.

[17]The flood was forty days[a] on the earth; the waters multiplied and lifted[b] the ark so that it floated[c] above the earth. [18][a]The waters triumphed[a] and multiplied greatly on the earth and the ark traveled[b] on the face of the waters. [19][a]The waters triumphed[a] exceedingly on the earth and all the high mountains under the whole heaven were covered.[b] [20][a]To a depth of fifteen cubits[a] the waters triumphed, so that the mountains were covered. [21]All flesh which moved on the earth expired, among[a] the birds, domesticated animals, wild animals, all swarming things which swarm on the earth and all mankind. [22]Everything which has the breath of the spirit of life in its nostrils, namely[a] everything on the dry land, died. [23]He wiped[a] out all existence which is on the surface of the land, from man to animals to creeping things to birds of the sky, and they were wiped out from the earth. There was left[b] only Noah and what was with him in the ark. [24]The waters triumphed over the earth for a hundred and fifty days.

[8:1]God remembered Noah and all the wild animals and all the domesticated animals that were with him in the ark, so God caused a wind to pass[a] over the earth and the waters receded.[b] [2]Then the springs of the great deep and the windows of heaven were sealed[a] and the heavy rain from heaven was restrained.[b] [3]Then the waters [a]gradually receded[a] from the earth, and the waters had declined by the end[b] of a hundred and fifty days. [4]Then in the seventh month on the seventeenth[a] day of the month the ark rested[b] on the mountains[c] of Ararat. [5]The waters [a]continued to decline[a] until the tenth month: in the tenth month on the first[b] day of the month the mountain tops appeared.[c]

[6]After forty days Noah opened the window of the ark which he had made [7]and sent[a] out a[b] raven [c]and it went [d]to and fro[d] until the water dried[e] out on the earth.

[8][a]Then he sent out a dove from him to see [b]if the waters had gone down[b] on the land. [9]But the dove did not find anywhere for its foot to rest, so it returned to him in the ark, for there was water all over the earth. Then he put out his hand, took it, and brought it into him in the ark. [10]He then waited[a] another seven days and then sent the dove out of the ark again.[b] [11]The dove came back to him at evening time, and there[a] in its beak was a plucked olive leaf![a] Then Noah knew that the waters had gone down on the earth. [12]He then waited[a] yet another seven days and then sent out the dove, but it did not return to him again.

[13]So in the six hundredth and first year,[a] in the first month on the first day of the month, the waters were drying up on the earth and Noah removed[b] the covering of the ark and saw that the surface of the land was dry. [14]In the second month on the twenty-seventh day of the month, the earth was dried out.

[15]God spoke to Noah as follows: [16][a]"Go out of the ark, you and your wife, your sons and their wives with you.[a] [17][a]All the wild animals that are with you, some of all flesh among the birds and the domesticated animals, and all the moving creatures who move on the earth, bring[b] them out with you that they may swarm in the earth, be fruitful and multiply in the earth."

[18]So Noah, his sons, his wife, and his sons' wives with him went[a] out; [19][a]all

the wild animals, ᵇand all the creeping things,ᵇ and all the birds and all the moving things that move on the earth went out of the ark by their clans.

²⁰Then Noah builtᵃ an altar to the LORD and took some of all the clean domesticated animals and some of all the clean birds and offeredᵇ burnt offerings on the altar. ²¹Then the LORD smeltᵃ the soothing aroma, and the LORD said to himself, "I shall notᵇᶜ curse the land again any further because of man, for the ideas of man's mind are evil from his youth, and never again shall Iᶜ smiteᵈ every living thing as I have done. ²²As long as the earth exists, sowing and harvest, cold andᵃ heat, summer andᵃ winter, day andᵃ night shall not cease."

⁹:¹God blessed Noah and his sons and said to them: "Be fruitful and multiply and fill the earth.ᵃ ²The fear of youᵃ and the dread of youᵃ will beᵇ on every wild animal of the earth,ᶜ and onᵈ every bird of the sky, onᵈ everything which moves on the land and onᵈ all the fishes of the sea: into your hands they have been given.ᵇᵉ ³Every moving thing that is alive shall beᵃ yours to eat: as I gave you the green vegetation, I have now givenᵃ you everything. ⁴Butᵃ flesh withᵇ its life, ᶜits blood,ᶜ you must never eat. ⁵But I shall require your blood for your lives, from the hand of every wild animal I shall require it; and from man's hand, ᵃfrom each man his brother's life,ᵃ I shall require the life of man. ⁶ᵃᵇWhoever sheds the blood of man,ᵇ byᶜ a man his blood shall be shed.ᵃ Because in the image of God he made man. ⁷But as for you,ᵃ be fruitful and multiply, ᵇswarm in the earth and multiplyᶜ in it."

⁸God said to Noah and his sons with him, ⁹"I myselfᵃ am about to confirm my covenant with you and with your descendants after you, ¹⁰and with every living being that was with you, among the birds, ᵃthe domesticated animals, and with all the wild animals of the earth who were with you, all who came out of the ark, ᵇall the animals of the earth.ᵇ ¹¹I shall confirmᵃ my covenant with you, so that never again shall all flesh be cutᵇ off byᶜ the waters of a flood, and there will never again be a flood to ruin the earth."

¹²Then God said to Noah,ᵃ "This is the sign of the covenant which I am making between me and you and every living being which was with you for farthest generations.ᵃ ¹³My bowᵃ I have put in the cloud, and it shall be a sign of the covenant between me and the earth. ¹⁴Whenever I bringᵃ clouds over the earth and the bow is visibleᵇ in the cloud, ¹⁵then I shall remember my covenant which is between me and you and every living being among all flesh, so that never again willᵃ the waters become a flood to ruin all flesh. ¹⁶My bow shall be in the cloud and I shall see it to remember an eternal covenant between God and every living being among all flesh which is on the earth." ¹⁷Then God said to Noah, "This is the sign of the covenant which I have confirmed between me and all flesh which is on the earth."

¹⁸The sons of Noah who came out of the ark were Shem, and Ham, and Japhet: and Ham was the father of Canaan. ¹⁹These three were the sons of Noah and from them the whole earth was populated.ᵃ

²⁰Noah, ᵃthe man of the land,ᵃ was the firstᵇ to plant a vineyard. ²¹He drankᵃ some wine, became drunk, and uncoveredᵇ himself inside hisᶜ tent. ²²Ham, Canaan's father, saw his father's nakedness and toldᵃᵇ his brothers outside. ²³Then Shem and Japhet tookᵃ a cloak, put itᵇ over the shoulders of them both, went backwards and coveredᶜ their father's nakedness: they faced backwardsᵈ and did not see their father's nakedness. ²⁴And Noah wokeᵃ up from his wine and realized what his youngestᵇ son had done to him. ²⁵Then he said, "Cursed be Canaan; the lowest of

slaves[a] *to his brothers shall he be."* [26] *He said: "Blessed is the* Lord, *the God of Shem: let Canaan be a slave to him."*[a] [27] *"May God enlarge*[a] *Japhet, and may he dwell in the tents of Shem and may Canaan be a slave to him."*[b]

[28] *Noah lived three hundred and fifty years after the flood.* [29] *Noah's whole life lasted nine hundred and fifty years, and then he died.*

Notes

6:9.a-a. Three clauses in apposition, the second and third specifying the nature of Noah's righteousness, his blamelessness with men, and his walk with God (*SBH*, 55–56.) It is therefore unnecessary with SamPent Vg to insert "and" before "faultless."

9.b. Cf. 5:22, 24.

10.a. Cf. n. 5:3.c. etc.

11.a. Waw consec + 3 fem sg impf niph: מלא, שחת.

12.a. והנה, lit., "and behold," emphasizes the element of surprise and discovery when God looked (*SBH*, 94–95.)

13.a. Lit., "has come before me," like the ratification of a royal decision. Cf. Esth 9:11.

13.b. The verb "to be full" can take the accus of the filling, here "violence," (GKC, 117z).

13.c-c. הנה + 1 sg suff followed by ptcp of imminent action (Joüon, 119n; Lambdin, 169).

13.d. Hiph ptcp of שחת + 3 masc pl suffix.

13.e. *BHS* emending to מאת "from" is unnecessary.

14.a-a. The general command is explicated by three long sentences (14b–16) in apposition to it. See *SBH* (50–51) for detailed analysis of the syntax of these verses.

14.b. Note the double accus following the verb "to make": "the ark, reeds" (GKC, 117ii). See Cassuto, 2:62, and *SBH*, 50–51.

14.c. *BHS*'s suggested repetition of קנים is unnecessary and so are its proposed transpositions of various phrases in vv 14–16. See *Comment* for justification of pointing קָנִים "reeds."

15.a-a. Three verbless clauses in explanatory apposition to the lead clause, "This . . . make it" (cf. *SBH*, 51, 99).

16.a. 2 masc sg impf piel of כלה + 3 fem sg suff. Many MSS put daghesh in ל, as would be expected.

16.b-b. See *Comment* on this obscure phrase.

17.a. Use of independent pronoun before הנה + pronom suff "is especially emphatic" (*EWAS*, 140). It emphasizes the contrast between what God is doing and what Noah must do, vv 14–16, 21.

17.b. הנה + suff + ptcp (hiph of בוא) used for imminent future (Joüon, 119n; Lambdin, 169).

17.c. Often regarded as a gloss explaining rare word "flood."

17.d. Piel inf. SamPent has hiph inf שחת. Same meaning.

17.e-e. Sentence in epic apposition to preceding one; cf. similar pattern in 7:21–22 (*SBH*, 39).

18.a. Waw consec + 1 sg pf hiph קום.

18.b-b. Note chiasmus with v 19a (*SBH*, 132).

18.c. Subj "you" repeated because of multiple subj "you . . . wives" governing verb "enter" (Joüon, 146c).

19.a-a. Chiastic apposition to 18b highlights simultaneity "At the same time." Cf. n. 6:18.b-b.

19.b. 2 masc sg impf hiph בוא

19.c. Inf hiph חיה

19.d. N.B. unusual pointing (הָחַי instead of הַחַי). SamPent reads החיה "the wild animals." G has a longer text.

19.e. G S apparently read שנים שנים "in twos" as in 7:9, 15 possibly correctly.

19.f-f. Specifying pairs: in apposition to previous sentence (*SBH*, 47, 55).

20.a. Some MSS SamPent S Vg *Tg. Ps.-J.* read ומכל "*and* some of all."

21.a. Pron brings out contrast with v 17 "I myself" (*SBH*, 151).

21.b. Lit., "which may be eaten": 3 masc sg impf niph אכל. On the nuance of potentiality in niphal, see Lambdin, 177.

22.a-a. Apposition clause marking end of paragraph (*SBH,* 42).

7:1.a. SamPent reads "God"; G "the Lᴏʀᴅ God."

1.b. Putting obj pron "you" before the verb probably emphasizes it: Noah as opposed to other men was righteous. Cf. 6:9 (*EWAS,* 38–39).

2.a-a. SamPent G S Vg have "male and female."

2.b. SamPent G S Vg "pairs" i.e. שנים שנים possibly original.

3.a. SamPent G insert "clean." To emphasize parallel with v 2, G also states that pairs, not seven pairs, of unclean birds entered the ark.

3.b. Inf piel of חיה (SamPent להחיות = hiphil inf),

4.a. ל "in," to denote the close of a period (BDB, 517a).

4.b. Hiph ptcp of מטר for imminent future (Joüon, 119n; 121e).

4.c-c. Accus for duration of time (GKC, 118k).

6.a-a. Episode-initial circumstantial clause (*SBH* 80).

6.b-b. Note chiasmus "flood was" with "was flood," v 17a, and rhetorical analysis of vv 6–17 in *SBH* (124–25).

6.c-c. Phrase explaining "flood was" (Gispen, 1:269).

7.a-a. Note the chiasmus between this verse "came . . . Noah" and vv 8–9 "the animals . . . came" and the use of epic apposition linking vv 7 and 8 (*SBH,* 124, 39).

8.a. Probably read with SamPent, G, S, Vg ומכל "and some of all."

9.a. SamPent, Vg read "the Lᴏʀᴅ."

10-12. On the use of apposition and chiasmus here see *SBH,* 41, 124–26.

11.a. Note the repetition שנה . . . שנת "year." On this construction see GKC, 134o; Joüon, 142o.

11.b. G, "twenty-seventh."

13.a. שלש, not שלשת, would be more usual grammar (GKC, 97c).

13.b. G S *Tg. Ps.-J.* read "with him," the more usual expression in this narrative.

14.a-a. Omitted by G.

15.a-a. Note chiasmus wi.h v 16a.

16.a-a. Chiasmus with v 15.

17.a. G adds "and forty nights": unnecessary harmonization with v 12.

17.b. Waw consec + 3 masc pl impf of נשא "to lift."

17.c. Waw consec + 3 fem sg impf of רום "to rise."

18.a-a. Note chiasmus with v 19a.

18.b. Waw consec + 3 fem sg impf of הלך "to go."

19.a-a. Note chiasmus with v 18a (*SBH,* 41).

19.b. Waw consec + 3 masc pl impf pual of כסה "to cover."

20.a-a. Accus of extent (GKC, 118h).

21.a. "Among," "consisting of": on this use of ב, see GKC, 119i.

22.a. מן "namely," "that is to say" (GKC, 119wN).

23.a. Waw consec + 3 masc sg impf apoc qal מחה "he wiped out." No need to repoint as niph as *BHS* suggests.

23.b. Waw consec + 3 masc sg impf niph שאר "to leave."

8:1.a. Waw consec + 3 masc sg impf hiph עבר "pass over."

1.b. Waw consec + 3 masc pl impf qal שכך "decrease."

2.a. Waw consec + 3 masc pl impf niph סכר "shut up."

2.b. Waw consec + 3 masc sg impf niph כלא "restrain."

3.a-a. The coupling of the inf abs of הלך "to go" with that of שוב "to return, recede" emphasizes the long time in which the waters continued to decline (GKC, 113u; Lambdin, 232).

3.b. SamPent reads מקץ, which is more usual in temporal phrases than MT מקצה; cf. 8:6. However, SamPent's preference for uniform spelling makes MT more likely.

4.a. As in 7:11, G has 27th day of the month.

4.b. Waw consec + 3 fem sg impf qal נוח "to rest."

4.c. Or "one of the mountains of Ararat." Here the pl "mountains" may be used for an indefinite sg (GKC, 124o); cf. Exod 21:22; Deut 17:5.

5.a-a. On this construction cf. n. 8:3.a-a.

5.b. On the use of cardinal for the day of the month see GKC, 134p.

5.c. 3 masc pl pf niph of ראה "to see."

7.a. Waw consec + 3 masc sg impf piel of שלח "to send."

7.b. Lit., "the raven." Heb. uses the definite article for a specific single obj, where English would use an indefinite (GKC, 126q-r).

7.c. G inserts "to see if the water had dried," assimilating to v 8.

7.d-d. Pair of inf abss following verb to express simultaneous or quasi-simultaneous acts (Joüon, 123m); cf. 1 Sam 6:12.

7.e. Inf constr of יבש "to be dry."

8.a. *BHS's* proposed insertion "and Noah waited seven days" would spoil the symmetry of the account; see below.

8.b-b. הקלו *he* interrogative (GKC, 150i) + 3 pl pf קלל "to be slight."

10.a. *BHS* suggests reading the commoner 3 masc sg impf piel form וייחל here and in v 12 from root יחל "to wait." The MT form is 3 masc sg impf qal from חול or חיל, usually "to writhe." Since the root means "to wait anxiously" in Mic 1:12, Gispen (1:283) argues for retaining the MT here.

10.b. ויסף = waw consec + 3 masc sg impf hiph יסף "to do again."

11.a. והנה, lit., "and behold," expresses Noah's surprise at the development (*SBH*, 94–95).

12.a. Waw consec + 3 masc sg impf niph יחל "to wait." Typically SamPent assimilates to v 10 ויחל. On *BHS's* suggested emendation, cf. n. 8:10a.

13.a. G adds "in the life of Noah."

13.b. Waw consec + 3 masc sg impf hiph of סור "to turn aside"; hiph, "to remove."

16.a-a. Note use of epic apposition between vv 16 and 17, and between 18 and 19 (*SBH*, 39).

17.a. SamPent, G, S unnecessarily add "and."

17.b. The K reading הוצא is the normal 2 masc sg impv hiph יצא "to go out." The Q הַיְצֵא is unusual, possibly impv formed like a I-yodh verb such as ישׁ (GKC, 69v, 70b).

18.a. Note the singular verb "he went out" with the pl subj "Noah . . . wives." With a composite subj the verb frequently agrees with only part of it; cf. 3:8; 7:7; 9:23 (GKC, 146f).

19.a. SamPent, G, S, Vg unnecessarily insert "and"; cf. v 17.

19.b-b. *BHS* following G, Vg suggests וכל־הבהמה "and all domesticated animals." But MT may be preferable. Had Noah let out all the domesticated animals and birds, he would have had none to sacrifice. Cf. v 17 where he is instructed to release some of the birds and domesticated animals.

20.a. Waw consec + 3 masc sg impf apoc בנה "to build."

20.b. Waw consec + 3 masc sg impf apoc hiph עלה "to go up."

21.a. Waw consec + 3 masc sg impf hiph ריח "to smell."

21.b. אסף 1 sg impf hiph of יסף "to do again" (Lambdin, 238).

21.c-c. Note the chiasmus, verb + עוד : עוד + verb (*SBH*, 113, 131).

21.d. Inf constr hiph (נכה) "to strike."

22.a. Note the punctuation of "and" ו before tone syllable in a pair of words (GKC, 104g; Joüon, 104d).

9:1.a. G adds "and subdue it," harmonizing with 1:28.

2.a. Suff acting as obj gen (GKC, 135m).

2.b. Note vv 2-3 consist of four clauses in apposition alternating the verbs "to be" and "to give" (*SBH*, 56).

2.c. G MSS add "and over all domesticated animals."

2.d. With Gispen and Westermann ב alternative to על "over"; cf. 1:28b.

2.e. 3 pl pf niph נתן "to give"; SamPent, G read "I have given it" נתתיו.

3.a. Note alternating "be," "give"; cf. n. 2.b.

4.a. In legal texts אך often introduces important restrictions or exceptions (*EWAS*, 130).

4.b. On ב "with," see GKC, 119n.

4.c-c. In apposition to and explaining "its soul/life" (GKC, 138b).

5.a-a. The brevity of the Heb. has caused difficulty: מיד איש אחיו stands for מיד איש את־נפשׁ אחיו (Skinner, 170–71; cf. GKC, 139c).

6.a-a. Note chiastic structure "shed, blood, man : man, blood, shed."

6.b-b. On use of ptcp for the protasis of a conditional sentence, see GKC, 116w.

6.c. ב "by" for agent of passive verb (GKC, 121f).

7.a. "You" contrasts with "I" "for my part," v 9 (*SBH*, 151).

7.b. SamPent, G, Vg insert "and" unnecessarily (*SBH*, 99).

7.c. *BHS* emendation of רבו "multiply" to רדו "rule" (cf. 1:28) is unjustified; cf. B. Porten and U. Rappaport, "Poetic Structure in Genesis IX 7," *VT* 21 (1971) 363-69.

9.a. Pron + הנה + suff especially emphatic (*EWAS*, 140); cf. 6:17. Heightens contrast with v 7.

10.a. SamPent, G, S, Tg insert "and."

10.b-b. G omits, perhaps because it appears redundant.

11.a. Waw consec + 1 sg pf hiph קום "to rise."

11.b. 3 masc sg impf niph כרת "to cut."

11.c. Unusually, מן "from" expresses the agent of the passive (GKC, 121f). The more-used ב is perhaps avoided here to avoid the ambiguity "in/by the waters"; Jouön, 132d. Cassuto (2:132) says מן here means "because of."

12.a-a. Opening title in apposition to detailed exposition in vv 13–16 (*SBH*, 54).

13.a. Putting the obj first emphasizes it (so *EWAS*, 38–39).

14.a. Piel inf + 1 sg suff עננ "to make clouds."

14.b. Waw consec + 3 fem sg pf niph ראה "to see." On the potential sense of niph "be visible" see Lambdin, 177.

15.a. The sg verb "will become" with the pl subj "waters" may be explained by the verb's preceding the subj (Gispen, 1:301); cf. 1:14.

19.a. BDB (659a), KB (671) agree this is 3 fem sg pf qal נפץ "disperse, be scattered"; cf. 1 Sam 13:11; Isa 11:12; 33:3. But GKC, 67dd, followed by Westermann, think 3 fem sg pf niph of פוץ. The former is more likely.

20.a-a. It is uncertain whether "man of the land" should be taken as complement of "begin," i.e., "Noah began to be a man of the land and planted" (GKC, 120b; Gispen, 1:304), or with the majority of commentators to take "man of the land" as in apposition to Noah. The latter seems more likely as the definite article before אדמה is most likely to include איש as well.

20.b. Waw consec + 3 masc sg impf hiph חלל "to begin," "was the first to" (cf. 4:26; 10:8).

21.a. Waw consec + 3 masc sg impf apoc שתה "to drink."

21.b. Waw consec + 3 masc sg impf apoc hithp גלה "to uncover."

21.c. SamPent as usual replaces archaic ה 3 masc sg suff by ו (Waltke, 214).

22.a. Waw consec + 3 masc sg impf hiph (נגד) "to tell."

22.b. As in English the direct obj "it" may be omitted in Heb. (GKC, 117f; Jouön, 146i).

23.a. Waw consec + 3 masc sg impf לקח. On sg verb with pl subj see GKC, 146f; Jouön, 150q.

23.b. On omission of obj "it," cf. n. 9:22.b.

23.c. Waw consec + 3 masc pl impf piel כסה "to cover."

23.d. Note use of adverb "backwards" as predicate. Lit., "their faces were backwards" (Jouön, 154d).

24.a. Waw consec + 3 masc sg impf יקץ "to wake" (GKC, 70a).

24.b. With the article, adjectives may express superlative (GKC, 133g).

25.a. Lit., "slave of slaves": on this idiom for the superlative see GKC, 133i; Jouön, 141l.

26.a. More often למו is poetic alternative to להם "to them," but here and in v 27 to לו "to him"; also Isa 44:15 (Jouön, 103f).

27.a. 3 masc sg juss (impf apoc) hiph פתה "be open."

27.b. Cf. n. 26.a.

Form/Structure/Setting

The story of Noah clearly begins with this phrase, the so-called *toledot* formula "This is the family history . . . " in 6:9. It has sometimes been argued on source-critical grounds that the story of Noah and the flood really begins in 6:1 or 6:5, but for reasons stated earlier it seems preferable to regard 6:1–8 as giving a preview of the next stage in the drama. Editorially, "This is the family history of Noah" unambiguously signals a new major section (cf. 2:4; 5:1; 10:1; 11:27, etc.).

Relying on a similar cue in 10:1, the end of "the family history of Noah" must be in 9:29, which ultimately derives from the old genealogical source preserved in chap. 5. However, modern commentators usually hold that 9:17 is the end of the Noah story and that a new section "Noah and his sons" begins in 9:18. Thematically, there is clearly a sharp division between 6:9–9:17, dealing with Noah the saved saint, and 9:18–29, telling of Noah the drunkard. Whether the stories of the flood and wine-making were once independent is uncertain. Drewermann (*Strukturen des Bösen*, 231–36) draws attention to a similar conjunction of themes in Greek mythology and suggests that this combination of motifs antedates J. Yet it is characteristic of the editor's method to bring together a variety of stories under the opening rubric "This is the family history of . . . ." Thus the story of Cain and Abel (chap. 4) supplements the garden of Eden story in chaps. 2–3, and the divine-human marriages topic (6:1–4) supplements the genealogy of Adam in chap. 5. Furthermore, 9:18–19 mentions the way Noah's sons spread out to populate the earth and introduces us to the fact that Shem is chosen and Ham rejected. Again, as elsewhere in Genesis, the close of one section acts as a preview of the next: in this case the curse on Ham (9:20–27) explains the arrangement of the table of nations (10:1–32).

The theme and general plan of the flood story (6:9–9:17) is quite clear. Three elements go to make up the basic theme: (1) God saves Noah and his companions by having them embark in an ark; (2) God sends a flood which destroys the rest of the world; (3) he promises never to send another such flood.

The story itself follows a favorite pattern of Hebrew narrators, the palistrophe or extended chiasmus, perhaps because a flood narrative lends itself to such a schema so easily. B. W. Anderson (*JBL* 97 [1978] 38) put forward the following analysis:

Transitional introduction (6:9–10)
1. Violence in creation (6:11–12)
  2. First divine speech: resolve to destroy (6:13–22)
    3. Second divine speech: "enter ark" (7:1–10)
      4. Beginning of flood (7:11–16)
        5. The rising flood (7:17–24)
          God remembers Noah
      6. The receding flood (8:1–5)
    7. Drying of the earth (8:6–14)
  8. Third divine speech: "leave ark" (8:15–19)
9. God's resolve to preserve order (8:20–22)
10. Fourth divine speech: covenant (9:1–17)
Transitional conclusion (9:18–19)

Note how each feature in the first half of the story matches a corresponding feature in the second half to create a mirror-image structure (3 // 8, 4 // 7, 5 // 6, etc.) with its center "God remembered Noah" in 8:1. I have also noted the palistrophic structure of this story (*VT* 28 [1978] 337–39) and drawn attention to fifteen verbal echoes in the second half of the story that match elements in the first half. Most striking is the way the number of days is inverted after 8:1.

> 7 days of waiting for flood (7:4)
> > 7 days of waiting for flood (7:10)
> > > 40 days of flood (7:17a)
> > > > 150 days of water triumphing (7:24)
> > > > 150 days of water waning (8:3)
> > > 40 days' wait (8:6)
> > 7 days' wait (8:10)
> 7 days' wait (8:12)

Similarly, R. E. Longacre (*JAAR* 47 Sup [1979] 89–133) has shown how the flood narrative builds up to a peak in 7:17–24 and then declines.

Palistrophic writing is particularly suited to telling a flood story: the literary structure closely resembles the real-life situation. Noah enters the ark and later leaves it. The waters rise and then fall. In other words, the story falls naturally into two halves that ought to resemble each other to some extent. The surface structure of the narrative mirrors the deep structure of the event being described.

Nevertheless, there is certainly an element of artificiality involved in creating a palistrophe on such a grand scale, particularly in mentioning the number of days in reverse order as here (see *VT* 28 [1978] 338–39). The structure itself helps to draw attention to the nature of the flood and the water's rise and fall, and to pinpoint the real turning point, God's remembering Noah (8:1). It was divine intervention that saved Noah, and the palistrophic pattern reminds the reader of the fact.

SCENE DIVISION

The flood story is a carefully integrated whole, so it is hardly surprising that there has been some difference of opinion between writers about where episodes and paragraphs within it open and close. If it is analyzed by scenes (cf. Walsh's methodology in Gen 2–3, *JBL* 96 [1977] 161–77), the narrative breaks up as follows:

> 1) 6:9b–21: Divine monologue addressed to Noah, preceded by reflections on Noah and mankind's behavior
> > 2) 6:22: Narrative: Noah main actor
> > > 3) 7:1–4: Divine monologue addressed to Noah
> > > > 4) 7:5–16: Narrative: Noah and animals main actors, God minor role
> > > > > 5) 7:17–24: Narrative: the rising waters main actor, Noah et al. passive
> > > > > 6) 8:1–5: Narrative: the falling waters main actor, God minor role
> > > > 7) 8:6–14: Narrative: Noah and birds main actors
> > > 8) 8:15–17: Divine monologue addressed to Noah
> > 9) 8:18–19: Narrative: Noah main actor

10) 8:20–9:17   Divine monologue addressed to Noah, preceded by reflections
      on Noah's, and mankind's, behavior

Again the palistrophic organization of the material is very obvious in this
division by scenes. There is a close correspondence in character and content
between scenes 1 and 10, 2 and 9, 3 and 8, etc.

Scenes 1 and 10 are alike in that both are lengthy divine monologues
addressed to Noah, and both are preceded by God's reflections on the character
of Noah and of mankind. Though Noah is present in both scenes, he is,
apart from the initial activity, entirely passive, a recipient of the divine word.
The vocabulary of both scenes is distinctive. The phrases "to ruin all flesh,"
"confirm my covenant," "fill the earth," "to eat" (לאכלה) occur only in these
two scenes, and only they are concerned with violence (6:11, 13) and bloodshed
(9:5–6). And finally, of course, there is the striking inversion that characterizes
the whole flood story: before the flood the whole world is doomed to destruction; afterward its preservation is guaranteed.

Scenes 2 and 9 correspond in that both describe Noah's obedience to the
preceding injunction, in the first case to build the ark and in the latter to
leave it.

Scenes 3 and 8 correspond in that both give God's instructions to Noah,
first to enter the ark with the animals and then to leave it. Here the inversion
is very exact, extending even to the motive clauses which emphasize the
importance of preserving life on earth.

Scenes 4 and 7 match each other in being purely narrative, with Noah
and the animals the principal actors in scene 4 and Noah and the birds the
principals in scene 7. This pair of scenes contains the long date formulae
specifying the date of the flood's onset (7:6, 11) and its termination (8:13, 14)
by reference to Noah's life. Both scenes mention the covering of the ark by
the LORD in 7:16 and its uncovering by Noah in 8:6, 13. These two references
to Noah's activity form a loose inclusion framing this scene, whereas in scene
4 the repetition of the phrase "as the LORD (God) had commanded him"
(7:5, 16) makes a much clearer frame to the scene, emphasizing Noah's obedience to God. Further, whereas the action in scene 7 takes place over a period
of weeks, scene 4 deals with essentially one event, the entry into the ark
and the coming of the flood which is described with many details repeated
so as to emphasize the significance of the event (so Andersen, SBH, 124–
25, and Jacob).

Finally, scenes 5 and 6 closely correspond in that both are narratives in
which the waters of the flood and the ark are the principal actors: in scene
5 the doomed dwellers on earth and in scene 6 God are only briefly mentioned.
Again, as is the case between scenes 4 and 7, there is a great difference of
pace. In scene 5 the tale reaches its climax with the destruction of all life on
earth and the triumph of the waters everywhere. The use of repetition and
other rhetorical devices, e.g., the preponderance of m and other labials to
convey the sound and feel of the waters of the flood (mym, mabbul) rolling
around the ark is prominent and helps to draw attention to the greatness of
the event whereas in scene 6 the tension relaxes and the style reverts to
patterns more typical of Hebrew prose in a series of simple waw-consecutive
clauses.

ANCIENT PARALLELS TO FLOOD STORY

Bibliography

See also the bibliography in *Introduction* on ancient Near Eastern parallels.

Fisher, E. "Gilgamesh and Genesis: The Flood Story in Context." *CBQ* 32 (1970) 392–402. **Freedman, R. D.** "The Dispatch of the Reconnaissance Birds in Gilgamesh XI." *JANESCU* 5 (1973) 123–29. **Frymer-Kensky, T.** "The Atrahasis Epic and Its Significance for Understanding Gen 1–9." *BA* 40 (1977) 147–55. **Heidel, A.** *The Gilgamesh Epic and Old Testament Parallels*. 2d ed. Chicago: University of Chicago Press, 1949. **Jacobsen, T.** "The Eridu Genesis." *JBL* 100 (1981) 513–29. **Keel, O.** *Vögel als Boten*. OBO 14. Freiburg: University Press, 1977. **Killmer, A. D.** "The Mesopotamian Concept of Overpopulation and Its Solution as Reflected in the Mythology." *Or* 41 (1972) 160–77. **Kramer, S. N.** "'The Sumerian Deluge Myth' Reviewed and Revised." *AnSt* 33 (1983) 115–21. **Lambert, W. G.,** and **A. R. Millard.** *Atrahasis*. Oxford: Clarendon Press, 1969. **Lang, B.** "Non-Semitic Deluge Stories and the Book of Genesis: A Bibliographical and Critical Survey." *Anthropos* 80 (1985) 605–16. **Tigay, J. H.** *The Evolution of the Gilgamesh Epic*. Philadelphia: University of Pennsylvania Press, 1982. ———. "The Stylistic Criteria of Source Criticism in the Light of Ancient Near Eastern Literature." In *Essays on the Bible and the Ancient World: I. L. Seeligmann Vol. III*, ed. A. Rofé and Y. Zakovitch. Jerusalem: Rubinstein, 1983. 67–91.

Stories of a great flood are known from cultures around the world (Lang, *Anthropos* 80 [1985] 605–16), but as might be expected, the closest parallels to the biblical account come from Mesopotamia: "The most remarkable parallels between the Old Testament and the entire corpus of cuneiform inscriptions from Mesopotamia are found in the deluge accounts" (Heidel, *Gilgamesh Epic*, 224). Quite how these similarities are to be evaluated is another matter; the number of uncertainties is such that firm conclusions are hard to reach.

It will perhaps be best to begin by quoting part of the fullest, though latest, Mesopotamian version of the flood story found in the Gilgamesh epic, tablet 11. The standard late recension of the Gilgamesh epic dates from the neo-Assyrian period (*ca.* 650 B.C.), although it was compiled in the Cassite period. An earlier version was composed in the early second millennium. However, it seems probable that the full account of the flood was not incorporated into the Gilgamesh epic until about 1600 B.C. and may be based on the flood story told in Atrahasis. (So Lambert; cf. his review of Tigay, *The Evolution of the Gilgamesh Epic*, in *JBL* 104 [1985] 115–17. Tigay holds that the flood story was inserted into Gilgamesh in the late second millennium.)

The translation of Gilgamesh Tablet 11 by E. A. Speiser *ANET*, 93–95 goes as follows:

[23] "Man of Shuruppak, son of Ubar-Tutu,
     Tear down (this) house, build a ship!
     Give up possessions, seek thou life.
     Forswear (worldly) goods and keep the soul alive!
     Aboard the ship take thou the seed of all living things.
     The ship that thou shalt build,
     Her dimensions shall be to measure.
[30] Equal shall be her width and her length.
     Like the Apsu thou shalt ceil her."

I understood, and I said to Ea, my lord:
"[Behold], my lord, what thou hast thus ordered,
I will be honored to carry out

. . . ."

⁵³The little ones [carr]ied bitumen,
While the grown ones brought [all else] that was needful.
On the fifth day I laid her framework.
One (whole) acre was her floor space,
Ten dozen cubits the height of each of her walls,
Ten dozen cubits each edge of the square deck.
I laid out the contours (and) joined her together.
⁶⁰I provided her with six decks,
Dividing her (thus) into seven parts.
Her floor plan I divided into nine parts.
I hammered water-plugs into her.
I saw to the punting-poles and laid in supplies.
Six sar [measures] of bitumen I poured into the furnace,
Three sar of asphalt [I also] poured inside.
Three sar of oil the basket-bearers carried,
Aside from the one sar of oil which the caulking consumed,
And the two sar of oil [which] the boatman stowed away.
⁷⁰Bullocks I slaughtered for the [people],
And I killed sheep every day.
Must, red wine, oil, and white wine
[I gave the] workmen [to drink], as though river water,
That they might feast as on New Year's Day. . . . .
⁸⁰[Whatever I had] I laded upon her:
Whatever I had of silver I laded upon her;
Whatever I [had] of gold I laded upon her;
Whatever I had of all the living beings I [laded] upon her.
All my family and kin I made go aboard the ship.
The beasts of the field, the wild creatures of the field,
All the craftsmen I made go aboard.
Shamash had set for me a stated time:
"When he who orders unease at night,
Will shower down a rain of blight,
Board thou the ship and batten up the entrance!"
That stated time had arrived:
⁹⁰"He who orders unease at night, showers down a rain of blight."
I watched the appearance of the weather.
The weather was awesome to behold.
I boarded the ship and battened up the entrance.
To batten down the (whole) ship, to Puzur-Amurri, the boatman,
I handed over the structure together with its contents.

With the first glow of dawn,
A black cloud rose up from the horizon.
Inside it Adad thunders,
While Shullat and Hanish go in front,
¹⁰⁰Moving as heralds over hill and plain.
Erragal tears out the posts;
Forth comes Ninurta and causes the dikes to follow.

The Anunnaki lift up the torches,
Setting the land ablaze with their glare.
Consternation over Adad reaches to the heavens,
Who turned to blackness all that had been light.
[The wide] land was shattered like [a pot]!
For one day the south-storm [blew],
Gathering speed as it blew, [submerging the mountains],
¹¹⁰Overtaking the [people] like a battle.
No one can see his fellow,
Nor can the people be recognized from heaven.
The gods were frightened by the deluge,
And, shrinking back, they ascended to the heaven of Anu.
The gods cowered like dogs
Crouched against the outer wall.

. . . .

¹²⁴The gods, all humbled, sit and weep,
Their lips drawn tight, [...] one and all.
Six days and [six] nights
Blows the flood wind, as the south-storm sweeps the land.
When the seventh day arrived,
The flood(-carrying) south-storm subsided in the battle,
¹³⁰Which it had fought like an army.
The sea grew quiet, the tempest was still, the flood ceased.
I looked at the weather; stillness had set in,
And all of mankind had returned to clay.
The landscape was as level as a flat roof.
I opened a hatch, and light fell upon my face.
Bowing low, I sat and wept,
Tears running down on my face.
I looked about for coast lines in the expanse of the sea:
In each of fourteen (regions)
There emerged a region (-mountain).
¹⁴⁰On Mount Nisir the ship came to a halt.
Mount Nisir held the ship fast,
Allowing no motion.
One day, a second day, Mount Nisir held the ship fast,
Allowing no motion.

. . . .

When the seventh day arrived,
I sent forth and set free a dove.
The dove went forth, but came back;
Since no resting-place for it was visible, she turned round.
Then I sent forth and set free a swallow.
¹⁵⁰The swallow went forth, but came back;
Since no resting-place for it was visible, she turned round.
Then I sent forth and set free a raven.
The raven went forth and, seeing that the waters had diminished,
He eats, circles, caws, and turns not round.
Then I let out (all) to the four winds
And offered a sacrifice.
I poured out a libation on the top of the mountain.
Seven and seven cult-vessels I set up,

Upon their pot-stands I heaped cane, cedarwood, and myrtle.
The gods smelled the savor,
[160] The gods smelled the sweet savor,
The gods crowded like flies about the sacrificer.
When at length as the great goddess arrives,
She lifted up the great jewels which Anu had fashioned to her liking:
"Ye gods here, as surely as this lapis
Upon my neck I shall not forget,
I shall be mindful of these days, forgetting (them) never.
Let the gods come to the offering;
[But] let not Enlil come to the offering
For he, unreasoning, brought on the deluge
And my people consigned to destruction."
[170] When at length as Enlil arrived,
And saw the ship, Enlil was wroth,
He was filled with wrath over the Igigi gods:
"Has some living soul escaped?
No man was to survive the destruction!"
Ninurta opened his mouth to speak,
Saying to valiant Enlil:
"Who, other than Ea, can devise plans?
It is Ea alone who knows every matter."
Ea opened his mouth to speak,

. . . .

[186] "It was not I who disclosed the secret of the great gods.
I let Atrahasis see a dream,
And he perceived the secret of the gods.
Now then take counsel in regard to him!"
Thereupon Enlil went aboard the ship.
[190] Holding me by the hand, he took me aboard.
He took my wife aboard and made (her) kneel by my side.
Standing between us, he touched our foreheads to bless us:
"Hitherto Utnapishtim has been but human.
Henceforth Utnapishtim and his wife shall be like unto us gods.
Utnapishtim shall reside far away, at the mouth of the rivers!"

Though not as full as the epic of Gilgamesh just quoted, the version found in the Atrahasis epic (old Babylonian version, ca. 1600 B.C.) is particularly interesting in making the flood one of a sequence of primeval events somewhat akin to the opening chapters of Genesis. Despite its fragmentariness this also appears to be true of the Sumerian version (see T. Jacobsen, *JBL* 100 [1981] 513–29). Another text from Ras Shamra, ca. 1400 B.C. shows that the story was also known in the West. (For these texts see W. G. Lambert and A. R. Millard, *Atrahasis*.) Regrettably, though these texts are earlier than Gilgamesh Tablet 11, they contain many gaps making systematic comparison with Gen 6–9 difficult.

Our purpose in comparing the Mesopotamian accounts of the flood with Genesis is exegetical. Comparison should shed light not only on the biblical writer's method, but on his theological purpose in relating the flood story. Again problems arise, however, since it is difficult to be sure what version of the flood story Genesis knew. Is he simply repeating, more or less unchanged, an earlier version of the flood story? Is he taking an earlier account of the flood story, somewhat different from any of the existing versions, and giving it a theological interpretation of his own? Does he actually know something like the Mesopotamian versions, and is he self-consciously rewriting them to express Hebrew theology instead of Babylonian mythology?

The minimalists argue that the differences between the Mesopotamian and the biblical accounts are too great to suppose dependence of the latter on the former. Both must be independent developments of an earlier common tradition. On this view those features in common between the biblical and extrabiblical accounts must represent the common tradition used by Hebrew and Babylonian scribes. A comparison of Genesis with this reconstructed pre-biblical tradition should shed light on the standpoint of Genesis.

Maximalists argue that the Genesis editor was in fact familiar with Mesopotamian traditions in something like their present form. They point out that there was ample opportunity for Israel to learn the myths of Mesopotamia in various periods from the time of Abraham to the exile. Elsewhere in Gen 1; 4; 5; 6:1–4; 11:1–9, the writer seems to be aware of other ancient Near Eastern ideas and to be deliberately opposing or commenting on them, and it may be presumed that similar policies are being followed here.

It is not of crucial importance which view is correct. The maximalist approach turns the editor of Genesis into a more aggressive self-conscious opponent of his contemporaries' ideas, whereas the minimalist plays down the polemical intent of Gen 6–9. As argued earlier, in the *Introduction,* I suspect that the truth lies somewhere between the minimalist and maximalist positions and that the biblical writer did know something like the traditions enshrined in Atrahasis and Gilgamesh, though not in precisely their present shape. Yet here it seems wisest to begin from the minimalist position and simply list those points in common between biblical and Mesopotamian tradition. On the minimalist assumption, these common elements go back to an earlier account utilized by Hebrews and others. On the maximalist view, they represent those features of the Mesopotamian account that the Hebrew writers found acceptable and compatible with their theology.

1. Divine decision to destroy mankind	Gen 6:6–7(J); G 14–19; A 2:7:38–52; 2:8:34; RS 1, 3; S 3:15–4:1 (140–51)
2. Warning to flood hero	Gen 6:13(P); G 20–23; A 3:1:13–21; RS 12, 14; S 4:2–12 (152–62)
3. Command to build ark	Gen 6:14–21 (P); G 24–31; A 3:1:22–33.
4. Hero's obedience	Gen 6:22; 7:5(P/J); G 33–85; A 3:2:10–18
5. Command to enter	Gen 7:1–3(J); G 86–88
6. Entry	Gen 7:7–16(P/J); G 89–93; A 3:2:30–51
7. Closing door	Gen 7:16(J); G 93; A 3:2:52
8. Description of flood	Gen 7:17–24(P/J); G 96–128; A 3:2:53–4:27; S 5:1–3 (201–3)
9. Destruction of life	Gen 7:21–23(P/J); G 133; A 3:3:44, 54
10. End of rain, etc.	Gen 8:2–3(P/J);G 129–31;S 5:4–6 (204–6)

11. Ark grounding on mountain   Gen 8:4(P); G 140–44
12. Hero opens window   Gen 8:6(J); G 135; S 5:7 (207)
13. Birds' reconnaissance   Gen 8:6–12(J); G 145–154
14. Exit   Gen 8:15–19(P); G 155; A 3:5:30
15. Sacrifice   Gen 8:20(J); G 155–158; A 3:5:31–33; S
     5:11 (211)
16. Divine smelling of sacrifice   Gen 8:21–22(J); G 159–161; A 3:5:34–
     35
17. Blessing on flood hero   Gen 9:1–17(P); G 189–96; S 6:4–11 (254–
     61); RS r. 1–4

A = epic of Atrahasis
RS = Ras Shamra version (see Lambert and Millard, *Atrahasis*)
G = epic of Gilgamesh Tablet 11 (*ANET*, 93–95)
S = Sumerian version "Eridu Genesis" (*JBL* 100 [1981] 522–25)

Old but detailed discussions of the points of contact between the biblical account of the flood and Near Eastern parallels may be found in Heidel, *The Gilgamesh Epic and Old Testament Parallels*, and Cassuto, vol. 2. Here we shall simply focus on the main differences in presentation between Gilgamesh and Atrahasis on the one hand and Genesis on the other which shed light on the theological interests of Genesis. Points of peripheral interest—the length of the flood or the types of birds sent out on reconnaissance—though of value in determining the genetic relationship of Genesis and other accounts, will not be discussed here.

The opening of the story in Genesis brings immediately to the fore the difference between the monotheistic theology that informed the approach of the Hebrew writer and the polytheistic mythology of his contemporaries. According to the extrabiblical accounts, the heavenly council of the gods led by Anu and Enlil decided to destroy mankind, for multiplying too much and making too much noise. However, this decision was not unanimous, and the god Ea or Enki went so far as to tip off the flood hero about the divine decision. This was how he managed to escape, much to Enlil's subsequent annoyance.

The plurality of divinities creates uncertainty about the future as far as mortals are concerned, and the pettiness of the gods' motives in destroying mankind contrasts starkly with the stern moral tone of the biblical account. Man is damned in the latter not for making noise but because of his incorrigible evil for ruining the earth and committing violence. The divine decree admits of no exception but Noah, who was delivered not because he happened to worship a god sympathetic to his plight, but because of his perfect righteousness.

If the sending of the flood shows the capricious nature of Mesopotamian deities, its effects demonstrate their weakness. When the storm arrived they were unable to control it; they were frightened and "cowered like dogs." Genesis too gives a dramatic account of the rise of the floodwaters and their destructive powers. Yet as soon as "God remembered Noah" and caused a wind to pass over the earth (compare God's breath in creation), the waters receded. The omnipotence and control of Yahweh is again demonstrated. He who brought order out of chaos at the beginning does so again after the flood.

The closing scenes after the flood again serve to point up the differences between biblical and Babylonian attitudes to the divine: the points are made more sharply in that Genesis, like the Gilgamesh epic, has the flood hero offer sacrifice which is acceptable to God. "The gods smelled the sweet savor" (GE 11:160) sounds very like "The Lord smelt the soothing aroma" (Gen 8:21); yet the divine reaction is very different. Gilgamesh continues by describing the gods "crowding like flies around the sacrifice," greedily jostling for places at the open-air barbecue. Since mankind had been created to feed the gods, obviously the latter had gone hungry while there were no men around to present offerings. Then Enlil, chief executive among the gods, arrives and is surprised to discover survivors of the flood. Clearly he is neither omnipotent nor omniscient. The recriminations that follow underline the fact that the gods do not agree or act in concert, whereas in Genesis the divine speeches that follow the sacrifice reassert the creator's lordship over his creatures and his determination to uphold the cosmic order and his mercy towards mankind.

Through the flood story, then, Genesis paints a completely different portrait of God from the standard ancient theology. Most obviously, there is only one God. This means that all power belongs to him: it is not shared out unequally among different members of a pantheon. But just as important is the character of the divinity revealed by the flood story. He is still personal: anthropomorphic language is freely used to describe God's thoughts and attitudes. But the failings that too often characterize humanity and the Babylonian deities are eliminated. God is not fearful, ignorant, greedy, or jealous. He is not annoyed by man's rowdiness, but by his depravity. Not partiality but justice dictates the salvation of Noah.

While Genesis builds up the character of God, it very much reduces the dimensions of the flood hero. Indeed, Noah is hardly a heroic figure at all. His name, "Noah" ("rest") simply expresses his father's hopes (5:29), whereas the names "Ziusudra," or "Utnapishtim" ("finder of [eternal] life") and "Atrahasis" ("exceedingly wise") clearly refer to the achievements of the survivor of the flood. We are simply told over and over again that Noah obeyed God: clearly he believed the divine warnings and acted on them and so could be described as a man of faith. When the flood subsided, he patiently waited until the earth was dry. Then he offered a sacrifice. But he never speaks. We are given no insight into his feelings at any point. He could simply be a well-programmed robot responding to the divine instructions.

In contrast, Utnapishtim is a very active figure, hurrying hither and thither building his ship, spinning a yarn to his neighbors as to why he is doing it. Besides animals, he loads on board a large crew and all his gold and silver. At the appointed time he enters the ark and shuts himself in, whereas "the Lord shut Noah in." Utnapishtim describes what it was like to be in the eye of the storm, and tells of his own grief when he looked out and saw "all mankind had returned to clay. . . . I sat and wept, tears running down my face." These techniques of graphic description are frequently used elsewhere in the Bible. Speech is often employed to give an insight into characters' motives and attitudes (Gen 2–3; 4). Here Genesis appears to be self-consciously avoiding this kind of description: Noah's obedience is all that matters. Who he was and what he felt are irrelevant.

Noah is also cut down in another way. Ziusudra, the Sumerian Noah, and apparently Utnapishtim and Atrahasis are kings. Noah is simply a commoner. Admittedly, other antediluvian heroes in Mesopotamian tradition are also called kings, whereas their Hebrew counterparts are not, so the absence of royal traits with Noah may be coincidental. However, in the closing scene Ziusudra/Utnapishtim joined the ranks of the gods by being made immortal in the full sense, a privilege akin to that conferred on a few Mesopotamian kings who were deified on death and lived in the netherworld. Noah certainly did not gain eternal life by surviving the flood: the last thing we hear of him is his disgracing himself through drinking too much. May it be that Genesis is, in passing, quietly protesting about Mesopotamian kingship ideologies in recounting the flood story? Human greatness is to be found neither in heroic feats nor in an exalted social station but in faithfully obeying God's word.

Finally, it has been argued that Gen 6–9 is opposing the Babylonian belief in population control. According to Atrahasis, the flood was sent to destroy man who was breeding too fast and making too much noise. After the flood the gods decreed that certain women should be celibate, others infertile, and some infants should die soon after birth (A 3:7:1–8). The thrice-repeated divine command to "be fruitful and multiply" (Gen 8:17; 9:1,7) echoing the earlier commands in 1:26, 28 "makes it probable that the Bible *consciously rejected* the underlying theme of the Atrahasis Epic, that the fertility of man before the flood was the reason for his near destruction" (T. Frymer-Kensky *BA* 40 [1977] 150). Cf. A. D. Killmer, *Or* 41 (1972) 174–75; W. L. Moran, *Bib* 52 (1971) 51–61.

Though Genesis' retelling of the flood story is antagonistic to many aspects of Babylonian thought, it should be recognized that in some ways there is much continuity between the two traditions. It is not simply that the plots are similar. In Atrahasis and the Sumerian account, the flood forms part of a sequence of primeval events covering the creation of man, the long-lived antediluvians, and the universal flood, which is in outline remarkably similar to Gen 1–9: "This arrangement along a line of time as cause and effect is striking, for it is much the way a historian arranges his data" (Jacobsen, *JBL* 100 [1981] 528). Furthermore, Genesis, Atrahasis, and the Sumerian flood story as reconstructed by Jacobsen are all remarkably interested in primitive chronologies, albeit very extended ones. But myths and folktales are not generally concerned with time at all. That is the prerogative of annals and historiographers. For this reason, Jacobsen wishes to term these stories, both Mesopotamian and biblical, mytho-historical accounts. In that many of the typical features of myth have been eliminated from the biblical account of the flood, we can perhaps stick with our own preferred description of these chapters as proto-historical narratives.

SOURCES IN GEN 6–9

Traditionally these chapters have been held up as a parade example of the value of the documentary hypothesis. Gunkel terms the source analysis of this story "a masterpiece of modern criticism" and suggests that beginners may learn how source criticism is done by studying these chapters. First assign to J passages mentioning Yahweh, and to P passages mentioning God. This criterion alone serves to distinguish 6:5–7:5 from 8:15–9:17, leaving only the middle of the story source-critically problematic. But these verses can be distributed between J and P by examining the differences between the sources in the opening and closing sections of the narrative and tracing through the central part the same distinctions in chronology and vocabulary. The following analysis of the material is widely accepted:

	J	*P*	*Editor*
Flood announced/ark built		6:9–22	
Command to enter ark	7:1–5		7:3a
Noah's age		7:6	
Entry into ark	7:7	7:13–16a	7:8–9
Flood comes	7:10,12	7:11	
Noah shut in	7:16b		
Flood continues	7:17b	7:17a	
Flood destroys	7:22, 23a,c	7:18–21, 24	7:23b
Flood abates	8:2b, 3a	8:1–2a, 3b–5	
Ark rests on mountain		8:4	
Window opened	8:6		
Birds depart	8:7–12		
Earth dry	8.13b	8:13a, 14	
Exit from ark		8:15–19	
Sacrifice	8:20–22		
Covenant with all life		9:1–17	

In support of the above analysis the following differences between J and P are cited:

J	*P*
Yahweh: divine name and other linguistic differences	Elohim: divine name and other linguistic differences
7 pairs of clean animals, 1 pair of unclean (7:2–3)	Pairs of all animals (6:19–20; 7:15–16)
40 days of rain after 7 days of waiting (7:4,10,12 cf. 8:6–12)	Water rises 150 days, falls 150 days; chronology makes flood last over a year (7:11, 24; 8:3, 5, 13, 14)

Furthermore, both narratives run in parallel forming a series of doublets:

	J	P
Corruption of man	6:5	6:11–12
Decision to destroy	6:7	6:13
Command to load ark	7:1–3	6:18–21
Entry to ark	7:7	7:13
Arrival of flood	7:10	7:11
Destruction of creatures	7:22–23	7:20–21
End of flood	8:2b; 3a	8:3b–5
Promise of no future flood	8:21b–22	9:11–17

Though there is wide agreement about the demarcation of the sources in the flood story, there is much less unanamity about their relationship. The classical view saw J and P as basically independent sources, both nearly completely preserved in Gen 6–9. But McEvenue (*Narrative Style of the Priestly Writer*, 23–27) argues that P runs sufficiently parallel to J to suppose that P must be built on J. An alternative theory (see Cross, *Canaanite Myth*, 293) holds that P is not a separate source but merely an editorial supplement to J.

However attractive this supplementary hypothesis may seem elsewhere in Genesis, it faces grave difficulties in chaps. 6–9. Westermann correctly observes that "at first glance it is clear that . . . J has been worked into the basic P document" (1:533; cf. ET, 1:396). In these chapters P consists usually of long blocks of material, e.g., 6:9–22; 9:1–17, whereas J consists of quite short fragments that often appear as very brief comments in P contexts, e.g., 7:16b, 17b, 22–23a. Furthermore, the whole flood story is prefaced by a J introduction (6:5–8) and followed by a J appendix (9:20–27). Though Westermann has correctly analyzed the relationship between the J and P material in these chapters, he has not drawn the obvious conclusion that J is reworking P, because he assumes that J antedates P. But it is noticeable that the elements he picks out as editorial glosses all occur within J contexts: 7:3a, 8–9, 23b.

Though these chapters then present further evidence of a J-type redaction of earlier sources, I think it would be wrong to regard the J/P analysis of these chapters as final. In the light of Mesopotamian parallels to the flood story it is strange that certain elements from the flood tradition are missing from P and J. P omits the command to enter the ark, the closing of the door, the opening of the window, the bird's reconnaissance, the sacrifice, and God's smelling it, whereas J omits the building of the ark, the ark landing on a mountain, and the exit from the ark.

The relationship between the biblical flood story and the Mesopotamian parallels, it was pointed out above, can be explained either on the assumption that both go back to a common tradition (the minimalist view) or that the Genesis account is a deliberate rewriting of the Mesopotamian versions of the flood story (the maximalist view). On both views, then, the Hebrew storyteller must have known all those features that are found in both Mesopotamian and Genesis versions of the flood. Only those features unique to Genesis may be presumed to come from other sources or to be the writer's own contribution. It is therefore strange that both J and P versions should lack features of the common tradition, but when combined create an account which resembles it. It would seem more probable that the source used by the J editor contained all the elements of the common tradition, i.e., it consisted of P + command to enter ark + closing of door + opening of window + the bird's reconnaissance + the sacrifice scene. In other words, those features usually assigned to J must, along with the P elements, belong to the source used by the final editor. That is not to say that the present wording of any of these sections goes back to the earlier source. Throughout the flood story it is very difficult to distinguish minor verbal changes introduced by the final editor as opposed to the major theological innovation discussed earlier. Much of the apparent repetitiousness of the account can be explained in terms of Hebrew epic style and need not be explained as the juxtaposition of two sources. Furthermore, though two different chronologies of the flood have been postulated on the basis of the J/P analysis, this is unnecessary, as all the dates and periods mentioned fit together quite coherently (see Wenham, *VT* 28 [1978] 342–45; cf. G. Larsson, *ZAW* 97 [1985] 325). In the exposition that follows we shall take the flood story as a substantial unity from the hand of the final redactor, pointing out, where possible, how he has modified earlier sources.

Comment

6:9a "This is the family history of Noah." The standard editorial introduction to a new section of Genesis; cf. *Comment* on 2:4; 5:1, and remarks under *Form/Structure/Setting.*

9b–21 The first scene in the flood story matches the final scene (8:20–9:17) and is a divine monologue (6:13–21), preceded by reflections on Noah's character (9b–10) and the corruption of the earth (11–12); cf. 8:20–22.

9b "Noah was a righteous man. He was blameless among his contemporaries." Literally, the accented Hebrew says, "Noah, a man righteous, perfect was he among his contemporaries" and so most commentators ancient and modern understand two clauses, the second, "he was blameless . . . ," being in apposition to the first. Ramban, König, and Cassuto prefer to ignore the accents and understand "perfect" as an adverb modifying "righteous man. . . ." For a clear example of this usage, see Job 12:4 and possibly Num 19:2, "a perfectly red heifer." Cassuto's interpretation is grammatically simpler in that there is only one verb, but the sense is only slightly modified by it.

"Righteous" צדיק. The LORD describes Noah as "righteous" in 7:1. Here the editor anticipates the divine judgment (cf. Job 1:1,8). The word "righteous" is a very common term in the OT (used 206 times, most frequently in Psalms and Proverbs). It is nearly always used of persons, either men or God, and often stands in contrast to "wicked," רשע. Near synonyms include "innocent" and "upright." In legal contexts, "righteous" means "innocent" or "acquitted" of specific offenses, e.g., Exod 23:7–8; Deut 25:1. More generally, a righteous person is one who keeps the moral law: Ezekiel defines the righteous man as one "who does what is lawful and right" and then goes on to give examples of sins he avoids and good acts he does, e.g., clothing the naked and feeding the hungry, 18:5–9. Ezekiel's definition seems to fit very well the many references to the righteous in the Psalms. Negatively, a righteous man avoids sin; positively, he does good to his neighbors. In short, it is the most general Hebrew term to describe good people. טוב, which is usually translated "good" in the OT, is used relatively rarely of men, much more frequently of things and situations. Someone called "good" in English would be described as "righteous" in Hebrew. So in describing Noah as righteous, he is being pointed to as a good man who lived according to God's standards of behavior (cf. *EM* 6, 678–79).

"Blameless," תמים, is a term much more rarely applied to people than "righteous." The root idea is that of wholeness or completeness. Most frequently it describes blemish-free sacrificial animals (e.g., Lev 1:3, 10, etc.). Probably the same idea is carried over into the human realm. According to Ps 15:1–2, only the blameless may dwell in God's holy hill. The blameless are characterized by their abstaining from iniquity (2 Sam 22:24; Ezek 28:15) and walking in the law of the LORD (Ps 119:1). Job is described as being blameless (12:4; cf. the similar term תם in 1:2, 8; 2:3), and Abraham (Gen 17:1) and all Israel (Deut 18:13) were told to be blameless. Blamelessness is the prerequisite for close fellowship with God. Every Israelite was expected to be righteous. Though Deuteronomy encourages the whole people to be blameless, this was actually achieved by few.

"His contemporaries": cf. 7:1; here the plural, there the singular of דור is used.

"Walked with God." This phrase puts Noah on a par with Enoch (5:22, 24), the only other named individual to have walked with (התהלך את) God. Abraham, Isaac and godly kings "walked before" God (17:1; 48:15; 2 Kgs 20:3). It thus appears that there is a progressive build-up in Noah's characterization: he was a good man (righteous, like the majority of Israelites). More than that, he was blameless, the goal of all but achieved by few. Finally, he walked with God like Enoch, the only man in Genesis to have been translated to heaven. Utnapishtim went to dwell with the gods after the flood, but Noah enjoyed God's close presence beforehand.

10 Repeats 5:32b and serves to remind us of the other passengers on the boat. Having three sons may be viewed as confirming Noah's righteousness; cf. Job 1:2; 42:13; Pss 127, 128. It also links him with Adam and Terah (Gen 4:1–2, 25; 11:27), who also fathered three sons and stand at turning points of history. Noah's sons are presumably considered righteous, as they are mentioned before the general corruption of the rest of the world in vv 11–12. Cassuto (2:51) plausibly argues that this is Ezekiel's understanding, for in 14:14–20 he says that Noah, Daniel, and Job would only deliver themselves by their own righteousness and would not have saved their children. As Ezekiel must have known of Noah's sons surviving, he must have believed they were righteous. However, it is certainly Noah's righteousness on which Genesis concentrates; it is not much interested in his children's behavior at this point.

11–12 Noah's character stands out even more brightly against the blackness of the rest of humanity. These two verses, by repetition of key words, underline the gravity of the situation. The opening of God's speech again reinforces the diagnosis by echoing the same sentiments.

11 "The earth was ruined." "The earth" is mentioned six times in vv

11–13 and the verb "to ruin," five times. Here and in v 12, "ruin" is the niphal of שחת, a stem used to describe the spoiling of a garment, or a pot in Jer 13:7; 18:4. The hiphil in vv 12–13 is frequently used to describe the sudden destruction of peoples and cities in war, or through divine judgment (e.g., Gen 18:28, 31, 32). Here Genesis brings together the ideas of "being spoilt" and "destroy," so "ruin" has been adopted to translate שחת because it covers both senses.

"The earth was filled with violence." Animals and men had been intended to fill the earth (1:22, 28); instead, "violence" (חמס) fills it. This important term (see H. J. Stoebe, *THWAT,* 1:583–87; H. Haag, *TDOT,* 4:478–87) is most often paired with שד "oppression." "Violence" denotes any antisocial, unneighborly activity. Very often it involves the use of brute force, but it may just be the exploitation of the weak by the powerful or the poor by the rich (e.g., Amos 6:1–3), or the naive by the clever (Prov 16:29). Cassuto goes too far in suggesting that it covers any action that is not righteous. "*Chamas* is cold-blooded and unscrupulous infringement of the personal rights of others, motivated by greed and hate and often making use of physical violence and brutality" (*TDOT,* 4:482). In this context, Gen 4 well illustrates the meaning of "violence," although the word itself is not used here. The post-flood decrees in 9:4–6 attempt to limit human and animal violence.

12 "And God saw. . . ." The last use of these exact words is found in 1:31 (but cf. 6:5) where "God saw all that he had made was very good." The deliberate echo of 1:31 here heightens our sense of the tragedy that has overtaken the world since its creation. Then God was pleasantly surprised by his creation: here he is shocked by its corruption. Left to itself the world has ruined itself: "All flesh had ruined its way." The divine judgment announced in the following verse merely completes the self-destruction that has already begun.

"All flesh" (כל בשר.) Most commentators recognize that "all flesh" here and throughout the flood story (cf. 6:19; 7:16; 8:17; 9:16) includes both man and the animals. However, Westermann, following A. R. Hulst ("Kol Basar in der priesterlichen Fluterzählung," *OTS* 12 [1958] 28–68), thinks that "all flesh" here, as often in the prophets, e.g., Jer 25:31, means only "all mankind," because it is hard to see how animals can have corrupted their way. This narrower meaning, however, is hard to justify in Gen 6–9. It should be noted that the covenant of 9:9–16 is made with man and the animals (Oberforcher, *Flutprologe,* 461–78). Furthermore, chap. 3 does describe one of the animals, the snake, usurping divine prerogatives in telling man how to act. It is true that chap. 3 does not use the terminology of 6:12 in describing the fall, but it does suggest that other creatures were involved apart from man.

13–21 It is important to grasp the structure of the divine speech.

A	13	God's proposed action: to destroy world
B	14–16	Hence, command to Noah to build ark
A¹	17–20	God's plan further explained
B¹	21	Hence, command to Noah to victual the ark.

The train of the thought is clear in vv 13–14. However, vv 18–20 are often mistakenly supposed to be commands to Noah, when they are simply part

of the exposition of the divine plan. The personal pronouns "I myself" (v
17) and "[But as for] you" (v 21) show clearly the break between the divine
plan and the divine commands. Furthermore, the only imperatives occur in
vv 14 and 21; elsewhere (e.g., v 18), perfects prefixed by *waw,* or imperfects
are used. Vv 17–20 should therefore be understood as predictions, not commands.

13   The divine speech begins with a divine summing up of the situation
described in vv 11–12. The same terms—"the earth," "full of violence,"
"ruin"—reappear. But now Noah is told of God's assessment and of the divine
plan to end "all flesh" and "ruin them with the earth," for this is the reason
he must build the ark and gather animals together for their survival.

The phrasing of the divine decree "The end of all flesh has been determined
by me" (literally, "come before me"), suggests its irrevocability. The issue
has been brought before the divine king and he has decided to act (cf. Esth
9:11). "I am about to ruin them" again highlights the immediacy and certainty
of the coming judgment. הנני (I am about to) plus participle is most often
used to announce an imminent divine judgment or blessing (cf. Oberforcher,
Die Flutprologe, 453). The flood is described as "ruining the earth" which
earlier has been said to have ruined itself. This is a clear case of a punishment
fitting the crime, a favorite principle of biblical law; cf. 9:6; Exod 21:23–25.
It should also be noted how Ezek 7 echoes the terminology of this verse
("end," "violence," "coming," "is full") in announcing the fall of Jerusalem.

14–16   Instructions for building the ark are telegraphically brief in style.
If the word "ark" marks the beginning of a new sub-paragraph, these verses
may be analyzed as follows (cf. *SBH,* 52):

> v 14   General instruction: Make ark of gopher wood.
> Specific instruction: 1. Make it with reeds and seal it with pitch.
> v 15   2. Make it 300 cubits long, 50 broad, 30 high.
> v 16   3. Make a roof and complete it.
>   4. Put a door in the side, and make decks.

Leaving aside their obscurity at some points, these instructions are much
too short to serve as a practical blueprint for construction. Rather they give
the minimum details required for making sense of the flood story. Comparison
with the parallel commands in Gilgamesh 11:24–34 (see above) suggests that
both accounts at least go back to common tradition. The account of the
building of the ark, much fuller in Gilgamesh 11:50–75, furnishes other
interesting points of contact (discussed below) with Genesis. In Exod 25–31,
there are also parallels in phraseology with the directions for building the
tabernacle and its furniture that suggest that both ark and tabernacle were
seen as a sanctuary for the righteous.

14   "Ark" (תבה). Apart from the flood story the only other OT uses of
the word are Exod 2:3, 5, where it signifies the basket of bulrushes in which
baby Moses was hidden. It is probably an Egyptian loan word (*tbt*) meaning
box or chest.

"Gopher" (גפר). The word occurs only here in the OT. The identity of
this tree is uncertain. *Tg. Onq.* understands it to be "cedar," whereas LXX

translates it "squared" timber, and Vg, "smoothed" timber. Modern commentators usually suppose some sort of conifer suitable for shipbuilding must be meant (*EM* 2:544–45).

"Reeds." Though "compartments" is the traditional understanding of קִנִּים, literally, "nests," the context leads us to expect details of the building materials at this point, sandwiched as it is between wood and pitch. So it is attractive to repoint קָנִים "reeds" with Jacob (188), G. R. Driver (*VT* 4 [1954] 243), NEB, and McEvenue (*Narrative Style of the Priestly Writer*, 45, n. 36). Westermann objects that the traditional interpretation is proved by the Gilgamesh parallel 11:61–62, which divides Utnapishtim's boat into seven decks, each with nine cabins. But this is hardly sufficient, for it seems likely that Utnapishtim pulled down his reed hut (21–24) to provide building materials for his ship (cf. W. G. Lambert and A. R. Millard, *Atrahasis*, 12). Thus both views can claim support from Mesopotamian parallels. How the reeds could have been employed in Noah's ark is unclear, perhaps to fill gaps between the woodwork.

"Pitch," כפר. Used only here in the OT; elsewhere, e.g., 11:3; 14:10, חמר is the term. However, *kupru* "bitumen," a common Akkadian term, is used in the Gilgamesh epic (11:65, which is a remarkable parallel with the biblical tradition). "Inside and outside" is a technical phrase in construction texts; cf. Exod 25:11; 37:2; 1 Kgs 7:9.

15 The dimensions of the ark—length, breadth, height—are given according to the standard construction formula found in Exod 25:10, 17, 23, etc. At 18 inches or 45 centimeters to the cubit (for precise equivalents, see R. de Vaux, *Ancient Israel*, 197), the ark was a huge box about 450' (135 m) long, 75' (22 m) broad, and 45' (13 m) deep. It is usually supposed to have been flat-bottomed. The surface area of the ark was thus three times as much as that of the tabernacle courtyard, 100 x 50 cubits (Exod 27:9–13). The Babylonian ark, on the other hand, was a perfect cube, 120 cubits in each direction, in volume nearly five times as large as the Hebrew vessel. Cassuto (2:63) suggests that Genesis is scaling down Mesopotamian tradition, just as it does with the ages of the antediluvian patriarchs. He also points out that the dimensions of the ark are multiples of 60 or 10, just as many of the patriarchs' ages are. Gispen (1:254) notes that the largest boats known from the Egyptian old kingdom period must have been about 63 meters long and 22 meters broad. He also describes the building by a seventeenth-century Dutchman, Peter Janssen, of an ark two-fifths of the size of the Genesis ark to demonstrate its seaworthiness (1:257–59).

16 "Roof." צהר is another word that only occurs here in the OT and is a subject of much debate. Older translators and commentators generally associated it with the window mentioned in 8:6. Modern commentators, on the basis of Semitic cognates meaning "back," suppose the "roof" or "covering" of the ark (8:13) is referred to.

"And complete it to a cubit upwards." This is the most obscure remark in the flood story. Of the multitude of interpretations, two seem more plausible than the others. Either it means "complete the ark (or the roof) to leave a gap of one cubit between the roof and the walls of the ark" (18", 45 cm; Gispen, Cassuto), or it could mean "complete the ark or roof so that the roof overhangs the walls of the ark by one cubit." On the latter view (Jacob), the roof was made of cloth or skins like the cover of the tabernacle, which was draped over the top of the ark. Jacob connects this remark with 8:13, where the covering is removed by Noah.

"Door" is mentioned, because entering and leaving the ark is central to the subsequent narrative (cf. 7:16.) It is also mentioned in Gilgamesh 11:93.

"Decks." Whereas the biblical ark had three decks, the Babylonian had seven (GE 11:60–61). Jacob (192) notes that if each deck were further subdivided into three sections (cf. Gilgamesh's nine sections GE 11:62), the ark would have had three decks the same height as the tabernacle and three sections on each deck the same size as the tabernacle courtyard. While the last point is speculative, it is true that the ark and the tabernacle are the only structures described in the law. This prompts Westermann to comment that P looks to the tabernacle, the place where God meets with his people, as the goal of history.

> The place where God allows his glory to appear is the place whence the life of the people is preserved. The ark corresponds to this in the primeval event where the concern is for the preservation of humanity. . . . Such is the significance of the construction of the ark because by means of it God preserved humanity from destruction. The parallel between the ark and the tabernacle has a profound meaning. The people of Israel, which alone has in its midst the place where God reveals his glory, is part of the human race which exists now because it has been preserved by this same God (1:421).

17 Up to this point in the narrative there have simply been general warnings of doom. Though a command to build an ark has been given, its precise purpose has not been disclosed. Now everything is made brutally clear.

"I myself." The repetition of the personal pronoun makes it perfectly clear that God is author of the flood. It is not a force that gets out of divine control as in Babylonian tradition; cf. Ps 29:10: "The LORD sits enthroned over the flood."

"Flood" מבול is a technical term for Noah's flood used only in Gen 6–11 and Ps 29:10. Here used for the first time it is further explained as "water over the earth. . . . " Its etymology is uncertain: most probably it comes from the root יבל "to flow." In Gen 6–9 "flood" appears to refer to the first destructive phase of the flood: after 7:17 the narrative simply speaks of waters.

"To ruin all flesh . . . " repeats the warning of v 13, but makes it more specific: "in which there is the spirit of life." God the giver of life (cf. 2:7) is now taking it away.

"Beneath the heaven" may be a poetic alternative to "upon the earth," but Delitzsch and Cassuto may be correct to see it contrasting with "beneath the waters" (cf. Exod 20:4), thereby excluding fishes and other water creatures from destruction.

"Expire," גוע; cf. 7:21. This is a rarer word for dying, often used in poetry, also of the death of the patriarchs (e.g., 25:8; 35:29; 49:33), and sometimes in the context of dramatic divine judgment (e.g., Num 17:27–28 [12–13]; Josh 22:20).

18–20 These verses, which further expound the divine plan, are not to be understood as commands to Noah but as additional explanations of the divine purpose in having the ark built and loaded with food; see above on 6:13–21.

18 "Confirm my covenant." This is the first appearance of the key theological term בְּרִית, *bĕrît*, "covenant." For discussions of this term see E. Kutsch, *THWAT*, 1:339–51; M. Weinfeld, *TDOT*, 2:253–79; D. J. McCarthy, *Treaty and Covenant* (AnBib 21A, 2d ed. [Rome: Biblical Institute Press, 1978]); P. Kalluveetil, *Declaration and Covenant* (AnBib 88 [Rome: Biblical Institute Press, 1982]); W. J. Dumbrell, *Covenant and Creation* (1984); E. W. Nicholson, *God and His People* (Oxford: Clarendon Press, 1986).

As Israel's relationship with God is most frequently seen in terms of covenant, there has been much discussion as to whether covenants are basically one-sided pledges or two-sided agreements. Here the phrase "confirm my covenant" suggests that divine obligations are uppermost, that God will maintain his special relationship with Noah. The confirmation of the covenant is found in 9:9–17, but this presupposes the commands in 9:1–7.

The phrase "confirm [הֲקִים] my covenant" is often held to be P's phrase for *initiating* a covenant, language synonymous with כרת "to cut a covenant." But this is not so. Whereas "to cut" describes the point of entry to a covenant, "to confirm" is used of ratifying pre-existing "words" (Deut 9:5), "promises" (2 Sam 7:25), "threats" (Jer 30:24), "oaths" (Gen 26:3), "vows" (Num 30:14), as well as "covenants" (Dumbrell, *Creation and Covenant*, 25–26; cf. *TDOT* 2:260).

It should be noted that "I shall confirm my covenant with you" shows that Noah is viewed as already in a covenant relationship with God. He is not simply a perfectly righteous man; there is a covenant between him and God. This makes a further parallel between him and later Israel.

This is the first mention of a covenant in the OT. Here the chief consequences of the covenant are mentioned: the deliverance of Noah, his family, and selected animals.

Now the paradox inherent in the instructions about building the ark is resolved. Noah had been told to build it for himself (v 14), but the structure was far too vast for one man, or even for himself and his family alone. The phrase "you, your sons, your wife, and your sons' wives" runs like a refrain through the narrative (cf. 7:7, 13; 8:16, 18), illustrating that the basic unit of biblical society consisted of a man, his wife, his married sons and daughters-in-law and their children, rather than the modern nuclear family.

19–20 The chiastic ordering of the verbs "come," "bring" in vv 18 and 19 emphasizes that the animals are to board the ark at the same time as Noah and his family. Note how the list of animals, at first very general, is gradually made more specific with many echoes of the creation account. "Male and female" (cf. 1:27); "according to their types" (1:11, 12, 21, 24, 25). Note too the same sequence "birds," "land animals," "creeping things" (1:20–24). Though "you shall bring into" could suggest that Noah had to round up the animals, "will come to you" (v 20) shows that the animals would arrive spontaneously. The twice-repeated verb "to stay alive, preserve life" stresses the point of Noah's heroic efforts and looks forward to the mission of Joseph (45:7; 50:20).

21 The second command given to Noah in the opening scene (the first was "build an ark," vv 14–16) follows the explanation for these injunctions in vv 17–20. The wording of the command echoes both the creation injunctions about eating: cf. "you and they will have it to eat," היה ל . . . לאכלה, with 1:29–30 and with the garden of Eden story. "Take some of every edible food" seems to make allusion to the *taking* and *eating* of the fruit which was not to be *eaten* (3:6), terms which run as leitmotifs throughout Gen 3. Noah, like Adam (2:16–17), was told to eat only of divinely permitted food. 7:2 shows that Noah is presumed to be able to distinguish clean (edible) and unclean (inedible) animals.

22 Scene 2: In contrast to the Gilgamesh epic which gives an elaborate and colorful description of the building and loading of the ark (GE 11:54–82), Genesis gives this brief bald statement about Noah's obedience. Similar summaries are found in 7:5, 9, 16, but they do not constitute a complete scene as here (cf. Exod 12:28,50): "did exactly as God commanded him, so he did." The phrasing "exactly as," literally, "according to all," and the repetition "did . . . so he did" make this a very emphatic declaration of Noah's total obedience. Similar formulae recur rarely in the Pentateuch, except at the erection of the tabernacle (Exod 39:32, 42; 40:16) and at some other high-points in the wilderness wanderings (Num 1:54; 2:34; 9:5.) Within the context of the primeval history, verbal allusions to the refrain of Gen 1:3, 9,-11, 15, 24, 30 "and it was so" and to Gen 2:16; 3:11, 17 may be detected, implying that Noah's acts were more like God's than Adam's.

7:1–4 Scene 3: A divine monologue addressed to Noah instructing him to enter the ark corresponds to that of scene 8 (8:15–17) telling him to leave. Like scene 1, this scene contains two commands, "Enter" (v 1) and "You must take" (v 2), separated by an explanation.

1 "The Lord said to Noah." The use of the divine name "Yahweh," here and in v 5, has led to the ascription of 7:1–5 to J. However, in the present context "because you I have seen are righteous in this generation" clearly points back to 6:9 (P), for the same words "righteous" and "generation/contemporaries" appear. See on 6:9 for their meaning. W. M. Clark's attempt (*VT* 21 [1971] 261–80) to prove that in 7:1 Noah's righteousness is prospective, not actual, does not suit the present context of 7:1. Nor is he justified in arguing that "I have seen" refers to royal election ideology; cf. 1 Sam 16:1. In context "I have seen" echoes "God saw . . . the earth was . . . ruined" (6:12), so that there is a long-range chiasmus between 6:9, 11, and 6:12 and 7:1, viz.:

> 6:9   Noah was righteous . . . among his contemporaries
> 6:11 The earth was ruined
> 6:12 God saw the earth was ruined
> 7:1   The Lord said . . . "you I have seen are righteous in this generation."

2–3 According to 6:19–20, pairs of all kinds of creatures would come to the ark to preserve life on earth. Here Noah is told specifically to admit additional clean land animals, seven pairs of each, and seven pairs of birds. The purpose of this measure becomes clear only after the flood. Birds are let out to reconnoiter the earth (8:7–12), and clean animals and birds are offered in sacrifice (8:20.) Without extra pairs of these creatures sacrifice would have entailed the extinction of the clean birds and animals, the only types permitted to be sacrificed (cf. G. J. Wenham, *Leviticus*, 164–80). It is characteristic of Gen 1–11 to trace back the fundamental religious institutions to primeval times: Sabbath (2:1–3); the Garden of Eden, the ideal sanctuary (2–3); sacrifice (4:1–8); and here the difference between clean and unclean. As a righteous and blameless man, Noah knew the difference between clean and unclean and the necessity of sacrifice. Furthermore, the timetable of the flood with its seven-day periods of waiting may indicate that he observed the Sabbath. Atrahasis seems to have included clean animals and the winged birds of heaven among his cargo (3:2, 32–35), so mentioning these items is not an innovation of Genesis.

As the Genesis account stands, there is no conflict between the general announcement in 6:19–20 that pairs of all animals will embark and the more detailed injunctions of 7:2–3 about added clean animals. If 6:19–20 (P) and 7:2–3 (J) were once independent, it would be possible to view their remarks as contradictory. But there is no inherent incompatibility between them as they stand at present. 7:2–3 simply is more precise than 6:19–20 about the types and number of animal passengers.

4 Earlier when instructed to build the ark (6:17), Noah had been warned of the impending flood; now with the command to "enter," more specific details are given about its timing, "in seven days' time," and its nature, "rain for forty days and nights." The Gilgamesh epic seems to envisage that seven days were needed to *build* the ship (11:76) and that the storm lasted seven days (11:128). The biblical time frame is clearly more appropriate to the scale of the events described. "Forty days and forty nights" is a conventional expression for a long time (cf. Exod 24:18). The mention of "seven days" here forms part of the palistrophic sequence in counting the days (7, 7, 40, 150, 150, 40, 7, 7) mentioned under *Form/Structure/Setting*. The mention of "40 days and 40 *nights*" falls outside this pattern, though. "Wipe out" echoes the phraseology of 6:7 and looks forward to 7:23. "Existence," קוּם, occurs only here, in 7:23, and in Deut 11:6, another situation of total destruction.

5–16 Scene 4 is narrative that relates the complete and total obedience of Noah and the animals to God's command to enter the ark and the onset of the flood. The fullness of description, the use of epic apposition, and repeated mentions of the date give this scene weight and solemnity. The day when the old creation died is described with a gravity befitting the occasion. The threefold refrain "as God (the LORD) had commanded him" emphasizes the other central fact: Noah's fidelity to God led to his salvation.

This scene, like scenes 1 and 3, falls into two main parts, each concluding with "as God had commanded Noah/him" (vv 9, 16).

Date in Noah's life	6a	10a (11a)
Flood comes	6b	10b, 11b–12
Noah and family enter	7	13
Animals enter	8	14
In pairs	9a	15–16a
"As God commanded"	9b	16b

This is a good example of panel-writing. (For definition of the term see McEvenue, *Narrative Style of the Priestly Writer*, 158–59. He notes an example in Gen 17 but overlooks this one.) It should be noted that the second panel does not simply repeat, but is more precise than the first. V 6a dates the flood to the "600th year of Noah's life"; v 11a dates it to the day. V 7 mentions Noah's sons; v 13 names them.

Andersen (*SBH*, 124–25) has also shown that there are elaborate chiastic patterns spanning these verses, demonstrating that the coming of the flood and the entry into the ark are viewed as essentially one event.

> The whole of Gen 7:6–16 is an elaborate piece of epic composition, in which there are only two events both already stated at the beginning, namely, the onset of the flood and the entry into the ark. Descriptions of these events alternate— flood (v 6), entry (vv 7–9), flood (vv 10–12), entry (vv 13–16a), flood (v 17). A third event (the closing of door) is mentioned only once (v 16b).

These repetitions are generally appealed to as proof that the two sources J and P are present here. The analysis does not follow the panel division just mentioned, but vv 7, 10, 12, 16b are assigned to J; vv 6, 11, 13–16a to P; and vv 8–9 to an editor. It is evident that if this source analysis is right, the redactor has drastically modified his sources. Furthermore, within P there is still substantial repetitiveness (cf. vv 6 and 11), whereas J either lacks any reference to the animals entering the ark, or if vv 8–9 belong to him, his account is full of P-phraseology (see further M. Kessler, "Rhetorical Criticism of Genesis 7," 2–9).

It therefore seems prudent to recognize the impossibility of distinguishing with certainty the Hebrew sources underlying the present account. If the final editor is the Yahwist, his hand may be discerned in the opening and closing verses of the scene where the LORD is mentioned by name (vv 5, 16).

5 is almost identical with 6:22 with the replacement of "the LORD" for "God," and the omission of "so he did." Instead of the latter clause we have the long and detailed description in vv 6–16 of the arrival of the flood and Noah's embarkation. Clearly the narrator wishes to insist that the latter events were much more important than the actual building of the ark. Yet, from a human perspective, boarding the ark was much easier than building it! The Gilgamesh epic plays up the heroic achievement of the flood hero by describing the construction of the boat in some detail. Genesis plays down Noah's effort, merely mentioning his obedience.

Cassuto gives another reason for the detail in 7:6–16 compared with the brevity of 6:22:

> Here we have a mighty and amazing spectacle: the tremendous endless procession of all the creatures streaming from all parts of the earth to Noah's abode. . . . This time a brief and anaemic expression, such as 6:22, would have been inadequate; a detailed description was necessary. Hence the matters on which Noah was previously instructed are repeated here, and this reiteration presents us, as it were, with a magnificent and graphic picture of that wondrous scene, the mass pilgrimage from all parts of the world to the one place that promised salvation to every kind of creature (2:80).

6 Apart from creation, the flood is the only event in the primeval history to be dated. In the absence of any fixed chronological base-line, it is necessary to date events by reference to regnal years (cf. 1–2 Kgs) or to a well-known figure's age. Noah was 500 years old when he fathered his sons (5:32). It has been suggested that an age of 600 years may be related to the Sumerian *ner* which equals 600 (so Skinner), a learned loan word in Babylonian, or to Ziusudra, who according to one tradition ruled 600 *ner* until the flood came (Cassuto), but this may be just coincidence. On the term "flood" see 6:17.

7 Fulfills the command in 7:1, though the terminology is closer to 6:18.

8–9 Records the fulfillment of 7:2–3. No mention is made of the seven pairs of clean animals, but the use of 7:2–3, the remark "as God had commanded Noah," and the rest of the story (8:20) indicate additional clean animals were embarked. The list of animals here and throughout the flood story clearly echoes Gen 1.

10 The second part of this scene goes over the same events as vv 6–9 in rather more detail, especially as concerns the flood. "In seven days" looks back to 7:4 and "waters of the flood . . . the earth" to 7:6. Note that God is pictured as working according to a seven-day cycle. In waiting for the flood to subside, Noah too follows a weekly cycle of activity (8:10,12). These seven-day periods contribute to the palistrophic structure of the narrative (see above on *Form/Structure/Setting*).

11 "In the 600th . . . on the 17th day." The fullness and precision of the dates in the flood narrative are astonishing (7:12, 17, 24; 8:3, 4, 5, 6, 10, 12, 13, 14); only Ezekiel in dating his prophecies (e.g., 1:1; 3:16, etc.) approaches Gen 7–8 in this regard. These dates have therefore attracted much inconclusive study (cf. S. E. McEvenue, *Narrative Style of the Priestly Writer,* 55–59; G. Larsson, *VT* 27 [1977] 490–92; *ZAW* 97 [1985] 323–25; N. P. Lemche, *JSOT* 18 [1980] 52–62; F. H. Cryer, *Bib* 66 [1985] 241–67). Given our ignorance of the calendars used in OT times, it is impossible to be dogmatic about the significance of the dates in the flood story. The dates may of course simply be mentioned to underline the factuality of the flood, to give assurance that it really happened. However, various suggestions have been made to find symbolic significance behind the numbers, since ancient peoples believed they held the key to the mysteries of the universe.

Thus the first and last dates given (7:11; 8:14) make the flood last exactly one year and eleven days. Now the difference between the lunar and solar years is 11 days (365 - 354), and it is surmised that Genesis wanted to have the flood last an exact solar year. But this observation does not explain why the flood began and ended on these particular days (17.2.600; 27.2.601). If the writer simply wanted to say the flood lasted a solar year, why not have the flood begin on, say, 15.2.600 and end on 25.2.601? Cassuto suggests the narrative has omitted to say that it took forty days to build the ark. If Noah started on 1.1.600, then spent forty days in building and seven waiting (7:10), we arrive at 17.2.600. Even if this surmise is correct, it offers no explanation for the other dates in the flood story.

Source criticism postulates that our present narrative combines two independent chronologies. J held that the flood lasted forty days and was preceded by a week of waiting (7:10) and followed by two weeks of waiting afterwards (8:10, 12). P, on the other hand, spread the flood over a whole year; all the references to dates and the 150–day period come from P. If on other grounds the presence of J and P can be demonstrated within the flood story, one might accept that two chronologies have been amalgamated. But that still leaves the problem of understanding the redactor's chronology, which, as has often been pointed out, is quite coherent (e.g., A. Heidel, *The Gilgamesh Epic*, 246–47; E. Nielsen, *Oral Tradition*, SBT 11 [London, SCM, 1954] 93–101; Wenham, *VT* 28 [1978] 343–45).The events may be dated as follows:

1)	Announcement of the flood	(7:4)	10.2.600 Sunday
2)	Flood begins	(7:11)	*17.2.600* Sunday
3)	Flood lasts 40 days and ends	(7:12)	27.3.600 Friday
4)	Waters triumph and abate (including flood for 40 days) for 150 days = 5 months till ark grounds	(8:4)	*17.7.600* Friday
5)	Mountain tops appear	(8:5)	*1.10.600* Wednesday
6)	Raven sent out (after 40 days)	(8:6)	10.11.600 Sunday
7)	Dove's second flight	(8:10)	24.11.600 Sunday
8)	Dove's third flight	(8:12)	1.12.600 Sunday
9)	Waters dry up	(8:13)	*1.1.601* Wednesday
10)	Noah leaves ark	(8:14)	*27.2.601* Wednesday

The italicized dates are those given in the text itself: the others are deduced from other remarks. The only problem with the chronology is fitting the forty days (7:12) and the 150 days (7:24) into the five months between 7:11 and 8:4. Evidently the editor of Genesis and certainly the early versions understood the forty days of flood to constitute part of the 150 days during which the waters triumphed.

Jaubert offered a possible explanation of the significance of the dates in the flood narrative, as well as various other great events in the OT. She suggested that these dates presuppose the use of the calendar used by the book of Jubilees (probably 2nd century B.C.). This calendar has 364 days to the year, and this means that every year a particular date always falls on the same day of the week. Thus New Year's Day is always a Wednesday. This may explain the special prominence given to Wednesday, the fourth day in the creation narrative (so P. Beauchamp, *Création et séparation* [Paris: Desclée, 1969] 113–14).

On this hypothesis, most of the dates in the flood story are seen to be highly significant. Creation began on a Sunday according to Gen 1. Gen 7:11 makes the flood, the agent of creation's destruction, arrive on Sunday too. Creation was completed on Friday. If we regard the five months when the ark floated as the period of de-creation, then de-creation concluded on a Friday. Alternatively, one could say the ark ceased traveling on Friday in order not to violate another Sabbath! The appearance of mountains (8:5), the drying of the waters (8:13), and the exit from the ark (8:14) all fell on a Wednesday, the day of new beginnings (A. Jaubert, *La Date de la cène* [Paris: J. Gabalda, 1957] 33).

Jaubert's hypothesis may be developed further, using the other periods mentioned in Gen 7–8. Then the flood, the destructive phase of the waters, also seems to be over on a Friday (7:12), and Noah, like God, begins a new phase of activity on Sundays (8:6, 10, 12; cf. 7:10, 11). This suggests that he observed the previous day as a Sabbath, a mark of his righteousness perhaps.

This hypothesis is somewhat fragile (cf. Baumgarten, *VT* 32 [1982] 485–89) and depends on the assumption that Genesis actually knew and used the Jubilees calendar. It is usually assumed that pre-exilic Judaism, like later Judaism, used a lunar calendar, and that the Jubilees calendar was a sectarian pipe-dream. It could be, though, that the Jubilees calendar was really a relic of pre-exilic practice (so P. R. Davies, "Calendrical Change and Qumran Origins," *CBQ* 45 [1983] 80–89).

"All the springs . . . burst open . . . and the windows of heaven were opened." Once again the expanded description of the flood's arrival is more explicit than previous remarks; "springs of the great deep" and "windows of heaven" are poetic phrases (e.g., Amos 7:4; Ps 78:15; Isa 24:18; Mal 3:10) suggesting water gushing forth uncontrollably from wells and springs which draw from a great subterranean ocean ("the great deep") and an unrestrained downpour from the sky. The same pair of terms ("great deep/windows of heaven") recurs in 8:2. In Babylonian mythology, Adad the weather god controls the rain and, occasionally, the water from the abyss so that the idea of the flood involving disruption of both goes back to pre-Hebrew sources (cf. M. Weinfeld, *WO* 9 [1978] 242–48).

The terminology and the frequent use of parallelism in this section has led Gunkel, Cassuto, and Westermann among others to postulate that the present account of the flood is, at this point at least, based on an earlier poetic Hebrew version. This may well be so. However, it is precarious to attempt to reconstruct a verse account of the flood based on the use of poetic vocabulary and parallelism. Parallelism is not confined to Hebrew poetry (cf. J. L. Kugel, *The Idea of Hebrew Poetry* [New Haven: Yale UP, 1981]); indeed, it is quite common in Hebrew epic prose (cf. *SBH*, 39–53). But just as in Gen 1, where the excitement of creation led to the use of an elevated, quasi-poetic prose style, so here the writing is characterized by various features commonly regarded as poetic which help to evoke the tension and emotion associated with creation's destruction. In releasing the waters pent-up below and above the earth, God is undoing his great acts of separation whereby the dry land was created and the waters were confined in the seas (Gen 1:9). The earth is going back to Gen 1:2, when the waters covered its face.

12 "Heavy rain" (cf. 8:2), גשׁם (cf. Ezra 10:9,13), is "commonly used of the heavy winter rain" (Skinner, 154); "*gešem*, unlike *māṭār*, signifies abnormal rainfall" (Speiser, 53). "Forty days and forty nights"; cf. 7:4,17.

13–16 The entry into the ark is here described again (cf. vv 7–9), but with extra details giving the whole occasion "a festive tone" as befits an act which marks one of the turning points in human history. Noah's great act of obedience not merely saved himself but made possible the new world order, whose safety would be guaranteed by covenant. These verses thus portray the founders of the new humanity and new animal kingdom processing in a double column into the ark. As each group embarks, its name is called and recorded for posterity.

13 "On this very day": a fairly rare phrase used to stress the memorableness of a particular occasion, e.g., Abraham's circumcision (17:23, 26), the exodus (Exod 12:41, 51), Moses' death (Deut 32:48).

"Shem, Ham, and Japhet," named only here and in 6:10 and 9:18. Elsewhere in the story always "his sons."

"Noah's wife" only here. Elsewhere "his wife" (7:7; 8:18) or "your wife" (6:18; 8:16).

"The three wives of his sons." Another unique phrase: elsewhere "the wives of his sons." Cassuto (2:93) suggests the unusual grammatical form (see *Notes*) draws attention to the wives being a distinct group.

14 The full roll call of all the creatures echoes Gen 1. Note especially the refrain "according to their types." Similar lists omitting the refrain occur again at 7:21 (the flood victims) and 8:17 (those who left the ark). Again the narrative makes the point that only through boarding the ark does creation survive.

15–16 Repeats v 9, but more fully. "Of all flesh in . . . life": cf. 6:17; 7:22. Note the threefold repetition of "come in," "enter". A great stream of male and female creatures enters the ark invisibly controlled. These last two clauses, "as God had commanded him . . . the LORD shut him in," point to the divine director behind the operation.

Gilgamesh (11:93) mentions that Utnapishtim shut the door. Genesis, by ascribing this action to the LORD, reiterates that Noah was saved by divine grace, not by his wisdom or heroic efforts.

17–24 Scene 5: The waters triumphant. Here the drama reaches its climax with the destruction of creation by the waters. Alliteration and repetition combine to describe a scene of watery chaos from which all life has disappeared beneath the waves. The absence of any personal names, apart from a parenthetic mention of Noah in v 23, enhances the atmosphere of desolation. The effects of the rising waters are portrayed by focusing on different aspects in turn. The ark floats (17–18), then the high mountains are covered (19–20), and all living creatures die (21–23). A brief cut to the ark again in 23b reminds the viewer that there is still a glimmer of hope, but the sequence closes with a final shot of the waters triumphing over the earth (24).

The phrases "on the earth," עַל הָאָרֶץ, and "waters," מִים, occur six times in this paragraph, often in close conjunction. Both these phrases produce a strong resonance with Gen 1, but are hardly heard again until the flood story which recounts the undoing of creation. There also appear to be an above-average number of words containing the sound *m* and the phonetically adjacent *b*, for example, *mabbul*, "flood." This alliteration perhaps suggests the presence of water, *mayim*, even when the word is not used.

17 Here "the flood," מבול, i.e., the first stage of heavy rainfall (v 12), is said to have lasted forty days. The consequences are then elaborated. The waters "multiplied," a baleful echo of the injunction given to the first creatures to be fruitful and multiply (1:22, 28). As if to reinforce the echo, the word reappears in v 18. The phraseology again reminds us that creation has been put into reverse by the waters of the flood. Note the use of "on the earth" and "waters" once each, and the very similar "above the earth" and "flood."

18 A stage further. The waters do not merely multiply greatly; they triumph. גבר, which occurs four times in this scene (vv 18, 19, 20, 24) is a military word for succeeding in battle (e.g., Exod 17:11). The ark does not merely lift off, but it travels over the waters.

19 Yet further victory by the waters over the earth. Note the repetition of the key words, and the way the remark "the waters triumphed and multiplied greatly" in v 18 is heightened here to "the waters triumphed exceedingly [greatly greatly]." Just how deep the water was is indicated by the high mountains' being submerged.

20 In fact the mountains were covered by at least 15 cubits (22 feet or 7 meters) of water, allowing the ark to float over them. Apparently the story assumes the ark's draft was half its height of thirty cubits (6:15).

21–23 The narrator's camera lingers longest over the destruction of life by the flood. Elsewhere in Genesis "expire and die" are used in quick succession to describe the process of dying (25:8, 17; 35:29). To "expire" "signifies the moment of transition from life to death." "To die" "indicates the condition obtaining after that moment" (Cassuto, 2:96). Here the members of this standard word pair are spaced out, standing at opposite ends of sentences in chiastic apposition. Such slowing of pace regularly marks the climax of a narrative (cf. J. Licht, *Storytelling in the Bible*, 113–14).

21–22 "all flesh . . . expired . . . the breath of the spirit of life" fulfills 6:17 and contrasts with 7:15. But as usual, at this point in the story the phraseology is much more detailed. The dying creatures are listed in the order of creation, and therefore the list ends with a mention of man.

22 "Everything . . . nostrils." Though similar to 6:17 and 7:15, the mention of "breath" and "nostrils" echoes 2:7. God who gave man the breath of life, thereby making him a living being, now removes it, and so man dies.

23 Life did not simply die. It was wiped out. The threats of 6:7 and 7:4 were fulfilled. Only Noah and those with him in the ark survived. The contrast between those wiped out *mḥh* and Noah *nḥ* is deliberately highlighted by using the similar verb with the proper name; cf. *Comment* on 6:5–8.

24 "The paragraph closes, with an awe-inspiring picture of the mighty waters covering the entire earth. We see water everywhere, as though the world had reverted to its primeval state at the dawn of Creation, when the waters of the deep submerged everything. Nothing remained of the teeming life that had burst forth upon the earth" (Cassuto, 2:97).

"One hundred and fifty days." On the role of this phrase in the palistrophe, see *Form/Structure/Setting*. Chronologically the 150 days must cover the five months from the coming of the flood (7:11) to the grounding of the ark (8:4). Evidently the first forty days of heavy rain (7:12) were followed by 110 days of the waters' triumph. 8:4 makes plain that at least toward the end of the five months, the waters had begun to fall.

8:1–5 Scene 6 opens the second half of the flood story. All the different analyses make the opening sentence of this scene, "God remembered Noah," the turning point of the narrative. The floodwaters have done their worst in the previous scene with the total annihilation of all life outside the ark. Now divine intervention begins the reestablishment of order and life on earth.

In various ways this scene closely corresponds to the previous one. The water continues to be the principal actor. The same period of 150 days is mentioned. But the whole atmosphere is changed by the opening sentence. Whereas in scene 4 the impersonal waters of destruction triumphing everywhere dominate the whole picture; here "God remembered Noah" sets the narrative in a new, optimistic, personal direction. There the waters triumph; here they retreat. There the ark floats over the earth; here it lands on the mountains. There the high mountains are covered; here they reappear above the waves. The tension relaxes and the pace of the action quickens. Whereas Scene 4 moves very slowly, with repeated action-replays holding back the development of the plot, in scene 5 the tempo accelerates: the only repeat draws attention to the gradualness of the waters' retreat.

The chronology makes it clear that the 150 days mentioned in both scenes 4 and 5 fall between the 17.2.600th day of Noah's life and 17.7.600th day, i.e., a period of about five months. In other words, although the waters appear to triumph for 150 days, they were actually falling well before the period elapsed, or else the ark would not have grounded on 17.7.600. Presumably, then, we are meant to understand that God remembered Noah and blew this wind long before 17.7.600. Yet to an ordinary observer, the waters appeared to be triumphing throughout this time. In reality, however, the stormy wind was bringing Noah's salvation. It was driving back the waters, so that after five months afloat the ark landed on the mountains of Ararat.

1 "God remembered Noah." Similarly, God "remembered" Abraham after the destruction of Sodom (19:29); he "remembered" Rachel (30:22), and he "remembered" his covenant made in 9:15, 16, etc. Man is bidden not simply to "remember" the past but the future (e.g., Isa 47:7; Eccl 11:8), which suggests that the word is more equivalent to "think about" than to a concept of recall. However, since its usual reference is to the past, "remember" suits most passages. When God remembers, he acts, e.g., saving Lot, giving Rachel children, bringing Israel out of slavery (Exod 2:24; 6:5). This is the first time God is said to have remembered someone, and this passage is a paradigm of what that means in practice; cf. H. Eising, *TDOT* 4:64-82. Note God's concern for the animals as well as Noah (cf. Jon 4:11; Matt 6:26; 10:29). "A wind": cf. the wind of God at creation which hovered over the waters, Gen 1:2.

2 "The springs . . . sealed," reversing 7:11. The verb סכר "seal, block" is common in Akkadian: *sekēru* for blocking waters (*AHW*). "The rain was restrained," reversing 7:12. Hebrew כלא "restrain" is cognate with Akkadian *kalû*, which is found in Gilgamesh 11:131: *abūbu ikla* "the flood ceased," a similar context.

3 "The waters . . . receded," reversing 7:17, 24. Exactly the same description is given of the Red Sea returning to its place in Exod 14:26, 28, and the Jordan likewise, in Josh 4:18, the other great saving acts associated with water in the OT. Here the waters are pictured as returning to their normal place, above the sky and below the earth.

"150 days," i.e., after the coming of the flood, the retreat of the waters was evident (cf. 7:24).

4 Exactly five months after the start of the flood (7:11), the ark comes to rest, a Friday, according to the Jubilees calendar. Evidently the water level has fallen enough that the ark no longer has fifteen cubits clearance above the mountain tops (7:20).

"Rested" (*wattānaḥ*), clearly a paronomastic allusion to Noah's name (*nōăḥ*; cf. 5:29).

"On the mountains of Ararat" does not mean on a mountain called Ararat, but on the mountains in the area called Ararat. Ararat is the Hebrew term for Urartu, a kingdom north of Assyria (2 Kgs 19:37; Isa 37:38; Jer 51:27) later called Armenia, now part of eastern Turkey, southern Russia, and north-western Iran. Various mountains in Armenia have been identified with the one on which the ark landed (see Cassuto for full discussion). Early Jewish tradition called them the mountains of Qardu, apparently Jebel Judi, south of Lake Van. Other suggestions include Great Ararat, called by locals the mountain of Noah, and Little Ararat. The Epic of Gilgamesh names the landing place of the ark Mount Nisir, probably Pir Omar Gudrun south of the lower Zab, i.e., much further south than Ararat. But it should be repeated that the biblical text does not give a precise location.

5 Over two months later, after a gradual decline, the water had fallen sufficiently for the mountain tops to be seen. "The withdrawal proceeds in steps: v 4 corresponds to 7:18 (ark floats— ark touches bottom): v 5 corresponds to 7:19–20 (hills are covered—tops of hills become visible" (McEvenue, *Narrative Style*, 65). Note also the correspondence with the account of creation: "on the third day dry land appeared" (1:9). The third dated event in the flood story is the appearance of the mountains.

8:6–14 Scene 7 matches scene 4 in that both are straight narratives with Noah and the animals as the principal actors, but whereas the earlier scene concentrates on one event, the entry to the ark, this one spans a long period during which the waters gradually subside. In the earlier scene repetition is used to bring out the hustle and bustle before the impending flood; here the repetition helps to convey the monotony of waiting inside the ark for the earth to dry out. The scene falls into 3 parts:

8:6–7 Noah opens the window and dispatches the raven
8:8–12 The dove makes three journeys
8:13–14 Noah sees the earth is dry

There are interesting similarities between the first and last sections. Both begin with a temporal clause introduced by ויהי and follow it by an explicit mention of Noah uncovering part of the ark, and both close with a reference to the earth drying out. Thus vv 6–7 and vv 13–14 serve as a frame for the central section vv 8–12, the dove section.

The whole scene is dominated by Noah's concern to discover whether the waters have retreated. The raven episode is then essentially an unsuccessful experiment: it brings back no evidence of any change in the situation. The dove does bring back some evidence, the fresh olive leaves, so that Noah concludes that the waters had lessened. But only when he removes the cover of the ark does he himself see that the surface of the soil is dry (8:13). Finally on the 27th day of the second month the earth has dried out. Thus the whole scene progressively builds to a climax. At the end there seems no further reason for Noah to remain in the ark.

The central section dealing with the dove is a fine example of an episode told in three parts (vv 8–9, 10–11, 12) a favorite format with Hebrew story-tellers. Jacob observes that the story suggests the dove was Noah's pet, and

Strus (*Nomen-Omen*, 160–62) has pointed to the phonetic affinity between Noah (*nōaḥ*) and the dove (*hayyônāh*). Clearly the dove represents Noah. When the dove leaves the ark, it is time for Noah to do so as well.

Commentators from Dillmann to Westermann have suggested that since the raven episode spoils the neat arrangement of three journeys by the dove alone, it is a later insertion or from a variant tradition. It is impossible to be sure, but in that the Gilgamesh Epic also mentions a raven among the reconnoitering birds, the episode is unlikely to have been added to the story later. The Gilgamesh Epic sends out a dove, a swallow, and a raven (11:146–54), so the precise relationship between the accounts at this point is obscure.

6 "After forty days." If this is not a round number, it makes Noah start work on a Sunday (10.11.600), the day after the Sabbath. Certainly the narrative implies that he worked according to a weekly cycle (like God in 7:10) in that repeated seven-day periods are mentioned here (8:10, 12). These forty-day and seven-day periods form part of the palistrophic pattern of the narrative already mentioned (cf. 7:4, 10, 17).

Apparently the window must have been in the roof of the ark; at least it did not allow Noah to see the waters receding, which is why he resorts to sending out the birds. Gispen notes that before the electronic era sailors used to use birds in this way to discover if land was close.

7 The raven is not only black but unclean (Lev 11:15; Deut 14:14), so it is little surprise that it brought Noah no consolation. The reference to its flying to and fro may simply be paraphrasing Mesopotamian tradition (cf. GE 11:152–54) or perhaps pointing out that it did not die. Since they were unclean, there were only two ravens on the ark, so both had to live if the species was to survive. Note that the raven kept on flying till the earth "dried out." Only then did Noah disembark (8:14).

8 The dove was an altogether different bird. It is white, a clean animal often used in sacrifice (e.g., Lev 1:14; 12:6, etc). Like other sacrificial animals, it is sometimes seen as a symbol of Israel (Hos 7:11; 11:11), and therefore within this story it is an ideal representative of Noah himself. Here the stated purpose of her mission is "to see if the waters had gone down." Nothing is said here about how long Noah waited after sending out the raven before sending out the dove, but v 10 "*another* seven days" implies a week.

9 Again initial success is nil. There is not an inch anywhere for the dove to rest. In translation, part of this verse is remarkably close to GE 11:148, but the Hebrew makes a pun on Noah's name that has no parallel in the Akkadian. Literally, "the dove found no *mānôaḥ* (resting place)." She looked for another Noah outside the ark, but finding none, she returned to the Noah she knew. But the last half of the verse is without extrabiblical parallel: "he put out his hand, took it, and brought it into him." Skinner (156) comments, "The description of the return and admission of the dove is unsurpassed even in the Yahwistic document for tenderness and beauty of imagination." But there is more to the comment than this. It shows the sort of relationship that ought to exist between man and the animal world (cf. 1:26–28; 2:19–20). Prov 12:10, "A righteous man has regard for the life of his beast," and various injunctions in the law show a similar concern (Exod 23:4–5; Deut 25:4). Noah illustrates his righteousness not only by his piety toward God but by his devoted concern for the animals; he was an archetypal conservationist. This is another respect in which he is an imitator of God (cf. 8:1).

10–11 The second week of impatient waiting climaxes with the return of the dove at evening, when birds normally retire to their nests, with a freshly picked olive leaf in her beak. The discovery of an olive was no doubt highly auspicious. One of the commonest trees in Palestine and source of the invaluable oil, the olive was regarded as a symbol of beauty and fertility. Like many other ingredients of sacrifice (Lev 2), the olive also symbolized Israel (Jer 11:16; cf. *EM* 2:913–18 and M. Zohary, *Plants of the Bible* [Cambridge: Cambridge UP, 1982] 56–57). The find was the more significant in that it was "freshly plucked" (טרף, only here; cf. Aram. *ṭarufa* fresh), indicating that plants were growing again ready to feed man and beast (cf. 1:30), and that "the waters had gone down on the earth." The last remark shows that the dove has fulfilled her mission (cf. 8:8) and anticipates her non-return next time she is dispatched.

12 On each previous flight both the dove's return and the depth of water on the earth are mentioned. This time she does not come back and nothing is said about the water.

13–14 Eventually Noah sees for himself that the earth is dry. The double date formula and the threefold mention that "the earth (land) was dry (dried out)" emphasizes the importance of this development. A new world is born from the watery grave of the old; a new era has begun. Nevertheless, it was a slow delivery: nearly two months elapsed between Noah's looking out of the ark to see the earth is "drying" חרב till it was "dried out" יבש. This distinction between the two roots is also attested in Isa 19:5; Job 14:11; and Jer 50:38. The significance of the two dates (1.1.601 and 27.2.601) is not clear, unless we suppose the Jubilees calendar to be in use, in which case both days would be Wednesdays—the day the sun, moon, and stars were created. Cassuto thinks, however, that the explanation for the second date is that it makes the flood last one (lunar) year (354 days) and 11 days (17.1.600–27.2.601) which exactly equals a solar year of 365 days. This presumes Genesis' familiarity with both lunar and solar methods of reckoning.

"Removed the covering of the ark." מכסה "covering" is used elsewhere of the hide cover of the tabernacle (e.g., Exod 26:14; 35:11). A different term is used in 6:16. The Sumerian account assumes a much harder surface, for "Ziusudra drilled an opening in the big boat and the gallant Utu sent his light into the interior of the big boat" (5:7–8). In the Gilgamesh Epic, Utnapishtim looks out before he sends out the birds, and he sees the great desolation, that "all mankind had turned to clay" (GE 11.133), whereas Noah is cheered up to see dry land.

15–17 These verses constitute scene 8, which corresponds to scene 3 (7:1–4). Both scenes consist of divine commands to Noah: the first to enter the ark, the last to leave it. But the passenger list is closest to that in 7:7–14. Earlier Noah had been instructed to take the animals on board to preserve life (6:19; 7:3); now he must send them out "to swarm, be fruitful and multiply." The commands given originally just to the fish and the birds (1:20, 22) are here extended to all the land animals, one of many hints in this story that the post-flood era represents the start of a new creation.

18–19   Scene 9, corresponding to Scene 2 (6:22). Both scenes tell of Noah's obedience to the divine command just given, this time to disembark. As in v 17, "wild animals" head the disembarkation list. The animals are pictured leaving in large groups of similar types "by their clans." In human society "the clan," מ שׁפ חה, is a sub-unit of a tribe and consists of a number of extended families, "father's houses" (e.g., Josh 7:14–17).

8:20–9:17   Scene 10. Like the first scene, 6:9b–21, this is basically a divine monologue most of which is addressed to Noah, though 8:21–22 are God's own thoughts. As in the first scene, mankind's acts, and Noah's in particular, are merely the cue for the ensuing speech (cf. 8:20 with 6:9b–11). Scene 10 falls into four sections:

> 8:20–22   God's intention: the continuance of the created
> order.
> 9:1–17   God's blessing
> 1–7   "Be fruitful . . . Fill the earth"
> N.b. the inclusion between v 1 and v 7.
> 8–11   The eternal covenant
> 12–17   The sign of the covenant,
> N.b. the inclusion between v 12 and v 17.

Clearly the emphasis in this scene lies on the divine promises in 9:1–17. Here the echoes of and contrasts with scene 1 are most marked. There the earth was filled with violence (6:11, 13); now Noah is told to "fill it" (9:1, 7), reaffirming the mandate given to man at his creation (cf. 1:28), and measures are introduced to curb the growth of violence among all creatures (9:3–6).

An even stronger contrast between God's action then and now is evident in 9:8–11, which takes up the phraseology of 6:17a, 18a ("I myself am about to bring the flood, water over the earth to ruin all flesh. But I shall confirm my covenant."): "I myself am about to confirm my covenant . . . so that never again will all flesh be cut off by the waters of a flood, and there will never again be a flood to ruin the earth."

Finally, in 9:12–17 God's seeing of the rainbow contrasts with his seeing the corruption of the earth in 6:12. The rainbow reminds him of his covenant not to destroy all flesh again, whereas the corruption prompted the flood.

The second half of the flood narrative consistently reverses the action of the first half. But in this final scene we have God's own public change of heart expressed. The slate is wiped clean; man is given a fresh start. The commands given at creation are renewed. But why should there be this new divine attitude toward mankind? 9:1–17 gives no explanation. Without the introduction in 8:20–22, and especially the divine soliloquy in 8:21–22, we would have no clue. Usually because 8:20–22 is assigned to J and 9:1–17 to P, commentaries fail to observe the gaping theological *non sequitur* in P as it jumps from 8:19 to 9:1. Something like 8:20–22 is required to explain God's change of attitude, and since the offering of sacrifice after the flood is also mentioned in the Mesopotamian flood stories, we must suppose that at least 8:20–21a is also integral to the Hebrew flood narrative. 8:21b, with its very close parallel in 6:5–7, therefore demands the closest attention to discover whether it provides the key to the great turnround in divine-human relations that characterizes the post-flood era.

20 records the first building of an altar in Scripture (one is evidently presupposed but not mentioned in 4:3–5) and the first offering of "burnt offerings" (עלה). This is the commonest and most basic sacrifice prescribed in the law; in it the whole animal was burnt on the altar (see Lev 1 and G. J. Wenham, *Leviticus*, 47–66, for interpretation).

"He took some of all the clean domesticated animals . . . clean birds" echoes 7:2–3. Here Noah is shown to be acting in accord with later Israelite sacrificial norms which permitted only the offering of clean domesticated animals and birds in sacrifice. The earlier insistence that seven pairs of clean animals be taken on the ark shows that the narrative presupposes the necessity of sacrifice. For definitions of "clean" animals, see Lev 11 and Deut 14.

21 "The LORD smelt the soothing aroma"; cf. GE 11.160 "The gods smelled the sweet savor." This is the only time the LORD is actually recorded as having "smelt" a sacrifice. David prays that he will (1 Sam 26:19), while Lev 26:31 (cf. Amos 5:21–22) declares that God will not "smell" the offerings of the disobedient. For God to "smell" a sacrifice implies his acceptance of it and the offerer.

"Soothing aroma": in the sacrificial law, this is a regular term for the smell produced by burning the sacrifices (cf. Lev 1:9; 2:2; 3:5, etc). "Soothing" (ניחח) sacrifices have a restful (נוח), soothing, pacifying effect on God. That God's anger at sin is appeased by sacrifice is the clear implication of this phrase. Here, however, it is also a deliberate pun on Noah's name. We might even paraphrase it, "The LORD smelt the Noahic sacrifice." Lamek called his son "Noah" because he hoped he would bring him rest from the labor of his hands (5:29): here God implies that Noah's sacrifice has soothed him.

"And the LORD said to himself." The obvious implication of the sequence of verbs "the LORD smelt . . . said" is that God's thoughts about mankind were prompted by his appreciation of the sacrifice. This was a common view among older commentators. Indeed, Gunkel, Skinner, and von Rad hold that the sacrifice was essentially propitiatory: "He offered . . . to quiet the remains of his wrath" (Gunkel, 65). "Noah's first act is to offer a sacrifice, not of thanksgiving but as v 21 shows of propitiation: its effect is to move the Deity to gracious thoughts towards the new humanity" (Skinner, 157). However, Cassuto sees no need for further atonement after all the suffering and death in the flood: the sacrifices were simply an expression of thanks for deliverance and trust in God for the future. Westermann and Gispen concur.

It is, however, wrong to see propitiation and thanksgiving as mutually exclusive interpretations of the burnt offering. It both made atonement (Lev 1:4) and served as an act expressing the total dedication of the worshiper to God (the whole animal ascended to God in the smoke; see J. Milgrom, *IDBSup* 769; G. J. Wenham, *Leviticus*, 48–63). Both ideas are appropriate here. But whatever significance the burnt offering had at this point, it can hardly be denied that it was God's appreciation of the sacrifice's "soothing aroma" that prompted the promises of v 22.

The reluctance of some to admit that this offering changed God's attitude to mankind springs partly from an aversion to allowing any significant role to ritual, and the overlooking of the very clear interest in cultic and priestly concerns that runs through Gen 1–8 (Sabbath, Garden of Eden // sanctuary, acceptable sacrifice [chap. 4], aversion to mixtures [6:1–4], clean/unclean, Sabbath observance earlier in the flood story). But a more serious objection is that God's attitude to Noah has already been seen to be gracious from the moment he "remembered Noah" (8:1). It can hardly be said that the offering of the sacrifice changed God's attitude to Noah.

However, this is not exactly what 8:21 is asserting. From the very start "Noah found favor in the eyes of the LORD" (6:8). It is God's attitude to mankind in general that is turned around: 8:21 stands in particular contrast to 6:5: "The LORD saw that the evil of man was great in the earth and every idea . . . of his mind was nothing but evil all the time." Now, for the very same reason, the LORD declares he will not curse the ground further. And the only hint the narrative gives for this change of heart is "God's smelling of the soothing aroma." Skinner (158) states: "That the pleasing odour is not the motive but merely the occasion of his gracious purpose (Knobel) may be sound theology, but it hardly expresses the idea of the passage." Ultimately, of course, the acceptance of every sacrifice depends on God's antecedent gracious purpose, whereby he appointed the sacrificial system as a means of atonement for reconciliation between God and man. A fundamental principle of the Levitical law is "I have given (the blood) for you upon the altar to make atonement for our souls" (Lev 17:11; cf. B. Janowski, *Sühne als Heilsgeschehen*, WMANT 55 [Neukirchen: Neukirchener Verlag, 1982] 242–47; N. Kiuchi, *The Purification Offering in the Priestly Literature*, JSOTSS 56 [Sheffield: JSOT Press, 1987] chap. 4). But this is not to deny sacrifice's importance; rather it is to assert its real efficaciousness, because God has declared it so and promised to respond to it.

Looked at in this light, we can view Noah's offering of sacrifice as a prototype of the work of later priests, who made atonement for Israel, or of Job, who offered burnt offerings for his sons and for his "friends" (Job 1:5; 42:8). Here, however, Noah's sacrifice is effective for all mankind.

"I shall not curse the soil any further." It is important to note the position of עוֹד in this sentence, coming after לְקַלֵּל to "curse," not after אֹסִף "do again" as in the parallel clause "Never again shall I smite." This shows that God is not lifting the curse on the ground pronounced in 3:17 for man's disobedience, but promising not to add to it. The flood was a punishment over and above that decreed in 3:17. This is further confirmed by the milder word for "curse," קלל "treat lightly, disdain," used here as opposed to the graver term אָרַר, used in 3:17; cf. J. Scharbert, *TDOT* 1:405–18; C. A. Keller, *THWAT* 1:236–40. Both terms are found in 12:3 (q.v.). Furthermore, it is also quite apparent that the curses pronounced in Gen 3—weeds, toil, pain, death, enmity with serpents—are part of man's present experience, so that 8:21 cannot be stating they are lifted after the flood. For these reasons, Rendtorff's (*KD* 7 [1961] 67–78) argument that the curse on the earth is lifted after the flood cannot be accepted. Nor is he right in holding that J's primeval history with its account of the curse on the earth ends here: the curses that affected man since the fall still continue. It is simply the threat of another flood that is lifted. The seasons, and even day and night (cf. chap. 1), were disrupted by the flood, and this will not happen again (v 22) "for the ideas of man's mind are evil from his youth." Though the statement is not as severe as 6:5, note the omissions: "*every* (idea)," "*nothing but* (evil)" are omitted, while "from his youth" replaces "all the time." There can be no doubt that man's nature has not changed since before the flood. The milder language simply reflects his creator's more lenient attitude after the flood. R. W. L. Moberly (*At the Mountain of God,* JSOTSS 22 [Sheffield: JSOT Press, 1983] 89–93, 113–15) has noted a similar example in Exod 33:3; 34:9 of a reason for divine judgment, "for you are a stiff-necked people," being subsequently cited as a justification of his mercy.

> The striking similarity between the flood and Sinai, between Noah and Moses, is of great theological significance for the interpretation of each story. . . . The world, while still in its infancy, has sinned and brought upon itself Yahweh's wrath and judgment. Israel has only just been constituted a people, God's chosen people, yet directly it has sinned and incurred Yahweh's wrath and judgment. Each time the same question is raised. How, before God, can a sinful world (in general) or a sinful people, even God's chosen people (in particular), exist without being destroyed? Each time the answer is given that if the sin is answered solely by the judgment it deserves, then there is no hope. But in addition to the judgment there is also mercy, a mercy which depends entirely on the character of God and is given to an unchangingly sinful people.

Furthermore, in both narratives the role of the mediator is vital, whether it be Noah or Moses. "This mercy is shown through a man who is chosen by God and whose right response to God, whether through sacrifice or prayer, constitutes the necessary medium through which this mercy is shown" (Moberly, 92).

22 "As long as the earth exists": literally, "all the days of the earth." Elsewhere in Genesis "all the days" is only used of human life (cf. 3:17; 9:29) and therefore here intimates earth's mortality.

But though not eternal, the regular alternation of the times and seasons is assured. The first three pairs may be contrasting the hot season (harvest, heat, summer) with the cold season (sowing, cold, winter), but this leaves "day and night" somewhat isolated. Westermann therefore asks whether "cold and heat" might be an alternative way of expressing "night and day," but since elsewhere (Jer 17:8; Job 24:19) "heat" refers to the hot season, this is not proven.

Perhaps then it is simply best to take these pairs as referring to the diurnal and seasonal rhythms of nature on which all life depends. God's assurance that these rhythms will be maintained is a mark of his continuing providential blessing on the world.

BLESSING ON THE NEW HUMANITY (9:1–17)

Bibliography

Abir, S. "Denn im Bilde Gottes machte er den Menschen (Gen 9:6 P)." *TGl* 72 (1982) 79–88. **Barré, L. M.** "The Poetic Structure of Gen 9:5." *ZAW* 96 (1984) 101–4. **Boer, P. A. H. de.** "Quelques remarques sur l'arc dans la nuée." *Questions disputées d'Ancien Testament,* ed. C. Brekelmans. BETL 33. Leuven: Leuven UP, 1974. 105–14. **Dequeker,**

L. "Noah and Israel: The Everlasting Divine Covenant with Mankind." *Questions disputées d'Ancien Testament,* 1974. 115–29. **Diebner, B.,** and **H. Schult.** "Das Problem der Todestrafe an Tier und Mensch in Gen 9:5–6." *DBAT* 6 (1974) 2–5. **Dumbrell, W. J.** *Covenant and Creation.* Exeter: Paternoster Press, 1984. 11–46. **Fox, M. V.** "The Sign of the Covenant." *RB* 81 (1974) 557–96. **Gross, W.** "Bundeszeichen und Bundesschluss in der Priesterschrift." *TTZ* 87 (1978) 98–115. **Kloos, C. J. L.** "The Flood on Speaking Terms with God." *ZAW* 94 (1982) 639–42. **Porten, B.,** and **U. Rappaport.** "Poetic Structure in Gen 9:7." *VT* 21 (1971) 363–69. **Stachowiak, L.** "Der Sinn der sogenannten Noachitischen Gebote (Gen 9:1–7)." VTSup 29. Leiden: E. J. Brill, 1978. 395–404.

9:1–7 God's blessing is now verbalized. His blessing on the new humanity repeats almost verbatim his blessing on the old pre-flood humanity; cf. 9:1 with 1:28a. The section closes with an inclusion, 9:7, repeating God's basic injunction to mankind. Indeed, 9:1–7 can be seen not simply as reasserting 1:28–29 but as modifying the food law (cf. 1:29) and reasserting the sanctity of human life in the light of chap. 4.

9:2	"The fear of you . . . upon everything"	// 1:28	"rule . . . every living creature."
9:3	". . . yours to eat: as I gave you the green vegetation"	// 1:29	"I have given you . . . for food."
9:5–6a	"your blood . . . his brother's life."	// 4:8–24	
9:6b	"in the image of God he made man"	// 1:27	"God created man in his image" (cf. 5:1).

This section must then be read as commentary on the antediluvian history.

1 This is the third time God has blessed mankind (1:28; 5:2), and the third time man has been told to be "fruitful and multiply" (1:28; 8:17). The subsequent chapters will relate its fulfillment.

2 Superficially, this verse simply repeats 1:28b with slight variation in wording and order. However, "the fear of you and the dread of you" is distinctly military terminology (cf. Deut 1:21; 11:25; 31:8). With Keil and Gispen, this seems more likely to reflect the animosity between man and the animal world that followed the fall (3:15) than the animals' unpleasant experiences in the flood (Cassuto). "Into your hands they have been given" implies that man has the power of life and death over them (Deut 19:12; 20:13, etc).

3 Again part of 1:29 is quoted word for word; the new element is the first phrase, "every moving thing that is alive." In 1:29 man had been permitted to eat plants and their produce; now he can eat meat as well: "every moving thing" is defined by the categories in the previous verse, i.e., animals, birds, and fish, all of which had been given into his hand.

"That is alive" precludes the consumption of animals that have died of natural causes (cf. Lev 11:40; Deut 14:21). Whether this permission to eat meat meant that Noah could eat unclean as well as clean creatures is uncertain. The silence of the text on this issue is usually taken to mean that he was not restricted just to clean creatures. However, the frequent mention of the difference between clean and unclean animals elsewhere in the story makes it problematic to assert that total freedom is being given here (7:2,8; 8:20). Admittedly these passages are usually ascribed to J, whereas 9:1–17 is P, but since P is generally dated after J, it might well assume the clean/unclean distinction of J. This passage's keen concern with other food rules, e.g., no consumption of blood or cadavers, suggests that the unclean/clean distinction may be taken for granted. Be that as it may, the food laws certainly view the prohibition of the consumption of blood as more important than not eating unclean animals. Consuming blood leads to "cutting off," i.e., sudden death (Lev 17:10), but no such threat is attached to eating unclean animals.

4 God's provision of animal life to sustain human life is paradoxical. To preserve man's respect for life, he is forbidden to eat "flesh with its life, i.e., its blood." Westermann, following Jacob, wants to take this phrase in its most literal sense, viz., that one is not to eat animal flesh with the blood still pulsating through it. (The fondness of certain Abyssinian tribes for eating raw meat freshly cut from a living animal is sometimes cited.) In other words, this verse is not prohibiting the consumption of blood itself.

Such a narrow interpretation does, however, seem unlikely in the light of the numerous passages insisting that blood should be drained out of the animals before they can be eaten (Lev 3:17; 7:26–27; 19:26; Deut 12:16–24; 1 Sam 14:32–34). Genesis is interested in tracing back the fundamental principles of ethics and worship to earliest times, so it is likely that it is here prohibiting any consumption of blood. It is easy to see why blood is identified with life (on נפש "life," see 2:7): a beating heart and a strong pulse are the clearest evidence of life. Respect for life, and beyond that, respect for the giver of life, means abstaining from blood. Indeed, in the sacrificial law animal blood is given by God for the atonement of human sin (cf. Lev 17:11).

5 No sin shows greater contempt for life than homicide. Whereas an animal's blood may be shed but not consumed, human blood cannot even be shed. Three times God says he will require it, i.e., demand a reckoning "for your lives" (cf. Ps 9:13 [12]; Ezek 33:6). What that reckoning is will be clarified in v 6.

"From the hand of every wild animal." Divine retribution is threatened on wild animals who kill men. Exod 21:28–29 illustrates this principle by prescribing that an ox which gores a man to death should be executed.

"From each man his brother's life." "How much more so shall I require a reckoning for the blood of man in this instance, seeing that the slain person is the *brother* of the slayer" (Cassuto, 2:127). "Not the animal, but man is the brother, the relative, of man. Humanity is a family" (Gispen 1:295). This is the first time אח "brother" has been used since Gen 4 (cf. 4:8–11), where the term is harped on to highlight the incongruity of Cain's action, so it seems likely that here this story is being alluded to.

6 "Whoever sheds the blood of man, by a man shall his blood be shed." A concise poetic formulation of the principle of talion (whether its origin is legal or proverbial is indeterminable). The tight chiastic formulation (shed, blood, man, man, blood, shed) repeating each word of the first clause in reverse order in the second emphasizes the strict correspondence of punishment to offense; cf. Lev 24:16–22 (Wenham, *Leviticus,* 311–12).

"Because in the image of God he made man" reasserts the unique status of man and explains why human life is specially protected, but animal life is not.

It is because of man's special status among the creatures that this verse insists on the death penalty for murder. "A community is only justified in executing the death penalty in so far as it respects the unique right of God over life and death and in so far as it respects the inviolability of human life that follows therefrom. Every single violation of this limit, be it based on national, racial or ideological grounds is here condemned" (Westermann, 1:469).

7 Mention of the image of God in which man was made (1:27) leads back to the first command given to man, "Be fruitful and multiply." But in 1:28 the injunction continued to "subdue" and "rule," while here the emphasis is to "swarm and multiply." Originally just the sea creatures had been told to *swarm* and multiply (1:20). On emerging from the ark all creatures were told to be prolific (8:17). Finally mankind receives similar encouragement.

8–18 The confirmation of the covenant between God and all creation, mankind and the animals, involves God's putting the rainbow in the clouds and making three speeches, vv 9–11, 12–16, 17. These are arranged concentrically:

a)	9–11	"confirm the covenant"	
b)	12a	"sign of the covenant"	
		12b	covenant "for farthest generations"
		13–16 "my bow"	
		16 "eternal covenant"	
c)		17 "sign of the covenant"	
	17	"confirm" the covenant	

The first speech, vv 9–11, introduces the topic of the covenant and its content, the future stability of the cosmos. The second and most important speech, vv 12–16, equates the confirmation of the covenant with setting the rainbow in the clouds. The sign of the covenant is its confirmation. The third and final speech, v 17, sums up the significance of the whole event.

8–11 But will man's efforts to multiply again be brought to naught by a flood? No. These verses give Noah and his descendants after him an assurance that this will not happen again. The promises here are not a doublet of 8:21–22, which only express God's thoughts to himself. Here the terminology of the first scene is most clearly echoed, but the phraseology of 6:17–18, warning of an imminent flood, is here transformed into a promise of permanent security.

9–10 "I myself am about to confirm." Cf. the similar use of suffixed הנה + participle to announce the impending flood in 6:17: "I myself am about to bring."

"Confirm." The hiphil of קום is used to ratify legal agreements already initiated; cf. comments on 6:18. How God confirms his covenant to Noah is not immediately apparent, though the use of the past "I have confirmed" shows that it has happened by 9:17. Note that whereas in 6:18 it was simply "my covenant with you." here the covenant includes "your descendants after

you" and all the animals who accompanied Noah in the ark (v 10), the last
list of the ark's passengers in the flood narrative.

11 "I shall confirm my covenant" both makes an inclusion with v 9 and
harks back to 6:18.

"Never again shall all flesh be cut off." Contrast "The end of all flesh,"
6:13. "Be cut off" (כרת, niphal) is a frequent threat in the law (17:14; Lev
7:20; 17:4) against sin, probably indicating a sudden mysterious death. Here
the assurance is given that at least such a fate will not befall the world through
the agency of a flood. Cf. 6:17 for the content and 8:21 for the grammatical
construction (עוד + impf + לא).

12–17 Here the story of the flood is brought at length to a triumphant
and hopeful conclusion. The terminology of the first scene—"covenant" (6:18;
9:12, 13, 15, 16, 17), "generations" (6:9; 9:12), "see" (6:12; 9:14,16), "confirm"
(6:18; 9:17), "a flood to ruin all flesh" (6:17; 9:15)—is echoed and rewritten
in a joyful major key. Its theme is "the sign of the covenant" (vv 12, 13, 17;
note the inclusion between v 12 and 17) the rainbow in the cloud (vv 13, 14, 16).
Repetition with variation is very characteristic of this passage. Note how the
partners to the covenant are referred to in five different ways:

v 12   "between me and you and every living being which was with you"
v 13   "between me and the earth"
v 15   "between me and you and every living being among all flesh"
v 16   "between God and every living being among all flesh which is on
         the earth"
v 17   "between me and all flesh which is on the earth"

As Westermann says, it is hardly possible to ascribe this repetition to different
sources. Rather, they serve to underline the message, pealing out like bells
reverberating into the future (1:471).

12 "This is the sign of the covenant." "Signs" (אות) take various forms
in the Bible, from miracles (Deut 6:22; Isa 7:11) and striking coincidences
(Exod 3:12) to national customs (Exod 31:13) or items of clothing (Deut
6:8). But "signs" are all appointed by God: it is his word or consecration of
these sometimes ordinary events or customs that make them significant, point-
ers to his activity and purposes. Circumcision is also called "a sign of the
covenant" (17:11), and Exod 31:13–17 implies that the Sabbath is too. These
signs remind *man* of God's presence and God-given obligations, but here,
most unusually, the rainbow is a sign that is seen by man but serves to remind
God of his promises. (On אות, cf. F. J. Helfmeyer, *TDOT* 1:167–88, M. V.
Fox, *RB* 81 [1974] 557–96; also cf. *Comment* on 4:15.)

"Which I am making. . . ." Comparison with v 17 "which I have confirmed"
shows that this relative clause refers to the covenant, not the sign of the
covenant.

"For farthest generations": literally "for generations of eternity." Cf. 6:9;
17:7–8.

Underlying the history of nature and the history of mankind is an unconditional
divine Yes, a divine Yes to all life, that cannot be shattered either by any catastrophes

in the course of this history—and what is most important for P—by the mistakes, corruption or rebellion of man. God's promise remains rock certain as long as the earth exists (Westermann 1:633–34; cf. ET, 473.)

13 "My bow I have put in the cloud." Since Hebrew קֶשֶׁת means both "bow" and "rainbow," it has often been suggested that originally this phrase was speaking of God's hanging up his bow and arrows in the heavens as a sign that he would no longer be at war with mankind. The storms of the flood were the "arrows" he had hurled at the earth. Though the Bible sometimes uses imagery like this to describe divine wrath (e.g., Deut 32:23, 42; Hab 3:9–11; Ps 18:15 [14]) there is no reason for taking Gen 9 this way. Jacob, Westermann, and Gispen have rightly abandoned this interpretation of the rainbow as God's weapon of war.

The rainbow has attracted all sorts of explanations among primitive people, but none are as appropriate as the biblical. Delitzsch comments:

> It is indeed a phenomenon that may be accounted for by natural laws; but the laws of nature are truly the appointment of God (Ecclus 43:11ff) and it is just in its conformity to natural law that the rainbow is a pledge that the order of nature shall continue. And is there not to every law of nature a background pointing to the mysteries of the Divine nature and will? The label of the rainbow is sufficiently legible. Shining upon a dark ground, . . . it represents the victory of the light of love over the fiery darkness of wrath. Originating from the effect of the sun upon a dark cloud, it typifies the willingness of the heavenly to penetrate the earthly. Stretched between heaven and earth, it is as a bond of peace between both, and, spanning the horizon, it points to the all-embracing universality of the Divine mercy (1:289–90).

"I have put in the cloud." "From these words certain eminent theologians have been induced to deny that there was any rainbow before the deluge: which is frivolous. For the words of Moses do not signify, that a bow was then formed, which did not previously exist; but that a mark was engraven upon it, which should give a sign of the divine favour towards man" (Calvin, 299).

14–15 V 14 is the protasis to v 15. Not every time that clouds come is the rainbow visible. But whenever the rainbow appears, God is reminded of his covenant.

"Then I shall remember." This is the second time God is said to "remember" in this story. At the height of the flood "God remembered Noah" (8:1). Here is a pledge for the future: because God will remember his covenant (identical phraseology in Lev 26:42, and cf. Exod 2:24; 6:5), there will never be a repeat of the flood.

16 Reemphasizes the message of vv 14–15 using slightly different phraseology. This time the covenant itself is described as "eternal"; cf. v 12; Gen 17:7, 13; Lev 24:8.

17 In a final fanfare the section closes with a restatement of God's merciful guarantee addressed to "all flesh which is on the earth"; cf. 9:12.

CODA TO THE NOAH STORY (9:18–29)

Bibliography

Bassett, F. W. "Noah's Nakedness and the Curse of Canaan: A Case of Incest?" *VT* 21 (1971) 232–37. **Bastomsky, S. J.** "Noah, Italy and the Sea-Peoples." *JQR* 67 (1976–77) 146–53. **Cohen, H. H.** *The Drunkenness of Noah*. Alabama: University of Alabama Press, 1974. **Hoftijzer, J.** "Some Remarks to the Tale of Noah's Drunkenness." *OTS* 12 (1958) 22–27. **Luria, B. S.** "The Curse of Noah and His Blessing." (Heb) *BMik* 15 (1970) 298–306. **Phillips, A.** "Uncovering the Father's Skirt." *VT* 30 (1980) 38–43. **Rice, G.** "The Curse That Never Was (Gen 9:18–27)." *JRT* 29 (1972) 5–27. **Ross, A. P.** "Studies in the Book of Genesis. Part 1: The Curse of Canaan." *BSac* 137 (1980) 223–40.

This section falls into three distinct parts:

18–19 Introduction of characters
20–27 Noah's drunkenness and subsequent reaction
28–29 Noah's epitaph

Vv 28–29 clearly conclude the genealogy of Noah which opened in 5:32. They follow the standard formulae of the genealogical table in chap. 5 (cf. vv 7–8, 10–11, etc.). Indeed, between 5:32 and 9:28 only a remark like 7:6, "Noah was six hundred years old when the flood came, water on the earth," is needed to secure a smooth transition. The flood story and this concluding episode form a giant insertion into the genealogical record found in chaps. 5 and 10–11. Vv 18–19 may well be editorial as they provide a neat transition from the flood to Noah's viticulture and a preview of his sons' future role: "and from them the whole earth was populated" (cf. chaps. 10–11). It is their destiny and interrelationships that are foreshadowed in this closing scene. Noah's only recorded words predict the interaction between Shem, Ham, and Japhet. The story of Noah's drunkenness gives the background to these momentous words. As we have already noted, the editor of Genesis tends to use the final scene of a section to adumbrate the next stage of the story, which begins in 10:1, "This is the family history of the sons of Noah. . . ."

Vv 20–27 pose a problem for exegetes and critics. While it is Ham who sins against his father's honor in v 22, it is his son Canaan who was cursed. How is this to be explained? From Wellhausen to von Rad, many commentators suggested that "Ham, father of" was a gloss. Thus v 22 originally read, "Canaan saw his father's nakedness . . .," and this explains why Noah cursed him in vv 25–27. It does, however, create the problem that, whereas everywhere else in the Noah story and also in chap. 10 the sons of Noah are identified as Shem, Ham, and Japhet, in this passage alone are they named as Shem, Canaan and Japhet. As Westermann points out, it is unlikely that Canaan was ever supposed to be Noah's son. He thinks that the identification of Ham's descendants with Canaan's descendants was so obvious that it was not felt strange that Noah should have cursed Canaan as opposed to Ham, for the blessings and curses pronounced were essentially addressed to the descendants of Shem, Ham and Japhet, not to the men themselves.

18 Noah's sons have already been named in 5:32; 6:10; 7:13. Here they are reintroduced by way of background information to clarify the subsequent story. For the same reason Ham's son, Canaan, is also mentioned, for he figures in the curse and blessing; cf. 9:25–27.

19 "From them the whole earth was populated." Understanding "was populated" from the root of נפץ links this verse with 1 Sam 13:11, Isa 33:3, where it means "scatter." However, it must also be associated with another similar root, פוץ, which is frequent in Gen 10–11; cf. 10:18; 11:4, 8, 9, again meaning to "scatter." So this remark anticipates the dispersal of mankind throughout the world as related in Gen 10–11. The obvious contrast with the small number who emerged from the ark shows that the command to "be fruitful and multiply and fill the earth" (9:1, 7) was indeed carried out by Noah's descendants.

20 "Noah, the man of the land, was the first to plant a vineyard." This seems to mark a step forward in agriculture. Whereas Noah's ancestors raised only the most basic foodstuffs (cf. 3:18–19; 4:2), Noah introduces the cultivation of luxury items so that he can produce "wine that maketh glad the heart of man" (Ps 104:15). It is interesting that the vine comes originally from Armenia, which is where the biblical ark landed. According to Mesopotamian tradition, however, viticulture antedated the flood, for Utnapishtim plied the ark builders with wine (GE 11:72–73).

"The man of the land" is an unusual phrase. If "tiller of the land" were meant, עבד האדמה would be the normal expression (cf. 4:2; Isa 30:24). So Cassuto suggests it really means "master of the earth," because Noah as the head of the one family on earth was *ipso facto* lord of the whole earth. Were this the meaning, though, a more specific term than איש would be expected, and ארץ "earth" would be a more appropriate term than אדמה "land," at least in this agricultural context (cf. *Comment* on 2:5). But Cassuto's observation that this title may be connected with Lamek's aspiration that his son Noah would "bring us relief from our work and from the pain of our hands because of *the land* which the LORD has cursed" has more merit. Maybe describing Noah as "the man of the land" is an ironic reference to 5:29. Noah's grape-growing certainly brings comfort, but the fruit of the vine proves to be something of a mixed blessing!

21 "He drank some wine, became drunk, and uncovered himself inside his tent." Brief and to the point, as often when Scripture disapproves of certain actions, this verse does not go into elaborate and lurid detail.

But does the writer really disapprove of Noah's actions, for earlier Noah is described as "righteous, blameless among his contemporaries" (6:9)? So striking is the contrast between Noah the saint who survived the flood and Noah the inebriated vintner that many commentators argue that the two traditions are completely incompatible and must be of independent origin. Westermann, on the other hand, argues that in fact Noah's behavior was regarded as quite acceptable in biblical times: only Ham's voyeurism and his subsequent recounting of what he had seen is censured. Ham's actions show clear disrespect for his father and this merited his father's wrath. Uncovering oneself was dishonorable, and Noah's son should have quietly covered him up, not gossiped about it to his brothers. Others have felt that Noah's reaction indicates that Ham must have done something worse than is actually described. Seeing his father's nakedness must be a euphemism for a more serious offense. Overindulgence in alcohol and sexual misconduct go hand in hand in Scripture and in modern society (cf. 19:32–35). Is this what is being hinted at here? These are some of the major questions posed by this story.

"He drank some wine." It is certainly most unlikely that Noah is being censured for this. Wine is seen as one of God's gifts to man (Ps 104:15). Every burnt or peace offering had to be accompanied by a libation of wine (Num 15:5–10), and Deut 14:26 encourages its purchase at the festivals. Indeed, the vine was one of Israel's national symbols (Isa 5:1–7; Mark 12:1–11).

However, running through the same literature there is frequent mention of the dangers of wine. A key element of the Nazirite vow (the Nazirites were the holiest laymen in ancient Israel) was abstinence from any alcohol or product of the vine (Num 6:3–4). Priests were forbidden drink before officiating in the sanctuary "lest you die" (Lev 10:9). Clearly, insobriety was regarded as incompatible with holiness. And the ordinary laity are warned about the dangers of drinking too much wine (Isa 5:22; Prov 21:17; 23:20–21, 29–35). Men "are confused with wine . . . they err in vision" (Isa 28:7). Drunkenness in particular is deprecated (1 Sam 1:14), especially when it leads to self-exposure (Hab 2:15; Lam 4:21), and its punishment is used by the prophets as an image of divine judgment (Isa 63:6; Jer 51:57). To uncover oneself is regarded as not merely publicly demeaning (e.g., 2 Sam 6:16), but incompatible with living in the presence of God (Exod 20:26; Deut 23:13–15 [12–14]; cf. Gen 3:21). Drewermann draws parallels between Noah's consuming wine and Adam's eating the forbidden fruit, and also with the drunken orgies that accompanied Canaanite fertility cults: "The humanity that begins with Noah fully parallels the humanity that preceded the flood" (252).

To equate Noah's sin with Adam's in this way is a little harsh. Undoubtedly, though, Genesis views it as a fall from grace for one who was "blameless among his contemporaries and walked with God" (the highest accolade that Scripture gives to a man) to have become drunk and exposed himself.

22 However, Westermann is right to see the chief thrust of the story as blaming Ham for his improper, quite unfilial behavior. Throughout the ancient world, and even today in traditional societies, honoring parents is a most sacred duty. The OT certainly underlines and reinforces this attitude in the decalogue ("Honor your father and mother"), and in Deut 27:15–26 this is the first of the manward commandments, coming immediately after the Godward commands and before the prohibitions on murder and adultery. The case law backs this up with dire threats of capital sentences on those who strike or curse their parents (Exod 21:15, 17; cf. Deut 21:18–21; cf. Mark 7:10). The book of Proverbs repeatedly urges devotion to parents and their instruction.

Admittedly, the OT nowhere states how sons should handle situations where parents are disgracing themselves. But no doubt Israelites would have agreed with the Ugaritic Aqht epic which states that a son should take his father "by the hand when he's drunk, carries him when he's sated with wine" (A 1.32–33, *ANET,* 150). In other words, he must try tactfully to cover up his father's folly. But this is precisely what Ham did not do. With total lack of discretion he publicized it to his brothers. Proverbs warns against unkind gossip that "he who repeats a matter alienates a friend" (17:9). How much more serious when that gossip adds to one's parent's disgrace!

Though this is the natural way to understand ths text, Westerners who are strangers to a world where discretion and filial loyalty are supreme virtues have often felt that there must be something more to Ham's offense than appears on the surface (cf. Gunkel, von Rad). Bassett (*VT* 21 [1971] 232–37) suggested that Ham actually committed incest with Noah's wife. He would equate seeing (ראה) someone's nakedness with uncovering (גלה) someone's nakedness, which certainly does denote sexual intercourse (Lev 18:11, 20, 21). Furthermore, Reuben lost his first-born's rights for lying with his father's concubine (35:22; 49:3–4), and later Absalom attempted to secure his hold on the kingdom by going in to his father's concubines (2 Sam 16:20–23). H. H. Cohen (*The Drunkenness of Noah,* 14–16) suggests on the basis of some far-fetched etymologizing and passages such as Exod 33:20, "man shall not see me and live," that looking was much more than a sense experience; it transferred power. By looking on his naked father, Ham had acquired Noah's potency: that was why he had to tell his brothers about it.

23 But these and other suggestions are disproved by the next verse, "Then Shem and Japhet took a cloak . . . went backwards and covered their father's nakedness." As Cassuto (2:151) points out: "If the covering was an adequate remedy, it follows that the misdemeanor was confined to seeing." The elaborate efforts Shem and Japhet made to avoid looking at their father demonstrate that this was all Ham did in the tent. As for Cohen's theory, it has no support elsewhere in the OT, and clearly neither Noah nor his sons recognize any transfer of potency from father to son as a result of his action.

In contrast to the terse brevity with which Ham's deed is described, the description of Shem and Japhet's response is distinctly repetitious and long-winded. The narrative is slowed down so that the listener can appreciate their meritorious deeds and their utter propriety. Notice how it is twice said that they went "backwards," and that they covered and did not see "their father's nakedness." This slower pace allows the listener not only to reflect on these sons' modesty, but to visualize the awkwardness of their task. Backing into a tent trying to cover their sleeping father without looking at him must have been quite a tricky operation! They used "a cloak" to cover Noah, that is, the outer daytime garment also used as a blanket at night (Exod 22:26). Though "cloak," שמלה, is here preceded by the definite article, it is not necessary to suppose that it was actually Noah's cloak and that Ham had brought it outside as proof of his story. The article simply indicates it was the cloak Shem and Japhet used on this occasion. "Put it over their shoulders" is another detail that helps slow down the story-telling. Perhaps we are to envisage the sons backing into the tent until Noah's toes are seen in front of the cloak, and then their letting it down over him.

24 "And Noah woke up." The soporific effect of drink is often mentioned (e.g., Ps 78:65). How Noah discovered what had happened to him is not related, since it is not relevant to the story. However, the phrase "his youngest son," literally, "his little son," is a surprising epithet for Ham, since the usual order of names "Shem, Ham, and Japhet" leads to the supposition that Ham was the second in the family. It could of course have been taken as further evidence that this drinking tale was originally independent of the flood story. Yet if this is correct, it might have been expected that the redactor who is credited with so many other changes in integrating the traditions overlooked this rather obvious point. It seems likely that the phrase "youngest son" should be explained differently. The LXX and Vulgate translate "younger son," i.e., younger than Shem. Rashi suggested "little" here means "contemptible" (cf. Jer 49:15; Obad 2). Probably the best solution is Cassuto's, who holds that the order Shem, Ham and Japhet is not chronological but euphonic. In pairs of words Hebrew tends to put the short word first, e.g., יום ולילה "day and night," חן וחסד "grace and mercy"; hence "Shem, Ham, and Japhet" came more easily than "Japhet, Shem, and Ham" or "Shem, Japhet, and Ham." Whether Shem or Japhet is the eldest depends on the interpretation of 10:21.

25 "And he said 'Cursed be Canaan, the lowest of slaves to his brother shall he be.'" On the term "cursed," ארור, cf. above on 3:14. This is the first time a man is recorded as uttering a curse. Though it is not stated, Noah's words evidently have divine authority and affect the future. Why should Noah have cursed Canaan, Ham's son, and not Ham himself? The question has baffled commentators for centuries, and there is no obvious answer. Indeed, there may be elements of truth in several of the explanations that have been offered. Leaving aside those explanations which presuppose some dislocation of the text, whether deliberate or accidental (e.g., Canaan was actually involved in his grandfather's disgrace), three explanations have merit. First, *Ber. Rab.* 36:7 points out that God had recently pronounced his blessing on Noah and his sons (9:1), so that Noah could not really unsay that promise. Second, there may well be an element of mirroring punishment: here Noah's youngest son, Ham, sinned against him; therefore it was appropriate that Ham's youngest son, Canaan, should be punished for his father's wickedness (so Delitzsch, Gispen). Third, the sons of Noah embody and personify the character of their descendants. From Ham descended Cush, Egypt, Put, and Canaan (10:6). Now the Canaanites are notorious throughout the Old Testament for their aberrant sexual practices, and Lev 18:3 links both Egypt and Canaan as peoples whose habits are abominable: "You shall not do as they do in the land of Egypt . . . and . . . as they do in the land of Canaan." Ham's indiscretion towards his father may easily be seen as a type of the later behavior of the Egyptians and Canaanites. Noah's curse on Canaan thus represents God's sentence on the sins of the Canaanites, which their forefather Ham had exemplified. Westermann denies that this story links Ham's offense with the sins of the Canaanites; rather, he views it just as another family-quarrel-type story such as are found in Gen 3–4. But even he admits that the blessings on Shem and Japhet (9:26–27) look beyond the horizon of Noah's time to the subsequent interactions of their descendants, so it seems most likely that this is true of this curse on Canaan as well. In the post-flood stories there is thus a distinct change of perspective. The antedi-

luvian chapters tell of events that affected all mankind: these post-flood narratives tell of happenings that molded the lives and characters of the peoples
of the world.

"The lowest of slaves," literally, "slave of slaves": cf. the expressions "leader
of the leaders" (Num 3:32), "King of kings and Lord of lords" (Rev 19:16).
"To his brothers," i.e., Shem and Japhet, as vv 26, 27 made clear, "Let
Canaan be a slave to them." How and when this prediction of Canaan's
subjection to Shem and Japhet was fulfilled is another subject of disagreement.
Skinner sums up the problem neatly: "Three points may be regarded as
settled: that Shem is that family to which the Hebrews reckoned themselves;
that Canaan stands for the pre-Israelitish inhabitants of Palestine; and that
the servitude of Canaan to Shem at least *includes* the subjugation of the Canaanites in the early days of the monarchy. Beyond this everything is uncertain"
(186). Though many fulfillments of Shem's dominance over Canaan can be
seen, it is more difficult to know when Canaan was subject to Japhet.

26 "Blessed is the LORD, the God of Shem." This is an unusual way to
express a blessing, in that it makes the LORD rather than Shem the object of
blessing. One might rather have expected "Blessed of the LORD is Shem,"
and this and other textual emendations have been proposed. However, since
they are purely conjectural, it is better to attempt to understand the text as
it stands as a doxology to God. Normally it would continue with an explanation
of what the LORD has done which led to this expression of thanks, e.g., 24:27,
"Blessed be the LORD, the God of my master Abraham, who has not forsaken
his steadfast love . . . toward my master." Here the omission of any specific
explanation must mean that Noah is blessing the LÓRD for being the God
of Shem. This is then the first intimation that the line of God's election
blessing is going through Shem (cf. 4:26). The phrase "the LORD, the God
of Shem," indeed anticipates many similar expressions in later texts, e.g.,
"the LORD, the God of Abraham [your fathers, Israel, etc.]" (24:27; Exod
3:15; 32:27; 34:23).

"Let Canaan be a slave to him." Note the reiteration of the curse on Canaan
yet again.

27 "May God enlarge Japhet." An obvious play on the name Japhet.
Indeed, in biblical times, Japhet was probably pronounced *yapt,* the same as
יפת "may he enlarge." The only other example of the root פתה meaning
"to open" is Prov 20:19: "Do not associate with one who opens his lips wide,"
i.e., with a chatterbox. Here, though, the word has a positive sense: it expresses
the hope that God will make Japhet grow (cf. 26:22). This may well be the
traditional etymology of Japhet.

"May he dwell in the tents of Shem." Who is to dwell in Shem's tents? Is
it God or Japhet? That God should dwell there is a very old Jewish interpretation attested in the book of Jubilees and the Targums, for example. While
there was an obvious fulfillment of this prayer in that God did dwell in Israel
(Shem; שכן "dwell" is used of God camping in Israel [Exod 25:8; 29:45;
Lev 16:16; Num 35:34, etc.]) it seems more likely that Japhet must be the
subject of "dwell" for several reasons: (1) it is hard to construe God's dwelling
with Shem as a blessing on Japhet; (2) the use of the plural "tents of Shem"
suggests that a group of people is dwelling among Shem, not a singular

God; (3) if God were the subject of "dwell," one might have expected his personal name "the LORD" to be used as in v 26.

Attempts to find a historical situation in which Shem and Japhet were in league against Canaan are legion. Gunkel suggested it referred to the mid-second millennium when he believed both Aramaean peoples and Hittites were moving into Canaan. However, according to 10:15, Heth is a son of Canaan. Skinner prefers to think of a situation in the Amarna period when the Habiru were oppressing Canaan, but he gives no precise identification of Japhet. Neiman identifies the situation with the conquest/judges period, with the Israelites invading Canaan from the East and the sea peoples from the West. The most popular view (for detailed defense, see G. Rice *JRT* 29 [1972] 14–17) is that it refers to the period of the united monarchy when David finally subdued the Canaanites and may have incorporated Philistia (Japhet) into his empire as a vassal state. Again, however, 10:14 apparently links the Philistines with Ham rather than Japhet. So yet later fulfillments have been suggested: Japhet's dwelling in the tents of Shem refers to the Assyrian or Babylonian conquest of Israel and Judah (Hoftijzer), but 10:10–11 links Assyria and Babylon with Ham, not Japhet. Even later fulfillments have been suggested, e.g., Alexander the Great's conquest of the East in the fourth century, or the adoption of the Greek language by the Jews, or the incorporation of Gentiles into the Jewish fold (so Tg and the Fathers). "Gentile Christians are for the most part Japhetites dwelling in the tents of Shem" (Delitzsch, 1:298).

The difficulty with all of these interpretations is that they are beyond the horizon of Genesis itself. It would be better to find a situation which Genesis itself envisages. This is the chief merit of Cassuto's proposal. He points out that, according to 10:22, Elam was the eldest son of Shem, and according to 14:4, the Canaanite cities "served" (were slaves to, עבד) Elam. Among Elam's allies (14:1, 9) were the Goiim, a Japhetic group (10:5). The obvious objection to this view is that Gen 14 seems a somewhat isolated episode to link with such a wide-ranging prophecy. If the Philistines could be identified with Japhet, one could point to 26:26–33 as a possible fulfillment of these words, but again comparing chap. 26 with 20 makes it likely that Genesis regards Philistines as Hamitic (cf. 10:14).

We are therefore forced to admit to a certain agnosticism about the primary application of Noah's words. It is certainly attractive to see the incorporation of Gentiles into the Shemite fold as a *sensus plenior* of this saying, but I doubt whether this was the fulfillment envisaged by the human author of Genesis.

"May Canaan be a slave to him." For a third and final time Canaan's future slavery is predicted. This threefold repetition of the curse makes it unusually emphatic: there can be no doubt about its fulfillment.

28–29 The record of Noah's life is here completed in the style of the genealogy of 5:3–32, although the usual phrase "he fathered other sons and daughters" is omitted to make it clear that all mankind is descended from Ham, Shem, or Japhet. "After the flood": Since the flood began in the 600th year of Noah's life and finished in the 601st year, evidently "flood" (מבול) here refers to the first destructive phase of the inundation (cf. *Comment* on 6:17), for otherwise Noah would have been 951 years old at his death, not

950, as v 29 asserts. Within the genealogies of Genesis the flood is the only event used to mark the passage of time apart from human births and deaths. As in Mesopotamian tradition, the flood is the great break between the first and the second creations.

"Then he died." Unlike the Mesopotamian flood hero Utnapishtim who was granted immortality after the flood, Noah suffered the fate of all his ancestors save Enoch.

Explanation

From the third millennium b.c. to the present day, the story of the great flood has captured man's imagination. And no wonder, for it is the story of a universal catastrophe that engulfed all humanity, except for one man and his family who were saved by the grace of God. Genesis and Mesopotamian tradition alike see the flood as the great turning point in the history of the world. Up until the flood, Genesis deals with proto-history, those remote and distant events, often related in richly symbolic language, which have affected all mankind. But after the flood, we enter a new era, which might perhaps be termed prehistory, where the events related affect not all mankind but only those branches of humanity who are descended from the actors mentioned. Thus the sin of Ham determines directly the destiny of the Canaanites, and only indirectly other groupings who happen to profit from Ham's punishment.

Gen 6–9 uses various devices to draw attention to the way the flood closed one epoch of world history and opened another. Noah's death and Arpachshad's birth are dated by the flood. And the narrative goes to extraordinary lengths to date every phase of the flood exactly. No other event in Genesis is dated at all (excluding births and deaths)—not creation, the fall, Abel's murder, the tower of Babel, nor the call of Abram—and usually only the vaguest indications are given as to how long particular episodes lasted. The flood story is unique. Five times it gives a very specific date, not simply to the nearest year, but to the very day of the month, that a particular stage of the flood developed (7:11; 8:4, 5, 13, 14), and it also mentions periods of seven, forty, and a hundred and fifty days for different phases of the flood. The phrase "on this very day" links the onset of the flood to other decisive events like Abraham's circumcision (17:23), the exodus from Egypt (Exod 12:41), or Moses' death (Deut 32:48). Being father of three sons puts Noah on a par with Adam and Terah, other men who inaugurated new eras.

In stressing the epoch-dividing character of the flood, Genesis is at one with Mesopotamian tradition. Indeed, many of the narrative features, the universality of the flood, the ark, the birds and the sacrifice, are astonishingly similar. At no other point do Genesis and oriental tradition appear so close. Yet, equally, at no point are they so divergent and the differences between biblical and Mesopotamian theology so sharply defined.

In Gen 1 a clear polemic against oriental notions of divinity and ancient creation myths was noted. The God of Genesis is shown as supreme and omnipotent, not struggling against various rival deities such as the sun and moon or the monsters of the deep. God's word alone calls the cosmos into existence. Man is the apex of God's creative activity in Genesis, whereas Mesopotamia viewed him as an afterthought to relieve the gods of working and to supply them with food.

These contrasts between biblical and other Near Eastern attitudes are even sharper in the accounts of the flood. In Genesis there is but one God who plans and executes the flood and delivers Noah. In the Gilgamesh Epic it is a committee decision to flood the world, and one of the dissenting gods plots the escape of his devotee, Utnapishtim. In Gilgamesh the gods are scared by the deluge they have unleashed, "cowering like dogs against the wall," a trait wholly alien to the God of Genesis. Indeed, most striking of all, when Enlil arrives at the sacrifice he is surprised to find that Utnapishtim survived the flood. Though one of the supreme gods in the pantheon, he neither controlled nor knew what was happening in the world. But the LORD of Genesis is the God who sent the flood, shut in Noah and the animals, remembered Noah, brought him out on dry land, and gave him a guarantee that never again would the earth be destroyed by a flood. The Mesopotamian deities do not make such a pledge, and by their very nature would seem incapable of ensuring its fulfillment.

The God of Genesis is not only omniscient and omnipotent, properties the Babylonian gods clearly lack, but he is himself moral and just in dealing with his creation. Mankind is not destroyed for noisiness or excessive fertility but for his depravity.

"Every idea . . . of his mind was nothing but evil all the time" (6:5). "The earth was ruined, because all flesh (that is, both man and animals) has ruined its way on earth" (6:12). It therefore fitted the offense when God declared, "I am about to ruin them with the earth" (6:13).

Whereas spite or partiality dictated the Babylonian deities' treatment of mankind, the God of Genesis is portrayed as loyal and a rewarder of the righteous. He confirmed his covenant toward Noah by preserving him through the flood. Noah himself is described as "blameless among his contemporaries; Noah walked with God." He did not survive because he had the luck to pick the LORD as his patron deity. He walked with the only Sovereign God and was a loyal upholder of his law.

Whereas Utnapishtim is portrayed as a sharp, energetic organizer, Noah's character is barely described. Genesis is primarily interested in Noah's relationship with God, particularly his obedience to divine directions, though it also implies that he behaved as one who put the requirements of the law into practice in his daily affairs. The initial description "righteous" (6:9) implies that he was a good man who did what was lawful and right. More striking still, he is described as "blameless," as one who "walked with God." The subsequent narrative emphasizes his total and complete obedience to God's instructions. He built the ark and stocked it with food "exactly as God commanded" (6:22). He gathered the animals and embarked "exactly as the LORD commanded him" (7:5, 16). He finally left the ark at God's behest, offered sacrifice, and was assured of God's continuing blessing on him and on all creation.

Noah's erection of an altar and his offering of sacrifice is just one of several features in the story that suggest that Noah was a righteous and God-fearing man. He knows the difference between clean and unclean animals. He cares for the animals under his charge. His great task is "to preserve life" (6:19, 20;

7:3). Yet although he has such a multitude on board with him he does not forget the lonely dove but brings her lovingly back into the safety of the ark. Indeed, this bird scene seems to imply by its seven-day cycle that Noah observed the Sabbath as well.

The narrative thus places great emphasis on Noah's righteousness, at least during the flood itself. But it would be too crude to say that the story portrays Noah as earning his salvation by good works. Rather the narrative implies that Noah was linked by a pre-existing covenant with God. It repeatedly talks of God confirming his covenant with Noah (6:18; 9:9,17), and the rainbow reminds God of his covenant. And at the peak of the flood we are told "God remembered Noah" (8:1), a phrase subsequently used of those with whom God has entered into covenant. Noah's righteous conduct appears to ensure that he continued to enjoy God's covenant blessings, not least his preservation in the flood, and led to God confirming his covenant with the sign of the rainbow and the extension of the covenant to all mankind.

The other feature of the story that emphasizes God's mercy is the promise of earth's preservation and the blessing pronounced on her inhabitants after the flood. The LORD's assurance that "never again shall I smite every living thing as I have done" is prompted by his smelling the burnt offering and the observation that the "ideas of a man's mind are evil from his youth" (8:21). What previously had been cited as the reason for the extinction of all flesh is now declared to be God's motive for its preservation. Evidently the priestly-mediatorial role of Noah and his sacrificial offering has profoundly influenced God's attitude to mankind. These divine reflections on the nature of man form the backdrop to the fanfare of blessing on Noah and his sons in which the commission first given to Adam "to be fruitful and multiply; fill the earth and subdue it" (1:28; 9:1) is reaffirmed afresh.

The world seems all set for a new start. The slate has been wiped clean, and we hope that the mistakes of the antediluvians will not be repeated. But no sooner is the blessing pronounced and the eternal covenant confirmed than man lapses again. The righteous and blameless Noah, who had walked with God for six hundred and one years, falls victim to demon drink and disgraces himself in his tent. Worse still, his youngest son, instead of covering up his father physically and metaphorically, shows total lack of filial piety, prattling about the situation to his brothers. In this last tragicomic scene, the truth that the "ideas of man's mind are evil from his youth" is starkly exhibited for all to see. Even the most righteous and their offspring may fall from grace in an unguarded moment. And such falls do have long-term consequences, as the curse on Ham's descendants the Canaanites makes clear. Lack of filial piety and sexual indiscretion lead to bondage. But more important still, this last scene reminds us that were it not for the changed logic of God, in that he now cites man's depravity as a ground for his mercy rather than for his judgment, the descendants of Noah would be heading for extinction in another deluge. However, even sinful man is now sustained by grace and can face the future not with complacency but with security. The world will indeed be filled and subdued by man.

The flood destroyed the old world, God's original creation, and out of it was born a new world. Genesis brings out fully the correspondences and contrasts between creation and the flood. The long lists of creatures that perished in the flood—"man and land animals and creeping creatures and birds of the sky" (6:7), "birds, domesticated animals, wild animals, all swarming things which swarm on the earth" (7:21)—echo the classification of the creatures in Gen 1:20–26, while the phrase "everything which has the breath of life in its nostrils" (7:22) harks back to 2:7. The flood itself involved the bursting of the springs of the great deep and the opening of the windows of heaven (7:11), thus reversing the process of separating the waters above and below the firmament and the dry land from the seas. Indeed, through the upsurge of water from the great deep, the situation of Gen 1:2, when "darkness was upon the face of the great deep," reappears. Furthermore, on one interpretation of the chronology, it would appear that just as creation began on a Sunday and ended on Friday, so did the destructive phase of the flood. This would make the parallel between creation and decreation even more pointed.

But just as obvious is the parallel between the original process of creation and the world's re-creation described in Gen 8–9. The turning point of the story is the text "God remembered Noah . . . so God caused a wind to pass over the earth and the waters receded." Here the divine-sent wind echoes the wind of God hovering over the waters before the first act of creation. And, as in Gen 1, there follows the progressive separation of water from the land: first the mountain tops appear, then the fresh growth of the trees, and eventually the earth was dried out (8:1, 5, 11, 14). As God created the animals to swarm and multiply in the earth, so Noah is directed to send them out to do the same again (1:20–22; 8:17).

God's first words of blessing to Noah after he left the ark repeat almost exactly his original commission to Adam, "Be fruitful and multiply" (1:28; 9:1). Noah is obviously seen to be father of the new humanity just as Adam was head of the old order. But while in some ways their roles are similar, the narrative makes it plain that the situation has changed. While God promises not to add to the curse on the ground, he does not lift it. Though the threat of another flood is removed, the ground is still cursed. Furthermore, the remark that "the fear of you and the dread of you will be on every wild animal" indicates a degree of enmity between man and the animal kingdom that was lacking in the original mandate "have dominion over them" (9:2; 1:26), but which may, however, be expressed by 3:15. Likewise the original permission to eat only plants (1:29–30) is referred to and modified to allow the consumption of meat (9:3). But the less than ideal state of affairs is hinted at by the warnings against homicide: the stories of Cain and Lamek and the violence of the antediluvians has brought to light what man's capabilities are. The inveterate sinfulness of humanity is a fact of life to Noah, the second Adam. Thus although in some ways his fall looks like a rerun of Adam's (both were caused by eating a fruit or its product), it is not really comparable. This is seen by the fact that it is Noah's son Ham who is regarded as most culpable and the fact that his fall only disadvantages one group of his descendants, not his whole family.

Noah's experiences do not just look back to Adam's, they also look forward. He is described in terms that befit a model Israelite: "righteous, blameless, he walks with God." He is in covenant relationship with God, observes the Sabbath, distinguishes clean and unclean, does not eat flesh with blood in it, and offers sacrifice. His sacrifice, like Moses' intercession, brings God's blessing on others. Possibly, too, Noah's salvation in the floodwaters may be compared to Israel's passage through the Red Sea: in both a wind from God was instrumental in their preservation.

Unlike other episodes in the primeval history, the story of Noah and the flood story are subjects for comment in the prophets. Ezek 14:14, 20 puts Noah on a par with Job and Daniel as men famed for personal righteousness who, for all that, could not avert judgment's falling on others. Isa 54:9–10, on the other hand, focuses on God's oath never to destroy the earth again as a model of his enduring love for Israel:

> As I swore that the waters of Noah
>   should no more go over the earth
> so I have sworn that I will not be angry with you
>   and will not rebuke you.
> For the mountains may depart
>   and the hills be removed,
> but my stedfast love shall not depart from you.

The NT also regards Noah as an example of faith and hero of righteousness (Heb 11:7; 2 Pet 2:5; cf. 1 Pet 3:20). Jesus compares his second advent to the coming of the flood: it too will take most men by surprise and only a few will be saved (Matt 24:37–38; Luke 17:26–27).

These quotations focus on two different aspects of the flood story. It is indeed a tale of catastrophic destruction that proves God's hatred of sin, a picture of the wrath of God that will be finally revealed at the last day on all who ignore his demands and go their own way. But it also offers comfort: God will continue to uphold the present natural order "as long as the earth exists," despite man's incorrigible perverseness of heart. More than that, it gives assurance to the righteous, those who walk with God and keep his commandments, that in the last great day, or in the natural disasters that presage it, they too will be preserved unto eternal life.

From Flood to Babel (10:1–11:9)

Form/Structure/Setting

10:1–11:9, "The family history of the sons of Noah," consists of two quite heterogeneous items—the table of the nations (10:1–32) and the story of the tower of Babel (11:1–9)—that on first sight have very little to do with each other. Were it not for the fact that the next major editorial heading, "This is the family history of Shem," does not occur until 11:10, it would seem more natural to take chap. 10 as a discrete unit. Such an analysis could be supported by the observation that 10:32, "These are the clans of the sons of Noah by their descendants (לתולדתם) . . . after the flood," forms an inclusion with 10:1, "This is the family history (תולדת) of Noah's sons . . . after the flood."

Nevertheless, from the point of view of content, 11:1–9 does cohere with chap. 10. Chap. 10 affirms that all mankind has descended from a single family and describes the interrelationships that exist among the nations of the world. Several times it mentions that these peoples "spread out" (vv 5, 18, 32), that "the earth was divided" (v 25), that different peoples had their own "languages" (vv 5, 20, 31), and that Ashur went out from Shinar and founded Nineveh, Rehobot-Ir, and Calah (v 11). But no explanation of the spread of mankind is offered in chap. 10: one might surmise (cf. chap. 5), that it simply reflects man's being fruitful and multiplying. But that would hardly explain the reference to the variety of languages.

11:1–9, which might better be described as the dispersal of the nations, puts mankind's dispersal and divisions in an entirely new light. They represent God's judgment on man's attempts to make himself a name and to reach the heavens. Though not as catastrophic a sentence as that announced in 6:1–8, after the somewhat similar description of antediluvian man's fertility, the tower of Babel again puts man's intentions in question. He is not master of his own destiny. Indeed, in rebellion he must suffer God's displeasure curtailing his grandiose dreams.

10:1–32 and 11:1–9, despite their differences, are linked by a number of key words and phrases, most obviously, פוץ "scatter" (10:18; 11:4, 8, 9; cf. פרד "spread out," 10:5, 32), "country of Shinar" (10:10; 11:2), בנה "build" (10:11; 11:4, 5, 8). The word ארץ occurs fourteen times in all: eight times with the meaning "earth, world" (10:8, 25, 32; 11:1, 4, 8, 9 [2x]), and another seven times meaning "land, country" (10:5, 10, 11, 20, 31, 32; 11:2). בני "sons of" occurs fourteen times in chap. 10. Furthermore, it seems likely that the number of peoples listed as descendants of Noah's sons totals seventy (see below). This use of key terms in multiples of seven is reminiscent of the techniques in earlier sections of Genesis (cf. *Form/Structure/Setting* on 1:1–2:3; 4:1–26; 5:1–6:8) and tends to confirm the view that 10:1–11:9 is an editorial unit. Finally, 11:1–9 is full of pre-echoes of the name of Babel (see below), and 10:1 contains an even clearer one, "after the flood," *mbl*; cf. "Babel," *bbl*. For this reason the whole section could be entitled "from flood to Babel."

In fact, it is characteristic of Gen 1–11 to juxtapose very different types of material as occurs here. The most obvious parallel is 5:1–6:8, where the genealogy from Adam to Noah is followed by the angel marriages and the intimation of the flood. But also in 2:4 to 4:26, there is the juxtaposition of obviously diverse material (2:4–3:24, the garden of Eden, is followed by 4:1–26, Cain's family story) all under the one heading "This is the history of the heaven and the earth." So although the editorial organization seems odd to us, it is quite congruent with the method to be observed elsewhere in the primeval history. But since the material in chaps. 10 and 11 is so different, the sections will be discussed separately until we reach the *Explanation* section.

The Table of the Nations   (10:1–32)

Bibliography

Abramsky, S. "Nimrod and the Land of Nimrod." (Heb.) *BMik* 25 (1980/81) 237–55, 321–40. **Archi, A.** "The Epigraphic Evidence from Ebla and the Old Testament." *Bib* 60 (1979) 556–66. **Astour, N. C.** "Sabtah and Sabteca: Ethiopian Pharaoh Names in Genesis 10." *JBL* 84 (1965) 422–25. **Bastomsky, S. J.** "Noah, Italy, and the Sea Peoples." *JQR* 67 (1976–77) 146–53. **Berger, P. R.** "Ellasar, Tarshish und Jawan, Gen 14 und 10." *WO* 13 (1982) 50–78. **Coppens, J.** "Une nouvelle date pour le document yahviste?" *ETL* 42 (1966) 567–71. **Grau, J.** *The Gentiles in Genesis: Israel and the Nations in the Primeval and Patriarchal Histories.* Ph.D. Dissertation: Southern Methodist University, 1980. **Hidal, S.** "The Land of Cush in the Old Testament." *SEÅ* 41–42 (1976/77) 97–106. **Ishida, T.** "The Structure and Historical Implications of the Lists of the Pre-Israelite Nations." *Bib* 60 (1979) 461–90. **Lipinski, É.** "Nimrod et Aššur." *RB* 73 (1966) 77–93. **Loretz, O.** *Habiru-Hebräer: Eine sozio-linguistische Studie über die Herkunft des Gentiliziums.* BZAW 160. Berlin: de Gruyter, 1984. 183–94. **Los, F. J.** "The Table of Peoples of the Tenth Chapter of Genesis." *Mankind Quarterly* 7 (1967) 144–52. **Luke, K.** "The Nations of the World." *BibBh* 8 (1982) 61–80. **Neiman, D.** "The Two Genealogies of Japhet." In *Orient and Occident: Essays Presented to C. H. Gordon,* ed. H. A. Hoffner. AOAT 22. Kevelaer: Butzon and Bercker, 1973. 119–26. **Oded, B.** "The Table of Nations (Genesis 10)—A Socio-cultural Approach." *ZAW* 98 (1986) 14–31. **Parunak, H. V. D.** "Oral Typesetting: Some Uses of Biblical Structure." *Bib* 62 (1981) 153–68. **Rainey, A. F.** "Toponymic Problems (cont.)." *TA* 9 (1982) 132–36. **Ross, A. P.** "The Table of Nations in Genesis 10—Its Structure." *BSac* 137 (1980) 340–53. ———. "The Table of Nations in Genesis 10—Its Content." *BSac* 138 (1981) 22–34. **Sasson, J. M.** "*Reḥōvōt ʿîr.*" *RB* 90 (1983) 94–96. **Savasta, C.** "Alcune considerazioni sulla lista dei discendenti dei figli di Noè." *RivB* 17 (1969) 89–102, 337–63. **Simons, J.** "The 'Table of Nations' (Gen 10): Its General Structure and Meaning." *OTS* 10 (1964) 155–84. **Speiser, E. A.** "In Search of Nimrod." *Oriental and Biblical Studies.* 41–52. **Tengström, S.** *Die Toledotformel.* ConB 17. Lund: Gleerup, 1981. **Thompson, J. A.** "Samaritan Evidence for 'All of Them in the Land of Shinar' (Gen 10:10)." *JBL* 90 (1971) 99–102. **Winnett, F. V.** "The Arabian Genealogies in the Book of Genesis." *Translating and Understanding the Old Testament: Essays in Honor of H. G. May,* ed. H. T. Frank and W. L. Reed. Nashville: Abingdon, 1970. 171–96. **Wiseman, D. J.** ed. *Peoples of Old Testament Times. (POTT)* Oxford: Clarendon Press, 1973. **Yamauchi, E. M.** "Meshech, Tubal and Company: A Review Article." *JETS* 19 (1976) 239–47. **Zadok, R.** "The Origin of the Name Shinar." *ZA* 74 (1984) 240–44.

Translation

¹ This is the family history of Noah's sons, ᵃ Shem, ᵇHam, and Japhet.ᵃ Children were bornᶜ to them after the flood.

² The sons of Japhet wereᵃ Gomer, Magog, Madai, Yavan,ᵇ Tubal, Meshek,ᶜ and Tyras. ³ The sons of Gomer wereᵃ Ashkenaz,ᵇ Riphat and Togarmah. ⁴ The sons of Yavan wereᵃ Elishah,ᵇ Tarshish, Kittim, and Dodanim.ᶜ ⁵ From these the nations of the coastlands spreadᵃ outᵇ in their countries, eachᶜ with his own language, by their clans among the nations.

⁶ The sons of Ham were Cush, Egypt, Put, and Canaan. ⁷ The sons of Cush were Seba, Havilah, Sabtah, Raamah, Sabteca. The sons of Raamah were Sheba and Dedan. ⁸ᵃ Now Cush fatheredᵇ Nimrod,ᵃ who began to be a champion in the earth. ⁹ He was a champion hunter before the LORD. Therefore it used to be said,ᵃ "Like Nimrod a champion hunter before the LORD." ¹⁰ The prime of his kingdom wasᵃ Babylon, Erech,ᵇ Akkad, and Calneh in the country of Shinar. ¹¹ᵃ From that country went out Ashur,ᵃᵇ and he builtᶜ Nineveh, Rehobot-Ir, Calah, ¹² and Resen between Nineveh and Calah, ᵃthat is the big city.ᵃ ¹³ᵃ Egypt fatheredᵃ Ludim, Anam-im,ᵇ Lehabim, Naphtuhim,ᶜ ¹⁴ Pathrusim and Casluhim, ᵃwhere the Philistines came from,ᵃ and the Caphtorim. ¹⁵ᵃ Canaan fatheredᵃ Sidon his firstborn and Heth, ¹⁶ the Jebusites, the Amorites, the Girgashites, ¹⁷ the Hivites, the Arkites,ᵃ the Sinites, ¹⁸ the Arvadites, the Zemarites, the Hamathites. Afterwards the clans of the Canaanites scattered.ᵃ ¹⁹ The boundary of the Canaanites came to be ᵃfrom Sidon as far asᵇ Gerar up to Gaza, as far asᵇ Sodom, Gomorrah, Admah, and Zeboim up to Lasha.ᶜᵃ ²⁰ᵃ These are the sons of Ham according to their clans and their languages in their countries among their nations.ᵃ

²¹ᵃ Now to Shem also (children) were bornᵇᵃ (he was father of all the sons of Eber and ᶜthe oldest brother of Japhetᶜ). ²² The sons of Shem were Elam, Ashur, Arpachshad, Lud, and Aram.ᵃ ²³ The sons of Aram were Utz,ᵃ Hul,ᵇ Gether, and Mash.ᶜ ²⁴ᵃ Arpachshad fatheredᵇ Shelah, and Shelah fathered Eber.ᵃ ²⁵ To Eber were bornᵃ two sons: ᵇthe name of the one was Peleg, because in his days the earth was divided,ᶜ and the name of his brother was Yoqtan.ᵇ ²⁶ Yoqtan fathered Almodad, Sheleph, Hasarmaveth, Yerah, ²⁷ Hadoram, Uzal,ᵃ Diqlah, ²⁸ Obal,ᵃ Abi-mael, Sheba, ²⁹ Ophir, Havilah, and Yobab. All these were sons of Yoqtan. ³⁰ Their settlement went from Mesha to the approachᵃ to Sephar, the eastern mountain. ³¹ These are the sons of Shem according to their clans and languages, in their countries by their nations.ᵃ

³² These are the clans of the sons of Noah by their descendants among their nations, and from theseᵃ the nations spreadᵇ out in the world after the flood.

Notes

1.a-a. In 7:13 the names "Shem, Ham, and Japhet" precede "Noah's sons"; hence Cassuto makes "Shem . . ." begin a new clause, and Westermann inserts "The sons of Noah were," בני נח having been omitted by haplography. This is unnecessary (for this word order, cf. 6:10; 9:18 and Joüon, 131i-j), so the traditional punctuation may be retained.

1.b. Some MSS insert "and" before "Ham," וחם.

1.c. Waw consec + 3 masc pl impf niph ילד.

2.a. Here and in vv 3, 4, 6, 7, the verb "to be" must be understood. The context suggests a past tense is appropriate.

2.b. G inserts "and Elisa," although he is also mentioned in v 4 as son of Yavan.

2.c. SamPent spells it מוֹשֵׁךְ; cf. G Μόσοχ.

3.a. Cf. n. 2.a.

3.b. *BHS* conjectures אשׁכנו on extrabiblical comparisons; see *Comment*.

4.a. Cf. nn. 2.a, 3.a.

4.b. SamPent spells it אֱלִישׁ.

4.c. For MT דּוֹדָנִים, some MSS, 1 Chr 1:7, S G have רוֹדָנִים; *BHS* offers a conjectural alternative, דָּנָנִים ("Danaeans"). See *Comment*.

5.a. 3 pl pf niph, פרד.

5.b. *BHS*, Westermann, Savasta conjecturally insert "These are the sons of Japhet" to match similar concluding statements in vv 20, 31.

5.c. On the distributive use of אִישׁ "each," see GKC, 139b.

8.a-a. It is anomalous to have a sequential clause with the subj preceding the verb. Waw consec וילד + subj would be normal. *SBH* (87–88) calls it a pseudocircumstantial sequential. Cf. vv 13, 15, 24, 26.

8.b. SamPent has הוֹלִיד, typical substitution of hiph for qal; cf. Waltke, *New Perspectives*, 216.

9.a. 3 masc sg impf niph, אמר. On this use of impf, see GKC, 107g.

10.a. Waw cons + 3 fem sg impf, היה.

10.b. G reads Ὀρεχ.

11.a-a. In apposition to "land of Shinar," v 10 (*SBH*, 59); cf. 10:14.

11.b. Some, e.g., Westermann, Cassuto, take Ashur to be accus of place, "to Ashur" (cf. GKC, 118d, f) and would translate it "he [i.e., Nimrod] went out to Ashur." Further see *Comment*.

11.c. Waw consec + 3 masc sg impf (apocopated), בנה; cf. 8:20.

12.a-a. Appositional clause instead of a relative clause introduced by אשׁר (*SBH*, 59).

13.a-a. Pseudocircumstantial sequential clause; cf. n. 8.a-a.

13.b. SamPent עינמים; G Ἐνεμετιείμ.

13.c. G Νεφθαλιείμ.

14.a-a. Because elsewhere, e.g., Amos 9:7, the Philistines are said to have come from Caphtor, this clause is often transferred to the end of the sentence, i.e., after "Caphtorim."

15.a-a. On this construction cf. vv 8, 13.

17.a. SamPent העֲרוּקִי. On the unusual MT punctuation הָ instead of הַ see GKC, 35g. But 1 Chr 1:15 has the same spelling.

18.a. 3 pl pf niph, פוץ.

19.a-a. SamPent substitutes a simpler summary of the boundaries of Canaan; see *BHS*, "from the river of Egypt to the great river, the river Euphrates to the Western Sea." Cf. Num 34:1–12.

19.b. Inf constr בוא "to come" + 2 masc sg suff, lit., "your coming"; cf. עַד בֹּאֲךָ, Judg 6:4, "until you come to . . ."; cf. GKC, 144h. Speiser (*Oriental and Biblical Studies*, 124–28) suggests the ך is really a frozen obsolete ending.

19.c. *BHS* suggests בלע as in 14:2. *Tg. Ps.-J.* (and Jerome) קלרה = Kallirhoe.

20.a-a. Appositional sentence serving as colophon to preceding paragraph (*SBH*, 54).

21.a-a. Pseudocircumstantial clause; cf. vv 8, 13, 15.

·21.b. 3 sg pf qal pass ילד; cf. 4:26.

21.c-c. This translation supposes that הגדול qualifies "brother"; it could qualify "Japhet." In that case it would be translated "the brother of Japhet the oldest."

22.a. G adds καὶ Καινάν.

23.a. SamPent חוץ.

23.b. SamPent וחויל.

23.c. SamPent וּמַשָּׁא; cf. G καὶ Μόσοχ; cf. 1 Chr 1:17 וּמֶשֶׁךְ.

24.a-a. Pseudocircumstantial sequential clauses; cf. vv 8, 13, 15, 21.

24.b. G inserts "Kainan, and Kainan fathered."

25.a. On this form, cf. n. 10:21.b. SamPent has pl ילדו, eliminating the lack of concord between subj and verb. Typical change (Waltke, *New Perspectives*, 218).

25.b-b. On this construction see *SBH*, 33.

25.c. 3 fem sg pf niph, פלג.

27.a. SamPent אִיזֹל; G Αἰζήλ.

28.a. 1 Chr 1:22 and SamPent עיבל.

30.a. Cf. n. 10:19.b.

31.a. *BHS* unnecessarily amends to בגויהם; cf. Savasta, *RivB* 17 (1969) 348–53.
32.a. SamPent G insert איי "islands of."
32.b. 3 pl pf niph, פרד.

Form/Structure/Setting

The structure of chap. 10 expresses in its tripartite arrangement the three-fold division of mankind. Each section deals with one of Noah's sons and opens and closes with regular formulae (vv 2, 6, 20, 22, 31): "The sons of X were . . ."; "These are the sons of X according to their clans and languages in their countries among/by their nations." The closing formula of Japhet (v 5) is somewhat different: not only does it not mention the sons of Japhet, it rearranges the order of countries, language, clans, and nations. The introductory formula for the sons of Shem is prefaced by v 21, "Now to Shem also were born . . . ," which echoes 4:26; cf. 10:25. As already noted, the introduction to the whole (v 1) is neatly matched by the conclusion in v 32. Thus, despite some occasional irregularities, the structure of chap. 10 is clear.

1	Introduction: "This is the family history [תולדת] of Noah's sons . . . after the flood"	
2–5	Japhet's descendants:	2 "The sons of Japhet were . . . (7 names)" (vv 3–4 mention 7 grandchildren)
		5 Concluding formula
6–20	Ham's descendants:	6 "The sons of Ham were . . . (4 names)" (vv 7–18 mention 24 grandchildren and 2 great-grandchildren, Sheba and Dedan)
		20 Concluding formula: "These are the sons of Ham . . . nations"
21–31	Shem's descendants:	21 Prefatory remark: "Now to Shem were born . . ."
		22 "The sons of Shem were . . . (5 names)" (vv 23–29 mention 21 more distant descendants)
		31 Concluding formula: "These are the sons of Shem . . . nations"
32	Conclusion: "These are the clans of the sons of Noah by their descendants [תולדת] . . . after the flood"	

Within this table a fondness for seven-numbered lists is evident. Japhet's sons total seven (v 2), as do his grandsons in vv 3–4. V 7 lists seven sons and grandsons of Cush. Vv 13–14 mention seven sons of Egypt. It seems likely that the total number of nations descended from Shem, Ham, and Japhet comes to seventy. Cassuto omits Nimrod (vv 8–12) to arrive at this total. It would seem preferable to leave out of the reckoning the Philistines (v 14), who are only connected geographically with the Casluhim, there being no genealogical link with Ham adduced in this chapter. Seventy was a traditional round number for a large group of descendants. Asherah had seventy sons according to Canaanite tradition (II AB, 6.46; *ANET,* 134), and so did Jacob (46:27; Deut 10:22), Gideon (Judg 8:30), and Ahab (2 Kgs 10:1). It seems likely, therefore, that listing seventy descendants of Noah's sons is

not a matter of chance. This list does not purport to be an exhaustive list of
the nations of the world (cf. 10:5); rather it mentions the major peoples
known to Israel and their relationship to each other and to Israel. In particular,
it is probably significant that this chapter lists seventy peoples, whereas Jacob's
family comprised seventy souls. Israel is thus a microcosm of the wider family
of humanity described in this chapter. The table of nations begins with the
descendants of Japhet, the group of peoples with which Israel had least contact.
They are thus handled first and dealt with most briefly. Afterward, and more
fully treated, are the Hamites, among whom were the Babylonians, Egyptians,
and Canaanites, Israel's most influential neighbors. Finally come the Shemites,
who include the forefathers of Israel herself. This pattern of dealing with
non-elect lines before the chosen line is often to be observed in the organization
of Genesis; cf. the Cainites before Sethites (chaps. 4–5); Esau (chap. 36)
before Jacob (chaps. 37–50).

Wiseman remarks: "The origin of this material is unknown. It is impossible
to be dogmatic as this chapter remains unique in ancient literatures" (*Peoples
of Old Testament Times,* xviii). Its cosmopolitan outlook suggests an author
well informed about world affairs and possibly connected with a royal court,
whether fourteenth century Egypt (so Wiseman) or tenth/seventh century
Jerusalem (so Westermann, 1:503). The majority of scholars prefer a first-
millennium date for the composition of this chapter, because some of the
peoples listed here are not mentioned in extrabiblical texts until then (see
comments below). Oded (*ZAW* 98 [1986] 16) has argued that this chapter is
based on much earlier material which divided mankind into three groups:
nomadic peoples (Shem), urban dwellers (Ham), and seafarers (Japhet).

According to documentary theory, this chapter is composed of J and P.
To P are assigned vv 1a, 2–7, 20, 22–23, 31–32, and to J the rest, i.e. vv
1b, 8–19, 21, 24–30. In other words, most of the formulae used to structure
the chapter, e.g., "The sons of X were . . ."; "These are the sons of . . ."
as well as the introduction (v 1a) and conclusion (v 32), are P, whereas the
digressions about Nimrod (8–12), Canaan (15–19), and Eber (25–30) are
ascribed to J. Apart from the observation that the J passages expand the
brief lists that constitute P, there is little to demarcate or identify the sources.
In that v 9 twice mentions "the LORD," and vv 8, 13, 15, 26 use the qal of
יָלַד "fathered" instead of the hiphil as in chap. 5 (P), it seems plausible to
ascribe these passages to J. Savasta (*RivB* 17 [1969] 89–102, 337–63) has,
however, persuasively argued that vv 4c–5, 20, 31–32 should be ascribed to
J rather than P. The sudden mention of Kittim and Dodanim, v 4c, a plural
name for peoples, is akin to vv 13–14. The mention of the dispersal of the
nations (vv 5a, 32) is a J theme (cf. 10:25; 11:1–9). The four key terms
"country," "language," "clan," "nation" which reappear in vv 5, 20, 31–32
all have closer affinities with the J material in chap. 10 than with P. Savasta
points out that vv 5, 20, 31 all act as colophons to the immediately preceding
sections, vv 2–4, 6–19, 21–30 respectively, while v 32 is a colophon to the
whole of vv 2–31. The phrase "after the flood" also suggests that v 32 and
at least part of v 1 also belong to J.

On the usual analysis of chap. 10, the J material does not constitute a
real parallel to the P material, at least if one is looking for a duplicate genealogy

of the sons of Noah. It includes nothing about any descendants of Japhet and only a truncated account of Ham's (vv 8–19); of the three brothers only Shem is explicitly mentioned in the J material (v 21). So here, as in chap. 5, it would be easier to regard the J verses as an expansion of the P material than as a duplicate source. Savasta's analysis confirms that J is the major editor at work in this chapter. But obviously J is doing more than making editorial comments on P; he has so much fresh material that he must be presumed to have access to alternative sources. However, it might well be better to see all of v 1 as editorial, not P (so Savasta), because אלה תולדת "This is the family history of" clearly links onto the repeated refrain in the J material, "X fathered Y," ילד (vv 8, 13, 15, 26).

If then we regard the J material as deliberately added by an editor, his special interests become clearer. He is particularly interested in the flood, in the dispersal of the nations into different language groups, in the origins of Babel and Shinar (10:8–12; cf. 11:1–9), Egypt and the Canaanites (vv 13–20), and the Arabian tribes descended from Shem (vv 25–30). As Ross says,

> These are peoples with whom the new nation of Israel would have dealings in accord with the oracle of Noah in Gen 9.
> According to Genesis, the new nation of Israel was to be blessed as God's people in the land of Canaan. God's plan to bless Israel involved the movement, displacement and subjugation of other peoples. The oracle of Noah in Gen 9 anticipated the blessing for Shem, along with Japhet, and the cursing of Canaan, a son of Ham. This table in Gen 10 gives direction to that oracle. It presents the lines of Shem and Japhet as pure tribal groups around the promised land; it also presents the old block of Hamites, especially the mixed races in the land of Canaan, as the predominant powers on the earth. The ילד sections identify these tribes for Israel and signify their relationship to the blessing and cursing (A. P. Ross, *BSac* 138 [1981] 30–31).

Though this table of the nations appears on first sight to be very similar to the genealogies in the primeval history (cf. chaps. 5, 11), there are important differences that should make us chary of assuming that all the names refer to specific individuals. First, no ages are mentioned, unlike 5:1–32 and 11:10–32. Second, while many names are personal—e.g., Japhet, Nimrod—others are obviously place names—e.g., Sidon, Sheba—names of peoples—e.g., Ludim, Caphtorim—or gentilics—e.g., Amorites, Girgashites. Third, the terms used to express the relationship between those listed are more flexible than in genealogies: "The sons of . . . were . . ." alternates with "X fathered. . . ." These observations make it unlikely that all the names in this list should be regarded as eponyms, i.e., the putative ancestor of the group that bears the name. Some fit such a description; others do not. Fourth, "sonship" and "brotherhood" could be used in ancient times to refer to a treaty relationship as well as blood-based kinship. So here "sons of" or "fathered" might well be referring to a people's political or geographical affiliation, not its genealogical links. Nevertheless, while the terminology of this chapter does not demand that all the names be personal eponyms, the phrases "sons of" and "fathered" do express the idea that all mankind known to Israel is descended from a single stock. All men are sons of Noah as well as sons of Adam.

Comment

1 "This is the family history of Noah's sons" is the standard editorial formula introducing a new section; cf. 2:4; 6:9, etc. This is the only time it occurs in a family history of someone's *sons*. Elsewhere it is always "the family history of X," or, once, "heaven and earth" (2:4). "After the flood" echoes 9:28, thus providing a link backward and a look forward to 10:32, the conclusion of this table of nations. It probably also anticipates Babel/Babylon in 10:10 and 11:9, since the Hebrew for "flood" (*mbl*) and for "Babel" are so close phonetically. This makes it probable that this part of the verse is also editorial and not from a source different from that of the first half. From a narrative viewpoint, it reminds us that Noah's sons brought only their wives with them into the ark: no children were born until after the flood.

2–5 The table of nations begins with the descendants of Japhet, the group of surrounding nations with whom Israel had least to do. Their distance from Israel explains the brevity of this section compared with the treatment of the Hamites and Shemites later in the chapter.

2 "The sons of Japhet were." The Hebrew clause is without a verb, and it is problematic whether this sentence should be translated as above with Westermann, or whether the copula should simply be omitted, as in most English versions. Since the verb "to be" is often omitted in Hebrew, it can legitimately be supplied here. The context requires a past tense.

"Japhet": cf. above on 5:32; 9:27. In connection with this passage, commentators have often noticed that one of the Greek titans was called Iapetos. Despite the similarity in names, it is doubtful that there is any historical connection between them. The LXX transliterates Japhet Ἰάφεθ, not Ἰαπετός (cf. *EM* 3, 745–46; *OCCL*, 432).

Japhet's Family Tree

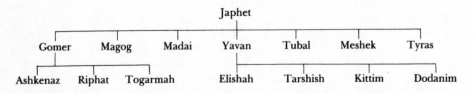

"Gomer," also mentioned in Ezek 38:6, is identified with *Gimirray* of Assyrian and Κιμμέριοι of Greek sources. The Cimmerians were a powerful group of Indo-European origin who came from southern Russia and posed a considerable challenge to Assyria in the eighth and seventh centuries. They eventually settled in Asia Minor (Cappadocia).

"Magog" is mentioned again in Ezek 38:2; 39:6, led by a king named Gog. But it is impossible to identify Magog with any certainty or even to be sure whether a people or a land is meant. Magog is not mentioned in any cuneiform texts. It could be that Ezekiel's Gog is Gyges, the king of Lydia (685–52 B.C.), called *Gugu* in the Assyrian texts. The difficulty with this identification is that Gyges' territory did not include eastern Anatolia (Anatolia =

approximately modern asiatic Turkey), the territories of Meshek and Tubal.
Josephus (*Ant* 1.vi.1 [1:123]) identified Magog with the Scythians. *Tg. Neof.*
identifies Magog with Germania, possibly the Germanicia of southern Anatolia
(so M. McNamara, *Targum and Testament* [Shannon: Irish UP, 1972] 194–
95). It has been conjectured that the name "Magog" is derived from Gog by
prefixing it with *m* (מ), a typical Hebrew way of making a place name, or
that it is an Akkadian formation from *mat gûgi*, "land of Gog," but neither
suggestion is proven. Given our ignorance, it is prudent to suggest that Magog
may be located somewhere in Anatolia.

"Madai" or "Medes": cf. Isa 13:17; 21:2; Dan 5:28; 6:16 [15]; Ezra 6:2.
Another Indo-European people that is first mentioned in Assyrian texts in
836 B.C. during the reign of Shalmaneser III. The date when they first arrived
in the Iranian plateau is disputed. Though it used to be held that they arrived
in about 1000 B.C., T. C. Young (*Iran* 5 [1967] 11–34) has argued that they
settled there in about 1300 B.C.

"Yavan" (cf. Ezek 27:13; Isa 66:19) refers in the first instance to the Ionian
Greeks who lived on the coast of Turkey. But later in the OT it denotes all
the Greeks, e.g., Dan 8:21; 10:20. However, contacts between Greece and
the Middle East stretch back at least into the third millennium B.C. (E. M.
Yamauchi, *Greece and Babylon* [Grand Rapids: Baker, 1967] 27–46).

"Tubal" and "Meshek" are also mentioned in Ezek 27:13; 32:26; 38:2–3;
39:1. Cuneiform texts locate *Muški* and *Tabāl* in central and eastern Anatolia. The Mushki are firs. mentioned *ca.* 1100 B.C. fighting with Tiglath-Pileser I
on the upper Tigris. Their capital was at Mazaca (modern Kayseri). Tabal
was a region north of Cilicia. In the eighth century, the Mushki and Tabal
fought together against Assyria. In 709 B.C., however, the famous King Midas
(called Mita by the Assyrians) became an Assyrian ally in order to fight off
the Cimmerian invasion. Herodotus (1.14) describes Midas as a Phrygian. It
seems that the Phrygians entered Asia Minor from Europe, whereas the Mushki
came from the east. They merged to form a single kingdom known by one
name to the Greeks and by the other to the Assyrians. The Persian empire
incorporated the remains of the Mushki and Tabal into the nineteenth satrapy
in northeast Anatolia, and in the Greek sources they are called the Moschoi
and Tibarenoi (Herodotus 3.94; 7.78).

"Tyras." These people are mentioned only here and in 1 Chr 1:5. They
are not named in cuneiform sources. They may be identified with the *Turuša,*
one of the sea peoples who attacked Egypt in the late thirteenth century. It
is often surmised that they are to be identified with Aegean pirates, the Tyrseni-
ans mentioned by Herodotus, and the Etruscans (Tyrrhenians) who were
well established in Italy in the eighth century. They are said to have originated
in Lydia in Asia Minor, but this is uncertain. It is possible therefore that
Genesis locates Tyras in Asia Minor, and maybe reflects a time before the
Tyras were finally driven out from there, perhaps by the Cimmerian invasions
(cf. Gispen 1:319).

3   "Ashkenaz." Here and in 1 Chr 1:6, Ashkenaz is a son of Gomer. In
Jer 51:27, Ashkenaz, Ararat, and Minni are summoned to attack Babylon.
It is generally agreed that Ashkenaz is to be equated with the Aškuza, the
classical Scythians, mentioned in Assyrian texts. Why the Hebrew word for

them should include an *n* is hard to account for: it seems unlikely that it is simply a scribal mistake of ‍נ *n* for ‍ו *w* because it occurs in three different books. The Scythians came from southern Russia, driving the Cimmerians ahead of them, and may have eventually settled in Media in the seventh century. In that the Scythians displaced the Cimmerians from their homeland, one can understand why this table of nations regards them as descendants of Gomer.

"Riphat" (Diphat in 1 Chr 1:6) is not mentioned in other ancient Near Eastern texts. Josephus (*Ant* 1.6.1. [1:126]) identifies Riphat with the Paphlagonians, who lived between the Black Sea and Bithynia. This fits in well with the geographical location of the other peoples mentioned here, but Josephus' grounds for making this identification are unclear.

"Togarmah" (cf. 1 Chr 1:6) is associated in Ezek 27:13–14; 38:3–6 with Yavan, Meshek, Tubal, and Gomer. Second- and first-millennium Assyrian as well as Hittite texts mention a *Tegarama*, the name of a city and its surrounding district north of Carchemish on the trade route between Assyria and Kanish. Its name survives in modern Gurun. It may be identified with the area between the upper Halys and the Euphrates. Again, this roughly fits geographically with the other peoples related to Gomer (cf. *EM* 8,430–31).

4 "Elisha" (cf. 1 Chr 1:7; Ezek 27:7) is probably to be identified with Alašiya of Akkadian, Hittite, and Ugaritic inscriptions. *Alašiya* is usually supposed to be either the island of Cyprus or at least part of it. A Mycenaean (Greek) colony was established on Cyprus in the mid-second millennium B.C. and this could explain Elisha's being regarded as a son of Yavan. Berger (*WO* 13 [1982] 59), however, holds that Elisha is a city in the southern foothills of Crete, whose ruins are to be found at Haghio Kyrko. This avoids the problems posed by the mention of Kittim below, which is also generally identified with Cyprus. Greek settlement of Crete is well known.

"Tarshish." Although frequently mentioned in the OT, it is difficult to locate. It was reached by traveling west across the Mediterranean (Jon 1:3; 4:2), and it was a supplier of many of the luxuries at the Solomonic court (1 Kgs 10:22): gold, silver, ivory, apes, and peacocks are mentioned. It has usually been identified with Tartessos in western Spain, but modern commentators doubt whether the OT horizon stretched quite that far. Similarly, when Esarhaddon claimed to have subdued "all the kings who dwell in the midst of the sea, from Cyprus and Yaman as far as Tarshish" (Berger, 65), it seems unlikely that he actually meant Tartessos in Spain. Nor is it probable that Gen 10 would have regarded the Phoenician colony at Tartessos as a descendant of the Greeks. So various alternatives have been proposed, including Tunis, somewhere in Sardinia, or Rhodes, or western Anatolia. But none of these suggestions is totally convincing. More plausible is Berger's suggestion that Tarshish could be Carthage, the famous Phoenician colony in North Africa (*WO* 13 [1982] 64).

"Kittim" is usually identified with the island of Cyprus. It is surmised that the town Kition (*kty* in Phoenician inscriptions) near modern Larnaca gave its name to the whole area, for elsewhere in the OT Kittim always refers to an area or people, not a town (cf. Num 24:24; Isa 23:1; Ezek 27:6). However, it is odd that Kittim should be mentioned in such close proximity to Elisha, which is also usually identified with Cyprus. Westermann holds that Kittim and D(R)odanim are an independent addition to the list and that this explains the mention of both Elisha and Kittim. But both terms appear together in Ezek 27:7. So Speiser supposes that here Kittim does mean just the town Kition (cf. the city of Tarshish) while Elisha applies to the whole island. Even this is not completely satisfactory. If, though, Berger's suggestion that Elisha is a town on Crete and Kittim is Cyprus may be accepted, this problem would be eliminated.

"Dodanim." Some MT manuscripts, SamPent, LXX, and 1 Chr 1:7 have "Rodanim" instead. ר and ד are so similar that confusion is not surprising, and it is difficult to be sure which is the original reading. It is obviously simplest to accept Rodanim and identify them with the inhabitants of Rhodes. This is what most commentators do. According to the *lectio difficilior potior* principle, however, "Dodanim" should be preferred. On this basis Dodanim might be identified with the land of Danuna mentioned in the Amarna letters, apparently north of Tyre. Inscriptions of Rameses III mention a people *Dnn* among the invading sea peoples. And Homer sometimes gives the name Danaeans to those who besieged Troy. Sargon II's inscriptions mention the *Yadanāna,* apparently Greek-speaking inhabitants of Cyprus. Despite the widespread mention of *"dnn"* peoples in antiquity, it cannot be certain that the Dodanim are identical, given the variant spelling (cf. *EM* 2:626–27). Another possibility is that they are the Dodanoi, i.e., the inhabitants of Dodona, home of the oldest Greek oracle (so D. Neiman, *AOAT* 22 [1973] 121, and Berger, *WO* 13 [1982] 60).

5 "From these the nations. . . ." Similar though not identical remarks round off the sections devoted to the sons of Ham and sons of Shem (vv 20, 31) and the verse anticipates the final closing statement, v 32. For this reason it seems more likely that "these" refers to the sons of Japhet as opposed to just the sons of Javan. Admittedly, not all sons of Japhet can be described as coastland nations (the Hebrew term אי refers not just to islands but to lands adjoining the sea); but some obviously can be, and others are sufficiently distant from Israel that the description is intelligible. "Spread out" anticipates the decisive dispersal at Babel (11:1–9); "in their countries each with his own language by their clans" specifies the three main constituents of nationhood, territory, language, and race. (cf. *TDOT,* R. E. Clements, 2:426–27).

To sum up: so far as these Japhetic peoples can be identified, they seem to represent the nations furthest removed from Israel geographically. Some of them are described in Ezek 38:6 as coming "from the uttermost parts of the north." Others reflect Israel's western horizon, in Asia Minor and the Greek islands. Others, e.g., the Medes and Cimmerians, are those people beyond Israel's closer neighbors in Syria and Assyria. But from an Israelite perspective, these too are powers from the far north.

6–20 "The sons of Ham": the sheer length of this section indicates its importance. Among the sons of Ham are some of Israel's closest neighbors, who exercised a profound influence on her political and cultural life. This section sets these relationships in context.

The quite simple family tree of Japhet in vv 2–5 is unlike those of Ham in vv 6–20 and Shem in vv 21–31, which are much fuller. The latter two

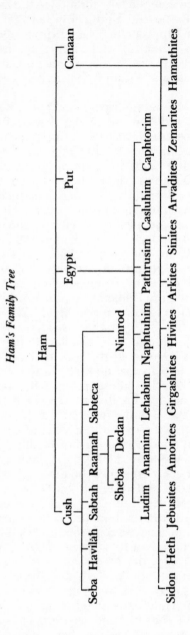

Ham's Family Tree

genealogies contain long expansions in a style different from the genealogy of Japhet, or their own opening sections of vv 6–7, 22–23. The source-critical implications of these observations have already been discussed (*Form/Structure/ Setting*). Here it may be noted that the family trees of Ham and Shem are arranged similarly.

Primary descendants	"The sons of Ham (Shem) were"	6–7,	22–23
Refrain	"X_1 fathered Y_1"	8,	24
Historical comments		9–12,	25
Refrain	"X_2 fathered Y_2"	13a,	26a
List of descendants		13b–14,	26b–29
Refrain	"X_3 fathered Y_3"	15	
List of descendants		16–18	
Definition of territory		19,	30
Closing formula (cf. v 5)	"These are the sons of Ham (Shem)"	20,	31

6 Note the similar introductory formulae in vv 2, 22. The list begins with four great nations listed in order from south to north. "Cush" lies to the south of Egypt, and is traditionally translated "Ethiopia," following LXX, but it probably covers a variety of dark-skinned tribes (cf. Jer 13:23) living beyond the southern border of Egypt. Note that most of Cush's descendants listed in the next verse seem to be located in Arabia.

"Egypt": Israel's well-known neighbor.

"Put." Though it has sometimes been suggested that this term is equivalent to Egyptian *Punt*, possibly in Somali, the equation is linguistically difficult. The traditional identification with Libya poses few problems; the two are associated in Nah 3:9 as Egypt's allies.

"Canaan" here includes the various peoples that inhabited the territory of modern Israel, Lebanon, and part of Syria. A more precise definition follows in vv 15–19. For a discussion of Canaan's boundaries, see Num 34:2–12 and Y. Aharoni, *The Land of the Bible* (London: Burns and Oates, 1966) 61–70.

7 These sons of Cush are all to be found in Arabia or close to it. "Seba" was clearly an important trading center (cf. Ps 72:10; Isa 43:3), but it is uncertain whether Josephus' location of it (*Ant.* 2.10.2 [2:249]) in upper Egypt at Meroe is correct. Recent commentators have suggested that it has been confused with the better known Sheba, others that it should be located in Arabia. But none of the evidence is decisive (*EM* 5:993–95).

"Havilah" is the same word as in 2:11, but whether the same place is meant is uncertain. If its root meaning is "sandy" (cf. "sand" חול), it could fit a number of places. Gen 25:18 and 1 Sam 15:7 encourage the supposition that it is somewhere in Arabia. Gispen suggests Haulan in South Arabia.

"Sabtah": the name is found only here and in 1 Chr 1:9. Josephus (*Ant* 1.6.2 [1:134]) identified it with Astaboras, modern Abare, but the popular modern suggestion is that it refers to Sabota, the capital of Hadramaut, nearly 270 miles north of Aden. For other suggestions see *EM* 5:996–97.

"Raamah," a trading center associated with Sheba in Ezek 27:22, is often identified with Ragmah, mentioned in Minaean and Sabaean inscriptions.

This would be near Negram in northern Yemen. However, it is unusual for
Hebrew ע to appear as *g* in Arabic. This leaves Raamah's relationship to
Sheba and Dedan (see below) as the only clue to its location, i.e., somewhere
in Arabia (cf. *EM* 7:388).

"Sabteca." No firm consensus about its location has emerged. Comparison
with the name of the Egyptian pharaoh Shebiktu (M. C. Astour, *JBL* 84
[1965] 422–25) does not help. However, Rabin (*EM* 5:997–98) points out
that several places in Arabia have names similar to the LXX version of the
name, Σαβακαθά, e.g., Aššabbak, near Medina, and Sembrachate, a trading
center mentioned by Pliny (*Natural History* 12:69), located in north Yemen
near the coast.

"Sheba." Yoqtan (10:28) had a son, and Abraham, a grandson (25:3), called
Sheba. This indicates the richness of Sabean tradition and its close associations
with Israel, especially in the days of Solomon (1 Kgs 10:1–13). Sheba was a
leading exporter of gold, frankincense, and other luxuries (cf. Ps 72:10, 15;
Isa 60:6). The kingdom of Sheba was apparently established at the beginning
of the first millennium B.C. and had its capital at Marib, about two hundred
miles north of Aden in southwest Arabia. It is also mentioned in Assyrian
inscriptions.

"Dedan." Like Sheba, Dedan is also said to be a descendant of Abraham
(25:3) and an important trading center (e.g., Ezek 27:20; 38:13). An inscription
has assured its precise location at Al-Alula, seventy miles southwest of Tema.
The settlement there dates from the first millennium B.C.; but Dedan is also
mentioned in cuneiform texts of the early second millennium.

8–12 This short narrative dealing with Nimrod is obviously different in
style from the preceding list-like material that constitutes the framework of
the table of nations. That it is an addition to the brief genealogy is indicated
by the narrative's backtracking in v 8. Five sons of Cush have already been
mentioned, then two grandsons, but now unexpectedly a sixth son of Cush,
Nimrod, is mentioned. The clause "X fathered (ילד) Y" occurs twice more
in the genealogy of Ham. Each time it introduces further details about Israel's
most influential neighbors: v 8, Mesopotamia; v 13, Egypt; and v 15, Canaan.
The description of Nimrod as a warrior links this passage back to 6:4, while
the mention of Babylon anticipates 11:1–9.

8 "Nimrod." The Bible gives no explanation of the name, though it could
be simply translated "We shall rebel," possibly foreshadowing 11:1–9. However, more recherché etymologies have frequently been offered. It has been
connected with Marduk, the patron god of Babylon, and with Ninurta, the
god of hunting and war. Others have attempted to find a historical king or
mythological figure lying behind the figure of Nimrod. Among suggested
royal figures, Sargon I of Akkad (D. J. Wiseman, *NBD*, 888), and Tukulti-
Ninurta I of Assyria (Speiser) have both found protagonists. Several (e.g.,
Gunkel and Skinner) have seen the figure of Gilgamesh behind Nimrod.
None of these suggestions is totally convincing, and it may be best to regard
Nimrod as an archetype of Mesopotamian ideals of kingship (cf. Abramsky,
BMik 25 [1980/81] 237–55). According to their inscriptions, the kings of Meso-
potamia were especially fond and proud of their achievements in building
and fighting, and some boast too of their hunting exploits. A few, e.g., Gilga-

mesh, were credited with divine blood in their veins, a point possibly hinted at here by the description of Nimrod as a champion (cf. 6:4). Though Mesopotamian ideals are here allowed full play, their nemesis is described in 11:1–9.

"Who began to be a champion in the earth." "Began," הֵחֵל, is used in 4:26; 6:1; 9:20 of other significant innovators in world history . "Champion," גִּבּוֹר, is the usual term to describe a great soldier, e.g., 1 Sam 9:1. Whether it has here the suggestion of supernatural parentage as in 6:4 is unclear.

9 "Champion hunter" is literally "champion of game," צַיִד, a term used frequently in the story of Esau, the other great hunter in Genesis (e.g., 25:27–28). The epic of Gilgamesh relates his hunting triumphs, and Assyrian kings also display their prowess in palace reliefs. "Before the LORD" is probably no more than a superlative. The phrase does not necessarily imply God's approval or otherwise of Nimrod's activity, simply that it stood out as remarkable (cf. 6:11; 7:1). "It used to be said" suggests that "Like Nimrod, a champion hunter before the LORD" was a traditional proverb (cf. 1 Sam 19:24) though it may mean that a written source is being quoted (cf. Num 21:14).

10 "The prime," רֵאשִׁית, has both chronological and qualitative significance. The word refers to the beginning of time in 1:1, and it is regularly used in the law of firstfruits (e.g., Lev 2:12; Deut 26:2). And because something is first, it is expected to be the best: Gen 49:3, Deut 21:17. If "Babylon" (בָּבֶל, Akk *bâb-ili*, "gate of the god") was not the earliest foundation of Mesopotamia (it goes back at least to the third millennium), by the first millennium it was certainly the most prestigious.

"Erech," known as Unu(g) by the Sumerians and Uruk by the Babylonians, is present-day Warka, forty miles northwest of Ur. It was one of the earliest Sumerian cities, and Gilgamesh was once its king.

"Akkad." Under Sargon I, a powerful Semitic dynasty flourished here *ca.* 2350, but the site of the city has not been located. It gave its name to the Semitic language of Mesopotamia, Akkadian.

"Calneh" is probably different from that mentioned in Amos 6:2 and Isa 10:9, modern Kullan Koy in northern Syria. No town with this name is known in Babylonia (the land of Shinar), but the proposal to revocalize Calneh as *kullānāh* "all of them" to avoid the problem is questionable.

"The country of Shinar" is mentioned several times in the OT, but its etymology and boundaries are uncertain (cf. 11:2; 14:1; Isa 11:11; Dan 1:2; Zech 5:11). The term "Shinar" is not used in Mesopotamian documents, only in biblical and western texts, e.g., Egyptian, *Sangar*; Hittite, *šanḫar;* also El Amarna (24:4,95; 35:49), for the Cassite kingdom of Babylon. From its usage in extrabiblical texts it can be seen to be an old term originating before 1500 B.C. and possibly derived from an archaic pronunciation of Sumer (*EM* 8, 225–28). Recently R. Zadok (*ZA* 74 [1984] 240–44) has suggested that Shinar comes from *Samḫarû*, apparently the name of a Cassite tribe who lived in Babylonia.

11 "Went out Ashur." This, it is admitted, is the more natural way to construe the Hebrew, though if necessary, it could be understood "he [i.e., Nimrod] went out to Ashur." In support of the latter interpretation it is argued that, since the first of Nimrod's deeds is mentioned in v 10, this

verse must give further details of his career. The description of Assyria as
the "land of Nimrod" in Mic 5:5 [6] may support this. However, since ראשית
"prime" may not refer to strictly chronological precedence, this argument is
not conclusive. But whether Nimrod or Ashur is construed as the subject of
"went out," this verse contains an interesting reflection on the cultural relationship between northern and southern Mesopotamia. Sumerian civilization
spread from the south (Shinar) to the north, i.e., Assyria.

"Nineveh" (Assyrian *Ninua*) was the most important city of Assyria after
Ashur. It was founded *ca.* 4500 B.C., and its ruins are opposite modern Mosul.

"Rehobot-Ir": literally, "city-squares." This may be the name of a suburb
of Nineveh, a description of Nineveh itself (so Sasson, *RB* 90 [1983] 96), or
even an interpretation of the name of the city of Ashur (cf. *NBD*, 1083).

"Calah" (Assyrian *Kalḫu*) is identified with modern Nimrud, twenty-four
miles south of Nineveh, and was first settled in the early third millennium.
It is not, however, mentioned in historical records until *ca.* 1250 B.C. It was
made the capital of Assyria in the ninth century B.C.

12 "Resen" is probably equivalent to Akk *rēš-ēni* "fountainhead." A number
of places called this are known in Assyria, but none of them lies between
Nineveh and Calah. Wiseman suggests that Hamam Ali, on the right bank
of the Tigris eight miles south of Nineveh, might be a suitable location (*NBD*,
1085).

"The big city." Both Nineveh and Calah deserve this epithet, but although
it is more natural grammatically to apply it to Calah, the frequent description
of Nineveh (e.g., Jonah 1:2; 3:2, 3, etc.) as a "great city" makes most commentators suppose it refers to Nineveh.

13–14 "Egypt fathered" introduces the second main expansion of the
basic genealogy of Ham (cf. vv 9–12, 15–19). In that all the sons of Egypt
are really names of peoples with the characteristic ending *-im*, it seems likely
that the editor is drawing on a different tradition from that of Nimrod. The
inclusion of this material about Egypt fits in with the concern evident in
this table to clarify Israel's relations with her most important neighbors. Note
that the shortest names are listed first, e.g., "Ludim"; the triliterals "Anamim,"
"Lehabim" next; and the longest, e.g., "Casluhim" last.

"Ludim" are also mentioned in Jer 46:9. The singular Lud is a son of
Shem according to 10:22. This form reappears in Isa 66:19; Ezek 27:10;
30:5; and may well refer to the Lydians. However, the "Ludim" cannot be
identified, but it would seem likely that they lived in or near Egypt.

"Anamim." There is no clue to their identity unless *Tg. Ps.-J.* is justified
in its rendering "Maryutai," which might point to a home in Egypt west of
Alexandria (*EM* 6, 309).

"Lehabim" is generally regarded as an alternative spelling of "Lubim,"
the Libyans, inhabitants of North Africa west of Egypt.

"Naphtuhim." *Tg. Ps-J.* translates "Pentaskinai," which would place them
in the northeast delta region of Egypt (*EM* 5:905). Kitchen (*NBD*, 865) offers
three different Egyptian etymologies of "Naphtuhim," i.e., "the men of Lower
(i.e., northern) Egypt"; "they of the Delta," "they of the Oasis land."

14 "Pathrusim": the people of Pathros (cf. Jer 44:1, 15; Ezek 29:14; 30:14),
the Egyptian name for upper Egypt, i.e., the southern part of the country
which stretches from Cairo to Aswan.

"Casluhim." Attempts to identify the Casluhim are little more than guesses. *Tg. Ps.-J.* translates "Pentapolitai," i.e., from Cyrene. Other possibilities mooted include the inhabitants of Mount Casios (east of the Nile Delta), or Scylace in Asia Minor or the Tjekker, one of the sea peoples.

"Where the Philistines came from." At first glance it looks as though this comment ought to follow "Caphtorim" (the Cretans), for elsewhere the OT states the Philistines came from Caphtor (Amos 9:7; cf. Jer 47:4), but given our ignorance about the identity and location of the Casluhim, we cannot be so dogmatic. That the Philistines are linked both with the Cretans and the Casluhim suggests a close association between these two groups. Or it may be that the Philistines of Genesis represent a different group from the Philistines of the post-conquest period (so Cassuto 2:207-8; Kitchen, *POTT*, 56.)

"Caphtorim," i.e., Cretans. Some of them settled in southwest Canaan (cf. Deut 2:23). Were racial kinship the only governing principle in the table of nations, one might have expected the Caphtorim to be classed as a son of Japhet. But as has often been noted the principles governing the arrangement of this list are manifold: geographical, linguistic, social, and political as well as racial characteristics determine the arrangement of the peoples.

15–19 The relevance of Canaan to Israel explains the amount of detail included here. As with the two earlier expansions of Ham's genealogy, this begins "X fathered Y"; cf. vv 8, 13. The boundaries of Canaan as defined in Num 34 and in Egyptian texts take in the Phoenician coastline (modern Lebanon) as well as southwest Syria, so Westermann's observation that Israel never claimed this territory is mistaken.

"Sidon his first-born" reflects tradition that this was the most ancient Phoenician settlement. The Phoenicians certainly regarded themselves as Canaanites. Sidon lies halfway between Tyre and Beirut.

"Heth." In the OT, Heth, or the Hittites, must be distinguished from the great empire whose capital, Hattušas, was in Turkey. The "land of the Hittites" and "the kings of the Hittites" refer to certain Syrian kings who once belonged to the Hittite empire in Asia Minor. However, in the OT "Hittites" usually refers to some of the pre-Israelite inhabitants of the hill country in the days of the patriarchs and somewhat later. All those named in the OT have good Semitic names, which makes their affiliation to Canaan the more intelligible here (cf. H. A. Hoffner, "The Hittites and Hurrians," *POTT*, 197–228).

16–17 "Jebusites, . . . Hivites": four of the pre-Israelite inhabitants of the land. "The Jebusites" dwelt in and around Jerusalem. Indeed, the OT several times calls Jerusalem "Jebus" (e.g., Judg 19:10–11), but this name is not used in extra-biblical sources. To judge from the personal names of the Jebusites that have been preserved, e.g., Abdiḥepa, Araunah, Ornan, the Jebusites were not a Semitic people, but possibly Hurrian.

"Amorites": another group of the pre-Israelite dwellers in Canaan according to the OT, often mentioned in extrabiblical texts. They spoke a west-Semitic language akin to Canaanite. Not only were some of the most famous dynasties of Babylon, Mari, and Ashur of Amorite descent, there was also an Amorite kingdom just north of the border of Canaan. The OT, however, seems to use the term rather loosely, either of any of the pre-Israelite inhabitants of Canaan (Josh 10:5) or Transjordan (Og and Sihon are called Amorites in

Deut 3:8), or specifically of certain people who dwelt in the hill country as opposed to Canaanites who tended to live in the cities on the coastal plain (Josh 11:3; see further M. Liverani, "The Amorites," *POTT*, 100-33).

"Girgashites." Apart from being regularly mentioned in lists (15:21; Deut 7:1; Josh 3:10; 24:11) we know very little about the Girgashites. They were apparently known at Ugarit, for someone is called *grgš* and another *bn grgš*. Kitchen (*NBD*, 471) doubts whether they are to be identified with the Karkisa in Hittite and *krkš* in Egyptian sources.

17 "Hivites." Though they are often mentioned, we again have little precise information about these people. Their main centers seem to have been well north in Lebanon and Syria (Josh 11:3; Judg 3:3), but some are found as far south as Shechem and Gibeon (Gen 34:2; Josh 9:1,7). Occasionally there is textual confusion of Hivite with Horite, which has led to the suggestion that the groups should be identified. But this seems unlikely.

That the Hivites lived mainly in the north may be confirmed by the next five peoples named: the first four, the inhabitants of Arqa, Sin, Arvad, Ṣumur, are on the Phoenician coast, while Hamath is somewhat inland.

"Arqa," twelve miles northeast of Tripoli, has archeological remains dating back to the Early Bronze Age. It is mentioned in various oriental sources of the second and first millennia. It was called by the Romans Caesarea Libani.

"Sin." A town *Siannu/a* is mentioned in Ugaritic and neo-Assyrian texts. It was evidently a Phoenician coastal town near Arqa, but its precise location is uncertain.

18 Arvad, modern Ruad, an island city lying two miles off shore, fifty miles north of Byblos. The most northerly Phoenician city, it was a famous and flourishing center in the second and first millennia B.C. It is mentioned in the Amarna letters, neo-Assyrian texts, and in Ezek 27:8, 11.

"Zemarites." Ṣumur is the name of this city in the Amarna letters, and slightly different spellings are found in later Assyrian texts. Tiglath-Pileser I locates it three double-hours south of Arvad. But though various suggestions have been made (see *EM* 6:740–42), there is no obvious candidate for this important site.

"Hamath": modern Hama on the Orontes. A city has been on this site from about 4000 B.C. For a while, it was a vassal of David and Solomon (2 Sam 8:9–10; 2 Chr 8:4), and later it was reconquered by Jeroboam II (2 Kgs 14:28). It is most often mentioned in the OT as being near the northern border of the promised land of Canaan (e.g., Num 34:8; Josh 13:5).

"Afterwards the clans of the Canaanites scattered." Cf. the similar remark in v 5: "From these the nations . . . spread out." "Afterwards" means after the birth of all the peoples listed in vv 15–18; "scattered" or "were scattered" may both appropriately translate the niphal of פוץ. This is the first time this key term of 11:1–9 appears (9:19 is from a different root). Though the term is apparently used in a neutral, innocent sense, it may yet be foreshadowing the judgment to befall all mankind at Babel. The Canaanites are often viewed in the Pentateuch as *the* sinful nation who deserve God's wrath.

19 For their sins the Canaanites lost their native land, so the text goes on to define the boundaries of their territory, the first definition of the not-yet-promised land in Genesis. It is the significance of the land in Genesis that explains the apparently unnecessary details being provided here.

This definition of the borders of Canaan is less precise than that found in Num 34:2–12, but it nevertheless seems to have much the same entity in mind. Though some of the places cannot be certainly located, this would not seem to justify the postulation of two traditions as Westermann does. The most northerly coastal town of importance in Canaan is "Sidon." Its western border is defined by the Mediterranean as far south as "Gerar." The preferred modern identification of Gerar is Tell Abu Hureira, eleven miles southeast of Gaza, rather than Tell Jemmeh, eight miles south of Gaza (cf. *EM* 2:561–64). It is not clear why Gaza should be mentioned after Gerar, since Gerar is the further south. It may be that because it is better known, it has been added as a clarifying gloss. Rainey (*TA* 9 [1982] 132) suggests that Gaza is mentioned here as the most influential town on the southern coast of Canaan, corresponding to Sidon on the northern coast.

"Sodom, Gomorrah, Admah, and Zeboim" are the cities of the plain overthrown in the destruction of Gen 19. Whether they lie south, east, or north of the Dead Sea is a matter of dispute (see further discussion on Gen 14). However, that the Dead Sea and Jordan Valley mark the eastern boundary of Canaan is clear in Num 34:12. The area of these four cities, then, evidently indicates the southeastern extremity of Canaan.

The final phrase, "up to Lasha," is mysterious. On the analogy of "up to Gaza," it might be supposed that Lasha is the better-known place, clarifying the uncertain location of Sodom, etc. However, this word occurs only here in the OT, so it has been proposed to emend it to Bela (cf. 14:2) or Laish (cf. Judg 18:7; this would make Lasha/Laish the northeastern corner of Canaan). Traditionally, Lasha has been identified with Kallirhoe, east of the Dead Sea. None of these conjectures will carry conviction until the location of Sodom and Gomorrah is more certain.

It should be noted that Gerar, as well as the cities of the plain, occupies a prominent place in the subsequent patriarchal narratives (cf. Gen 20–21, 26, Gerar; 13–14, 18–19, cities of the plain). Thus this apparently irrelevant note about Canaan's boundaries serves to set the scene for the subsequent promise narratives.

20 On this formula, cf. vv 5, 31–32. Here the framework of the genealogy is resumed, as the important digressions about Babylon, Egypt, and Canaan are complete.

21–31 The genealogy of Shem is also framed by the typical opening and closing formulae (vv 22, 31). It is placed last because Shem fathers the elect line, and the chosen line is always dealt with last. Theological dead-ends (cf. Cain's line) are mentioned before the main highway is described. There is obviously some overlap between the account of Shem's descendants here and in 11:10–26 (cf. the two genealogies of Adam 4:1–26; 5:1–32). Though the presence of two overlapping genealogies may be due to the existence of two sources, it is also characteristic of Genesis to adumbrate the contents of the next section of the book toward the end of the previous section; cf. 6:5–8 before 6:9–9:29. Furthermore, this account of Shem's descendants mentions various theological cul-de-sacs among the Shemites, whereas 11:10–26 is solely concerned with tracing through the holy line from Shem to Abram. A similar relationship subsists between Gen 4 and 5.

The importance of the genealogy of Shem is indicated not simply by its

being placed last and by its repetition in Gen 11, but by its various expansions
that are made apparent by comparing it with the genealogy of Japhet in
10:1–5. Comparison of the two genealogies shows that vv 21, 24–30 are supplementary to the basic framework of vv 22–23, 31.

21 "Now to Shem also (children) were born. . . ." This extra introductory
sentence sets off Shem's descendants from those of Ham and Japhet; cf.
4:26. Despite the hesitation of Skinner and Westermann, an explicit subject
of "were born" is not indispensable. If one is required, "the sons of Shem"
could serve, since several times ילד (qal passive), singular, takes a plural
subject (e.g., 10:25; 35:26).

"Father of all the sons of Eber." Since 10:24 and 11:13–14 make Shem
the great-grandfather of Eber, "father" must be understood here in the looser
sense of "forefather, ancestor." "Sons of Eber" occurs only here in the OT.
"Hebrew" (עברי) is the gentilic of Eber (עבר), so presumably this remark
looks forward to the emergence of the Hebrews from Shem's line.

"The oldest brother of Japhet" reflects the modern consensus translation
of אחי יפת הגדול. The adjective "oldest" modifies "brother." LXX, Symmachus, Rashi, possibly the MT, and Cassuto suppose, however, that "oldest"
modifies "Japhet." Combined with the comment that Ham is the youngest,
the former view makes the order in the family "Shem, Japhet, Ham" whereas
the latter makes it "Japhet, Shem, Ham"; cf. *Comment* on 9:24.

22–31 Shem's family tree is shown on the following page.

22 "Elam." The powerful eastern neighbor and rival of Mesopotamia
from earliest times. Elamite is not a Semitic language, and the classification
of Elam as a son of Shem probably reflects cultural and geographical considerations. From the later third millennium B.C. Semites lived in Elam. Chedorlaomer (14:1, 9) was king of Elam, and in later times Assyrians deported
Israelites to Elam (Ezra 4:9; Isa 11:11; *EM* 6:189–99).

"Ashur." or Assyria is the name of the people and country of northern
Mesopotamia that is often mentioned in the OT. Its old capital was also
called Ashur (2:14 cf. 10:11), as was its national god. Why it should be mentioned both here and 10:11 under Ham is not clear. There was another
Ashur, apparently a northern Sinaitic tribe (cf. 25:3, 18; Num 24:22, 24; 2
Sam 2:9; Ps 83:9 [8]). This might be the reference here. Or in the light of
the positive attitude to Ashur implied by calling him "son of Shem," it may
be that this list originated long before Assyria threatened Israel.

"Arpachshad." From Josephus (*Ant* 1.6.4 [1:144]) to Westermann, many
have argued that this must be a reference to Babylon. The only supports
for this notion are (a) the theory that the last three letters of Arpachshad,
kšd, could spell *kaśdîm*, i.e., Chaldaeans, and (b) the conviction that somewhere
Babylon must appear among the sons of Shem. But since Babylon has already
been mentioned explicitly in v 10, would it have been essential for the final
redactor to mention it again here? Another possibility is that Arpachshad
represents a corruption of *Arrapḫa* (modern Kirkuk) in northern Iraq. It is
unusual for *ḫ* to appear in Hebrew as *k*, and the last two letters remain
unexplained. "For the present . . . the problem remains insoluble" (Speiser,
70).

"Lud"; cf. v 13, "Ludim." The identification of both groups is difficult;

Shem's Family Tree

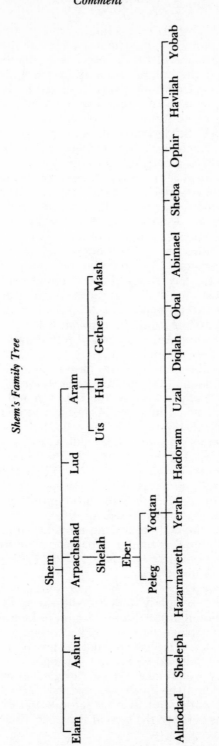

cf. *Comment* on v 13. Possibly Lud is the Lydians of Asia Minor (so Josephus, *Ant.* 1.6.4 [1.144]), known in Assyria as *Luddu*. Admittedly, they were not a Semitic people, but since Elam was not either, this does not prove much. Another possibility is the Lubdu who lived on the upper Tigris.

"Aram." This name in various forms is attested from the third millennium onwards. Indeed a settlement in the eastern Tigris region, north of Elam and east of Assyria, called Aramu, is known. This has been linked with Amos 9:7, which associates the Syrians with Kir, and with Isa 22:6, which links Kir and Elam (K. A. Kitchen, *NBD*, 56). However, the Aramaeans only became significant historically as a people at the end of the second millennium, when a series of Aramaean states in Syria became important. The patriarchs are portrayed as having particularly close relations with Aramaeans (25:20; 31:20; Deut 26:5), which may explain why four descendants of Aram are listed in the next verse. (See also A. Malamat, "The Aramaeans," *POTT*, 134–55).

23 Very little is known about any of these groups either from elsewhere in the Bible or outside, which according to Cassuto and Gispen argues for the antiquity of this data. "Utz" could be the same as Job's home (Job 1:1). However, this is so vaguely located that it does not really help. Furthermore, Job's Utz seems close to Edom, i.e., southeast of Israel (Job 2:11; cf. Lam 4:21), whereas one would expect an Aramaean tribe of Utz to be found somewhere to the north. A connection between Utz and Aram is also hinted at in Gen 22:21, which makes Utz a son of Nahor and uncle of Aram. "Hul" and "Gether" are otherwise unknown.

"Mash." Two possible identifications have been advanced—Mount Masius in northern Mesopotamia (Tur Abdin) or the *Mâšu* mountains of the Gilga- mesh Epic (9:2, 1–2) which could be the Lebanon and anti-Lebanon ranges. The Samaritan Pentateuch here reads Masha, which is the name of one of the sons of Ishmael (25:14).

24–30 These verses constitute the major expansion of the basic genealogy of Shem in vv 22–23, 31. It is arranged like the similar expansion of Ham's genealogy; see *Comment* on 10:6–20. Vv 24–25a parallel and summarize the data found more fully in 11:12–17. V 25b looks forward to 11:1–9. The sources of the rest of the material cannot be so readily identified.

24 Shelah normally means "weapon, missile." But it seems very unlikely that a personal name should have this meaning. Less improbable is the sugges- tion that Shelah is a god's name (a Canaanite underworld deity, according to M. Tsevat, "The Canaanite God Šälaḥ," *VT* 4 [1954] 41–49) applied to a man. But even this is uncertain.

"Eber." Cf. *Comment* on v 21. The name probably means "the one who crosses over." That it is rightly understood as an individual personal name is confirmed by mention at Ebla of an Ebrium as king there.

25 "Peleg" comes from the root פלג "to divide"; as a common noun it means "canal, channel." Here the etymology gives it a more abstract sense, "division." Like many biblical names this is prophetic, in that it foreshadows the great events that would take place in Peleg's lifetime.

"Because in his days the earth was divided." Here "the earth" denotes the peoples of the world. But in what sense was it divided? Some suggest that the division was between the sons of Peleg, i.e., sedentary agriculturalists who depended on irrigation channels (*pĕlāgîm*), and the sons of Yoqtan, wandering Arab tribes (e.g., D. J. Wiseman, *NBD* 957; cf. *EM* 6:481–82). More likely it refers to the dispersal of the nations at Babel (11:1–9). Admittedly the verb used there, "disperse" (פוץ), is not "to divide" (פלג). But פלג can be used of confusing speech (Ps 55:10 [9]). Peleg could also be taken as a place name. Falga on the Euphrates is mentioned in hellenistic writings.

The descendants of Peleg are not mentioned here, as they will be taken up in 11:18–26. The genealogy therefore concludes by dealing with Peleg's brother Yoqtan and his offspring.

"Yoqtan." The etymology and meaning are obscure. KB (411) compares Arabic *juqẓān* "wakeful." The most obvious Hebrew root to compare it to is קטן "to be small": Yoqtan was younger than Peleg. Tribes in southern Arabia claim that pure Arabs are descended from *Qaḥṭān* Yoqtan. The connection of Yoqtan with South Arabia seems to be confirmed by the names of his sons. They lend themselves to Arabic etymologies, and some at least may be located in Arabia.

26 "Almodad" could mean "the (*al*) friend (*modad*)," or if the LXX ('Ελμωδάδ) is correct "God (El) is friend," but it is otherwise unknown outside the Bible.

"Sheleph" has been identified with a district Silf, and with Yemenite tribes called Salf or Sulf, all near Aden.

"Hasarmaveth" (literally, "enclosure [oasis] of Mot [god of death]"; *EM* 3:279) is the well-known district of Hadramaut east of Yemen.

"Yerah," literally, "moon." The moon was the leading deity in the South Arabian pantheon.

27 "Hadoram" (literally, "[the god] Hadad is exalted,") was also a personal name (1 Chr 18:10; 2 Chr 10:18). It is attested as a personal or tribal name in a Sabaean inscription.

"Uzal." Probably = Azal, which, according to Arabic tradition, was the old name of Sanaa, the capital of Yemen. (The Uzal mentioned in Ezek 27:19 may well be in northeast Syria; A. R. Millard, *NBD,* 1307).

"Diqlah," literally, "date palm," is presumably the name of some date-growing oasis in Arabia.

28 "Obal" could be equated with ʿUbal, a place between Hodeida and Sanaa, or a Yemenite tribe Banū ʿUbal (KB, 750).

"Abimael," literally, "my father, truly, is god." The infixed *ma* ("truly") suggests that it could be a Sabaean formation although it is also found in west Semitic. Apart from 1 Chr 1:22, the name is otherwise unknown.

"Sheba." Cf. *Comment* on 10:7.

29 "Ophir." The source of the best gold in biblical times, evidently reached by ships sailing from the southern port of Ezion-geber ("Eilat"; 1 Kgs 9:26–28; Ps 45.10[9]). It has been located in various sites between South Africa and India. However, assuming that Ophir, the gold producer, is the same as the son of Yoqtan, it would seem most probable that, like the other names here, it is to be located in southwest Arabia (cf. D. J. Wiseman, *NBD,* 911).

"Havilah." Cf. *Comment* on v 7. This is another region famed for its gold (2:11).

"Yobab" ("wilderness"?; KB 381). Four other Yobabs are mentioned in the OT (36:33; Josh 11:1; 1 Chr 8:9, 18). Cassuto mentions a tribe called Yuhaybib in southern Arabia.

30 "Their settlement. . . ." "Their" refers to all the sons of Yoqtan discussed in the previous verses. As in v 19, this verse defines the territory of the peoples just discussed. Unfortunately, it is extremely obscure. Neither "Mesha," "Saphar," nor "the eastern mountain" can be positively identified. Sephar might be the coastal town of Ṣaphar in southern Arabia, but the different initial sibilant makes this questionable. Most commentators guess that Mesha represents the western limit of the Yoqtanites and Sephar the eastern, and that the territory lies within southern Arabia, but certainty is impossible.

31 This verse closes the discussion of the sons of Shem; cf. similar formulae in vv 5, 20.

32 The table of nations is rounded off with neat inclusions with v 1. Note the echoing phraseology—"These," "sons of Noah," "descendants/family history" (תולדת), "after the flood"—that links vv 1 and 32. But whereas v 1 says "children were born," v 32 states that "the nations spread out," anticipating the great dispersal at Babel about to be discussed.

The Tower of Babel (11:1–9)

Bibliography

Alster, B. "An Aspect of 'Enmerkar and the Lord of Aratta.'" *RA* 67 (1973) 101–9. **Anderson, B. W.** "Unity and Diversity in God's Creation: A Study of the Babel Story." *CurTM* 5 (1978) 69–81. **Auffret, P.** *La sagesse a bâti sa maison.* Fribourg: Editions Universitaires, 1982. 69–90. **Banon, D.** "Babel ou l'idolâtrie embusquée." *BCPE* 32 (1980) 5–30. **Cohen, S.** *Enmerkar and the Lord of Aratta.* Ph.D. Dissertation: University of Pennsylvania, 1973. 419–29. **Couffignal, R.** "La Tour de Babel: Approches nouvelles de Gen 11:1–9." *RevThom* 83 (1983) 59–70. **Dahood, M.** "Northwest Semitic Notes on Genesis." *Bib* 55 (1974) 76–82. **Fokkelmann, J. P.** *Narrative Art in Genesis.* Assen: Van Gorcum, 1975. **Frentz, A.** "Der Turmbau." *VT* 19 (1969) 183–95. **Gelb, I. J.** "The Name of Babylon." *Journal of the Institute of Asian Studies* 1 (1955) 1–4. **Gurney, O. R.,** and **S. N. Kramer.** *Sumerian Literary Texts in the Ashmolean Museum.* Oxford: Clarendon Press, 1976. **Kikawada, I. M.** "The Shape of Genesis 11:1–9." In *Rhetorical Criticism: Essays in Honor of J. Muilenburg,* ed. J. J. Jackson and M. Kessler. Pittsburgh: Pickwick Press, 1974. 18–32. **Kramer, S. N.** "The 'Babel of Tongues': A Sumerian Version." *JAOS* 88 (1968) 108–11. ———. "Enki and His Inferiority Complex." *Or* 39 (1970) 103–10. **Laurin, R. B.** "The Tower of Babel Revisited." In *Biblical and Near Eastern Studies: Essays in Honor of W. L. Lasor,* ed. G. A. Tuttle. Grand Rapids: Eerdmans, 1978. 142–45. **Margulis, B.** "A 'Weltbaum' in Ugaritic Literature?" *JBL* 90 (1971) 481–82. **Pury, A. de.** "La Tour de Babel et la vocation d'Abraham." *ETR* 53 (1978) 80–97. **Röllig, W.** "Der Turm zu Babel." *Der babylonische Turm: Aufbruch ins Masslose,* ed A. Rosenberg. Munich: Kösel Verlag, 1975. 35–46. **Ross, A. P.** "The Dispersion of the Nations in Gen 11:1–9." *BSac* 138 (1981) 119–38. **Sasson, J. M.** "The 'Tower of Babel' as a Clue to the Redactional Structuring of the Primeval History." In *The Bible World: Essays in Honor of C. H. Gordon,* ed. G. Rendsburg, R. Adler, M.

Arfa, and N. H. Winter. New York: Ktav, 1980. 211–19. **Seybold, K.** "Der Turmbau zu Babel: Zur Entstehung von Gen 11:1–9." *VT* 26 (1976) 453–79. **Soden, W. von.** "Etemenanki von Asarhaddon nach der Erzählung vom Turmbau zu Babel und dem Erra-Mythos." *UF* 3 (1971) 253–63. ———. "Zum hebräischen Wörterbuch." *UF* 13 (1981) 157–64. **Speiser, E. A.** "Word Plays on the Creation Epic's Version of the Founding of Babylon." *Or* 25 (1955/56) 317–23. = *Oriental and Biblical Studies*, 53–62. **Strus, A.** "La poétique sonore des récits de la Genèse." *Bib* 60 (1979) 1–22. **Van Dijk, J.** "La 'confusion des langues': Note sur le lexique et sur la morphologie d'Enmerkar." *Or* 39 (1970) 302–10. **Wallis, G.** "Die Stadt in den Überlieferungen der Genesis." *ZAW* 78 (1966) 133–48. **Witt, D. S. de.** "The Historical Background of Gen 11:1–9: Babel or Ur?" *JETS* 22 (1979) 15–26.

Translation

[1] *The whole earth had*[a] *one language and one kind of speech.*[b]

[2] *When they journeyed*[a] *in*[b] *the East, they found a plain in the country of Shinar and they settled there.*

[3] *They said to each other, "Come,*[a] *let us make*[b] *bricks and bake*[b] *them*[c] *thoroughly."* [d] *So they had bricks for stone and asphalt for mortar.*[d] [4] *Then they said, "Come,*[a] *let us build for ourselves*[b] *a city and a tower*[c] *with its top in the sky*[c] *to make for ourselves*[b] *a name, lest we are scattered*[d] *over the face of the whole earth."*

[5] *Then the* LORD *came down to*[a] *see the city and the tower which mankind had built.*

[6] *The* LORD *said, "Since*[a] *they are one people and they all*[b] *have one language and this is the beginning*[c] *of their activity, now*[d] *lest nothing they plot*[c] *to do be beyond*[f] *them,* [7] *come,*[a] *let us*[b] *go down and mix*[c] *up their language there so that*[d] *they cannot understand each other's language."*

[8] *Then the* LORD *scattered*[a] *them from there over the face of the whole earth and they stopped building the city.*[b]

[9] *Therefore its name was called*[a] *Babel, because there the* LORD *mixed up the language of the whole earth and from there the* LORD *scattered*[b] *them over the face of the whole earth.*

Notes

1.a. The verb, 3 masc sg impf היה, does not agree with the term "earth." So Gispen suggests it agrees with כל "whole"; Westermann, that it anticipates ויהי at the beginning of v 2.

1.b. G adds πᾶσιν "for all."

2.a. ב + inf constr נסע + 3 masc pl suff.

2.b. G, Vg take מקדם as *from the* East," but many modern commentators cite 13:11 in support of translating it "eastward." The former translation is more natural, but clearly the issue depends on where the people are supposed to have come from before arriving in Babylon: "in the East" leaves the issue undecided.

3.a. הבה, probably impv from יהב "to give," has become purely hortatory (*SBH*, 57).

3.b. 1 pl coh שׂרף/לבן.

3.c. "Them" understood from previous clause. Note how the two clauses complement each other (*SBH*, 98).

3.d-d. Note chiasmus "was . . . bricks // asphalt . . . was," tying the two aspects of the event together (*SBH*, 20).

4.a. הבה; cf. 11:3a.

4.b. וֹנּ: the doubled letter *l* is euphonic, *daghes̆ forte conjunctivum*, and is found following *eh* on words whose first syllable is stressed (GKC, 20f; Lambdin, 208). "For ourselves": so-called ethical dative, used to emphasize the significance of an action for a particular subject (GKC, 119s).

4.c-c. Verbless circumstantial clause (*SBH*, 85).

4.d. 1 pl impf qal, פוץ.

5.a. ל + inf, expressing purpose (GKC, 114g).

6.a. Cf. use of הנה to introduce subordinate clause (Lambdin, 169–71), and parallel construction in 3:22.

6.b. כל + 3 masc pl suff.

6.c. Inf constr hiph חלל + 3 masc pl suff.

6.d. On use of ועתה, cf. H. A. Brongers (*VT* 15 [1965] 289–99).

6.e. 3 masc pl impf qal, זמם (GKC, 67 dd).

6.f. 3 masc sg impf niph, בצר.

7.a. Cf. use of הבה in vv 3, 4.

7.b. "Let us," echoing v 4 and analogous usage to 1:26; cf. discussion there.

7.c. 1 pl coh, בלל (GKC, 67 dd).

7.d. Unusual for אשר to introduce final clause, but cf. Exod 20:26 (Joüon, 186f).

8.a. Waw consec + 3 masc sg impf hiph פוץ.

8.b. SamPent, G add "and the tower," assimilating to vv 4–5.

9.a. Lit., "one called," 3 masc sg "he called" being used for indefinite subj (GKC, 144d, Joüon, 155e) cf. 16:14; 19:22.

9.b. 3 masc sg pf hiph פוץ + 3 masc pl suff.

Form/Structure/Setting

The tower of Babel is a short but brilliant example of Hebrew story telling. The compositional techniques have been thoroughly explored by Cassuto, Fokkelmann, Kikawada, and Auffret. Word play, chiasmus, paronomasia, and alliteration are just some of the devices used to unify and accentuate the message of the tale.

Its beginning and end are marked by an inclusion—"the whole earth had one language" (v 1) . . . "the language of the whole earth" (v 9)—and semantically "a plain in the country of Shinar" (v 2) corresponds to "Babel" (v 9). The overall arrangement of the story has parallels elsewhere in the primeval history. The double ויהי opening of vv 1–2 matches 4:2b–3, while הן "since" plus ועתה "now" plus a final clause (vv 6–7) parallels the similar conclusion in 3:22. The etiological "therefore" על־כן (v 9) echoes the concluding comment of 2:24. These features of the narrative show that the tower of Babel narrative is very much at home in the primeval history and bears several of the hallmarks of the style of these chapters.

Furthermore, the narrative builds towards the explanation of the name of Babylon, Babel. As elsewhere in Genesis (cf. Adam, Noah, Eve), a proper name is pre-echoed in the story long before the word itself is heard. As soon as the men of Babylon start speaking they use words that contain the consonants *b* and *l*, or *p* and *m*, phonetically close to *b*, e.g., *nilbĕnāh lĕbēnîm* "let us make bricks," *nibneh-llānû* "let us build for ourselves," and *nābĕlāh* "let us mix up." Some words just rhyme with *bābel*, e.g., *lāhem*, *'āreṣ*, *wayyāpeṣ*, *yibbāṣer* (though it should be remembered that the Masoretic pronunciation may not be identical with that in use in biblical times). It should be noted that many of these phonetic allusions to Babylon also contain *n*. This makes the contrast between man's *nilbĕnāh* "let us make (bricks)," v 3, and God's *nābĕlāh* "let us mix up," v 7, the more dramatic. The LORD literally mixes up *nilbĕnāh* through his judgment. Indeed, *nābĕlāh* sounds very like *nĕbālāh* "the folly of the impious." The name "Babel" thus stands forever as a reminder of the failure of godless folly (cf. Ps 14:1).

Other key words that lend unity to the narrative are *šām* "there," *šēm* "name," and *šāmayim* "heaven" (vv 2, 4, 7, 8, 9). The phrase "face of the earth" also seems to echo the word "scattered," and the people's fear anticipates God's judgment (vv 4, 8, 9) for "face . . . the earth" *pĕnê . . . hā'āreṣ* begins with *p* and ends in *ṣ*, just as does *pûṣ* "scatter" (vv 4, 8, 9).

The narrative itself falls into an introduction, five brief scenes, and a conclusion.

v	1	Introduction
v	2	Scene 1: The travels of mankind
vv	3–4	Scene 2: Human plans to build a city and tower
v	5	Scene 3: Divine inspection visit
vv	6–7	Scene 4: Divine plans to frustrate mankind
v	8	Scene 5: Mankind is scattered: building stopped
v	9	Conclusion: What Babel means

It is particularly obvious how scene 2 (human plans) matches scene 4 (divine plans). Note the introductory הבה "come" in vv 3, 4, 7. Similarly, in scene 1 mankind's journeyings halt, but in scene 5 they resume. Scene 3, God's inspection visit, is the turning point in the sequence.

As already noted, verbal inclusions link the introduction (v 1) and the conclusion (v 9). A similar use of key words enhances the scenic parallelism. The whole narrative can be viewed as cast in parallel panels.

v 1	"one language"	v 6	"one people"
	"one kind of speech"		"one language"
v 2	"there"	v 7	"there"
v 3	"each other"		"each other"
v 4	"build . . . a city"	v 8	"building the city"
	"name"	v 9	"its name"
	"lest we are scattered over the face of the whole earth"	vv 8, 9	"the LORD scattered them over the face of the whole earth"

But it is possible also to see the narrative as a palistrophe, or extended chiasmus.

A	"The whole earth had one language" (v 1)
B	"there" (v 2)
C	"each other" (v 3)
D	"Come let us make bricks" (v 3)
E	"let us build for ourselves" (v 4)
F	"a city and a tower"
G	"the LORD came down . . ." (v 5)
F¹	"the city and the tower"
E¹	"which mankind had built"
D¹	"come . . . let us mix up" (v 7)
C¹	"each other's language"
B¹	"from there" (v 8)
A¹	"the language of the whole earth" (v 9)

This simultaneous use of parallel panels and palistrophe is remarkable and unusual. Another good example is Gen 17 (cf. S. E. McEvenue, *The Narrative Style of the Priestly Writer*, 157–59). It should be noted that v 5 stands right outside the parallel panels and constitutes the turning point in the palistrophe. This verse, scene 3 on our analysis, is the hinge or crossover point in the story. It both looks back to what has been done and forward to what is to come.

> Scenes 1–2:   Human deeds
> Scene 3:   Inspection of the city and tower which mankind had built
> Scene 4–5:   Divine actions

Scene 3 is the decisive divine intervention that reverses the tide of human history. It is comparable to "And God remembered Noah" in 8:1. Like 8:1, v 5 occurs at the midpoint of a story and heralds the undoing of what has gone before: there the flood waters start to fall; here the building stops. In both stories the palistrophic pattern serves to underline the fundamental inversion that takes place in the events; but whereas in 8:1 God intervenes to save mankind in Noah, here the LORD steps in to frustrate human scheming. The similar phraseology in the human and divine speeches and particularly the exchange of וְֽלִבְּנָה "let us make bricks" into נָבְלָה "let us mix up" also serve to express most vividly the total reversal that has taken place.

Unlike the case with the flood story, no good Near Eastern parallel to the tower of Babel story is known. But as with Gen 2–3, certain oriental motifs seem to have been drawn on to create our present narrative. The great ziggurats of Mesopotamia were a well-known feature of its landscape. In particular *Enuma Elish* celebrates the building of Babylon and its temple tower, and Sumerian tradition tells of a time when all men spoke or will speak the same language. Nowhere else do we know of a story that combines these ideas in the way that Genesis does, nor do extra-biblical sources look on these events with the biblical perspective.

The mention of the universal world language comes in the Sumerian epic "Enmerkar and the Lord of Aratta." As translated by Kramer and Cohen, lines 136–40 look back to a golden age when "there was no snake, . . . no scorpion . . . no fear, no terror. Man had no rival." In that period "the whole universe, the people in unison, to Enlil in one tongue spoke" (ll. 145–46). But it continues:

> Enki . . . the leader of the gods
> changed the speech in their mouths
> brought contention into it,
> Into the speech of man that (until then) had been one (ll. 150–56).

Though Kramer held that this text "puts it beyond all doubt that the Sumerians believed there was a time when all mankind spoke one and the same language," Alster (*RA* 67 [1973] 101–9) and H. Schmökel (*NERTOT*, 87) argued that this text is really looking forward to a time when all mankind would speak the same language, the Sumerian language. This would be closer to Zeph

3:9 which looks forward to an age when God "will change the speech of all peoples to a pure speech."

The interpretation of this Sumerian text is fraught with difficulty, but on either view the tower of Babel story can be seen as an interesting comment on earlier tradition. On Kramer's interpretation, the OT is offering an alternative explanation of the diversity of languages. Genesis is affirming that the diversity of languages represents a divine judgment on mankind and is not the product of rivalry between the gods Enlil and Enki. Here, as in the flood story, Genesis explains things in terms of a moral monotheism, whereas Mesopotamia saw things in terms of polytheistic competitiveness.

Alster's view of the earlier tradition suggests that Genesis may be making a different point: the Sumerian gods saw the diversity of languages as undesirable because men were thereby prevented from joining in the worship of the great god Enlil, but Genesis holds that the confusion of languages is a divine antidote to human arrogance. Whereas Mesopotamia saw the human condition as improving, Genesis sees it as deteriorating. On Alster's view, the Sumerian epic is vaunting the superiority of Sumerian civilization because one day the Sumerian language, the chief expression of that culture, will be adopted by all peoples. And certainly the Hebrew story is adamant that this is not so. Far from being a cultural and religious Mecca, Babylon epitomizes the folly of humanistic culture. This comes out very clearly in its comments on the tower-building. According to the Babylonians, their temple was constructed as "a likeness on earth of what he has wrought in heaven" (EE 6:113). Indeed, the Esagil was built by the lesser gods, the Annunaki, as a dwelling place for the great gods Marduk, Enlil, and Ea.

> The Annunaki wielded the hoe;
> For one whole year they moulded its bricks.
> When the second year arrived
> they raised the head of Esagil, a replica of the Apsû.
> They built the lofty ziggurat of the Apsû
> and established its . . . as a dwelling for Anu, Enlil and Ea.
> (EE 6:59-64, W. G. Lambert's unpublished translation)

According to Speiser (*Genesis* 75) the mention of brick-making and a "tower with its top in the sky" in Gen 11:3–4 echoes *Enuma Elish*'s description of the building of the Esagil. But as already pointed out (see *Introduction*, p. xliv, and *Form/Structure/Setting*, p. 8), it is unlikely that Genesis is directly dependent upon *Enuma Elish*. Nevertheless, it was a commonplace of Babylonian thought that temples had their roots in the netherworld and their tops reached up to heaven (W. G. Lambert, *Babylonian Wisdom Literature*, 327, nn. 83-84). So although Gen 11 is unlikely to be addressing *Enuma Elish*'s account of the building of the Esagil, it may well be mocking Babylonian boasts about their temples. Their fancy brickwork and their vaunted height are something to laugh at. Babylon shows man's folly, not his wisdom, man's impotence before the judgment of God.

When the present story could have been composed is uncertain. The temple tower called Etemenanki, which was associated with the Esagil, was built in

the neo-Babylonian period by Nebuchadnezzar. It is therefore usually surmised that Genesis is referring to an earlier structure, perhaps erected in
the old Babylonian period, which fell into ruin under the Cassites. Another
possibility, suggested by von Soden, is that the Genesis story reflects the
earlier building efforts of Nebuchadnezzar I (1123–1101 b.c.), whose great
constructions came to an abortive end and hence became an occasion for
jest and legend. Clearly, a number of motifs have been integrated in this
narrative, which is usually assigned to J on the grounds of its obvious similarities
with other J material in Gen 2–10. But whether it is possible to recover any
earlier literary sources within 11:1–9 is doubtful. Gunkel's view that two parallel
accounts, one of city-building (vv 1, 3a, 4a, 6a, 7, 8b, 9a), the other of tower-
building (vv 2, 4a, 3b, 5, 6b, 8a, 9b), have been combined in this chapter is
now generally abandoned. However, Seybold (*VT* 26 [1976] 453–79) has suggested that one basic story (vv 2–4a, 5–6aαβ, 6aδ–7, 8b–9aα) has undergone
two slight expansions. The first (1, 6aγ, 9aβ) he attributes to J; the second
(4b, 8a, 9b) to the redactor who integrated chap. 11 into the rest of Gen 1–
11. Basically, he wishes to attribute most of the remarks about the confusion
of language to J, though this is already mentioned in v 7, and the remarks
about the dispersal of the nations to the final editor. While such a view of
the editorial process is less unlikely than Gunkel's, it does scant justice to
the careful arrangement and the interplay of ideas and sounds that make
this narrative such a finely crafted piece. In this passage it seems difficult to
distinguish between author and editor, and the sources of his composition
can only be indicated in the most general fashion by comparing it with other
oriental traditions.

Comment

1 As introduction, "The whole earth had one language and one kind of
speech" sets the scene for the subsequent narrative. "The whole earth," here,
as in 9:19, denotes all the inhabitants of the world. "One language" is literally
"one lip," שׂפה. For a Sumerian parallel to the idea that at one time all mankind
spoke the same language, see above *Form/Structure/Setting*. "One kind of
speech" is literally "words, one." The plural of אחד "one" occurs in only
four other passages. In 27:44; 29:20; Dan 11:20 it means "a few" (days); in
Ezek 37:17, "one." The latter sense seems more likely here. The narrative is
not drawing attention to mankind's limited vocabulary, "few words," but to
their unity of speech. It essentially parallels "one language."

2 Scene 1, mankind's journey, "When they journeyed in the east." "Journey" נסע is often used of the patriarchal and Exodus wanderings (cf. 12:9;
33:17; Exod 12:37; 14:19). "In the east": the parallel with 13:11 suggests
that "eastward" would be an apt translation here. This would be a possible
rendering, if we suppose that mankind is seen as emigrating from Ararat to
Mesopotamia (cf. 8:4), though in this case "southward" would have been
more exact geographically. However, elsewhere in Genesis מקדם, when used
adverbially and not as a preposition, means "in the east" (2:8; 12:8; cf. Isa
9:11[12]). Here and in 2:8, the people are "east of Canaan." Traveling east
of Eden was the judgment on Adam, Eve, and Cain (3:24; 4:16), and the

mention of similar journeyings here may be intended as a reminder of mankind's earlier sentence. "They found" probably expresses their relief that they can now settle down (cf. 26:17; Judg 17:8–9). "Plain," בקעה, is usually a broad flat valley, like the Jordan valley near Jericho (Deut 34:3) or Esdraelon near Megiddo (2 Chr 35:22); here it refers to the even broader, flatter plain of Mesopotamia. "Shinar": cf. *Comment* on 10:10. "They settled there": cf. 11:31. As in Terah's case, settling down is but the prelude to great upheaval!

3–4 The second scene allows us to hear the people planning their project. Nowhere is the fulfillment of their dreams described, although v 3b, "they had bricks for stone . . . mortar," and v 5, "which mankind had built," indicate that they did make some progress.

3 The builders' words are replete with ironic hints of the ultimate failure of their project. As already noted, the Hebrew words for "make bricks," "for stone," and "build for ourselves" contain the consonants *n, b, l,* which spell "mix up" (v 7) or "Babel" (v 9) and evoke the word "folly," *nēbālāh.* In particular, the people's express purpose in building, "to make a name, lest we are scattered over the face of the whole earth," is precisely what they fail to achieve. For ultimately the LORD does scatter them (vv 8, 9), and the name given to their construction commemorates their failure, not their success.

"Let us make bricks." Elsewhere this phrase is used only of the Hebrews making bricks in Egypt (Exod 5:7), but it is common in Akkadian. Indeed, *Enuma Elish* talks of molding bricks for a year to build the Esagil. The second clause, "bake them thoroughly," while not such a clear pre-echo of Babel as the previous clause, contains the consonants *n, l,* and *p* (close to *b*).

"So they had bricks for stone and asphalt for mortar" is a brief aside introducing the narrator's point of view and the approach of Israelites to building material. It is, of course, an accurate comparison of building techniques in Israel and Mesopotamia. The former used stone and mortar (חמר denotes potter's clay as well as mortar), whereas the latter used bricks (usually sun-dried, but here no doubt special kiln-baked bricks are meant) and asphalt, produced by exposing crude oil to the air. But this is more than a technical note on differences in ancient building methods; there is also an implied disparagement of Babylonian materials (we use stone; they have only brick!). And the whole comment combines a tight chiasm: "for them brick" // "asphalt for them," with ingenious word play: *lĕbēnāh/lĕʾāben // hahē-mār/lahōmer.* Again it makes use of the significant *n, b, l.*

4 The focus returns to the deliberators in Shinar. The purpose of their brick manufacture now becomes clear—to build a city with a tower ("city and tower" is probably hendiadys). The tower is to be so high that "its top is in the sky or heavens." Here the allusion to Babylonian theology is most obvious. Not only does their mutual exhortation "let us build for ourselves" contain those letters *n, b,* and *l,* but the main temple in Babylon was called the Esagil, i.e., the house with the raised head. From a purely human viewpoint, building a tower as high as the sky is an audacious undertaking, but it seems likely that Genesis views it as a sacrilege. For the sky is also heaven, the home of God, and this ancient skyscraper may be another human effort to become like God and have intercourse with him (cf. 3:5; 6:1–4).

"To make for ourselves a name." Again the people's ambition suggests

impiety. God promised to make Abram's name great (12:2) and also David's
(2 Sam 7:9, fulfilled in 2 Sam 8:13). But elsewhere in Scripture it is God
alone who makes a name for himself (e.g., Isa 63:12, 14; Jer 32:20; Neh
9:10). Mankind is again attempting to usurp divine prerogatives.

"Lest we are scattered over the face of the whole earth." Cf. *Form/Structure/
Setting* above on the use of *p* and *ṣ* in this clause. Possibly the desire to congregate
in one place should be seen as a rejection of the divine command "to be
fruitful, multiply and fill the earth" (1:28; 9:1). But from a dramatic point
of view, the irony of the story is certainly heightened: what man did his
utmost to prevent, he is condemned to suffer by the decree of heaven (vv
8, 9).

5 Scene 3. The action now switches to heaven. Structurally and thematically, this scene marks the turning point in the story. With heavy irony we
now see the tower through God's eyes. This tower which man thought reached
to heaven, God can hardly see! From the height of heaven it seems insignificant,
so the LORD must come down to look at it! "He sits above the circle of the
earth, and its inhabitants are like grasshoppers" (Isa 40:22). God's descent
to earth to view the tower is no more proof of the author's primitive anthropomorphic view of God than is God's asking Adam and Eve where they were
hiding in the garden an indication of his ignorance. It is simply a brilliant
and dramatic way of expressing the puniness of man's greatest achievements,
when set alongside the creator's omnipotence.

6–7 Scene 4. The LORD's words are an obvious take-off on man's words
in vv 3–4. Man says, "Come, let us make bricks" (*nilbĕnāh*): God says,
"Come, . . . let us mix up" (*nābĕlāh*). In v 3 the people speak "to each other":
in v 7 the LORD prevents them from understanding "each other." Man tries
to build "a tower with its top in the sky" (*šāmayim*) to make "a name" (*šēm*).
God descends "there" (*šām*) to confuse their "language" (*śĕpātām*). Men fear
they will be "scattered over the face of the whole earth" (v 4), while the
LORD is concerned that "nothing they plot to do will be beyond them" (v 6).

6 The structure (note the introductory הן "since" and ועתה "now") and
sentiments closely resemble 3:22, "Since man has become like one of us,
knowing good and evil, now lest he reach out . . . and live for ever."

"Since they are one people." "People" עם are characterized by common
racial descent, whereas a "nation" גוי is more of a political entity with common
institutions, land, and, usually, language binding it together (*TDOT* 2:426–
27). To say that "they are one people" is to underscore the message of the
previous chapters that all mankind is descended from Noah and Adam.

But having "one language" makes this narrative prior to chap. 10, when
the various nations of the world were established, each with their different
tongue (10:5, 20, 31), a situation already intimated by the narrator in 11:1.

"This is the beginning of their activity." As eating of the tree of knowledge
could have been just the prelude to eating from the tree of life, so building
the tower, an arrogant undertaking in itself, may be the forerunner of yet
further trespass on the divine prerogatives: "nothing they plot" will "be beyond
them." "Be beyond them": the niphal of בצר is used in only one other
passage, Job 42:2—"no purpose of thine can be thwarted"—again in conjunc-

tion with the root נמם "to plot, purpose." This Job parallel suggests that only God may plan without limit. Man is not supposed to emulate his creator in this way. Indeed, the verb "to plot" tends either to be used of God (e.g., Jer 4:28; 51:12) or of nefarious human scheming (Deut 19:19; Ps 31:14[13]; 37:12).

7 "Come, let us go down and mix up." On the use of "us," cf. *Comment* on 1:26 and, in a very similar context, 3:22. It would be particularly appropriate for the LORD to invite the angels to assist in confusing the nations, for to their care were entrusted all the nations except Israel, the LORD's special possession (Deut 32:8–9). "Go down": it is pedantic to see this as contradicting v 5. Compare the similar remark in 18:21, "I will go down to see whether they have done according to the outcry." In both passages the LORD knows what has been going on. Coming down to Babel or Sodom is a prelude to judgment.

"Mix up" (*nābělāh*): see earlier discussion of the word play with *nilběnāh/ něbālāh/bābel*. "Each other": cf. v 3.

8 Scene 5 describes the final frustration of mankind's plans. What they most feared—dispersal (v 4)—befalls them, and their grandiose construction project is halted. Expulsion from one's former home marks the conclusion to the fall and to the Cain and Abel narratives as well (cf. 3:24; 4:16). "They stopped building the city." The tower is not mentioned because it is the name of the city that is the focus of the narrative. To see the cessation of building and the dispersal of the nations as incompatible motifs is to miss the profound grasp of culture that this story exhibits. Without mutual communication through a common language it is impossible for men to cooperate either commercially or socially. Towers cannot be built nor communities live together unless those concerned can understand each other.

9 This is the conclusion to which the whole narrative has been driving: "Therefore its name was called Babel." For similar concluding "therefores," cf. 2:24; 4:15. Though this looks like a typical etiological formula rather loosely tacked onto the preceding narrative, the repeated phonetic allusions to Babylon in the previous verses makes this an untenable view. The whole story is built up to explain the word "Babel" and to characterize it as under divine judgment.

The Babylonians understood Babel to mean "the gate of the god." The Hebrews liked to suppose it to mean "mixed up, confused." Here, as often in the OT, it is clear that the etymology offered is a popular one, an interpretation of a name based on a similar sounding word, not a scientific etymology explaining the verbal roots; cf. Moses (Exod 2:10), Samuel (1 Sam 1:20). The same is probably true of the Babylonians' own etymology "gate of the god" (so Gelb). בלל "mix up" occurs only here and in v 7 with this meaning: in the sacrificial law it apparently means "smear" "moisten" with oil, e.g., Lev 2:4 (KB, 128).

The narrative is rounded off with a double reference to "the language of the whole earth . . . the whole earth," which makes a literary inclusion and striking contrast to its opening, "the whole earth had one language." The tower of Babel was intended to be a monument to human effort: instead it became a reminder of divine judgment on human pride and folly. Similarly, the multiplicity of languages and man's dispersal across the globe points to the futility of man setting himself against his creator.

Explanation

The modern interpreter finds the juxtaposition of the table of nations (chap. 10) and the tower of Babel story incongruous. On the face of it, they offer two incompatible accounts of the origins of the nations and their different languages. But the very fact that the author of Genesis included both shows that he regarded the material as complementary, not contradictory. The dual mention of "flood" (*mbl*) and "Babel" (10:1, 10, 32; 11:9) and the other key-words, e.g., "scatter," "build," "land," shows how the two narratives have been brought into mutual relationship and shed light on each other.

The table of the nations, unique in world literature, paints a basically positive, or at least neutral, picture of the relationships between the nations. All are linked genealogically to the sons of Noah, so all men are ultimately brothers of each other. Were that the end of the story, the reader would conclude that the sons of Noah lived in brotherly concord, fulfilling God's command to fill the earth and subdue it.

The very much shorter tower of Babel story corrects this interpretation. Mankind is seen organizing and arrogating to himself essentially divine prerogatives: he builds a tower to reach to God's dwelling in heaven; he tries to make himself a name and he schemes on his own account. Whereas God wanted man to fill the earth, he seeks to congregate in one town, Babel. And it is in Babel that the LORD confuses human speech, so that all the descendants of Noah can no longer live together and cooperate on anti-God projects. The tower of Babel story is the last great judgment that befell mankind in primeval times. Its place and function in Gen 1–11 may be compared to the fall in Gen 3 and the sons of God episode in Gen 6:1–4, both of which triggered divine judgments of great and enduring consequence.

There is a recurring pattern in Gen 1–11 of a positive episode's being succeeded by a negative. The creation of the earth, which was very good (Gen 1), is followed by the fall and Abel's murder (chaps. 3–4). The prosperity of the long-lived antediluvians (chap. 5) is followed by intermarriage with divine beings and the flood (chaps. 6–8). The renewed covenant with Noah is succeeded by his drunkenness and the curse on Canaan (chap. 9). The same sequence is evident here in the quite positive table of nations and the highly judgmental account of Babel.

The table of nations falls into three sections, dealing in turn with the descendants of Japhet, Ham, and Shem. It would be wrong to imagine that this table lists all the nations known to ancient Israel, for it cannot be coincidence that exactly seventy descendants of Noah's sons are listed here, on a world scale prefiguring the seventy sons of Jacob who went down to Egypt (46:27).

Within this table, the nations farthest removed from and of least consequence to Israel, the sons of Japhet, are mentioned first (10:2–5). No details of these peoples or their history are included, just their names. Insofar as they can be identified, the sons of Japhet seem to lie to the north and west of Israel, e.g., Cyprus, Greece, and Turkey.

The second group, the sons of Ham, includes nations of much greater consequence to Israel. There are a number of peoples listed of whom we know as little as some of the Japhetites, e.g., Raamah, Anamim, but they also include Israel's most dangerous rivals in the ancient world, the Babylonians, the Egyptians, and the Canaanites. Linguists and anthropologists, on grounds of race and language, would describe as Semitic (i.e., sons of Shem) some of the people listed here as sons of Ham. But as often observed, race and language do not make up the most important principle underlying the classification of the nations in Gen 10: the sons of Ham are those who are under Noah's curse (9:26–27). Though Canaan was the primary target of that curse, it was Ham, the wayward son, who prompted the curse, and consequently Israel's greatest enemies are listed here. Their classification as Hamites indicates that the table of nations is not really so uncommitted as it may first appear.

Further examination of the sons of Ham section reveals that the author of this chapter has a particular interest in them. Two verses (vv 6–7) list with telegraphic brevity eleven descendants of Ham; then the genealogy backtracks to introduce Nimrod (vv 8–12), another of Ham's grandsons. This notice about Nimrod, "a champion hunter before the LORD" and founder of the major cities of Mesopotamia, takes a full four verses, an indication of the prime importance of this area as far as Genesis is concerned. Nimrod's achievements as warrior, city-builder, and hunter epitomize the ideals of Mesopotamian heroes, particularly their kings. The epithet "champion" may suggest a claim to supernatural parentage (cf. 6:4) which would be another point of contact with Mesopotamian ideology. Nimrod's name is not explained here, but it may be translated "we shall rebel," an apt characterization of the motives of the builders of Babel according to 11:1–9. Here Babel/Babylon is simply called "the prime of his kingdom," not necessarily reflecting the antiquity of Babylon, but certainly its status as the first city of Mesopotamia.

Southern Mesopotamia, Ur of the Chaldaeans, was the original home of Terah and Abram (11:28,31). Harran in northern Mesopotamia (cf. Nineveh, Ashur, Calah [10:11]) was the area to which Terah migrated and where he subsequently died (11:32). To this latter area the patriarchs returned to find wives among other members of their clan (24:4, 10; 28:2, 10). The other pole of the patriarchal wanderings was Egypt, which is also picked out for extended treatment in 10:13–14. Finally, the goal of the patriarchal wanderings, the promised land of Canaan, is mentioned among the descendants of Ham. Vv 15–20 list first some of the traditional inhabitants of the land, including Hittites, Jebusites, Amorites, Girgashites, and Hivites. Then a brief definition of the boundaries of the land is added, from Sidon in the north and Gerar in the southwest, to Sodom and Gomorrah in the southeast. In the context of 9:25–26 (the curse on Canaan) and chaps. 18–19 (the overthrow of Sodom and Gomorrah), the inclusion of these details must be seen as deliberate. They explain just who are the Canaanites on whom judgment will fall.

Finally, the table deals with the elect line of Shem. By and large, the sons of Shem are peoples with whom Israel has good and positive relations. The Aramaeans (v 23) provide several brides for Abraham's family (cf. chaps. 24, 28). Arpachshad, Shelah, and Eber were ancestors of Terah. Indeed, vv 24–25 are a typical trailer for the next section of Genesis, the genealogy of Shem (11:10–26), and the mention of Peleg in whose "days the earth was divided" anticipates and serves to place the tower of Babel episode chronologically. Finally, the sons of Yoqtan (vv 26–30), insofar as they can be identified, seem to be Arab tribes. Sheba is listed in 25:3 among Abraham's grandsons and was of course one of Israel's allies in the reign of Solomon (1 Kgs 10:1–13). These descendants of Shem then appear to be Israel's future allies. The inclusion of Assyria and Elam is unexpected, if the classification of a people as a son of Shem implies a positive attitude toward them by Israel. Either a different Assyria is meant, or a Sinaitic tribe perhaps, or its inclusion may indicate the early date of this material.

"From these the nations spread out in the world after the flood" (10:32) rounds off the table of nations and, by echoing its opening (10:1) with another mention of the flood, frames the whole account with a double reference to universal judgment. Despite all its progress and expansion recorded in chap. 10, mankind is still haunted by the specter of divine wrath. The word "flood" (*mabbul*) evokes these associations and adumbrates the key word of the next story, "Babel."

With the tower of Babel we come to the last of the great tales of universal judgment that punctuate the primeval history. Its content, literary structure, and terminology parallel at many points the other stories of this genre in Gen 1–11. We have noted the palistrophic arrangement of material, its dramatic scenes, and the vivid anthropomorphisms used to express an exalted view of an omnipotent and sternly moral creator, features that are just as obvious in the garden of Eden and the flood stories.

As elsewhere in Gen 1–11, there is in this narrative a strong polemic against the mythic theology of the ancient world. Often this polemic is implicit rather than explicit. Only ancient hearers and modern scholars familiar with Mesopotamian accounts of the flood can appreciate the world of difference between the characterizations of Noah and Utnapishtim or between the LORD and the gods of Mesopotamia who cower before the flood and swarm like flies around the sacrifice. But Gen 11 throws discretion to the winds: the assault on Babylonian pretensions is open and undisguised. The tower of Babylon stands as a monument to man's impotence before his creator, and the multiplicity of human languages is a reminder of divine retribution on human pride.

With a knowledge of Mesopotamian mythology, Genesis' attack can be seen as even sharper. Man's inability to speak a common language is, according to one understanding of the Enmerkar epic, to be ascribed to the mischief-making of Enki, the leader of the gods. The moral motivation of the Hebrew account is completely missing. Texts like *Enuma Elish* make it clear that the tower of Babel story is also a spoof on oriental beliefs about the Mecca of Mesopotamia, the Esagil. The temple of Marduk in Babylon was supposed to have been built by the Annunaki gods with specially prepared bricks. Its name, "house with the uplifted head," reflects its claim to have reached the heavens. But Genesis unmercifully batters these claims. It was, first, only a human building, and who would chose brick in preference to good Palestinian stone? And as for its vaunted height, so far short of heaven did this so-called skyscraper fall that God could hardly see it: he had to come down to look at it!

But though man's highest achievement was pathetic in God's eyes, the motives that prompted his efforts were horrific. The desire to displace God from heaven, to make a name for oneself rather than allow God to do this, and to scheme without reference to his declared will, prompts one final judgment that will hobble man's attempts at cooperation once and for all. The confusion of languages prevents community living and technological cooperation: people cannot trust or work with those they do not understand. The name "Babel/Babylon" does not mean "gate of the god," as the Babylonians held, but "confusion," and it evokes the similar sounding words "folly" and "flood." Far from being the last word in human culture, it is the ultimate symbol of man's failure when he attempts to go it alone in defiance of his creator.

On this note of fierce condemnation of mankind's sinful folly, focused in Babylon, the primeval history is virtually at an end. The genealogy of Shem 11:10–26 is usually assigned to the primeval history, but it serves more as an interlude, bridging the gap between those primeval events that have shaped and continue to shape the destiny of every man and the patriarchal history. We still live in a world where language differences impede cooperation and curb man's repeated attempts to achieve technological mastery of his fate and the totalitarian control of other men. But after the flood there was a new beginning for mankind: the mandate to be fruitful and multiply was renewed. The rainbow shone in the sky as a guarantee that the earth would never again be destroyed in a flood. But the tower of Babel is not followed immediately by a hopeful sequel; the years roll on without a hint of renewal. The last word is Babel. It is as if to say, man must leave Babel, its proud dreams and its God-defying ways, if there is to be hope. And it is with Terah and Abram departing from Ur in southern Babylonia that the saving history of the patriarchs begins.

Throughout Scripture, Babylon is seen as the embodiment of human pride and godlessness that must attract the judgment of almighty God.

Isaiah seems to recall the Genesis story when he says of the king of Babylon,

> "You said in your heart,
> I will ascend to heaven;
> above the stars of God
> I will sit on the mount of assembly in the far north
> [i.e., in the divine council]
> I will ascend above the heights of the clouds
> I will make myself like the Most High.
> But you are brought down to Sheol,
> to the depths of the pit" (14:13–15).

Genesis links the fate of Sodom with that of Babylon, first, by making both sons of Ham, via Canaan and Nimrod respectively, and, second, by saying in both instances that God came down to see what was going on (10:10–19; 11:7; 18:21). This comparison is made more directly in Isa 13:19 where it is said:

> And Babylon, the glory of kingdoms,
> the splendor and pride of the Chaldaeans
> will be like Sodom and Gomorrah
> when God overthrew them.

Isaiah's prophecies against Babylon are taken up and reapplied to the neo-Babylonian empire in Jer 50–51. Similarly, the book of Daniel paints a picture of the glamour of Babylon, the head of gold (Dan 2:38), the tree whose top reached to heaven (4:8 [11], 19 [22]). But the image with the golden head was smashed and the tree was hewn down. At Belshazzar's feast the hand wrote, "Mene, Mene, Tekel and Parsin . . . God has numbered the days of your kingdom and brought it to an end. . . . That very night Belshazzar the Chaldaean king was slain" (5:25–30).

If Babylon symbolizes the accumulated wickedness and impiety of mankind (cf. Zech 5:5–11), final salvation comes only through its destruction, but in the meantime the righteous must escape from it. Isa 47 proclaims the desolation of Babylon, while 48:20 urges

> Go forth from Babylon, flee from Chaldea,
> declare this with a shout of joy . . .
> The LORD has redeemed his people Jacob.

Primarily this return from Babylon is viewed as a second exodus, a deliverance from a latter-day Egypt, but the imagery of Abraham's pilgrimage is also evoked in these prophetic appeals. No doubt those who returned from exile in 537 B.C. and subsequently were inspired by such prophecy.

The NT also takes up the picture of Babylon, the great harlot, the persecutor of the people of God and the incarnation of human pride and vice. The saints are encouraged both to "come out of her" (Rev 18:4) and to rejoice at the prospect of her destruction (Rev 18:20), for her fall will immediately herald the last judgment and the establishment of the kingdom of God (Rev 20–22). In that day all the redeemed will unite in the worship of God. Zephaniah 3:9 seems to envisage an end of the confusion of Babel when he says,

> At that time I will change the speech of the peoples
> to a pure speech
> that all of them may call on the name of the LORD
> and serve him with one accord.

And Luke evidently looked on the day of Pentecost when all could understand each other's speech as a sign of the last days when all who call on the name of the LORD shall be saved (Acts 2:8–21). The hopelessness of man's plight at Babel is not God's last word: at least the prophets and NT look forward to a day when sin will be destroyed and perfect unity will be restored among the nations of the world.

The Family History of Shem (11:10–26)

Bibliography

See also Bibliography on 5:1–32.

Cryer, F. H. "The Interrelationships of Gen 5:32; 11:10–11 and the Chronology of the Flood." *Bib* 66 (1985) 241–61. **Liverani, M.** "Un'ipotesi sul nome di Abramo." *Hen* 1 (1979) 9–18. **Prewitt, T. J.** "Kinship Structures and the Genesis Genealogies." *JNES* 40 (1981) 87–98. **Thompson, T. L.** *The Historicity of the Patriarchs.* BZAW 133. Berlin: de Gruyter, 1974. 22–36, 298–314.

Translation

¹⁰ *This is the family history of Shem. Shem was a hundred years old and he fathered*[a] *Arpachshad two years*[b] *after the flood.* ¹¹ *Shem lived*[a] *five hundred years after he had fathered*[b] *Arpachshad fathering sons and daughters.*[c]

¹² *Arpachshad lived*[a] *thirty-five years and then he fathered Shelah.*[b] ¹³ *Then Arpachshad lived four hundred and three years after he had fathered Shelah*[a] *fathering sons and daughters.*[b]

¹⁴ *Shelah lived thirty years and then he fathered Eber.* ¹⁵ *Then Shelah lived four hundred and three years after he had fathered Eber fathering sons and daughters.*

¹⁶ *And Eber lived thirty-four years and then he fathered Peleg.* ¹⁷ *Eber lived four hundred and thirty*[a] *years after he had fathered Peleg fathering sons and daughters.*

¹⁸ *Peleg lived thirty years and then he fathered Reu.* ¹⁹ *Then Peleg lived two hundred and nine years after he had fathered Reu fathering sons and daughters.*

²⁰ *Reu lived thirty-two years and then he fathered Serug.* ²¹ *Then Reu lived two hundred and seven years after he had fathered Serug fathering sons and daughters.*

²² *Serug lived thirty years and then he fathered Nahor.* ²³ *Then Serug lived two hundred years after he had fathered Nahor fathering sons and daughters.*

²⁴ *Nahor lived twenty-nine years and then he fathered Terah.* ²⁵ *Then Nahor lived one hundred and nineteen years after he had fathered Terah fathering sons and daughters.* ²⁶ *Terah lived seventy years and then he fathered Abram, Nahor, and Haran.*

Notes

10.a. Waw cons + 3 masc sg impf hiph ילד.

10.b. Dual of שנה "year." On construction see GKC, 118i.

11.a. Waw cons + 3 masc sg impf apoc חיה.

11.b. Inf constr hiph ילד + 3 masc sg suffix.

11.c. SamPent inserts here and in vv 13, 15, 17, 19, 21, 23, 25 a summary of the patriarch's life like the summaries found in 5:5, 8, 11, etc., e.g., "And all the days of Shem were six hundred years and he died." G more briefly just adds "and he died." For fuller discussion of the textual variants between MT, LXX, and SamPent, especially of patriarchal ages, see *Comment* below.

12.a. For this form, cf. 3:22; 5:5.

12.b. G Καινάν.

13.a. G Καινάν; cf. 12.b.

13.b. G adds "And Cainan lived 130 years and fathered Shelah. And Cainan lived 330 years after he had fathered Shelah fathering sons and daughters and he died." Note these figures for Cainan are identical with G's figures for Shelah in vv 14, 15.

17.a. SamPent 270; G 370. Usually G agrees with MT and SamPent is 100 less: the deviation from this pattern suggests G's originality here. MT's 430 could be the result of confusion with "34" in v 16; so Klein (*HTR* 67 [1974] 258).

Form/Structure/Setting

The beginning of this new section is marked by the editorial formula "This is the family history of Shem" (11:10). The next editorial formula, "This is the family history of Terah," appears in 11:27, so it is evident that the previous section must conclude with 11:26. This is not to deny that the source used in 11:10–26 may not continue to be drawn on in 11:27–32 (cf. vv 27, 32 in particular), but the editor of Genesis clearly intended a new section to begin with 11:27, as the introductory formula shows. Another indication that 11:26 marks the end of a section is the mention that Terah had three sons, Abram, Nahor, and Haran. The very similar genealogy of Gen 5 ends with the same phenomenon, the last man in that list, Noah, also has three sons (5:32). Fathering three named sons links Adam, Noah, and Terah.

Apart from the introductory verse "This is the family history of . . ." and possibly the closing mention of Terah's three sons, nothing in this genealogy is suggestive of editorial intervention. Unlike the genealogy of Gen 5, this genealogy has within it no digressions giving interesting snippets of information about certain figures. About each person there is an almost invariable pair of statements:

A lived x years and then he fathered B.
A lived y years after he had fathered B fathering sons and daughters.

The first statement is slightly different for Shem, and the second statement is not found for Terah. In chap. 5 there is a third statement made about each member of the family tree: "A lived a total of x + y years and then he died," but no similar comment is found in 11:10–26; but cf. 11:32.

The sparseness of this genealogy invites comparison not only with 5:1–32 but with 25:12–18 and 36:1–8 [9–43], other genealogies opening with "This is the family history of" and characterized by telegraphic brevity of narrative.

The patriarchal history is arranged so that a terse genealogy like this one alternates with a long family history of one of the key characters.

11:10–26	Genealogy of Shem:	"This is the family history of Shem"
11:27–25:11	Story of Abraham:	"This is the family history of Terah"
25:12–18	Genealogy of Ishmael:	"This is the family history of Ishmael"
25:19–35:29	Story of Jacob and Esau:	"This is the family history of Isaac"
36:1–43	Genealogy of Esau:	"This is the family history of Esau"
37:2–50:26	Story of Joseph:	"This is the family history of Jacob"

So this genealogy of Shem serves as a preface to the story of Abraham in the overall pattern of Genesis. However, its formulation, particularly its chronological details, links it much more strongly with Gen 5. It is a noteworthy feature of the primeval history that it dates events, e.g., the flood, and records men's ages more fully and precisely than does the patriarchal history. However we look at it, 11:10–26 stands very much as a bridge passage between the primeval history and the patriarchal stories. The contents too point in the same direction. It traces the chosen line from Shem, the son of Noah, down to Abram, son of Terah. Like chap. 5, which links Adam and Noah, this chapter runs from Noah's sons to Abram. Each stands at the head of a new epoch in world history: Adam, the first man; Noah, head of the new post-flood humanity; Abraham, father of Israel the chosen people.

The source of this genealogical material is dubious. There are certainly Mesopotamian connections. Several of the names in the list are known either as personal or place names in this region, notably Eber, Serug, Nahor, Terah, and Peleg. It is also significant that the Sumerian king list tells of certain kings reigning astronomical lengths of time before the flood, then of the flood, then of kings reigning shorter but still extraordinarily lengthy periods after the flood. This pattern of very long-lived antediluvians, flood, long-lived postdiluvians corresponds to the sequence Gen 5, flood, Gen 11:10–26. The names are quite different. Genesis deals with commoners, not kings, and Genesis' periods are much shorter. Nevertheless, a similar pattern is apparent, which suggests some sort of common tradition behind Genesis and the Sumerian king list, but the two accounts are much too far apart to build anything on them.

Attempts to determine the immediate source of Genesis 11:10–26 are also problematic. Source critics generally assign the section to P, but whether P is preserving, more or less intact, part of the *Toledot* book that begins in 5:1–32 or is creating another genealogy in imitation of chap. 5 is disputed. Stylistically, the chapters are almost identical: the summary statements of 5:5, 8, etc., are not found in 11:10–26, but that hardly demonstrates whether it is an original source or an editorial composite. Nor does the fragment of Shem's genealogy preserved in 10:22–25 decide the issue, any more than the parallels between 4:25–26 and 5:1–8 prove that chap. 5 is dependent on 4:25–26. If both chap. 5 and 11:10–26 come from a very old source antedating P, the dependency could be the other way round. The arguments are finely balanced and certainty is unattainable. It would, though, seem to be the simpler solution to regard 11:10–26 as the continuation of the *Toledot* book which forms the basis of chap. 5. This conclusion could claim support from other fragmentary formulae that suggest the *Toledot* book has been broken up, e.g., 5:32; 9:28–29; 11:32, to allow for the insertion of the flood story and the table of nations. On this hypothesis it would be preferable to see the briefer formulae of 11:10–26, which omits the sum totals of the individual lives, as an abridgement of longer statements like those contained in chap. 5. Equally, however, it could be that chap. 5 has been expanded from something shorter into its present form.

Comment

10 On the names "Shem" and "Arpachshad," cf. 5:32; 10:22.

"Two years after the flood." This is the last mention of the flood in Genesis (cf. 9:28; 10:1,32). The narrative is now entering a new phase, leaving the primeval history behind.

The mention of "two years" creates a problem for which there is no obvious solution, though many have been offered (cf. Cryer). According to 5:32, Noah was 500 years old when he fathered Shem, Ham, and Japhet, and 7:6 states that he was 600 years old when the flood came. This would appear to mean that Shem was 100 years old in the year of the flood, whereas here Shem is said to be 100 years old two years after the flood. Gunkel suggested that some of these figures are approximations—this is Cryer's (*Bib* 66 [1985] 247) approach to 5:32. Skinner held that this remark, "two years after the flood," is a gloss; Jacob, that ancient methods of computation explain it; Cassuto, that Japhet, being the oldest, was born in Noah's 500th year, and Shem, the second, about two years later. This would be the neatest solution, but whether 9:24 and 10:21 will bear this interpretation is uncertain (see *Comment* on these verses above).

The birth of Arpachshad, the first after the flood, shows that Shem has fulfilled the renewed mandate to mankind to "be fruitful and multiply" (8:17; 9:1, 7). Shem's obedience is seen as another ground for the blessing on his descendants. At all events, Arpachshad's birth marks the advent of a new era. And by the MT's chronology, 365 years elapse between his birth and Abram's arrival in Canaan.

11 Shem's age of begetting, 100, and death, 600, makes him transitional between the antediluvians of chap. 5, whose ages at these points average 156 and 858, and the postdiluvians listed here, whose corresponding ages average 36 and 300.

12 "Arpachshad lived thirty-five years and then he fathered Shelah." Though the postdiluvians still live hundreds of years, their life spans are much less than those of their pre-flood ancestors, and their ages of begetting are similar to those known in historical times. This reduction in longevity after the flood may be compared with the Sumerian king list's much shorter reigns after the flood and with 6:3, which decrees that man's life will be reduced to one hundred and twenty years (cf. *Comment* on 6:3).

The Septuagint and the Samaritan Pentateuch, however, offer a quite different set of ages for these postdiluvians.

	First son born			Remaining years		
	MT	SamPent	LXX	MT	SamPent	LXX
Shem	100	100	100	500	500	500
Arpachshad	35	135	135	403	303	430
(Kainan)			130			330
Shelah	30	130	130	403	303	330
Eber	34	134	134	430	270	370
Peleg	30	130	130	209	109	209
Reu	32	132	132	207	107	207
Serug	30	130	130	200	100	200
Nahor	29	79	79	119	69	129
Terah	70	70	70	135	75	135

The inclusion by the LXX of Kainan stands out as a secondary addition. It was probably prompted by the desire to produce a list of ten ancestors like that in chap. 5 as well as to stretch out the period from Shem to Abram as much as possible. Its secondary nature is also suggested by the identity of Kainan's ages with those of Shelah who succeeds him.

The other obvious feature of this table is the way the SamPent and LXX usually increase by 100 years the age at which the first child is born (only 50 in the case of Nahor). SamPent then usually compensates by deducting 100 (or 50) from the remaining years of the patriarch's life. LXX is not so systematic; its deviations from MT usually seem to be scribal errors (Klein *HTR* 67 [1974] 258).

Very similar phenomena are found in chap. 5. There LXX regularly adds 100 to the age at which the first child is born, and then deducts 100 from the remainder. Explanations offered for the changes there also seem to work here. On the MT figures, Abram was born 290 years after Arpachshad, and all his ancestors were still alive then. Indeed Shem died 35 years after Abram! Making each of his forefathers 100 (or 50) years older when they fathered their first child reduces this problem. According to LXX, only Abram's father, grandfather, and great-grandfather were alive at the time of his birth. SamPent, by reducing the subsequent years of his ancestors, has only Abram's father, Terah, witness his birth. And by reducing Terah's subsequent years of life from MT's 135 to 75, SamPent ensures that Terah died before Abram left Harran (cf. 11:32). (For fuller discussion, see R. W. Klein *HTR* 67 [1974] 255–59).

The consensus among commentators, then, is that because of their difficulty the MT figures have here the best claim to originality. However, their size still poses formidable problems if they are intended to be taken as history, although the difficulties are not as extreme as those in chap. 5. They are comparable indeed to Abraham's fathering Ishmael at the age of 86 and dying aged 175, or Isaac's dying at the age of 180. It may be that all these figures are meant to be taken symbolically, even though a totally convincing explanation of the symbolism has yet to be proposed (cf. Gevirtz, "The Life Spans of Joseph and Enoch," *JBL* 96 [1977] 570–71; also see our earlier discussion on chap. 5). But the comparability of the ages of Shem's descendants with those of the patriarchs is another indication that we have moved from the primeval period into the more historical era that forms the background to the patriarchs.

"Shelah": cf. *Comment* on 10:24.

14 "Eber": cf. *Comment* on 10:24.

16 "Peleg": cf. *Comment* on 10:25.

17 The original reading here could be "three hundred and seventy years." See *Notes*.

18 "Reu." The name is mentioned only here in the OT. There may be a connection with the name Reuel, son of Esau (36:4, 10, 13) and also Moses' father-in-law (Exod 2:18). Reuel may mean "Friend of God." Others have suggested a connection with the Ru'u, an Aramaean tribe, mentioned in neo-Assyrian inscriptions. Or it could be a place name, Til Raḥaua, like Peleg, Nahor, Serug, Terah.

20 "Serug." If it comes from the root שׂרג "intertwine" (cf. שׂריג "twig, tendril"), it could mean "offshoot, descendant" (BDB, 974b). It is associated generally with the place Sarugi about twenty miles west-northwest of Harran which is mentioned in neo-Assyrian texts. N. Schneider "Patriarchennamen in zeitgenössischen Keilschrifturkunden," (*Bib* 33 [1952] 521–22) cites one example (*šarugi*) of its use as a personal name from the Ur 3 period.

22 "Nahor" is the name both of Abram's grandfather and also of one of his brothers; see v 26. The latter appears as the head of a group of Aramaeans in 22:20–24. Nahor is known as a personal name from the Ur 3 period (*naḥarum*) down to late Assyrian times. It may be derived etymologically from the root נחר "to snort, blow out." A place near Harran (Naḥur/Til Naḥiri) is mentioned in old Assyrian, Mari, and neo-Assyrian texts, though it has not yet been definitely located (cf. *EM* 5:805–9).

24 "Terah" is Abram's father. It is under Terah's aegis that all the stories about Abram are related, for the next introductory formula, "This is the family history of Terah," covers all the material from 11:27 to 25:11. This is not so anomalous as may appear at first sight, for according to 11:32 (MT) Terah did not die until 135 years after Abram's birth, so he witnessed most of the events described in chaps. 12–25. Terah is also the name of an Israelite encampment in the wilderness (Num 33:27–28). It is usually compared with the place name *Til ša turāḥi* (Tell of Terah), a place mentioned in neo-Assyrian texts *ca.* 900 B.C., situated on the Baliḥ river near Harran. Though not mentioned in second millennium texts, the prefix *Til*, common in neo-Assyrian place names, probably indicates that the city was reestablished on an old ruined site, i.e., on a tell (cf. *EM* 8:932; 5:808). Etymologically, Terah may mean "ibex," or it may be related to יָרֵחַ "moon." Several of Abram's relations have names that suggest adherence to lunar worship (cf. Sarah, Milcah, Laban), a cult that was prominent in Ur and Harran.

26 Like the genealogy of Adam in chap. 5, this one ends with the birth of three sons to one man. Noah and Terah each stand at the beginning of a new age. But whereas Noah was the hero of the subsequent narrative, here it is Terah's son Abram that takes the limelight.

"Abram" is well attested as a personal name in both the second and first millennia B.C., but not as a place name. The name *Abarâma* (and variants) appears in old Babylonian texts, *Abiramu* at Ugarit, and *Abarama* again in neo-Assyrian times. The name is clearly composed of two elements, *Ab* "father" and a verb *rûm* which means "be high, exalted" in west-Semitic contexts, though in Akkadian the root *râmu* means "to love." Assuming a west-Semitic interpretation, *Ab-ram* may mean "he is exalted as to his father," i.e., he is of noble birth, or, more probably, "the father [i.e., God] is exalted." Later Abram's name is changed to Abraham (17:5). Probably this is just a phonetic variant of Abram, with the insertion of *h* into the weak root *ram*, a change attested in Aramaic, Ugaritic, and Phoenician. Liverani (*Hen* 1 [1979] 9–18) has suggested that Abraham is the name of the eponymous ancestor of the *rhm*, a nomadic group living in northern Palestine *ca.* 1300 B.C. However, the popular explanation offered in Gen 17:5 understands it to mean "father of a multitude." Though רהם, *raham*, "multitude," is unattested in biblical Hebrew, one must assume that this or a very similar-sounding word was known in Hebrew for this explanation to be offered (cf. A. Strus, *Nomen-*

Omen, 45–48, on the character of biblical etymologizing and Thompson, *Historicity*, 22–36, on Abraham).

"Nahor": naming a child after his grandfather (cf. v 24) is called papponymy, a well-attested practice of biblical and much later times.

"Haran": הרן, "mountaineer" (BDB) or "sanctuary" (KB). Note that this is not the same as the place name חרן, *ḥārān*. It is surmised that the personal name is theophoric: הר *har* "mountain" may be a divine epithet like צור "rock." Personal names compounded with *har* are attested at Mari and among the Hyksos kings of Egypt.

Explanation

With this short genealogy from Shem to Abram, the Genesis narrative steps from the primeval period, whose events have a cosmic significance directly affecting all mankind, into the patriarchal period. Genesis affirms that in the long term the lives of the patriarchs also have universal significance, but for the most part the narratives describe the everyday world of ordinary Near Eastern folk concerned with birth, marriage, family quarrels and death.

In just nine generations, and a mere 365 years from Arpachshad's birth to Abram's migration to Canaan, the narrative moves us from one world to the other, from the dim and distant past into the nearly contemporary world of the patriarchs (at least it must have seemed nearly contemporary to the narrator and first readers of Genesis, however remote it is from us).

The information given about Shem, Arpachshad, Shelah, Eber, Peleg, Reu, Serug, and Nahor is extremely brief. We are told nothing about them save their names, the ages at which their first child was born, and how much longer they lived. Other extra-biblical material that we use to build up a picture of them—the etymology of their names, the fact that many of their names are apparently places in northern Mesopotamia, Sumerian king list parallels—is evidently peripheral to the narrator's purpose. All he was concerned about was tracing the line of election from Shem to Abram, pointing out that man continued to be fruitful and that his life span was somewhat curtailed, as 6:3 predicted. Indeed these postdiluvians' ages are not much larger than those of the famous patriarchs from Abraham to Joseph.

With 11:26 the scene has finally been set for the patriarchal history to unfold. The opening chapters of Genesis have provided us the fundamental insights for interpreting these chapters properly. Gen 1 revealed the character of God and the nature of the world man finds himself in. Gen 2 and 3 portrayed the relationship between man and woman, and the effects man's disobedience has had on man-woman and divine-human relations. Chap. 5 sketched the long years that passed before the crisis of the great flood (chaps. 6–9), which almost destroyed all humanity for its sinfulness. The table of the nations (chap. 10) started the process of Israel's geographical and political self-definition with respect to the other nations in the world, but Gen 11:1–9 reminded us that the nations were in confusion and that mankind's proudest achievements were but folly in God's sight and under his judgment.

However, according to 11:10–26, just five generations after Peleg, whose lifetime according to 10:25 saw the confusion of languages at Babel, Abram arrives. As 12:3 will declare, it is through him that all the families of the earth will be blessed. Man is not without hope. The brevity of this genealogy is a reminder that God's grace constantly exceeds his wrath. He may punish to the third or fourth generation but he shows mercy to thousands (Deut 5:9; 7:9). Though we may find names like Serug or Reu quite irrelevant, this genealogy states that they were most significant, for they were forefathers of the one who was to bring salvation to Israel and ultimately blessing to all mankind, a point Luke makes later by including these men in the genealogy of our Lord (Luke 3:34–36).

Patriarchal History (Gen 12–50)

Bibliography

See also Main Bibliography on Genesis 1–50.

Blum, E. *Die Komposition der Vätergeschichte.* WMANT 57. Neukirchen: Neukirchener Verlag, 1984. **Carmichael, C. M.** *Women, Law, and the Genesis Traditions.* Edinburgh: University Press, 1979. **Donaldson, M. E.** "Kinship Theory in the Patriarchal Narratives: The Case of the Barren Wife." *JAAR* 49 (1981) 77–87. **Emerton, J. A.** "The Origin of the Promises to the Patriarchs in the Older Sources of the Book of Genesis." *VT* 32 (1982) 14–32. **Fisher, L. R.** "The Patriarchal Cycles." In *Orient and Occident: Essays Presented to C. H. Gordon on the Occasion of His Sixty-fifth Birthday,* ed. H. A. Hoffner. AOAT 22. Neukirchen: Neukirchener Verlag, 1973. 59–65. **Frymer-Kensky, T.** "Patriarchal Family Relationships and Near Eastern Law." *BA* 44 (1981) 209–14. **Hauge, M. R.** "The Struggles of the Blessed in Estrangement." *ST* 29 (1975) 1–30, 113–46. **Hoftijzer, J.** *Die Verheissungen an die drei Erzväter.* Leiden: Brill, 1956. **McKane, W.** *Studies in the Patriarchal Narratives.* Edinburgh: Handsel Press, 1979. **Millard, A. R.,** and **D. J. Wiseman,** eds. *Essays on the Patriarchal Narratives.* Leicester: IVP, 1980. **Oden, R. A.** "Jacob as Father, Husband and Nephew: Kinship Studies and the Patriarchal Narratives." *JBL* 102 (1983) 189–205. **Reventlow, H. G.** "'Internationalismus' in der Patriarchenüberlieferungen." In *Beiträge zur Alttestamentliche Theologie: FS für W. Zimmerli zum 70. Geburtstag,* ed H. Donner, R. Hanhart and R. Smend. Göttingen: Vandenhoeck und Ruprecht, 1977. 354–70. **Seebass, H.** "Gehörten Verheissungen zum ältesten Bestand der Väter-Erzählungen?" *Bib* 64 (1983) 189–209. ———. "Landverheissungen an die Väter." *EvT* 37 (1977) 210–29. **Selman, M. J.** "The Social Environment of the Patriarchs." *TB* 27 (1976) 114–36. ———. "Comparative Methods and the Patriarchal Narratives." *Them* 3 (1977) 9–16. **Silberman, L. H.** "Listening to the Text." *JBL* 102 (1983) 3–26. **Thompson, T. L.** *The Historicity of the Patriarchal Narratives.* BZAW 133. Berlin: de Gruyter, 1974. **Wallis, G.** "Die Tradition von den drei Ahnvätern." *ZAW* 81 (1969) 18–40 **Wander, N.** "Structure, Contradiction, and 'Resolution' in Mythology: Father's Brother's Daughter's Marriage and the Treatment of Women in Gen 11–50." *JANESCU* 13 (1981) 75–99. **Weizman, Z.** "National Consciousness in the Patriarchal Promises." *JSOT* 31 (1985) 55–73. **Westermann, C.** *Genesis 12–50.* Erträge der Forschung 48. Darmstadt: Wissenschaftliche Buchgesellschaft, 1975. ———. *The Promises to the Fathers.* Tr. D. E. Green. Philadelphia: Fortress Press, 1980. **Zakovitch, Y.** "A Study of Precise and Partial Derivations in Biblical Etymology." *JSOT* 15 (1980) 31–50.

The Story of Abraham (11:27–25:11)

Genesis 12–25 Bibliography

See also bibliographies on Genesis 1–50, 12–50.

Alexander, T. D. *A Literary Analysis of the Abraham Narrative in Genesis.* Ph.D. Dissertation: University of Belfast, 1982. **Golka, F. W.** "Die theologischen Erzählungen im Abraham-Kreis." *ZAW* 90 (1978) 186–95. **Hunter, A. G.** "Father Abraham: A Structural and Theological Study of the Yahwist's Presentation of the Abraham Material." *JSOT* 35 (1986) 3–27. **Kilian, R.** *Die vorpriesterlichen Abrahamsüberlieferungen, literarkritisch und traditionsgeschichtlich untersucht.* BBB 24. Bonn: Hanstein, 1966. **Muilenburg, J.** "Abraham and the Nations." *Int* 19 (1965) 387–98. **Nobile, M.** "Il ciclo di Abramo (Gen 12–25): Un exercizio di lettura semiotica." *Antonianum* 60 (1985) 3–41. **Rose, M.** "'Entmilitarisierung des Kriegs'? (Erwägungen zu den Patriarchen-Erzählungen der Genesis)." *BZ* 20 (1976) 197–211. **Seters, J. van.** *Abraham in History and Tradition.* New Haven: Yale UP, 1975. **Sutherland, D.** "The Organization of the Abraham Promise Narratives." *ZAW* 95 (1983) 337–43. **Wcela, E. A.** "The Abraham Stories: History and Faith." *BTB* 10 (1980) 176–81.

Form/Structure/Setting

The limits of the story of Abraham are clearly defined by the editorial formulae, "This is the family history of Terah" in 11:27 and "This . . . of Ishmael" (25:12). As with the stories of Jacob and Esau in chaps. 25–35 and the story of Joseph in chaps. 37–50, it is the father of the principal hero of the succeeding tales who gives his name to the family history. Some, most recently Coats, have suggested that the story of Abraham really begins in 11:10 with the genealogy of Shem, rather than in 11:27. This view rests on the observation that fragments of this genealogy appear to be preserved in 11:27–32. However, the same appears to be true of the genealogy of 5:1–32, the last elements of which are found in 9:28–29. That in both cases the editor of Genesis has used a pre-existing genealogy and split it up into various parts does not mean that everything from a particular source belongs to the same editorial unit at the end. Source-critical considerations cannot override redactional indicators. As already argued, the genealogy of Shem (11:10–26) seems essentially to be a bridge between the primeval history of chaps. 1–11 and the patriarchal stories.

Chaps. 12–50 of Genesis contain three long connected cycles of narrative:

11:27–25:11	the story of Abraham
25:19–35:29	the story of Jacob
37:1–50:26	the story of Joseph.

Genealogically, the narratives are connected by Abraham's being father of Isaac, Jacob's being Isaac's son, and Joseph's being Isaac's grandson. But there are many parallels between the plots of each group of stories, and these tend to highlight the similarities between the careers of the leading patriarchs and, more loosely, with the subsequent history of Israel, for example:

1. All these heroes leave their home-land	(12:1; 28:2; 37:28)
2. All quarrel with their brothers	(13:7; 27:41: 37:4)
3. Three go down to Egypt, one to Gerar, i.e., toward Egypt	(12:10; 26:1; 37:28; 46:6)
4. Two patriarchal wives are seduced or nearly so; an Egyptian wife attempts to seduce Joseph	(12:14–16; 20:1–14; 26:1; 39:6–18)
5. Their wives are barren and quarrel (in Abraham's and Jacob's cases)	(16:1–6; 29:31–30:8)
6. The younger sons are divinely favored (also Joseph's sons)	(17:18–19; 25:23; 48:14; 49:8–12, 22–26)
7. Brides met at well	(24:15; 29:9)
8. Promises of children, land, divine blessing	(e.g., 12:1–3, 26:2–5; 28:13–14)
9. Gentiles acknowledge God's blessing on the patriarchs	(21:21–22; 26:28–29: 41:39–40)
10. Buried in cave of Machpelah	(23:1–20; 25:9; 35:27–29; 49:29–32)

These parallels between the patriarchs seem to be rather more than coincidence. Obviously, in a family where traditions run strong, it is not surprising that everyone is buried in the same ancestral grave. But the stories do seem to lay special emphasis on this point, and a whole chapter of the Abraham cycle is devoted to recording the purchase of the family tomb. Other features, though, like the seduction of the patriarchs' wives and Joseph's experience, meeting one's bride at a well, or the acknowledgment of divine blessing by foreigners, can hardly be put down to family tradition. These parallels are being consciously drawn and even accentuated so that the analogy with the experiences of different generations can be observed. Therefore the stories should not be interpreted in isolation. They were written to shed mutual light on each other, and if we are to recapture and appreciate the original writer's motives and intentions, each cycle of stories must be read in the light of the others and each episode ought to be compared with other similar episodes. The slight differences from one version to another help to enhance the portrait of the actors. For example, while Jacob and, later, Moses both personally encounter their future brides at the well and then negotiate terms of marriage with their fathers-in-law, Isaac stays at home. Abraham's servant meets Rebekah, negotiates with Laban, and brings her to Isaac. This suggests that Isaac is a rather retiring, unforceful person, an impression that is confirmed later in his dealings with the Philistines and in his manipulation by Rebekah and Jacob.

If these parallels among the narratives give them depth and interest, they also illustrate the theological principle of typology. There is already in the parallels between Cain's and Adam's sin in Gen 3 and 4 a rudimentary typology. We see men acting in similar fashion in similar situations. But typology is not merely a result of human nature's unchanging weaknesses; it also reflects the constancy of God's character. God always punishes sin and always keeps his promises, so it is not surprising that the accounts of his dealings with one generation resemble in some degree those of the next. And man's propensity to disobedience only makes it more likely that history will repeat itself to some extent.

Yet we must not exaggerate the similarities among the cycles: there is a real development from one story to the next in the tightness of the plot, the depth of characterization, and in theological sophistication. The differences between the primeval history and the patriarchal stories are most marked. The stories of Adam and Eve, or the flood, are little more than episodes set in a framework of genealogies. These stories are more like isolated snapshots than an album of photographs which would allow a multifaceted, developed depiction of the characters and their motives. The flood story gives us hardly any insight into Noah's character apart from his strict obedience to God. The Lord is not simply producer of the play but also the principal actor in the primeval history. Gen 1–11 offers frequent and immediate access into the mind of God by recording his innermost thoughts.

But in the patriarchal stories the Lord retreats farther into the background. Though he frequently appears to Abraham, his direct encounters with Isaac and Jacob are fewer, while Joseph learns God's will through dreams. At the level of human characterization, however, the personalities of the patriarchs become more sharply delineated as the cycles unroll. In Gen 12–25 we have a number of pen portraits of Abraham, but they are not really integrated so as to make a coherent developing biography. Chaps. 25–35 are all dominated by the theme of struggle between Jacob and Esau as announced to Rebekah before their birth. Finally the Joseph story offers a perfectly harmonious, beautifully coherent account of one family and the interaction of its different members. The personalities of the father and his sons all come vividly to light in this absorbing tale.

Running through all the patriarchal stories is the theme of the promises. Descendants, land, and divine blessing are the goals to which the stories press, but the means that the patriarchs use to obtain these ends vary. Abraham, though praised for his faith, descends to allowing his wife to enter an Egyptian harem just to protect himself. Jacob deceives his father and cheats his brother to ensure that God's blessings fall on him. But with Joseph we see a more mature faith. In the most difficult of circumstances he finds that God is with him, and without stooping to the dubious devices employed by his father and great-grandfather, he reaches a most exalted position in Egypt, the superpower of his day. So there seems to be not only a greater depth of literary quality and characterization, but also a deeper moral awareness in the patriarchs as the generations pass. A balanced interpretation of the patriarchal stories should therefore attempt to take account both of the parallels between the stories and the developments within them.

Before examining individual episodes in the Abraham cycle, it is necessary to look at the whole story, its construction and inner logic.

By and large, the Abraham story falls into clearly defined episodes. At some points the analysis is uncertain, but provisionally the following division is adopted. Controversial points in the analysis will be discussed later, where appropriate.

11:27–32	Genealogical introduction
12:1–9	Call of Abram and first journey
12:10–20	In Egypt
13:1–18	Abram and Lot separate
14:1–24	Abram rescues Lot
15:1–21	Covenant with Abram
16:1–16	Birth of Ishmael
17:1–27	Covenant of circumcision
18:1–15	Divine visitation
18:16–33	Abraham's intercession for Sodom
19:1–29	Destruction of Sodom and Gomorrah
19:30–38	Lot's daughters' incest
20:1–18	Abraham and Abimelech
21:1–21	Isaac born; Ishmael leaves
21:22–34	Covenant with Abimelech
22:1–19	Testing of Abraham
22:20–24	Genealogy of Nahor
23:1–20	Purchase of burial ground
24:1–67	Betrothal of Rebekah
25:1–11	Conclusion

Some of this material hangs together so closely, particularly chaps. 18–19, that it is often surmised that they have come from an Abraham-and-Lot tradition that was originally independent of the other episodes. Other themes that are particularly prominent within the Abraham stories are the promises of land and descendants and the problem of the birth of the child. It is Westermann's belief that these themes were once independent of each other and have been brought together over a period until the narrative reached its present form.

It is the present form of the Abraham story that must occupy our attention first. All earlier forms of the narrative are hypothetical reconstructions. Even though they are sometimes very plausible, their definition and interpretation should take second place to understanding the final form of the text. We shall therefore give first a sketch of the main themes and plot of the Abraham story.

The opening expanded genealogical section (11:27–32) introduces the main characters of the story—Abram, Sarai and Lot. Sarai's big problem, her barrenness, is mentioned, and also Lot's close relationship with his uncle Abram, who appears to have adopted him after Lot's father died.

Then 12:1–3 sums up the LORD's call to Abram. He must leave his homeland and his family, for he is promised a new land, many descendants, divine protection, and that he will be a source of blessing to the nations. The promises of land, descendants and protection dominate the subsequent story, but the blessing to the nations theme is also highly significant. It relates the patriarchal to the primeval history, and it also explains various elements in the Abraham story that have no obvious relationship to the promise of son and land.

Immediately after his call, Abram leaves Haran with Lot, and shortly arrives in Canaan, where he is told that this is the land of promise (12:7). But instead of his journey terminating here as might be expected, famine drives him to

Egypt as later it was to drive Jacob. And despite the promise of divine protection, Abram fears for his life, pretends his wife is his sister, and allows her to enter Pharaoh's house. This is the first of three occasions in which a patriarch acts this way. Clearly the fear that prompts such a course of action is regarded as unjustified by the narrator, but it also seems to place in jeopardy the promise of descendants. However, although the patriarch appears to doubt the promises, he nevertheless prospers and leaves Egypt a richer man.

Chap. 13 explains that the very wealth of Abram and Lot is the cause of their separation. The land of promise is therefore divided between them, and Lot goes to live in Sodom, which according to 10:19 was on the borders of Canaan. The departure of Lot posed the problem of who Abram's heir would be, Lot hitherto having been the obvious candidate. So the promise to Abram that his descendants would inherit the land is particularly apposite in 13:14–17.

The battle of the kings, chap. 14, serves to keep Abram on the world stage (his career has potential blessing for all the nations) and to confirm that Lot has dropped out of the running to be Abram's heir. The narrative is notable for having no scene of reunion between Lot and Abram. Instead, the episode closes with Melchizedek blessing Abram in terms that echo the original promise in 12:3.

After the interlude of Melchizedek, the main problem, Abram's heir, is raised again, this time by Abram himself in 15:2. He is assured his own son will be his heir and that eventually his descendants will inherit the land. The night vision (15:12–21) which underlines so emphatically the land promise, here called a covenant, also shows that its fulfillment is hundreds of years hence. From now on, therefore, the promise of a son becomes all-important.

Chap. 16 puts forward Sarai's solution to the problem of childlessness, the traditional Near Eastern one of having a child by one's maid. Abram consents and Hagar conceives Ishmael. But now Sarai, whose idea it was, rejects the potential heir and Hagar flees. However, an angel reiterates the promises of numerous descendants and Hagar returns. It certainly looks as though Sarai's solution to childlessness may also be God's.

Chaps. 17 and 18 are both concerned with the LORD's personally appearing to Abram and Sarai to disabuse them of this notion that Ishmael is the promised son. As chap. 17 opens, the LORD appears to Abram to renew his covenant with him. The promise of numerous descendants is expanded and reiterated in striking fashion, as well as the promise of Canaan, and circumcision is prescribed. Then God announces that Abram and Sarai's names will be changed in token of the promise that she will bear a son. This Abraham finds hard to believe: Ishmael is good enough for him. But God insists that Sarah will give birth to Isaac who will father the chosen line, though Ishmael too will be blessed.

At the beginning of chap. 18, a three-man/angel delegation comes to Abraham's tent to confirm the promise that Sarah herself will bear a son. Sarah's incredulous laughter prompts the LORD himself to rebuke her and assure her that she will soon be a mother. The twofold announcement of the imminent birth of Isaac makes it a certainty. (Cf. 41:32: "the doubling of Pharaoh's dream means that the thing is fixed by God, and God will shortly bring it to pass.") But having sped over the first ninety-nine years of Abraham's life, the narrative now slows to a crawl, spending a long while on other matters apparently peripheral to the main plot. This keeps the listener in suspense. One wonders, When will this great promise eventually be fulfilled?

But the supernatural visitation has another purpose: to discuss the destruction of Sodom and Gomorrah, a cataclysm that in many respects resembles the flood. That the LORD is ready to discuss this great judgment with Abraham shows the latter's standing, an impression enhanced by the LORD's acceptance of Abraham's plea not to destroy Sodom if only ten righteous people are found there. The narrative implies there were not even that number of righteous in Sodom, but the angelic evacuation of Lot and his family from Sodom shows that Abraham's plea was not forgotten. The story's account of the behavior of Lot and his family makes clear that even their righteousness had been tarnished by their residence in Sodom. Nevertheless they escape, and the final episode, in which Lot incestuously fathers Moab and Ben-Ammi, gives conclusive evidence that his claim to be Abraham's heir is now completely void. The destruction of Sodom also foreshadows and explains the fate that one day will befall all the Canaanite inhabitants of the promised land. They too will be destroyed for their sins by Israel acting as the agent of divine judgment.

Chap. 20 brings Abraham and Sarah back on stage. There is still no mention of Sarah's conceiving. Instead, incredible as it may seem, she enters the harem of Abimelech, the king of Gerar. However, the story is most insistent that this time she had no sexual relations with the king, and with heavy irony it mentions that Abimelech ticks off Abraham for his godless immorality in permitting this situation to arise. Yet again Abraham is greatly enriched by his encounter with a royal harem. The effectiveness of his intercession for others is illustrated by the answering of his prayers for the barren women of Gerar. But why were they not answered for Sarah? That is the unasked question posed by chap. 20.

Finally, after all the diversions and delays, "the LORD visited Sarah as he had said" (21:1). The long-awaited Isaac is born. Quite naturally, the birth of Isaac leads to tension between Sarah and Hagar, mother of Ishmael, Abraham's heir apparent hitherto. And this time Hagar and Ishmael leave for good. There is only Isaac left to inherit the promises of land, descendants, and divine blessing.

The short episode that follows (21:22–34, telling of Abraham's covenant with Abimelech) provides another brief interlude in the development of the main plot, and shows Abraham being a source of blessing to the nations.

Suddenly, after this low-key section, the whole Abraham story rises to its point of highest tension. God himself demands the life of Isaac, the only son (22:2). In a superb dramatic narrative the Abraham story reaches its climax. At the last minute the angel of the LORD holds Abraham back from slaying his son and commends him: "For now I know that you fear God, seeing that you have not withheld your son, your only son, from me" (22:12). The second message from heaven reiterates the divine promises of a multitude of descendants, the land, and blessing to the nations. The future of Isaac now seems guaranteed.

It is Isaac's future that is the central concern of the closing chapters of the Abraham cycle. 22:20–24, a short genealogical note on Nahor's descendants, traces the family of Rebekah, Isaac's future wife. Chap. 23 tells of Sarah's death and Abraham's acquisition of a tomb for her, a grave that was to serve as the last resting place for Abraham, Isaac, and Jacob as well. As the first permanent real estate acquired by Abraham in the promised land, this purchase stands as a pledge that ultimately all Canaan will be theirs, just as the Sodom story foreshadows the annihilation of the pre-Israelite inhabitants of the land for their sins.

Finally, Abraham arranges for the marriage of his only son, Isaac, to ensure that his line will continue. The expansiveness of this account in chap. 24 underlines the significance of Isaac's marriage for saving history and allows Abraham's servant to describe from the perspective of an outsider the blessings that the LORD has granted Abraham. Then, after a brief mention of Abraham's marriage to Keturah, the Abraham cycle concludes with his burial in the family tomb at Machpelah.

Clines has described the theme of the Pentateuch as the *partial* fulfillment of the promises made to the patriarchs. Whatever that description's weaknesses as a summary of the whole Pentateuch, it can most aptly be applied to the Abraham story. For by the time of his death, Abraham has acquired only a small plot of land as a burial ground in Canaan, and only one of his children, Isaac, counts towards the numberless company of descendants as numerous as the stars of heaven that Abraham had been promised. That the promises of land, descendants, and blessing to the nations are but very partially fulfilled in the story of Abraham is quite obvious. The promise of divine protection appears to have been fulfilled in much larger measure, though Abraham so often goes in fear that at times he seems to have forgotten it.

It is the promise of a son that is central to the Abraham story, and most of the episodes are related in some way or another to that promise. Thus what appears on first sight to be a collection of rather heterogeneous stories is in fact seen to be carefully integrated into a well-constructed narrative in which little is irrelevant to the promised son and his inheritance. The episodes such as those dealing with Sodom or Abimelech, which do not bear immediately on the promise of a son, serve to create suspense when the promise of a son seems on the brink of fulfillment and to recall those other aspects of the promises, land, protection, and international blessing that are part of the original package of promises that Abraham received.

Several attempts have been made to discover in the Abraham cycle a palistrophic arrangement of the material comparable to that displayed in the flood story. Westermann sees in Gen 12–25 five broad blocks of material, dealing with the birth of a child, with Lot, and with the promises; he suggests that the material may be roughly analyzed as follows:

Chap. 12	Birth of a child
Chap. 13	Lot
Chaps. 15–17	Promises
Chaps. 18–19	Lot
Chaps. 20–25	Birth of a child

Westermann omits chap. 14 as a much later element in Gen 12–25. He is of course much more concerned with the diachronic development of the material than with its final arrangement.

Coats offers a more detailed analysis:

A	11:10–12:9	Exposition
B	12:10–20	Threat to ancestress
C	13:1–14:24	Family novella: Abram-Lot
D	15:1–21	Covenant
	(16:1–16)	(Tale of family strife)
D¹	17:1–27	Covenant
	(18:1–15)	(Tale of family strife)
C¹	18:16–19:38	Family novella: Abraham-Lot
B¹ᵃ	20:1–18	Threat to ancestress
	(21:1–21)	(Tale of family strife)
B¹ᵇ	21:22–34	Beersheba etiology
A¹	22:1–19	Abraham legend

This analysis does bring out some of the most obvious parallels within the Abraham cycle, e.g., 12:10–20 // 20:1–18; chap. 15 // chap. 17; 13:1–14:24 // 18:16–19:38. But the three tales of family strife interrupt this palistrophe somewhat, and it is not obvious how 11:10–12:9 matches 22:1–19. Coats calls 22:20–25:26 death reports and regards it as a sort of appendix to the main palistrophic structure in 11:10–22:19.

For these reasons Alexander's less ambitious analysis of the material may be preferable. He analyzes 12:10 to 20:18 as follows:

A			Sarah endangered; Abraham in Egypt	12:10–13:1
	B		Lot episodes I	13:2–14:24
		C	Covenant with Abraham	15:1–21
			D Birth of Ishmael	16:1–16
		C¹	Covenant with Abraham	17:1–27
	B¹		Lot episodes II	18:1–19:38
A¹			Sarah endangered; Abraham in Gerar	20:1–18

Alexander also observes (*Literary Analysis,* 24) that the Lot episodes B and B¹ correspond to each other in some degree. It may be further noted that the testing of Abraham (22:1–19) clearly echoes his call (12:1–9), while the genealogy of Milcah (22:20–24) corresponds to that of Terah (11:26–32). These correspondences enhance the palistrophic arrangement of 12:10–20:18 noted by Alexander.

Within individual episodes palistrophic arrangement and parallel panel writing have been noted by several authors (e.g., S. E. McEvenue, *The Narrative Style of the Priestly Writer*), but how significant this is for exegetical understanding of the material remains open.

Classical source criticism has found three main documentary sources in Gen 12–25; the J (Yahwist) source and P (Priestly) source are also found in Gen 1–11, but the third source E (Elohist) appears for the first time in chap. 15. As earlier in Genesis, the grounds for source division are the names for

God ("Yahweh" or "Elohim"), the presence of doublets (e.g., chap. 15 // chap. 17; chap. 16 // chap. 21) and other supposed theological and chronological differences between the narratives. Driver S. R. (*An Introduction to the Literature of the Old Testament*, 5th ed. [Edinburgh: T. & T. Clark, 1894]), who is representative of this school of thought, assigned to P 11:27, 31–32; 12:4b–5; 13:6, 11b–12a; 16:1a, 3, 15–16; chap. 17; 19:29; 21:1b, 2b–5; chap. 23; 25:7–11a. To E he assigned 15:1–5, 12–16, 19–21; 20:1–18; 21:6–32, 34; 22:1–14, 19. The rest belongs to J except for chap. 14, which, Driver held, came from an independent source.

This view held sway until the 1970s, when it became common to admit only two main documentary sources in these chapters, namely, J and P. Van Seters, Westermann, and Coats contend that the E material is at most an expansion of J and does not constitute a separate document. This view has received strong endorsement from Radday, who has shown that J and E are stylistically homogeneous.

But though there is a tendency to regard all the J and E material as belonging to one document and the P material to another, few attempts are made to question the basic J/P analysis (see, however, Radday, Alexander, and Rendtorff) or to see the relationship between the material assigned to J and that assigned to P. This is much closer than most commentators recognize. Though a case can be made for an editor like J being the chief and final redactor of Genesis (see Alexander's [*Literary Analysis*, 1982] introduction and detailed discussion on each section), this exegesis is not based on this standpoint. Rather our primary aim is to understand the text as it is in its final form, and then look at the possible sources that the final editors may have employed.

The Call of Abram (11:27–12:9)

Bibliography

Auffret, P. "Essai sur la structure littéraire de Gen 12:1–4a." *BZ* 26 (1982) 243–48. **Braulik, G.** "Durch dich sollen alle Geschlechter der Erde Segen erlangen: Vom Segen nach dem Alten Testament." *BL* 52 (1979) 172–76. **Coats, G. W.** "The Curse in God's Blessing." *Die Botschaft und die Boten: FS für H. W. Wolff*, ed. J. Jeremias and L. Perlitt. Neukirchen: Neukirchener Verlag, 1981. 31–41. **Crüsemann, F.** "Die Eigenständigkeit der Urgeschichte." *Die Botschaft und die Boten: FS für H. W. Wolff*, ed. J. Jeremias and L. Perlitt. Neukirchen: Neukirchener Verlag, 1981. 11–29. **Diedrich, F.** "Zur Literarkritik von Gen 12:1–4a." *BN* 8 (1979) 25–35. **Gutt, E.-A.** "Literalness in Modern Translations of OT Texts: Why?" *BT* 33 (1982) 406–9. **Habel, N. C.** "The Gospel Promise to Abraham." *CTM* 40 (1969) 346–55. **Jenkins, A. K.** "A Great Name: Gen 12:2 and the Editing of the Pentateuch." *JSOT* 10 (1978) 41–57. **Kikawada, I. M.** "The Unity of Gen 12:1–9." *Proceedings of the Sixth World Congress of Jewish Studies* 1 (1977) 229–35. **Miller, P. D.** "Syntax and Theology in Gen 12:3a." *VT* 34 (1984) 472–76. **Roche, M. de** "Contra Creation, Covenant and Conquest (Jer 8:13)." *VT* 30 (1980) 280–90. **Ruprecht, E.** "Vorgegebene Tradition und theologische Gestaltung in Gen 12:1–3." *VT* 29 (1979) 171–88. ———. "Der traditionsgeschichtliche Hintergrund der einzelnen Elemente von Gen 12:2–3." *VT* 29 (1979) 444–64. **Scharbert, J.** "'Erwählung' im Alten Testament im Licht von Gen 12:1–3." *Dynamik im Wort: FS aus Anlass des 50 jährigen Bestehens des katholischen Bibelwerks in Deutschland.* Stuttgart: Katholisches Bibelwerk, 1983. 13–33. **Schedl, C.** "Berufung Abrahams, des Vaters der Gläubigen: Logotechnische Analyse von Gen 12:1–9." *BZ* 28 (1984) 255–59. **Schmidt, L.** "Israel ein Segen für die Völker? (Das Ziel des jahwistischen Werkes— eine Auseinandersetzung mit H. W. Wolff)." *TV* 12 (1975) 135–51. ———. "Überlegungen zum Jahwisten." *EvT* 37 (1977) 230–47. **Schreiner, J.** "Segen für die Völker in der Verheissung an die Väter." *BZ* 6 (1962) 1–31. **Steck, O. H.** "Gen 12:1–3 und die Urgeschichte des Jahwisten." *Probleme biblischer Theologie: G. von Rad FS*, ed. H. W. Wolff. Munich: Kaiser Verlag, 1971. 525–54. **Tournay, R.** "Abraham et le Cantique des Cantiques." *VT* 25 (1975) 544–52. **Vriezen T. C.** "Bemerkungen zu Gen 12:1–7." *Symbolae Biblicae et Mesopotamicae: F. M. T. de Liagre Bohl dedicatae*, ed. M. A. Beek. Leiden: Brill, 1973. 380–92. **White, H. C.** "The Divine Oath in Genesis." *JBL* 92 (1973) 165–79. **Wolff, H. W.** "Das Kerygma des Jahwisten." *EvT* 24 (1964) 73–98. **Yarchin, W.** "Imperative and Promise in Gen 12:1–3." *StudBT* 10 (1980) 164–78.

Translation

[27ab]*Now this is the family history of Terah.*[b] [c]*Terah fathered Abram, Nahor, and Haran. Haran fathered Lot.*[c]

[28]*And Haran died before his father Terah in his homeland in Ur*[a] *of the Chaldaeans.* [29]*Abram and Nahor married*[a] *wives:* [b]*the name of Abram's wife was Sarai and the name of Nahor's wife was Milcah, the daughter of Haran.*[b] (*He was father of both Milcah and Iskah.*) [30]*Sarai was infertile: she*[a] *had no children.*[ab]

[31]*Terah took his son Abram,*[a] *his grandson Lot, the son of Haran, and his daughter-in-law Sarai,*[b] *the wife of Abram his son,*[c] *and they*[d] *left Ur*[e] *of the Chaldaeans with them to go*[f] *to the land*[g] *of Canaan. They came to Harran and stayed there.* [32]*Terah was*[a] *two hundred and five*[b] *years old when he died in Harran.*

[12:1]*The LORD said to Abram, "Go by yourself*[a] *from your country, your clan, and your father's house to the country that I shall show*[b] *you.* [2]*I will*[a] *make you into a great nation, and bless*[a] *you, and make*[a] *your name great, and you shall*[b] *be a blessing.* [3]*And*[a] *I will bless*[b] *those who bless you*[c] *and he who disdains*[d] *you I shall curse,*[ae] *and all the families of the earth will find blessing*[f] *in you."*

[4]*Then Abram went*[a] *as the LORD had told him and Lot went*[a] *with him.* [b]*Now Abram was seventy-five years old when he left*[c] *Harran.*[b] [5]*Abram took Sarai his wife, Lot his nephew, the property and the persons which they had acquired in Harran, and they left to go to the land*[a] *of Canaan. Then they came to the land*[a] *of Canaan.* [6]*Abram passed through the land*[a] *as far as the place of Shechem as far as the oak*[b] *of Moreh:*[c] [d]*the Canaanite was then in the land.*[d]

[7]*The LORD appeared*[a] *to Abram and said:*[b] *"To your descendants I shall give*[c] *this land." Then he*[d] *built*[e] *an altar to the LORD, who had appeared*[f] *to him.* [8]*From there he moved camp*[a] *to the hills*[b] *east of Bethel, pitched*[cd] *his tent*[e] [f]*with Bethel on the west and Ai on the east.*[f] *There he built an altar for the LORD and called on*[g] *the name of the LORD.* [9]*Then Abram went*[a] *on traveling*[b] *toward the Negeb.*[c]

Notes

27.a. SamPent reads אלה instead of MT ואלה.

27.b-b, c-c. Title (b-b) followed by coordinate clauses (c-c) in apposition (*SBH*, 54).

28.a. G reads ἐν τῇ χώρᾳ for באור.

29.a. Sg verb ויקח "and he took" with multiple subj; cf. 7:7; 9:23 (GKC, 146f).

29.b-b. Clauses in apposition to "wives," naming them; cf. 4:19 (*SBH*, 32).

30.a-a. Antithetic apposition clause for emphasis (*SBH*, 43).

30.b. SamPent has the more common ילד for unique ולד; cf. Ugaritic *wld* "child."

31.a. Some G MSS add "and Nahor."

31.b. SamPent adds "and Milcah, his daughter-in-law."

31.c. For "his son," SamPent reads "and Nahor his sons."

31.d. For ויצאו waw consec + 3 masc pl impf qal יצא "they went out," SamPent has ויוצא, waw consec + 3 masc sg impf hiph of יצא "he brought out." This is followed by G, Vg. MT אתם "with them" must then be pointed אתם "them." However, MT may probably be retained as the harder reading.

31.e. G ἐκ τῆς χώρας "from the land"; cf. n. 28.a.

31.f. Inf constr הלך "to go."

31.g. ארץ + directional ending ה.

32.a. LXX inserts "in Harran."

32.b. SamPent reads 145 for 205; cf. Acts 7:4. SamPent assumes that Abram did not leave till his father's death and so corrects 205 to 145 on the basis of 11:26 (70) and 12:4 (75).

12:1.a. לך "to you." This dative construction (the ethical dative) emphasizes "the significance of the occurrence in question for a particular subject" (GKC, 119s). "This particular usage of the preposition . . . conveys "the impression . . . that the subject establishes his own identity, recovering or finding his own place by determinedly dissociating himself from his familiar surrounding. Notions of isolation, loneliness, parting, seclusion or withdrawal are often recognizable" (*EWAS*, 122). Used with the verb "to go," it suggests that the person mentioned is going alone and breaking away from the group (Cassuto, 2:310); cf. 21:16; 22:2; Exod 18:27; Cant 2:10, 13; 4:6.

1.b. 1 sg impf hiph ראה + 2 masc sg suff.

2.a. The cohortative following an imperative expresses consequence, "so that," or intention, "I will" rather than "I shall" (Joüon, 116b).

2.b. SamPent, as at 17:1, reads והוי for וְהְיֵה (*waw* + 2 masc sg impv היה). *BHS* and some commentators (e.g., Skinner, Gunkel, Speiser) repoint וְהָיָה "and it [your name] shall be (a blessing)." This repointing is unnecessary. The impv (as in MT) expresses the same mood in the 2d person as the coh does in the 1st person (Joüon, 116h). Following a coh, the impv frequently expresses "a consequence which is to be expected with certainty . . . or . . . an intention" (GKC, 110i).

3.a-a. Chiasmus: note word order "verb-object // object-verb," frequently used in Heb. for two sides of a single action (*SBH*, 119–37).

3.b. Waw + 1 sg impf coh ברך.

3.c. Masc pl piel ptcp ברך + 2 masc pl suff.

3.d. Masc sg piel ptcp קלל + 2 masc sg suff. Some MSS and versions (G, Vg, SamPent, S) read masc pl ptcp + suff מקלליך, i.e., "those who disdain you." Without the vowel points, the MT could be interpreted this way, defective spelling.

3.e. 1 sg impf qal ארר "curse."

3.f. Waw consec + 3 masc pl pf niph ברך. This understands the niph as a middle. Possible alternatives: passive "be blessed" or reflexive "bless themselves." See *Comment* for further discussion.

4.a. Waw consec + 3 masc sg impf הלך.

4.b-b. Circumstantial clause (*SBH*, 41).

4.c. ב + inf constr יצא + masc sg suff.

5.a. Cf. n. 11:31.g.

6.a. G adds εἰς τὸ μῆκος αὐτῆς "throughout its length," imitating 13:17.

6.b. Tg, Vg read "plain." "The Aramaic versions of the Pentateuch consistently render MT אלון by מישר (or slight variations of the same noun)—evidently because terebinths and oaks were used for idolatrous worship. . . . *Tg. Onk.*'s rendering . . . may have been designed to remove Abraham from any association with centers of tree worship" (M. Aberbach and B. Grossfeld, *Targum Onkelos to Genesis,* 79).

6.c. For מורה (hiph ptcp ירה "teacher"), G has τὴν ὑψηλήν "high"; S σ' "Mamre." Cf. 18:1.

6.d-d. Circumstantial verbless clause (*SBH,* 85).

7.a. Waw consec + 3 masc sg impf (apoc) niph ראה.

7.b. SamPent adds לו "to him," apparently also read by G, Vg, S.

7.c. 1 sg impf נתן.

7.d. G adds Ἀβράμ.

7.e. Cf. 2:22; 8:20.

7.f. Niph ptcp ראה + definite article. Ptcp may express past time in relative clauses; cf. 16:13; 32:10; 35:1, 3 (GKC, 116o).

8.a. Waw consec + 3 masc sg impf hiph עתק.

8.b. ההר "the mountain" + ה, directional ending.

8.c. Waw consec + 3 masc sg impf (apoc) qal נטה.

8.d. G, Vg add "there."

8.e. SamPent has the more usual suff, ו "his." MT's אהלה is more archaic (F. M. Cross and D. N. Freedman, *Early Hebrew Orthography* [New Haven: American Oriental Society, 1952] 57).

8.f-f. A circumstantial clause (GKC, 156c), in expository apposition to "pitched his tent" (*SBH,* 49-50).

8.g. Cf. n. 4:26.e.

9.a. Waw consec + 3 masc sg impf נסע.

9.b. Inf absolutes נסע and הלך; cf. 8:3, 5. Inf abs of הלך expresses continuing action (GKC, 113u; Lambdin, 158).

9.c. הנגב + directional ending ה.

Form/Structure/Setting

The beginning of this unit is clear. 11:27, "This is the family history of Terah," opens the Abraham cycle, which is not completed until 25:11. But it is not so clear where the first unit ends. Though most commentators make 11:27-32 the first section of the Abraham cycle and 12:1-9 the second, it seems preferable, with Westermann, Coats, and Alexander, to see 11:27–12:9 as the opening section which sets out the background to and theme of the patriarchal narratives in general and the Abraham cycle in particular. 11:27–32 deals primarily with the family background, while 12:1–9 focuses on the divine promises.

12:1, with its brusque mention of Abram, presupposes some knowledge of his identity, and the command "Go by yourself from your country" implies some understanding of the location of his original homeland. This information is supplied in 11:27–32. It therefore seems unlikely that 12:1–3 was ever an independent, self-standing introduction to the Abraham stories. The whole pericope is dominated by Abram's journey from his homeland in Ur of the Chaldaeans (11:28) via Harran (11:31; 12:4) to the land of Canaan (12:5), from Shechem in the north, Bethel in the center, and on to the Negeb in the south (12:6, 8, 9).

The section is essentially an itinerary (11:31; 4–6, 8a, 9), expanded with genealogical details (11:27–30, 32), divine promises (12:1–3, 7), and notes about Abram's responses (12:4, 7–8). These asides, however, are quite long and include indispensable background information for understanding the subsequent stories. They introduce Lot (11:27, 31; 12:4–5), the subject of chaps. 13–14, 18–19; Sarai and her barrenness (11:29–31; 12:5), the theme of 12:10–20 and chaps. 15–18, 20, 21, 23; and Milcah (11:29), grandmother

of Rebekah, Isaac's future bride (chap. 24). 11:28, 31–32; 12:4–9 set the
scene geographically and chronologically for the following story, while the
promises enunciated here for the first time serve to explain the significance
of Abraham's whole career as well as that of his successors. The fourfold
promise of land, descendants, covenant, and blessing to the nations is gradually
fulfilled in Genesis and the succeeding books of the Pentateuch. Very properly,
12:1–3 has been the subject of close scrutiny because these verses are so
central to the understanding of the whole of Genesis. The genealogy and
the promises link the primeval history with the patriarchal stories. Verbal
and ideological connections with the primeval history are numerous. Land
(ארץ and אדמה), descendants, nation, name, greatness, curse and blessing,
Canaan and the Canaanites have all already been broached in chaps. 1–11
and are here reintroduced with pregnant brevity.

The section may be analyzed as follows:

11:27a	Heading: "This is the family history . . ."		
27b–30	Terah's family:	27b	his sons
		28	death of Haran
		29–30	his other sons' marriages
31	Terah's journey from Ur to Harran		
32	Terah's death		
12:1–3	Divine promise to Abram		
4–6	Abram's journey from Harran to Canaan (Shechem)		
7a	Divine promise		
7b	Altar built by Abram		
8–9	Abram journeys from Shechem to Negeb		

Though the emphases of 11:27–32 differ from those of 12:1–9, there are
some notable parallels between the two passages, most particularly "they left
Ur . . . to go to the land of Canaan . . . They came to Harran and stayed
there" (11:31) and "they left to go to the land of Canaan . . . they came to
the land of Canaan" (12:5). Interestingly, both parts subdivide into two sections: 11:27–32 contains two death reports (11:28, 32), and 12:1–9 two divine
revelations followed by two journeys by Abram.

Though 11:27–12:9 is united by Abram's journeys, 11:27–32 forms a discrete unit within this longer section. As elsewhere in Genesis (most obviously
5:32 to 9:28–29), genealogical statements have been fragmented: 11:27b is
an abridged resumption of 11:26 (a typical opening of a genealogy), and
11:32 is a typical close (cf. 5:5, 8, etc.). As in 6:8, here in 11:27a the editor
has apparently split apart an originally compact genealogical statement about
Terah's life to underline with the *toledot* formula "This is the family history
of . . . " the fact that a new phase in human history has begun. Like Adam
and Noah, Terah had three named sons, which may suggest that his life
marks another great turning point in the history of mankind.

It is nevertheless somewhat surprising at first sight that the stories of Abraham are headed "This is the family history of Terah," when "This is the
family history of Noah" (6:8) introduces the history of Noah and the flood.
This is the more anomalous in that 11:32 relates the death of Terah, all the
subsequent narratives making no mention of him.

Yet it is characteristic of the patriarchal narratives that the heading should mention the father, while the stories focus on the sons. Thus "This is the family history of Isaac" (25:19) introduces the stories of Jacob and Esau, and "the family history of Jacob" (37:2) heads the Joseph story. In these cases it is clear that it is because Isaac was the head of the extended family throughout the period covered by 25:19 to 35:29 that the stories of Jacob and Esau have this introductory formula. Similarly, Jacob was still head of the family from 37:2 to 49:33, so the formula fits there too. A similar logic may explain the formula "This is the family history of Terah."

According to the MT, Terah died at the age of 205, when Abraham was 135 (11:32; cf. 11:26). Yet Abraham was only two years older (137) when his wife Sarah died (23:1; cf. 17:17). In other words, Terah was alive and notionally head of the family throughout most of the period covered by the Abraham cycle. Thus the use of the introductory phrase "This is the family history of Terah" in 11:27 matches similar usage in 25:19 and 37:2.

Having said this, though, it must also be acknowledged that it is strange that Terah's death should be recorded so early. There is doubtless reason for this departure from chronological order. It is characteristic of Genesis to deal with less significant points first: Ishmael's family history precedes Isaac's, and Esau's precedes Jacob's (25:12, 19; 36:1; 37:2). It could be that, because Terah plays no subsequent part in the story after the family reaches Harran, his death is recorded prematurely in 11:32. There may also be some symbolic significance: true life is to be found only in Canaan, and Terah, who set out for Canaan but settled in Harran, died there.

12:1–9 continues the journey begun in 11:31. But whereas 11:27–32 gives background information about Abram's family and homeland, 12:1–9 sets out the divine word that prompted his journey (12:1–3) and describes his response (12:4–9). The tersely worded itinerary with which it concludes, "And Abram went on traveling toward the Negeb," expresses the unsettled nature of Abraham's existence, an alien in the land of promise. Thus this section is at once an introduction to and a summary of Abraham's career.

Formally the section falls into two main parts:

A	divine word	vv 1–3
B	Abram's response	vv 4–9

Both subdivide into three paragraphs:

A	Divine word	v 1	command
		v 2	promise
		v 3	promise
B	Response	vv 4–5	journey
		vv 6–7	journey
		vv 8–9	journey

Each part begins with the keyword "go," הלך (vv 1, 4), and this is also almost the final word of v 9. Inclusions mark the beginning and end of paragraphs (e.g., ארץ, v 1, with אדמה, v 3; יצא, vv 4, 5). The fulfillment (v 4) inverts the word order of the command (v 1):

```
        v 1   The LORD
                 to
                    Abram
                           "Go"
        v 4                   he went
                    Abram
                 to him
              The LORD
```

These and other devices (cf. Auffret, *BZ* 26 [1982] 243–48; Ruprecht, *VT* 29 [1979] 171–88, 444–64) show that this section has been carefully composed and that each verse is integral to it. Within it the play on the name "Abram" is very obvious. Every mention of the term "bless," "blessing," ברך, evokes the name "Abram," אברם, as does probably "he passed through," עבר (v 6), if not his title "Abram the Hebrew," עברי (14:13). Doubtless it is also deliberate that the promises to Abram fall into seven clauses in vv 2–3, just as do the promises to Isaac and Jacob in 26:3–4; 27:28–29: seven is the OT holy number. Maybe too the fivefold use of the root ברך "bless" in vv 2–3 consciously negates the five curses on man and his world pronounced in the preceding chapters (3:14, 17; 4:11; 5:29; 9:25).

11:28–30; 12:1–4a, 6–9 are usually assigned to J, and 11:27, 31–32; 12:4b–5 to P. The grounds for this analysis are clear. The P sections contain various typical P words—"family history" (תולדת), "to father" (הוליד), "land of Canaan"—as well as genealogical and chronological details typical of his style. The J sections use the divine name "Yahweh" repeatedly (12:1, 4, 7, 8). Where these criteria do not decide the matter, the necessity of finding material to support two parallel sources is invoked.

Recent work has tended to question this analysis more or less radically, however. Westermann, while accepting that 11:28–30 are J, argues that in fact this genealogical fragment must begin with 27b, for without it the subsequent genealogy starts in mid-air. He is followed by Coats. Both insist that we have here an amalgam of sources and we cannot be overprecise about distinguishing them. Westermann observes that 12:4a (J) presupposes knowledge of Lot's identity defined in 11:27–32. He thinks 12:5c, "they came to the land of Canaan," must be J and P (not just P), for otherwise there is a hiatus in J. Rendtorff (*Pentateuch*, 122) and Kikawada (*Proceedings*) argue that 12:1–9 is a coherent unit; only the chronological notice (12:4b) would be assigned to a later P editor by Rendtorff. Van Seters (*Abraham*), while accepting a traditional analysis of 12:1–9, argues that all 11:27–32 is P, since v 28 presupposes v 27 and v 31 presupposes v 28: "All of these verses fit together as a unity."

12:1–3 is usually seen as expressing the quintessence of the Yahwist's theology (e.g., Wolff, *EvT* 24 [1964] 73–98; Steck, *Probleme;* Coats). It binds together the primeval and the patriarchal history by presenting the call and blessing of Abram as the answer to the calamities that have befallen mankind in Gen 1–11. However, Crüsemann (*Botschaft*) has pointed out that the terminology of 12:1–3 is subtly different from that found in the J sections of Gen

1–11. For instance, in 12:3 the world is called אדמה, not ארץ as before, e.g., 6:5. The terms "nation" (גוי), "family" (משפחה), "homeland" (ארץ) link it with P's table of the nations in Gen 10. He therefore argues that 12:1–3 presupposes that J and P were already combined in Gen 1–11, and that it therefore represents a late redactional element in Genesis. Alexander (*Literary Analysis*) has also argued that 11:27–12:9 is the work of the final editor of Genesis, whom he identifies with J. This is not incompatible with Crüsemann's observations if, as we argued above, the J elements in Gen 10 represent an expansion of the earlier P material.

The question of the sources used by the editor of this section is even more moot. As already observed, 11:32 seems to be the close of a genealogical notice about Terah, the opening of which is found in 11:26. It may be that the other genealogical remarks in 11:27–29 come from this same source. Elements of an itinerary are to be found in 11:31b and 12:4b–9, and this suggests that another source may have been used by the editor. On the other hand, the remarks about Sarai's barrenness have the appearance of an editorial comment anticipating the theme of the forthcoming stories. Most controversy surrounds the antiquity of the divine command and promises in 12:1–3, 7. It is widely maintained that the promises in Genesis represent a late theological interpretation of the narratives. But the methodology behind such an approach is open to question (H. Seebass, *Bib* 64 [1983] 189–210). Certainly it is widely admitted that some elements of the promises expressed here are pre-J (vv 1a, 4a, 6a, 7, according to Kilian [*Abrahamsüberlieferungen*] and van Seters [*Abraham*]; v 7, Emerton [*VT* 32 (1982) 14–32]). V. Maag ("Malkut Jhwh," *Congress Volume*, VTSup 7 [Leiden: E. J. Brill, 1960] 137–42) also argued that the command to migrate reflects the needs of nomads for new pasture, so that vv 1–3 could reflect an early tradition. Ruprecht and, more circumspectly, Westermann admit that this may indicate that these promises are early. Seebass on the basis of the parallel with 46:1–5 thinks that 12:2 is surely old (*Bib* 64 [1983] 189–209).

Certainty is impossible. Given the substantial integrity of this section (cf. Kikawada), it is doubtful to what extent earlier and later elements can be successfully distinguished. Early patriarchal tradition and later theological interpretation are not mutually exclusive: by including certain stories and promises rather than others the biblical writers draw attention to their significance. By placing the promises to Abram right at the beginning of the patriarchal narratives the redactor is asserting their fundamental importance for the history of Israel and the world and indicating how the stories that follow ought to be understood.

Comment

27–29 These verses introduce Terah's extended family, most of whom have some role to play in the Abraham story. We may set out the family tree thus:

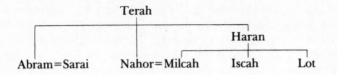

27 "This is the family history of Terah"; cf. 2:4; 5:1; 6:9. This is the editorial title to the whole Abraham cycle of 11:27–25:11. On why the stories of Abraham should be titled "the family history of Terah," see *Form/Structure/Setting* above; cf. 25:19; 37:2.

"Terah fathered . . . Haran" resumes 11:26b and adds a detail about Lot, "Haran fathered Lot." Lot is therefore Terah's grandson and Abram's nephew. He is introduced here because of the important role he plays in chaps. 13–14, 18–19. Apparently at least unofficially adopted by Abram, he was his presumptive heir until the acrimonious separation described in chap. 13.

On the etymologies of "Terah," "Abram," "Nahor," and "Haran," see *Comment* on 11:24, 26.

"Lot": the meaning and etymology of his name are unknown. Some would connect it with "Lotan," 36:20, 22, 29, but this is uncertain.

28 "And Haran died before his father Terah." עַל פְּנֵי "before" most frequently means "on the surface of." Why this prepositional phrase is used here instead of more usual expressions for "before," "in the lifetime of," is unclear. The closest parallels seem to be Num 3:4 and Deut 21:16, and the present phrase may have a quasi-legal significance suggesting that Lot was now regarded as Terah's son in place of Haran (cf. Jacob). At any rate, the death of Haran explains Lot's subsequent adoption by Abram. The early death of Haran and his daughter's marriage to his brother Nahor may suggest that he was the oldest of the three brothers. Though the order of names, Abram, Nahor, Haran, would naturally be taken as their order of birth, it need not. The order Shem, Ham, and Japhet seems to be euphonic rather than chronological; see above on 9:24.

"Ur of the Chaldaeans." Though this area used to be identified with Urfa (Edessa) in northern Mesopotamia, it is now usually agreed that the well-known Ur (el-Muqayyar) in southern Iraq is meant. Ur was already an important political and religious center in the early third millennium B.C. But the epithet "of the Chaldaeans" is probably anachronistic in Abram's day, since the Chaldaeans (Assyrian *Kaldu*) did not penetrate Babylonia till about 1000 B.C. It therefore most likely represents a gloss on the old tradition. (On Ur, cf. D. J. Wiseman, *NBD*, 1304–5; T. L. Thompson, *Historicity*, 303–4. On the Chaldaeans, cf. W. G. Lambert, *POTT*, 179–96. For identifying Ur with Urfa in northern Mesopotamia see C. H. Gordon, "Abraham of Ur," *Hebrew and Semitic Studies: G. R. Driver FS* [Oxford: Clarendon, 1963] 77–84; see also "Where is Abraham's Ur?" *BAR* 3 [1977] 20–21, 52.) Ur is called "his homeland," אֶרֶץ מוֹלַדְתּוֹ, literally, "land of his family." But LXX renders it "land in which he was born." Though it may be that Haran was born in Ur, the phrase is probably less precise. The point being made is that the family home was in Ur when Haran died. The names of Terah and his family suggest they were western Semites, possibly of Amorite stock. It is known that many Amorites settled in Mesopotamia both before and after 2000 B.C., and Terah's family could well have been among them. However, Abram's journey from Ur to Harran to Canaan took him against the mainstream of Amorite migration.

29 Abram married Sarai (according to 20:12, his half-sister; i.e., she had the same father Terah as Abram, but a different mother) and Nahor married Milcah, his niece. Marrying a half-sister is forbidden by Lev 18:9; 20:17; Deut 27:22, but not one's niece. Simultaneous bigamy with two sisters is also forbidden (Lev 18:18); contrast Gen 29, where Jacob marries Leah and Rachel. This suggests that Leviticus is introducing incest rules that were unknown in patriarchal times. That the patriarchs are portrayed as flouting later legal norms argues for the antiquity of the tradition here.

Sarai's name was later changed to Sarah. Both forms are probably from שרה, *śārāh,* "princess," while "Milcah" comes from מלכה, *malkāh* "queen." *Šarratu* was the wife of the moon god Sin, and *Malkātu* was his daughter. Both Ur and Harran were important centers of moon worship. It may be that Terah's family were once involved in such worship (cf. Josh 24:2, 15), though there is no trace of it in the following stories.

Nahor's marriage was compared by Speiser with the Nuzi *ṭuppi mārtūti u kallatūti* contracts in which, he alleged, a girl was simultaneously adopted and married by her uncle. However, both Speiser's interpretation of the Nuzi evidence (S. Greengus, *HUCA* 46 [1975] 5–31) and the appropriateness of the parallel (T. L. Thompson, *Historicity,* 230–34) have been rightly questioned.

"Iscah" is mentioned only here. The etymology and meaning of her name are unknown. Suggestions that Iscah is an alternative name for Sarah or that she was Lot's wife are purely speculative.

30 With stark brevity the bitterness of the childless wife is summed up (cf. Judg 13:2–3; 1 Sam 1:2–8; Isa 54:1). Digressions within a genealogy are of special significance, and this is no exception. The whole Abraham cycle is an eloquent witness to the desperate desire for children in primitive society (cf. Pss 127, 128). Without children the man had no one to perpetuate his name and the wife enjoyed little prestige and much frustration, for she had no alternative career to motherhood. Further, in old age, childless couples had no children to care for them, and after death, none to carry out the funerary rites regarded as vital to the soul's well-being in the afterlife. This traditional motif is given a peculiar piquancy in the Abraham stories in that this barren couple are repeatedly promised a child by God, but there is great delay in the fulfillment of that promise.

31 Terah, as head of the family, led the migration from Ur. His reasons are not given. He took the three chief actors in the subsequent stories with him: Abram, Lot, and Sarai. Nahor and his wife are not mentioned, as they play little part in the narrative. But from 22:20–24 and 24:10 it appears that Nahor and Milcah also moved to northern Mesopotamia.

"Harran" (Assyrian *ḫarrānu* "main road"), often mentioned in Mari texts as a center of Amorite activity, lies on the river Baliḥ, twenty miles southeast of Urfa (Edessa). By the Romans it was called Carrhae.

32 The formulation of this verse is typical of concluding statements in the genealogy of chap. 5; cf. 5:11, 14, 17, etc. This suggests that we have a fragment of the genealogy of Terah, the opening of which is 11:26. The Samaritan reading makes Terah 145 years old at his death, and therefore allows Abram to leave Harran after Terah died. However, the MT reading assumes Terah to be alive throughout most of Abraham's life. On the MT chronology, Terah died only two years before Sarah (23:1). This would explain why the Abraham cycle is headed "the family history of Terah" (11:27). But since he takes no further part in the action, his life is briefly summed up here, so that it does not distract from the main theme, the call of Abram.

1–9 The call of Abram is related in vv 1–3, while vv 4–9 tell of his obedience. More precisely, v 1 is answered in v 4, "Abram went as the LORD had told him." The divine speech consists of a command "Go . . . to the country . . . " followed by a series of promises (vv 2–3) that heavily outweigh the command, showing where the chief interest of the passage lies. Indeed, the command itself contains within it an implied promise of the land. These verses are of fundamental importance for the theology of Genesis, for they serve to bind together the primeval history and the later patriarchal history and look beyond it to the subsequent history of the nation.

1 "The LORD said to Abram," though marking a new development, presupposes some knowledge of Abram's identity and situation as already set out in 11:27–32; it is not therefore the beginning of a completely new narrative. The command is crisp and stark in its formulation. The ethical dative, "go *by yourself*" (see n. 1.a.), the use of rhyme (five words in v 2 end in *kā* "your/ you"), and the climactic development—"country . . . clan . . . father's house"—add punch to the command and emphasize the uncompromising nature of God's words. Abram must leave "his country"; in context (cf. 11:31) this must mean Harran rather than Ur. Coming from Ur, Abram presumably felt less attached to Harran than to his "clan," מולדת, a grouping intermediate in size between the tribe and extended family, here and elsewhere in the OT called his "father's house" בית אב, his closest relations. The quick progression from "land" to "father's house" draws attention to the costliness of obedience.

Most commentators have regarded this divine imperative as a test of faith: Abram is to give up all he holds dearest for an unknown land promised by God. This is confirmed by 22:2, where a very similar command to Abraham is explicitly prefaced by the comment that God tested Abraham (22:1). Westermann argues, though, that for a nomad it was easy to leave land and family and that we must postulate some crisis situation in which the divine command saved the situation. There is nothing in the text to support this suggestion. The fact that Terah stayed in Harran (11:31–32), whereas only Abram went on to Canaan (12:4), suggests that the traditional interpretation is preferable. This view is further supported by the policy of sending Isaac, and later, Jacob, back to Harran to find wives: the family base was in northern Mesopotamia. Most of the patriarchs are uprooted from their native land and their family for a while (cf. Jacob and Joseph). The phrasing of 15:7 in particular suggests that Abram's migration prefigures Israel's exodus from Egypt.

2–3 These two verses are generally regarded as the key to the Yahwist's interpretation of the patriarchal history and have consequently attracted much scholarly attention. Whatever one's critical position (cf. Crüsemann [*Botschaft*] and discussion under *Form/Structure/Setting*), there is no doubt about their cardinal importance for the understanding of Genesis.

Grammatically, the main verbs—"make," "bless," "make great," "be," "bless," "curse," "find blessing"—are all subordinate to the imperative "Go" (v 1). Most of them are imperfects or cohortatives prefixed by weak *waw* which indicates purpose or consequence. (The other grammatical forms used here have the same function). The divine intentionality could also be expressed by translating these verses "Go . . . so that I may make you . . . bless you . . . etc."

Within these verses the promise of blessing is central: five times the verb or the noun derived from ברך "bless" is used. The root ברך occurs more frequently in Genesis than in any other part of the OT: 88 times in Genesis as against 310 times elsewhere. God's blessing is manifested most obviously in human prosperity and well-being; long life, wealth, peace, good harvests, and children are the items that figure most frequently in lists of blessing such as 24:35–36; Lev 26:4–13; Deut 28:3–15. What modern secular man calls "luck" or "success" the OT calls "blessing," for it insists that God alone is the source of all good fortune. Indeed, the presence of God walking among his people is the highest of his blessings (Lev 26:11–12). Material blessings are in themselves tangible expressions of divine benevolence. Blessing not only connects the patriarchal narratives with each other (cf. 24:1; 26:3; 35:9; 39:5), it also links them with the primeval history (cf. 1:28; 5:2; 9:1). The promises of blessing to the patriarchs are thus a reassertion of God's original intentions for man.

Behind the fourfold promise of nationhood, a great name, divine protection, and mediatorship of blessing, E. Ruprecht (*VT* 29 [1979] 445–64) has plausibly detected echoes of royal ideology. What Abram is here promised was the hope of many an oriental monarch (cf. 2 Sam 7:9; Ps 72:17).

First, Abram is to become a "great nation" (גוי גדול). This promise is repeated in slightly different words in 18:18, and also to Ishmael in 17:20; 21:18; and to Jacob in 46:3. But the closest parallel is the offer made to Moses that his descendants instead of Abraham's should become a great nation (Exod 32:10). Apart from 10:5, 20, 31, 32, where גוי is used in summarizing formulae in the table of nations, this is the first use of the term in Genesis. A "nation" (גוי) is a political unit with a common land, language, and government, whereas "people" (עם) primarily draws attention to the consanguinity of the group (E. A. Speiser, "People and Nation of Israel," *JBL* 79 [1960] 157–63; R. E. Clements, *TDOT* 2:426–33; A. R. Hulst *THWAT* 2:290–325). A large population, a large territory, and a spiritual character make a nation great (cf. 12:7; 13:14–17, etc.; Deut 4:7–8). Thus this very first word to Abram encapsulates the full range of divine promises subsequently made to him.

"Make your name great" has its closest parallel in the promise to David in 2 Sam 7:9: "I will make for you a great name." Otherwise only the name of God is described as "great" (Josh 7:9; 1 Sam 12:22; Ps 76:2 [1]; Mal 1:11). However, royal aspirations for a "great" or "high" name long antedate David. Ruprecht (*VT* 29 [1979] 452) quotes several royal inscriptions from early second-millennium Mesopotamia promising a great name to kings. Wester-

mann rightly observes that the promise of great nationhood and name are
"one of the clearest links between the story of the patriarchs and the history
of Israel" (2:150).

"Bless you"; cf. 26:3. Every mention of the root "to bless" in this passage
is a paronomastic allusion to Abram's name. Here it is unmistakable (cf.
ʾăbārekěkā "I will bless you" and *ʾabrām*).

"You shall be a blessing." (Note another play on Abram's name: *běrākāh*
"blessing"). This is an unusual construction. ברכה היה "be a blessing" occurs
in only two other passages, Isa 19:24 and Zech 8:13. Its precise interpretation
is uncertain. The versions take it to be virtually equivalent to the passive
participle "you shall be blessed." This is the view too of Dillmann, Procksch,
and L. Schmidt (*TV* 12 [1975] 135–51), who would render it "you will be
the embodiment of blessing." Keil, Delitzsch, Wolff (*EvT* 24 [1964] 73–98),
and Westermann, however, give it a more active sense: because Abram has
been blessed, "he will be a source of blessing to others." But the most likely
interpretation is that suggested by Zech 8:13, "As you have been a byword
for cursing among the nations . . . so will I save you and you shall be a
blessing." In other words, people will say, "May God make me as blessed as
Abram" (cf. the use of names of Ephraim and Manasseh, 48:20). The use
of Abram's name in such a blessing of course implies that he is already blessed,
and as the next verse makes clear, those who bless Abram in this way will
themselves be blessed. So the alternative interpretations are rightly implied
by this passage, though they do not express the precise nuance of "you shall
be a blessing."

3 "I will bless those who bless you / and he who disdains you I shall curse."
The chiasmus and parallelism make this a poetic couplet. In 27:29 and Num
24:9 we have a more balanced but less personal formula: "Blessed are those
who bless you / and cursed are those who curse you." Similar formulae are
also found in extrabiblical literature (cf. E. Ruprecht, *VT* 29 [1979] 454–
57). Because they sound more like formulas, the versions of this saying in
27:29 and Num 24:9 are often adjudged more primitive than the form here,
and it is suggested that 12:3a represents a literary reworking of an older
saying. While the evolution of our text remains speculative, comparison of
this form with its variants is revealing.

This passage differs from its parallels in three striking ways. In each case
it accentuates the closeness of the relationship between the LORD and Abram
more strongly than the parallel. (1) 12:3 employs the first person, "I will
bless/I shall curse," instead of the more impersonal passive participle "blessed/
cursed" found in 27:29; Num 24:9. This emphasizes God's concern for Abram's
welfare. Retribution and justice are not left to the impersonal operation of
fate. The LORD himself will actively intervene on Abram's side.

(2) 12:3 uses a milder term קלל "disdain" instead of ארר "curse" to describe
those opposed to Abram. Traditional English translations fail to bring out
the difference between these words, usually translating both "curse." However,
קלל "disdain" generally covers illegitimate verbal assaults on God or one's
superiors, e.g., Exod 21:17; Lev 24:11; 2 Sam 16:5–13, whereas the latter
term ארר refers to a judicial curse pronounced on evildoers (3:14, 17; 9:25;
Deut 27:15–26). Balak wanted Balaam to "curse" Israel (Num 22:6), but in

the event he merely "disdained" Israel (Deut 23:5 [4]; Josh 24:9). כבד "make heavy, honor" is the opposite of קלל "disdain," whereas ברך "bless" is the antonym of ארר "curse."

The formula used elsewhere, "cursed are those who curse you," preserves a balance between evildoers and their reward. The cursers are cursed, just as the blessers are blessed: this is a literary formulation of the talion principle ("eye for eye", etc., as in Exod 21:24; Lev 24:20) which makes the punishment fit the crime. Here, however, the punishment is heightened. Those who merely "disdain" Abram will be "cursed" by God himself.

(3) Finally, the standard formula uses the plural participle "*those* who curse you," while here we have the singular "*he* who disdains you," at least if the MT punctuation is followed (see *Notes*). This appears to imply that those who disdain Abram will be far fewer than those who bless him. He will flourish to such an extent that few will fail to recognize that God is indeed on his side.

"Find blessing": נברכו. The niphal of ברך occurs only three times in the OT (here; 18:18; 28:14). The hithpael is more common (7 times), and apparently has the same meaning as the niphal in 22:18; 26:4. The rarity of its usage has led to uncertainty about the precise meaning of the verb here. Three interpretations have been advocated. The first sees it in a passive sense, "be blessed"; so the versions (LXX, *Tg. Onq.*, Vg), Sir 44:21; Acts 3:25; Gal 3:8, kjv, and more recently, König, Jacob, Cassuto, and Gispen. A second possibility is a middle "find blessing"; so Procksch, Keller, Schreiner, Wolff, Schmidt, nab. Or, third, it may have a reflexive sense, "bless themselves" (Speiser, Delitzsch, Skinner, Gunkel, Westermann, rsv, neb): the reflexive sense would mean that all the clans of the earth will say, "May we be blessed like Abram." In support of a reflexive meaning, "bless themselves," it is urged that this is the natural way to interpret a hithpael. Some of the instances of this stem of ברך clearly have this meaning, most obviously, Deut 29:18 [19], "one who . . . blesses himself in his heart," and Isa 65:16. It is argued that since the hithpael has a reflexive meaning outside Genesis, it must have the same sense within Genesis. Further, since there is no apparent difference between, say, 22:18 (hithpael) and 18:18 (niphal), the niphal must also have the same reflexive sense.

That a reflexive sense is possible may be conceded; that it is required is another matter. If the niphal and hithpael of ברך are totally interchangeable within Genesis, it could also indicate that the hithpael may sometimes have the sense of the niphal.

Grammatically, the basic sense of the niphal is medio-passive, that is, it may either be translated as a middle ("find blessing," as here), or as a passive, "be blessed." (For a clear general discussion of the meaning of the niphal see T. O. Lambdin, *Introduction to Biblical Hebrew*, 175–77; cf. "The engine stopped" [middle]; "The engine was stopped [by s.o.]" [passive]; "The engine stopped itself" [reflexive].) However, since the pual or qal passive participle is usually employed for the passive of ברך, a middle sense is more likely here. Furthermore, a middle sense here complements and completes the earlier remarks. Already it has been stated that Abram will be a blessing, which presupposes both the passive sense, "Abram has been blessed," and the reflexive sense, men will use his name in blessing each other. Then it was stated that all individuals who bless Abram will themselves be blessed. Finally, this clause brings the passage to a triumphant and universal conclusion: "all the families of the earth will find blessing in you." There is thus a progressive buildup in the good that will result from obeying God's command:

1) Abram alone is blessed →   2) Abram's name used as a blessing →
3) Abram's blessers are blessed → 4) all families find blessing in Abram.

The use of the hithpael "bless themselves" in 22:18 and 26:4 may, as König suggests, be a way of combining two ideas, that Abram's name will be used in blessing and that all clans will be blessed in him.

Finally it should be noted that even if a reflexive "bless themselves" is preferred here, it would also carry the implications of a middle or passive. For if those who bless Abram are blessed, and all families of the earth bless Abram, then it follows that "all families will be blessed/find blessing in him."

"All families of the earth": משפחה "family," translated "clan" in 10:5, 18, 20, 31, 32 is a grouping intermediate between a tribe and a father's house (cf. the rarer term מולדת, 12:1), Josh 7:14–18. "Earth" here and in 28:14 (cf. Amos 3:2) is אדמה. Elsewhere the phrase is "all the nations of the world [ארץ]" (18:18; 22:18; 26:4). Not every individual is promised blessing in Abram but every major group in the world will be blessed. The subsequent stories in Genesis illustrate these principles in action. Groups well disposed to Abram and his descendants prosper: those that oppose them do not.

4 וילך "Then Abram went," fulfilling the divine command in v 1: "Go." "As the Lord had told him" emphasizes Abram's obedience (cf. 6:22; 7:5; 17:23; 24:51). "Lot went with him" presupposes the knowledge about Lot already given in 11:27–31 and prepares the way for the stories in chaps. 13–14. "Seventy-five years old" implies that Abram left Harran sixty years before his father died; cf. 11:26, 32. Without spelling it out explicitly, this remark shows Abram putting the call of God above loyalty to his family (cf. Deut 13:7–11 [6–10]; Matt 10:37). Cassuto notes that Abram's life shows an interesting symmetry:

75 years with his father
25 years without father or son
75 years with his son.

5 Although the verse closely parallels 11:31, also note the contrasts. Whereas Terah set out for Canaan but settled and died in Harran, Abram actually reached Canaan. Both took various relatives with them, but Abram also acquired "property" (רכוש is movable property, including herds; cf. 14:11, 12; 31:18; Num 35:3) and slaves, literally, "persons" (נפש). His acquisition of wealth in Harran foreshadows his profitable visits to other foreign parts (cf. 12:16; 20:14). The fact that Lot accompanied Abram is again mentioned, drawing attention to the close relationship between them.

"Canaan." Its boundaries, loosely defined in 10:19 and more precisely in

Num 34:2–12, seem to correspond fairly closely to those of the Egyptian province of the same name in the fifteenth–thirteenth centuries B.C. (cf. *Comment* on 10:19 and R. de Vaux, "Le Pays de Canaan," *JAOS* 88 [1968] 23–30; M. Weippert, *IDBSup,* 126).

6 "Abram passed through the land." "The land" is short for "the land of Canaan." The most likely route for Abram to have followed would have taken him south through Damascus, along the shore of the Sea of Galilee, and then on to Shechem. This has been positively identified with Tell Balata, just east of modern Nablus (see G. E. Wright, *Shechem* [London: Duckworth, 1965]). Shechem was a very important center in the second millennium B.C. and is often mentioned in the OT (e.g., 33:18; 35:4; 37:12–13: Josh 24:1; Judg 9:6; 1 Kgs 12:1). Josh 20:7 indicates that it was regarded as lying in the center of the land.

"The place" probably suggests a holy place; cf. the deuteronomic "place which the LORD will choose" (Deut 16:7).

"The oak of Moreh." The identity of אֵלוֹן is disputed. Most commentaries translate it "terebinth," but M. Zohary (*Plants of the Bible* [Cambridge: University Press, 1982] 108–11) is convinced that אלון is an oak, either the Tabor oak (*Quercus ithaburensis*) or the common evergreen oak (*Quercus calliprinos*) while אלה should be interpreted "terebinth." He suggests that the greater height of the Tabor oak makes it likely that it was the one preferred for worship.

"Moreh": מורה is literally "teacher," which suggests it was a place where divine oracles could be obtained; cf. "the palm of Deborah" (Judg 4:5). Here the very name "Moreh" anticipates that the LORD will appear (niphal of ראה) there. Possibly the same tree is mentioned in Judg 9:37. De Moor (*TDOT* 1:443) notes that "trees and stones were specifically connected with the oracle at Ugarit" and similar associations are found in Gen 28:18–22; 35:8; Josh 24:26; Judg 6:11,19–20. Sacred trees are still known today in the Near East.

"The Canaanite was then in the land." Though the writer may be making a historical point, contrasting the situation in his day with that of the patriarchal age, his primary concern is to explain why Abram could not take immediate possession of the land about to be promised to him: it was already occupied.

7 "The LORD appeared to Abram." This is the first recorded appearance of the LORD to a patriarch (cf. 17:1; 18:1; 26:2, 24; 35:9; 48:3), which in turn foreshadows his appearances at Sinai and in the tabernacle (cf. Exod 3:2, 16; 16:10; Lev 9:4). What form the theophany took is not made clear. Here it introduces the first explicit promise of land and descendants, promises certainly implied in 12:1–2, but not spelled out.

"To your descendants I shall give this land." Jacob (344) comments: "This monumental statement, the shortest of all the promises, yet names both people and land and unites them by the verb give, here uttered for the first time." Cf. 13:14–15, 17; 15:7, 13, 16, 18; 17:8; 26:2–3. The promise of descendants and land are central to Genesis. Whether they represent merely the editor's interpretation of the stories or are really integral to the narratives themselves is much disputed. Westermann (*The Promises to the Fathers* [Philadelphia: Fortress Press, 1980] 146–47) argues that in this case the land promise is secondary, because the mention of descendants and the term "give," involving a solemn act of conveyancing, are too remote from Abram's situation. It addresses a later situation "when *possession* of the land had become a vital question for the tribes beginning to settle in Canaan." On the other hand, J. A. Emerton (*VT* 32 [1982] 22) argues that a promise of land fits in well with the context, in that 12:1–13:18 portrays Abram visiting the major sanctuaries of Canaan, Shechem, Bethel, and Hebron. Clearly both positions depend heavily on assumptions about what the LORD could or would do in various situations. If we incline to the authenticity of the promises here and elsewhere in Genesis, it is because the editors of Genesis seem in general to have a high regard for the divine words they record. (See G. J. Wenham, "The Religion of the Patriarchs," in *Essays,* ed. A. R. Millard and D. J. Wiseman, 157–88).

"Then he built an altar to the LORD." Abram's first act on being informed that he had reached his goal was to build an altar and presumably offer sacrifice, just as Noah did as soon as he came out of the ark (8:20). Subsequently Abram built altars at Bethel, Hebron, and Mount Moriah (12:8; 13:18; 22:9); Isaac at Beersheba (26:25); Jacob at Luz (35:7); and Moses at Rephidim and Sinai (Exod 17:15; 24:4). Sacrifice was the normal mode of worship in the OT, and theophanies often prompted it (22:14; Exod 20:24; Judg 13:16; 1 Kgs 3:15). However, Jacob, Cassuto, and Westermann argue that since sacrifice is not mentioned here, it was not offered. Abram built an altar to show that he believed the promise of the land. In building it, he symbolically demonstrated his conviction that one day it would belong to his descendants. This denial that Abram offered sacrifice seems a little perverse in the light of Noah's example and chap. 22. Both building an altar and offering sacrifice were expressions of faith in the promise and were integral to the worship of God. Presumably only the altar-building is mentioned here because it survived longer than the sacifice as a witness to God's promise and the patriarchs' response.

8 "Moved camp." The phrase is used with this sense also in 26:22. "Leaving" Shechem, which lies in a valley, Abram moved on "to the hills east of Bethel." Bethel was once called Luz (28:19). Its newer name is used here in anticipation of the later change (cf. 14:14; Judg 18:29). It is usually identified with Beitin, 10 miles (17 kilometers) north of Jerusalem (*EAEHL* 1:190–193).

"Ai" is usually identified with Et-Tell, one and a half miles (2 kilometers) east of Beitin (*EAEHL* 1:36–52). However, this creates problems, for, according to Josh 8, it was conquered by Joshua, and Et-Tell contains no remains between the Early Bronze Age and the Iron Age. Unless Josh 8 originally referred to another site (so W. F. Albright, *BASOR* 56 [1934] 11) or is fictional (so R. de Vaux, *The Early History of Israel* [London: DLT, 1978] 617–20), the identification of Et-Tell with Ai must be at fault (so Simons, *GTOT,* 270). It might possibly be at Khirbet Nisya, a mile southeast of El-Bireh (so J. J. Bimson, *BAR,* forthcoming). However, the last solution also requires the relocation of Bethel, perhaps at El-Bireh, 2 miles south of Beitin (Livingston, *WTJ* 33 [1970] 20–44; *WTJ* 34 [1971] 39–50; J. J. Bimson, *Redating the Exodus and Conquest* [Sheffeld: JSOT Press, 1978] 219–25).

"Pitched his tent." Since presumably Abram pitched his tent wherever he went, the mention of the fact here probably suggests that he settled near Bethel for some time; cf. 26:25; 33:19; 35:21; Judg 4:11.

"Built an altar": cf. v 7.

"Called on the name of the LORD." Again this deliberate mention of calling on the LORD implies more than simple prayer: it suggests that Abram worshiped in a regular formal way (cf. 4:26; 21:33; 26:25; Zeph 3:9). 13:4 records that Abram returned to this altar and called on the name of the LORD there. Despite the brevity of the remarks, their tenor suggests that Abram stayed a good while near Bethel.

9 "Went on traveling toward the Negeb" summarizes several stages in Abram's journey southward. The grammatical construction (see *Notes*) suggests a series of encampments. The root נסע "travel" is particularly common in descriptions of Israel's wilderness wanderings (e.g., Num 33), and it may not be coincidental that the term is introduced when Abram reaches the area closely associated with them, viz., "the Negeb." The Negeb (literally, "the dry land") is the area lying between the hills of Judah and Kadesh-Barnea. Its rainfall is generally too low for normal agriculture, and in consequence it has always been sparsely populated except for a period in the early Middle Bronze Age *ca.* 2000 B.C. It roughly marks the southern border of Canaan (Num 34:3–5), so in traversing it Abram found himself at the border of the promised land.

Thus the brief itinerary of Abram described in vv 5–9 takes him from the northern to the southern border of the land. He not only sees what has been promised to him; he walks through it, and he lives and worships in it. Symbolically he has taken possession of it. However, the end of his journey in the Negeb at the southern boundary prepares for the next episode, which takes place in Egypt (12:10–20).

Explanation

Within the book of Genesis no section is more significant than 11:27–12:9. It serves both as an introduction to and summary of Abraham's career. It looks forward to the later patriarchs and beyond them to the nation of Israel and the Davidic monarchy, the great nation that will inherit the land of Canaan. It also looks back to the primeval history, announcing the divine intervention that will bring blessing to all the families of the world, whose history hitherto has been overshadowed by divine judgments from Eden to the flood to Babel. But in Abraham all the nations of the world will find blessing. Abraham's obedience to the divine call, forsaking his homeland and family for the worship of the LORD in the land of promise, stands as an example and an incentive to all his descendants to follow suit. This will bring blessing on themselves and to the world.

The link between the primeval and patriarchal history is achieved not only in the word of promise; the opening biographical details (11:27–32) also contribute to this end. They serve to introduce us to Abraham and his family, so that we know who we are meeting in the following chapters, in particular Sarah, Lot, Nahor and Milcah. It highlights the central concerns of the patriarchal stories: Sarah's childlessness and Abraham's willingness to leave home and family in response to God's call.

At the same time, 11:27–32 is the last, albeit expanded, element in the genealogy of Shem. Abraham, we are reminded, is not merely the father of the faithful, but a son of Shem, who was in turn a son of Adam. This passage, then, by linking the patriarchs with the primeval history, gives the call of Abraham a cosmic setting: the LORD who summoned him to leave Ur of the Chaldaeans is also the creator and judge of the universe revealed in the opening chapters of Genesis. The promise of universal blessing to the nations is given by the sovereign LORD who had determined their times and their habitations (Acts 17:26; cf. Gen 10).

In this oblique but quite deliberate way the theological significance of Abraham is emphasized. If to human eyes he appears only as a landless wanderer, the divine call and his obedient response gives his life story an abiding importance that surpasses even the imagination of the author of Genesis.

The divine call and Abraham's response are eloquently summarized in 12:1–9. Briefly and simply, these paragraphs tell of the LORD's command to Abraham to leave home, the journey that Abraham undertook in obedient faith, and the acts of worship that followed his later experiences. He is portrayed as traversing the land of promise from end to end. Symbolically taking possession of it, lingering at the holy places, he has time to build altars and pitch his tent, and to call on the name of the LORD.

These words of promise and acts of faith set the tone for the whole Abraham story: they are at once programmatic and typological, that is, they reveal the divine plan for Abraham. He is to father children, inherit a land, enjoy divine protection, and be a source of blessing to the world. This story is typological in that it is the first in a series of episodes in which God speaks and the patriarch usually responds in faithful obedience, a pattern repeated many times in Genesis, not just in the Abraham cycle but also in the Isaac and Jacob cycles as well.

The divine word begins with a summons to Abraham to leave his family for an as-yet-unspecified land: "Go by yourself . . . to the country I shall show you." Here as in 22:2, "Go to . . . one of the mountains of which I shall tell you," Abraham is bidden to do something of which God is the sole guarantor of its successful outcome. Like his grandson Jacob and great-grandson Joseph, he had to leave his home to find God's blessing in a foreign land.

The later patriarchs were in many respects following in their forefather's footsteps. It was Abraham who first set out on this pilgrimage of faith. And the narrative draws attention to the new epoch that is inaugurated by a number of allusions to the primeval history. Five times in vv 2–3 Abraham is said to be "blessed" or a "blessing" to others. This harks back to the first great blessing of mankind at creation (1:28) and its renewal after the flood (9:1). Moreover, Abraham is to become "a great nation," comparable presumably to the seventy nations listed in Gen 10. His name will also be "great," whereas the men of Babel who tried to make themselves "a name" were frustrated (11:4–9).

Abraham's God-given success will be so evident to others that he will become "a blessing," that is, men will invoke blessings on themselves: "May the LORD bless me as he blessed Abram." Those who so invoke God's aid are assured by him: "I will bless those who bless you." So Abraham will become a source of blessing to all who seek it. Indeed, in him "all the families of the world will find blessing." However, the few who disdain to acknowledge God's working in Abraham are warned: "He who disdains you [Abraham] I shall curse." Succeeding episodes begin to illustrate these principles: kings like Melchizedek and Abimelech, who acknowledge God's blessing of Abraham, prosper, whereas Hagar, who despises Sarah, is cut off from Abram's family.

The narrative quickly moves on to relate Abraham's obedience. Unlike his father, Terah, who stays in Harran, he goes on to Canaan. There in its heartland of Shechem the LORD appears to him; indeed, this is the first time in Scripture the LORD is said to have appeared to anyone. He promises Abraham: "To your descendants I shall give this land." Abraham's response is immediate: he builds an altar. Briefly it is related that he moves on to another important holy site near Bethel, and there he stays, pitching his tent, building an altar, and worshiping the LORD. The scene closes with him moving towards the southern border of Canaan, the Negeb. His actions, however briefly related, are an acted prophecy. They foreshadow the day when Israel will take possession of the whole land and worship the LORD there.

This narrative thus looks forward to the conquest of the land, and beyond that, to the establishment of the Davidic empire. David himself was promised "a great name" (2 Sam 7:9), and he made Israel "a great nation." But that did not exhaust the scope of these promises. Ps 47:10 [9] encourages all the princes of the peoples to acknowledge the God of Abraham. The prophets, of course, look forward to a day when all men will recognize God's presence in Israel (e.g., Isa 2:2–4), when the curse of Babel will be reversed so that "all of them may call upon the name of the LORD" (Zeph 3:9). But most interesting are the specific allusions to Gen 12 in Isa 19:24, where Israel is going to be a blessing in the midst of the earth alongside her archenemies Egypt and Assyria. Jer 4:2 also makes reference to these promises. If Israel repents, he says, "then nations shall bless themselves in him, and in him shall they glory." The NT looks on the advent of Christ as ushering in the age in which all the nations will be blessed through Abraham (Acts 3:25; Gal 3:8). And his faith is held up as a model of God's dealings with all men (Rom 4; Gal 3); in particular his willingness to forsake his homeland is an example to us who should look for "the city . . . whose builder and maker is God" (Heb 11:8–10).

Abram in Egypt (12:10–20)

Bibliography

Aharoni, R. "Concerning Three Similar Stories in the Book of Genesis." (Heb.) *BMik* 24 (1979) 213–23. **Augustin, M.** "Die Inbesitznahme der schönen Frau aus der unterschiedlichen Sicht der Schwachen und der Mächtigen." *BZ* 27 (1983) 145–54. **Berg, W.** "Nochmals: ein Sündenfall Abrahams—der erste—in Gen 12:10–20." *BN* 21 (1983) 7–15. **Eichler, B. L.** "Please Say That You Are My Sister." (Heb). *Shnaton* 3 (1978–79) 108–15. **Greengus, S.** "Sisterhood Adoption at Nuzi and the 'Wife-Sister' in Genesis." *HUCA* 46 (1975) 5–31. **Keller, C. A.** "Die Gefährdung der Ahnfrau." *ZAW* 66

(1954) 181–91. **Miscall, P. D.** "Literary Unity in Old Testament Narrative." *Semeia* 15 (1979) 27–44. ———. *The Workings of Old Testament Narrative.* Philadelphia: Fortress, 1983. **Nomoto, S.** "Enstehung und Entwicklung der Erzählung von der Gefährdung der Ahnfrau." *AJBI* 2 (1976) 3–27. **Petersen, D. L.** "A Thrice-Told Tale: Genre, Theme and Motif." *BR* 18 (1973) 30–43. **Polzin, R.** "'The Ancestress of Israel in Danger' in Danger." *Semeia* 3 (1975) 81–97. ———. "Literary Unity in Old Testament Narrative: A Response." *Semeia* 15 (1979) 45–49. **Pratt, R. L.** "Pictures, Windows, and Mirrors in Old Testament Exegesis." *WTJ* 45 (1983) 156–67. **Schmitt, G.** "Zu Gen 26:1–14." *ZAW* 85 (1973) 143–56. **Speiser, E. A.** "The Wife-Sister Motif in the Patriarchal Narratives." In *Oriental and Biblical Studies.* 62–82. **Weir, C. J. M.** "The Alleged Hurrian Wife-Sister Motif in Genesis." *TGUOS* 22 (1967/68) 14–25. **Williams, J. G.** "The Beautiful and the Barren: Conventions in Biblical Type Scenes." *JSOT* 17 (1980) 107–19.

Translation

[10] *There was a famine in the land so Abram went down to Egypt[a] to settle[b] there, because the famine was severe in the land.*

[11a] *Shortly before he[b] entered Egypt,[a] he[b] said to Sarai his wife, "Since[c] I know[d] that you[e] are a beautiful[f] woman,* [12] *when the Egyptians see you, they will say;* [a] *'This is his wife,'[a] and* [b] *they will kill me while sparing[c] you.[b]* [13] *Say[a] then[b] that[c] you are my sister,[c] so that it will go[d] well with me because of you, and my person[e] will survive for your sake."*

[14a] *When Abram entered Egypt[a] the Egyptians saw that the woman was very beautiful.* [15] *The princes of Pharaoh saw her, sang her praises to Pharaoh, and the woman was taken[a] into Pharaoh's house.* [16a] *Meanwhile Abram was well treated[b] because of her,[a] and he acquired sheep, cattle,[c] donkeys, slaves, slave-girls, she-asses, and camels.*

[17] *Then the LORD struck[a] Pharaoh and[b] his household[b] with severe[c] plagues on account of Sarai, Abram's wife.* [18] *So Pharaoh summoned Abram and said: "What[a] have you done to me? Why did you not tell[b] me that[c] she was your wife?[c]* [19] *Why did you say,* [a] *'She is my sister,'[a]* [b] *so that I took[b] her to be my wife? Now here[c] is your wife. Take[d] her[e] and go."[f]*

[20] *And Pharaoh put him in the charge of men and they sent away him, his wife, and all who belonged to him.[a]*

Notes

10.a. Directional ה suff (acc case ending) "towards Egypt,"; cf. vv 11, 14.

10.b. ל + inf constr גור "to settle, be an immigrant [i.e., a potentially permanent resident in a foreign land]" (D. Kellerman, *TDOT* 2:439–49; R. Martin-Achard, *THWAT* 1:409–12).

11.a-a. ויהי + temporal clause often marks new episode; cf. v 14 (GKC, 111g; *SBH*, 63).

11.b. G adds "Abram."

11.c. הנה־נא "Since" gives the reason for the command "Say then" in v 13 (Lambdin, 170–71; Jacob, 348).

11.d. Perfect with present meaning; cf. 20:6; 48:19 (GKC, 106g).

11.e. SamPent has alternative form, אתי; cf. v 13.

11.f. Fem constr יפה "beautiful."

12.a-a. The Hebrew word order, predicate-subject ("his wife" . . . "this"), is typical of verbless classifying clauses and is therefore not especially emphatic (F. I. Andersen, *Verbless Clause*, 42, 61; cf. *EWAS*, 15–16).

12.b-b. The chiastic construction (ABBA "kill" . . . "me" : "you" . . . "spare") indicates that killing and sparing are here seen as different aspects of one action.

12.c. 3 masc pl impf piel חיה "make live."

13.a. 2 fem sg impv אמר.

13.b. נא links back to הנה־נא; cf. 11.c.

13.c-c. G makes this direct speech: "I am his sister." On Hebrew word order, cf. n. 12.a-a.

13.d. 3 masc sg impf יטב "be good."

13.e. נפש "person, soul." On this term cf. C. Westermann, *THWAT* 2:71–96.

14.a-a. Cf. n. 11.a-a.

15.a. Waw consec + 3 fem sg impf qal passive לקח "to take": cf. 3:19, 23 (GKC, 53u).

16.a-a. Circumstantial clause, more probably episode-final than episode-initial (*SBH*, 80–82; Westermann, 2:192–93).

16.b. 3 masc sg pf hiph יטב "be treated well." "He" is more likely impersonal than a reference to Pharaoh.

16.c. SamPent adds מקנה כבד מאד "very much livestock" here and puts "donkeys" after "slave girls." MT is preferable as the more difficult reading.

17.a. Waw consec + 3 masc sg impf piel נגע "to touch."

17.b-b. Despite *BHS*, 20:17 offers no grounds for supposing this to be a gloss.

17.c. G adds καὶ πονηροῖς "and evil."

18.a. The demonstrative מה־זאת is often used enclitically to make questions more pointed or to express surprise or shock; cf. 3:13 (BDB, 261).

18.b. 2 masc sg pf hiph נגד.

18.c-c. Cf. n. 12.a-a.

19.a-a. Cf. n. 12.a-a.

19.b-b. Waw consec may express result (Joüon, 118h).

19.c. הנה expresses immediacy in space or time (Lambdin, 168–69).

19.d. 2 masc sg impv לקח.

19.e. Object omitted since there is no ambiguity (GKC, 117f; Joüon 146i).

19.f. Waw (pointed ו immediately before tone syllable at end of sentence [GKC, 104g]) + 2 masc sg impv הלך.

20.a. SamPent, G add "and Lot with him," assimilating to 13:1.

Form/Structure/Setting

With this episode the detailed account of Abraham's career begins, 11:27–12:9 being more in the nature of background information and introduction to the story. Here, by contrast, a specific incident in Abram's life is recounted, in which his wife is temporarily parted from him and enters the royal harem in Egypt. Subsequent parallels with this narrative (20; 26) show that the abduction of a patriarch's wife is a type scene, a conventional situation in which the character of the actors can be clearly revealed.

The episode begins in v 10. The phrase "famine in the land" forms an inclusion and links the beginning and end of the verse, emphasizes the reason for Abram's journey, and makes the verse into a title of the subsequent section.

However, it is more difficult to determine the close of the section. There are three possibilities—13:4 (so Cassuto and Weimar, *Untersuchungen*, 48–51), 13:1 (Gunkel, Skinner, von Rad, Peterson [*BR* 18 (1973) 30–43], Alexander [*Literary Analysis*]), or 12:20 (the majority view).

In favor of the scene's ending at 13:4, it is pointed out that the wealth of Abram (כבד: 13:2) matches the severe (כבד) famine in 12:10, and the remarks about Bethel and Ai (13:3–4) make this scene conclude in a similar way to the previous scene (12:8–9). These observations certainly show that the episodes are carefully linked and that there are similarities between the separate incidents in Abram's life, but they are not sufficient to prove that the scene ends at 13:4. In fact, the opening of v 5, "And also (גַּם) to Lot," ties it closely to 13:2, showing that a new scene begins no later than 13:2.

But it is more difficult to decide whether our episode ends at 13:1 or at 12:20. The main arguments in favor of 13:1 are that Abram's going up from Egypt matches his going down to Egypt in 12:10 and that the verbal parallels (12:20 // 13:1) "him, his wife, and all who belonged to him" tie these two verses tightly together. However, it seems slightly more natural to view the expulsion from Egypt as marking the conclusion of one scene, and the journeying to the Negeb as signaling the start of a new episode. In confirmation of this reading is the fact that the final verb in 12:20, "sent away," has no explicit subject, whereas 13:1 reintroduces Abram. Thus I prefer to take 12:10–20 as a discrete unit.

The episode may be analyzed as follows (cf. Weimar, Coats):

A	Exposition: Entry	10
B	1st scene: Abram's speech	11–13
C	2nd scene: Fulfillment of Abram's fears	14–16
B'	3rd scene: Pharaoh's speech	17–19
A'	Conclusion: Exit	20

The story is thus organized concentrically, as is common in biblical narrative. The symmetry is further enhanced by the surrounding material; cf. the references to Bethel and Ai (12:8; 13:3), Negeb (12:9; 13:1), and Egypt 12:10; 13:1.)

Van Seters (*Abraham,* 168–83) has pointed out that this story follows the pattern of a typical folk tale quite closely: problem (v 10), plan to solve it (vv 11–13), execution of plan with complications (vv 14–16), unexpected intervention (v 17a), consequences (17b–20.) Furthermore, the story has just three principal characters—Abraham, Sarah, and Pharaoh—and it focuses attention on them two at a time— Abraham and Sarah, Sarah and Pharaoh, Pharaoh and Abraham. These features are wholly characteristic of oral folklore. By contrast, the other parallels to this story in 20:1–18 and 26:1–11 lack the typical ingredients of oral literature and appear to be literary compositions that consciously allude to this first story of a patriarch's passing his wife off as his sister. The view that chap. 12 is the oldest of the three stories has also been argued by Gunkel, Skinner, Procksch, G. Schmitt, Petersen, Westermann, Coats, and Alexander.

Among recent writers, however, the primitiveness of Gen 26 has been maintained by Noth, Kilian, Nomoto, Rendtorff, Zimmerli, and Weimar. They hold that when those features common to all three narratives are isolated so as to reconstruct their common source, Gen 26 appears closest to the common source. It is also urged that Isaac is more likely to have been the original hero, that Gerar is a more likely scene of action, and that the intervention of God in Gen 12 and 20 is a late feature of the narrative that is absent from chap. 26. Allusions to the earlier episode in chaps. 20 and 26 can be explained as later redactional modifications of the primitive stories. The subjective nature of these arguments is evident, and they do not account for the apparently oral character of 12:10–20 over against the markedly literary form of chaps. 20 and 26, which does suggest the originality of chap. 12. Nor can comparison of the form of these stories actually prove whether they are versions of the same incident, as assumed by most writers, or whether they go back to three different incidents (cf. Keller, *ZAW* 66 [1954] 186). The allusions to Gen 12 in chaps. 20 and 26 show that the Genesis editors understood them to refer to three separate occasions.

Vv 10–20 of chap. 12 are ascribed to J, but it is uncertain how far they represent just older material incorporated by J as opposed to J's own reworking of tradition. In favor of the former possibility are the apparent closeness of the section to oral literature and its terse style over against the more discursive style of, say, chaps. 18 or 24. On this hypothesis only the mention of Yahweh in v 17 may be ascribed to the Yahwistic editor.

Comment

10 "There was a famine in the land . . . famine was severe." Very similar terminology is used in 26:1; 41:54, 56; 43:1, etc. Famine compelled all the patriarchs to leave Canaan at different times (26:1; 47:4; cf. Ruth 1:1). Its fluctuating rainfall made it susceptible to food shortages until the advent of modern methods of irrigation, and Egypt was the standard refuge in this situation, as the Nile provided a much more certain food supply (cf. Deut 11:10.) Egyptian texts also mention the arrival of hungry foreigners. The inscription on the grave of Horemheb reads: "Certain of the foreigners who know not how they may live have come. . . . Their countries are starving" (*ANET*, 251).

Canaan is hilly, whereas the Nile valley is flat and low-lying, so the Bible regularly speaks of going down to Egypt (26:2; 43:15, etc.) or going up from Egypt (e.g., 13:1; 45:25; Exod 1:10.) It is striking that Abram is said to have gone to "settle in" Egypt, to be an immigrant there. To live as an immigrant (גור) suggests the intention of long-term settlement, which is somewhat alien to Abram's wandering lifestyle. It also comes as quite a surprise to hear that Abram is ready to settle in Egypt so soon after he has been promised "this land" (12:7.) The reader is disconcerted to learn that Abram is deserting the land of promise: to underline the fact that he had no other option, the famine is again mentioned, and this time is said to be "severe." Abram's action on this occasion makes for a parallel between his Egyptian journey and the later Israelite sojourn there (cf. 15:13). Both were prompted by severe famine that threatened the survival of the chosen people (47:4).

11–13 The first scene, set on the borders of Egypt, focuses on Abram and Sarai. Abram explains his fears and puts his plan to Sarai. No comments of hers are recorded, implying her consent to his scheme.

Escaping the danger of famine in Canaan, Abram fears that in Egypt he will run another sort of risk. As an immigrant there he would lack the support and protection afforded by the wider family network. The danger of immigrants being exploited is frequently harped on in the law, e.g., Exod 22:20(21); 23:9. Why Abram should have felt secure in Canaan but exposed in Egypt is not explained, though of course strange environments often do give rise to unfounded fears. It may be that having to hear and speak a non-Semitic language, Egyptian, would have made a Hebrew feel less at home there than elsewhere in the fertile crescent.

Stranger still is Abram's supposition that Sarai, aged about 65 (cf. 12:4; 17:17), should be regarded as outstandingly attractive. The narrative insists that this is not merely the opinion of a neurotically jealous husband, for the Egyptians heartily concurred (vv 14–15.) Source criticism mitigates the problem by assigning the chronological data to P (e.g., 12:4; 17:17) and this story to J. This does not eliminate the problem entirely, however, for it still must be explained how an editor who linked the supposed sources understood Sarai at her advanced age to be so beautiful. Various suggestions have been put forward. Calvin observed that childless women preserve their beauty longer than mothers. Gunkel suggested there was a natural tendency to glorify the national mother figure (cf. 24:16; 29:17.) Cassuto argues that if Sarai could bear her first child at 90, the narrator must have believed she was still pretty at 65. Finally, it should be borne in mind that ideas of feminine beauty in traditional societies differ from ours: well-endowed matronly figures, not slim youthful ones, tend to represent their ideal of womanhood. By such criteria, Sarai might well count as very beautiful even at her age.

Abram feared that Sarai's looks would prove irresistible to the Egyptians, and since he had no family in Egypt to protect his interests, they might simply kill him so that they could marry her. He therefore proposed that she should describe herself as his sister. Speiser argued that there was here an allusion to a Hurrian custom whereby a man could take a woman to be both wife and sister at the same time, a special high-status marriage. This view is rejected by more recent writers (Greengus, van Seters, Thompson, Weir) for two main reasons. First, as Speiser himself pointed out, it is clear that Genesis does not understand the patriarchal marriages this way. Second, Speiser's interpretation of the Nuzi documents, on which his theory of wife-sister marriages is based, is now rejected.

Whatever the historical and legal background to the incident, there still remains the question of what Abram hoped to achieve by calling his wife his sister. Many writers assume that he was thereby committing himself to allowing her to marry any suitor who sought her hand, and that by implication he was prepared to sacrifice his wife's honor for his own skin and financial gain. Though this is a possible interpretation of v 13, in the light of subsequent events (cf. vv 15–16), Cassuto (and van Seters) are right to question it. Oriental attitudes to adultery were much sterner than ours (cf. 20:2–9), and it seems unlikely that Abram would have contemplated with equanimity his wife's being guilty of that sin. Indeed, his silence following the Pharaoh's rebukes shows that all parties recognized he was at fault. Cassuto follows those medieval commentators who suggested that Abram hoped that by claiming to be Sarai's brother he could fend off suitors by promises of marriage without actually giving her away. This suggestion is confirmed by other stories in Genesis where brothers try to delay their sisters' marriages (24:55, Laban and Rebekah; 34:13–17, Dinah and her brothers.)

Sarai's silence indicates her consent to her husband's scheme. The narrative concentrates our attention on the essential features of the story by cutting out unnecessary dialogue. Her silence here matches her husband's at the end of the episode when harangued by the Pharaoh.

14–16 In this second scene in Egypt, the leading actors are Abram and the Egyptian princes. Sarai and the Pharaoh play more passive roles.

14 At first Abram's plan works well. As he anticipated the Egyptians noticed her beauty (v 14; cf. v 12) and nothing untoward happened.

15 But then an unforeseen complication occurred: her beauty was reported to the Pharaoh. His advances could not be staved off, and Sarai "was taken into Pharaoh's house." Pharaoh is the Hebrew equivalent of Egyptian *pr-o* "great house." In the Old and Middle Kingdom periods it retains this basic meaning, "royal palace," but from the eighteenth dynasty onward (from *ca.* 1500 B.C.) it denotes the Egyptian king himself. This verse's terminology "house of Pharaoh" then reflects the usage of the term in the writer's period rather than the patriarchal age (Gispen, 2:44).

"Was taken," לקח. In the context of marriage this phrase properly denotes the formal taking of a woman as a wife and is distinguished from the act of marital intercourse (cf. 20:2–4; 34:2; 38:2; Deut 22:13–14). However, it can be used more loosely to describe all aspects of marriage (25:1; 34:9, 16; Lev 21:7, 13; Deut 20:7). It is not clear in which sense the word is used here. We are left wondering whether Sarai just became a member of Pharaoh's harem or whether she was actually introduced to the king himself. The latter is probably implied, but the story refrains from saying so directly. That plagues were sent seems to indicate that Pharaoh did actually commit adultery.

16 It was customary for large presents, bride money (מהר), to be given to the bride's family at betrothal (24:52–53; Exod 22:15–16 [16–17]; 1 Sam 18:22–28). It is quite likely that the bounty bestowed on Abram represented this sort of payment, though it may have been simply a mark of Pharaonic goodwill toward Sarai's "brother." The strange order of gifts, "slaves, slave-girls" interrupting the list of animals, has led some commentators to conclude that either "slaves and slave-girls" is a later addition to the list (e.g., Gunkel) or that "she-asses and camels" is an addition (e.g., Skinner), while Weimar (*Untersuchungen,* 14) thinks that both phrases are additional and the work of two different redactors. "Camels" have also been objected to on the grounds that they did not come into common use until the end of the second millennium B.C. However, there is evidence of their domestication much earlier (see *NBD*, 181–83); their rarity no doubt made them somewhat of a luxury, one of several features in the tradition emphasizing the wealth of the patriarchs. Each of the wife-sister episodes mentions the enrichment of the patriarch as a result of his deception (20:14–16; 26:12–14).

These two first scenes have several terms and ideas in common with Gen 2–3. Both Sarai and the trees of the garden are described as "beautiful"/ "pleasant" in appearance (2:9; 12:11). Subsequently there is a seeing and a taking of the desirable person or fruit (3:6–7; 12:15–16).

17–20 The third and climactic scene tells of the LORD's intervention and brings the Pharaoh into face-to-face confrontation with Abram. The royal anger is conveyed in the rapid succession of accusatory questions and the brusque expulsion order. Abram offers no justification of his conduct. He and his wife are quickly escorted out of Egypt.

17 God's intervention marks the turning point. The nature of the punishment of the Egyptians is not precisely defined. נגע often refers to skin diseases, e.g., Lev 13–14; 2 Kgs 15:5, and these were generally regarded as the consequence of serious sin as is shown by the rule that a healed leper had to offer a guilt offering (Lev 14:12). This sacrifice is also required after adultery with a slave-girl (Lev 19:20–22). This could suggest that the Egyptians suffered from some sort of skin disease; cf. the plague of boils, Exod 9:9.

18 "So Pharaoh summoned Abram." קרא, "summon, call" immediately suggests the seriousness of Pharaoh; cf. the use of קרא in a similar context (3:9).

A triplet of accusations couched as questions follow: "What . . . Why . . . Why?" Pharaoh's sense of grievance and surprise is detectable in the Hebrew phrasing.

מה זאת עשית "What have you done?" The enclitic זאת gives the ordinary מה "what" a little more emphasis. Exactly the same question was put to Eve (3:13); without the enclitic it was put to Cain in 4:10, and again in 20:9; 26:10. Foreign kings are always shocked by the patriarchs' dishonesty in such a grave matter.

19 ועתה "now" customarily introduces a decision based on the immediately preceding statements, often judicial sentences on sin (e.g., 3:22; 4:11; 11:6; 20:7). The accusations were short. The sentence on Abraham is barked out in four Hebrew words. "Here . . . wife . . . take . . . go." The very abruptness expresses Pharaoh's anger. In the event, however, Abram is only sentenced to deportation. Considering that he had feared death at Egyptian hands and that his dishonesty had involved the king in adultery, which was regarded throughout the ancient world as the "great sin" deserving the death penalty, the royal leniency is remarkable. Pharaoh implicitly acknowledges that God is protecting Abram (cf. 12:3), and he therefore takes no revenge on him. Nor does Abram respond to the rebuke. He leaves the last word to the Pharaoh, thereby acknowedging his own guilt and the justice of the royal anger.

20 "Sent away" (שלח, piel) may have the mild sense of "setting someone on their way," "accompanying them on the first part of their journey" (cf. 18:16). But it also carries overtones of expulsion (cf. 3:23), and it is the verb used most often to describe Israel's exodus from Egypt (Exod 3–11). The Pharaoh's overriding concern is that the troublemaker should leave.

Explanation

After the great expectations aroused by the first episode in the Abraham cycle, this second one surprises us by the unheroic performance of the hero. Though it was argued by Gunkel that the story does celebrate both the beauty of Sarai, which attracted the attention of all Egypt, and the cunning of Abram, who enriched himself at the Pharaoh's expense, this is an unlikely interpretation. It was the LORD who saved Sarai from the plight in which her husband's cleverness had landed her (v 17), and Abram's silence in the face of Pharaoh's remonstrations shows that the author did not approve of his conduct. This is confirmed by comparing this tale with the similar ones in Gen 20 and 26. It becomes plain that for an individual to acquire both wealth and offspring is a mark of divine blessing: one without the other is not. Here, despite the promises of vv 1–3, Abram acquires wealth (v 16), but no children. This does suggest that the writer is not here endorsing Abram's conduct or holding it up for imitation. The echoes of the garden of Eden story also point in the same direction. The justice of the royal anger is underlined by the way Pharaoh asks the same question after the offense that the LORD asked Adam, and Pharaoh expels Abram from his land just as God expelled Adam from his garden.

What then is the purpose of this story? Von Rad sees it as an illustration of the fulfillment of God's promise despite Abram's weakness; Zimmerli, as an example of the frailty of God's elect; Westermann, that even in apparently hopeless situations God can deliver. There are elements of truth in all these suggestions, but they are truths of such generality that they do not really illuminate the details of this particular story. Cassuto and Weimar, by drawing attention to the parallels between this story and the later sojourn of the Israelites in Egypt, and Polzin and Miscall, by contrasting the Pharaoh's concern for morality with Abram's apparent indifference, have brought into focus the specific features of the story that demand interpretation.

Abram, like Jacob, was driven into Egypt because of famine. There Abram feared that he would be killed but that his wife would be spared. The policy of a later Pharaoh involved killing boy babies but sparing the girls (Exod 1:16). The Israelites were given gold and jewelry on leaving Egypt (Exod 12:35), and Abram too was enriched by his stay there. In both cases a heaven-sent plague (נגע) prompted the release of the Israelites, and similar instructions were given by the Pharaohs for both departures (Exod 11:1; 12:32) and the same verb (שׁלח piel) describes the expulsion. These parallels show that "Scripture wished to foreshadow in the tales of the patriarchs the history of their descendants. . . . In the account of how Abram went down to Egypt, what befell him there and how he went forth from there, the Torah presages as it were, the migration of the Israelites to Egypt after they had settled in the land of Canaan, their servitude and their liberation" (Cassuto, 2:336). This interpretation of Abram's experiences in Egypt as prefiguring those of Israel seems to be confirmed by 15:13–16, where the Egyptian bondage is specifically prophesied.

In one very obvious respect, however, there is a total contrast in the roles of the characters here and in Exodus. In Exodus the Pharaoh is implacably opposed to God despite the plagues: here the Pharaoh is shown to be highly respectful of Abram and his God and indeed to speak and act like God (cf. Gen 3). All three wife-sister stories in Genesis (chaps. 12, 20, 26) have in common that the foreign monarch is more concerned about morality than is the patriarch. Whereas Abram showed no faith in God, the Pharaoh did. Abram had been told he would be a blessing to the nations (12:2–3): in this case he patently was not. The story shows he could not attain security by his own intelligence: only God could save in such circumstances. The scene ends with Abram's leaving Egypt in silent ignominy, leading us to anticipate rather different behavior when his faith was next put to the test.

This story, foreshadowing as it does the later bondage in Egypt and the exodus, is an example of the typology that patterns many OT narratives.

This typological paralleling of Abraham with the exodus from Egypt is especially clear in Isa 40–55. Here the return from Babylonian exile is repeatedly compared with the exodus on the one hand and with the call of Abram on the other (Isa 41:8–9, 18–19; 43:1–2, 14–16; 48:20–21; 49:8–12; 51:2–3, 9–11; 52:3–12). Similar typological thinking is found in the NT by Matthew, who explicitly compares Israel's exodus from Egypt with Jesus' return to Palestine from there (Matt 2:15). Paul compares the exodus to the church's experience in Christ (1 Cor 10:1–12), and since Abram was also in Egypt, the believer is thus invited to look back to the life of Abraham and see in it not only an adumbration of his Lord's experiences but his own (Rom 4, Heb 11:8–19). Here Abram's failure in the face of hostility, like Israel's sinfulness in the wilderness, is surely recorded as a warning for later generations (cf. 1 Cor 10:11) and as an illustration of the invincibility of the divine promises (cf. Rom 11:29).

Abram and Lot Separate   (13:1–18)

Bibliography

Ben-Yashar, M. "And Lot Journeyed East." (Heb.) *Sefer Y. Braslavi*, ed Y. Ben-Shem, H. M. Y. Gevaryahu, and B. Z. Luria. Jerusalem: Kiryat-Sepher, 1970. 94–98. **Coats, G. W.** "Lot: A Foil in the Abraham Saga." In *Understanding the Word: Essays in Honor of B. W. Anderson*, ed. J. T. Butler, E. W. Conrad, and B. C. Ollenburger. JSOTSS 37. Sheffield: JSOT Press, 1985. 113–32. **Fisch, H.** "Ruth and the Structure of Covenant History." *VT* 32 (1982) 425–37. **Helyer, L. R.** "The Separation of Abram and Lot: Its Significance in the Patriarchal Narratives." *JSOT* 26 (1983) 77–88. **Kilian, R.** "Zur Überlieferungsgeschichte Lots." *BZ* 14 (1970) 23–37. **Schaub, M. M.** "Lot and the Cities of the Plain: A Little about a Lot." *Proceedings, Eastern Great Lakes Biblical Society* 2 (1982) 1–21. **Vogels, W.** "Abraham et l'offrande de la terre (Gen 13)." *SR* 4 (1974) 51–57. ———. "Lot, père des incroyants." *EgT* 6 (1975) 139–51. ———. "Lot in His Honor Restored: A Structural Analysis of Gen 13:2–18." *EgT* 10 (1979) 5–12.

Translation

[1] *Then Abram went[a] up from Egypt, he[b] and his wife and all who belonged to him, including Lot, to the Negeb.* [2a] *Now Abram[b] was very rich in livestock,[c] silver[c] and[d] gold.[a]* [3] *From the Negeb he moved[a] his camp by stages to Bethel, to the place where his tent[b] had been at the beginning between Bethel and Ai,* [4] *to the site of the altar which he had made the first time; and there Abram called on the name of the LORD.* [5] *Lot too,[a] who was traveling with Abram, had sheep, cattle, and tents.*

[6] *But the land would not sustain[a] them, dwelling[b] together, because their possessions were too numerous for them to dwell[b] together.* [7] *And a dispute broke out between Abram's herdsmen and Lot's herdsmen. The Canaanites[a] and Perizzites[a] were then dwelling[b] in the land.*

[8] *So Abram said to Lot, "Let there be[a] no argument between me and you, between*

my herdsmen and yours, for we[b] *are men*[c] *and brothers.*[c] [9]*Is not the whole land open to you? Separate*[a] *then from me. If* [b]*you take*[b] *the left, I shall go to the right.*[c] *If* [b]*you take*[b] *the right, I shall go to the left."*[c]

[10]*Then Lot looked*[a] *around and saw that all*[b] *the plain of the Jordan valley* [c]*as far as*[c] *Zoar was well watered like the garden of the LORD and the land of Egypt; this was before the LORD destroyed Sodom and Gomorrah.* [11]*So Lot chose for himself all the plain of the Jordan valley, and Lot journeyed*[a] *eastward and they separated*[b] *from each other.* [12]*Abram*[a] *dwelt in the land of Canaan but Lot*[a] *dwelt in the cities of the plain and camped towards Sodom.* [13]*Now the men of Sodom were evil, great sinners against the LORD.*[a]

[14]*The LORD,*[a] *however, spoke to Abram after Lot had separated*[b] *from him. "Look*[c] *around and see from where you are, northward, southward, eastward, and westward,* [15]*for* [a]*the whole land which you see*[a] *I shall give*[b] *to you and your descendants forever.* [16]*And I shall make your descendants like the dust of the earth, so that,*[a] *if one could*[b] *count*[c] *the dust of the earth, your descendants will be countable.*[d] [17]*Come on,*[a] *walk*[b] *to and fro throughout the length and breadth of the land, because I shall give it to you."*[c]

[18]*So Abram camped and came and dwelt among the oaks*[a] *of Mamre*[b] *which are in Hebron. He built there an altar to the LORD.*

Notes ·

1.a. Waw consec + 3 masc sg shortened impf עלה.

1.b. Resumptive use of subj pron (Joüon, 146c; *EWAS*, 63).

2.a-a. Verbless circumstantial clause, a parenthesis supplying background information (*SBH*, 85).

2.b. Vg omits "Abram."

2.c. The definite article is used with names of materials (GKC, 126n).

2.d. In groups of three, sometimes only the last two are linked by the conjunction (GKC, 154a¹ᵃ).

3.a. וילך; cf. 12:4a.

3.b. MT אהלה, archaic orthography; SamPent אהלו, modernized. Cf. 12:8.e.

5.a. וגם looks back to v 2 and draws attention to similarities between Abram and Lot (*SBH*, 160).

6.a. SamPent corrects נשא "he sustained" to נשאה "she sustained" to agree with "land," fem. Typical SamPent change (Waltke, 218). Retain MT.

6.b. ל + inf constr ישב "to dwell."

7.a. Lit., "The Canaanite/Perizzite," collective singular for a whole class (GKC, 126m).

7.b. SamPent has ישבים (pl) instead of ישב, to agree with composite subject; cf. n. 6.a.

8.a. 3 fem sg juss היה.

8.b. The subject "we" comes at the end of the clause, the normal position in classificatory clauses; cf. 12:12, 13, 19 (Andersen, *Verbless Clause*, 43).

8.c-c. Lit., "men brothers." In apposition the second word clarifies the first (GKC, 131b; *SBH*, 46–50).

9.a. 2 masc sg impv niph פרד "separate."

9.b-b. The Hebrew is elliptical, omitting the verb פרד; cf. 24:49; 1 Sam 2:16 (GKC, 159 dd). SamPent inserts השמאלה/הימינה.

9.c. 1 sg coh hiph of ימן/שמאל (GKC, 56).

10.a. Waw consec + 3 masc sg impf נשא "to raise."

10.b. SamPent alters כלה "all of her" to כלו "all of him" to agree with ככר "valley," masc; cf. n. 12.8.e.

10.c-c. Lit., "your coming" (inf of בוא + ך suffix). But as elsewhere, the pronominal suffix has lost its force. Cf. n. 10:19.b.

11.a. Cf. n. 12:9.a.

11.b. Waw consec + 3 masc pl impf niph פרד.

12.a-a. The unusual preverbal position of the subjects (Abram/Lot) contrasts their different careers (*SBH*, 151).

13.a., 14.a. G has "God" instead of "LORD."

14.b. Inf constr niph פרד "separate."

14.c. 2 masc sg impv נשא "lift" (eyes).

15.a-a. Putting the object "the land" first in the sentence makes it quite emphatic (GKC, 143c; Joüon, 156c; cf. *EWAS*, 38–39).

15.b. 1 sg impf נתן + 3 fem sg suff "it."

16.a. אשר introducing consecutive clause (GKC, 166b).

16.b. 3 masc sg impf יכל "be able."

16.c. Inf constr מנה "to count."

16.d. 3 masc impf niph מנה. As here, niph may have potential meaning "be countable" (Lambdin, 177).

17.a. קום, lit., "stand up." Verbs of motion can be prefixed to other verbs in the impv as an introductory exhortation (GKC, 120g; *SBH*, 56–57).

17.b. Cf. 3:8.

17.c. Some G MSS add "and to your descendants for ever."

18.a. G, S read singular.

18.b. S adds "the Amorite"; cf. 14:13.

Form/Structure/Setting

The new episode opens with an explicit mention of Abram leaving Egypt, and a list of his fellow-travelers almost identical with 12:20. This repetition serves to link the Egyptian affair with this following one. The one difference in the list of travelers is the addition of Lot's name, last mentioned in 12:5. The episode closes with Abram building an altar in Hebron (13:18).

The chapter divides into the following scenes:

vv 1–5	Background itinerary: Egypt to Bethel
vv 6–7	The Dispute
vv 8–9	Abram's proposed solution
vv 10–13	Lot's choice of Sodom
vv 14–17	The land promised to Abram
v 18	Abram settles in Hebron

Some commentators have held that this episode really begins with v 2. My reasons for dissent have been set out in *Form/Structure/Setting* on 12:10–20. After a note of Abram's return to Canaan (v 1), there is an episode-initial circumstantial clause (13:2) coordinated with v 5. Using elements from an itinerary, vv 2–5 set the background to this story and bring its two central figures, Abram and Lot, into focus. The contrast between them is carefully sustained throughout this chapter (cf. vv 7, 8, 10–11, 12, 18).

The problem and its resolution are the theme of vv 6–14. This begins with a double statement of the problem "(they could not) dwell together," an inclusion comparable to 12:10. The solution of the dispute is described in vv 11–12, and this phase of the episode is rounded off by a circumstantial clause (v 13) commenting on the character of Sodom.

The third main section reiterates the promises of land and descendants. The concentric arrangement of the promise in vv 15–17 may be noted:

v 15   I shall give it to you
             your descendants
v 16   dust of the earth
             dust of the earth
             your descendants
v 17   I shall give it you

The parallels between this section and vv 9–13 also deserve notice:

separate	vv 9, 11		v 14
look around	v 10		v 14
see	v 10		v 14
all the plain	vv 10–11 all the land		v 15
camped	v 12		v 18

With the exception of vv 6, 11b–12a (P), the whole story is usually ascribed to J. Rendtorff (*Pentateuch,* 122–23) and Alexander (*Literary Analysis,* 219–20) dispute the assignment of these verses to P, for neither vocabulary nor content suggests that they derive from a separate source. The question of the pre-literary sources used by J remains problematic. Kilian (*BZ* 14 [1970] 23–37) regards most of the material as pre-J, with Yahwistic expansions in vv 3–4, 7b, 10b, 14a. Westermann thinks fragments of an old itinerary underlie vv 1–5, 18, and an old account of patriarchal disputes (cf. chap. 21, 26), vv 5–12. However, he holds that the promises in vv 14–17 represent later editorial additions. Against this dissection of the story into earlier and later elements must be set the verbal parallels between the divine promises in vv 14–15 and the description of Lot's choice in vv 10–11. As already noted, vv 14–18 run on lines similar to vv 9–12. Other writers—von Rad, van Seters, Coats, Alexander—are indeed sceptical whether this episode can really ever have existed as an independent tale. It is so much a part of the series of stories about Abram and Lot that to suppose it once was transmitted separately seems too speculative. Most verses either look back to what has already been said (e.g., v 1 to 12:20; v 2, 12:16; vv 3–4, 12:8–9) or forward to future developments (v 10, 19:29; v 12, 14:12; 19:1; v 13, chaps. 18–19), or forward and backward simultaneously (e.g., v 7, 12:6; 15:19–21; vv 15–17, 12:7; 15:8–9, 18). Further points of contact are noted in *Comment* below.

Comment

1–5 These verses describe Abram's journey from Egypt to the heart of Canaan near Bethel.

1 וַיַּעַל "He went up" is the usual term to describe journeys from Egypt to Canaan. One goes down to Egypt (12:10) and up to Canaan.

"He and his wife. . . ." This phrase summarizing Abram's entourage in 12:20 is here expanded to include an explicit mention of Lot ("including Lot"), who is to figure so prominently in the next episode. He was last referred to in 12:5.

"To the Negeb." Cf. 12:9 when Abram approached from the north. In the Middle Bronze Age 1, there was more settlement in the Negeb than in

subsequent eras, and it has been noted that the only references to the patriarchs'
presence there is in the Abraham cycle (J. J. Bimson, "Archaeological Data
and the Dating of the Patriarchs," in *Essays on the Patriarchal Narratives,* ed
A. R. Millard and D. J. Wiseman, 59–92).

2 כבד "Rich, severe." The use of the same term in speaking of Abram's
wealth and of the famine (12:10) invites the comparison of his situation at
the beginning of the two episodes. מקנה "livestock" covers all sorts of animals
that are herded (cf. 47:16–17; 12:16). "Silver and gold" is the first mention
of patriarchal financial assets. It seems likely that Abram is reckoned to have
acquired this as a result of his Egyptian sojourn, perhaps by way of compensa-
tion for the pharaonic adultery (cf. 20:16; 12:16). The Israelites were also
given silver and gold before leaving Egypt (Exod 12:35–36). So in this respect
too, Abram's departure from Egypt foreshadows the exodus.

3 למסעיו "By stages" is a term used elsewhere in the Pentateuch only
of the stopping places of the Israelites in the wilderness, e.g., Exod 17:1;
Num 10:12, etc.

3b–4 These verses are a detailed and repetitive reminder of 12:8. By its
very fullness and the twofold reference to "the beginning/the first time,"
the narrator is surely suggesting that Abram is trying to recapture his previous
experience of God. The only difference this time is that he does not need
to build an altar: the old one is still there, perhaps implying that the promises
still stand too.

5–6 Here the origin of the conflict is described. Paradoxically, it is the
blessing of God on Abram and Lot that creates the problem. The patriarchs
are portrayed as semi-nomadic herdsmen living on the fringe of the settled
population, indeed, in process of settling down themselves. The verb ישב
"dwell" is a key word in this chapter, vv 6, 7, 12, 18. Their movements were
dictated by the need to find pasture for their flocks in areas that were already
partially settled and cultivated. Given the large increase in the patriarchal
herds in Egypt (12:16), genuine problems of sharing the limited pasturage
would have arisen. Similar problems precipitated wrangles between Isaac and
the Philistines (26:12–22), Jacob and his uncle Laban (30:43), and Jacob and
Esau (36:6–7).

6 The inclusion לשבת יחדו "dwelling together," using the key word of
this episode, "dwell," makes this verse a fitting opening to the next scene. It
also makes its assignment to a different source (P) unlikely; cf. 12:10 with
its double reference to "famine in the land," introducing a new stage in the
action.

7 ריב "dispute" may have the technical sense of legal dispute (e.g., Exod
23:3), but here it simply means "quarrel, complaint"; cf. Prov 15:18; 26:21.

"The Canaanites and the Perizzites." The addition of the Perizzites to the
list of earlier inhabitants of the land (cf. 12:6) explains why the herdsmen
felt congested in the land and anticipates the fuller list of pre-Israelite inhabitants found in 14:5–7; 15:19–21. The Perizzites are mentioned 23 times in
the OT, and once in the Amarna letters. Their racial affiliation and the etymology of their name is unknown, though the latter is often connected with
פרז "village." However, it seems likely that the term designates an ethnic
grouping.

8 "Men and brothers." It is unusual to have "men, brothers" in apposition like this. It would have made good sense to say simply, "We are brothers." The wording seems to imply, "Men should not quarrel, let alone brothers." "Brothers," אחים, is used here in the sense of "kinsmen"; cf. 31:32; Lev 10:4. Lot was in fact Abram's nephew, his brother's son. Abram's ideal is no doubt summed up by Ps 133:1: "How good and pleasant it is when *brothers dwell* [ישׁב] *in unity* [יחד]" (cf. v 6).

9 However, when peaceful community is impossible, Scripture prefers amicable separation (Acts 15:39; 1 Cor 7:12–15). Abram invites Lot to share the promised land with him, either to "take the right," often used of the south, or "the left," i.e., the northern part of the country.

10 From a hill southeast of Beitin (generally identified with Bethel; see *Comment* on 12:8), a good view may be had of the southern end of the Jordan valley and the northern end of the Dead Sea. The broad southern part of the Jordan valley is apparently the area denoted by the Hebrew term ככר הירדן (only here and 1 Kgs 7:46; 2 Chr 4:17). Elsewhere it is abbreviated to הככר "the plain" (v 12; 19:17, 25, 28–29; Deut 34:3; 2 Sam 18:23; see Skinner, 252; Simons, *GTOT*, 222–25). If, however (with most scholars), Sodom is located near Gebel Usdum on the western shore of the Dead Sea, the plain would have to include the southern end of the Dead Sea. Until the sites of Sodom and Gomorrah are positively identified, the question of the southern limit of the plain, "as far as Zoar," must remain open (see further discussion on chap. 14).

"The garden of the LORD" is evidently an allusion to Eden: Gen 2:8–14, Isa 51:3. "Well watered": cf. 2:10–14. "The land of Egypt": throughout Genesis, Egypt is the place to which the patriarchs resort in times of food shortage. The Nile ensured more reliable harvests than Canaan enjoyed. Powerful springs in the Jordan valley and beside the Dead Sea create very fertile areas, e.g., at Jericho, Ain Feshka, and Engedi. According to Genesis, the whole area was much more fertile before the destruction of Sodom and Gomorrah (cf. chap. 19).

"Before the LORD destroyed Sodom and Gomorrah." This ominous anticipation of chaps. 18–19 casts a shadow over Lot's decision which is about to be announced. Things are not necessarily as good as they look (cf. 1 Sam 16:7). שׁחת "destroy": this root, apart from 38:9, is used in Genesis only of the destruction of the flood and of these cities.

11–12 The theological geography of Lot's decision is particularly interesting. The boundaries of the promised land of Canaan are defined in Num 34:2–12. It appears that the eastern frontier coincided with the Dead Sea and the river Jordan, i.e., what Gen 13 terms "the plain of the Jordan." So in picking this area to live in, Lot is moving to the edge of Canaan, if not beyond it: 10:19 certainly suggests that Sodom and neighboring cities mark the borders of the land. Lot is stepping out toward the territory that his descendants, the Moabites and Ammonites, would eventually occupy in Transjordan. Though offered a share of Canaan, he is here depicted turning his back on it. "Eastward" describes his direction of travel, but it may echo Adam, Eve, and Cain, who went east after sinning (3:24; 4:16), and the men of Babel who journeyed "in the east" before commencing their ill-fated tower

(11:2). The very direction Lot takes suggests divine judgment, and apprehension is reinforced by the remark "[he] camped toward Sodom." Note too the deliberate contrast between Abram living in the land of Canaan and Lot in the cities of the plain.

13 The verse hints at the terrible fate of Sodom to be revealed in chap. 19. רע "evil" also described the generation of the flood (6:5; 8:21) who were blotted out. חטאים מאד "great sinners" is used only here. "Sinners" in the Pentateuch face sudden death (cf. Num 17:3 [16:38]). The rare phraseology implies the extreme seriousness of Sodom's sin. Thus obliquely the future fate of the city is indicated and the folly of Lot's choice is underlined. "Lot, when he fancied he was living in paradise, was nearly plunged into the depths of hell" (Calvin, 1:373).

14 This great reaffirmation of the promises of land, and descendants, is introduced by a deliberate evocation of the immediately preceding incident. The key words in v 14—"separate," "look around," "see"—are the same as in vv 9–11. In addition, the LORD's invitation to look to the four points of the compass recalls Abram's invitation to go to the right or to the left, v 9.

According to the Genesis Apocryphon (21:8–15), Abram went northward from Bethel to Ramat-Hazor, from where he had a panoramic view of the land. M. Noth (*ZDPV* 82 [1966] 266) has found a place to the northeast of Beitin from which it is possible to see the Mediterranean in the west, the mountains of Transjordan in the east, Mount Hermon in the north and the Dead Sea to the south.

15–17 The promises of land and descendants are much fuller than any earlier statements.

Cf. v 15, "all the land which you see I shall give to you and your descendants for ever" with 12:7   "this land   I shall give to   your descendants."

This reaffirmation of the promise of the land differs from the earlier formula by its much greater explicitness. First, the land is more precisely defined: "all . . . which you see." Second, it is given to Abram as well as to his descendants. And third, it is given in perpetuity, "forever."

16 Earlier statements about Abraham's descendants had been rather general. 12:7 assumes that he will have them, and 12:2 that God will make him a "great nation." Here again v 16 is very much more explicit. They will not constitute merely a nation, which in ancient times could be a relatively small group, but they will be uncountable, like the dust of the earth. Thus both aspects of the promise, the land and descendants, are made more explicit.

17 The command "walk to and fro" (hithpael הלך; cf. 3:8; 6:9; 17:1; 24:40; 48:15) throughout the land probably represents a symbolic appropriation of the land. By so doing Abram would legally take possession of it (Jacob, 365; D. Daube, *Studies in Biblical Law* [New York: Ktav, 1969], 37). This corresponds to the remark first made in v 15 that the LORD would give the land to Abram.

18 Here is resumed the itinerary style characteristic of 12:6–9; 13:1–4. "Abram camped . . . Hebron" contrasts with v 12, "Lot camped toward Sodom." Obeying the divine command to walk throughout the land (v 17), Abram moved south, whereas Lot had gone east.

"Oaks": on אלון, cf. 12:6.

"Mamre" in 14:13, 24 is the name of an Amorite, but elsewhere it is a place name: 18:1; 23:17, 19; 25:9, etc. It is not mentioned outside Genesis. It is generally identified with Ramat el-Khalil, some two miles north of Hebron, where remains dating back to the Middle Bronze Age have been found. However, S. Applebaum (*EAEHL*, 776–78) believes an alternative site in the town of Hebron itself, or just north of it, is more likely.

From a narrative viewpoint, Mamre and Hebron are central to the Abrahamic story, for it is here that the central episodes (chaps. 14–19) are set and all the patriarchs were buried. The cave of Machpelah is the first piece of real estate purchased by Abraham in Canaan, 23:1–20. The religious significance of this site is emphasized by the final note, "He built there an altar to the LORD"; cf. 12:7, 8.

Explanation

The central topic of this episode is the separation of Abram and Lot. Hitherto Abram and Lot have worked together amicably, as relatives should, and Lot is presumed to share in the promise of divine protection and blessing which comes to those who identify themselves with Abram (12:2–3). It may be that Lot was originally regarded as Abram's heir.

But here, as a result of a quarrel between Abram and Lot's herdsmen, Lot moves out of Abram's orbit. Indeed, he moves out of or at least to the very frontier of the land of promise, to the cities of the plain, whose inhabitants were great sinners (vv 12–13). Thus what he viewed as a great step forward was to be his ruin, for these cities were destined to destruction.

Abram's self-effacing generosity was, however, greatly rewarded. The promises of the land and numerous descendants are now reiterated categorically: "The *whole* land which you see I shall give to you and your descendants *forever*." Furthermore, "your descendants will be like the dust of the earth" for uncountability (v 16).

So in this episode the promise theme is again central, both positively and negatively. The explicit promises to Abram are the positive side, but the fate of Lot in edging away from Abram toward the city of destruction hints at the negative aspect: "He who disdains you I shall curse" (12:3). There is no position of neutrality: "He who is not with me is against me" (Matt 12:30). Conversely, "He that is not against us is for us" (Mark 9:40).

Abram's generosity toward his nephew Lot in allowing him to pick the best of the land for himself is recognized by most commentators as being set out as a model for his descendants to imitate. This intuitive judgment is confirmed by many detailed features in the narrative.

It begins with Abram returning to the altar near Bethel where he had last called on the LORD prior to his departure to Egypt (v 3; cf. 12:8). That he is intent on worship is underlined by its designation. "The site of the altar," v 4, is a phrase frequently employed for sanctuaries where men hope to meet with God (cf. 22:3, 9; 28:11, 16; Deut 12:5, 11, 21, etc.). And it is in the neighborhood of this altar that the promises of land and seed are confirmed more fully than on any previous occasion (vv 14–17).

The reiteration of the promises puts the divine seal of approval on Abram's treatment of Lot. Indeed, there are close parallels between Lot's actions in response to Abram's suggestions and Abram's in obedience to the LORD. Both look around and see (vv 10, 14). Both are offered all the land (vv 9, 15–17). Both travel to their allotted portion (vv 11–12, 18). But whereas Lot chooses an area that is to be destroyed by the LORD, Abram is assured that his inheritance will be forever (vv 10, 15).

Not only is the land promised to Abram and to his descendants; there are again clear anticipations of the latter's actions in their father's behavior. Isaac found his herdsmen disputing with the men of Gerar (26:12–33). When Jacob left Canaan, he had a vision at Bethel that reaffirmed the promises, and he built an altar there when he returned (28:11–17; 35:1–15). He too had to separate from his brother Esau, owing to the size of their flocks (36:6–7). Finally, Abram's experiences anticipate those of Israel after the exodus. Rich in silver and gold acquired in Egypt, they too journeyed by stages to "the place." On the way they encountered the sons of Lot, the Moabites and Ammonites, and like their forefather they were treated generously by the sons of Abram (Exod 12:35–38; 17:1; Num 10:29; Deut 2:8–19). Thus the principle of typology that is so important in 12:10–20 is evidently present in this section as well, and it may be that Lot is seen as typical of the wrong attitudes within the nation. His choosing of a territory like the land of Egypt foreshadows the off-repeated desire of the wilderness rebels to return to Egypt (Exod 16:3; Num 11:5; 14:2–3). Both ended in destruction.

But the promises that the land will belong to Abram's descendants for ever and that these descendants will be numberless as the dust of the earth look even further into the future. That the land will be Israel's everlasting possession is reaffirmed in 17:8; 48:4, and is the presupposition informing the jubilee year legislation and the inheritance laws (Lev 25:25–34; Num 36:5–9). The God-givenness of the land is a central theme of Deuteronomy (e.g., 3:18–21; 30:3–5) and the basis of the prophetic hope that Israel will return there after exile (e.g., Jer 31:2–21).

The uncountability of Abram's descendants is a perennial theme of Genesis: 15:5; 16:10; 28:14; 32:12. Balaam, the prophet hired by the king of Moab to curse Israel, said Israel was already beyond counting in his day (Num 23:10). Solomon said the same thing some centuries later (1 Kgs 3:8), though of course both eras were famed for their censuses. The NT sees believing Gentiles as well as faithful Jews as being counted as Abram's descendants (Rom 4:16–18; Gal 3:29), so that in heaven there will be "a great multitude which no man can number, from every nation, from all tribes and peoples and tongues" (Rev 7:9).

Finally of course the generosity and peaceableness displayed by Abram on this occasion is applauded from one end of Scripture to the other (e.g., Lev 19:17–18; Pss 122; 133; Prov 3:17, 29–34; Heb 12:14; Jas 3:17–18). Indeed, peacemaking and reconciliation are so central to God's character revealed in Christ (cf. Matt 5:22–26; 43–48) that Paul often calls God "the God of peace" (e.g., Rom 15:33; 2 Cor 13:11; Phil 4:9; 1 Thess 5:23; cf. Eph 2:14–17). It may be that, as elsewhere in the patriarchal story, this reaffirmation of the promises (cf. 22:16–18) is viewed as a blessing given to Abram in virtue of his prior faith and good works, illustrating the principle summed up in our Lord's well-known words "Blessed are the peacemakers, for they shall be called sons of God" (Matt 5:9).

Abram Rescues Lot   (14:1–24)

Bibliography

Andreasen, N-E. A. "Gen 14 in Its Near Eastern Context." *Scripture in Context*, ed. C. D. Evans, W. W. Hallo, and J. B. White. Pittsburgh: Pickwick Press, 1980. 59–77. **Archi, A.** "The Epigraphic Evidence from Ebla and the Old Testament." *Bib* 60 (1979) 556–66. **Astour, M. C.** "Political and Cosmic Symbolism in Gen 14 and in Its Babylonian Sources." *Biblical Motifs: Origins and Transformations*, ed. A. Altmann. Cambridge: Harvard UP, 1966. 65–112. **Ben-Yashar, Y.** "Night Warfare." (Heb.) *BMik* 17 (1971/72), 362–64. **Berger, P. R.** "Ellasar, Tarshish und Jawan, Gen 14 und 10." *WO* 13 (1982) 50–78. **Biton, G.** "The Meaning of the Root *mlk*." (Heb.) *BMik* 29 (1983/84) 85–87. **Dahood, M.** "Eblaite and Biblical Hebrew." *CBQ* 44 (1982) 1–24. **Delcor, M.** "Melchizedek from Genesis to the Qumran Texts and the Epistle to the Hebrews." *JSJ* 2 (1971) 115–35. **Doré, J.** "La rencontre Abraham-Melchisédech et le problème de l'unité littéraire de Gen 14." *De la Tôrah au Messie: Études H. Cazelles*, ed. M. Carrez, J. Doré, and P. Grelot. Paris: Desclée, 1981. 75–95. **Emerton, J. A.** "Some False Clues in the Study of Gen 14." *VT* 21 (1971) 24–47. ———. "The Riddle of Gen 14." *VT* 21 (1971) 403–39. **Fisher, L. R.** "Abraham and His Priest-King." *JBL* 81 (1962) 264–70. **Gammie, J. G.** "Loci of the Melchizedek Tradition of Gen 14:18–20." *JBL* 90 (1971) 385–96. **Garner, G.** "Cities of the Dead Sea Plain." *BurH* 18 (1982) 35–48. **Grelot, P.** "Ariok." *VT* 25 (1975) 711–19. **Habel, N. C.** "'Yahweh, Maker of Heaven and Earth': A Study in Redaction Criticism." *JBL* 91 (1972) 321–37. **Howard, D. M.** "Sodom and Gomorrah Revisited." *JETS* 27 (1984) 385–400. **Jones, G. H.** "Abraham and Cyrus: Type and Anti-Type?" *VT* 22 (1972) 304–19. **Kirkland, J. R.** "The Incident at Salem: A Re-examination of Gen 14:18–20." *StudBT* 7 (1977) 3–23. **Lack, R.** "Les Origines de *Elyon*, le Très-Haut, dans la tradition cultuelle d'Israel." *CBQ* 24 (1962) 44–64. **Lubsczyk, H.** "Melchisedek: Versuch einer Einordnung der Melchisedek-Perikope (Gen 14) in den jahwistischen Erzählungszusammenhang." In *Einheit in Vielfalt: Festgabe für H. Aufderbeck*, ed. W. Ernst and K. Feiereis. Leipzig: St Benno Verlag, 1974. 92–109. **Mazar, B.** "*Ba'al Šamēm* and *El Qōneh 'Ares*." (Heb) *Eretz-Israel* 16 (1982) 132–34. **Miller P. D.** "El, the Creator of Earth." *BASOR* 239 (1980) 42–46. **Moor, J. C. de.** "Rāpiūma-Rephaim." *ZAW* 88 (1976) 323–43. ———. "El, the Creator." In *The Bible World: Essays in Honor of C. H. Gordon*, ed. G. Rendsburg, R. Adler, M. Arfa, and N. H. Winter. New York: Ktav, 1980. 171–87. **Muffs, Y.** "Abraham the Noble Warrior: Patriarchal Politics and Laws of War in Ancient Israel." *JJS* 33 (1982) 81–107. **Olyan, S.** "Zadok's Origins and the Tribal Politics of David." *JBL* 101 (1982) 177–93. **Peter, M.** "Wer sprach den Segen nach Gen 14:19 über Abraham aus?" *VT* 29 (1979) 114–20. ———. "Die historische Wahrheit in Gen 14." In *De la Tôrah au Messie: Études H. Cazelles*, ed. M. Carrez, J. Doré, and P. Grelot. Paris: Desclée, 1981. 97–105. **Rast, W. E.,** and **T. R. Schaub.** "Preliminary Report of the 1979 Expedition to the Dead Sea Plain, Jordan." *BASOR* 240 (1980) 21–61. ———. *The Southeastern Dead Sea Plain Expedition: An Interim Report of the 1977 Season*. AASOR 46. Cambridge: American Schools of Oriental Research, 1981. ———. "Preliminary Report of the

1981 Expedition to the Dead Sea Plain, Jordan." *BASOR* 254 (1984) 35–60. **Schatz, W.** *Genesis 14: Eine Untersuchung.* EHS 23. 2. Bern: Herbert Lang, 1972. **Seebass, H.** "Der Ort Elam in der südlichen Wüste und die Überlieferung von Gen 14." *VT* 15 (1965) 389–94. **Shiloh, Y.** *Excavations at the City of David.* Qedem 19. Jerusalem: Institute of Archaeology, The University of Jerusalem, 1984. **Smith, R. H.** "Abram and Melchizedek (Gen 14:18–20)." *ZAW* 77 (1965) 129–53. **Soleh, A.** "The Structure of Gen 14's Story about the War of the Kings." (Heb.) *BMik* 29 (1983/84) 361–66. **Uffenheimer, B.** *"El Elyon,* Creator of Heaven and Earth." (Heb.) *Shnaton* 2 (1977) 20–26. **Weippert, M.** "Kedorlaomer." *RLA* 5 (1980) 543–44. **Wieder, A. A.** "Ugaritic-Hebrew Lexicographical Notes." *JBL* 84 (1965) 160–64. **Wojciechowski, M.** "Certains aspects algébriques de quelques nombres symboliques de la Bible." *BN* 23 (1984) 29–31. **Zeron, A.** "Abraham's 318 Retainers (Gen 14)." (Heb.) *Tarbiz* 52 (1982/83) 129–32. **Zimmerli, W.** "Abraham und Melchisedek." *Das ferne und nahe Wort: FS L. Rost,* ed. F. Maas. BZAW 105. Berlin: Töpelmann, 1967. 255–64.

Translation

14:1 *In the days*[a] *of Amraphel, the king of Shinar,*[b] *Arioch, the king of Ellasar,*[c] *Chedorlaomer, the king of Elam,*[d] *and Tidal, the king of Goyim,*[e] 2 *made*[a] *war with Bera, the king of Sodom, Birsha, the king of Gomorrah, Shinab,*[b] *the king of Admah, and Shemeber,*[c] *the king of Zeboim*[d] *and the king of Bela, that is, Zoar.* 3 *All*[a] *these came as allies to the Vale of Siddim, that is, the Dead Sea.*[a] 4 *For twelve years they had served Chedorlaomer, but in*[a] *the thirteenth they rebelled.*

5 *In the fourteenth year Chedorlaomer and the kings with him came and defeated*[a] *the* [b] *Rephaim in Ashtaroth-Qarnaim, the Zuzim*[c] *in Ham,*[d] *the Emim in Shave-Qiryathaim,* 6 *the Horites in the mountains*[a] *of Seir as far as El-Paran on the edge of the wilderness.* 7 *Then they turned and came to Ein-Mishpat, that is, Kadesh, and subdued the whole territory*[a] *of the Amaleqites as well as the Amorites, who dwelt in Hasason-Tamar.* 8 *Then the kings of Sodom, Gomorrah, Admah, Zeboim,*[a] *and Bela (that is, Zoar) came out*[b] *to do battle in the Vale of Siddim with them,* 9 *with Chedorlaomer, the king of Elam,*[a] *Tidal, the king of Goyim, Amraphel, the king of Shinar, Arioch, the king of Ellasar; four kings against five.*[b]

10 *Now the Vale of Siddim was full of bitumen pits,*[a] *so when the kings*[b] *of Sodom and Gomorrah fled*[c] *they fell in, but the remainder fled to the mountains.*[d] 11 *They took all the property of Sodom and Gomorrah and all their stocks of food and left.* 12 *They*[a] *took Lot,* [b] *Abram's nephew,*[b] *and his property and left,*[a] *for he had been living in Sodom.*

13 *Someone*[a] *escaped and came and told*[b] *Abram the Hebrew, while he was dwelling near the oaks*[c] *of Mamre the Amorite, kinsman of Aner*[d] *and Eshcol, allies of Abram.* 14 *When Abram heard that his kinsman had been taken*[a] *prisoner, he mustered*[b] *his trained men, three hundred and eighteen men born in his household, and gave chase as far as Dan.* 15 *During the night he and his slaves split*[a] *up against them, and he defeated*[b] *them and pursued them as far as Hobah, which is north of Damascus.* 16 *He*[a] *brought*[b] *back all the property, including Lot his kinsman and his property,*[a] *and also the women and people.*

17 *The king of Sodom came out to meet him in the Vale of Shaveh, the King's Vale, after he had returned*[a] *from defeating*[b] *Chedorlaomer*[c] *and the kings with him.* 18 *But Melchizedek, the king of Salem, brought*[a] *out bread and wine, for he was a priest*[b] *of El-Elyon.* 19 *And he blessed him,*[a] *and said, "Blessed be Abram*

by[b] *El-Elyon, creator of heaven*[c] *and earth.*[c] [20] *And blessed be El-Elyon, who has delivered your oppressors into your hand." And he gave*[a] *him a tenth of everything.*
[21] *Then the king of Sodom said to Abram,*[a] *"Give*[b] *me the people, but take*[c] *the property for yourself."*[a] [22] *Abram said to the king of Sodom, "I* [a]*solemnly swear*[a] *to the* LORD,[b] *to El-Elyon, creator of heaven and earth,* [23] *not*[a] *a thread or shoelace will*[a] *I take from you, so that you cannot say, 'I*[b] *have made Abram rich.'* [24] *Not I:*[a] *only what the young men have consumed, and the share for the men who went with me, Aner, Eshcol, and Mamre; let them*[b] *take their share."*

Notes

1.a. G "kingdom of," Vg "in that time" explain the Hebrew but do not presuppose any variant.
1.b. *Gen. Ap., Tg. Onq.* read בבל "Babylon"; *Tg. Ps.-J.* "that is, Nimrod."
1.c. σ′ Vg "Pontus." Also *Tg. Ps.-J.* in 14:9. *Gen. Ap.,* "Cappadocia."
1.d. σ′ "Scythians."
1.e. σ′ "Pamphylia."
2.a. After introductory ויהי clause (v 1), impf with waw most common, but simple pf as here also possible;, cf. 8:13; 40:1.
2.b. G Σενναάρ.
2.c. *Gen. Ap.* שמיאבד. Some SamPent MSS confusing d and r read שם אבד.
2.d. The Q reading.
3.a-a. Epic apposition to v 2 (*SBH*, 40–41).
4.a. MT without ב (GKC, 118i). SamPent and versions regularize by adding or understanding "in." Here and in v 5 the cardinal "13" is used for the ordinal "13th," for Hebrew has ordinals only up to 10.
5.a. Waw consec + 3 masc pl impf hiph נכה "to strike."
5.b. SamPent G add definite article.
5.c. *Gen. Ap.* זומזמיא; cf. Deut 2:20.
5.d. G, Vg, S point בָּהֶם "in them." Some SamPent MSS and Jerome read בחם. *Gen. Ap.* בעמן "in Ammon."
6.a. הררם: constr pl הררי + enclitic mem (KB, 244; Freedman, *ZAW* 64 [1952] 193). SamPent typically eliminates the rare form and reads constr without enclitic (Waltke, 217).
7.a. G, S "princes of," probably reading שרי for שדה.
8.a. Reading Q as in v 2.
8.b. Sg verb with composite subj (GKC, 145o).
9.a. Cf. variants in the names in v 1; see *BHS* apparatus.
9.b. Lit., four kings against *the* five: on use of article, see GKC, 134k.
10.a. Lit., "pits, pits of bitumen." On repetition to express intensity, plurality, see GKC, 123e; Joüon, 129r, 135e.
10.b. Sam, G, S read the more usual phrase "the king of Sodom and the king of Gomorrah."
10.c. Waw consec + 3 masc pl impf נוס "to flee."
10.d. SamPent has the more usual phrase ההרה. MT הרה only here.
12.a-a. Note the unusual use of waw consec with "took" and "left" after similar clauses in v 11. This epic repetition marks the episode climax (*SBH*, 42). Cf. 7:23; 21:1.
12.b-b. *Pace BHS*, no textual ground for supposing this is an addition.
13.a. Heb. uses the definite article, lit., הפליט "the fugitive" to indicate a specific person in this context (GKC, 126r; Joüon, 137n).
13.b. Cf. n. 9:22a.
13.c. G, S have sg "oak."
13.d. For variant spellings of Aner see *BHS*.
14.a. 3 masc sg pf niph שבה.
14.b. Waw consec + 3 masc sg impf hiph רוק. But SamPent וידק from דוק. Possibly also read by G "he numbered." Meaning of Heb. roots uncertain here; see *Comment*.
15.a. Waw consec + 3 masc sg impf niph חלק "to divide."
15.b. Waw consec + 3 masc sg impf hiph נכה + 3 pl suff.
16.a-a. Chiastic construction, lit., "he brought back property . . . Lot . . . he brought back," used to draw attention to different aspects of a single event (*SBH*, 128).

16.b. Waw consec + 3 masc sg impf hiph שוב "to return."

17.a. Inf constr שוב + 3 masc sg suff.

17.b. מן + inf constr hiph נכה "to strike."

17.c. Elsewhere one word; cf. vv 1, 4, 5 and 9. Here hyphenated.

18.a. 3 masc sg pf hiph יצא "to go out."

18.b. כהן ל means "*a* priest of" whereas constr + abs could mean "the priest of" (GKC, 129c).

19.a. Sam, G read "Abram": typical change for sake of clarity (Waltke, 220–21).

19.b. ל introduces agent in passive construction (GKC, 121f).

19.c. Unusually "heaven and earth" lack definite article; solemn discourse according to Joüon, 137hN, but more probably reflects underlying Canaanite phraseology.

20.a. Waw consec + 3 masc sg impf נתן.

21.a-a. Chiastic sentence in impv mood: "Give . . . people, property take." Two aspects of one action (*SBH*, 134).

21.b. 2 masc sg impv נתן.

21.c. Cf. n. 12:19.d.

22.a-a. Lit., "I have lifted my hand," 1 sg pf hiph רום. Perfect verb with present meaning (GKC, 106i). Especially frequent with verbs of speaking, where at the moment of action the punctiliar event is felt to belong to the past (Joüon, 112f).

22.b. Omitted by G, S, *Gen. Ap.* SamPent reads "God."

23.a-a. On אם to introduce oaths, see GKC, 149; Joüon, 165g. אם is repeated here (cf. Joüon, 165i), perhaps for emphasis (Gispen 2:96).

23.b. Note the use of the pronoun "I" for emphasis (*EWAS*, 55).

24.a. I.e., "I claim nothing" (BDB, 116a); cf. 41:16, 44.

24.b. Use of the personal pronoun contrasts Abram receiving nothing, and the others taking their share (*EWAS*, 55).

Form/Structure/Setting

The limits of this section are quite clear. A new departure in the Abram cycle is clearly marked by the opening clause (ויהי) of v 1. It is brought to an equally clear close in v 24. The style and subject matter of this story set it apart from the rest of the patriarchal material. Only here in Genesis do we have the account of a military campaign with various kings named. Though this is one of several stories dealing with Abram and Lot, neither is mentioned till halfway through (vv 12, 13). The story is marked by a large number of explanatory glosses, verbless clauses explaining old place names—e.g., "that is, Zoar," v 2; cf. vv 3, 7, 17—and background information—e.g., "for he was dwelling in Sodom," v 12; cf. vv 13, 18.

The arrangement of the material is also clear:

vv 1–16   Three battle reports:
            1–4   Eastern kings vs Westerners: round 1
            5–12 Eastern kings vs Westerners: round 2
            13–16 Abram vs Eastern kings
vv 17–24 Confrontation between Abram, the king of Sodom, and Melchizedek:
            17   King of Sodom meets Abram
            18–20 Melchizedek blesses Abram
            21   King of Sodom's demand
            22–24 Abram's reply

The story thus falls into two main parts: three accounts of battle, and the subsequent confrontation between Abram and the king of Sodom. The three battle reports conform to a regular convention in Hebrew narrative of telling a story in three scenes, and they serve to heighten Abram's final victory. In the first battle, Chedorlaomer and his allies defeat the king of Sodom and his allies. In the second campaign, Chedorlaomer defeats various inhabitants of Canaan and the Dead Sea kings. This double victory underlines the invincibility of Chedorlaomer and his allies. But in the third battle, Abram defeats the all-conquering Easterners and rescues the captives. Abram's military prowess is shown to be superior, not simply to that of the king of Sodom, twice defeated by Chedorlaomer, but also to that of Chedorlaomer.

Abram's victory forms the backdrop to the centerpiece of the story, the three-way discussion between Abram, the king of Sodom, and Melchizedek. The grudging attitude of the king of Sodom toward his great benefactor Abram (v 21) stands in sharp contrast both to Melchizedek's open acknowledgment of divine blessing on Abram (vv 18–20) and also to Abram's generosity to those he has saved (vv 22–24).

The story uses a variety of stylistic devices to integrate the various scenes within it. The lists of opponents in the first two battles are arranged chiastically (ABBA):

v 1, Chedorlaomer and allies   v 2, Sodom and allies

v 8, Sodom and allies   v 9, Chedorlaomer and allies

The closing remarks about the third battle echo those at the end of the second. "They took [לקח] the property [רכוש] . . . food [אכל] and left [הלך]. They took Lot . . . and his property and left" (vv 11–12). Similar terminology reappears in vv 15–16 "split up [חלק], brought back all the property including Lot." Note that Abram returned property whereas Chedorlaomer took it. It may be too that the word חלק "splitting up" is a deliberate play on לקח "to take."

The closing speeches of the king of Sodom and Abram make ready use of these key words, combining ideas of vv 11–12 and 15–16: cf. v 21, "take," "property"; v 23, "take"; v 24, אכל "consume"; חלק "share," הלך "went," "take," "share." Abram's final speech not only alludes to the military campaigns, but to Melchizedek. He says, "I solemnly swear to the LORD, *El-Elyon, creator of heaven and earth*," v 22; cf. vv 18–20. His remark about making rich (עשר, v 23) could be a covert allusion to his giving a tithe (v 20).

Melchizedek's remark "Blessed be El-Elyon, who has delivered your oppressors into your hand" presupposes knowledge of Abram's victory (vv 14–17). The repeated use of the verb ברך "to bless" is another example of paronomastic allusion to Abram's name; cf. 12:2–3; 22:17–18. Lastly, Melchizedek's "bringing out bread" (הוציא לחם v 18) may deliberately contrast with the king of Sodom's going out (יצא, vv 8, 17) to make war or do battle (מלחמה, vv 2, 8). This would accentuate the benevolence of Melchizedek and the hostility of the king of Sodom.

These elaborate cross-linkages within the story show that from a literary viewpoint it is a well-integrated piece despite its unique character within the patriarchal literature.

The idiosyncracies of this chapter have led to very diverse evaluations of its historical worth, some regarding it as based on an old written source, others holding that it was one of the last parts of Genesis to be composed. Generally it has been held that it does not belong to any of the usual penta-teuchal sources, but that it comes from a special source. Its annalistic style and international perspective set it apart from J, E, D, or P. Some possible P words, e.g., רכוש "property" are insufficient to prove its derivation from that source. Nor do its lists of place names and inhabitants of Canaan or its reports of battle prove its affinity with D (so Astour, *Biblical Motifs*).

In the nineteenth century Hupfeld and Delitzsch argued that Gen 14 is an integral part of J. This view has been revived recently by Lubsczyk, and independently by Vawter, Alexander, and Coats, who argue that chap. 14 forms part of the Lot-Abram traditions found in chaps. 13, 18–19. Since these other chapters also belong to J, it follows that chap. 14 does too. Radday and Shore (*Genesis: An Authorship Study*, 188) arrive at similar conclusions on statistical grounds. The most obvious links concern Lot and Sodom, which are of course the focus of chap. 14; cf. vv 12–16. What is more, this chapter is an indispensable stepping stone between chap. 13 and chap. 18. In 13:12 Lot was camping near Sodom. In 19:1 he is a respected citizen of the town, sitting in the gate. 14:12 notes the transitional stage "dwelling in Sodom." Similarly, that Lot was actually dwelling in Sodom explains Abram's concern for the town here and in 18:23–33. And Abram's rescue of Lot and the women by military intervention (14:16) adumbrates his later intercession for the city which led to the deliverance of Lot and his women from the doomed city. No doubt too, the churlish attitude of the king of Sodom toward his savior Abram hints at the subsequent doom that is bound to befall those who oppose the elect.

The parenthetic comment about Abram, "he was dwelling near the oaks of Mamre the Amorite" (14:13), explicitly connects this story back to 13:18 and forward to 18:1. The remark of Melchizedek "who has delivered [מגן] your oppressors" anticipates 15:1 "I am your shield [מגן]." These cross-refer-ences to other parts of the Abram-Lot cycle and the use of the divine name "the Lord" (v 22) certainly make it plausible that in its present form this chapter is an integral part of J. It is possible that the parenthetical comments in vv 12b, 13b, 18b are to be ascribed to the J editor: they clarify the sense of the story without adding to it. It may be too that the glosses on place names in vv 2, 3, 7, 17 and the use of the divine name in v 22 are also to be ascribed to this hand. These editorial revisions simply update and clarify the account: even after they are removed there is left a coherent and well-integrated narrative, as has been argued above.

However, it is often held that this is not so: chap. 14 is compiled from two or three originally independent traditions. Most commentators regard the Melchizedek episode as a later insertion into the narrative. It is admittedly strange that with the king of Sodom having been introduced to Abram in v 17, Melchizedek should suddenly appear, bless Abram, receive a tithe, and the king of Sodom say nothing until v 21. On first reading it does look like an insertion. But as we have already observed, there are several remarks in Abram's speech to the king of Sodom that are inexplicable without the Melchizedek interruption. Melchizedek's enthusiasm for Abram also serves to heighten our sense of the other king's surliness towards Abram. Furthermore, the introduction of Melchizedek is neatly done in v 18 with a conjoined chiastic clause "Melchizedek brought [הוֹצִיא]" linking back to v 17 "came out (יצא) . . . king of Sodom." The *taw-aleph* link between the two verses מלך מלכי־צדק also bespeaks its unity. The case for seeing vv 18–20 as an insertion does not therefore seem proven.

Several recent commentators (e.g., Emerton, Schatz, Westermann) have argued not only that vv 18–20 are an insertion into a tale of Abram, but that vv 1–11[12] have also been tacked on later. Originally the story told only of Abram's defeat of Chedorlaomer and rescue of Lot. Later the campaigns of the Eastern kings were added to the narrative (vv 1–11). In favor of this view, it is noted that Abram is not mentioned before v 13 and that the style of the opening is much terser, more annalistic than later in the chapter. Comparisons with Babylonian and Assyrian campaign reports are sometimes made (e.g., Shalmaneser III, *ANET*, 276–80).

However, these observations do not add up to proof that vv 1–11 are from a different source from the rest of the chapter. Unlike Mesopotamian annals, which use the first person, this is a third-person account. The brevity of the opening verses may be dictated by dramatic considerations as much as any other: the focus of interest is Abram's confrontation with the king of Sodom. The background details are therefore passed over more quickly.

The story would, however, lose much of its punch were the introductory verses omitted. Abram's victory would no longer be the climactic third in a series of battles, and as already noted, triadic patterns are beloved by Hebrew narrators. Furthermore, the phraseology of Abram's speech in vv 22–24 seems to use terminology drawn from vv 1–11 as well as vv 12–16 (see earlier discussion). For these reasons it would seem rash to distinguish three separate sources within chap. 14. Rather the chapter is a substantial unity, part of the larger Abram-Lot cycle, with a number of glosses that may be ascribed to a J-editor.

This conclusion, that the chapter consists largely of pre-J material, excludes those approaches to the chapter which see it as a later post-exilic midrash with no claim to historicity. Rather it represents old tradition. The presence of various glosses and some stylistic idiosyncracies suggests that it may be based on an older written source. But beyond this we cannot confidently go. Its claim to historicity must be assessed on the same basis as other parts of Genesis. Where possible, the kings and events mentioned must be identified to discover whether they fit into what else is known of Near Eastern history.

Comment

1–4 The report of the first battle is quite vague, simply a remark that four Eastern kings campaigned against five Western kings in the Vale of Siddim, and that the latter served the former for twelve years. Though the names seem authentic and the route of the campaign possible, no extrabiblical sources attest that these kings reigned simultaneously, let alone campaigned together in the West. This has frustrated hopes of being able to date Abram's career using this incident.

1 "Amraphel, king of Shinar." "Shinar" is Babylonia; cf. 10:10. "Amraphel": various plausible Akkadian or Amorite equivalents have been suggested, e.g., *Amurru-ipul*, "[the god] Amurru paid back" or *Amur-pi-el*, "The mouth of God has spoken." For other suggestions see Schatz (85). However, no king with this name is known from extrabiblical sources. The identification of Amraphel with Hammurapi is etymologically and historically unlikely. Amraphel is only a minor actor here, whereas Hammurapi was a powerful emperor.

"Arioch, king of Ellasar." Arioch is most simply equated with Hurrian names such as *Ariwuku* or *Ariukki*. These forms are not attested after the second millennium, according to Speiser. "Its appearance in the present context thus presupposes an ancient and authentic tradition" (Speiser, 107). However, another Arioch is mentioned in Dan 2:14, 15, although the etymology of this name could be different (R. Zadok, *VT* 26 [1976] 246).

The identity of Ellasar is uncertain. The former identification of it with Larsa rests largely on misreading the name of one of its kings, Warad-Sin, as *Eri-aku* (= Arioch). It may possibly be a town mentioned in the Mari texts, Ilanzura, between Carchemish and Harran, or less likely, an abbreviation of Til-Asurri on the Euphrates. A better suggestion (P. R. Berger, *WO* 13 [1982] 50–78) identifies Ellasar with eastern Asia Minor on the basis of etymology, versional support, and intrinsic probability. Ellasar could be related to אלסרין "hazelnuts," for which Pontus, on the southern coast of the Black Sea, was famous. The Vulgate and Symmachus translate it "Pontus," while the Genesis Apocryphon says "Cappadocia." An alliance of a ruler of this area with kings of these other areas is not out of the question.

A prince of Mari was called *Ariwuku*, but it seems unlikely that he is to be identified with Arioch. If they were the same, that would date our episode to about the eighteenth century B.C.

"Chedorlaomer, king of Elam." Chedorlaomer is made up of an authentic Elamite term (*kudur*, "son") and an Akkadian divine name (*Lā-gamāl*, "the unsparing"), but no king of this name is attested among Elamite records. The suggestion that Chedorlaomer should be identified with Kutir-naḫḫunte I (*ca.* 1730) is improbable, or with Kutir-naḫḫunte III (*ca.* 1170) is even less likely. On "Elam" see note on 10:22. Chedorlaomer emerges as the leader of the Eastern kings in vv 4, 5, 17. Though knowledge of the history of Elam is very fragmentary, it was a powerful state in the Middle East in the early second millennium B.C. It is therefore possible that an Elamite king could have led a coalition of kings on a raid against Canaan. (See *CAH* 1:2, 644–80; 2:1, 256–88.)

"Tidal, king of Goyim." Tidal represents Hittite *Tudḫaliya*. Three or four Hittite kings of this name are known between about 1750 and 1200 B.C. A private person of this name is also known in the nineteenth century Cappadocian tablets. However, it seems unlikely that "Goyim," literally, "nations," is another name for the Hittites. A people with this name is unknown. It may be the Hebrew equivalent of Akkadian *Ummān-Manda* (Manda people), barbarian invaders of Mesopotamia from the late third millennium B.C. They are occasionally associated with Elamites, "which could be pertinent to the present passage" (Speiser, 107). Another possibility is that the term covers a "federation of Indo-European (Hittite and Luvian) groups; hence Hebrew *goyim* nations" (Kitchen, *NBD*, 1276). But Berger (*WO* 13 [1982] 76) compares Greek Pamphylia "rich in peoples" with Goyim and thinks Hittites the best identification.

2 מלחמה "war." This is its first mention in the Bible; cf. Josh 11:18.

"Bera." The meaning and etymology of the name are uncertain. KB suggests a possible derivation from Arabic *baraʿa*, "to conquer." Birsha is possibly related to Arabic *biršiʿ* "hateful." "Shinab" could be from Babylonian *Sin-abušu.* "Sin (the moon god) is his father." "Shemeber" from *Šem* "name" or "son" and *ʾabāru* "be mighty." It therefore may mean "the [divine] name is mighty" or "the son is mighty."

It is striking that the kings of Sodom and Gomorrah have names compounded with רע "evil" and רשע "wicked." It is not surprising that from the targumists onward, commentators have suggested that "Bera" and "Birsha" are pejorative nicknames given to these kings. However, the more authentic sounding "Shinab" and "Shemeber" suggest that the names probably rest on an older tradition. Deliberate Hebrew mispronunciation of these kings' names from early times with a view to emphasizing their sinfulness seems quite likely; cf. Nabal, "fool," in 1 Sam 25:25. The Samaritan Pentateuch and Genesis Apocryphon, by reading שמאבד for Shemeber, seem to be deliberately reinterpreting it as "the name is lost," and Shinab has been understood as "hating the father."

The location of the five towns (Zoar's king is not named) remains problematic. The next verse makes it clear that the towns were near the Dead Sea. Though it has been suggested that they lay at the northern end of the Dead Sea, it has usually been supposed that the cities lie under or near the shallow southern end where interesting salt formations and the reek of sulphur remind the visitor of Sodom's end (19:24–26). In favor of this location are the hints in Genesis about the cities being well-watered like the land of Egypt (13:10). On the southeastern banks of the Dead Sea basin there are abundant springs feeding into streams. Furthermore, near the cities was the valley of Siddim, which was full of bitumen pits (14:10). Asphalt deposits are most abundant at the southern end of the Dead Sea, but some are also to be found at the northern end. These hints seem to support the southern location. However, no cities dating from the right period were known in this area, so it has been widely surmised they must be hidden under the relatively shallow waters (about 20 feet) of the southern Dead Sea. Recent explorations have noted five sites on the eastern shoreline of the Dead Sea, towns occupied in the Early Bronze Age *ca.* 3100–2350 B.C. Bab ed-Dhra is the largest and most northerly: those to the south are all between 4 and 8 miles apart. The furthest is only 25 miles from Bab ed-Dhra. Bab ed-Dhra (Sodom?) and Numeira were both destroyed about 2350 B.C. and then reoccupied for a short while. They were finally abandoned about 2200 or 2100 B.C. These dates are somewhat early for Abram, and the archeological evidence published to date suggests that a military attack rather than some (super)natural disaster led to the destruction of these sites. Further archeological work is planned. Only then will it be possible to say how closely it matches the Genesis accounts. (See *EM* 5, 998–1002, and the articles by Schaub and Rast, Garner, in the bibliography.)

"Sodom and Gomorrah" are frequently mentioned together in the law and the prophets. The pair "Admah and Zeboim" is rarer (only in this chapter and 10:19; Deut 29:22[23]; Hos 11:8). "Bela" occurs only in this chapter, but "Zoar" in 13:10; 19:22, 23, 30; Deut 34:3; Isa 15:5; Jer 48:34. Though it has been conjectured that Bela is actually the name of the otherwise anonymous king of Zoar, this is unproved. Rather the explanatory phrase "that is, Zoar" (vv 2, 8) is the first of several glosses in this chapter, indicating that this chapter is based on an old source which has been updated (cf. v 4). Zoar, according to 19:20–23, is the name given to the city in recollection of Lot's plea to be allowed to take refuge there. Isa 15:5; Jer 48:34 show that Zoar is in the territory of Moab, i.e., southeast of the Dead Sea. A possible site is Safi on the river Zered (Wadi Hesa). Though no pottery from biblical times has been found on this site, it might have been eroded away (*EM* 6, 695–96). The fact that five towns so close together each had its own king fits in with what is known of the political structure of pre-Israelite Palestine. It was a collection of independent city states, not a unified nation; cf. Josh 12:7–24.

3 "The Vale of Siddim." The name occurs only here and in vv 8, 10. The etymology of Siddim is obscure. Suggestions include "deep," "fields," "demons" (see lexica). Siddim sounds like Sodom, which helps to make the latter one of the key words of this chapter. "That is, the Dead Sea." It is doubtful whether this implies that the Vale of Siddim is where the Dead Sea is now. Geologically this is most unlikely. The shallow southern end could be a recent feature of the Dead Sea, but not the northern. More likely the phrase is just identifying the Vale with this region. The reference to bitumen pits (v 10) makes the area just to the south of the sea the most likely area.

4 This verse implies that the Dead Sea kings had been defeated in battle. The sequences "serve" . . . "rebel" "twelve years" . . . "thirteenth" are not necessarily poetic (*pace* D. N. Freedman, *ZAW* 64 [1952] 193–94): rather they are typical of campaign reports in royal inscriptions. Cf. 2 Kgs 18:7; 24:1, 20.

5–12 The passage describes the second East-West conflict. This time Chedorlaomer's conquest of various other peoples is mentioned, vv 5–7. It is unnecessary to see this as an insertion from another source. More details are given to show that this campaign prompted Abram's, and to underline Chedorlaomer's military strength. Note how he is now seen as leader of the Easterners, "Chedorlaomer and the kings with him."

5 "Rephaim" are among the traditional pre-Israelite inhabitants of Canaan (cf. 15:20). They were renowned for their height, as were the Anakim: Og their king had a nine-cubit bed! The largest concentration of them was found in Bashan, northern Transjordan (Deut 2:11, 20; 3:11). They were called Emim by the Moabites, and Zamzummim by the Ammonites. The relationship of these Rephaim and the souls of the dead, also called Rephaim (e.g., Isa 14:9) has been much discussed but remains obscure (*EM* 7:404–7; N. Y. Tromp, *Primitive Conceptions of Death and the Nether World in the Old Testament* [Rome: Pontifical Biblical Institute, 1969] 176–80; J. C. de Moor, *ZAW* 88 [1976] 323–45.)

"In Ashtaroth." Given their strong presence in Bashan, it is not surprising that Chedorlaomer clashed with the Rephaim in Ashtaroth, modern Tell

Aštara. Ašterot is mentioned in a fifteenth-century list of Tuthmosis III (*ANET*, 242) and in the Amarna letters, and also in a nineteenth-century text (Schatz, 169–70). Qarnaim (cf. Amos 6:13) is near Ashtaroth, so probably the compound phrase means Ashtaroth near Qarnaim. It could be Schech-Saʿd, three miles north of Ashtara.

"Zuzim" are mentioned only here. Genesis Apocryphon and Symmachus equate them with the Zamzummim of Deut 2:20. The meaning of their name and their affinity is unknown.

"Ham." This name survives today in a site south of Ashtaroth along the King's Highway, and 4 miles southwest of Irbid.

"Emim" are also mentioned in Deut 2:10–11, where they are equated with the Rephaim. Their name could be related to the root אֵים "awesome." They are described as the pre-Moabite inhabitants of Moab, i.e., the area east of the Dead Sea.

"Shave-Qiryathaim." Shave has not been identified. It could mean simply "valley." Or it could be a place name with its unfamiliar location clarified by the better-known Qiryathaim (cf. Num 32:37; Josh 13:19; Jer 48:1). The exact location of Qiryathaim is uncertain too: evidently it is situated between Ham and Mount Seir, i.e., somewhere in northern Moab. However, there are too many places in this area with names akin to Qiryathaim to be sure which is meant. Two places near Madeba present least difficulties, Khirbet el-Qureiyeh and Qaryet el-Mekhairet (cf. Y. Aharoni, *The Land of the Bible*, 2d ed., [Philadelphia: Westminster, 1979] 307; Schatz, 170–71).

6 "The Horites in the mountains of Seir." According to Deut 2:12, 22, the Horites lived in Seir, the mountainous region east of the Arabah between the Dead Sea and the gulf of Akaba, before the Edomites settled there. It is tempting to identify the Horites with the Hurrians, a very influential group of non-Semitic inhabitants of the fertile crescent from the end of the third millennium. Egyptian texts often refer to Palestine as Huru. Nevertheless, it is questionable whether the Hurrians penetrated into southern Transjordan, and the Horites of Gen 36 have Semitic names, which also tells against identifying them with the Hurrians. (See further *POTT*, 221–30; de Vaux, *History*, 64–66, 136–38.)

"El-Paran" (tree of Paran) is mentioned only here. However, the southward thrust of Chedorlaomer along the king's highway must have brought him toward Eilat (Deut 2:8; 1 Kgs 9:26) at the head of the gulf of Akaba. Since the next verse speaks of their turning, it seems most likely that Eilat is meant here. Paran is the largest of the wildernesses south of Canaan, covering much of the Sinai peninsula and part of the Negeb and Arabah (cf. 21:21; Num 10:12; so M. Harel, *Masei Sinai* [Tel Aviv: Am Oved, 1968] 208–9). Aharoni (*EM* 6:433–34) believes the whole Sinai peninsula is meant.

7 "They turned. . . ." From Eilat they headed in a northwesterly direction toward Kadesh-Barnea, usually identified with the large oasis Ain Hudeirat. Only here is it called Ein-Mishpat, apparently an older name for the site, as the gloss "that is, Kadesh" (cf. vv 2, 3) makes clear. It was an important center for the Israelites during the forty years of wilderness wanderings: Kadesh seems to have been their base (Num 13:26; 20:22). It also represented the southern border of Canaan (Num 34:4).

"Territory of the Amaleqites." The Amaleqites were a Bedouin-like people who lived in the Sinai peninsula and northern Negeb. Several clashes with them are recorded in the exodus and early monarchy period, which led to great animus against them in Israel (Exod 17:8, 14; Num 13:29; Deut 25:17, 19; 1 Sam 15:2–8). It certainly fits that Chedorlaomer should have encountered them near Kadesh.

"The Amorites": these are one of the peoples most commonly mentioned in lists of the pre-Israelite inhabitants of Canaan and Transjordan. Sometimes the designation is used as a blanket term for all the earlier residents (cf. 48:22; Deut 1:44; *POTT*, 100–33).

"Haṣaṣon-Tamar" ("Gravel dump with palms"; so KB, 330) is identified by 2 Chr 20:2 with Ein-Gedi, a settlement on the western side of the Dead Sea. The wadi Haṣaṣa six miles north of Ein-gedi could also support this identification. Others think Haṣaṣon-Tamar should be identified with Tamar in southern Judah (1 Kgs 9:18; Ezek 47:18–19). Still other possible identifications include Kasr ejuniyeh or Ain Kusb (20 miles southwest of the Dead Sea; Schatz, 174–75; *EM*, 8:607–8). Whichever is the correct location, it is clear that from Kadesh the kings turned northwest back toward the Dead Sea region and the cities of the plain.

8–9 Though the second encounter between the Eastern kings and the cities of the plain is described more fully than the previous battle (vv 2–3), it is still tantalizingly brief. That the king of Sodom and his allies are here mentioned before the Easterners suggests that the former are still taking the initiative and maintaining their rebellious attitude. In v 9 Chedorlaomer heads the list of Eastern kings, as opposed to v 1 where he was third. This confirms his leadership of their coalition. Finally, although v 8 describes the battle lines being drawn and v 10 the rout, there is no account of the fight itself, perhaps suggesting that it was over very quickly. The summarizing phrase "four kings against five" is typical of royal campaign records (cf. Josh 12:24; 2 Sam 23:39).

10 "Bitumen pits." In certain places in the Middle East petroleum oozes to the surface and can then be dug out. "They fell in." Were it not for the reappearance of the king of Sodom in v 17, it would be simplest to suppose he died falling into a bitumen pit. Clearly, however, this cannot be the understanding of the writer. So either we must suppose "falling in" is a way of saying they jumped into a pit to hide (cf. 24:64; Josh 10:16; so Junker, Muffs). Or we should suppose that it is a general comment on the troops of Sodom and Gomorrah, that they are the ones who fell in and perished there, though as v 17 makes plain, the king himself survived (so Delitzsch, Driver, Westermann.)

"To the mountains." The ground rises very steeply both to the east and the west of the Dead Sea.

11–12 The repetitiveness "took . . . property . . . left" is no sign that v 12 is necessarily an editorial addition. Repetition at climactic points in the story (cf. 7:18–19, 23; 21:1) is a regular feature of Hebrew epic prose style (*SBH*, 42). The next scene closes in very similar fashion, though it is arranged chiastically instead of being simply coordinated (cf. v 16). Here we have a general statement of the sacking of Sodom and Gomorrah, then a more detailed remark about the capture of Lot, who, we are reminded, was Abram's nephew and lived in Sodom. The last point is new: when last heard of, Lot was simply camping near Sodom (13:12). A similarly structured account of the taking of captives is 1 Sam 30:1–5 (first, a general statement; capture of women, v 1; then capture of David's wives, v 5). Though the reader already knows of Lot's relationship to Abram, the information is repeated here because it is the motive for Abram's intervention in the next scene.

13–16 The third battle report follows naturally from the previous two. Here, however, Chedorlaomer and his allies, after two victorious campaigns, are now defeated by Abram. The two previous victories put this one into perspective. It was an astute and able man that Abram defeated. Chedorlaomer's great victories are now overshadowed by Abram's. Throughout this episode Abram appears in quite a different light from elsewhere in Genesis, yet the differences are mentioned in passing, quite unselfconsciously. In the OT, survivors of a battle are often recorded as bringing reports back (cf. 1 Sam 4:12; 2 Sam 1:2; 18:19). Often, messengers give fairly detailed accounts of the battle. Here all that is mentioned is that Abram's kinsman had been taken.

13 העברי "the Hebrew." It is quite striking that Abram should be termed "the Hebrew" here. This is not a term used by Israelites of themselves, but only by non-Israelites of Israelites (39:14; 41:12). The Ḥabiru/Apiru were well known in the ancient Near East, being referred to in a wide variety of texts from the late third millennium on. It seems to be more of a social categorization than an ethnic term. The Apiru are usually on the periphery of society—foreign slaves, mercenaries, or even marauders. Here Abram fits this description well: he is an outsider vis à vis Canaanite society, and he is about to set out on a military campaign on behalf of the king of Sodom as well as Lot. He is "a typical hapiru of the Amarna type" (H. Cazelles, *POTT*, 22). The phrase "enhances the flavor of antiquity of which this chapter is redolent" (Vawter, 196) and could indeed support the view that an originally non-Israelite source lies behind this account, since Israelites did not describe themselves as Hebrews (see further *POTT*, 1–28; O. Loretz, *Habiru-Hebräer*, BZAW 160 [Berlin: De Gruyter, 1984]).

שכן "dwelling." This term is more common than אהל (13:12, 18) and suggests fairly long-term dwelling in a tent; cf. 9:27; 26:2; 35:22. It is often used to describe God's dwelling in the tabernacle (e.g., Exod 25:8; 40:35). Muffs (*JJS* 33 [1982] 102) notes that the Habiru preferred living in the forested highlands of Palestine, such as "the oaks of Mamre."

"Mamre," here and in v 24, is a personal name; elsewhere a place name. "The Amorite"; cf. v 7.

"Eshcol" occurs only here and in v 24 as a personal name. The common noun means "bunch of grapes," but it is also the name of a valley near Hebron (Num 13:23, 24), an area noted for grape-growing.

"Aner": cf. v 24. This is the name of a Levitical city in 1 Chr 6:55 [70], but it could be a corruption for Taanak; cf. Josh 21:25. The SamPent reading, ענרם, would make it a theophoric name, *ram* being a divine name. Otherwise its meaning is obscure.

It is notable that at least two of Abram's allies are also place names. It suggests that the clans who lived there gave their name to the locality or, vice versa, that their names were derived from their home ground. It also may be remarked that they are described as בעלי ברית "allies"; only here is this phrase found. (On ברית, cf. *Comment* on 6:18.) Elsewhere Abram is depicted as making agreements with Philistines (21:22–34) and with Hittites (chap. 23). Here he is in league with Amorites.

14 The brevity with which the capture of Lot and the Sodomites is described conveys the speed with which Abram reacted to the crisis. נשבה "taken prisoner" is most frequently used of being taken captive following military defeat (cf. 31:26; 34:29; 1 Sam 30:2, 3, 5).

חניכיו "his trained men." The term only occurs here. חנך is most frequently used of dedicating buildings, once of training a child (Deut 20:5; Prov 22:6). This Hebrew etymology explains the term adequately, though an Egyptian origin with the meaning "retainer" is possible (T. O. Lambdin, *JAOS* 73 [1953] 150; KB, 320; cf. S. C. Reif, *VT* 22 [1972] 495–501).

ויֶרק "he mustered." The context makes the meaning clear, though ריק hiphil usually means "to empty" or "to draw" (a weapon out of its sheath) (42:35; Lev 26:33). So the SamPent reading וידק may be preferred; it appears to be related to Akk *dekû* "to muster troops."

ילידי ביתו "born in his household." The phrase recurs four times in Gen 17—vv 12, 13, 23, 27; also Lev 22:11; Jer 2:14. Those "born in the house" are slaves (cf. v 15) who have grown up in Abram's clan rather than those more recently acquired, and are therefore the most reliable ones. It is surprising that Abram could field so many fighting men. If he had that many young men, his total group must have numbered well over a thousand. Nevertheless, the narrative has already implied that large groups were involved in the squabble between Abram and Lot. There was insufficient pasturage for them to dwell together. By the standards of the Canaan portrayed in the El-Amarna tablets, a fighting force of three hundred men was a sizable army (cf. *ANET*, 485). It was with a group this size that Gideon conquered the Midianites, a story with some parallels to this one (Judg 7). The fact that Abram could defeat the Eastern kings with this number suggests their campaign was more like a raiding expedition than a full-blooded conquest. Though the number 318 equals the numerical value of Eliezer's name (15:2), this appears to be coincidence.

"Dan" is often regarded as the northernmost point of the promised land (cf. the phrase "from Dan to Beersheba") and may be identified with Tell el Qadi. Its older name was Laish, by which it is known in the Egyptian execration and Mari texts. It was changed to Dan when the Danites overran it in the judges' period (Judg 18:29). Settlement at the site goes back to the Early Bronze Age 2, when a large city was already in existence there (*EAEHL*, 1:313–21).

15 ויחלק "split up." 1 Kgs 16:21; Job 38:24 support this rendering of the niphal of חלק rather than "surround" (so D. J. Kamhi, *VT* 23 [1973] 238). Here the text suggests Abram employed similar tactics to those of Gideon who defeated much larger forces than his own by a surprise night attack from three sides (Judg 7:19–23; cf. 1 Sam 11:11). ויכם "defeated": Chedorlaomer had defeated the Rephaim and the Amaleqites (vv 5, 7). Now the tables are turned and Abram defeats him. Indeed, he drives them north of

Damascus to Hobah, a site mentioned nowhere else in the Bible or in other ancient texts. Attempts to equate Hobah with Apum or Upe, the area in which Damascus lies, are misguided. The northern border of Canaan ran some way north of Damascus, so perhaps Abram is being pictured driving the invaders out of the land of promise; cf. his symbolic driving off of the birds, Israel's enemies, in 15:11. Damascus was from prehistoric times a very important center on the Near Eastern trade routes.

16 This victory scene concludes with Abram bringing back all the property taken at the end of the previous scene. Note the twice-repeated רכוש "property" and the double use of השיב "bring back," corresponding to the double לקח "take" in vv 11–12. Lot is specifically mentioned at both points too. Here the importance of Abram's victory is underlined by the final phrase, "also the women and people." Previously the capture of Sodom's food supplies had been noted (v 11) but not the loss of the women and other inhabitants. In rescuing the womenfolk Abram foreshadows David's later action (1 Sam 30:17–18). But the taking of women in war is often remarked on in biblical law and narrative (cf. Deut 21:10–14; 2 Kgs 5:2). And who should take the spoils of victory was also a recurrent problem (cf. Num 31:25–54; Josh 7; 1 Sam 30:21–25) which the next scene focuses on.

17–24 The final climactic scene is well constructed, with just three principal actors on stage—Abram, the king of Sodom, and Melchizedek. It is so arranged that the kings' appearance and speeches are in chiastic contrast, and then Abram is given the last word.

v 17	King of Sodom comes	A
v 18	Melchizedek King of Salem brings out bread and wine	B
v 19–20	Melchizedek speaks	B¹
v 21	King of Sodom speaks	A¹
v 22–24	Abram replies	

In both words and deeds Melchizedek appears more generous than the king of Sodom. Whereas Melchizedek gives Abram bread and wine, the king of Sodom gives him nothing. Indeed, to start with he says nothing, and when he does speak he is very grudging, considering all that Abram has done for him.

17 The last time the king of Sodom "came out," it was to do battle with Chedorlaomer (v 8). This time it is to greet Abram, who has rescued those taken captive by Chedorlaomer. It is not said where the king came out from, but the story seems to presuppose that he had returned to his home in Sodom. "The vale of Shaveh": the meaning of Shaveh is uncertain. It may be simply "valley" (cf. v 5), or it may be "ruler" (cf. A. A. Wieder, *JBL* 84 [1965] 161), as the root apparently means "to rule" in Ugaritic. If the latter is correct, then the gloss "the King's Vale" is an apt Hebrew translation of an earlier Hebrew term. "A king's vale" is mentioned in 2 Sam 18:18 and is located by the Genesis Apocryphon in Beth-Hakkerem, probably Ramat Rachel, two and a half miles south of Jerusalem (*Gen. Ap.* 22:14). Whether the same King's Vale is meant here is unclear, but if Salem (v 18) is Jerusalem, it is possible. But apart from the location of Abram's encounter with the king of

Sodom, we are told very little new: almost everything else repeats information given earlier in the narrative.

18 The chiasmus and taw-aleph links (cf. *Form/Structure/Setting*) with v 17 as well as the remarks by the king of Sodom in v 21 show that, at least as far as the editor is concerned, Melchizedek and the king of Sodom met Abram simultaneously. In their present context, vv 18–20 may not be viewed as a separate episode.

The name "Melchizedek" may be understood in three different ways: "My king is Ṣedeq," "Milku is righteous" or "my king is righteous [i.e., legitimate]." The first two interpretations presuppose that either Melek or Ṣedeq is the name of a god. The third does not: if it were correct, it would be the equivalent of Akkadian *Šarru kēn* (Sargon). Since theophoric names are frequent in the ancient orient, the first or second explanation is to be preferred. It is noteworthy that a king of Jerusalem mentioned in Josh 10:1 is called Adonizedek ("my lord is Ṣedeq"), and David's high priest was called Zadok. This seems to corroborate the narrator's assumption that Melchizedek was king of Jerusalem. This is certainly the oldest understanding of the episode. Ps 110 associates the king in Zion with Melchizedek, and Ps 76:3 [2] puts Zion and Salem in parallel. The Genesis Apocryphon (22:13) and Josephus (*Ant.* 1.10.2 [1:180]) also affirm the identity of Salem with Jerusalem.

Here Melchizedek is simply said to be the "king of Salem," and it is not made clear where Salem is. If Jerusalem is meant, it is strange that an otherwise unattested abbreviation of the name is used here. Already in non-biblical second-millennium texts Jerusalem is called Rushalimum/Urusalim. So it has been suggested that Salem near Shechem (cf. Gen 33:18) could be meant, and that a tradition associated with this town has been transferred to Jerusalem (so Smith, Gammie, Kirkland). Though this is possible, it seems clear that Genesis views Melchizedek as a southern figure, in that he appears on the scene with the king of Sodom.

"Brought out bread and wine." The precise significance of this gesture is uncertain. Clearly it was a token of goodwill, but can one be more precise? Vawter has suggested that this remark shows that Melchizedek and Abram had a covenant meal together. Melchizedek as the dominant ally provided the bread and wine. This seems to be going beyond the evidence. What is being portrayed, however, is the generosity of Melchizedek. Bread and water would have been the staple diet. Bread and wine is royal fare (1 Sam 16:20) and regularly accompanied animal sacrifice (Num 15:2–10; 1 Sam 1:24; 10:3). Melchizedek, who in traditional Near Eastern fashion combined the offices of king and priest, should have had ample supplies of bread and wine. Here he is portrayed as laying on a royal banquet for Abram the returning conqueror.

"He was a priest of El-Elyon." Note that Melchizedek is the first priest named in Scripture. El-Elyon is one of the titles of the God worshiped by the patriarchs. Others include El-Olam, El-Shaddai, El-God of Israel. El, the supreme god of the Canaanite pantheon in the second millennium, often has his name qualified by some epithet, such as Elyon, Shaddai or creator of earth. In late texts Elyon appears as the name of a different deity, so it has been suggested that El-Elyon is a synthesis of two divine names. However, with R. Lack (*CBQ* 24 [1962] 44–64) and F. M. Cross (*Canaanite Myth and Hebrew Epic*, 50–52), it seems most likely that Elyon ("most high") is an ancient epithet of El. It certainly suits his character and situation in the pantheon. (For further discussion, see M. H. Pope, *El in the Ugaritic Texts*, VTSup 2 [Leiden: Brill, 1955].)

19 "He blessed him." Three times the important root ברך appears. This not only alludes to Abram's name, but looks back to 12:1–3 where Abram was promised that he would be a blessing and that all families would find blessing in him. Here is the first fulfillment of that promise, as Melchizedek, one of the family of men, blesses Abram. The expected corollary of his goodwill is that he himself will be blessed. In contrast, the attitude of the king of Sodom seems to be that of disdain, and that has grave implications (cf. 12:3).

"Maker of heaven and earth." El is regularly called "maker of earth" and also "father of mankind," but doubts have been raised as to whether he was also viewed as creator of the whole cosmos, as the phrase "maker of heaven and earth" implies. But J. C. de Moor ("El the Creator," in *The Bible World*, 171–87) has plausibly argued that as El is also called "father of the gods," like Enlil in Mesopotamia, so, like Enlil, he was regarded as creator of heaven and earth. "It is hardly imaginable that the god who created the whole cosmos would have been a minor deity in Ugarit. No other Ugaritic god than El, the head of the pantheon, qualifies for this role" (ibid., 186). In the light of these considerations, the phrase "creator of heaven and earth" could well be early. Later Hebrew poets (Ps 115:15; 121:2; 124:8; 134:3) record the epithet, applying it to the God of Israel. Perhaps because of its associations with procreation (e.g., Gen 4:1) the verb used here, קנה, was later changed to עשה "to make." This avoids any suggestion that God's creativity was in any way sexual.

20 "Who has delivered your oppressors into your hand." The verb "deliver" (מגן) occurs in only two other passages (Hos 11:8; Prov 4:9), both times in parallel with נתן "to give." Here too, giving is mentioned immediately afterwards (vv 20–21). The cognate term מָגֵן "shield," used in 15:1, seems to look back to this passage. "Oppressor" צר is a common word for enemies: etymology (cf. צר/צרה "narrow," "distress") and usage make it particularly apt where enemy aggression has caused suffering, as in this case.

"He gave him a tenth of everything." Tithing was an old and widespread custom in the ancient orient. Tithes were given to both sanctuaries and kings. Melchizedek qualifies on both counts. Here, however, it is probably in virtue of his priesthood that Abram gives him a tithe. For as Abram has received a priestly blessing from Melchizedek, it is fitting that he should respond in the customary fashion. Here Abram (cf. Jacob 28:22), father of the nation, sets an example for all his descendants to follow (cf. later legislation on tithing: Num 18; Lev 27:30–33). "Everything" in context must refer to all the booty captured from the fleeing kings, since it was on his way home that Abram met Melchizedek. (On tithes see *EM* 5:204–12). Here and in vv 21–24 it is presupposed that Abram, the victor, has a right to keep the spoils for himself. But having given a tenth to Melchizedek, he gives the rest to the king of Sodom. To see a conflict between v 20 and vv 21–24 is oversubtle. That victors had a right to the spoils of battle, yet might forgo it, is illustrated in a treaty from Ugarit: the obligation to supply allied troops with food is illustrated in a number of texts, mainly from the second millennium (see Muffs, *JJS* 33 [1982] 83–92).

21 The meanness of the king of Sodom stands in stark contrast to Melchizedek's warm generosity. Sodom brought nothing, whereas Melchizedek brought out bread and wine. Melchizedek blessed Abram. Sodom makes a short, almost rude demand of just six words: "Give me people; take property yourself." There is none of the customary courtesy here. The word order (note how he mentions "giving" before "taking") reflects Sodom's ungracious self-centeredness. As their rescuer, Abram presumably had a right to both the people and the property that he had recovered. Certainly he does not expect his allies to forfeit their share; cf. v 24.

22 "Solemnly swear": literally, "I have raised my hand." Raising the hand when swearing an oath seems to underline its solemnity (cf. Deut 32:40; Dan 12:7). Note that when Abram swears by Melchizedek's God El-Elyon, this deity is identified with the LORD. With the majority of commentators, it seems likely here at least that an earlier version of the story simply said El-Elyon: this Yahwistic gloss indicates that the patriarchs did indeed worship the same God as later Israel (cf. G. J. Wenham, "The Religion of the Patriarchs," in *Essays*). The mention of El-Elyon links this verse with v 18.

23 Similarly, the verb "I have made . . . rich" uses an almost identical root, עשר, to that found in "tithe" (v 20), עשר. "Thread or shoelace": Abram swears he is not interested in keeping for himself even the smallest items of booty, let alone anything of value. It seems to correspond to the Akkadian phrase *lu ḫāmu lu ḫuṣābu* "be it a blade of straw or a splinter of wood" used in legal texts to renounce property rights (Muffs, *JJS* 33 [1982] 83–84).

24 In forgoing his normal share of the booty, Abram speaks only for himself. What has already been consumed by the campaigners cannot be given back to the king of Sodom, nor does Abram expect his allies Aner, Eshcol, and Mamre to give up their share. This is the first explicit mention that these men accompanied Abram on the campaign; cf. v 14. That they were not asked to give up any of their booty underlines Abram's generosity toward Sodom: just as in the previous episode where Abram allowed Lot the pick of the land, so here he allows the surly king of Sodom more than his due.

THE HISTORICITY OF GENESIS 14

In Gen 14 the issue of the historicity of the patriarchal narratives is most sharply focused. Throughout most of Genesis the chronology of events is fairly vague, locations are imprecise, and interaction between the patriarchs and Gentiles is rare. There is little for either defenders of patriarchal historicity or sceptics to take hold of. The arguments must necessarily rest on fairly general considerations. But Gen 14 is different in that many names of kings, peoples, and places are given. There are also precise itineraries of several military campaigns. Here the claim that Abram was part of the international history of the ancient orient is very explicit. Yet here critical assessments of the material are at their most diverse. On the one hand, there are those who claim that this chapter is one of the latest parts of Genesis and that it is highly fictitious. On the other, many have claimed that this chapter goes back to a very old account, probably pre-Israelite and possibly of Babylonian origin. Despite a century of discussion, the different sides are still miles apart and show little sign of reaching agreement. Here I do not profess to offer any new proof of the material's historicity or otherwise; I simply aim to set out some of the most pertinent considerations, briefly summarizing the evidence already listed and adding some other points.

The names of the Eastern kings have a ring of authenticity about them. Arioch (Hurrian), Tidal (Hittite) are well-attested second-millennium names, and Amraphel and Chedorlaomer, while unknown, have quite plausible Amorite and Elamite etymologies. However, there is no extrabiblical text that brings these kings into temporal conjunction to enable a precise date to be placed on these events.

The route of the invasion is also plausible, with a string of place names set out along the trade route called the King's Highway in Transjordan. The names of the kings of the Dead Sea pentapolis, and indeed some of the city names, are not attested outside the Bible, but this proves little. The presence of glosses explaining some of the names seems to imply the antiquity of the information presented here, as does the old term, חניכים "trained men." This is found not only here in the Bible, but also in a nineteenth-century Egyptian text and in a fifteenth-century Taanak letter.

The reference to Melchizedek, priest of El-Elyon, also seems to fit in with what is known of second-millennium Canaanite religion. The legal phraseology "not a thread or a shoelace" and Abram's giving up his rights to booty find parallels in second-millennium Hittite and Canaanite texts. The description of Abram as "the Hebrew dwelling near the oaks of Mamre" also fits the life style of the Habiru mentioned in many second-millennium texts. All these archaic features of the narrative seem to support the view that the narrative is based on an archaic text. On literary grounds I have argued that the original text must antedate the J-editor of Genesis, for the story as it stands has been carefully integrated into the Lot-Sodom cycle. This makes it unlikely that the text is a late midrash: the evidence rather suggests that this chapter is based on one of the oldest literary sources in Genesis.

But to admit its antiquity is not to prove its historicity. The greatest objections to this being a historical account are of a more general sort. First, the picture of Abram in this story is quite different from that found elsewhere in the narratives. Here he is a powerful warrior taking on some of the major kings of the orient. Elsewhere he appears as an almost solitary figure wandering through Canaan with his wife and a few slaves. Second, "it is historically quite impossible for these five cities south of the Dead Sea to have at any one time during the second millennium been the vassals of Elam" (R. de Vaux, *The Early History of Israel*, vol 1 [London: DLT, 1978] 219).

Let us take these points in reverse order: Despite the difficulty of suggesting a time when Elam ruled the Dead Sea area, our knowledge of second-millennium history is still sufficiently patchy to make Elamite rule of this area a possibility. Furthermore, the history of the late third millennium is also very skimpy, and if recent suggestions about the identity of Sodom and its neighboring cities are correct, it is perhaps in this period that the conflicts should be placed.

Second, the contrast between Abram the great warrior in chap. 14 and Abram the lone bedouin elsewhere is probably overdrawn. Certainly other stories rarely mention Abram's fellow travelers, but they do give hints that a substantial company followed him. Though the Pharaoh of Egypt expelled Abram, he did not summarily execute him, which may imply that Abram had his own protectors, and he left Egypt with vast herds and slaves and slave-girls (12:16). Soon after their arrival in Canaan, Abram and Lot had to split up because their herdsmen were quarreling, "because the land could not support both of them dwelling together" (13:6). So already the narratives have suggested that Abram had many people accompanying him. Later stories portray Abram negotiating a treaty with Abimelech, a king in the coastal plain (21:22–34), and being described by the Hittites of Hebron as "a great prince" (23:6). Both episodes show that Abram was a force to be reckoned with from a military point of view. Indeed to have 318 retainers, as 14:14 says he had, does not seem extravagant in the light of the other stories. What is surprising is that with such a modest force he could defeat a four-king coalition. It is akin to Gideon's defeat of the Midianites with just three hundred men (Judg 7). No doubt this is seen by the narrator as a heroic achievement, but again it would be unwise to read too much into the story of the Eastern kings. Armies in ancient times were often quite small, and it could be that what is described here is more in the nature of a raid by relatively limited forces than a full-scale attempt at conquest. The suggestion of Andreasen that the story originally told only of a political delegation accompanied by armed men seems to overlook some clear statements in the account. However, it would seem fair to claim that the contrast between the figure of Abram in this chapter and elsewhere in the narrative is less than appears at first sight. The other stories do give hints that Abram had a sizable retinue, while the mention of kings and their armies here should not mislead us into thinking of vast forces ranged against Abram.

To sum up, the account of Abram's battle with the Eastern kings has many archaic features which suggest that an old source underlies the present version. However, it is not yet possible to pin down the events described to a specific period, for correlation with non-biblical accounts remains elusive. In these respects Gen 14 resembles other parts of Genesis: at many points they bear the hallmarks of antiquity, but to prove that the events happened just as recorded is impossible. While the reasons often adduced for doubting the historical character of these narratives are weak, it is also true to say that neither can it be proved that the events described are historical. The evidence is open to various interpretations in which preconceptions play a large part.

Explanation

In style and content the invasion of the Eastern kings shatters the air of calm that characterized the close of the previous episode. That left Lot progressing toward prosperous living in Sodom, and Abram, reassured by the divine pledge of land and offspring, dwelling contentedly in Hebron. Suddenly the tranquility of Canaan is overturned by an invasion led by Chedorlaomer of Elam (part of modern Iran) and Amraphel of Babylon (part of modern Iraq) and two other kings, probably from Turkey. For twelve years the cities of the Dead Sea plain submitted to this Eastern alliance, and then rebelled.

This rebellion led to a punishment raid by the Eastern kings. Their campaign of retribution took them along the main trade route of Transjordan and down to the gulf of Akaba before they swung west toward Kadesh-Barnea. A second defeat of the Dead Sea kings involved the rout of their forces, the pillaging of their towns, and the deportation of many of their inhabitants, including Lot, Abram's nephew.

This led to Abram's intervention. As the Eastern kings were retreating northward, Abram caught them near Dan, defeated them, and then chased them out of Canaan. He brought back the loot, including his relative Lot and the women of Sodom.

On his return, Abram was met near Salem, probably Jerusalem, by Melchizedek, its priest-king, and the king of Sodom. The attitudes of the two kings stand in marked contrast. Melchizedek, for whom Abram has done but little, greets him warmly, laying on a banquet for him. He further blesses Abram in the name of the high god of Canaan, El-Elyon. Here the promise of blessing upon Abram and those who bless him (12:1–3) starts to be fulfilled. By implication Melchizedek, who blesses Abram, is himself blessed. Indeed, Abram shows his benevolence toward Melchizedek by giving him a tenth of the booty. But the king of Sodom, by his cool, if not surly, reception of Abram, shows that he disdains Abram, an attitude that is both unjustified, considering Abram's rescue of the people of Sodom, and, in the light of 12:3, a response that will evoke the divine curse. Yet despite Sodom's coolness, Abram treats him generously, returning to him all the people and booty that the Eastern kings had carried off, a trait already shown in his treatment of Lot (13:8–12).

This episode does not therefore add many new elements to the picture of Abram already painted. It reinforces earlier hints about the large retinue that accompanies him, when it mentions over three hundred born in his household. It underlines his generosity, already shown in his attitude to Lot, by his remarks to the king of Sodom. The dire fate awaiting Sodom, already hinted at in 13:13, here becomes more certain. Not only is the city sacked by human hands, which suggests divine displeasure, but its king's brusque treatment of Abram, his deliverer, suggests antipathy to one who evidently enjoys divine blessing and support. Even without the explicit warning that "he who disdains you I shall curse," the narrative suggests that it is dangerous to despise those through whom God works.

It is the demonstration of divine support for Abram that is the clearest thrust of this story. The Dead Sea cities are twice defeated by the coalition of Eastern kings. Yet Abram, who has much smaller forces at his disposal, smashes the invaders, expelling them from Canaan, and rescues Lot and the captured women. For those with eyes to see, such as Melchizedek, this is proof that "El-Elyon, God most high, has delivered your oppressors into your hand." And with his verdict on the situation the narrator doubtless concurs. Here the LORD's promise—to make Abram's name great and for him to be a blessing—begins to be fulfilled. Indeed, were it not for his antipathy to Abram, the king of Sodom, the narrative implies, could have found blessing too. But his rejection of Abram's ministry puts him on the path to doom. On the other hand, Melchizedek, who blessed Abram, is himself blessed.

The figure of Melchizedek, the god-fearing Canaanite priest-king, has naturally fascinated succeeding generations. Ps 110, often seen as a coronation liturgy, declares the Davidic king to be a priest "after the order of Melchizedek" (v 4): "He was the type of that that union of civil and religious life, which must be the ideal of the perfect state" (A. F. Kirkpatrick, *The Psalms* [Cambridge: CUP, 1902] 668). The Davidic king was priest, at least in the sense that he belonged to a priestly nation (Exod 19:6), mediated between God and Israel, and participated in worship (2 Sam 6:14), both directing sacrifice and blessing the people (2 Sam 6:17–18; 1 Kgs 8:14, 55, 62–63). Gen 14 implies that because Melchizedek blessed Abram, divine blessing would rest on his successors, the priest-kings in Jerusalem.

Already in Jesus' day, Psalm 110 was interpreted messianically, as the Qumran texts and the Gospels show. It is the most quoted psalm in the NT, and Jesus assumes a messianic interpretation of it in his dispute with the Pharisees (Matt 22:41–45). This implicitly compares Melchizedek to the Christ, a theme taken up very fully in Heb 5–7. Here the superiority of our Lord's priesthood to the Aaronic Jewish priesthood is argued on the basis of Abraham's giving of tithes to Melchizedek. Tithe-giving implies acknowledgment of superior status. Thus if Aaron's great ancestor Abraham acknowledged Melchizedek's priesthood, so implicitly did Aaron himself. This is just one of several arguments deployed by Hebrews to demonstrate how Christ's ministry has made obsolete the institutions of the old covenant, such as the priesthood and sacrifices. At any rate, as Jesus did in the gospels, Hebrews makes Melchizedek a type or forerunner of the messiah, an idea that early Christian exegetes developed further, seeing, for instance, in the bread and wine brought out by Melchizedek a type of the eucharist.

Within Genesis, however, Melchizedek is primarily an example of a non-Jew who recognizes God's hand at work in Israel: like Abimelech (21:22), Rahab (Josh 2:11), Ruth (1:16) or Naaman (2 Kgs 5:15). Similarly, he may be seen as a forerunner of the Magi (Matt 2:1–12), centurions (Matt 8:5–13; Mark 15:39; Acts 10), or the Syro-Phoenician woman (Mark 7:26–30), let alone the multitude of Gentile converts mentioned in Acts. They are those who have discovered that in Abram all the families of the earth find blessing.

The Covenant Promise *(15:1–21)*

Bibliography

Anbar, M. "Abrahamic Covenant: Gen 15." (Heb) *Shnaton* 3 (1978–79) 34–52. ——
—. "Additional Notes to *Shnaton* 3." (Heb) *Shnaton* 4 (1980) 275–79. ———. "Gen

15: A Conflation of Two Deuteronomic Narratives." *JBL* 101 (1982) 39–55. **Boyd, J.** "Two Misunderstood Words in the Ras Shamra Akkadian Texts." *Or* 46 (1977) 226–29. **Caquot, A.** "L'Alliance avec Abram (Gen 15)." *Sem* 12 (1963) 51–66. **Cazelles, H.** "Connexions et structure de Gen 15." *RB* 69 (1962) 321–49. **Clements, R. E.** *Abraham and David.* SBT 2.5. London: SCM Press, 1967. **Dion, H. M.** "The Patriarchal Traditions and the Literary Form of the 'Oracle of Salvation.'" *CBQ* 29 (1967) 198–206. **Ginsberg, H. L.** "Abram's 'Damascene' Steward." *BASOR* 200 (1970) 31–32. **Gross, H.** "Glaube und Bund—Theologische Bemerkungen zu Gen 15." *Studien zum Pentateuch: W. Kornfeld zum 60. Geburtstag,* ed. G. Braulik. Vienna: Herder, 1977. 25–35. **Hahn, F.** "Gen 15:6 im NT." *Probleme biblischer Theologie: G von Rad FS,* ed. H. W. Wolff. Munich: Kaiser, 1971. 90–107. **Hasel, G. F.** "The Meaning of the Animal Rite in Gen 15." *JSOT* 19 (1981) 61–78. **Jaroš, K.** "Abraham, Vater des Glaubens; Glaube als Vertrauen." *BLit* 49 (1976) 5–14. **Kaiser, O.** "Traditionsgeschichtliche Unter-suchung von Gen 15." *ZAW* 70 (1958) 107–26. **Kessler, M.** "The 'Shield' of Abraham." *VT* 14 (1964) 494–97. **Kline, M. G.** "Abraham's Amen." *WTJ* 31 (1968) 1–11. **Loewen-stamm, S. E.** "Zur Traditionsgeschichte des Bundes zwischen den Stücken." *VT* 18 (1968) 500–506. ———. "The Divine Grants of Land to the Patriarchs." *JAOS* 91 (1974) 509–10. **Lohfink, N.** *Die Landverheissung als Eid.* SBS 28. Stuttgart: Verlag Katholisches Bibelwerk, 1967. **Loretz, O.** "Mgn—'Geschenk' in Gen 15:1." *UF* 6 (1974) 492. **Naor, M.** "And They Shall Come Back Here in the Fourth Generation (Gen 15:16)." (Heb) *BMik* 27 (1981/82) 40–45. **Oeming, M.** "Ist Gen 15:6 ein Beleg für die Anrechnung des Glaubens zur Gerechtigkeit?" *ZAW* 95 (1983) 182–97. **Petersen, D. L.** "Covenant Ritual: A Traditio-Historical Perspective." *BR* 22 (1977) 7–18. **Polak, F.** "Gen 15: Theme and Structure." (Heb.) In *Studies in the Bible and the Ancient Near East Presented to S. E. Loewenstamm,* ed. Y. Avishur and J. Blau. Jerusalem: Rubinstein, 1978. 319–27. **Pomponio, F.** "*Mešeq* di Gen 15:2 e un termine amministrativo di Ebla." *BeO* 25 (1983) 103–09. **Rad, G. von.** "Faith Reckoned as Righteousness." In *The Problem of the Hexateuch and Other Essays.* Tr. E. W. T. Dicken. Edinburgh: Oliver and Boyd, 1965. 125–30. **Rendtorff, R.** "Gen 15 im Rahmen der theologischen Bearbei-tung der Vätergeschichten." *Werden und Wirken des ATs: FS für C. Westermann zum 70. Geburtstag,* ed. R. Albertz, H. P. Müller, H. W. Wolff, and W. Zimmerli. Göttingen: Vandenhoeck und Ruprecht, 1980. 74–81. **Rickards, R. R.** "Gen 15: An Exercise in Translation Principles." *BT* 28 (1977) 213–20. **Rogers, C. L.** "The Covenant with Abraham and Its Historical Setting." *BSac* 127 (1970) 241–56. **Schmid, H. H.** "Ge-rechtigkeit und Glaube: Gen 15:1–6 und sein biblisch-theologischer Kontext." *EvT* 40 (1980) 396–420. **Seebass, H.** "Zu Gen 15." *Wort und Dienst* 7 (1963) 132–49. ———. "Gen 15:2b." *ZAW* 75 (1963) 317–19. **Snijders, L. A.** "Gen 15: The Covenant with Abram." *OTS* 12 (1958) 261–79. **Uffenheimer, B.** "On Gen 15." (Heb) *Hatsevi Israel:* I. & Z. Bodie, 1976. 15–21. **Weinfeld, M.** "The Covenant of Grant in the Old Testament and the Ancient Near East." *JAOS* 90 (1970) 184–203. **Weingreen, J.** "הוצאתיך in Gen 15:7." In *Words and Meanings: Essays presented to D. W. Thomas,* ed. P. R. Ackroyd and B. Lindars. Cambridge: Cambridge UP, 1968. 209–15. **Wenham, G. J.** "The Symbolism of the Animal Rite in Gen 15: A Response to G. F. Hasel, *JSOT* 19 (1981) 61–78." *JSOT* 22 (1982) 134–37.

Translation

[1]*After these things the word of the LORD came to Abram in a*[a] *vision: "Do not be afraid,*[b] *Abram.* [c]*I am your shield.*[c] [d]*Your reward will be exceedingly great."*[de] [2]*Abram replied, "Sovereign LORD,*[a] *what will you give me, since I depart*[b] *childless and* [c]*my heir*[c] *is Eliezer from Damascus?"* [3]*Abram said, "Look,*[a] *you have not given me descendants, so that*[a] *one of my household will inherit from me."* [4]*The word of the LORD*[a] *came*[b] *to him: "This one will not inherit from you, but*[c] *one*

who comes out of your loins, he shall inherit from you." [5] *Then he brought*[a] *him outside and said: "Look*[b] *at the sky, and count the stars, if you can count them." Then he said: "Your descendants will be like that."*[c] [6] *And he believed*[a] *in the LORD*[b] *and it*[c] *was counted to him as righteousness.*

[7] *Then he said to him: "I am the LORD who*[a] *brought you out of Ur*[b] *of the Chaldaeans to give*[c] *you this land to inherit*[d] *it."* [8] *He replied, "Sovereign LORD, how am I to know that I shall inherit*[a] *it?"* [9] *He said to him, "Take*[a] *for me a three-year-old*[b] *calf, a three-year-old goat and a three-year-old ram, a dove, and a turtledove."* [10] *He took all these and split them down the middle*[a] *and he placed each split piece*[b] *opposite the other, but he did not split the birds.*[c] [11] *Then the birds of prey came down on the carcasses and Abram drove*[a] *them off.*

[12] *When the sun was about to set,*[a] [b] *and a deep sleep had fallen on Abram,*[b] [c] *a great dark fear overtook him.*[c] [13] *He said to Abram: "You must*[a] *know that your descendants will be immigrants in a land that is not theirs; they will be slaves to them, and*[b] *they shall oppress them for four hundred years.*[b] [14] *But I am to judge*[a] *the nation which they serve, and afterwards they shall come out with much property.* [15] *But you*[a] *will come to your fathers in peace.* [b] *You will be buried in ripe old age.*[b] [16] [a] *And in the fourth generation*[b] *they will return here,*[a] *for as yet the iniquity of the Amorites is not complete."*

[17] *When the sun had set*[a] *and it was*[b] *dark, there appeared*[c] *a smoking pot and a torch of fire which passed between the pieces.* [18] *On that day the LORD made a covenant with Abram: "To your descendants I have given*[a] *this land from the river*[b] *of Egypt, to the great river, the river Euphrates,* [19] *the Kenite, the Kenizzite, the Qadmonite,* [20] *the Hittite, the Perizzite, the Rephaim,* [21] *the Amorite, the Canaanite, the Girgashite,*[a] *and the Jebusite."*

Notes

1.a. Definite article in Heb. because a particular vision is referred to (GKC, 126r).

1.b. 2 masc sg impf ירא "to fear."

1.c-c, d-d. Clause d-d in apposition to c-c. First gives speaker's point of view: second, addressee's viewpoint (*SBH*, 44). Cf. 3:16; 31:39.

1.e. Sam ארבה "I shall multiply" for הרבה "great." Inf abs hiph of רבה. SamPent frequently replaces inf abs (Waltke, 215–16).

2.a. Omitted by G.

2.b. Ptcp הלך, here used figuratively either meaning "live" or "pass away, die" (BDB, 234). The versions translate it "die"; cf. Ps 39:14.

2.c-c. The Hebrew is problematic; see *Comment*. The versions have various interpretations but appear to presuppose MT.

3.a. ה/הנה. The traditional translation "behold" is often inadequate. Expresses immediacy of thing portrayed. Frequent in description and visions (D. J. McCarthy, *Bib* 61 [1980] 340; *SBH*, 94–96; Lambdin, 168–69).

4.a. G "God."

4.b. הנה; cf. n. on v 3. G "immediately."

4.c. כי־אם "but" makes the following clause emphatic (BDB, 475a) as does the following pleonastic הוא "*he* shall inherit" (*EWAS*, 99).

5.a. Waw consec + 3 masc sg impf hiph יצא "to come out."

5.b. 2 masc sg impv hiph נבט "to look."

5.c. כה is usually prospective "thus." Here retrospective; cf. Num 22:30.

6.a. Waw consec + 3 masc sg pf hiph אמן. It is unusual for single events in past time to use pf + waw: impf + waw is usual (Joüon, 192). It may indicate repeated action in the past, "he kept on believing" (GKC, 112ss).

6.b. G, S and NT "in God."

6.c. Waw consec + 3 masc sg impf qal חשב + 3 fem sg suff. Lit., "one counted it (her) to him." Fem suff "her" has neutral sense here (GKC, 122q).

7.a. 1 sg pf hiph יצא + 2 masc sg suff. Verb in relative clause agrees with main clause "*I* the LORD . . . *I* brought" (GKC, 138d; Joüon, 158n).

7.b. G has "country"; cf. 11:28, 31.

7.c. ל + inf constr נתן.

7.d. ל + inf constr ירש + 3 fem sg suff.

8.a. 1 sg impf ירש + 3 fem sg suff.

9.a. 2 masc sg impv לקח + ה ending.

9.b. Fem sg pual ptcp שלש "do a third time." *Tg. Onq.* "three."

10.a. SamPent inf abs בתור "splitting" for MT בתוך "down the middle."

10.b. SamPent adds def obj marker את. Typical (Waltke, 221).

10.c. SamPent reads plural "birds" for collective "bird." Typical (Waltke, 218–19).

11.a. For MT וַיַּשֵּׁב אֹתָם "he drove them off" (3 masc sg hiph נשׁב) G reads וַיָּשֶׁב אֶתָּם "he sat with them"; *Tg. Onq.*, וַיָּשָׁב (from שוב) "he returned."

12.a. On this idiom היה + inf constr (GKC, 114i; Joüon 124l), cf. Josh 2:5.

12.b-b. Circumstantial clause modifying initial temporal clause *SBH*, 87; cf. Gen 15:17.

12.c-c. On main clauses introduced by הנה see *SBH*, 96; particularly in visions, D. J. McCarthy, *Bib* 61 (1980) 332–33. Cf. 29:25; 38:27, 29.

13.a. On this nuance of inf abs "expressing absolute obligation," see *EWAS*, 87.

13.b-b. Note the chiasmus with 16.a-a: "Oppress . . . 400 years . . . 4th generation . . . return" (*SBH*, 133).

14.a. Ptcp with future meaning (GKC, 116p). On word order, object-verb-subject, probably for emphasis, see *EWAS*, 38–51.

15.a. Note use of pronoun making obvious contrast with previous verse (*EWAS*, 56).

15.b-b. In apposition to first part of verse and clarifying it (*SBH*, 47).

16.a-a. See n. 13.b-b.

16.b. Adverbial accusative (GKC, 118i-q).

17.a. Perfect with pluperfect meaning (GKC, 111g); cf. 24:15; 27:30.

17.b. Lit., "darkness was." Masc verb, fem subject (GKC, 145o).

17.c. והנה expresses the vividness of the experience (McCarthy, *Bib* 61 [1980] 332–33).

18.a. Prophetic pf because gift, though future, is guaranteed (GKC, 106m).

18.b. There is no ms support for the conjectural emendation נחל "wadi" instead of נהר "river."

21.a. Sam, G add "and the Hivite"; cf. Exod 3:8, 17, etc. Supplementation of lists with the aid of parallel passages is characteristic of SamPent (Waltke, 221–22).

Form/Structure/Setting

The limits of this episode are clearly demarcated. Its opening words, "after these things" (v 1), in the present context refer to the victory over the kings recorded in chap. 14: later on in chap. 15, various allusions to the previous chapter confirm that these are the things referred to here. It reaches its climax in vv 18–21, which define the great extent of the promised land and list the ten peoples inhabiting it in Abraham's lifetime.

The episode falls into two scenes which run in close parallel:

Yahweh's word	v 1	Promise of reward	v 7	Promise of land
Abram's word	vv 2–3	Complaint about childlessness	v 8	Guarantee requested
Yahweh's reaction	v 4	Promise of heir	v 9	Oath rite commanded
Public act	v 5	Taken into open	vv 16–17	Oath rite carried out
Yahweh's word	v 5	Promise of many descendants	vv 13–16	Promise of land for descendants
Conclusion	v 6	Abram's faith	vv 18–21	Yahweh's covenant

Key words link together the two scenes: "Sovereign Lord," vv 2, 8; "descendants" (זרע), vv 3, 5, 13, 18; "inherit" (ירש), vv 4 (2 times), 7, 8; "bring out" (הוצא), vv 5, 7. Scenic construction is typical of Hebrew narrative, but here the scenes simply serve as a setting for the dialogue. For this reason Lohfink calls it an "imitation (nachgeahmte) narrative."

Literary critical discussions of this chapter tend to be elaborate, and proponents freely admit the hypothetical nature of their suggestions. Discussions center on the unity of the material and its date. Traditionally, it was customary to find elements of both J and E here, either arranged consecutively—vv 1–6 E, vv 7–21 J (cf. Wellhausen)—or interwoven, e.g., E = 1b, 3a, 5, 11, 12a, 13a, 14, 16 (Gunkel), with the rest J. Often vv 13–16, 18–21 were reckoned to be later editorial additions. Arguments in favor of two sources here include the twin self-introduction of God in vv 1, 7, and the double response by Abram vv 2–3, 8, as well as the contrasts between the night in v 5 and early evening in vv 12, 17; and between Abram's faith in v 6 and his doubt in v 8.

However, recent writers generally doubt the presence of E here, and indeed, many argue for or accept the substantial unity of the narrative (e.g., Lohfink, McEvenue [Narrative Style], van Seters [Abraham], Vawter). Vv 13–16 are perhaps a later insertion according to Lohfink, though this has been doubted by van Seters, Wenham, Anbar, and Alexander (Literary Analysis). These writers argue that the supposed evidence for separate sources can be better explained in terms of Hebrew literary conventions. See Comment below.

The date of the material is also a matter of dispute. Cazelles has pointed out that the leading ideas and terms in this chapter have many parallels in early second-millennium literature from the ancient Near East, which supports its antiquity. Weinfeld looked to early oriental land grants as an analogy for the covenant promise of land. Likewise, Lohfink argues that most of the material in this chapter is pre-J, though the editorial hand of the Yahwist is obvious.

Others claim that the material is much later than the putative date for J, i.e., the tenth century. Rendtorff and Westermann point to the centrality of the promises in this chapter, which, given their assumptions about the growth of the promise-material in Genesis (much of it represents a later development), indicates a seventh-century date for this section. Others (from Skinner to Anbar) point to the affinities between this chapter and deuteronomic literature: e.g., Abram's portrayal as a prophet, the covenant terminology, and the list of the inhabitants of the land.

The correctness of these observations may not be contested, but their interpretation is more uncertain. Westermann and Rendtorff's history of the promise tradition is hypothetical, and its datings are necessarily relative. To use the presence of certain promises here to date the chapter is circular argumentation. The same may be said of the deuteronomic affinities of the chapter. The assumption of many writers is that chap. 15's ideas and phrases are borrowed from deuteronomic literature. It could of course be the other way around. Certainly this chapter expresses most clearly and pungently some of the leading themes of the Pentateuch, and it could as easily be the source as the deposit of these promise traditions. In my view, Lohfink's general approach still has most to commend it.

Comment

1 "After these things." A similar formula occurs in 22:1, 20; 39:7; 40:1; 48:1. It indicates that some time has elapsed since the previous incident, and presupposes the existence of a cycle of Abraham narratives. The present context and the allusions to chap. 14 in this chapter—"deliver/shield" (מגן), 14:20 // 15:1; "go out," 14:17–18 // 15:4–5, 7, 14; "property," 14:11–12, 16, 21 // 15:14; cf. שלם ("Salem"/"complete"), 14:18 // 15:16)—make it likely that "these things" means the events described in the previous chapter.

"The word of the LORD came." This is a phrase typically introducing revelation to a prophet, e.g., 1 Sam 15:10; Hos 1:1; but in Genesis it is found only here and in v 4 of this chapter. Abraham is actually called a prophet in 20:7. It prepares the way for the prophecy of the Egyptian bondage in vv 13–16.

"Vision," מחזה, is rare in Hebrew and used only of Balaam (Num 24:4, 16) and contemporaries of Ezekiel (13:7). Second- and third-millennium Akkadian texts show that visions were a recognized and very ancient mode of revelation.

"Do not be afraid." This is a very common phrase in the OT, frequently introducing an oracle of salvation (e.g., Isa 7:4; 10:24; there are other examples in Gen 21:17; 26:24; 35:17; 43:23; 46:3; 50:19, 21). Given its ubiquity in Scripture, it would appear dangerous to use this formula to date the oracle. Cazelles (*RB* 69 [1962] 321–49) and Lohfink [*Landverheissung*] cite Mesopotamian and Egyptian parallels. Its use suggests that Abraham is viewed as a military warrior.

"I am your shield." Here the military metaphor is unmistakable (cf. 2 Sam 22:3, 31; Ps 3:4 [3]; 115:9–11, etc.). In view of the frequency of the idea that God is the shield of his faithful people (cf. Ps 84:12–13 [11–12]; Prov 30:5), particularly the protector of the king, and the parallel to this expression in an Assyrian text (Kaiser, *ZAW* 70 [1958] 113), it is superfluous to reinterpret מגן as "present" (so Dahood, *JBL* 38 [1957] 62–73; Kessler, *VT* 14 [1964] 494–97). More probably there is an allusion to 14:20, מגן "delivered." Yahweh himself now confirms Melchizedek's verdict.

"Your reward," שכר: Kaiser (cf. Cazelles, Lohfink) suggests that this is the term for a mercenary's pay. In Ezek 29:19 it refers specifically to a soldier's booty, although it is a broad term meaning "wage" or "fee" (Gen 30:32; Exod 22:14 [15]; Num 18:31). Nevertheless martial overtones would be quite appropriate in this context following chap. 14.

2 "Sovereign LORD." This formula occurs only here and in v 8 in Genesis. אדני "sovereign" is a characteristic mode of address to God in intercessory prayer; cf. 18:3, 27, 30–32; 19:18; 20:4. It is not found in Genesis outside the Abraham cycle. The traditional interpretation of אדני is "my Lord," the 1 sg suffix י being understood as a plural of majesty. However, Eissfeldt (*TDOT* 1:62–72; cf. E. Jenni, *THWAT* 1:31–38) argues on the basis of Ugaritic parallels that the suffix may serve to intensify the root meaning of the noun; hence "Lord of all, sovereign." While Eissfeldt allows that the word may well be translated "my Lord" in this passage, Gispen (2:101) thinks that in the light of 14:22 "sovereign" may be preferable. G Δέσποτα may also support this interpretation.

"What will you give me . . . childless" gives the substance of Abram's complaint. The barrenness of Sarah has already been mentioned, and three times Abram has been promised a multitude of descendants (12:2, 7; 13:16). "Childless," עֲרִירִי: the word also occurs in Lev 20:20–21 and Jer 22:30, where it is a divine judgment. Abram's situation contradicts not only the general view of Genesis that divine blessing leads to a man being fruitful and multiplying (1:28; 9:1; 26:24; 35:11), but also the specific assurances already made to him.

"My heir is Damascus, Eliezer." This phrase is very difficult and widely regarded as corrupt and impossible to correct. The major problem concerns the interpretation of בֶּן־מֶשֶׁק בֵּיתִי "my heir." The minor problem is the qualifying phrase ("he is Damascus, Eliezer") הוּא דַמֶּשֶׂק אֱלִיעֶזֶר. מֶשֶׁק is a *hapax legomenon* of uncertain meaning, and nowhere else is Abraham's heir called Damascus or Eliezer.

The sentence puzzled the early translators: G, "The son of Masek my steward, this is Damascus Eliezer." Vg θ′ "the son of the manager of my house that is Damascus Eliezer," α′ "the son of the cup-bearer of my house that is Damascus Eliezer." S "Eliezer the Damascene, the son of my house will be my heir." *Tg. Onq.* "This manager who is in my house, he is Eliezer of Damascus." *Gen. Ap.* equates Eliezer with "one of my household servants."

Modern commentators attempt to emend the text or reinterpret it. The simplest solution tentatively adopted in my translation is to understand מֶשֶׁק to mean "property" (so Gispen, 2:102, following BDB, 606b). Then בֶּן־מֶשֶׁק בֵּיתִי would mean "possessor of my house," i.e. "heir." Another possibility suggested by Snijders (*OTS* 12 [1958] 261–79) is to derive מֶשֶׁק from שָׁקַק "to rush, assault." Hence בֶּן־מֶשֶׁק means "assaulter, usurper." The sentence is then a complaint that a foreigner Eliezer from Damascus will usurp Abram's house. A third possibility proposed by Cazelles (*RB* 69 [1962] 321–49) is that בֶּן־מֶשֶׁק is "cup-bearer," from the root שָׁקָה "drink," i.e., someone like the royal official mentioned in Gen 40:2. C. H. Gordon ("Damascus in Assyrian Sources," *IEJ* 2 [1952] 174–75) has argued that הוּא דַמֶּשֶׂק "from Damascus" is an Aramaic gloss explaining בֶּן־מֶשֶׁק, both phrases meaning "servant." The sentence would then read "the servant of my house [i.e., *dammeseq* in Aramaic] is Eliezer." Though this is a neat solution, the context suggests there should be more to Abram's complaint than a reference to the name of his servant (cf. v 3). It seems more probable that הוּא דַמֶּשֶׂק is a gloss, but one that explains the name "Eliezer," not "my heir." There are several explanatory glosses in chap. 14 (e.g., vv 2, 7, 8), so it would not be surprising to find one here. Furthermore, theophoric names compounded with Ezer, e.g., Hadad-ezer, are well known among kings of Damascus, so it is quite likely that the text is explaining Eliezer's background. Hence my suggested translation "My heir is Eliezer of Damascus."

3 This verse is widely regarded as a gloss explaining the obscurities of the previous one. But the use of הִנֵּה/הֵן "look," "so that" adds a note of exasperation to the complaint.

"One of my household will inherit from me." Attempts have been made by W. F. Albright ("Abram the Hebrew," *BASOR* 163 [1961] 47), Gordon, and Speiser to explain Eliezer's right to Abram's inheritance in terms of a Nuzi custom whereby a man could adopt a slave as his heir. However, Thompson (*Historicity*, 203–30) demonstrates that there is no basis for this interpretation of the Nuzi text: those adopted were either minors or independent persons in their own right. But he goes too far in asserting that there is no parallel to this arrangement in non-biblical texts. Adoption was perfectly possible: the adopted person would be expected to look after the adopter in his old age, bury him, and could then expect the inheritance. If the adopter subsequently had children, the adopted "child" could not be totally disinherited, but would share the inheritance. Thompson can affirm that Genesis is flouting oriental practice only by reading into these verses ideas they do not entail. First, Eliezer is not said to be a slave (the servant is unnamed in chap. 24), simply a member of the household. Second, the text does not say he has been adopted. Abram says he will inherit: this could mean that Abram will have to adopt him, if he has no son of his own.

Outside this chapter "inherit," ירש, is rare in Genesis (21:10; 22:17; 24:60; 28:4). It is ubiquitous in Deuteronomy, referring to Israel's taking possession of the land.

4 Abram's exasperation is answered by an emphatic affirmation that a real son will inherit from him. "Not this one . . . but . . ."; cf. *Notes.*

"Loins," מעה, refers to the lower belly; cf. Jon 2:2 [1]; Cant 5:14; to the seat of reproduction, Num 5:22; Ps 71:6. In other words, Abram will have a real son, not simply a legal heir. A similar formula is found in 2 Sam 7:12 in the promise to David (cf. Gen 25:23).

5 "Look" suggests a long look; cf. 1 Kgs 18:43; Exod 3:6.

"Stars." For this comparison, cf. 22:17; 26:4; 37:9; Deut 1:10. On the numberlessness of Abram's descendants, cf. 16:10; 32:13 [12].

6 The editorial comment with which the first scene closes (cf. 2:24) points out that Abram's silence showed his faith in the promises just made to him (vv 4–5). Without this remark, an element of ambiguity would have surrounded Abram's reaction: indeed, then his question in v 8 could have been taken as an expression of doubt. The verbal form והאמין (*waw* + perfect) "he believed" probably indicates repeated or continuing action. Faith was Abram's normal response to the LORD's words.

האמן "he believed" can mean "he relied on someone, gave credence to a message or considered it to be true, trusted in someone" (Jepsen, *TDOT* 1:308). It occurs quite rarely in a positive context in the OT: much more often the texts speak of people not believing in God, or in someone, cf. 45:26; Exod 4:8; 14:31; Num 14:11; 20:12; Deut 1:32; 9:23. But *pace* Jepsen, this does not prove that faith is peripheral to OT theology. Rather faith is presupposed everywhere as the correct response of man to God's revelation. It is in crisis situations that faith or the lack of it is revealed, and therefore commented on, e.g., Isa 7:9; Jon 3:5; Ps 78:22, 32.

There appear to be two reasons why Abram's faith should be noted here: (1) because the word of promise had come to him in a crisis situation following the battle of chap. 14, and (2) it serves as a reminder of Abram's attitude to God, which should be a model for all his descendants to follow.

ויחשבה "It was counted to him." Here the imperfect qal of חשב is used. Similar constructions using the niphal are found in Lev 7:18; 17:4; Num 18:27, 30; Prov 27:14. But the closest parallel is Ps 106:31: "that has been reckoned to him [niphal] as righteousness." The legal texts quoted illustrate the meaning of "count": when Levites pass on a tenth of the tithes they receive, that counts as though they had given a tithe from their own produce (Num 18:27, 30). Similarly, killing a sacrificial animal outside the tabernacle compound counts as murder: "he has shed blood" (Lev 17:4).

Von Rad (*Problem*, 125–30) has postulated that a cultic setting lies behind this statement that Abram's faith counted as righteousness. Just as priests declared sacrifices acceptable (Lev 7:18), or men clean or unclean (Lev 13), so they could declare them righteous (Ezek 18:9). Here in Gen 15, von Rad says, there is a spiritualized idea of righteousness that is not dependent on cultic worship. His suggestion of cultic background for the term חשב has been widely endorsed by commentators, but Lohfink (*Landverheissung*, 59–60) is right to question the supposed contrast between the usage of Gen 15:6 and the legal texts. More radically still, Oeming (*ZAW* 95 [1983] 182–97) doubts whether the rarer niphal usage of חשב should control our interpretation of the qal stem. He thinks it has no connection with cultic usage. Within the Pentateuch, though, the niphal is twice as common as the qal, which weakens Oeming's case. It does seem likely that once again Abram's experiences are regarded as archetypal for later generations. Just as he exercised faith in God's revelation, so too must his offspring exercise faith in their situation by obediently carrying out God's will declared in the law; cf. Ps 119:66.

"Righteousness," צדקה. Within the Pentateuch צדקה always applies to human activity. This makes Oeming's proposal to apply the term to God's act unlikely, the more so in that all early Jewish as well as Christian exegesis is against such a view. The root צדק is rich in meaning, though fairly rare in Genesis outside chap. 18, where the righteous are constantly contrasted with the wicked. Abraham's intercession for Sodom rests on the impossibility of God's destroying the righteous (18:23, 25, 26). Abimelech makes the same point in 20:4. Similarly, Noah was saved from destruction in the flood because he was righteous (6:9; 7:1). In legal contexts the righteous are those who should be acquitted (הצדיק) by the judges (e.g., Deut 25:1). Thus in the spiritual realm the righteous are those acquitted by God, those who are saved (Ps 1:6; 75:11, etc.).

Normally righteousness is defined in terms of moral conduct, for example, Ezek 18:5: "If a man is righteous and does what is lawful and right." There then follows a list of actions prohibited in the Pentateuch which a righteous man refrains from doing (vv 6–9). God himself is frequently called "righteous" (e.g., Deut 32:4; Ps 7:10 [9], 12 [11]) and righteousness might well be paraphrased as God-like, or at least God-pleasing, action. This sense of God-approved behavior is apparent in Gen 18:19; 30:33; 38:26.

But here Abram is not described as doing righteousness. Rather faith is being counted for righteousness. Normally righteousness results in acquittal by the divine judge. Here faith, the right response to God's revelation, counts instead. As the rest of the story makes plain, this faith leads to righteous action (e.g., 18:19), but only here in the OT is it counted as righteousness.

7 The second scene, like the first, begins with a divine promise; cf. v 1: "I am the LORD who brought you out of Ur of the Chaldaeans." An almost identical formula introduces the decalogue (Exod 20:2; Deut 5:6), with the substitution of "land of Egypt" for "Ur of the Chaldaeans." On this term, see *Comment* on 11:28.

The continuation of the promise "to give you this land" parallels Lev 25:38, while its conclusion "to inherit it" is typically deuteronomic (e.g., Deut 3:18; 9:6; 21:1; 19:14). But this is hardly enough to demonstrate that this episode is the work of the deuteronomist (cf. Lohfink, *Landverheissung,* 62).

This is one of only four passages in Genesis where God refers to himself as Yahweh (the LORD). Here the use of this name helps to enhance the analogy between God's call of Abram and his subsequent redemption of Israel from Egypt. This is expressly prefigured in vv 11–18.

8 Abram's request for a sign parallels his petition in v 2. Note the same opening formula, "Sovereign LORD." To ask for a sign does not imply unbelief or any conflict with v 6 (cf. Judg 6:36–40; 2 Kgs 20:8–11). On the contrary, to refuse a proffered sign can indeed demonstrate lack of faith (Isa 7:10–14). On signs, cf. Gen 9:12–13.

9 In response to Abram's request God gives him an enigmatic command: "Take." This very common word often introduces a ritual such as a sacrifice, e.g., Lev 9:2,3. The list of animals that follows covers all those species that could be offered in sacrifice. There is some doubt about the identity of the last bird mentioned, "turtledove" (גוזל), as the only other example of its use is in Deut 32:11. However, it seems likely that it is equivalent to the בן־יונה "young pigeon" of the sacrificial texts.

10 Abram's fulfillment of the command is expounded in more detail. Again in an action reminiscent of a sacrifice, he cuts up the large animals but does not split the bird; cf. Lev 1:6, 17. Were this a sacrifice, the pieces would now be placed on the altar and burned. Instead, they are put in two rows. This unique feature of this rite must have been included in the divine command (v 9). For stylistic variation, the command is briefer than the description of its fulfillment: it is common for the command to be more detailed than the record of its fulfillment.

11 Most commentators see the attacks of the birds of prey as an ominous sign, but a more precise interpretation depends on the significance of the rite as a whole.

12 "When the sun was about to set and a deep sleep . . . Abram." Note the similar structure of v 17, with a double temporal clause preceding והנה. It has often been argued that since Abram was told to look at the stars in v 5, it must already have been dark then, and this reference to the sun setting therefore indicates that vv 1–6 and 7–21 are from different sources. However, the structure of the second scene mirrors that of the first too closely for them to be regarded as independent. Either the author is postulating a lapse of time between vv 6 and 7, and vv 7–21 take place the day following vv 1–6, or the second scene is expressing the promises in a different way.

Westermann holds that this verse marks the opening of an addition to the oath ritual. The majority opinion is that the expansion consists only of vv 13–16.

"The deep sleep," "fear" and "darkness" all suggest awe-inspiring divine activity (cf. Gen 2:21; Isa 29:10; Exod 10:21, 22; 14:20; 15:16; 23:27; Deut

4:11; Josh 2:9) and are closely associated with the exodus and conquest, appropriately introducing the prophecy in the next verses.

13–16 These verses prophesy the Egyptian bondage and the exodus after 400 years (v 13) in the fourth generation (v 16). Apparently the two periods are equated, so one generation equals 100 years. This suggests they are intended to be round numbers (cf. Exod 12:40). In this case the three-year-old animals (v 9) could well symbolize three generations of oppression in Egypt (so Keil, 215, following Theodoret).

14 "With much property": cf. Exod 12:35–39.

15 "In peace." This is the first occurrence of this word (שלום) in Scripture. The prophecy "You will be buried in ripe old age" is fulfilled in Gen 25:8. The same phrase is used also of Gideon (Judg 8:32) and David (1 Chr 29:28).

16 Here the Amorites stand for all the inhabitants of Canaan. Divine judgment, in the form of Israel's conquest, must wait until they are sufficiently wicked to deserve this fate; cf. Lev 18:24–27; Deut 9:4–5; Amos 2:9.

17 "Smoking pot." Since it is used for baking תנור may be translated "oven," but modern ovens are so different that this is rather misleading. The term seems to have been used for a large earthenware jar. The dough stuck to the side and was then baked by putting charcoal inside the jar or putting the jar near the fire (cf. *NBD,* 166). Smoke and fire are symbolic of the presence of God (cf. Exod 13:21; 19:18; 20:18).

The interpretation of this mysterious rite is much discussed; see Hasel (*JSOT* 19 [1981] 61–78) for a comprehensive survey. Most modern commentators take their cue from v 18, "The LORD made [literally, cut] a covenant with Abram," and from Jer 34:18, which speaks of the people passing between a dismembered calf. This act is then interpreted as an enacted curse. "May God make me like this animal, if I do not fulfill the demands of the covenant." A curse like this is actually attested in one of the eighth-century treaties (*ANESTP,* 532). In Genesis, of course, it is God himself who walks between the pieces, and it is suggested that here God is invoking the curse on himself, if he fails to fulfill the promise.

While this interpretation could explain the phrase "to cut a covenant," it leaves many features of this rite unexplained. It does not explain the choice of these particular animals. Why are only sacrificial types selected? Why must they be three years old? Why are the birds not cut up? Why does Abram drive off the birds of prey? Finally it must be asked whether a divine self-imprecation is really likely. Is it compatible with OT theology for God to say "May I die, if I do not keep my word"? Divine oaths generally take the form, "As I live, says the LORD" (cf. Num 14:21).

The use of sacrificial terminology in v 9 suggests that the rite should be interpreted using the categories underlying other OT rituals. It then becomes clear that the sacrificial animals must represent Israel or its priestly leaders (M. Douglas, *Purity and Danger* [London: Routledge, 1966]; cf. Jacob). The birds of prey represent unclean nations, Gentiles, possibly Egypt (so Cazelles). Thus Abram's actions in driving away the birds represent his defending his descendants against foreign attackers. This may look back to his defeat of the kings in chap. 14, but more probably it looks forward to their deliverance from Egypt. The rest of the Pentateuch insists that it is the promise to Abram that is the ground for the exodus (Exod 2:24; Deut 9:5). This scene portrays a time-lapse between Abram's falling asleep (v 12; cf. v 15) and God's walking between the pieces (v 17). If the pieces represent Israel, this action would appear to portray God as walking with his people. Whether the reference is to the pillar of fire accompanying them through the wilderness or the theophany of Sinai, or whether it portrays the fulfillment of the covenant promise "I will walk among you and be your God" (Lev 26:12; cf. Deut 23:15 [14]) is difficult to decide: indeed the possibilities are not mutually exclusive.

Every type of sacrificial animal is represented to underline the significance of the scene. All Israel is involved. Finally, there may be significance in the choice of three-year-old animals. Gideon sacrificed a seven-year-old bull to represent the seven years of Midianite oppression (Judg 6:1, 25). The use of three three-year-old animals makes it likely that some significance is attached to their age and the certainty of the events predicted (cf. Gen 41:32). This interpretation of the ritual is confirmed by the prophecy of Israel's future in vv 13–16: the congruence of the actions with this interpretation makes it less likely that the prophecy in vv 13–16 is a later addition.

18 "Covenant" (ברית; cf. 6:18; 9:9–17). Throughout the Abraham stories there is an implicit comparison with the later experience of Israel, and it has therefore been supposed that the patriarchal and Sinaitic covenants were similar. But this is not so. The Sinaitic and Deuteronomic covenants were agreements imposing obligations on both God and Israel: their closest extra-biblical analogy is found in the ancient international treaties made by great powers with their vassals. This covenant with Abraham is different: it is a promissory oath made by God alone. Weinfeld (*JAOS* 90 [1970], 184–203; *TDOT* 2:270–72) says the nearest parallel to this form is the royal land grant made by kings to loyal servants. These grants of land were typically made to a man and his descendants in perpetuity. In form and content they thus run in parallel to the patriarchal promises. It is doubtful, though, whether the land-grant parallels explain the animal rite of Gen 15 (so Loewenstamm, *JAOS* 91 [1971] 509–10; van Seters, *Abraham*, 102–3).

"From the river of Egypt to the great river." According to Weinfeld (*JAOS*, 90 [1970] 200): "Delineation of borders . . . constitute an important part of the documents of grant." The more usual term for the southern border of the promised land is the brook (נחל) of Egypt, which is to be identified with Wadi el Arish in northeastern Sinai (Num 34:5). It is not clear whether "river of Egypt" is an alternative name for Wadi el Arish (so Simons, *GTOT*, 27) or means the eastern branch of the Nile delta (so Aharoni, *Land of the Bible*, 59). Assuming there is no corruption of the text and that usage is consistent, the latter would be more probable. In that case, there is an element of hyperbole here, for the land of promise is identified with Canaan, whose boundaries are more restricted (see Num 34:2–12). Only in Solomon's day did Israel's boundaries approach the limits specified here (1 Kgs 5:1 [4:21]), but it seems unlikely that they extended as far west as the Nile even then (A. Malamat, *JNES* 22 [1963] 1–17).

19–21 This is the longest list of the pre-Israelite inhabitants of Canaan found in the OT. Usually six or seven groups are mentioned: here there are ten. Lohfink argues that this must be an old part of the tradition, because it omits certain groups who settled in the land about the same time as Israel (e.g., Philistines, Moabites) and includes other groups who were subsequently incorporated into the nation (e.g., Kenites and Kenizzites; *Landesverheissung*, 65–72).

19 "Kenites" mostly dwelt in the south of the land in the Negeb (e.g., Num 24:21; 1 Sam 27:10) though some lived further north (Judg 4:11–17).

"Kenizzite." Caleb is called a Kenizzite (Num 32:12) though it is not certain that he belonged to the same group as that mentioned here.

"Qadmonites" are mentioned only here.

20 "Hittites" are regularly mentioned in other lists of peoples. They lived near Hebron (23:10) and are probably to be distinguished from the people found in Asia Minor; cf. 10:15.

"Perizzite." This is another regular member of the lists; see 13:7.

"Rephaim": cf. 14:5.

21 "Amorite, Canaanite, Girgashite, Jebusite": see *Comment* on 10:16, 18.

Explanation

The chapter opens on a high note. Abram, like a great prophet, receives a word from the LORD assuring him of divine protection and reward (v 1). The content of this promise evokes images of Abram as a great and successful warrior enjoying the spoils of battle and alludes to his triumph in chap. 14.

Abram's reply is pitiful. Despite all his outward success and the repeated promises from God, he lacks a son and heir. Childlessness was viewed as an unmitigated disaster in the ancient world. Without children there was no one to carry on your family line or preserve the family inheritance, no one to look after you in old age, no one to carry out the funerary rites and secure your soul's rest in the life to come. The tragedy of Abram's situation was compounded by the fact that God had implicitly promised him children (12:2, 7; 13:16). If there is no change in his situation, Abram says, he will have to take action to preserve his interests (vv 2, 6 evidently presuppose that Abram is an old man): he will adopt Eliezer, one of his household, as his heir.

This prompts God to assure Abram that he will indeed have a child of his own, and that his descendants will be as numerous as the stars (vv 4–5). "And he believed in the LORD." The verbal form implies continued repeated acts of faith. The significance of the phrase does not lie here, though, nor in the existence of his faith as such, for the OT everywhere presupposes that men ought to exercise faith in God; faith means believing his promises or obeying his commands as the situation dictates. What is unusual is that the writer saw fit to draw attention to Abram's faith: if all men of the old covenant were expected to be men of faith, why mention it here? Possibly it was because of the staggering nature of the promise made to an old man, though in the light of the earlier somewhat vaguer promises along the same lines, this does not seem an entirely adequate explanation. More likely, there is an element of paradigm here. Abram is a model for all his descendants to imitate: whatever their circumstances, they must have faith in God. The importance of faith is underlined by the following clause, "it was counted to him as righteousness" (v 6). Righteousness is a guarantee of salvation, of acquittal in the day of judgment. It involves conformity to God's will set forth in the law. Here, however, faith counts for righteousness: it is the response of believing obedience to the word of God, not righteous deeds, that counted for righteousness. To be sure, such faith, when genuine, issues in righteous deeds, but that it is not what the text says: faith counts for (instead of) righteousness.

It is therefore natural and right for the NT writers to refer to this text in describing how salvation is available in Christ. Paul stresses that faith for Abram meant believing in God's promise of a child, an attitude to God that preceded his acts of obedience (Rom 4). While Genesis implies that the sons of Abram must be men of faith, Paul turns the words around and explains, "it is men of faith who are the sons of Abraham" (Gal 3:7). In the OT, faith involves both believing promises and obeying commands: it is the latter aspect that both Heb 11:8–19 and James 2:18–24 emphasize in their comments on the life of Abraham; "By faith Abraham obeyed" (Heb 11:8); "Faith was completed by works" (Jas 2:22). That the two sides of faith—belief and obedience—are not incompatible is recognized by Hebrews,which repeatedly links faith with receiving the promises.

Gen 15:7 continues with the divine reminder that the Lord had brought Abram out of Ur to inherit the land. The parallel with the exodus from Egypt emphasizes once again how the life of Abraham foreshadows the history of Israel, a theme that is explicit in the subsequent dialogue. Abram's question "How am I to know?" is a request for a sign to confirm the promise, not the expression of doubt.

The answer takes the form of a ritual and accompanying message. The action underlines the prophecy with great emphasis and is a guarantee of its fulfillment. The rite pictures Abram's descendants, in the form of sacrificial animals, protected by the Abrahamic promises from attacks by foreigners, the birds of prey. After Abram's death, his "falling asleep," the Lord (the smoking pot and torch of fire) will walk among them. The prophecy in vv 13–16 is more specific foretelling of 400 years' oppression in Egypt and their exodus in the fourth generation. They will then return to Canaan and expel the ten nations that inhabit it (vv 19–21). With this promissory oath or covenant, the scene reaches its climax, and Abram's questions are answered.

In these scenes Abram is portrayed not merely as the archetypal Israelite who has faith in God, but as a conquering king who has been promised victory over his foes and a great territory. As often noted, there are many resemblances in the form and content between the covenant with Abram and that with David (2 Sam 7). However, the paradigmatic character of the father of the nation is also seen in the way he is viewed as a prophet enjoying a vision (v 1) of God and insight into the future (vv 13–16). Finally Abram appears as a sort of priest: the description of the bird-rite suggests it, and the mention of his sacrifices and altar-building points in the same direction. Within the OT these same features reappear in the figure of Moses, and the NT sees our Lord as prophet, priest, and king. In exercising faith, the people of the new covenant both imitate Christ and also walk in the footsteps of our forefather Abram.

Index of Authors Cited

Index of Principal Subjects

Index of Biblical Texts

A. Old Testament

B. Old Testament Apocrypha and Pseudepigrapha

C. New Testament

Index of Key Hebrew Words